LARGE
PRINT

SINATRA

SINATRA

THE LIFE

Anthony Summers

and Robbyn Swan

Doubleday Large Print Home Library Edition

RANDOM HOUSE

Published in the United States of America
by Random House Large Print in association
with Alfred A. Knopf, New York.
Distributed by Random House, Inc., New York.

0-375-43549-2

This Large Print edition published in accord
with the standards of the N.A.V.H.

For Theresa Santore Swan
with love

"Right from the beginning, he was there with the truth of things in his voice."

—Bob Dylan

Contents

SINATRA

1

Debut

MARCH 18, 1939.

In a studio on West 46th Street in New York City, a band was playing Rimsky-Korsakov's "Flight of the Bumblebee." It was a simple place, a room with couches and lamps, hung with drapes to muffle the echo from the walls. This was a big day for the musicians, who were recording for the first time.

A skinny young man listened as they played. The previous night, at the Sicilian Club near his home in New Jersey, he had asked if he could tag along. Now, as the band finished playing, he stepped forward and spoke to the bandleader. "May I sing?" he asked.

The bandleader glanced at the studio clock to see if they had time left, then told the young man to go ahead. He chose "Our Love," a stock arrangement based on a melody from Tchaikovsky's **Romeo and**

Juliet. Standing at the rudimentary microphone, he launched into a saccharine lyric:

> Our love, I feel it everywhere
> Our love is like an evening prayer . . .
> I see your face in stars above,
> As I dream on, in all the magic of
> Our love.

Unseasoned, a little reedy, the voice was transmitted through an amplifier to a recording device known as a lathe. The lathe drove the sound to a needle, and the needle carved a groove on a twelve-inch aluminum-based lacquer disc. The result was a record, to be played on a turntable at seventy-eight revolutions per minute.

The bandleader kept the record in a drawer for nearly sixty years. He would take it out from time to time, with delight and increasing nostalgia, to play for friends. The music on it sounds tinny, a relic of the infancy of recording technology. Yet the disc is kept in a locked safe. The attorney for the bandleader's widow, an octogenarian on Social Security, says the singer's heirs have demanded all rights and the lion's share of any potential income derived from it, thus obstructing its release.

The disc is a valuable piece of musical history. Its tattered adhesive label, typed with an old manual machine, shows the recording was made at Harry Smith Studios, "electrically recorded" for bandleader Frank Mane. Marked "#1 Orig.," it is the very first known studio recording of the thousand and more that were to make that skinny young man the most celebrated popular singer in history. For, under "Vocal chor. by," it bears the immaculately handwritten legend:

Frank Sinatra

A year after making that first record, at twenty-five, Sinatra told a new acquaintance how he saw his future. "I'm going to be the best singer in the world," he said, "the best singer that ever was."

2

A Family from Sicily

"IO SONO SICILIANO . . ." I am Sicilian.

At the age of seventy-one, in the broiling heat of summer in 1987, Frank Sinatra was singing, not so well by that time, in the land of his fathers. "I want to say," he told a rapt audience at Palermo's Favorita Stadium, "that I love you dearly for coming tonight. I haven't been in Italy for a long time—I'm so thrilled. I'm very happy."

The crowd roared approval, especially when he said he was Sicilian, that his father was born in Sicily. Sinatra's voice cracked a little as he spoke, and he looked more reflective than happy. At another concert, in the northern Italian city of Genoa, he had a joke for his audience. "Two very important and wonderful people came from Genoa," he quipped. "One . . . **Uno: Christopher Columbus. Due: mia Mamma . . .**"

This second crowd cheered, too, though a little less enthusiastically when he mentioned that his father was Sicilian. "I don't think," he said wryly, "that they're too thrilled about Sicilia." It was a nod to northern Italians' feelings about the island off the southernmost tip of the country. They look down on its people as backward and slothful, and because, as all the world knows, it is synonymous with organized crime. It is the island of fire and paradox, the dismembered foot of the leg of Italy. Sicily: at ten thousand square miles the largest island in the Mediterranean, a cornucopia of history that remains more remote and mysterious than anywhere in Europe.

The island's story has been a saga of violence. Its ground heaved to earthquakes, and its volcanoes spat fire and lava, long before Christ. Its population carries the genes of Greeks and Romans, of Germanic Vandals and Arabs, of Normans and Spaniards, all of them invaders who wrote Sicily's history in blood.

"Sicily is ungovernable," Luigi Barzini wrote. "The inhabitants long ago learned to distrust and neutralize all written laws." Crime was endemic, so alarmingly so that a hundred years ago the island's crime rate was said to be the worst in Europe. By then, the outside world had already heard the spectral name that has become inseparable from that of the island—Mafia.

The origin of that word is as much a mystery as

the criminal brotherhood itself, but in Sicily "mafia" has one meaning and "Mafia"—with an upper case "M"—another. For the islanders, in Barzini's view, the word "mafia" was originally used to refer to "a state of mind, a philosophy of life, a concept of society, a moral code." At its heart is marriage and the family, with strict parameters. Marriage is for life, divorce unacceptable and impossible.

A man with possessions or special skills was deemed to have authority, and known as a **padrone.** In "mafia" with a small "m," those who lived by the code and wielded power in the community were **uomini rispettati,** men of respect. They were supposed to behave chivalrously, to be good family men, and their word was their bond. They set an example, and they expected to be obeyed.

The corruption of the code and the descent to criminality was rapid. Well before the dawn of the twentieth century, the Mafia with a capital "M," though never exactly an organization, was levying tribute from farmers, controlling the minimal water supply, the builders and the businessmen, fixing prices and contracts.

Cooperation was enforced brutally. Those who spoke out in protest were killed, whatever their station in life. The Mafia made a mockery of the state, rigging elections, corrupting the politicians it favored, and terrorizing opponents. From 1860 to 1924, not a single politician from Sicily was elected to the Italian parliament without Mafia approval. The island and its people, as one early visitor wrote, were "not a dish for the timid."

Frank Sinatra's paternal grandfather grew up in Sicily in the years that followed the end of foreign rule, a time of social and political mayhem. His childhood and early adult years coincided with the collapse of civil authority, brutally suppressed uprisings, and the rise of the Mafia to fill the power vacuum.

Beyond that, very little has been known about the Sinatra family's background in Sicily. The grandfather's obituary, which appeared in the **New York Times** because of his famous grandson, merely had him born "in Italy" in 1884 (though his American death certificate indicates he was born much earlier, in 1866). Twice, in 1964 and in 1987, Frank Sinatra told audiences that his family had come from Catania, about as far east as one can go in Sicily. Yet he told one of his musicians, principal violist Ann Barak, that they came from Agrigento on the southwestern side of the island. His daughter Nancy, who consulted her father extensively while working on her two books about his life, wrote that her great-grandfather had been "born and brought up" in Agrigento. His name, according to her, was John.

In fact he came from neither Catania nor Agrigento, was born earlier than either of the dates previously reported, and his true name was Francesco—in the American rendering, Frank.

SICILIAN BAPTISMAL and marriage records, United States immigration and census data, and interviews with surviving grandchildren establish that Francesco Sinatra was born in 1857 in the town of Lercara Friddi, in the hills of northwest Sicily. It had about ten thousand inhabitants and it was a place of some importance, referred to by some as **piccolo Palermo,** little Palermo.

The reason was sulfur, an essential commodity in the paper and pharmaceutical industries, in which Sicily was rich and Lercara especially so. Foreign companies reaped the profits, however, and most locals languished in poverty. The town was located, in the words of a prominent Italian editor, in "the core territory of the Mafia." The town lies fifteen miles from Corleone, a name made famous by **The Godfather** and in real life a community credited with breeding more future American mafiosi than any other place in Sicily. It is just twelve miles from the Mafia stronghold of Prizzi—as in **Prizzi's Honor,** the Richard Condon novel about the mob and the film based on it that starred Jack Nicholson.

It was Lercara Friddi, however, that produced the most notorious mafioso of the twentieth century. Francesco Sinatra's hometown spawned

Lucky Luciano. Luciano was "without doubt the most important Italian-American gangster," according to one authority, and "head of the Italian underworld throughout the land," according to a longtime head of the Chicago Crime Commission. One of his own lawyers described him as having been, quite simply, "the founder of the modern Mafia."

Luciano, whose real name was Salvatore Lucania, was born in Lercara Friddi in 1897. Old marriage and baptismal registers show that his parents and Francesco Sinatra and his bride, Rosa Saglimbeni, were married at the church of Santa Maria della Neve within two years of each other. Luciano was baptized there, in the same font as Francesco's first two children.

In all the years of speculation about Frank Sinatra's Mafia links, this coincidence of origin has remained unknown. Other new information makes it very likely that the Sinatras and the Lucanias knew each other. The two families lived on the same short street, the Via Margherita di Savoia, at roughly the same time. Luciano's address book, seized by law enforcement authorities on his death in 1962 and available today in the files of the Federal Bureau of Narcotics, contains only two entries for individuals who lived in Lercara Friddi: one a member of his own family and the other a man named Saglimbeni, a relative of the woman Francesco Sinatra married. Even if the Sinatras and the Lucanias did not know each other, Luciano's later notoriety makes it certain that the Sinatra family eventually learned that they and the gangster shared the same town of origin. Kinship and origins are important in Italian-American culture, and were even more so in the first decades of the diaspora.

As a boy, Frank Sinatra could have learned from any of several older relatives that his people and Luciano came from the same Sicilian town. He certainly should have learned it from Francesco, who lived with Sinatra's family after his wife's death and often minded his grandson when the boy's parents were out.

Francesco, moreover, survived to the age of ninety-one, until long after Luciano had become an infamous household name and Frank Sinatra an internationally famous singer. Sinatra himself indicated, and a close contemporary confirmed, that he and his grandfather were "very close." Late in life, he said he had gone out of his way to "check back" on his Sicilian ties. And yet, as we have seen, he muddied the historical waters by suggesting that his forebears came from Sicilian towns far from Lercara Friddi.

That the Sinatra family came from the same town as a top mafioso was not in itself a cause for embarrassment. The reason for the obfuscation, though, may be found in the family involvement with bootlegging in Frank Sinatra's childhood and, above all, in his own longtime relationship with Luciano himself, the extent of which can now be documented for the first time.

THERE WAS ONLY ONE SCHOOL in Lercara Friddi, and few people there could read or write. Francesco Sinatra was no exception, but he did have a trade—he was a shoemaker. He married Rosa, a local woman his own age, when both were in their early twenties, and by the time they turned thirty, in 1887, the couple had two sons. As the century neared its close, thousands of Sicilians were going hungry, especially in the countryside. There were food riots, and crime was rampant.

In western Sicily, the Mafia's power had become absolute. Palermo, the island's capital, spawned the first **capo di tutti capi**, Don Vito, who would one day forge the first links between the Sicilian Mafia and the United States. His successor, Don Carlo, operated from a village just fourteen miles from Lercara Friddi. Some of the most notorious American mob bosses—Tony Accardo, Carlo Gambino, Sam Giancana, Santo Trafficante—were, like Luciano, of western Sicilian parentage.

By 1889 Francesco and Rosa had moved to a working-class suburb of Palermo. Two more sons were born there, but died in infancy, possibly victims of the cholera epidemic that ravaged the neighborhood in the early 1890s. One and a half million Sicilians were to leave the island in the next twenty-five years, many going to Argentina and Brazil and, increasingly, to the United States.

Francesco Sinatra joined the exodus in the summer of 1900. At the age of forty-three, he said goodbye to Rosa and their surviving children—there were by now three sons and two daughters—and boarded a ship for Naples. There he transferred to the British steamer **Spartan Prince,** carrying a steerage ticket to New York. At Ellis Island, on July 6, he told immigration officials he planned to stay with a relative living on Old Broadway in Manhattan. He had $30 in his pocket.

Francesco found work, and soon had enough confidence to start sending for his family. His eldest son, Isidor, joined him in America, and Salvatore, just fifteen and declaring himself a shoemaker like his father, arrived in 1902. Rosa arrived at Christmas the following year, accompanied by Antonino, age nine, and their two daughters, Angelina and Dorotea, who were younger. Antonino—Anthony Martin or Marty, as he would become in America—was to father the greatest popular singer of the century.

The Statue of Liberty smiled, Frank Sinatra would say in an emotional moment forty years later, when his father "took his first step on Liberty's soil." For many Italian newcomers, however, the smile proved illusory.

IN FRANCESCO'S DAY, Italian immigrants were greeted with widespread hostility. They were at the bottom of the heap in New York, ostracized by those who had arrived before them, by the Germans and the Irish especially. Italians were said to be dirty, ignorant, and criminal, and were vilified as "wops," "dagos," "guineas." Early in the twentieth century, when blacks were being lynched in the South, some Americans considered Italians—immigrants from southern Italy and Sicily especially—"not even white." The Ku Klux Klan railed against them. They found themselves excluded from churches used by other ethnic groups, consigned to menial work, and persecuted by the police.

The accusation of criminality had some basis in fact. Mafia fugitives from Sicily had by then been active in the United States for some years. Palermo's mob chieftain Don Vito, describing himself to immigration officials as "a dealer," arrived from Europe the year after Francesco and during a two-year stay laid the foundation of what would eventually become the American Mafia.

To oppressed Sicilian immigrants, Vito and his kind were the **uomini rispettati** who had ruled the roost back home. They offered protection, loaned money, made many things possible—at a price. They extorted money from shopkeepers and workmen, and those who did not cooperate got hurt. To some immigrants, joining the ranks of the criminals was more attractive than legitimate work. "I realized Italians were considered dirt, the scum of the earth," recalled "Jimmy Blue Eyes" Alo, the son of a Calabrian tailor who was to become a senior American mafioso. "I quit . . . went the other way."

Lucky Luciano, who arrived in America from Lercara Friddi several years after the Sinatras, made the same choice. "We was surrounded by crooks," he recalled of his childhood years on Manhattan's Lower East Side, "and plenty of them were guys who were supposed to be legit. . . . All of them was stealin' from somebody. And we had the real pros, the rich Dons from the old country, with their big black cars and mustaches to match. . . . The only thing is, we knew they was rich, and rich was what counted."

Francesco, for his part, struggled. Many Italians were cobblers, apparently too many, for he found work as a boilermaker. He later landed a job at the American Pencil Company that paid $11 a week (about $200 today), and stayed with the company for seventeen years. Rosa, like Francesco already well into her forties, raised their children and eventually opened a small grocery. By that time, the couple had long since left New York City for the town now inseparably linked with the name Sinatra—Hoboken.

In the nineteenth century the town had been a resort for opulent New Yorkers like the Vanderbilts and the Astors. By the time the Sinatras arrived, however, it had become a grubby industrial town of sixty thousand people. Its waterfront, on the Hudson River, served oceangoing ships and backed onto a jumble of factories and railroad yards. The Irish ran the city, held the plum jobs, occupied the best housing. Italian newcomers, crammed into a few mean streets to the west, made the best of it in tenements.

The Italians stayed in their own territory, in part because they were unwelcome elsewhere and in part because it suited them. In the town's Little Italy they had the comfort of their own church and their own customs and rules, rules enforced by their own criminal protectors. Sicilians, especially, tended to gravitate to streets settled by earlier arrivals from their hometowns and villages. Close relatives often lived on the same block or even in the same building.

Hoboken was a tough town, and Italians straying into Irish territory after dark invited violent attack. Many men in the Italian section owned firearms, mostly antiquated handguns, and in 1909 some of them fought a battle against the Irish-dominated police force. The police, summoned to the scene of a fracas on Monroe

Street—an Italian child had been killed in an accident involving other Italians—came under heavy fire. "Excited Italians armed with revolvers," the **New York Times** reported, "were lurking behind windows and doors taking pot shots at the police. . . . A hundred or more shots were fired, and at a late hour last night quiet had not been entirely restored."

Francesco and Rosa raised their five children in Hoboken through a decade and more of freezing winters and sweltering summers. They had no central heating and, of course, no air-conditioning. Isidor worked with his parents in their grocery. Salvatore became a baker. Marty, who dropped out of school when he was ten or eleven, could neither read nor write nor speak much English. He turned fifteen the month of the Italian immigrants' battle with the police.

Marty was a small fellow, "the size of a mushroom," one acquaintance said. He soon had a prematurely receding hairline and, perhaps to compensate for his lack of stature, sported multiple tattoos. He was dogged by chronic asthma. Relatives recalled him as having been a gentle character, most of the time, but he was prone to long brooding silences and had an explosive temper. He also liked to drink.

Following in the steps of his father and his brother Salvatore, Marty started out as an apprentice shoemaker. For years, though, he had no steady job. At one point, when he was listing his occupation as "chauffeur," he was involved in a fatal accident. After running over and killing a five-year-old child on Newark Street, near the docks, Marty simply drove away. Tried for manslaughter, he told the court he had been "unnerved" and lost his head, and was acquitted. He also got into trouble for receiving stolen goods.

For a while he fought professionally, as a bantamweight. He called himself Marty O'Brien in the ring, after his sponsor, an Irishman from Philadelphia. Italian boxers often used Irish names to make themselves acceptable to a wider public. It was probably through a fellow prizefighter, Dominick "Champ" Garaventa, that he met the woman who was to become Frank Sinatra's mother.

Dolly Garaventa, one of Dominick's eight siblings, was also an immigrant—from northern Italy. Her father, a peasant from Rossi, a hamlet near Genoa, had brought his wife and children to the United States before the turn of the century. If he had high hopes for his sons, however, he was sorely disappointed.

Dominick was involved in bootlegging, and got arrested after a shooting incident involving his brother Lawrence. Lawrence, known as "Babe" because he was the youngest of the brood, turned out to be the worst of the lot. Also a boxer, he was arrested more than twenty times, convicted of loan-sharking and pulled in for bootlegging offenses and for two armed holdups that resulted in murder. Another brother, Gustavo, was arrested several times for running numbers.

Dolly, more properly Natalina, or Natalie, Garaventa, had been born the day after Christmas in 1896. She had blue eyes and light skin and, as a young woman, strawberry blond hair. Though tiny, she was formidable even as a teenager. Women were not allowed to attend fights, but Dolly dressed as a boy to see Marty Sinatra box. She talked tough—her foul mouth became legendary—and nonstop. She never forgot or forgave a perceived offense. She was literate, spoke fluent English, and could get by in several Italian dialects. She was a good organizer, and at some point trained as a nurse. She could also sing, a talent inherited from her father. She sang popular songs and operatic arias at weddings and family affairs, and at Hoboken's Clam Broth House—while standing on a table.

Marty Sinatra met Dolly in 1912 when he was eighteen and she sixteen. He could sing, too, and serenaded her with a sentimental ditty called "You Remind Me of the Girl Who Used to Go to School with Me." Dolly was brainier, bossy, and domineering, but love flowered. Defying opposition from her parents, she and Marty ran away—all of two miles—to Jersey City, where they were married at city hall on Valentine's Day 1913. Afterward, they returned home, made up with their families, and later married again in church.

They rented an apartment at 415 Monroe Street, on the block where four years earlier their fellow Italians had fought with the police. Salvatore Sinatra—he now called himself Charlie—and his wife moved in across the hall. Publicists would one day describe the building as having been a slum tenement. In fact it was a modern wood frame structure, four stories over a cellar, divided into eight apartments. There was no hot water and two families shared the single toilet on each floor, but in those days that was nothing out of the ordinary. Each family had three rooms, plus a kitchen with a stove. Dolly's brother Dominick remembered it as "a pretty good, lower-middle-class neighborhood."

WHILE DOLLY AND MARTY found each other, tied the knot, and set up house, the world had gone on turning. The **Titanic** was sunk by the iceberg. Woodrow Wilson was installed as president, avoiding as best he could a demonstration in Washington by women demanding the right to vote. A French aviator flew over the Mediterranean past Sicily, taking his airplane farther over water than any man before him. The Panama Canal opened, joining the Atlantic to the Pacific.

Henry Ford established a "moving assembly line" to build automobiles. Einstein refined his Theory of Relativity. Europe was engulfed by war, though for the time being the United States was staying out of it.

There was something else. Wind-up Victrolas—phonographs—were now on the market and easily available. For the first time, Americans could listen to music on rapidly spinning discs called records.

These seismic tremors impinged little on the newlyweds, though Dolly, who would one day immerse herself in local politics, may have cheered for the suffragettes protesting in the capital. For the time being, though, she was preoccupied, and so was Marty. Brides, especially brides with Sicilian husbands, were supposed to get pregnant.

3

The Only Child

"We were married for a long time," Dolly was to recall, "and we didn't think we were going to have any babies." Then in early 1915, after a wait of two years, she did become pregnant. She hoped for a girl.

The pains came in the second week of December. Midwives plodded through snow-covered streets to reach the Sinatra apartment, then summoned a doctor. Sprawled on the kitchen table, Dolly was in trouble. She was less than five feet tall and weighed just ninety pounds, and the baby was enormous. She was in agony.

Other women crowded around, shouting advice. There was Dolly's mother, Rosa, her sister Josie, and a neighbor from across the street. The labor was not progressing and the patient was becoming feeble. Fearing for Dolly's life, the doctor opted for forceps. The baby was literally torn from the birth canal, bleeding at the head and neck. It was not the girl Dolly had hoped for but a boy weighing thirteen and a half pounds, and he appeared to be dead.

"I don't think he'll live," Josie remembered the doctor muttering. "Let's take care of the mother." Then one of the women—Dolly's mother is usually given the credit—thought to hold the huge infant under the cold-water tap. He spluttered, was tapped on the back with the palm of a hand, and began to squall.

The trauma left Dolly unable to bear more children. The child's left earlobe, cheek, and part of his neck, torn by the doctor's forceps, would be scarred for the rest of his life. As an adult he would use makeup on occasion to cover the damage. A perforated eardrum, discovered far in the future, may also have been a result of the birth.

The grown man would talk publicly of his gratitude at having been revived. Privately, he had trouble accepting what he learned about the circumstances of his birth. At age eleven, he reportedly tried to attack the doctor who had delivered him. As an adult, he would astonish one of his lovers with an irrational outburst of resentment. "They weren't thinking about me," he said bitterly, "they were just thinking about my mother. They just kind of ripped me out and tossed me aside."

The birth certificate, registered with the state of

New Jersey on December 17, 1915, gave the newborn's name as "Frank Sinestro." "Sinestro" was a clerk's mistake, but the "Frank" made sense. It is the Italian custom to name a firstborn child after a paternal grandparent, in this case Francesco. A quarter of a century later, when the grown child had become a celebrity, the name would be reregistered as "Francis A. Sinatra." The "A.," the world was told, stood for "Albert."

"God loves you," family elders told the boy; "he saved you for something. You're meant to be somebody."

A baby photograph of Frank Sinatra, taken in his birthday suit against a painted backdrop of a rural scene, shows a plump child. "It wasn't until he was four or five that he got to be real skinny," recalled his aunt Josie. A tinted print that has been published shows him swaddled against the cold in his mother's arms, a cap hiding the scarred left side of his head. Nineteen-year-old Dolly looks as though she is finding it hard to smile, and Frank—Frankie, as he would be called until early adulthood—appears to be looking at her doubtfully.

That old family snapshot now seems symbolic of the childhood that followed. Dolly had a strange concept of motherhood, and Frank had all the problems of an only child and more. Having hoped for a girl, she had bought pink baby clothes, and that is what he wore. "I didn't care," she recalled. Later, she got her mother to make him Little Lord Fauntleroy suits. Frank played with dolls and was "a little bit of a sissy" far longer than is usual, according to a childhood acquaintance.

Staying at home with the baby was never a priority for Dolly. Frank spent most of his infancy being minded either by his grandfather Francesco or by his maternal grandmother. In 1917, when the United States entered World War I, Marty was exempted from the draft as a man with a dependent family. Dolly, however, volunteered for overseas service as a nurse. When her offer was not accepted, she went to work as a chocolate dipper in a candy store.

Dolly's sights were set higher than that. She became a midwife and plunged into local politics, both activities that made her a controversial figure. In 1919, in the final months of the campaign for women's suffrage, she was one of a number of women who chained themselves to the railings at Hoboken city hall. After the suffrage struggle was won, still in her twenties, she became a Democratic ward leader. "I was asked to run because I spoke all the dialects," she recalled.

When the Irish city bosses started to solicit Italian immigrant votes, they needed someone with influence in the neighborhood. Dolly won that influence by getting people jobs, securing welfare checks for the needy, giving advice on health problems, getting bags of coal distributed in the winter. "She was like a godmother," said Anthony Petrozelli, who grew up on Monroe Street. "They respected her. She was strong, and she didn't give a damn about nothing."

The politicians Dolly worked for ruled Hoboken and Jersey City for thirty years, a period infamous for corruption and thuggery. She was close to two mayors of the period, both notorious characters, and spent her spare time, in the words of her granddaughter Tina, "buying votes for the local Democratic machine."

Dolly wanted to get her husband into politics, too, but, as her niece Rose Paldino put it, "Marty wasn't smart enough." At home, he would tease his wife by pretending to favor the Republicans, and she would retaliate by refusing to cook. Frank was soon pressed into carrying placards for the Democrats. He grew up supporting the Democrats and would continue to do so until he was in his fifties.

Women in the Italian neighborhood knew about Dolly because of the entry in the city directory that read, in bold print: "DELLA SINATRA, Maternity Nurse and Midwife—Phone Hoboken 985." Writing about the family years later, Kitty Kelley made much of the fact that Sinatra's mother performed abortions, at a time when the procedure was an illegal, shameful affair. Dolly was arrested several times for performing abortions and convicted twice. Some knew her as "Hatpin Dolly," and her reputation would one day cause her son to be barred from performing in a local Catholic church.

Others were less condemnatory. "If someone got themselves pregnant by mistake it was a big disgrace," Petrozelli said, "so their mother called Dolly and begged her: 'Please, before my husband finds out, you've got to do something.' She did. No money involved, she just did it out of her own heart." Sinatra's mother delivered more babies than she performed abortions, others maintained, and sometimes did not charge for her services.

While Dolly worked and wheeled and dealed she continued to farm Frank out to relatives and neighbors. When not with Francesco or Dolly's mother, or one of her sisters, he might be with an old Jewish lady, Mrs. Golden, or a teenage baby-sitter, Rose Carrier. Rose took Frank to the movies, still silent then. Mrs. Golden fed him coffee cake and apples, and gave him an inscribed Jewish charm that he came to treasure. One day, in her memory, he would pledge to buy a quarter of a million dollars' worth of Israel bonds. Frank picked up more Yiddish from Mrs. Golden, it seems, than he did Italian from close relatives. He had some understanding of Italian, but never learned to speak it well.

Dolly tried to make up for her absences by showering her son with toys, more bikes than he needed, and holidays in the Catskills every summer. She dressed Frank in clothes so smart that his appearance became something of a local legend. "She would have had me wear velvet pants, I think," he said, looking back, "except that in that neighborhood I would have gotten killed." As he grew older and Dolly a little richer, Frank even had his own charge account at Geismar's, the local department store.

Clothes and toys, of course, were no substitute for affection. "Aunt Dolly was always busy," recalled one of the cousins, John Tredy. "I think Frankie was always underfoot a bit. He was always alone." Relatives and neighbors remembered a solitary figure, sitting forlornly on his tricycle on the sidewalk, hanging around outside his grandmother's front door.

When Dolly was at home, Marty and Frank could not relax. She whisked away her husband's ashtray every couple of minutes. She washed her son, in cold water with a scrub brush, far more than was necessary. Even as a grown man and a heavy smoker, Sinatra himself could not stand to see an ashtray filled with butts. He was forever washing his hands, a habit that fellow musicians mocked as his "Lady Macbeth bit," and was, a friend said, "a fanatic about his nails." The paper money in his pocket had to be in clean, brand-new bills. "I can't stand bureau drawers slightly open, knives and forks out of line, books in untidy heaps," Sinatra would say at the age of thirty. In restaurants, the glasses in front of him always had to be lined up just so.

Dolly had no patience with childhood fears. "We were on the beach," Frank remembered. "The waves leaping high terrified me. I kept crying: 'No! No!' but my mother laughed. I can still feel the cold fright that choked me when she ducked me under the water."

Dolly "always expected more of him," Frank's first wife, Nancy, would say, "it was never enough. . . . It was difficult to please her." When Frank failed to please, the punishments were severe—he was beaten, as he himself confirmed. Once, when he stood up on a horse at a merry-go-round, he got his head caught in the roof structure and was extracted only with difficulty. Far from being sympathetic, he recalled, "Dad took it out of my hide."

It was his mother, though, whose beatings he feared. The once petite Dolly had grown stout and intimidating, and her punishments were fearsome and sometimes unfair. She once punished him, according to family lore, for falling down stairs. As her granddaughter Tina heard it, it was a blow from Dolly that made Frank fall in the first place, and he was knocked unconscious. Dolly then fussed around her son for days afterward, "like a chastened mother hen."

"She used to beat Frankie up a lot," recalled

Rose, the niece who lived across the hall. "He used to run into my mother's apartment and go under the table and cry—she had those long tablecloths that touched the floor—so he could hide. He'd say: 'Lala Nanina'—that was my mother's nick-name, sort of like 'Little Auntie'—'she's got a baseball bat, she's gonna kill me.' "

It was sometimes difficult to distinguish between Dolly's rage and her affection. She would "give me a rap with that little club," Frank remembered, "then she'd hug me to her breast. . . . When she came close, I never knew whether I was going to get hugged or hit."

Dolly inspired a mix of obedience and resent-ment in her only child until well into his middle age. "Yes, mama. No, mama," people would hear him saying into the telephone. And wearily, when she was still ordering him around as late as the 1970s, he was heard to say, "Okay, mom, if you think so, mom."

The singer Peggy Connelly, one of Sinatra's lovers, remembered him "avoiding his mother like the plague. She was a pain in the neck and he found her embarrassing." "She was a pisser," Frank told the actress Shirley MacLaine after Dolly's death, "but she scared the shit outta me. Never knew what she'd hate that I'd do." All the same, he would be devastated by her passing.

Frank's upbringing fits a familiar pattern. Par-ents who cannot have more children classically spoil the child they have, exaggerate the importance of the child's mistakes, demand perfection. Only children, studies show, may turn out overaggressive, socially inept, and less successful in sustaining relationships. Or, with careful parenting and good luck, they may turn out just fine. Frank Sinatra, however, was not only prone to the problems of an only child. He grew up surrounded by lawbreakers in a time of lawlessness.

WORLD WAR I CHANGED both Hoboken and the lives of the Sinatra family. Troopships replaced passenger liners on the waterfront. "Heaven, Hell, or Hoboken by Christmas!" became the catchphrase of the million or more soldiers who embarked for Europe. In 1917, three years before Prohibition became law nationwide, the town's many bars were ordered to close in the interests of military propriety. A vain hope.

Hoboken became an entry point for shipments of foreign liquor, and bars sprang up everywhere. With the local administration failing to enforce the law, there would soon be 250 of them in the little town's square mile.

Marty and Dolly ran one such tavern. Using money borrowed from Dolly's mother, they opened a "bar and grill" on the corner of Fourth Street and Jefferson. They called it Marty O'Brien's—using the name Marty employed in the ring—which made good commercial sense in Irish-dominated Hoboken. As an Italian touch, they served pasta and sandwiches along with the booze.

A little of what went on at the bar has become family lore: Dolly helping to bounce drunks, wielding a billy club she kept behind the bar; Marty taking macabre revenge on a fellow saloon-keeper who tried to settle a $200 cash debt by delivering a horse. When Marty saw that the beast was on its last legs, he walked it to the door of the other man's bar one night and shot it dead. The carcass was found the following morning, blocking the doorway. Marty was "a quiet, gentle guy until you backed him into a corner," said a friend, "then he became the street guy that he was."

There was another, much more serious, side to the bar business. The Sinatras needed liquor and they needed protection, services only gangsters could supply. Prohibition meant a bonanza for the Italian and Jewish mobsters who would eventually join forces and control organized crime in America. The first big-name mobsters were now making fortunes and fighting bloody battles for territory: Meyer Lansky, Bugsy Siegel, Joe Adonis, Johnny Torrio, Longy Zwillman, Willie Moretti, Waxey Gordon, Dutch Schultz, Frank Costello—and Lucky Luciano.

Prohibition was "a whole new ball game," Costello recalled, "and we owned the ball." The gangsters were exceptionally active in New Jersey. The Hoboken docks were a key transit point for booze shipments, and Marty Sinatra was one local Italian who got involved. "He aided in bootlegging," his son would admit years later. "His job was to follow the trucks with the booze so they weren't hijacked. . . . I remember in the middle of the night—I was only three or four years old—I heard sobs, terrible crying and wailing. I think my old man was a little slow and he got hit on the head. And he came home and he was bleeding all over the kitchen. My mother was hysterical."

Frank admitted that his father's bootlegging activity was on behalf of "one of the tough guys" of the day. He did not say which tough guy, but in 1995 his daughter Nancy—in one of the books she wrote with her father's help—said her grandparents had been obliged to "rub elbows" with major criminals. One of them, she specified, was the bootlegger Waxey Gordon, who did business with Luciano. According to the writer Pete Hamill, who had rare access to Frank many years later, the story in Hoboken was that Gordon had been "a regular" at the Sinatras' bar.

Young Frank spent a good deal of time in the bar during Prohibition—he often did his homework there in the evenings. His parents' customers were among the first ever to hear him sing. "There was a player piano in the joint," he recalled, "a nickelodeon—put a nickel in, and the roller would play. I was about eleven years old or so. . . . Some of the guys would put me up on the piano, and I would sing along with the piano, and they'd give me a dime. . . . I had a voice like a siren—way up there. And I remember the song was called 'Honest and Truly.' " "Honest and truly," the little boy sang, "I'm in love with you. . . ." As a grown man he would say he remembered thinking, even then, "What a great racket this is!"

Dolly was close to her brothers Dominick and Lawrence, both of whom got into serious trouble during Prohibition. Lawrence's criminal record began with an arrest for selling liquor to soldiers. By 1921, when he was twenty and out on bail facing charges of murdering an American Express driver, he was wanted by police in connection with two New Jersey holdups and another murder. In 1922, he was arrested after yet another holdup in which a policeman was shot dead. Before dying, the policeman named as his killer a prominent associate of Waxey Gordon.

When Lawrence stood trial in the American Express case, Dolly appeared in court masquerading as his wife, carrying a baby borrowed for the occasion and sobbing. When he received a long jail sentence, she loudly denounced the judge as "an S.O.B. bastard." She visited Lawrence in prison regularly, then took him into her home when he was released. He lived with the Sinatras for several years, and Frank adored him.

Lawrence was arrested yet again in 1931, as was his brother Dominick, following a shootout in the street. In the aftermath, police cordoned off part of Hoboken in search of a car registered in the name Marty Sinatra used, O'Brien. Lawrence abandoned his own car, with a bullet hole in the windshield, on Madison Street two doors away from the home of his and Dolly's sister Josie Monaco. Frank had seen a lot of his aunt Josie, for her house backed onto the Sinatras' first apartment. Her father-in-law, who also lived on Madison, had been a defendant in a liquor violations case, and a gangster was gunned down outside Josie's house during fighting between rival bootleggers.

Lawrence, like Frank's father, was involved with a powerful bootlegger. "He was a hijacker with Dutch Schultz with the whiskey and stuff," Josie's son said, "and I think he got himself in a swindle by hijacking **from** Dutch Schultz." Schultz used Italians as hired guns and, like Waxey Gordon at one stage, did business with Lucky Luciano. As Tina Sinatra has said, "My dad grew up with gangsters next door. . . . They were his personal friends."

A family named Fischetti lived near the Sinatras on Monroe Street during Prohibition, and one of the Fischetti children was close to Frank. Members of the family, according to police sources, were truck operators involved in organized crime and in touch with the notorious Fischetti brothers associated both with Chicago's Al Capone and with Lucky Luciano. The brothers, Rocco, Charlie, and Joseph, lived in the New York area before relocating to the Midwest. They served Capone initially as bodyguards, but later rose high in his organization. The younger sibling, Joseph, Joe "Stingy," would eventually be categorized by the FBI as a "top hoodlum." He would specialize in the entertainment industry and become a close companion and associate of Frank Sinatra, whom he said he had known since they were "youngsters."

"Jimmy Blue Eyes" Alo, Meyer Lansky's right-hand man, kept a photograph of Marty and Dolly Sinatra on his coffee table as late as 2001. "I knew Frank Sinatra from when he was a kid," he said before his death. "He always wanted to be a gangster, this phony bastard."

BY THE TIME Frank turned twelve, in 1927, the Sinatras had accumulated enough money to move up in the world. They left Monroe Street and the Italian section and took a three-bedroom apartment in a German-Irish neighborhood. Marty, at thirty-three no longer fit enough to box or work on the docks, managed to get a job as a firefighter, work normally barred to Italians. It was Dolly who fixed that, reportedly by using her pull with the mayor himself. The joke in those days was that it took a bribe of $200 to get onto the police force and $300 to join the fire department—"because firemen get to sleep a lot."

The Sinatras kept Marty O'Brien's bar going, ensuring that they remained fairly well off when the Depression came. The family owned a radio—Americans had been enjoying that magical invention since 1920—and Frank got one of his own, a contraption that "looked like a small grand piano." It brought him what he would remember as the "blending saxophones and tightly knit brass" of the big bands, Guy Lombardo and Wayne King, the foot-stomping jazz of Louis Armstrong, the "serious" jazz of George Gershwin, the genius of Irving Berlin. And the crooners, too—the "tantalizing tonsils" of Rudy Vallee, "Prisoner of Love" Russ Columbo, and, solo on CBS as of 1931, a mellow Bing Crosby.

Marty's mother had died in 1925, her passing recalled long afterward because of the earth tremor that sent her coffin sliding across the room while relatives were viewing the body. His father, Francesco "Pops" Sinatra, lived on into the 1940s to be remembered fondly by Frank as a "sweet old gent with long curly mustachios" who offered exhortations in fractured English. "How are you going to grow up to be healthy man?" he would ask, as he cooked up a pot of spaghetti. "You gotta eat! Eat plenty! So your bones won't stick out!"

Frank and his young friends, said Lee Bartletta, who was always in and out of the house, were now "Pops's whole life."

Dolly continued to buy her son fancy clothes, which attracted the envy and mockery of other children. At ten he sported a fedora. At twelve he was photographed, outlandishly, in jodhpurs. By the time Frank went to high school he had more than a dozen sports jackets, and so many pairs of pants that friends called him "Slacksey." He sometimes gave clothes away, even bought clothing for poorer kids—and Dolly paid. He let others use his pass to the swimming pool and bought movie tickets for groups of pals. He was to be bountiful in that way all his life. "Frank doesn't know how to express friendship," the comedian Phil Silvers said thirty years later. "He does it with expensive gifts."

Astonishingly, when her son was fifteen, Dolly spent $35 to buy him a car—a secondhand Chrysler convertible. It made him "the prince of the neighborhood," recalled Nick Sevano, a younger Hoboken contemporary. Academically, however, he was no prince. At David E. Rue Junior High School, Frank had been in constant trouble. His report cards were bad, made worse by the fact that his cousin Sam across the hall brought home good ones. Frank got a certificate showing he had completed junior high, but that was his last graduation.

At Demarest High, he enraged his teachers. "A lazy boy," the math teacher called him years later, "absolutely no ambition at all." "No talent for anything," said the principal, and Frank's record card noted only his name, none of the usual information on his academic progress. "School was very uninteresting," he would say later. "Homework we never bothered with, and the few times we attended school we were rowdy." Frank frequently sneaked off with pals into New York City to visit the Hudson Burlesque House on 38th Street. After just over a year, depending on which source one accepts, he either dropped out of school or was expelled.

The expulsion, if that is what it was, was predictable. Frank had started with pranks, complicated ones that earned him another nickname, "Angles." He released pigeons in the school auditorium during assembly, caused a commotion by taking a cat into a movie theater and shooting it in the backside with a BB pistol, set off firecrackers under a manhole cover. In adult life, he would enjoy scaring people with cherry bombs.

Frank also did some petty stealing. He spoke later of a time when "a bunch of us decided to raid a fruit stand. We waited until it got pretty dark, then struck out across the street. When the old fruit man had his back turned we charged the stand with loud whoops. Then we grabbed anything we could lay our hands on." He told other stories—too numerous and too lurid to be entirely credible—of pocketing candy in stores, snatching change from cash registers, stealing bicycles. "All I knew," he said, "was tough kids on street corners, gang fights, and parents too busy trying to make enough money for food, rent, clothing. . . . The kids in the Irish, Negro, and Jewish neighborhoods ganged together . . . we found a release from our loneliness in vicious race wars."

The neighborhood wars of his childhood, Frank suggested, made him a lifelong champion of racial equality. While playing in undergrowth near the Hudson River, he said, he and friends once managed to eavesdrop on a Ku Klux Klan meeting. They ran home to tell their fathers, who rushed to attack the bigots with baseball bats. "I would hear the stories," he said, "things that happened because you were Italian. . . . I skirted some areas of town because the cry would go up: 'Kill the dago!' I heard the same kinds of things from my Jewish friends." Once, he recalled, "A big kid called me a wop. But a Jew kid and me creamed him."

Frank painted a lurid picture of "bitter, bloody block fights," of a childhood in which "everyone carried a twelve-inch pipe—and they weren't all studying to be plumbers." He bragged of his own pugnacity. "Sometimes with me it was a matter of if-you-got-the-name-you-might-as-well-have-the-game. You think I'm just some wop wise guy off the street? All right, I'll **be** a wop wise guy off the street and break your fucking head."

His boyhood buck teeth had been straightened, he said, not by the dentist but in a fistfight. A scar over his nose was the legacy of "a Coke bottle blow in a street fight," inflicted when he was nine. Another story suggested that it was a crack on the head with a bicycle chain that punctured his eardrum—not, as generally accepted, the forceps used to wrench him from the womb. "I was hit," he said, "more times than a fender in a parking lot."

His uncle Dominick witnessed one such encounter, after his nephew ran into another boy on his bike. "Pretty soon four or five kids were whacking the tar out of him. He just stood up to them and traded punches and never backed down. He had lots of fights as a kid, because he had a temper." With three onetime professional fighters in the family, Frank was taught early on how to use his fists.

His father, he recalled, "used to show me in the yard, you know, how to jab, how to throw a left hook, set your feet, that kind of thing. . . . I was five years old when I got my first pair of boxing gloves." In an era when heavyweights like Jack Dempsey and Gene Tunney stirred worldwide fervor, the young Sinatra became a lifelong enthusiast. "My favorite exercise is boxing," he told an early interviewer, and it was even reported that he had fought as a semipro in Hoboken clubs. He had publicity photographs taken showing him clad in trunks and wearing boxing gloves. In his early singing days, it would be said, he worked out backstage with gloves and a punching bag, or visited gyms to watch professional boxers sparring. He went on to share "ownership" of two heavyweights, Tami Mauriello and Chuck Crowell, as well as a welterweight, Ray Brown.

Fighting, temper, and braggadocio were to become lifelong characteristics that damaged Sinatra's reputation again and again. "Anybody hits you, call me!" he would scrawl at the bottom of a letter to songwriter Sammy Cahn. It was just a jocular postscript, but he was also prone to real, inexcusable violence.

Frank as a grown man would say that his "days of gang fights and petty thievery" led him to resent authority, especially in the shape of policemen. He described how one night "two big plainclothesmen" accosted him as he stood on a street corner and asked how he had come by his brand-new blue suit and black patent leather shoes. When he refused to answer, he said, the detectives "beat the stuffing out of me until I was a bleeding mess."

"Many of the kids I grew up with in Hoboken are serving time today," Sinatra told the columnist Lloyd Shearer. "A few even went to the chair." He told Anita Colby, then assistant to the movie producer David Selznick, "Everyone in my class either went to the electric chair or was hung." In another press interview, he said something less dramatic and more credible—that "some" of his old buddies landed in reform school and that just "one" went to jail.

Frank evidently invented much of his image as the abused wop with a violent childhood. "He was never picked on because of his heritage," said Nick Sevano. "When he was growing up he was known as the little thin rich boy, and people in our town, who were poor, would pick on him. . . . He got a little bored with it, and that's when he got into scraps." Frank's uncle Dominick said there were "no gang fights, just fighting, the way kids have always been fighting, and nobody ever really got hurt." If there was really a run-in with two policemen, Dominick never heard of it. As for boxing, said Dominick's son Buddy, Frank "never had a fight. He is excitable and he gets loaded and then thinks he can fight, but he couldn't knock your hat off with a ball bat." A major investigative article in **Look** magazine quoted a Hoboken resident as saying, "That stuff about him being a juvenile delinquent is a lot of baloney. He's just trying to make himself sound tough."

DOLLY HAD NOT BEEN GREATLY CONcerned when Frank's school career ended ignominiously in 1932. "Her way of thinking," her niece Rose remembered, "was that Italians didn't need an education to get a job." Marty was "terribly upset," however, and for good reason. Frank had shown himself adept at drawing—he liked to sketch bridges and tunnels—and his father had hoped he would become an engineer. The Stevens Institute of Technology is in Hoboken, and Frank had encouraged his parents in the notion that he would study there. Now their hopes were dashed.

"I didn't want to go to college," he recalled, but his father did want him to, as Sinatra put it, "in the worst way. He was a man who could never read or write his name and his big point was education." Marty had laid it on the line: "Do you want to get a regular job?"—"reggala" was the way he actually said it—"or do you wanna be a bum?"

"If I had the chance again," Sinatra was to say, "I would have been a little more patient about getting out into the world . . . seen to it that I had a more formal education." When his own boy came home with a high school diploma, the son remembered, he behaved as though "it was the greatest thing since cellophane. He thought I was Albert Einstein." The mature Sinatra would discover literature and history, collect works of art. "He craved to better himself, to learn," his actor friend Brad Dexter said. "He was hungry for knowledge."

In his mid-teens, though, Sinatra recalled feeling "that there was only one answer, to run away . . . more than once I hid out with an aunt for a week or two." When not running away, he went through the motions of getting a job. Because one of his few distinctions at school had been to win a model airplane competition, he tried out as a trainee technician at the Casey Jones School of Aeronautics in nearby Newark. When that did not work out, he enrolled briefly at Drake Business School.

An early Sinatra press spokesman would claim that Frank had been a sportswriter at the **Jersey Observer** newspaper. Not true. He had a menial job at the paper, obtained only thanks to Dolly's intervention with circulation manager Frank Garrick, who happened to be her son's godfather. "I remember Frank well," the city editor's widow said. "He worked at flinging bundles of newspapers onto the delivery trucks, but he was so frail that my husband gave him a job inside. He was an office boy."

Garrick later explained how the sportswriter myth started. The day after an actual sportswriter died in a car crash, he said, Frank "sat down at the dead boy's desk and acted as if he had the job." When someone inquired why Frank was there, he claimed falsely that it was on his godfather's instructions. Exposed and told he was to be let go, he threw a horrendous tantrum. "The filthy names he called me!" Garrick remembered. "Like he was going to kill me. . . . The words he used were hateful, awful. He called me every terrible name in the book and then he stormed out. He never said another word to me until fifty years later, after his mother died. She wrote me off, too."

Marty and Dolly went up another rung on the economic and social ladder in 1932, buying a sizable house close to the most desirable part of town. Dolly now had a backyard of her own, a bulldog and a turtle—and a son who was failing at everything. Frank, for his part, had had it with Hoboken, had had it with the limited world in which he had grown up.

"Be proud of your Italian lineage," his father is said to have told him. The son would eventually take that to heart, but that was in the future. He resented and rejected Marty's "old-fashioned ideas," the ideas of **la via vecchia,** the old European way. He wanted to explore the universe of new possibilities that he sensed was out there in America, if only he could reach it.

The Frank Sinatra who came out of Hoboken would be conflicted about his background. The day was not far off when, wishing to express contempt for men he despised, he would scornfully dismiss them as mere "shoemakers"—knowing well that his own grandfather and uncle had been cobblers. Far in the future, though, according to his friend Tony Oppedisano, he would express "an affinity for the working man, identify with people who break their back to keep a roof over the family's head."

Personally, though, the young Sinatra had no time for "those little town blues" he was to share with the world one day in the song "New York, New York." He wanted to leave behind Little Italy with its aging immigrants whose dreams had failed them, its old ladies in black clinging to the customs of a time gone by. The grown man would speak of Hoboken contemptuously, characterizing it as "a mudhole" and a "sewer." He told Pete Hamill he had "just wanted to get the hell out."

All through his childhood Frank had watched the trains coming and going at the Hoboken railroad terminus, had gotten into trouble for climbing up onto them, had badgered his mother to buy him a wind-up toy engine and a freight truck. In his days of wealth, he would install a train room at his home in California complete with a replica of the Hoboken railroad yards. The trains, the young Sinatra had seen, **went** somewhere, somewhere else.

So did the ferries, and the teenage Sinatra took the four-cent ride to Manhattan as often as possible. An evocative photograph, unearthed not long ago in a Hoboken basement, shows a gaunt teenage Sinatra sitting cross-legged on a Hoboken pier, staring out over the water. The figure in the picture looks solitary, but from the summer of 1931 the boy who would sing of loneliness was no longer entirely alone. There had been teenage flirtations before, a girl to show off at the junior high school dance, but this one would turn out to be special.

The girl was Nancy Barbato, just fourteen when they met. Frank's aunt Josie had a summer place near the ocean at Long Branch, an hour south of Hoboken, and he spent weekends there. Nancy's parents had a house across the street. "The first time I saw her," he remembered, "she was sitting on her porch steps manicuring her nails. When I whistled she slapped me down hard by ignoring me completely."

The rebuff was short-lived. Frank would wait for Nancy to complete her household chores, and they would head off for long strolls on the beach. "That summer was the beginning," he said. "I can still remember the way the moon shone on those little crimped wet rims on the sand where the waves had made a pattern, the salty smell of the sea when I'd leap down the wooden steps to meet her." By winter, he was walking through deep snow just to say hello and go home again.

Nancy was the fourth of seven children born to Michelangelo Barbato, a plasterer, and his wife, Giaraninna—Michael and Jenny in America. Her father was an Italian immigrant, her mother had been born in Hoboken. The Barbatos welcomed Frank to their home, and he enjoyed his visits greatly.

Nancy's household was very different from the one he had grown up in, without brothers and sisters, with his father's long, moody silences and his mother's interminable fussing. An evening at the Barbatos' was a cheerful, noisy affair, with the babble of children talking over each other around the table, Jenny Barbato presiding in the kitchen, and Verdi or Caruso on the Victrola.

There would be other girls in the seven years that were to pass before Frank married Nancy. Even so, she changed everything for him. "I was a poor, lonely and discouraged kid when I met her," he was to say. "In Nancy I found beauty, warmth and understanding. Being with her was my only escape from what seemed to me a grim world."

Nancy not only had faith in Frank as her beau. She also thought he could sing.

4

"I'm Going to Be a Singer"

FRANK SINATRA HIMSELF had trouble remembering how the singing began. "Sometimes I think I know," he said forty years later, "but then I shake my head and wonder. Am I remembering what really happened or what other people think happened? Who the hell knows, after a certain point?"

The idea of singing for a living, he thought, came to him when he was eleven, getting those nickels and dimes for singing in his parents' bar. Music was in his blood, for his was a musical family. Dolly sang at weddings and political meetings and sometimes picked up a guitar. A cousin who played the banjo sang with his own group. Ray Sinatra, a distant relative who had been acclaimed a child prodigy as a classical pianist, would eventually head his own band in Las Vegas.

By the time Frank sang in the family bar he was

a regular in the choir at St. Francis's church in Hoboken, and his treble tones were heard at summer picnics. He thought he first sang on his own in public "at some hotel in Elizabeth, New Jersey. Late twenties. I had a hairline down to here. I probably sang 'Am I Blue?' and I probably got paid a couple of packs of cigarettes and maybe a sandwich."

While living with the Sinatras, after getting out of jail, Frank's uncle Lawrence heard his nephew singing in the bathroom. He thought he would go far, but it was his uncle Dominick, who in 1931, when Frank was fifteen, gave him a ukulele. To the youngsters of the 1920s and 1930s, that four-stringed instrument was what the guitar was to be decades later. Those were the glory days of "Ukulele Ike" Cliff Edwards and "Wizard of Strings" Roy Smeck, and thousands of young imitators donned raccoon coats to plunk out tunes for their girls.

"He was the only kid in the neighborhood with a musical instrument," said his former baby-sitter Rose Carrier. "I remember very clearly how he used to sit on the curbstone under the lamppost on a summer night, strumming that uke and singing away. All the kids would be around him, fascinated by the idea that he was learning to play it."

Frank had his ukulele with him when he met Nancy Barbato, and he serenaded her with it. By fall, during the year he spent at Demarest High, he was confident enough to sing at halftime during a basketball game. "The cheers kept him singing," recalled referee Gerald Molloy. "The kids would not let him stop."

At New Year's 1933, when Dolly wanted to show off her new home, resplendent with baby grand and gold-painted telephone, she built Frank and his singing into the celebration. "A party was given at the home of Mr. and Mrs. M. Sinatra of upper Garden Street," noted an item on the society page of the local newspaper, "in honor of their son Frank. Vocal selections were given by Miss Marie Roemer and Miss Mary Scott, accompanied by Frank Sinatra."

Her seventeen-year-old could do something, Dolly seemed to be saying, even if he had been expelled from school and showed no sign of getting a steady job. He worked briefly as a riveter's laborer at the Teijent and Lang shipyards, as a loader for a book company, as a cleaner-fitter on ships laid up in dock. Nancy's father let him try his hand at plastering, but he was no good at that.

Music, it was now clear, was what mattered to Frank. Marian Brush, a girl with whom he was having a dalliance, suggested he get a group together to play at school dances. "In exchange for hiring the musicians," she said, "he'd get to sing a few numbers with the band. I'd take money at the door, and when we got enough we all went to the

Village Inn in New York so Frank could sing with the orchestra there. We'd go in and ask the manager beforehand to let Frankie sing. We said that's the only way we would come in, and he usually said yes."

Rehearsing at home was difficult, because Marty, who was irritated by his son's failure to hold down a job, allowed it only in the basement. Frank's aunt Josie, however, let the boys use a building on Madison Street, a former club that still boasted an old piano. Soon he was singing at social clubs—the Cat's Meow, the Comedy, Azovs—and for women's groups. Draped in the requisite raccoon coat and crooning into a megaphone like Rudy Vallee, he sang at parties. He sang for his mother at political meetings. "I performed anyplace," he recalled, "that people would listen to me." Told he was too young to perform at the local vaudeville theater, Fabian's Follies, he somehow managed to get on stage anyway. According to legend, he sang "Someday Our Names Will Be in Lights on Broadway."

Few, then, would have believed that. So badly was Frank's singing received at Cockeyed Henny's, a local poolroom, that he was unceremoniously ejected. Nor was he welcome when he tried to perform at a hall on Monroe Street. "Frankie would sneak in and try to sing, and they would throw him out," one of the owner's relatives recalled. A burly trombone player chased him off the stage at the Catholic Union in Newark's Little Italy when they could not make him stop singing.

Some were more encouraging. "People began to say: 'That's not bad!' " Sinatra remembered. "I wasn't sure. I didn't know at all." For a while, he said, he considered becoming "a monologist or a juggler." Then came a turning point. "A short time after Frank started going out with Nancy," said his aunt Josie, "he took her to see Bing Crosby. And after Crosby went off the stage Frank turned to Nancy and said: 'I'm going to be a singer.' When they got home that night he announced it, very seriously."

"Most people," Frank reportedly said of Crosby, "think he's just a crooner. But they're wrong. He's a troubadour. He tells a story in every song. . . . He makes you feel like he's singing just for you. I bet I could sing like that." "Someday," Nancy remembered him saying on the way home from the Crosby show, "that's gonna be me up there."

Family sources differ as to when and where Frank had this revelation, but it seems not to have been merely some publicist's invention. Sinatra recalled the moment. "From the time I first heard Bing on the radio," he said, "I thought he was in a class by himself. He was the greatest . . . the Will Rogers of song."

Radio, the most influential music vehicle of the day, played Crosby's hits constantly. "The Groaner" would soon eclipse Rudy Vallee, and Russ Columbo would die in a shooting accident. Crosby became the reigning crooner, entrancing audiences with "Million Dollar Baby" and "Just One More Chance," songs to which a generation made love.

Crosby was "the biggest thing in the country," Sinatra remembered. "On records. On the radio. In the movies. Everybody wanted to be Bing Crosby, including me. . . . Bing was my first singing idol." Musician and Hoboken contemporary John Marotta recalled seeing Frank "standing on street corners wearing a blazer, a sailing cap and smoking a pipe"—aping Bing Crosby.

"My father said that got him disliked by the kids, walking around like Bing," said another contemporary's son, James Petrozelli. Frank remained undeterred. The pipe, a Crosby trademark, can be seen jammed in the corner of his mouth in his first publicity photograph. Even in the first days of his own fame, years later, he would turn up for rehearsals sporting pipe and cap and a Crosby-style floral sports shirt.

Sinatra recalled thinking that Crosby "sang so easily it couldn't be very tough. . . . He was so relaxed, so casual. If he thought the words were getting too stupid or something, he just went buh-ba, buh-ba, booo. He even walked like it was no effort. . . . It was like Fred Astaire. Fred made you think you could dance, too. I don't mean just me. I mean millions and millions of people. Some people, they danced and sang right through the fucking Depression. Every time Bing sang, it was a duet, and you were the other singer."

Frank's determination to become a singer became evident at the very nadir of the Depression, when 13 million Americans were out of work. His parents despaired. Dolly found a picture of Crosby on the wall of Frank's room and "threw a shoe at me when I repeated my ambition." Marty thought him "obsessed," and lost patience.

"I remember the moment," Sinatra said. "We were having breakfast, and I was supposed to have gotten up that morning to go out and look for a job. . . . He said: 'Why don't you just get out of the house and go out on your own?' You know, 'Get out!' And I think the egg was stuck [in my throat] for about twenty minutes, and I couldn't swallow it or get rid of it. . . . We agreed it might be a good thing, and I packed up the small case that I had and I came to New York. My mother of course was nearly in tears. . . . He didn't speak to me for a year . . . one whole year."

Sinatra was seventeen when he left home, he said, which would date his departure to sometime in 1933. Two years would pass before he got a significant break, more than five before he really broke into the music business. "They call me an overnight success," he would say then. "Don't make me laugh!"

What followed is something of a lost period. It has proved impossible to identify any specific events between 1933 and the fall of 1935—surprising in an otherwise well-chronicled life. There are, however, a few clues. Dolly softened and gave Frank $65—a princely sum then—to buy a rudimentary sound system. It was a new device, much coveted by musicians, that gave him an entrée to aspiring bands. It was comprised of an amplifier, a speaker and, crucially, a microphone.

Up to that time, the only way singers could boost their voices had been by using a megaphone. Rudy Vallee used one and, a contemporary recalled, Frank had been toting one around "like it was part of his wardrobe." The megaphone brought humiliation. "Guys would throw pennies into it to see if they could get me to swallow them," he recalled. "Lots of fun." Bing Crosby, by contrast, had started using early-model microphones as soon as they became available in the late 1920s. Suddenly, performers with financial resources no longer had to project their voices. Some saw the microphone as a sort of deception. Not Sinatra.

"I discovered very early," he was to say, "that my instrument wasn't my voice. It was the microphone." One reporter in the early days wrote of Sinatra's hands "tightly gripping the microphone, as if to sustain a body too frail to stand alone." One night years later in Las Vegas, when he found his mike was dead, he simply dropped it on the floor and left the stage. He was not prepared to work without his secret weapon, because it made "speech-level singing" possible. It gave Sinatra intimacy with the audience.

Unlike many performers who have followed him, Sinatra sought to use the microphone "with great economy." "I usually try to have a black one," he said, "so that it will melt into my dinner-jacket and the audience isn't aware of it." With a microphone, he said, "you can sing as if you're singing in someone's ear, you can talk to a buddy at the bar, you can whisper sweet nothings to a woman."

This last, of course, above all. "To Sinatra," E. B. White thought, "a microphone is as real as a girl waiting to be kissed." Or as Gore Vidal put it: "Sinatra got the blood flowing. Bing Crosby put you to sleep."

In New York after his father sent him packing, though, there were more urgent priorities. He had a room to pay for, and he needed to eat. "I went around," he recalled, "singing with little groups. . . . Many's the time I worked all night for nothing. Or maybe I'd work for a sandwich and cigarettes—all night for three packets."

He had first come to the big city as a wide-eyed eleven-year-old, brought in by his parents to see the Christmas display at Macy's. More recently there had been sneak trips with school pals, to see the wonder of bare-breasted women at the burlesque houses. Now, at seventeen, he began hanging out at Roseland Ballroom to hear the big bands. Most important of all, he sampled the club scene.

A musicians' Shangri-la was coming into its own in New York at that very time on the Midtown block between Fifth and Sixth Avenues, remembered now as "Swing Alley," "The Street That Never Slept"—and as plain "52nd Street." The block was fast becoming the place to be for night people, actors, writers, and politicians, and the gossip columnists who fed on their activities. Above all, it was the home of jazz.

Bing Crosby had started as an obscure jazz singer, and jazz gave Sinatra his sense of rhythm and his lifelong readiness to improvise. Fifty-second Street was where the culture of Harlem met the white world, and Sinatra gave credit to more than a dozen black "jazzmen whose art helped to educate me musically." "Talent has a blindness to color," said Sinatra, and he championed racial equality when it was still controversial to do so. Billie Holiday, "Lady Day," was not yet performing regularly on the Street in 1933, but did appear occasionally. When he first heard her sing "standing under a spotlight in a 52nd Street jazz spot, swaying with the beat," said Sinatra, "I was dazzled by her."

A quarter of a century later, he offered the ultimate accolade. "Billie Holiday was and still remains the greatest single musical influence on me. . . . The depth of Lady's singing has always rocked me." It was from her, he said, that he learned "shading, phrasing, dark tones, light tones, and bending notes." Holiday, he thought, "lived inside the song." In time the admiration became mutual. Holiday would one day say she wished she could sound like a female Sinatra, and on her last album paid him the tribute of singing "All the Way," which he had made famous.

Many of the big names of the big band era, with whom Sinatra would eventually achieve national prominence, were familiar figures on 52nd Street. Benny Goodman was a regular at the Onyx Club, playing his clarinet. So was Tommy Dorsey, jamming on trumpet—surprisingly not on the trombone for which he is famous.

The Street had been home to more speakeasies than anywhere in the city during Prohibition, which was about to end in 1933. Prostitution was a feature in the area. Frank was among night people, who thought nothing of staying up till dawn. Among them were top gangsters, who had owned and frequented the speakeasies and dominated the clubs and restaurants that replaced them once drinking became legal again. They were also increasing their penetration of the entertainment industry.

Four powerful mobsters in particular frequented the nightspots of the New York area: Lucky Luciano, by now the de facto head of the national crime syndicate; his close friend Frank Costello of New York; Costello's cousin, New Jersey crime boss Willie Moretti; and Dutch Schultz, who owned a 52nd Street club, Club Abbey, until his murder by one of Luciano's henchmen. All figure in the Sinatra story.

FRANK RECALLED HIS EARLY ADVENTURES in New York City as having had "a kind of motion picture ending." "On Christmas Eve," he said, "I went home to visit my folks and there was hugging and kissing and making up." This was probably in December 1933, the month he turned eighteen. Marty was relieved to have his only son home, and Dolly had become his enthusiastic backer. Armed with more money from his parents, Frank started acquiring the sheet music for a wide selection of popular tunes. This gave him even more leverage with local bands, and he began to get more gigs.

At an amateur contest at the New York Academy of Music, he experienced the stage fright that unbeknownst to audiences would dog him far into the future. "I swear on my mother's soul," Sinatra would say on **The Larry King Show** in 1988, "I tremble every time I take the step and walk out onto the stage." At the Academy, as he waited in the wings, Frank could hear other competitors being subjected to catcalls and shouts of "Get the hook!"—the curved pole used to yank hopeless performers off the stage. "I'm standing there shaking," Sinatra remembered, "figuring that the moment they announce a guy from Hoboken, he's dead."

The audience did not sentence Frank to the hook, but nor did he win a prize. Closer to home, in a contest at the State Theater in Jersey City, he sang "That Old Black Magic" and did win a prize. He broke into radio in a modest way, too, when a contact of his uncle Dominick got him onto WAAT in Jersey City. Frank sang without pay, but any exposure helped. An old radio guide shows that he had a fifteen-minute slot in April 1935, under his own name. On other occasions, by one account, he was identified only as "The Romancer."

The next break came thanks to some young musicians who had been customers at the Sinatras' bar. Members of a trio called the Three Flashes had been hired to sing weekends at the Rustic Cabin, a roadhouse on Route 9W, fifteen miles outside Hoboken. "Frank hung around us like we were gods or something," according to Fred Tamburro, one of the Flashes. "We took him along for one simple reason: Frankie-boy had a car. He used to chauffeur us around."

"Then," Tamburro's widow said, "Dolly went

over to speak to Freddie and asked him to put Sinatra in the group." "His mother started pestering us," said Flashes' musician Jimmy "Skelly" Petrozelli. "Dolly was a big wheel in Hoboken. She kept throwing her weight around, and we finally took him." "She pushed and pushed Frankie and got him in," Dolly's niece Rose said recently. "There wasn't anybody who didn't know who she was. She knew all the gangsters, and all the politicians."

Dolly got her son into the Three Flashes just as they were about to try out for a radio show hosted by a popular impresario, Major Bowes. When Frank tagged along to the Bronx, for a first meeting with Bowes, Tamburro explained that they were now four. Bowes liked what he heard. He was swayed, according to Tamburro, by the group's rendering of "Shine"—"Shine away your bluesies"—to which Frank contributed some solo lines. Sinatra said it was his rendering of "Night and Day" that won Bowes over.

A few days later, in a competition at New York's Capitol Theater, they were introduced as the Hoboken Four, "singing and dancing fools." Fools, Bowes said, "because they're so happy." The audience applause meter, and call-ins by radio listeners, won them first prize—a six-month contract to perform on stage and radio around the country. It was September 8, 1935, a few months short of Frank's twentieth birthday.

The Bowes tour turned out to be more grueling than glamorous, and ended in bitterness. The boys' pay of $75 a week each ($1,000 today) was more than any of them had earned before, yet that seemingly munificent sum shrank when they found they had to pay their own living expenses. They were shunted by train and bus across thirty-nine states and beyond: to cities including Des Moines, Wichita, Los Angeles, San Diego, San Francisco, Oakland, Vancouver, then back down to Bellingham, Washington.

It became obvious during the trip that Frank had a special talent. Asked to perform at an Oakland nightclub, he got up and sang solo without rehearsal. "He got so good after just a couple of months on tour," Petrozelli remembered. "The bus would be packed, people talking, people necking, people reading—everything people do on a bus. Then Frank would start to sing from somewhere down back and everything stopped . . . he had his heart and soul in it. That kid really had it."

"Frank stood out as the best in the group," a former Bowes staff member said. "After the show people would flock backstage. . . . The others would be asked to sign an autograph or two, but Frank was practically torn apart. He'd have to fight off the nicest women you've ever seen. All the women wanted was to climb into bed with Frank Sinatra."

In Hoboken, so far as is known, his teenage sex life had been limited to flirtations with neighbors' daughters and the long-running romance with Nancy Barbato, still just eighteen in 1935 and very much under the wing of her family. On the road, far from home and treated like a mini-celebrity, he was the young stud. According to Tamburro, "He could get all the tail he wanted. This guy had an appetite for sex like no one I ever knew."

Frank's popularity, and especially the success with girls, did not go down well with his fellow singers. On occasion they took it out on him with their fists, and one of several fierce brawls ended with Tamburro knocking Frank unconscious. After three months, he quit and went home to New Jersey. The reason, he said later, was that he had "got homesick." The rest of the group completed the tour but broke up soon afterward. Two took jobs as waiters and Tamburro worked for a while as a car salesman. When Sinatra became famous and Tamburro asked him for a job, Sinatra offered to hire him as a valet. He turned the offer down.

Despite the unhappy ending, Sinatra remembered that first tour as the experience that "made me stick to singing as my lifetime ambition and work." Two more arid years were to pass before luck again came his way. He remembered this time as a "panic period." He tried out for a job as a singing waiter at Vaughan Comfort's restaurant on the Jersey Shore, but was not taken on. The pianist said he did not sing loudly enough. Things improved somewhat after the Sinatra family turned out in force for a Sicilian Cultural League function at Hoboken's Union Club. Marty and Dolly presented the league with an American flag and Sam Sinatra, the cousin who had frustrated Frank by doing well at school, was treasurer. Frank began getting some work at the club.

It was not enough, though, to make a living. On December 12, 1936, he sang in a "Minstrel Show" sponsored by his father's fire company at Malec's Plauderville Ballroom; he was listed on the program as just one of eighteen "Boys" in the chorus. It was his twenty-first birthday.

Frank took to haunting the lobbies of radio stations in New Jersey and New York. "I'd come out of my office," recalled Jimmy Rich, the staff pianist at WNEW in Manhattan, "and he'd be standing there to see me or anybody who would listen. . . . Somehow he'd get past the receptionist." He was prepared to sing for bus fare or "for no," no pay at all.

He performed on that basis on WNEW, WOR in Newark, and again, with a guitarist friend to accompany him, on Jersey City's WAAT. He especially liked WOR because the station boasted an orchestra with strings. "I had three songs that I did with the string section—I wanted to work with strings," he said later.

In the spring of 1937, Frank contacted Ray Sinatra, at that time a member of the NBC house orchestra. "He wanted to know whether we might be related," Ray recalled. "He mentioned that he wanted to be a singer." Ray checked, found they were cousins of some sort, and helped Frank get a stint on an NBC radio show.

This was a high point in a low time. "The cream cheese and nut sandwiches I ate when I was living on about thirty cents a day, working on those programs!" Sinatra remembered. "The coldest nights I walked three miles because I didn't have a dime bus fare. . . . But I worked on one basic theory—stay active, get as much practice as you can."

Staying active meant more trips into Manhattan, often with his Hoboken friend Nick Sevano. On a visit to a Broadway music publisher in search of sheet music, the pair were befriended by a young man named Hank Sanicola. He was a song plugger, one of an army of faceless musicians paid by publishers both to cultivate performers and to get new music played on the radio. Frank was not yet a good bet, but Sanicola took him under his wing.

Soon they were spending hours together, Frank trying out songs as Sanicola banged away on the piano. "Without his encouragement," Sinatra was to say, "I might very easily have tossed in the sponge." Sanicola had some musical talent, business savvy, and the physical build of a blacksmith. He recalled becoming Sinatra's "strong arm . . . I used to step in and hit guys when they started ganging up on him in bars." Sinatra later employed Sanicola as his manager and Sevano as his general factotum. For now, in the "panic period," Sanicola helped out by slipping him a little money each week.

Frank also got to know Chester Babcock, a song plugger at Remick Music. Babcock, who was keeping the wolf from the door by working as an elevator operator in a hotel, aspired to a career as a composer. Under the name Jimmy Van Heusen, the last name appropriated from the shirt manufacturer, he would find success sooner than Frank. "Come Fly with Me," "High Hopes," "My Kind of Town," and "Only the Lonely" are just a few of the dozens of songs he was eventually to write for Frank. When the good times arrived, Van Heusen was a natural to become a Sinatra intimate. He managed to combine a lifelong enthusiasm for flying—he later piloted both Sinatra and Bing Crosby—with a gargantuan appetite for sex and strong drink. At twenty, the nucleus of Frank's friendships was already taking shape.

In the late 1930s, though, these friends were still trying to make it and Frank was what the pluggers called a "kolo," a wannabe not yet established on a major radio network. He had become something of a 52nd Street regular, attending

Sunday afternoon jam sessions at the Hickory House jazz club. He hung around there in a back booth listening to Count Basie, Artie Shaw, Benny Goodman, Art Tatum, and Nat "King" Cole among others, waiting for a chance to sing.

Billie Holiday was appearing on the Street more often now, her trademark gardenia in her hair, bewitching listeners with her songs of love and hurt. When two men at the Onyx Club talked loudly during her performance one night, Frank laid into them—one of his earliest public displays of violent temper.

In those formative days, Sinatra said, he also paid close attention to two other black women singers. He felt "touched deep down" by the work of Ethel Waters, celebrated for her recording of "Stormy Weather." By then in her forties, Waters like Holiday had been reared in poverty, the daughter of a twelve-year-old mother who had been raped by a white man. And in about 1938 he would hear the British-born Mabel Mercer, just arrived from cabaret work in Paris. "He would be there almost every night," Mercer's press agent Eddie Jaffe remembered. "He would tell everybody how influenced he was by the way she sold the lyric."

People in the business, meanwhile, were telling Frank he could learn from opera. He was spending more and more time at Nancy's home, where opera was played all the time. He fantasized about singing the aria "Vesti la giubba"—"On with the Show"—from **I Pagliacci,** and envied those with the voice to do so. He thought his contemporary Robert Merrill "the greatest baritone I ever heard." If reincarnation were possible, Sinatra would one day say, he would like to return as Luciano Pavarotti. Both great singers would one day become his friends.

SOMETIME AFTER the Hoboken Four broke up, probably in 1936, the group's former leader, Fred Tamburro, noticed a change in Frank. "He didn't talk Hoboken anymore. He sounded like some Englishman or something. I asked him about it, and he told me he took lessons from some professor." At Sanicola's suggestion, Frank was seeing a voice coach. "His voice then was very thin," Nick Sevano recalled. "It didn't have range. We went to see a coach twice a week. He'd have him go through the scales on the piano. And then Frank would study at home, a couple hours a day, and learn rhythm and timing."

This first teacher passed Frank on to John Quinlan, a former Metropolitan Opera singer who had been fired for drunkenness. A series of forty-five-minute sessions began, at a dollar a time. Frank consulted Quinlan on and off for years, and later they would collaborate on a slim volume called **Tips on Popular Singing.** Sinatra thought the coach "a great teacher." Quinlan remembered Frank as "a boy who never stopped studying."

A business card Frank used about this time read:

FRANK SINATRA
VOCALIST
RADIO—STAGE—RECORDING ARTIST

The card carried the phone number Hoboken 3-0985, the same number pregnant women called to avail themselves of Dolly's midwifery and abortion services. Few potential customers responded, however. For all the voice lessons, for all the days and nights listening to the music of others, success was as elusive as ever. At twenty-two, Frank was getting desperate. "I wasn't going anywhere," he remembered. "I was giving up."

5

"Did I Know Those Guys?"

IT WAS DOLLY, characteristically, who came to the rescue. One night, probably in early 1938, a dejected Frank told her he had been turned down for a singing job. She said she did not want him staying out to all hours in clubs anyway. He gave her a withering look and went upstairs to his room. Soon, through the door, his mother heard him crying. The sobbing went on for hours.

"I suppose I realized then, for the first time, what singing really meant to Frankie," Dolly said later. She had never been opposed to his becoming a singer the way her husband was, and resolved to help once again.

The job he was after was at the Rustic Cabin, the nightspot near the George Washington Bridge where Frank had first hung out with the Three Flashes. Built to look like a log cabin, and advertised as having "true Western atmosphere," it was a steak-and-chop house with a dance floor and band platform. The Rustic Cabin would attract several hundred people on a good weekend. Sinatra remembered it as a "sneak joint . . . all the married guys would be there with their girlfriends, because there were little cabins inside the room itself . . . very private."

Frank was eager to work there for two reasons. The management of Hoboken's Union Club, where he sang sometimes, could not afford to install a link enabling radio stations to pick up and broadcast music played at distant venues. The Cabin did have a link, and bands performing there were featured Saturday nights on WNEW in New York.

"Working with a good band," Sinatra recalled, "was the end of the rainbow for any singer who wanted to make it." This was, of course, the era of the big bands, of Goodman, Jimmy and Tommy Dorsey, Artie Shaw, Duke Ellington, and Guy Lombardo. The radio link ensured that the musicians and managers who mattered, just across the river in Manhattan, could hear the music played there. Its proximity to New York also made it accessible to scouts looking for fresh talent. When Frank had heard there was an opening at the Rustic Cabin, he had jumped at the chance.

They were looking for someone who could wait tables and emcee on occasion—and sing. The job paid only $15 a week, but Frank wanted it. He badgered musicians who played at the Cabin to put in a word for him when he went for an audition, but bandleader Harold Arden, who remembered Frank from the days of the Three Flashes, did not like him. He was turned down flat.

Years later, when the press got interested, Dolly explained that she had contacted her acquaintance Harry Steeper, who was head of the New Jersey branch of the American Federation of Musicians and close to the man soon to be its president. The union man was a public official in the township of North Bergen, five miles from Hoboken, and knew the Sinatras. "As fellow politicians we used to do favors for one another," Dolly told a reporter. "I asked him to see to it that Frankie got another tryout. 'And this time,' I said, 'see to it that he gets the job.' " Steeper also received a written request from Marty. He told the Sinatras they could tell Frank he was as good as hired, and he was.

Some believed there was more to it. In a scathing article years later, **New York Daily Mirror** columnist Lee Mortimer wrote, "The mob got Sinatra a job at the Rustic Cabin."

"DID I KNOW THOSE GUYS?" Sinatra said late in life, referring to the Mafia. "Sure, I knew some . . . I spent a lot of time working in saloons. And saloons are not run by the Christian Brothers. There were a lot of guys around, and they came out of Prohibition, and they ran pretty good saloons. I was a kid. I worked in the places that were open. They paid you, and the checks didn't bounce. I didn't meet any Nobel Prize winners in saloons. But if Francis of Assisi was a singer and worked in saloons, he would've met the same guys. That doesn't make him part of something. They said hello, you said hello. They came backstage. They thanked you. They offered you a drink. That was it. It doesn't matter anymore, does it?"

Far from merely having had incidental encounters with "some guys" in his youth, Sinatra had intimate relationships with vicious murderers, thieves, and vice czars. His business would be entwined with their rackets for fifty years.

Sinatra avoided the mob issue whenever possible. In the mid-1960s, when he agreed to a CBS interview, he had his attorney stipulate that there were to be no questions about the Mafia. When Walter Cronkite broached the subject anyway Sinatra promptly interrupted the interview and, producer Don Hewitt remembered, "went ballistic." Over nearly five decades, various congressional committees and state bodies sought to question Sinatra about his mob connections. When forced to testify he was often truculent, always evasive.

In the wake of the attack by Lee Mortimer,

Sinatra responded with a lengthy article of his own. "I've met many undesirable characters in my years of nightclub entertaining," he wrote, "just as every nightclub star has at some time or other." That was his standard defense, and it was true, so far as it went. Singers' relations with the mob, however, sometimes had sinister consequences.

Italian-American gangsters had tried to extort money from the great tenor Enrico Caruso as early as 1909. He reportedly resisted at first, but later placated them with a secret payment. Bing Crosby, according to FBI files, caved in to demands for money and once, when one element of the mob threatened him, turned for help to a Capone hit man. Mario Lanza endured underworld pressure throughout his career, most often when he was in financial trouble. East Coast mobsters once told Lanza they could help in various ways provided they received a cut of his earnings. If he did not go along, they threatened, they would kill him.

Al Martino made a deal with criminals that he came to regret. "Underworld figures came to see my manager," he said, "to make him an offer he couldn't refuse. My manager stepped aside after he was threatened. So now these figures became my managers." Martino eventually fled to Europe because of debts to the mob, not to return until seven years later, after his principal tormentor had died.

"Serious business, giving yourself over to 'the Boys,' " Mel Tormé recalled. "Their power in the entertainment field was indisputable. The price a performer had to pay, though, was almost certainly unacceptable." Warned by his manager that the mobsters "would literally run your life," Tormé said, he managed to work without them.

Other entertainers close to Sinatra were manipulated by gangsters. Comedian Jimmy Durante had a tough guy and fringe underworld character as his manager, was bankrolled in a movie by Waxey Gordon, paid a fine for Mickey Cohen, and counted Bugsy Siegel as a friend. So did the actor George Raft, who had a good grounding for the gangster roles that brought him fame. He started out as a small-time hoodlum, riding shotgun on booze trucks being delivered to Dutch Schultz. Many years later, having fronted for organized crime as host and greeter at the Capri Casino in Havana, he was indicted for fraud. During the related IRS probe, the casino's former treasurer was shot dead. The mob also used him to front as an investor at the Sands Hotel in Las Vegas and at a gambling club in London, until he was barred from the United Kingdom.

Joe E. Lewis, remembered as a comic, was also a good tenor until he defied the owners of the Green Mill club in Chicago by leaving to perform at a rival nightspot. Assailants beat him senseless and slashed his face and throat with a hunting knife. Lewis's singing days were over. His fame as a comedian was achieved with a voice described as sounding like "two pieces of sandpaper being rubbed together." Lewis continued to work for gangsters even after that experience, a measure of the grip organized crime had on the nightclub business.

The entertainer Sonny King, born Louis Schiavone in Brooklyn, partnered Durante onstage for years. He was also close to Sinatra, who became godfather to one of his children. "There wasn't a nightclub in New York that wasn't owned by the Boys," King said. "Naturally you came into contact with them. They preferred Italian performers. If they liked you, you worked all the time. They dictated what you were paid. If they didn't like you, you just didn't work."

Just as mobsters sought out entertainers, so some entertainers sought out the mob, a pattern that continued for decades. "They want to be around mob people because they know the mob controls the better places," said Vincent Teresa, the first high-ranking mafioso to turn informer, "so they come in, they get cozy with you and they ask your help in getting them a spot."

Club owners, meanwhile, might start off clean but find themselves drawn into the rackets. "Most of these clubs operate on a thin line," said Teresa. "A mob guy finds out they're in financial trouble, and pretty soon he makes an offer to lend the owner some money. Before the club owner realizes it, he's in hock up to his eyes and suddenly he's got a new silent partner."

By the late 1930s there were more than 200,000 jukeboxes in bars and taverns across the country. They represented a multimillion-dollar industry, and it was dominated by gangsters. The criminals largely controlled what records were played, and thus what songs made the weekly hit parade of most popular songs. That gave them another hold over musicians. "They would get to you and say, 'We're gonna put you on every jukebox in the eastern United States,' " Artie Shaw recalled. "It was very tempting. They were into everything, the Boys."

Five years after the end of Prohibition, the mob bosses had their hooks into every facet of the music industry, as well as theatrical agencies and Hollywood studios. Their operation was indeed now "organized" crime, with disciplined leadership and rules enforced nationwide.

The acknowledged leader of this modernized crime network, with a personal interest in the entertainment world, was Lucky Luciano.

THREE DECADES AFTER his poor parents had brought him from Lercara Friddi, Luciano was wealthy and wielded unprecedented power. His beginnings, however, had not been auspicious. He was a shoplifter as a child, and at eighteen was jailed for six months on a narcotics charge. He was arrested in New Jersey for carrying a loaded revolver. There was also a string of armed robbery, larceny, and gambling charges that he beat or escaped with only a fine.

According to one of his biographers, Luciano progressed from beatings to no fewer than twenty murders to pioneering drug trafficking. One of his attorneys thought him "sadistic." Another observer described him as "wily, rapacious . . . savagely cruel, like some deadly King Cobra, coiled about the Eastern underworld." By 1928, having distanced himself from personal involvement in violence, he was ordering others to kill.

In the course of the next three years, the murders of three major criminals marked the end of the "old Mafia." Luciano, who was involved in at least two of those killings, emerged in 1931, at the age of thirty-four, as the head of the new national crime syndicate.

The face he showed to the world in the early 1930s was that of a wealthy businessman. He lived in style at the Waldorf Towers, going out at night to the restaurants and clubs he controlled. Durante was a dining companion, Lewis and Raft were friends. He invested in Broadway musicals and—to extend the crime empire to Hollywood—played a leading part in establishing mob control of the stage employees' union.

Then in 1936, having been declared New York's Public Enemy Number One, Luciano was arrested, convicted, and sentenced to a long prison term for running a chain of brothels. Behind bars, however, he would long remain, in the words of one scholar, "one of the most brilliant criminal executives of the modern age." Senior mob associates stayed in constant touch, consulting him regularly on important matters.

Prominent among those accomplices were Frank Costello and Willie Moretti. Moretti "idolized" Luciano and was his most loyal associate, according to a Federal Bureau of Narcotics document. He and Costello, like their leader, had committed juvenile crime—robbery and assault—then moved on to major-league crime during Prohibition. Moretti, whose neighbors in New Jersey saw him as a good family man, benefactor of local charities, and regular churchgoer, was a brute and a murderer. Costello, in New York, was a wise adviser to criminal associates and an effective corrupter of public officials. Less well known was the fact that he, too, was a killer.

Moretti controlled casinos and nightspots in northern New Jersey and elsewhere. The Riviera, high on a bluff near the George Washington Bridge, was his showpiece. It was popular for its nightclub, with a roof that slid back in summer so that couples could dance beneath the stars, and notorious for its Marine Room, where illegal gambling went on. Sinatra used to stop by on his way home from the Rustic Cabin, just three miles away, to listen to the music.

Costello's fiefdom was Manhattan, and like Luciano he had major show business interests. He was covert owner of the Copacabana nightclub, was said to have an interest in the Stork Club and, eventually, in the Tropicana in Las Vegas. He befriended and hired Joe E. Lewis, and took part in the attempt to lure Mario Lanza into a crooked deal. In Hollywood, Costello had influence with studio chiefs Harry Cohn and Jack Warner.

Sinatra said he did not set eyes on Luciano until 1947, and then only in a chance encounter that amounted to no more than a handshake and a drink. Had he heard the mobster's name, he asserted, he might even then not have connected it with the infamous Mafia boss. This of the most notorious gangster of his time, who came from Frank's own family's home village in Sicily.

Sinatra knew Costello. "Just to say 'Hello' " in nightclubs, he would one day tell Senate investigators. Others had different memories. Nick Sevano firmly recalled Costello as one of "those guys" with whom Frank "sat around and talked all night in the clubs." The columnist John Miller, Costello's intimate friend and Copacabana dining companion, said "Sinatra and Frank C. were great pals. . . . Sinatra would join us all the time."

As for Moretti, Sinatra said he never heard of him until the mid-1940s, when Moretti became his "neighbor." The mafioso did live around the corner from Frank in the 1940s. "Our backyards just about touched," Moretti's daughter Angela has said. Frank said he declined the invitation when Moretti asked him to dinner. "Later," he added, "he introduced himself at a restaurant, and I subsequently saw him five or six times over a period of years." On another occasion, he said someone—he claimed he could not recall the man's name—brought Moretti to see him at home. He knew him, he said, only "very faintly."

Yet Moretti was present, apparently in a group with Sinatra's parents, when Frank opened at the Copacabana in 1950. The Las Vegas restaurateur Joe Pignatello, the personal chef to another top mobster, said before his death in 2001 that Moretti was Sinatra's "longtime friend." Tina Sinatra has acknowledged that her father knew Moretti "all his life."

THERE IS NO EVIDENCE that Moretti or Costello had anything to do with getting the young Sinatra his job at the Rustic Cabin. If there was mob help at that stage, as claimed by Lee Mortimer and others, it was likely provided by a lesser figure. Three sources say that man was local mafioso Angelo "Gyp" De Carlo.

De Carlo was born and raised in Hoboken and in 1938, in his mid-thirties, was coming into his criminal prime. "He was a kind of laid-back, not a flamboyant, guy . . . never loud," an acquaintance recalled. "If you went into a bar you'd think he was your uncle." In fact he had done time for highway robbery, then moved on to gambling and loan-sharking. The FBI would eventually characterize him as "methodical gangland executioner."

De Carlo was a "made man," a formally inducted mafioso, and his family was in touch with Lucky Luciano at least from the 1940s to the early 1960s; there are entries for Gyp and his daughter Gloria in separate Luciano address books. "My grandfather would say, 'Lucky said this' or 'Lucky said that,' " Gloria's son Joe Sullivan said. "Everything was hush-hush." Locally, De Carlo answered to Moretti.

Dolly Sinatra knew De Carlo well. When they were young they had run dances together, and now they collaborated in local politics. Her nephew Sam Sinatra was soon to marry De Carlo's wife's sister. Gyp helped Sam when he needed cash, and Sam did a little work on the side for De Carlo. "He used to check places out for him," said his grandson. "These guys would send somebody like Sam to the West Coast . . . and Cuba, back and forth . . . to see if dealers were cheating them or not."

De Carlo took a proprietary interest in entertainers, singers especially. Anthony Petrozelli, brother of Hoboken Four member Jimmy "Skelly" Petrozelli, served time in jail with the mafioso and said De Carlo liked Frank and the other members of the group. "He loved all those guys," Anthony Petrozelli said recently. "They worked for him. He'd just snap his fingers and they would be at Gyp's no matter what occasion it was."

James Petrozelli, Jimmy's son, recalled his father telling him much the same thing, and got the impression from his father that "Gyp had a lot to do with getting" Frank the Rustic Cabin job. Sam Sinatra thought so, too, said his widow, Rose. Robert Phillips, a former police officer who had frequent contact with Frank years later in California, said "Sinatra was nowhere until Gyp De Carlo put the okay on him," basing his statement on what he saw in organized crime files. "Gyp De Carlo was his sponsor, his main man. His 'duke-in,' as they used to say on the street—meaning, the man who brought him in."

The indications are that, once Frank was given his start at the Rustic Cabin, Mafia fish bigger than De Carlo took an interest. Luciano, in prison at Dannemora in upstate New York, maintained a keen interest in his many "investments," which included saloons and gambling venues in New Jersey. Word now filtered through to him about the progress of a young singer named Frank Sinatra.

"When I was in Dannemora," he recalled years later, "the fellas who come to see me told me about him. They said he was a skinny kid from around Hoboken with a terrific voice—and one hundred percent Italian. He used to sing around the joints there, and all the guys liked him."

One of Luciano's visitors, a longtime friend from New Jersey named Mike Lascari, was especially knowledgeable about the music industry. Lascari, a kingpin of the burgeoning jukebox racket, was constantly on the lookout for fresh talent. Luciano's visitors also included Willie Moretti and, on a regular basis, Frank Costello. Reports in law enforcement files suggest the three of them played a role at the start of Sinatra's career.

A 1951 Bureau of Narcotics document on the Mafia states flatly that Frank was " 'discovered' by Willie Moretti after pressure from Frank Costello and Lucky Luciano." An FBI document quoted an informant as saying Sinatra "was originally 'brought up' by Frank Costello of New York." And a 1944 report on crime in New Jersey noted that Moretti "had a financial interest in Frank Sinatra." Later, engaged in conversation by agents on a pretext, the gangster "admitted his association" with Sinatra.

The son of the senior policeman who wrote the 1944 report, himself a former New Jersey investigator, recalled his father discussing the Sinatra-

Moretti matter. As Matthew Donohue Jr. remembered it: "Willie Moretti and big guys like Joe Adonis* used to go into the Rustic Cabin. People like that were often there. And Willie took a liking to Sinatra."

CHICO SCIMONE, a Boston-born pianist of Sicilian parentage, has confirmed Sinatra's early connections to the Mafia. Scimone had moved to New York on the advice of Rosario Vitaliti, an older Sicilian who had known him since childhood. Vitaliti had a butcher's shop in Brooklyn but, Scimone soon realized, "he was actually mixed up in the Cosa Nostra." Vitaliti was a lifelong friend of Lucky Luciano. At the butcher's shop, Scimone had been introduced to Luciano's brother Bartolo and to Luciano himself. He also met Costello, Moretti, and others, mobsters who hired him as a musician, not just in clubs but for their personal entertainment.

"Anytime they had meetings, secret meetings, they had fun afterwards," Scimone said. "They would have singers and dancers, and if there wasn't a piano I'd bring my accordion. Sometimes they would want me to go to their homes for family occasions, christenings and the like. Carlo

*Adonis was a longtime Luciano associate, and a power in gambling and waterfront rackets in New York and New Jersey.

Gambino had a grand piano, and he would have me go to his home once a month. He loved 'Come Back to Sorrento.' "

Scimone long stayed silent about his experiences with mobsters, innocent though they were. "They trusted me," he said. "I would never talk. Now the last of them has died—Joe Bonanno—and I can talk." In 1938 or 1939—Scimone could not date it more closely than that—Frank Costello made an unusual request. "The **amici** from New Jersey had contacted him about a young fellow. They said he had a good voice and they wanted to test him—a sort of audition—and asked me to play the piano."

Moretti was present at this audition, and the young fellow in question was Sinatra. "He was in his early twenties," Scimone remembered. "He had some sheet music. I asked him: 'What key are you gonna sing in?' . . . He did a couple of songs. I don't remember what now—one may have been 'Night and Day.' Someone had brought Sinatra there, and afterwards he left. They had been listening while he sang, and when they asked me my opinion of him I said, 'It's fine.' He had a nice voice. It was just a little audition."

Looking back, it seemed normal enough to Scimone that the mob bosses wanted to test Sinatra. "The Mafia controlled everything then," he said. "They could make somebody or they could destroy them." He learned, he said, that at some stage Sinatra and Luciano "had some friendship."

"THE BOYS GOT ON TO FRANK in part because he was a saloon singer, and they loved saloon songs, and they liked his cockiness," Sonny King said. "He was a young punk kid when he met them. They liked to think of him as their kid, or son. He was respectful, which was the right thing to do."

Frank maintained in testimony to the Nevada State Gaming Control Board in the 1980s that Willie Moretti "had nothing to do with my career at any time." The transcript of a much earlier closed session with U.S. Senate investigators, however, shows on that occasion Frank made a crucial admission:

ATTORNEY: "I will ask you specifically. Have you ever, at any time, been associated in business with Moretti?"

SINATRA: "Well, Moretti made some band dates for me when I first got started."

6

All, or Nothing at All

HOWEVER HE GOT THERE, working at the Rustic Cabin was less than glamorous. "Frank hated the place," said Fred Travalena, who worked there as a singing waiter. "But he said he knew how to put a plate in front of somebody, and he'd do **anything** to be able to sing. Some of the food orders weighed more than he did. If you got the orders messed up or spilled anything and the customer complained, they'd take it out of your check."

Sinatra remembered having to sweep the floor, show people to their tables, and "bow to the boss." It was worth it, though, because he got to sing. The tips rolled in, he recalled, when he and the pianist pushed a little "half piano" around and sang at individual tables. By the time a young girl singer arrived, a few months later, Frank "was the boy singer," said Lucille Kirk, who later married the resident trumpeter. "One of the best I ever heard. Every time he opened his mouth the audience went quiet. He could take control of an audience just by looking at them. There was a magic quality about him."

In a photograph Kirk kept, a white-tuxedoed Frank stands diffidently in front of a band playing the Cabin. In another picture he looks straight into the camera, shiny-haired, very youthful, intense.

Kirk remembered Frank as an incorrigible flirt. He dared to run his hand up and down her spine when she was wearing a backless dress, even in front of her husband-to-be. And "Oh, the women!" she said of Frank and the female customers. "There were a lot of women."

Sinatra rarely shared his thoughts about women and sex. But a Hoboken contemporary, Joey D'Orazio, remembered something Frank said at the Rustic Cabin. "We're animals," he said, "fuckin' animals, each and every one of us, that's what we are, and we're damn proud of it, too. . . . There's more to life than just Nancy, and I gotta have it." "I'm just looking to make it with as many women as I can," he told another friend, Tom Raskin.

Seven years into his relationship with Nancy Barbato, Frank's world was suddenly full of sexual opportunity. "He was a skinny guy, ordinary looking, his Adam's apple protruded, his ears stuck out," said D'Orazio, "but he had more charisma and magnetism than anyone. . . . The broads, they swarmed over him whenever he got off stage."

Frank discussed his good luck with Harry Schuchman, the regular saxophonist at the Cabin. "You got something, boy," shrugged Schuchman, "you look mattress oriented." Schuchman's wife watched the women in the audience as Frank sang. "His voice and little-boy charm got them," she said. "They were sent."

Nancy Venturi, barely into her teens, was one of those who fell. "He had sex on the brain," she recalled. "He would make love to anyone who came along. . . . There was something unusually intensive about his lovemaking, at least it was with me." She remembered Frank's seduction technique, his sexually direct lines. Other guys, she thought, "didn't talk like that back then."

Venturi contributed to the legend that Sinatra was hugely well endowed sexually. "There's only ten pounds of Frank, but there's a hundred and ten pounds of cock," Ava Gardner famously told Britain's colonial governor of Kenya years later, at a social occasion.

D'Orazio said Frank bragged about the size of his penis. Venturi, with a laugh, said he "would swing it around and call it 'Big Frankie.' . . . It sounds ridiculous now but back then—well, it was ridiculous back then, too."

Another lover said she went to bed with Frank in part to discover "what a bundle of bones like that could do. It wasn't very much in those days. I imagine he got better." He was a "cuddler," Venturi said. "I felt loved, completely loved . . . what did I know?"

At one point Venturi thought she was carrying Frank's baby. At a loss for anything else to do, she persuaded him to go to church with her and pray. "C'mon, God," she remembered him saying as they knelt in front of the altar. "Gimme a break, will ya? Make her not be pregnant. Okay? So, uh, thanks a lot, God. . . . That's it. So, amen, all right?" The deity apparently listened.

In the late spring of 1938, Frank danced at the Rustic Cabin with a twenty-seven-year-old Italian-American, Toni Della Penta. She was the daughter of a man involved in illegal alcohol rackets, separated from her husband and highly temperamental. According to Della Penta, she and Frank dated for months. Dolly, whom she met early on, called her "cheap trash" and tried to keep the couple apart. One summer night, however, Frank gave her a ring and asked her to marry him. She had not slept with him up to that point, but the proposal did the trick. They began going to hotels together, checking in as "Mr. and Mrs. Sinatra."

Della Penta said she became pregnant. For a while, in spite of Dolly's objections, Frank continued to say he would marry her. Then, she said, she miscarried and Frank "didn't come around anymore." She felt spurned and embittered.

At the time, Frank was still very much involved with Nancy Barbato. Now twenty-one, she would come into the roadhouse to hear Frank sing. "He was promising both women that he'd marry them," Travalena remembered. "It really got to be a mess."

Della Penta called the Cabin one night to speak to Frank, and Nancy picked up the phone. They had angry words, and then Della Penta arrived in a rage. She lashed out at Nancy, tearing her dress. Then she had a stand-up argument with Frank—who was trying to slip away—before storming out.

Della Penta filed a complaint, and on November 26, 1938, Frank was arrested at work and taken to the county jail. He found himself facing the outdated charge of "Seduction"—which he had allegedly committed twice that month—"under the promise of marriage" to "a single female of good repute for chastity, whereby she became pregnant." The mug shot taken the next day, showing Sinatra as prisoner No. 42799, later vanished from police files—only to reappear years later and go on sale as a poster.

Dolly swung into action once again, according to Della Penta, sending Marty Sinatra to see Toni's father. The two men tried to persuade Della Penta to back off. Frank was released on $1,500 bail, and then the complaint was withdrawn when it emerged that Della Penta was still legally married. When she in turn was arrested, after a fracas with Dolly at the Sinatras' home, she responded by filing a second complaint. The charge this time was for another arcane offense still on the statute book at the time—"Adultery."

Just before Christmas Frank was arrested again and again released on bail. The nonsense came to an end only when Della Penta withdrew the second complaint. Though ridiculous, the case provided early evidence of three traits in Frank's character: promiscuity, rage over press coverage of his private life, and a propensity to make violent threats.

The local press had reported both arrests, the second one under the headline "Songbird Held on Morals Charge." Frank "called up someone at the newspaper," a friend recalled, "and said: 'I'm coming down there and I'm gonna beat your brains out, you hear me? I'm gonna kill you and anyone else who had anything to do with that article. And I ain't no fucking songbird.' "

Meanwhile, there was music of another kind to face. "What Nancy don't know ain't gonna hurt her," Frank had told D'Orazio a few months earlier. Now she did know, and it hurt. "Nancy was crushed by the whole damn thing," a Sinatra acquaintance said. "There was a lot of screaming and hollering over that, let me tell you." Nancy asked whether the affair with Della Penta was the first time Frank had strayed. He confessed that it was not, but swore it would never happen again.

Early in January 1939, formal invitations were sent out inviting family and friends to the marriage of Nancy Rose Barbato to "Mr. Francis A. Sinatra." "I was quite taken aback," said Adeline Yacenda, who had long known the young couple. "I knew they hadn't planned on getting married so soon at all. That wedding was all very, very sudden." The invitation was for February 4, 1939, less than two weeks after Della Penta withdrew her charges.

Dolly hosted a shower for the bride-to-be and produced one of her own rings for Frank to give Nancy during the ceremony. Frank borrowed some cash from a friend and obtained a black tailcoat and striped pants. Nancy settled for a traditional white wedding dress that had previously been worn by one of her sisters.

She remembered the ceremony, at Our Lady of Sorrows church in Jersey City, as not large "but awfully nice." Nancy walked down the aisle on her father's arm, tears streaming down her face. The bridegroom had on his face what Nancy described as his "completely 'gone' expression. . . . I don't think I'd ever seen Frank so happy in his whole life." An old girlfriend, Marian Brush, who spent a few moments alone with Frank at the end of the reception, thought otherwise. To her, "He looked like the saddest man I'd ever seen."

The couple went straight from the wedding supper to their first home, which Nancy described as a "cheerful little apartment in Jersey City." Frank was "too busy," she said, to take a honeymoon. He turned out to be handy around the house, however, picked out curtains for the kitchen—yellow and brown—and hung them himself.

"Frank," Nancy told the press a few years later, "doesn't believe a wife—not his anyway—should have a separate career or her own independent income. As for me, I don't want my husband helping with the housework or darning his own socks." Yet Nancy did work in the first months of their marriage, as a secretary. Even with Frank's raise at the Rustic Cabin, to $25 a week, money was short.

"Our marriage started off with one strike against us," Sinatra recalled. "I was working most of the nights, and Nancy worked all day. We couldn't even have Sundays together." When they moved on to another apartment, moreover, Nick Sevano regularly stayed overnight. Frank spent much of his spare time out with Sevano and Hank Sanicola.

Before the wedding, a Sinatra family member had reportedly overheard Frank telling Nancy: "I'm going to the top, and I don't want anyone dragging on my neck." Nancy had responded meekly, promising not to get in his way. She was more worried about her husband's roving eye. Sevano, who thought Nancy was "a great lady," said Frank "spent very little time at home, and we spent more time with him than she did. She was very, very nervous about Frank and women he might meet." Frank realized within eighteen months that he should not have gotten married after all. "What I had mistaken for love," he admitted later, "was only the warm friendship Nancy had brought me."

When Sanicola had first heard about Frank's wedding plans, he had ruefully responded, "Poor Nancy . . ."

THE WORLD WAS IN TUMULT as Frank and Nancy began married life. Hitler grabbed Czechoslovakia and forged an alliance with Mussolini. Those for and against the Nazis demonstrated in New York. President Franklin Roosevelt hinted that America would not stand aloof from the war that now loomed. Eleanor Roosevelt resigned from the Daughters of the American Revolution when the organization prevented the black singer Marian Anderson from singing at Constitution Hall in Washington. In New Jersey, the popular right-wing radical priest Father Coughlin continued to blame the rise of communism on the Jews.

Orson Welles's radio program about Martians landing in New Jersey caused nationwide panic. Hollywood boomed with movies starring Spencer Tracy, Errol Flynn, Mickey Rooney, and Bette Davis. Judy Garland was flying over the rainbow. Humphrey Bogart and Jimmy Cagney had cornered the market on gangster pictures. The best-selling record of the moment was "Deep Purple," sung by Hildegarde.

At the Rustic Cabin, after a year of doubling as waiter and singer, Frank was becoming impatient. He took other singing jobs when he could, not just for the money but to get his name known. "I was running around doing every sustaining [unsponsored] radio show I could," he recalled. Six weeks after his wedding he was in that studio on West Forty-sixth Street in New York, when bandleader Frank Mane let him make his very first recording, "Our Love."

Frank's goal was to get where the action was, with the big bands. "I was segueing between Jersey and New York," he recalled, "trying to make a buck here and there. . . ." He managed to buttonhole Glenn Miller, who was just coming into his own. "I walked up to him," Sinatra remembered, "and I said, 'Glenn, I want a job!' I really did! . . . He said to me, in essence, 'Don't call me, I'll call you.' " The hugely popular Tommy Dorsey, whom Frank considered "a god," was persuaded to go hear him at "a club," perhaps the

Rustic Cabin, but was not impressed. When he got up to leave, Frank got his attention by holding up a sign reading: "We need the money!" Dorsey just laughed, and left.

Then Frank attended a rehearsal at the Nola Studios in New York at the invitation of another bandleader, Bob Chester, who himself had heard him at the Rustic Cabin. Dorsey happened by while he was singing. "When he saw us he got a little flustered," Dorsey remembered. "Right in the middle of the song, he forgot the lyrics." Even so, what the bandleader heard this time made him think "the kid's voice was appealing, real good. . . ."

Frank tried out with the Dorsey band about this time at Charlie's Grill, a New Jersey roadhouse operated by Willie Moretti, but still Dorsey did not hire him. Meanwhile, he suffered another setback. One night at the Rustic Cabin, the trumpet player leaned over and told Frank that Cole Porter was in the audience. "I dedicated the next song, 'Night and Day,' to Mr. Porter," Sinatra recalled, "and proceeded to forget all the words."

In the end it was the Cabin's radio link that brought a breakthrough. Late one night in June 1939, the young singer Louise Tobin was getting ready to leave on a trip. Tobin's husband was the brilliant trumpeter Harry James, who had just left the Benny Goodman Orchestra to form his own band. He was being helped to do so by the mafioso Gyp De Carlo. "I was packing and listening to the radio," Tobin remembered. "In those days they had those little speakers up in the corners of hotel rooms. Harry was trying to book his band, and that particular day he was looking for a boy singer. I heard this kid singing, and he sounded good to me. Harry was lying across the bed, and I woke him up and said: 'Honey, there's a kid singing here you might want to listen to.' "

James drove out to the Rustic Cabin the following night. "I asked the manager," he recalled, "where I could find the singer. 'We don't have a singer,' he told me. 'We do have an emcee, though, and he sings a little bit.' "

Sinatra claimed it was mere chance that he was working the night James came in—Lucille Kirk had asked him to swap nights off with her. "Oh, yeah?" Kirk said when told this recently. "It was he who asked **me** if I'd take off. I'm sure he knew James would be there." Frank had been trying to get James's attention since hearing he was forming a band. According to one former colleague, he had even persuaded someone to leave his photograph on James's desk.

Frank was waiting tables when he got word that James was in the audience. "Suddenly," James remembered, "he took off his apron and climbed onto the stage. He'd sung only eight bars of 'Night and Day' when I felt the hairs on the back of my neck rising." At James's request, Frank followed up with "Begin the Beguine." James knew right then, he said years later, that Frank "was destined to be a great vocalist." The bandleader offered him a job on the spot, at $75 a week for a year. It was none too soon, for the Rustic Cabin management had just told Frank he was to be let go. "I nearly broke his arm so he wouldn't get away," he said of that first talk with James. "I called Nancy and told her to quit her job. She was going to travel on the road with me and Harry James. . . . The world looked good, golden, glorious."

JAMES WAS A SKINNY SIX-FOOTER with dark wavy hair and blue eyes to rival Frank's. He was the son of circus performers, a bandmaster father and a trapeze artist mother, and at the age of five had been billed as "The Human Eel." At eight, he had started playing the trumpet with the circus band. Though only twenty-three when he hired Frank, he was way ahead of him in experience.

James drank heavily, smoked marijuana—as did many musicians then—and was a chronic gambler. His sexual promiscuity was legendary; one lover called him the "most faithless son of a gun who ever lived." He was a lonely man who went out of his way not to be alone. "I loved Harry James," Sinatra said years later, "loved him for a long time."

Joining James was a leap forward, but not to the

big time. Harry James and the Music Makers were suffering from poor bookings and sparse audiences. "We were struggling for money," Louise Tobin said, "and Harry wasn't the best businessman." He was a virtuoso musician, though, and for Frank he opened up a world of new possibilities.

The day after their meeting at the Rustic Cabin, Frank met with James at the Paramount Theater in New York. Inspired by the texture of Sinatra's voice, James wanted him to use the stage name Frankie Satin. Frank said no. "Can you imagine?" he once said. " 'Now playing in the lounge, ladies and gentlemen, the one and only **Frankie Satin.**' . . . If I'd've done that, I'd be working cruise ships today."

The girl singer on the first James tour, Yvonne Marie Jamais, had wisely agreed to take a new name, Connie Haines. Frank, Haines recalled of their appearance at the Baltimore Hippodrome, "was so new that he wasn't even billed. The fans didn't even know his name. And after the first show the screaming started in the theater, and those girls came backstage. . . . There were about twenty of them. We didn't have that many in the audience. But it happened, it was real."

Frank worked for James throughout the summer and fall of 1939. In Atlantic City, at the Steel Pier, he sang to a huge dance floor thronged with young couples. In New York, which was hosting the World's Fair, he sang at the Roseland Ballroom on Broadway. George Simon, who had played drums for Glenn Miller and was beginning a career as a music critic, heard him there. "He sounded somewhat like a shy boy out on his first date," Simon thought, "gentle, tender, but frightfully unsure of himself. His need of approbation was also reflected in a somewhat unusual routine by James's manager, Gerry Barrett, who—after I'd reviewed the band that night—jockeyed not for a good review of the band but for good notices for 'the boy.' "

Barrett told Simon that Frank wanted a good write-up "more than anybody I've ever seen. So give him a good write-up, will you, because we want to keep him happy and with the band and that's the only thing that will keep him happy." In the first known published review of the new singer's work, Simon noted "the very pleasing vocals of Frank Sinatra, whose easy phrasing is especially commendable."

James had spotted Frank's great strength. "He was always thinking of the lyrics," he remembered. "The melody was secondary. The feeling he has for the words is just beautiful. He could sing the wrong melody and it would still be pretty." Frank's breath control, however, needed work. James suggested he exercise more, learn to jump rope.

Several times that year, James took his band

into recording studios. Five records came out of the sessions, each earning Frank a $50 fee over and above his weekly pay. These were his first commercial records.

"It was new to him," recalled James's drummer, Mickey Scrima. "He was anxious, like everybody else is when we're recording, because if you're not anxious you don't give a shit. . . . I remember that on the playbacks Frank would sit there and be very critical, saying, 'Oh, I missed that . . .' or 'I should have done this or that.' We would do three or four takes on a tune, and he would ask if he could take one of the ones that wasn't used. Later, he would play them over and over."

None of the records became immediate hits, in part because a union dispute with broadcasters prevented their being played on the radio. Reissued four years later, though, one of them, "All or Nothing at All," would go to number two in the charts:

> All or nothing at all,
> Half a love never appealed to me.
> If your heart never could yield to me,
> Then I'd rather have nothing at all . . .

Glenn Miller, who a year or so earlier had abruptly rejected Frank, heard "All" and admitted he had missed out. Of the four times Sinatra was to record the song, which became a huge hit, its writer, Jack Lawrence, preferred that first youthful version.

James's future wife, Betty Grable, heard Frank sing at the Panther Room in Chicago and was captivated. "That guy," she said, "sings like Clark Gable makes love." Billie Holiday, who was also in Chicago, was gently critical of his singing style. "I went over to where he was," she recalled, "and they wouldn't let me in. But Frank and the others saw me, so four of us, we just went out and had a ball. I told him he didn't phrase right. . . . He says, 'Lady, you're not commercial.' "

A Panther Room customer recalled a touching encounter. "The male singer left the stage," Julie Paresich recalled, "and I proceeded to request his autograph. He was taken by surprise and seemed quite shy. He inquired why I would want it. I said, 'Because I enjoyed your singing.' He replied, 'Nobody has ever asked me for my autograph.' "

Perhaps not, but Frank was hardly modest. When a journalist asked about the "skinny little singer" who sang so well, James replied: "Not so loud. The kid's name is Sinatra. He considers himself the greatest vocalist in the business. Get that! No one ever heard of him. He's never had a hit record. He looks like a wet rag. But he says he is the greatest. If he hears you compliment him, he'll ask for a raise tonight."

On the West Coast, nothing went right for James and the band. The ballroom they were booked to play in burned to the ground, and the substitute venue, a Beverly Hills supper club called the Victor Hugo, proved totally unsuitable. "The place was so small," Sinatra remembered, "that the brasses in our band blew the dancers off the floor. There were canaries in cages around, in nooks. . . . After Harry's first blast they never chirped again."

The Victor Hugo management canceled the engagement, and the musicians found themselves stranded and broke. Frank and Nancy, who had joined her husband on the tour as planned, found themselves sharing an apartment with two band members and going hungry. "A number of times," a fellow musician recalled, "Frank was so depressed that the band wasn't shooting into the sky, that he wasn't becoming a big star, he actually talked about quitting." If he considered quitting James's band, he had no thought of abandoning his ambition. Mickey Scrima, one of the couple's Los Angeles roommates, said Frank talked constantly about what could be.

He aspired to singing with Count Basie, with whom Billie Holiday had worked. Most of all, he clung to the hope of singing with Tommy Dorsey because, he thought, singing with him would be "a better showcase." Dorsey had by now heard Frank's rendering of "All or Nothing at All," and the bandleader was at odds with his own lead singer.

In November 1939, when his band and James's were in Chicago at the same time, Dorsey acted. Frank found a scrawled note, on a torn piece of paper, on his dressing room door: "Mr. Dorsey would like to see you." At Dorsey's hotel an aide asked Sinatra to sing "Marie," one of the band's trademark songs. Frank listened to the Dorsey version on a record player, then sang a cappella. His performance, which ended with an impressive glissando, won him an audience with the bandleader himself.

"The moment I saw him I remembered him," Dorsey recalled. "I said, 'You're the kid who blew the lyrics.' He laughed and so did I. He told me he had always wanted to be in my band." Shrewdly, Dorsey gave Frank the impression the job might go to another singer—then offered him a long-term contract at $100 a week. Frank took the bait.

James reacted philosophically to the news. "Well," he said, "if we don't do any better in the next few months or so, try to get me on too." Sinatra never forgot James's generosity in letting him out of his obligations. He spoke of James as a friend and mentor, the man who "made it all possible."

Frank spent a miserable Christmas alone as he worked his last few weeks with James, then retreated to bed in Cleveland with pneumonia. Nancy, who was pregnant, was at home with her parents in Jersey City. She sent her husband a gift to cheer him up over the holidays, a pair of gloves—each finger symbolically stuffed with a dollar bill.

Frank sang with James for the last time in January 1940, in Buffalo, New York. The band played at the Shea Theater on a bill with Red Skelton and an acrobat named Burt Lancaster. After the show, around midnight, James and the other musicians left town. "The bus pulled out with the rest of the guys," Frank remembered. "I'd said goodbye to them all, and it was snowing. There was nobody around, and I stood alone with my suitcase in the snow and watched the tail-lights disappear. Then the tears started. . . . There was such spirit and enthusiasm in that band."

At home in New Jersey for a week or so, Frank let people know he was leaving town for good. Before he did, though, he and three friends got together at his parents' home in Hoboken. Using a home recording kit, they made a record featuring only Frank and Walter Costello, an accordionist he knew. Perhaps because war was raging in Europe, they chose to sing "Roses of Picardy," a haunting ballad of World War I:

> She is watching and longing and waiting,
> Where the long white roadway lies. . . .

Costello told his sister that Frank made the record as "a remembrance." "I think it was his way of saying goodbye to Hoboken," said Ed Shirak, a Sinatra enthusiast who stumbled on the record in the late 1990s. "He always had a way of knowing his destiny before he lived it."

One day, leaning out the window of the Waldorf Towers in Manhattan, Sinatra would look west toward his birthplace. "It's a lot farther than you think," he said to a colleague, "from Hoboken to the Waldorf."

7

“Let Him Go”

AT TWENTY-FOUR, seven years after vowing he would one day be as successful as Bing Crosby, Frank was on America’s musical radar. In January 1940, the month he signed with Dorsey, the trade magazine **Metronome** published the results of a new poll: Bing Crosby was best “boy singer,” with 637 votes; eleventh on the list was Frank Sinatra, with 21 votes.

Working with Tommy Dorsey would change those numbers. Frank had joined the band he considered “No. 1 in the United States, in fact in the world . . . the General Motors of the band business.” His drummer, Buddy Rich, thought Dorsey “the most beautiful and melodic trombone player who ever lived.” He was known in the business as “the Starmaker,” for with the talent came a flair for business.

Ten years older than Frank, Dorsey had grown

up in a home filled with the bright, bold sound of brass instruments. His father, a coal miner turned music teacher in a depressed region of eastern Pennsylvania, handed him his first instrument at the age of six. Tommy and his equally talented brother, Jimmy, formed their first musical group—a little jazz band—as teenagers, when Jimmy was an underage mineworker and Tommy a delivery boy.

After a long, hard apprenticeship, they triumphed briefly as the Dorsey Brothers Orchestra. When they had quarreled and split up, Tommy went on to find national fame as "The Sentimental Gentleman of Swing." "Sentimental" aptly described Dorsey's mastery of musical mood, of a sound both warm and easy to dance to. His personality was something else again.

"If you could put up with him, and he could put up with you," clarinetist Buddy DeFranco said, "you could learn a lot from him." He demanded total dedication, was intolerant of failure, and enforced strict discipline. He fined musicians who arrived late—one singer was fired for missing the start of rehearsal. He screamed at arrangers. He once chased his finest drummer, Buddy Rich, off the stage and into the street, and another time was said to have hit him over the head with his trombone.

Dorsey drove like a maniac and swore a blue streak. He was a womanizer. He drank too much, but was more irritable when not drinking. "I do what I fucking want," Dorsey said. "Nobody tells me how to live my life."

Sometimes he would show his sensitivity, as when he stopped the band's bus to ask plaintively: "Why don't you guys like me?" Yet a newcomer to the band would be met with a disconcerting baptism of abuse. "Well, shit heel," Dorsey might ask, "are you going to give me trouble or are we going to be okay?"

Sinatra joined Dorsey in January 1940, and probably first sang with the band at the Lyric Theater in Indianapolis. Though there had again been talk of altering his name—"Frank Sinatra will never mean much," one band member had said—there was no change. Frank's billing, in small print beneath Dorsey's in large capital letters, was "Frank Sinatra, Romantic Virtuoso."

"We knew we were going to have a new boy singer," the female vocalist Jo Stafford recalled, "but we didn't know anything about him . . . we didn't even meet him before the first show." There is some question as to what Frank sang that night, but none as to the reception he got. "Out came this rather frail looking young man with a whole bunch of hair," Stafford said. "I just thought, Hmm—kinda thin. . . . But he sang no more than a few bars of 'Stardust' and a great hush fell over the theatre. . . . Nobody had ever sounded like that before."

Dorsey's radio producer, Herb Sanford, heard the same song and thought: "Boy, this is something else." The press agent Jack Egan recalled how the newcomer "broke it up completely. . . . They kept yelling for more, but Frank had no encore prepared. . . . He and Tommy went into a huddle and Frank suggested they fake 'South of the Border.' . . . That broke it up even more.

"The kids started screaming," Egan said. "There was nothing rigged about it . . . those screams were real." After the show that night, according to a band member, Frank "actually looked into a mirror and pinched himself." Trumpeter Zeke Zarchy thought Sinatra seemed "in awe of being where he was." Frank himself recalled having been somewhat restrained for fear band members would think him an intruder. Others recalled no such reserve. "He just moved right in and took charge," said arranger Sy Oliver. "He had an awful lot of assurance for a youngster."

The band routine was grueling, as many as nine shows a day and bus rides as long as four hundred miles through the night to the next gig. Frank took it in his stride. To the amazement of colleagues who struggled to keep themselves presentable, he remained conspicuously well groomed. This was in part thanks to Nick Sevano, who months earlier, at eighteen, had joined him as valet and general gofer. Frank was extravagant, checking into fancy hotels while colleagues put up with humbler quarters. He picked up the tab in restaurants, threw money around. "Frank was always broke," said band manager Bobby Burns, "because he lent so much to the other guys."

Early on, noticing that Dorsey usually ate alone after the show, Frank and a friend asked him to dinner. Dorsey reciprocated by taking Frank to Patsy's, an Italian restaurant on 56th Street in New York, exhorting the owner to "fatten him up."

Frank became the liaison between the band members and their boss. "One time," he recalled, "there was a lot of unrest in the band because of traveling all night in Greyhound buses. I went to Tommy and said, 'Look, the boys are unhappy—hard seats, no air, no refreshments. When they come on the stand they're **out.** You won't get the best out of them.' After that there were always twelve cases of Coke on every bus—till [pianist] Joey Bushkin introduced the band to Pernod and all the Coke suddenly went green."

Once Frank took over the wheel of the bus and announced that he intended to pass Dorsey, who was driving in front of them in his car. "At first everyone yelled at him that he was nuts," Bobby Burns recalled. "Then they began to laugh. We rocketed along that road." Frank did manage to pass and Dorsey responded good-humoredly, even after learning that the engine of the bus needed expensive repairs.

Frank called the bandleader "the old man," and said he had been "almost like a father to me." Dorsey was a night person, as was Frank. "I'd sit up playing cards with Tommy until maybe 5:30 every morning," Sinatra remembered. "He couldn't sleep ever: he had less sleep than any man I'd ever known. I'd fall off to bed about then, but around 9:30 A.M. a hand would shake me awake and it'd be Tommy saying, 'Hey pally—how about some golf?' So I'd totter out on to the golf course. Tommy bought a baby carriage one time, filled it with ice and beer and hired an extra caddie to wheel it around after us. We'd have a beer after each shot. After nine holes, imagine—we were **loaded.**"

Both men had humble origins and minimal schooling. Dorsey sought out people who had an education, as would Frank. Both had rambunctious, protective mothers. Dorsey loved puerile pranks, as would Frank in the future. The bandleader would leave water-filled sponges on musicians' seats, or turn a garden hose on them from the wings. He would squirt seltzer down a female singer's cleavage.

Both men favored Courtley cologne. Both used Dentist Prescribed toothpaste. Dorsey collected elaborate toy trains, as would Frank. Both sought perfection and control over those around them. Both were ruthless toward perceived enemies. And the two men were in harmony on what mattered most to them, their music. Frank, Dorsey said, "sang a song like he believed every word of the lyrics. . . . I've had other singers in my band, perhaps many of them knew more about the technical part of music, but no one ever sang like Frank did. No one ever put into a song what he did."

Though Dorsey offered barely any coaching as such, Sinatra was to say that "Tommy taught me everything I know about singing." He ascribed to Dorsey his grasp of elocution and diction, which in his songs rarely betrayed his New Jersey upbringing. Frank learned most of all, though, from the way Dorsey played the trombone. He could hold a musical phrase for an extraordinarily long time, prolonging the mood of a musical moment, seemingly without needing to take a breath. If a singer could master the same degree of breath control, Frank thought, he could minimize the need to interrupt the sense of a song's lyrics. "I used to watch Tommy's back, his jacket, to see when he would breathe," he said. "I'd swear the sonofabitch was not breathing. I couldn't even see his jacket move. . . . I thought, he's gotta be breathing some place—through the ears?"

Dorsey eventually shared his secret. "He showed me," Sinatra said, "that he was breathing in the corner of his mouth so he could catch a breath. . . . But in holding the instrument he covered his mouth with his hand. . . . It made it **seem** like he played ten to twelve bars without breathing."

A singer could hardly cover his mouth, but Frank continued to focus on the problem not least because of a newfound enthusiasm that would have astonished many of the youngsters in his audience. A chance invitation to a concert at Carnegie Hall sparked in him a lasting love of classical music—Debussy, Brahms, Ravel, Rachmaninoff, Wagner. The violin of the Russian virtuoso Jascha Heifetz, whom Frank made a point of seeing often, strengthened his feeling that, for a singer, breath control was of paramount importance.

"Every time he came down with the bow," Frank said, "there was hardly any perception at all that it was going back up again. . . . You never heard a break. . . . I thought, If he's doing that with the bow, why can't I do it better than I do it now as one who uses my breath? . . . It was my idea to make my voice work in the same way as a trombone or a violin."

Frank set out to improve his breathing. "I did lots of exercises, breathing exercises. I did running and that kind of stuff." He used to swim "mostly underwater to keep the bellows as strong as I can." The physical training, Joe Bushkin reckoned, enabled Frank to increase his range by three notes. Sammy Cahn watched him at work with Dorsey and marveled. "Frank can hold a tremendous phrase," he said, "until it takes him into a sort of paroxysm—he gasps, his whole person seems to explode, to release itself."

Frank returned to his old singing coach, John Quinlan, to practice "calisthenics for the throat." Quinlan convinced him of the importance of vocalizing, singing without words, every day, a discipline to which Sinatra would adhere all his working life. Whenever possible before appearances, Frank rehearsed over and over, with Hank Sanicola playing piano.

Two years earlier, at the Rustic Cabin, another singing waiter had said he thought Frank was a **bel canto** singer. Now, with success beckoning, Frank decided **bel canto** might be the "something different" he needed. The Italian phrase, which dates back to the Middle Ages, simply means "beautiful singing." Articulating the full meaning of **bel canto** to laymen, however, tends to elude even the experts. The music writer Albert Innaurato has called it "never-never-land stuff . . . that impossible balance between word and tone . . . simultaneous sound and sense emerging from powerful emotion."

Innaurato thought Sinatra mastered the skills of **bel canto,** usually aspired to by opera singers, without pretending to operatic power. Both he and Ella Fitzgerald, he wrote, "have opera houses in their throats, and the breath of life courses through their voices . . . getting our souls to vibrate in response." Luciano Pavarotti thought the mature Sinatra came "very close to Italian **bel canto.**"

Less sophisticated listeners, a music critic pointed out, may have heard Frank's singing technique and thought it sounded like "moaning and mooing." Even Connie Haines, who also made the move from Harry James's band to Dorsey's, was at first nonplussed. "I didn't know if I cared for it," she remembered. "We had real 'trained voices' before that, you know. But Frank believed in the **words,** like an actor. He delivered the message. As a young singer I didn't understand. But when I hear him now I think he was the greatest singer in the business—ever."

Within three months of joining Dorsey, Frank was winning converts. A trio of musicians, including Frank's predecessor with the band, Jack Leonard, went to hear the "new kid" at a New York performance. "We all were sure he was gonna fall on his ass," pianist Joel Herron remembered, "but when he started to sing, I sunk down in my seat. I felt humiliated for the guy who was sitting next to me—Leonard—who had just become the oldest kind of news that there was in the world."

In May 1940, the Dorsey band played the nightclub at the Astor Hotel, near Times Square. A famous bar was reopening that night, and the place was filled with celebrities. When Frank sang "Begin the Beguine," Joe Bushkin recalled, "the place went bananas." When he followed up with "Polka Dots and Moonbeams," he remembered, "the people were still going nuts." That posed a problem, for the band had no more solo songs for Frank in its repertoire. "Just sing whatever you want to with Joe," Dorsey said, then Frank and Bushkin managed to get through several unrehearsed songs. Bushkin was thrown, though, when Frank called for "Smoke Gets in Your Eyes." "If you know the tune," Bushkin said, "you know you can really get lost in the middle. . . . I'm right out there without bread and water, man. . . . I couldn't find the chord change. Next thing I know, Frank was out there singing it all by himself." So helpless did Bushkin feel that for a few moments he actually walked away from the piano.

Yet Frank never lost the audience. That was the night, Bushkin thought, that "Frank Sinatra happened." Crowds flocked to the Astor, and the band's engagement was extended. The place was jam-packed all summer.

FRANK WAS ANXIOUS to make records, and with Dorsey he had ample opportunity. In the era before long-playing records, Frank recalled, the trick was to churn out "three hard-thrill minutes of commercial music" as often as possible. Eighty-four songs featuring Sinatra were released in the nearly three years he was with the band, more than forty of them in the first year alone. One of them was "I'll Never Smile Again."

The song was written by a young woman pianist mourning the death of her husband. It came to Dorsey as a demo record, but for some time he did not bother to listen to it. When he and colleagues finally did so, in his office at Rockefeller Center in Manhattan, they thought the song had obvious commercial appeal. Dorsey rushed to record it, but was dissatisfied with the result. Then he tried again with the Sentimentalists, a group consisting of Frank as lead singer and the Pied Pipers quartet. He urged them to sing "real easy, like five people sitting around a piano in the living room." Dorsey's trombone and a tinkling keyboard sustained the melancholy:

> I'll never smile again,
> Until I smile at you.

The song topped the charts for twelve weeks, beginning in mid-July 1940, receiving endless play on the radio and on jukeboxes across the country. Though Frank was credited on the record's label, his contribution earned him only a $25 bonus. Yet everyone involved knew that he had made a breakthrough, that "I'll Never Smile Again" was a career milestone.

Soon came more Dorsey-Sinatra hits focusing on loneliness: "Everything Happens to Me," the lament of a fellow whose girl has told him goodbye, "Stardust," and "I Guess I'll Have to Dream the Rest," a song of romance unfulfilled. Countless future Sinatra songs played on the same theme. Loneliness was to be his stock-in-trade.

Music programs aside, the radio was full of news about the war. Edward R. Murrow, broadcasting from London for CBS, brought the thud of exploding bombs and wailing sirens into American living rooms. Winston Churchill was promising resolute defiance of Hitler "until, in God's good time, the New World, with all its power and might, steps forth to the rescue." Though more than a year was to pass before the United States entered the war, the mood was established. In October 1940, President Roosevelt announced that 16 million American men were to register for the draft. Frank, who was one of them, filled out a Selective Service questionnaire stating that he had "no physical or mental defects or diseases."

Thousands of those already involved in the war were by now listening to Frank. "Young man," Churchill told him years later, "you belong to my people as well as your own. For yours was the voice that sang them to sleep in that infamous summer of 1940."

In the fall, when the band was performing at the Palladium ballroom in Los Angeles, they were recruited to appear in an undistinguished Paramount movie called **Las Vegas Nights.** Frank got to sing "I'll Never Smile Again" for an extra's fee of about $15 a day. The band members' fantasy, Bobby Burns remembered, was that their Hollywood sojourn would mean "lying in that warm sun, eating avocados, and walking with beautiful starlets in the moonlight." Frank lived the dream. He set himself up in a luxury suite, charging the bill to Dorsey, and installed in it a blond actress, Alora Gooding. Their affair continued for some time. Nick Sevano thought Gooding was Frank's "first big love away from home. . . . She was his first brush with glamour, and he was mad for her."

Nancy found out about the other woman, and had special reason to feel betrayed. Four months earlier she had given birth to a daughter, named Nancy after her mother. Frank had been excited by the news, and dubbed her "Miss Moonbeams." His song "Nancy" (with the laughing face)—not his idea but a colleague's several years later—would become a favorite among GIs. On the surface, the Sinatras' marriage appeared solid. In fact it had been shaky from the start, and all the more so now because of the infidelities of a young man constantly away from home.

Joe Bushkin, who liked Frank, watched him play the field from the vantage point of his piano. "Frank would tap me on the shoulder and say, 'Check the action out!' Some gal with a lot of booze in her would be shaking it up on the dance floor. . . . Whenever he could take a shot at a woman he would."

Taking a shot cannot have been difficult. "I used to stand there on the bandstand so amazed I'd almost forget to take my solos," Dorsey said. "You could feel the excitement coming out of the crowds when that kid stood up to sing. He was no matinee idol. He was a skinny kid with big ears. Yet what he did to women was something awful."

The columnist Liz Smith, then a seventeen-year-old in Fort Worth, Texas, savored the memory. "I looked up at him in the flesh and sighed," she remembered. "Our local boyfriends were livid that we looked over their shoulders longingly, failed to hear what they were saying."

Peggy Maley, a future actress, saw Frank at the Astor Roof while home from convent school. "There was this thin gentleman singing with this fantastic voice. His throat qui-i-i-ivered like . . . -like . . . I was spellbound. I fell in love with his voice."

Shirley Kelley, a fan who heard Frank in Montreal, thought it was "the way he caressed the song, phrasing the words so that each of us felt: He's singing to **me.** Half hypnotized, we paused and we swayed, drawing closer to the stage and to him. . . . I still cannot evoke anything about the young man who took me dancing on my first big date. When I try, what I remember is the powerful charisma of a young Frank Sinatra."

"I can have every dame I want," Frank said on a trip to Hoboken, according to his friend Joe D'Orazio. "I just can't help myself. I don't want to hurt Nancy. I just don't want to sleep with her no more."

In a conversation with Sammy Cahn, Frank

made it clear the marriage was in trouble. "A short time after we had little Nancy," he admitted much later, "I knew our marriage was going badly. We should have been very happy, but we weren't." As Bushkin put it, the woman Frank had married was "neighborhood serious," but Frank had quit the neighborhood.

On tour with Dorsey, Frank wrote his wife a letter freighted with contrition. She might doubt his sincerity, he wrote, "because of past happenings" but he promised to do better.

As the marriage continued its slow collapse, Frank collaborated with Hank Sanicola on a song called "This Love of Mine," one of only two to which he contributed lyrics over the years. He sang it in the style of "I'll Never Smile Again," and the words were painfully appropriate to his wife's situation:

> I cry my heart out—it's bound to break,
> Since nothing matters, let it break.

Nancy preferred the song, Frank said, over all his early work.

"NOTHING MEANT ANYTHING to him except his career," Nick Sevano said. "He had a drive like I've never seen in anybody." Dorsey had said repeatedly that Frank should take his lead from only one singer, Bing Crosby. By 1940, though, Frank remembered thinking, maybe the world didn't need another Crosby.

During the shooting of LAS VEGAS NIGHTS, Crosby had stopped by the studio and listened to Frank as he sang "I'll Never Smile Again." "This Sinatra," he said to Dorsey afterward, "very good, Tommy. I think you've got something there."

In the spring of 1941, six months and several hits later, Frank was picked as number one male singer in a survey of college students. By year's end, all three major music magazines would give him their top rating. Crosby's crown was no longer secure, and Frank was his closest rival. Americans passionately debated the two singers' relative merits.

Metronome critic George Simon, who saw a lot of Frank around this time, thought he had become "unbearably cocky." Frank told Sammy Cahn, as he had Harry James, that he expected to be "the best singer in the world." He said much the same thing during an encounter at a New Jersey ballroom with the show business writer Earl Wilson.

Frank was taking on airs and graces. "He didn't like me because I was from down south and wasn't New York–sophisticated like he thought he was," said Connie Haines. "He called me 'cornball,' 'squaresville.' He would be talking behind me while I was doing the jitterbug and singing. I would run off stage sometimes in tears. He got furious one time and said: 'I'm not going to sing on the same mike as her. I want two mikes.' "

Dorsey, who slapped down Frank on that occasion, remembered how he could "sulk like a kid." He was also prone to violent outbursts—a trait he had displayed in his days at the Rustic Cabin. "I was changing into another gown in the dressing room," Lucille Kirk recalled, "when he came rushing in angry about something. He picked up a makeup mirror and just threw it. It broke, and he rushed out again. He had some temper."

Sometimes Frank went looking for a fight. When Harry James's drummer Ralph Hawkins made a sarcastic remark about singers, he had wanted to settle the matter with his fists. If a drunk in the audience became a nuisance, Frank would attack him. When a customer threw popcorn onto the stage, Jo Stafford remembered, he "flew off the bandstand . . . ready to tear him to pieces." "The trouble with hanging around with Frank," said Milton Berle, who met him in 1940, was that "I always seemed to end up in fights."

Frank's spats with drummer Buddy Rich led to violence. Both were brilliant musicians endowed with colossal egos and hair-trigger tempers. They were friends—rooming together, sitting alongside each other on the tour bus—but then they began bickering. It started over trivial things, but the real conflicts were professional ones. Rich felt that the band's concentration on soft, Sinatra-style ballads gave him little chance to showcase his skills. As a star in his own right, he resented the fact that Frank got more prominent billing than he did. He found ways to irritate Frank, drumming too loud or at the wrong tempo, or talking in a raised voice when Sinatra was singing.

One night, during a quarrel backstage, Frank exploded. "Buddy was behind me screaming at Frank," Jo Stafford recalled. "Where Frank was standing there was a big tray with those old-fashioned pitchers full of ice water. . . . The next thing I knew there was this tremendous crash above my head. Frank had picked up one of those pitchers and had thrown it at Buddy. If it had hit him, it would have severely injured him and maybe even killed him." Sinatra and Rich began punching each other, then were separated by colleagues.

On September 1, 1940, **Down Beat** reported that Rich had been beaten up in the street by two men, sustaining injuries that left his face "as if it had been smashed in with a shovel." The assailants had been total strangers to Rich, according to his biographer Mel Tormé, and they had stolen nothing. The beating they administered, Tormé wrote, was "coldly efficient and professional."

Rich asked Frank if he was behind the attack. Frank hesitated, then confessed that "he had asked a favor of a couple of Hoboken guys." Even after that admission, amazingly, the pair later made up. When Rich wanted to form his own band, Frank lent him a large sum of money. They performed together far into the future, and Frank helped when Rich was seriously ill. The relationship encapsulated the extreme manifestations of Sinatra's character—from violent retaliation to lavish generosity. "He's the most fascinating man in the world," Tommy Dorsey famously remarked, "but don't stick your hand in the cage."

By early 1941, the bandleader's relations with Sinatra were deteriorating. Frank's tantrums and moodiness had become a nuisance to Dorsey, who himself had a short fuse. He sent Frank home the night he threw the jug at Rich. The band could function without a singer, he grumbled, but not without a drummer. He fired Frank when he made life unpleasant for Connie Haines, only to rehire him soon afterward. A real rift was opening up between the two men, one that deepened in proportion to Frank's success. Dorsey advance man "Bullets" Durgom, whose job it was to drum up interest at radio stations, found that "all they wanted to hear about was Frank." "This boy's going to be big," he told a reporter, "if Tommy doesn't kill him first. Tommy doesn't like Frank stealing the show—and he doesn't like people who are temperamental like himself."

Dorsey liked regimentation in his musicians—he outfitted the band in uniforms—and that did not suit Frank. The bandleader deplored the little curl on the forehead that Frank affected, and once ordered him to leave the stage and "go and comb your goddamn hair." Each night, like his fellow "vocalists," Frank had to sit with his arms folded until Dorsey signaled him to center stage. "We were like puppets," he remembered, "and Tommy was the guy who pulled the strings." Frank put up with working in Dorsey's shadow for many months, but he was restless. In the fall of 1941, by his account, he gave Dorsey a year's notice. "Tommy was very angry," he said, "refused to speak to me for months." Dorsey raised Frank's pay to $250 a month, but word spread in music circles that Frank might go "on strike."

In January 1942, Dorsey allowed Frank to record as a soloist. This was a major step forward, and he rehearsed intensively before the session at a Los Angeles studio. "It was a real nervous moment," recalled Dorsey arranger Axel Stordahl. "Frank didn't know what would happen—whether he would sell alone on a label. I'll never forget when we got the dubs [early copies]. We sat there in Frank's room in the Hollywood Plaza Hotel listening to them over and over. This was a turning point in his career."

Connie Haines recalled the scene as the band heard the first cut. "Frank sat on a stool. He had on one of those hats Bing Crosby had made popular. It was slouched down over his head at just the right angle, and he had a pipe in his mouth. I watched. . . . Little involuntary movements of his shoulders, eyes, fingers. . . . As the last note ended, we all knew it was a hit. The musicians rose to their feet as if one. They cheered. Then I heard him say, 'Hey, Bing, old man. Move over. Here I come.' "

The four songs Frank had recorded at the first solo session—"Night and Day," "The Night We Called It a Day," "The Song Is You," and "The Lamplighter's Serenade"—were well received. He continued to top popularity polls. At concerts crowds insisted on encore after encore. Dorsey reportedly raised his salary to $400 a week ($4,500 today).

Yet Frank was still miserable, a bundle of nerves. He picked at his food, flitted from doctor to doctor. "He started talking about death and dying," Nick Sevano recalled. "He'd tell me he didn't think he'd live long." Frank was in this state, he told Sevano and Sanicola, because he felt he had to leave Dorsey or be overtaken by other singers.

When Frank again told Dorsey he planned to quit soon, the bandleader reacted first with disbelief, then with a plea to stay on, then with anger. Frank, he insisted, had to stay on until the end of his contract—two more years. In the hope that Dorsey would give up on him, Frank began showing up late for broadcasts and walking out of recording sessions. It did not work.

Ever more desperate, Frank worked through the summer of 1942 on a breakneck schedule that took the band to New York, Montreal, Detroit, Philadelphia, Baltimore, Washington, and on to the Midwest. In Washington, he told Dorsey once and for all that he was leaving. The bandleader had him sign a severance agreement, then reportedly shrugged, "Let him go. Might be the best thing for me."

Frank sang with the band for the last time on September 10, 1942, in Minneapolis. As the drinks flowed after the show, according to Dorsey, Frank "was literally crying on my shoulder . . . depressed about what would happen to his career." Three months short of his twenty-seventh birthday, after nearly three years with the country's top band, he was on his own—but with horrendous strings attached.

"You're not gonna leave this band as easy as you think you are," Dorsey had said. Frank had ignored the stern clauses in the document that set him free. Under the terms of the release, Frank agreed to pay a third of all future earnings over $100 a week to Dorsey for the next ten years. Another 10 percent "off the top" was to go to Dorsey's manager. These deductions were to be made before expenses and taxes. It is possible, moreover, that the severance deal applied not for ten years but for an unlimited period of time. (Frank also had to pay 10 percent of all his earnings to the agent he had taken on to represent him as a solo performer.)

The following year, when the dollars were rolling in, Frank told the press it was "wrong for anybody to own a piece of him." He would dismiss the Dorsey severance deal as having been just a "ratty piece of paper." When he failed to honor the agreement, Dorsey and his manager sued. Then suddenly, two days after the Dorsey suit had been filed in California, it was settled out of court.

"I hired a couple of lawyers to get me out of it," Frank said a decade later. "They spoke to Dorsey, but he refused to budge. Finally I was referred to a noted theatrical attorney, Henry Jaffe, and he took me to Jules Stein, head of the biggest theatrical agency, Music Corporation of America. Mr. Stein was anxious to represent me and secured my release for $60,000, he contributing $35,000 and I paying $25,000 [$625,000 today]."

Sinatra offered more detail years later. Dorsey initially refused to give ground, he said, insisting: "No! No! No! No! I want one third of his salary for the rest of his life—as long as he lives." Using his clout as counsel for the American Federation of Radio Artists, according to Sinatra, Jaffe responded with a direct threat. The conversation went as follows:

Jaffe: "You enjoy playing music in hotel rooms and having the nation hear you on the radio? . . . You like broadcasting on NBC?"

Dorsey: "Sure I do."

Jaffe: "Not anymore you won't. . . . Well, how about we talk about Frank Sinatra and we'll see what kind of deal we can make—if you want to continue on radio."

As Sinatra told it, that was the exchange that broke Dorsey's resolve and persuaded him to cut a deal.

Dorsey's version of the episode began to emerge only a decade later, in a 1951 magazine article. He had surrendered, Dorsey was quoted as saying, only after "he was visited by three businesslike men, who told him out of the sides of their mouths to 'sign or else.' " Former Las Vegas casino entertainment director Ed Becker said Dorsey told him privately about the episode. "Tommy told me it was true," Becker recalled. "He said, 'Three guys from New York City by way of Boston and New Jersey approached me and said they would like to buy Frank's contract. I said "Like hell you will." . . . And they pulled out a gun and said, "You wanna sign the contract?" And I did.' "

Sinatra insisted that nothing remotely like that ever happened. A former attorney of Dorsey's, as well as a former aide, said they knew of no such intimidation. Frank's friend Brad Dexter, however, said Frank acknowledged to him that the story was true. Two of Dorsey's children said the threat was discussed in the family. "I'm sure it's fact," said his son, Tommy Dorsey III. Dorsey's daughter Patricia, who said she heard about the episode from her grandparents, said, "There was a threat that somebody was going to kidnap my brother and me. I assume that those were the kind of threats that made Dad decide to go on and let him out of the contract."

Before his death in 1956, Dorsey told Lloyd Shearer, then the West Coast correspondent for **Parade** magazine, "I was visited by Willie Moretti and a couple of his boys. Willie fingered a gun and told me he was glad to hear that I was letting Frank out of our deal. I took the hint."

The mobster Joseph "Doc" Stacher, who worked with Luciano's people, said, "The Italians among us were very proud of Frank. They always told us they had spent a lot of money helping him in his career, ever since he was with Tommy Dorsey's band."

Luciano himself spoke before his death of the time "when some dough was needed to put Frank across with the public. . . . I think it was about fifty or sixty grand. I okayed the money and it come out of the fund, even though some guys put up a little extra on a personal basis. It all helped him become a big star."

From the time the mob forced Dorsey to back down, a Federal Bureau of Narcotics document stated in the 1950s, Sinatra became "one of many in the entertainment world who knowingly collaborates with the Big Mob." According to his friend Sonny King, Luciano and Frank Costello "assigned" two specific mafiosi to handle Sinatra. Joe Fischetti, King said, was to "be around him all the time." Sam Giancana, the future Chicago Mafia boss, was there to step in "if major things came up." In the words of Giancana's mistress Phyllis McGuire, Frank remained "friends with the Boys for years, ever since he needed to get out of his contract with Tommy Dorsey."

"You don't know Italians the way Italians know Italians," said Gene DiNovi, an Italian-American pianist who worked with Sinatra. "Italians tend to break down into two kinds of people: Lucky Luciano or Michelangelo. Frank's an exception. He's both."

8

"F-R-A-N-K-I-E-E-E-E-E!"

"I HOPE YOU FALL ON YOUR ASS!" Tommy Dorsey told Frank as their dispute ended. He did not think Sinatra would last long on his own.

Frank should have been able to walk away from Dorsey and straight into a lucrative contract with Columbia Records. A top Columbia executive, Emanuel "Manie" Sacks, had long since recognized his talent and promised him recording work as a soloist the moment he was free. By the time he was, however, the recording industry was paralyzed by labor problems that effectively closed down the studios for two years.

So Frank headed for Hollywood. He made a brief singing appearance in a B movie called **Reveille with Beverly,** tried and failed to get a job as a staff singer with NBC, and then went back east. The comedian George Burns rejected him and picked instead a singing group the Three

Smoothies—a.k.a. Babs and her Brothers—for a weekly spot on his radio show. Sacks found him a fifteen-minute show on CBS Radio, which did provide some important exposure. By late 1942, though, Frank was back in New Jersey playing small-town theaters.

His luck turned on December 12, his twenty-seventh birthday, thanks to a persistent New York booker named Harry Romm. After weeks of trying, Romm got the attention of Robert Weitman, director of the Paramount Theater, Broadway's hottest music and movie venue. Weitman already had a surefire New Year's show, the musical comedy movie **Star Spangled Rhythm** starring Bing Crosby, coupled with Benny Goodman's band.

Nevertheless, Romm went on and on about Sinatra. "Take a chance. Come over and look for yourself," he recalled telling Weitman. "It's the damnedest thing you ever saw. A skinny kid who looks strictly from hunger is singing over in Newark and the she-kids are yelling and fainting all over the joint. You've got to see it to believe it." Weitman agreed to go to Newark's cavernous Mosque Theater to hear Sinatra perform. The place was less than half full. "Then," he remembered, "this skinny kid walks out on the stage. He was not much older than the kids in the seats. He looked like he still had milk on his chin. As soon as they saw him, the kids went crazy. And when he started to sing they stood up and yelled and moaned and carried on until I thought—excuse the expression—his pants had fallen down."

Weitman swung into action within hours. "He rang me at the house," Frank remembered, "and said, 'What are you doing New Year's Eve?' I said, 'Not a thing. I can't even get booked anywhere. . . .' He said, 'I'd like you to open at the joint.' He used to call the Paramount 'the joint.' I said, 'You mean on New Year's Eve?' He said, 'That's right.' . . . And I fell right on my butt!"

The Paramount was majestic, the tallest structure on Broadway north of the Woolworth Building. The illuminated glass globe at its top could be seen as far away as New Jersey. It was the model for the vast movie palaces of the day, and its plush red and gold auditorium could accommodate almost four thousand people. Bing Crosby, Rudy Vallee, Fred Astaire, Gary Cooper, Mae West, and Claudette Colbert were among the stars who had seen their names on the marquee beneath the Paramount's vast ornamental arch. At dawn on December 30, when Frank arrived to rehearse, there was his name beneath the title of the movie and "Benny Goodman and His Band" and alongside the billing for the Radio Rogues comedy act: "EXTRA—FRANK SINATRA."

That night was pivotal. For all his early success, he was still relatively unknown. When Weitman told Goodman that Frank would be appearing, Goodman asked: "Who's he?" The comedian Jack

Benny introduced Frank onstage as though he was a bosom pal—as a favor to Weitman. He had in fact never heard of him before.

As Sinatra's name was spoken, though, there came a reaction from the audience that no one present ever forgot. "I thought the goddamned building was going to cave in," said Benny. "People running down to the stage, screaming." As Weitman remembered it, there was a long call from the audience of "F-R-A-N-K-I-E-E-E-E-E!" Sinatra himself recalled a sound that was "absolutely deafening . . . a tremendous roar." Conducting with his back to the audience, Goodman could not imagine what was going on.

Frank froze in terror for a moment, then burst out laughing. He could not remember later whether he began by singing "For Me and My Gal" or "That Old Black Magic." "The devout," wrote the editor of **The New Republic,** Bruce Bliven, had recognized "a pleasant-appearing young man" who "with gawky long steps moves awkwardly to the center of the stage while the shrieking continues. . . . He has a head of black curls and holds it to one side as he gestures clumsily and bashfully, trying to keep the crowd quiet enough for him to sing."

Something unprecedented had begun. Vast throngs of people, most of them female and very young, began flocking to the theater. Frank was soon singing as many as a hundred songs a day—at least nine shows. "One Saturday I did eleven shows," he remembered. "We started at 8:10 in the morning and finished at 2:30 Sunday morning."

When his family came to the theater they became part of the spectacle. Nancy was swallowed up in the throng and Dolly was pawed by the fans. "I couldn't **hear**," Marty complained. "Who could hear?" It was all too much for Francesco Sinatra, by then in his late eighties. "I put him in the third row, in among the kids," Frank remembered. "He didn't know what the hell happened to him because when I came out on the stage everything broke loose and he just sat there. I could see his face. He was absolutely terrified. They brought him back in the dressing room after the performance, and he was so angry—that he had come that far and never heard me sing. He didn't understand that that was the game that the kids played."

The original one-week appearance at the Paramount was extended, first to a month, then to two months, a theater record. Frank agreed to return in the spring. His audience was made up overwhelmingly of schoolgirls in their early or mid-teens, typically dressed in sweaters, knee-length skirts, and white socks—bobbysoxers. **Webster's** defines a bobbysoxer as an "adolescent girl."

"The squealing yells reverberated," Bob Weitman's friend Armand Deutsch, the Sears, Roebuck heir, said of the fans. "It was a new sound, a screaming expression of adulation and curiously innocent eroticism. They were, Bob told me sadly, almost impossible to dislodge, fiercely fighting all eviction efforts and drastically cutting the grosses."

Few bobbysoxers stayed for only one performance. They came with food and drink and settled in. Theater staff often found that the girls had urinated on their seats, either out of fear of losing them if they went to the bathroom or out of sheer excitement.

"They would scream every time he sang a word like 'love,' " said Al Viola, who later became Frank's principal guitarist. "I used to think, 'Oh, here it comes!' " Sometimes, though, the fans were "as hushed as if they were in church."

Fans fell to their knees in the aisles. Girls lined up to kiss Frank's picture on billboards, begged for trimmings from the floor of his barber's shop, snatched the handkerchief from his jacket pocket as he passed. In the hope of forcing him to stop and sign autographs, some flung themselves in front of his car. They gave him teddy bears, heart-shaped flower arrangements, a loving cup, a golden key—said to fit the heart of its sender.

Soon enough, when somewhat older worshippers joined the fans, female underwear was thrown from the audience, brassieres thrust forward for signing while still on their wearers. A woman got into Frank's dressing room and opened her coat to reveal she was naked.

"He was my idol when I was in eighth grade," Marie Caruba, a former teacher, recalled half a century later. "I had his photos all over my locker at Ansonia High. I worked some days at Gardella's Ice Cream Shop, and the only way I'd work in the afternoons would be if Mr. Gardella let me listen to Frank on the radio. I knew, of course, that he was singing just to me. We lived in Connecticut, and a girlfriend and I would hop a train down to New York to go to matinees at the Paramount. I went as often as I could, but my mother never knew."

"Groups of little girls used to play hooky from school," said another former bobbysoxer, the journalist Martha Lear, "off to shriek and swoon through four shows live, along with several thousand other demented teenagers. . . . That glorious shouldered spaghetti strand way down there in the spotlight would croon on serenely, giving us a quick little flick of a smile or, as a special bonus, a sidelong tremor of the lower lip. I used to bring binoculars just to watch that lower lip. . . . Before going home we would forge the notes from our parents: 'Please excuse Martha's absence from school yesterday as she was sick.' "

The New Republic's Bruce Bliven thought the devotees at the Paramount were almost all "children of the poor." E. J. Kahn, in **The New Yorker,** thought them "plain, lonely girls from lower-middle-class homes." The Hearst journalist Adela Rogers St. Johns remembered the fans as "unkempt, wistful, neglected." In March 1943, though, Frank proved his audience was not all juvenile or poor.

As he ended his first Paramount run, he cast around for a nightclub booking. Several owners turned him down, including Arthur Jarwood, who ran the Riobamba on 57th Street. "Sinatra's for kids," he scoffed. With business down because of the war, though, he changed his mind. Privately, Frank fretted about how he would go down with an older, wealthier audience, but as things turned out he upstaged his fellow entertainers and packed them in. "We could hardly get through the crowd who had come to see Frank," said singer-comedienne Sheila Barrett, who shared the bill. "The club was so crowded the chorus girls couldn't go on. Nor could a dance team booked first. . . . The crowd was impatient for us to get off. They wanted Frank!"

The **Billboard** critic wrote such an effusive review that his editor assumed he had been drunk. Earl Wilson, now writing the **New York Post** column that was to become an institution, thought it "a wondrous night." Sammy Cahn, who saw him at the Riobamba, thought it "one of the most cosmopolitan, varied audiences you can imagine—the kept girls, the rich, the famous, the infamous sports figures, hoodlums . . . you name it."

"Three times an evening," **Life** magazine told readers, "Sinatra steps into the baby spotlight that splashes on to the dance floor. In a come-hither, breathless voice, he then sings such songs as 'You'd Be So Nice to Come Home To,' 'That Old Black Magic,' 'She's Funny That Way,' and 'Embraceable You.' As he whispers the lyrics, he fondles his wedding ring and his eyes grow misty. A hush hangs over the tables, and in the eyes of the women present there is soft contentment. The lights go on and Sinatra bows, slouches across the floor and is swallowed up by the shadows."

Two weeks into the Riobamba stint, Sheila Barrett and entertainer Walter O'Keefe were dropped. "When I came to this place," O'Keefe said, "I was the star and a kid named Sinatra was one of the acts. Then a steamroller came along and knocked me flat. Ladies and gentlemen, I give you the rightful star—Frank Sinatra!"

From the Riobamba it was back to the Paramount for another feverish month. Then, rare for a pop singer, he sang at concerts with the symphony orchestras of Washington, Cleveland, New York, and Los Angeles. In Washington, he sang to fifteen thousand people from a floating stage on the Potomac. Most wandered away when the orchestra moved on to Beethoven and Bach. Frank called the musicians of the New York Philharmonic "the boys in the band." In Los Angeles, highbrows were outraged that a "swing-shift

Caruso" was sullying the temples of classical music. Thousands of fans besieged the railroad station when he arrived, though, and conductor Vladimir Bakaleinikoff welcomed Frank warmly. The boost to the orchestra finances outweighed all objections. Classical musicians were often to work with Sinatra in the years that followed, in an atmosphere of mutual respect.

Frank had gone to Hollywood to make a musical comedy in which he would play himself. In **Higher and Higher,** he sang five songs and spoke the first line of dialogue of his movie career. "Good morning. My name is Frank Sinatra," he said on a doorstep, and a housemaid fainted in his arms. The film was forgettable.

Back in New York, he performed at the Wedgwood Room of the Waldorf-Astoria, for an audience even richer and classier than that at the Riobamba. Between engagements, he sang on national radio shows. He was on **Your Hit Parade** every Saturday night.

By the summer of 1944 he was again in Hollywood, to make a patriotic, big-budget wartime movie. **Anchors Aweigh** featured him improbably as a timorous bookworm and choirmaster who dialed the phone company for a time check when other sailors were calling their dates. Frank learned to dance for the film, with the help of Gene Kelly. "I couldn't walk, let alone dance," he recalled. "I was a guy who got up and hung on to a microphone. . . . And one of the reasons I became a 'star' was Gene Kelly." Frank progressed "from lousy to adequate," Kelly said, by working harder than anyone he had ever known.

On October 11, opening night at the Paramount in New York, Frank triggered a frenzy unprecedented in the history of music. Girls waited all night in the street to buy tickets. When the doors opened, a capacity crowd crammed into the theater and began chanting his name. The fans totally ignored the movie that was shown and then—when he appeared—their screaming made him virtually inaudible.

By five o'clock in the morning the next day, a veritable army of young people was already waiting outside and near the Paramount. "I ventured down to Times Square," wrote Earl Wilson, who had been working through the night at the **Post,** "and was literally scared away. The police estimated that 10,000 kids were queued up six abreast on 43rd Street, Eighth Avenue, and 44th Street, and another 20,000 were running wild in Times Square, overrunning the sidewalks and making traffic movement almost impossible.

"Over on Fifth Avenue, a Columbus Day parade was forming. Two hundred cops were taken off guard duty there and rushed over. . . . Eventually there were 421 police reserves, twenty radio cars, two emergency trucks, four lieutenants, six sergeants, two captains, two assistant chief inspectors, two inspectors, seventy patrolmen, fifty traffic cops, twelve mounted police, twenty policewomen and two hundred detectives, trying to control some 25,000 teenage girls. Girls shrieked, fainted—or swooned—fell down, were stepped on and pulled up by their companions and resumed screaming. They rushed the ticket booth and damaged it. Windows were broken."

Of the 3,600 fans admitted for the first performance, only a couple of hundred left when it ended. Angry thousands waiting outside swarmed the neighborhood all day, not dispersing until nightfall. There was similar chaos when Frank appeared in Chicago, Boston, and Pittsburgh. **The New Republic** described it as an "electric contagion of excitement . . . a phenomenon of mass hysteria that is seen only two or three times in a century."

The adulation of Elvis Presley ten years later, or of the Beatles in 1964, perhaps came close. The furor over Frank, though, was the first eruption of youthful idolatry in the twentieth century, and as great as any that has come since.

YOUNG GIRLS in World War II America were reported to be not just shrieking but swooning over Frank Sinatra. It had started at the first of the Paramount shows, according to the historian William Manchester. "A girl in the twelfth row who hadn't eaten lunch," Manchester wrote, "fainted—or 'swooned.' " Another girl "appeared at the theater daily, an unattractive, freckle-faced girl of about sixteen who wore glasses and her hair in pigtails. She could stand just so much of Sinatra's voice, and then she'd keel over in a faint."

"These dames come in night after night," said a waiter at the Riobamba. "When this guy sings, they actually swoon. We got to bring them water to keep them conscious. It's plain wacky." Bruce Bliven watched fans "slump in their seats, either fainting or convincing themselves that they are doing so." A girl wrote Frank to say that, after four swooning episodes, "I fell out of a chair and bumped my head. I decided to sit on the floor in the beginning when I listen to you."

"We loved to swoon," said Martha Lear. "We would gather behind locked bedroom doors, in rooms where rosebud wallpaper was plastered all over with pictures of The Voice, to practice swooning. We would put on his records and stand around groaning for a while. Then the song would end and we would all fall down on the floor."

The hysteria was encouraged by Sinatra's own people, perhaps started by them. "The whole sobbing business began with a wonderful press agent," said the actress Celeste Holm, who was playing in **Oklahoma!** at a nearby theater at the time. "He stood in the back of the house and said

'How many kids can you round up to come to tonight's show?' They said 'Why?' and he said, 'I'll let you in for nothing and I'll give you $10 apiece if you'll do just what you're doing, only ten times louder.' That's how it started."

Sinatra's first press agent, Milton Rubin, is said to have stood in the lobby of the Paramount handing out half-dollars—a more plausible figure than Holm's $10. He was replaced by George Evans, a master of invention who had represented Russ Columbo, Rudy Vallee, and Glenn Miller. Evans was to concede that "certain things were done. It would be as wrong of me to divulge them as it would be for a doctor to discuss his work." He denied having induced fans to "go in and screech" and pledged to donate $5,000 to charity should anyone prove otherwise. "I like to keep their wings flapping," he said of the bobbysoxers.

That meant, in part, distributing free tickets, stationing an ambulance and nurses near the theater to encourage would-be swooners, and arranging for girls to plant kisses on Frank—leaving him smeared with bright red lipstick. Evans assembled fans in the Paramount basement for coaching on when and how to squeal. According to Nick Sevano, Evans "had someone throw their panties on stage almost every show."

Jack Keller, Evans's assistant, said Frank's clothes were torn so often and so easily by the fans because he wore "breakaway suits" designed to fall apart if tugged. Keller said girls had indeed been "hired to scream when he sexily rolled a note." Years later, Evans himself admitted that "The Sinatra hysteria" had been "about 98% synthetic." Having heard a couple of "teenage honeys" moan, he said, had inspired him to get others to do the same. "Swooning became the newest craze," he said, "Frank rode to glory on it. . . . It was kind of comical turning this gawky guy into a love god, but I saw that he did have a certain effect on a lot of young girls. All I did was capitalize on it, enhance it a bit, and it worked."

Frank affected surprise at the frenetic display, said he disliked the girls' shrieking. He put it down to loneliness in wartime. "I was the boy in every corner drug store who'd gone off, drafted to the war. That was all." Yet he would stare into the eyes of individual fans, tease them by sticking his tongue out at them. "I never saw anything like the way he milks 'em and kicks 'em," a Broadway agent said.

Psychiatrists and psychologists prattled on about "mammary hyperesthesia," "mass hypnosis," speculated both that female fans wanted to mother Frank and be mothered by him, or saw him as a "father image." One psychologist, who thought Frank performed "a sort of melodic striptease," perhaps came closer to what was going on. A **Daily Variety** journalist put it another way: "To femmes of fifteen or thereabouts, he sang intimately, personally, like a guy parked with his girl in Lovers Lane."

"The young Sinatra," the music critic Francis Davis has written, "came across as a boy who might try to sweet-talk a girl into going all the way but wasn't going to be insistent—unlike the boys the girls knew in real life. . . . Often what young girls want in a boy is another girl, and the girls who swooned over Sinatra pressed him to their hearts as a young man who was as sensitive and, on some level, as self-conscious as they were."

"The sex element is the most important in this business," said Bobby Darin, a teen idol of the late 1950s. "You must sell sex." Sinatra, Darin thought, had the sort of magnetism that made a girl want to "park her shoes under the entertainer's bed." Martha Lear thought the psychologists and their theorizing ridiculous. "What yo-yo's!" she said. "Whatever stirred beneath our barely budding breasts, it wasn't motherly . . . the thing we had going with Frankie was **sexy.** It was exciting. It was terrific."

"What is it you've got," the actress Carmen Miranda asked Frank in 1944, "that makes the girls all cry over you?"

"It's not what I've got, Carmen," Frank replied, "it's what **they've** got. Imagination."

IT WAS HIS WORK on stage and on radio that had made Frank a star. Two days after the two-year union shutdown of the recording industry ended in 1944, though, Columbia executives rushed him into a studio for the first of several recording sessions. Seventeen songs were put on disc, including "Saturday Night (Is the Loneliest Night in the Week)," "Embraceable You," and "She's Funny That Way."

The Sinatra juggernaut rolled on and on. Frank had been making $400 a week when he left Tommy Dorsey. Now his agents could reportedly demand some $20,000 ($204,000 today) for an average week. In an especially busy seven-day period, Frank made $30,000. He made almost $1.5 million ($15,000,000 today) in both 1944 and 1945.

"I couldn't believe it," Nancy told the columnist Louella Parsons. "All I could think of was the time, six years before, when we had spaghetti without meat sauce because meat sauce was more expensive."

"I now own myself," Frank had said after extricating himself from the Dorsey contract, and he began to behave accordingly. He bought into a music publishing company, the Barton Music Corporation, and within three years would order construction of a Sinatra office building in Hollywood.

The Sinatra entourage had expanded. In addition to George Evans there was now a booking agent. Frank had filched Dorsey's arranger Axel

Stordahl, by more than quadrupling his salary. Stordahl was behind the lush sound and sheer quality that now marked Sinatra's work. Frank also hired Sammy Cahn and composer Jule Styne, who were to produce hit after hit for years. Jimmy Van Heusen, by now hugely successful in his own right, also wrote for Frank. Hank Sanicola doubled as manager, rehearsal coach, off-stage pianist, and, in Frank's words, as a sonofabitch who "would go down with the ship." Frank had fired Nick Sevano, though they would later reconcile. His role as general factotum was for a while filled by another Frank Sinatra, a first cousin from Hoboken who had been raised in the apartment across from the Sinatras'. According to the cousin's daughter, her father also functioned as a bodyguard. So did Sanicola.

Sinatra now openly cultivated a pugnacious image. "I'd like to see that guy backstage," he snarled at a heckler who flipped a penny onto the stage in Philadelphia. "If I can't lick him, I've got a big boy with me who can." Fred Tamburro, who had beaten up Frank when they were members of the Hoboken Four, was frightened off by a couple of heavies after pestering Sinatra for a loan. The professional trainer Al Silvani, with whom Frank worked out at Stillman's "muscle emporium" on Eighth Avenue in Manhattan, also became a bodyguard.

"I was intimidated," said George Avakian, a producer at Columbia Records. "Two [body]guards would come off the elevator. They'd look right and left. Then Frank would step out, and two other guys would step out, and they'd look right and left. They looked like five diamonds walking up the hall!"

Frank could also go out of his way to be caring and compassionate, as Peggy Lee discovered when she became ill while working with him at the Paramount. "He was my special nurse," she recalled. "First he brought me blankets to stop the shivering. Then, when it was possible, a little tea; later, a piece of toast. Meanwhile he was out there singing from six to eight shows a day." One night Frank shook hands with singer Ray Anthony, whom he knew was out of work, then hurried off. A moment later, Anthony realized he had been given $50. Frank drove out to New Jersey in a snowstorm to tell another hard-up musician about a job opening.

Such gestures were made without fanfare; others were bound to get attention. He liked throwing his money around. By the mid-1940s he had given three hundred gold cigarette lighters from Dunhill's—together costing nearly half a million dollars—to friends and acquaintances.

He sent a gold bracelet from Cartier's to Jule Styne, a gold watch to the comedian Rags Ragland. Others received gold cuff links. A friendly journalist got only a gold money clip, the same category of gift that Frank allotted to headwaiters. A bodyguard received a key chain, with letters attached spelling "Frank Sinatra" in gold. When Frank learned that the crew of a Navy PT boat had rechristened their ship the **Oh Frankie!**, he sent gold St. Christopher medals to the entire crew.

When not on stage Frank himself discarded the boyish sweaters, sports jackets, and "spaniel's ears" bowties familiar to his fans, and glittered with gold accessories. He favored sharply tailored dark suits and monogrammed shirts custom-made in New Jersey. It was said that he owned fifty suits, twenty-five sports jackets, a hundred pairs of slacks, and sixty pairs of shoes.

The Sinatras moved out of their Jersey City apartment and into a Cape Cod–style house in nearby Hasbrouck Heights. They did not stay there long. Frank now had a long-term contract with MGM, and decided to move to California. By Christmas 1944 the family was installed in a large pink house in the San Fernando Valley, at a superb waterside location on Toluca Lake. The previous owner had been the actress Mary Astor. Next door was the elite Lakeside Country Club, which turned up its nose at Jews, blacks, and some entertainers—including the upstart from Hoboken. Two members, Bing Crosby and Bob Hope, supported Frank's application in vain.

Snooty locals aside, Frank and Nancy had found an idyllic new home. They named it Warm

Valley—the same name they had given the Hasbrouck Heights house—and Nancy transformed the dark interior with creams, pastels, and flowered chintz. A fountain splashed on the patio. Frank improved the dock, bought a boat for expeditions on the lake, and built a raft. With a high stucco wall to one side, the water behind it, and a butler to keep out unwanted visitors, it was a perfect retreat for a star. Nancy called it the House That Music Built.

Almost all their friends were young and having fun. Nancy cooked spaghetti dinners for Mario Lanza, then still a fledgling tenor. Talented friends were recruited for home entertainment—Jule Styne on the piano, Sammy Cahn supplying patter and lyrics; Phil Silvers, Rags Ragland, and Danny Thomas producing the laughs; Frank in blackface singing "Mammy."

Sinatra formed a softball team that starred Styne and Cahn, Anthony Quinn, other actors and writers, and Hank Sanicola and Al Silvani. They called the team the Swooners.

During the day, the men played cards on the raft. At night there were endless games of gin rummy. "It was mostly the guys, except for Ethel Styne," recalled Cahn's first wife, Gloria, who met her husband at Warm Valley. "They played six or eight a side, for enormous stakes. Nancy and I were like the two maids or waitresses, feeding everybody, refilling the drinks, cleaning ashtrays."

To outsiders, the Sinatras appeared to be happy. George Evans, anxious to avoid the slightest whiff of scandal, made sure of that by orchestrating a succession of schmaltzy stories; the loving parents and their four-year-old daughter, Nancy, were even featured in a cartoon strip. This seeming bliss had been enhanced, just before the move to California, by the birth of a son, Franklin Wayne Emmanuel—Franklin for President Roosevelt and Emmanuel for Manie Sacks, the godfather. He came to be known as Frank Jr. This second child, Frank hoped, would cement the marriage. Instead, he said, "Little by little we drifted apart."

In New Jersey, when the tidal wave of publicity started, Nancy had tried to deal with the fan mail and handle the money herself. Frank's new staff took over those tasks, but she soon found that her house had become a goldfish bowl. Bobbysoxers had laid siege to it, scrawled messages of undying love for Frank in lipstick on doors and windowsills. Girls clambered on each other's shoulders to peer in bedroom windows, stole Frank's boxers off the clothesline. There were rumors of threats to kidnap the children.

In the pretentious world of California, Nancy was out of her depth. "People tried to get her not to dress like the little wife from New Jersey," recalled Gloria Cahn. "She got beautiful clothes made for her by Jean-Louis. But she was very much a homebody, a typical Italian who grew up to take care of her man and her family. She was very much 'real people.' I used to see her go by driving the huge wagon Frank had bought her, a Chrysler I think. It was a funny sight because she was such a tiny woman—I think she had to pack the seats with pillows so she could reach the pedals. . . . She was trying very hard to be what Frank needed as the star he had become, but . . ."

Virtually all of Nancy's family, her mother and father and her five sisters and their families, followed the Sinatras to California. One sister moved in with them. Frank complained to friends of coming home to find his home overrun with Barbato in-laws and their children.

"I was on edge and constantly irritable," Frank remembered. "Nancy and I found ourselves getting into terrible arguments." Frank often went out to parties on his own and now, at almost thirty, began to tipple more. He took a special liking to Jack Daniel's bourbon. "I began to drink it in the forties one night when I couldn't get to sleep," he was to say. "It's been the oil to my engine ever since."

The marriage to Nancy would produce a third child, but there was no passion left in it. Scuttlebutt about his dalliances with other women now increased. While working on **Anchors Aweigh**, it was said, Frank had a list in his dressing room of women at MGM he coveted. Makeup artist Gordon Bau said he saw the list pinned up on the inside of the door. Numerous names had been checked off by the time shooting ended.

The deterioration of the marriage was only one of a series of difficulties now looming, problems both of his own making and visited on him by enemies. To start with, he was having a difficult war.

9

Rejected for Service

When the Yanks go marchin' in.
I wanna be there boy . . .

WHEN HE OPENED AT THE PARAMOUNT again in October 1944, Frank chose to sing these lines from an unabashedly militaristic World War II song. It was not what his fans were used to, but they squealed anyway. In the barracks and mess halls, and on airfields and ships across the world, the men and women of American and Allied armed forces had been hearing the song for more than a year. The catalogue of V-Discs, records made exclusively for the military, includes more than ninety Sinatra songs.

Soldiers and airmen in the battles of Anzio and Monte Cassino had listened wistfully to "When Your Lover Has Gone" and "Falling in Love with Love." Troops braving German fire in Normandy had heard Frank sing "All the Things You Are" and "The Way You Look Tonight." Soldiers who crossed into Germany were familiar with his "Long Ago and Far Away" and "None but the Lonely Heart." His nickname, The Voice, was painted on the noses of American bombers. A newly released prisoner-of-war in Hong Kong, Alexander Shivarg, had a perplexing exchange with the first British servicemen he encountered after emerging from behind the wire. "I asked 'What's been happening?' And they said, 'Frankie Sinatra, that's what.'

" 'Sinatra' sounded a bit oriental, and I thought it must be some damn Pacific atoll I'd missed the name of, like Iwo Jima. But they laughed and said, 'No, he's a wop. He's skinny and unattractive, but he's got this wonderful voice that nobody can resist. He's an American singer, a kid just like us, and he makes girls' petticoats flutter and they wet their knickers when he sings. And sometimes he doesn't even have to sing. . . .' I couldn't believe it. I was shattered . . . all these people could talk about was Frank Sinatra. . . . Can you beat that damned Sinatra? More important to those kids than the war."

Even the enemy knew about him. The Japanese-American woman most identified with the Tokyo Rose propaganda broadcasts, Iga Toguri, had an interest in swing music from her student days in California. She made dark hints as to what that rascally Sinatra might be doing with the GIs' women while their men fought their way across the Pacific.

Frank's songs did smooth the way in American bedrooms. "Some women," Pete Hamill has written, "used that music, with its expression of sheer **need**, to seduce the available men. . . . He was singing to those women, of whatever age . . . for whom Saturday night truly was the loneliest night of the week." "I'll Be Seeing You" soothed husbands and wives, lovers and sweethearts, yearning to return to the old familiar places, to precious remembered embraces. Frank, former **Down Beat** editor Gene Lees wrote, "said for the boys what they wanted to say. He said for the girls what they wanted to hear."

Frank was in Hollywood, partying at Lana Turner's house, on the day that brought America into the war. The guests only learned of the attack on Pearl Harbor eight hours afterward, when a new arrival told them to turn on the radio. "As we listened," Turner recalled, "I looked around at the stunned young men in my living room, and thought how drastically our lives were going to change."

Professionally Frank energetically supported the war effort at home. The V-Disc program aside, he appeared on **Command Performance**, a radio show beamed to servicemen abroad. He sang at rally after rally, electrified a crowd in Central Park with his version of "God Bless America." He sang for military groups, including a curiously muted audience of WAVES, the women's naval auxiliary, who had been ordered not to behave like bobbysoxers. He asked fans to donate clothing for refugees. He raised money in a war loan drive by auctioning off his own clothes—a tie for $275, a shirt for $500, a pair of shorts for $1,000, a gold watch for $10,000.

Many musicians exchanged their civvies for uniforms. From the Dorsey band alone there were Joe Bushkin, Buddy Rich, trumpeter Ziggy Elman, arrangers Sy Oliver and Paul Weston, and manager Bobby Burns. Bandleaders Artie Shaw and Eddy Duchin enlisted in the navy. Glenn Miller insisted on joining up although he was too old to be drafted. Bands he organized for the Army Air Forces included musicians from his old band and those of James, Dorsey, Goodman, and Shaw. Miller died, six months after D-Day, while flying from England to France aboard a military aircraft.

Rudy Vallee was in the coast guard and Frankie Laine worked in an airplane factory. Jack Leonard, Frank's predecessor with Dorsey, was drafted into the army and awarded a Bronze Star for entertaining battle-weary troops. Mickey Rooney had a heart murmur, but got himself accepted by the army and went abroad as an entertainer. Gene Kelly enlisted in the navy and, though he asked for combat duty, was assigned to make propaganda movies. Others saw action. Clark Gable flew missions as a major in the air force, as did Jimmy Stewart, who was much decorated. The singer Jimmy Roselli served in combat in France. Frank, however, remained in the United States until the conflict ended, singing his way to fame and fortune. He would demonstrate his patriotism by flying the Stars and Stripes on a fifty-foot-high flagpole outside his home, and often played the soldier in movies. Yet he never donned a uniform during World II, stirring a controversy that was never satisfactorily resolved.

He had been one of 16 million young American men obliged to register for military service in late 1940, fulfilling what President Roosevelt called "the first duty of free citizenship." As "Frank Albert Sinatra," Serial No. 2615, he was granted a deferment on the grounds that he was married with a child. The deferment may have been accorded automatically, or in response to a request by him. It was subject to later review.

This was not an easy time for Italian-Americans. Though thousands were drafted and served with honor, their loyalty was suspect. Just as Japanese-Americans were interned, so too were some Italian-Americans who did not have American citizenship. They were released only in 1942, after government officials decided they posed no security risk. They were, Roosevelt quipped, only "a bunch of opera singers."

In the summer of 1943, in the full flush of his success, Frank applied to join the coast guard. There is no record of what became of the application. In the fall, though, with deferment for married fathers about to be abolished, he was reclassified 1-A—available for service. George Evans ensured that this fact received publicity. Frank passed a preliminary physical and, in December, was examined again. (The army medics noted his height as five feet seven and a half inches, about three inches shorter than he usually claimed.) He emerged from the induction center to announce that he had been rejected on medical grounds. The doctors, he said, had found a "hole in my ear I didn't know about" and "a few things I'd better take care of right away." He had been declared 4-F—"rejected for service for physical, mental or moral reasons." As fans rejoiced, rumors spread.

"Sinatra has no more ear trouble than General MacArthur," jeered a former Hoboken schoolmate. "How do you get a punctured eardrum?" a nightclub comic asked derisively. The young Pete Hamill heard his father dismiss Frank as a "draft dodger." At Camp Haan in California to entertain soldiers, Frank encountered Bobby Burns, now in uniform. "There's a lot of griping over your 4-F status," Burns told him. "The troops figure you're home living it up with the babes while they're away."

In October 1944, days after Frank was welcomed back to the Paramount by the bobbysoxers, someone in the third row hit him in the eye with an egg. Sailors threw rotten tomatoes at his picture on the marquee outside. During a showing of his movie **Higher and Higher,** marines got to their feet and booed. "It is not too much to say," wrote William Manchester, who served in the marines, "that by the end of the war Sinatra had become the most hated man in the armed services."

Frank's local draft board made things worse when it came up with a new and arcane classification. For a while in 1944 he became 2-A(F), defined as "qualified for limited military service" but deferred "in support of national health, safety or interest." One reporter's question, "Is crooning essential?," summed up the reaction. Then, in early 1945, Frank was summoned back to New Jersey for another medical examination.

The fans knew in advance that he was coming. Hundreds of them surged forward, tearing his clothes, as he arrived at the 113th Infantry Armory to see the doctors. Then, after Frank had been sent to Fort Jay for yet another examination, his file went to Washington "for review by high military officers under a ruling governing the reexamination of outstanding athletes and stage and screen stars." They decided once and for all that the "Frail Finch," as a New Jersey newspaper called him, would not be going to war. He was, once again, 4-F.

That was the end of the official process, but not of the suspicion and harsh criticism. "Can you tell me," a serviceman's mother asked in a letter to a newspaper within days, "why athletes or stage and screen stars are so important that there must be some special dispensation?" Conservative columnists had a field day. "The 4-F explanation is emotionally unsatisfactory," wrote George Sokolsky, deploring Frank's "opportunity to pursue his private business pursuits while other men of his age are forced to give up their careers and fight, even to death, for their country." Lee Mortimer, in the **New York Sunday Mirror**, derided Frank as a crooner who "found safety and $30,000 a week behind a mike" while others risked their lives. Hearst's Westbrook Pegler would still be sniping at "bugle-deaf Frankie Boy" years later.

Frank had told the **New York Times** before his first rejection that he would be "glad to serve," that he hoped to do "radio work or gunnery," perhaps in the marines. He expressed frustration at being excluded. According to Milton Berle's wife, Ruth, he had been "desperate" to serve.

The powerful Hedda Hopper, a columnist friendly to him, argued in his defense that he had supported the cause whenever possible, "singing night and day to win over those GI characters." She praised Frank, too, for having made a "war front tour." He had indeed made a seven-week tour singing for the troops in the Azores, North Africa, and Italy. Numerous entertainers had made similar trips early on, when there was significant risk. More than thirty "soldiers in greasepaint" had been killed during the war. Al Jolson and Joe E. Brown, both past fifty, had performed at forward bases on what was known as the Foxhole Circuit. Bing Crosby, Bob Hope, Merle Oberon, and Marlene Dietrich put themselves in harm's way before the German surrender in the spring of 1945. Yet only in June that year, after the guns had fallen silent, did Sinatra sing for the troops in Europe.

Frank's defenders have claimed he had wanted to do so all along but, as his daughter Nancy has put it, "the FBI denied him a visa because of the alleged Communist charges in the Hearst newspapers." The record, and the FBI file, tell a different story. Efforts to smear Frank for his political affiliations came only late in the war and he would be prevented from entertaining troops in Korea only ten years later.

Frank was not the only entertainer to stay out of the conflict. John Wayne went to extraordinary lengths to get out of war service. "He had his studio contrive ever-new exemptions for him," wrote

Garry Wills. Dean Martin had "the first real fright of his life" when he received his draft notice, according to one of his recent biographers. He did not want to serve, and was rescued by a double hernia. Jerry Lewis had hoped to get into the fight, but was exempted because of a heart murmur and, like Frank, a punctured eardrum. The **New York Times** referred laconically to the exemption Frank got as "another punctured eardrum case."

Weeks after the ear ailment was reportedly discovered, an anonymous letter was sent to a newspaper claiming that a Sinatra aide had paid doctors a huge bribe to ensure he got 4-F status. Ordered to investigate, FBI agents interviewed Captain Joseph Weintrob, the young army doctor who recommended the exemption. He denied that anyone had tried to influence him, and the FBI found no evidence to support the allegation. Weintrob said he had observed a perforation of the left eardrum consistent with previous disease, as well as scars consistent with mastoid surgery. X-rays, he and another doctor said, supported the finding. Yet draft board physician Dr. Alexander Povalski, examining Frank two months before Weintrob, had found no evidence of ear damage.

In three draft questionnaires, Frank had responded "no" to questions as to whether he had any physical defects. In Weintrob's formal report to his superiors, however, he said Frank drew attention to the ear. He volunteered that he had had "at least three mastoid operations in his youth," had since had repeated episodes of "running ear"—the most recent just months earlier—and "frequently suffered from 'head noises' on the left side."

Finally, Frank offered the military doctors information about himself that remained unknown until after his death. "During the psychiatric interview," Captain Weintrob noted in his report:

> the patient stated that he was "neurotic, afraid to be in crowds, afraid to go in elevator, makes him feel he wants to run when surrounded by people. He has somatic ideas and headaches and has been very nervous for four or five years. Wakens tired in the A.M., is run down and undernourished." The examining psychiatrist concluded that this selectee suffered from psychoneurosis and was not acceptable material from the psychiatric viewpoint.
>
> The diagnosis, of "psychoneurosis, severe," was not added to the list. Notation of "emotional instability" was made instead. It was felt that this would avoid undue unpleasantness for both the selectee and the induction service.

Weintrob's widow, Beverly, recalled that her husband had thought Frank "not physically able." Her knowledge was not contemporaneous, since she did not marry the doctor until much later. She remembered, though, that Sinatra had social contact with Weintrob after the war, and saw to it that he had tickets for his concert appearances.

A Sinatra friend, Maxwell House coffee heir Robert Neal, said their intimate times together led him to conclude that Frank "should have gone on in. He had something with the eardrum and he used it. He just used that, to escape. . . . He did not serve, and I think he was sorry he didn't."

IN THE MIDST of the furor about his draft status, Frank told journalists that he was just like any other young American. That had long since ceased to be true, especially given the way that, unusual for an entertainer in those days, he was now a figure on the political landscape.

He had been "indoctrinated" in Democratic politics, as he put it, when his mother took him to election parades as a small boy. In the wake of his first triumph at the Paramount, she had gotten him to sing at an election rally in New Jersey. As the war ended, he said in an interview that he was preparing himself for "some kind of public service." Meanwhile, the boy who had flunked out of school had started devouring serious books.

Frank had begun reading into the night while singing with Dorsey, the start of a lifelong habit. "He always had these big books, the sort of books he thought he should read," said the singer Peggy Connelly, who was one of his lovers in the 1950s. On planes and in rare moments of peace on transcontinental trains, he steeped himself in modern American literature. Asked in a wartime interview which books had most influenced him he mentioned: **One God,** by Florence Mary Fitch—"You'd never raise your hand or your voice against another man's religion after you read that"; **History of Bigotry in the United States,** by Gustavus Myers—"a great book"; **An American Dilemma,** by Gunnar Myrdal—"I read that one twice"; and **Freedom Road,** by Howard Fast—"sensational . . . everybody in the United States should read that one."

A postwar interviewer would notice in Frank's Hollywood dressing room—alongside **Webster's Dictionary**—Franz Werfel's **The Forty Days of Musa Dagh** and Margaret Deland's **The Way to Peace.** He read deeply in literature about racism, religious prejudice, and oppression. There was also **The Roosevelt I Knew,** by former Secretary of Labor Frances Perkins. The president's attitude toward Italy had alienated some older Italian-Americans, including Dolly Sinatra, in the 1930s. By 1944, to his mother's irritation, FDR's principled social policies inspired in Frank a devotion that, one observer thought, "almost amounted to worship."

He made gestures large and small, appearing at a huge war bond auction on Roosevelt's birthday, naming his son after the president, keeping two color photographs of him in his bedroom, letting it be known that he had voted as a Democrat in 1940. The very political George Evans encouraged Frank to involve himself directly in Roosevelt's 1944 reelection campaign, and Frank plunged in with enthusiasm. He offered his services to Democratic Party headquarters and to organized labor's Political Action Committee and, in the fall, asked an acquaintance to deliver a personal note to Roosevelt.

> My dear Mr. President,
> Are those guys [the Republicans] kidding? We're winning the war.
> Frank Sinatra

Days later, Frank received a last-minute invitation to an afternoon reception at the White House. He was one of many guests, but a pack of reporters was waiting for him when he emerged at the East Gate. "He kidded me about the art of how to make girls faint," he said then of his meeting with the president. The president had joshed with him, Frank recalled. "When I neared him in the line he cried 'Look who's here!,' and when we shook hands he laughed in his unforgettable way and whispered: 'How about telling me what's first on the Hit Parade this week. I won't tell.' " In private, though, Roosevelt seemed puzzled about the Sinatra craze. "Imagine this guy making them swoon," he murmured to an aide. "He would never have made them swoon in our day, right?" Yet the president reportedly received Frank on at least one other occasion.

Following the first White House visit, Republicans and conservative columnists derided FDR for meeting a mere crooner. In response, at one of his concerts, Frank sang a parody of the song "Everything Happens to Me":

> They asked me down to Washington
> To have a cup of tea:
> The Republicans started squawking
> They're mad as they can be!
> And all I did was say hello
> To a man called Franklin D.
> Everything happens to me!

Frank and Nancy contributed $7,500 ($75,000 today) to the Democratic campaign fund. One afternoon in New York, just by turning up outside the Waldorf as Roosevelt's opponent, Thomas Dewey, was speaking, Frank drew most of the crowd off along Park Avenue in his wake. Young people began sporting buttons reading: "Frankie's for FDR and so are we." "Roosevelt in 1944," a Democratic flyer solemnly quoted Frank as saying, "will make Young America's dream a reality."

Show business people across the country were becoming involved in politics as never before. The studio bosses made news with huge contributions. Humphrey Bogart, Danny Kaye, Charles Boyer, and Bette Davis were part of a Hollywood Is for Roosevelt committee. Edward G. Robinson chaired a union meeting. Rita Hayworth campaigned on the radio and her husband, Orson Welles, who was close to the president, traveled the country making speeches. It was Sinatra's star, though, that shone most brightly for the Democrats.

Frank made broadcasts supporting the president, and spoke at a Carnegie Hall meeting during the month of his tumultuous return to the Paramount. On October 29, a week before the election, he appeared at Madison Square Garden with FDR's running mate, Harry Truman, cabinet members, and the mayor of New York. He managed a moving little speech.

"I said I was for Roosevelt," he recalled, "because he was **good** for me. He was good for me, and for my kids and my country, so he must be good for all the other ordinary guys and **their** kids. When I got through I felt like a football player coming off the field—weak and dizzy and excited, and everybody coming over to shake hands or pat me on the back. I'm not ashamed to say it—I felt proud."

In the last days of the campaign Frank stopped working at the Paramount and appeared at two or three political events a day. According to his agent he also made several broadcasts in Italian, evidently prepared for him, since he was not fluent in the language. On election eve he was at the Astor Hotel addressing three thousand Democrats at a Broadway for Roosevelt rally. The following night he spent drinking with Orson Welles at Toots Shor's restaurant on West 52nd Street, waiting for the returns to come in. Welles and Shor celebrated Roosevelt's victory by hoisting the featherweight Frank in the air.

Such was the elation of those days, and Frank's sense that he had made a major contribution, that he imagined a future for himself in a very different sort of spotlight. "When I go someplace to talk," he told the magazine **PM** in the spring of 1945, "I'm Frank Sinatra **citizen**, not entertainer. . . . I guess I'll retire from show business some day. But when I do, I won't be sitting under any trees. I want to go into some kind of public service work. . . . If some wardheeler that didn't mean the community any good was running for an office, and I couldn't beat him any other way, then I'd run for an office. Sure."

Frank was not able to attend Roosevelt's inauguration. He and George Evans set off by plane from California only to be thwarted by airline delays. Three months later, he was one of millions stunned by the news that FDR was dead, felled by a cerebral hemorrhage. Frank was working at Columbia Records when he heard, and wept. Then, with a little group of bobbysoxers at his heels, he went to St. Patrick's Cathedral to light a candle. He would later travel to Roosevelt's home at Hyde Park, New York, to attend a memorial service.

There were those, of course, who did not grieve over Roosevelt's passing. His opponents had seen the president's economic and social reforms as betrayal, his talk of helping the "third of the nation, ill-housed, ill-clad, ill-nourished" as communism thinly veiled. They loathed some of his key supporters, including Frank.

"Poverty," Frank said in his **PM** interview, "that's the biggest thorn. It comes down to what Henry Wallace said, to what he meant when he said every kid, **every kid in the world,** should have his quart of milk a day." Frank admired Wallace, FDR's vice president during his third administration, who advocated advancement for women and blacks and increased public housing, favored closer relations with the Soviet Union, and doubted its commitment to world revolution. To the right, though, Wallace was a communist.

The Political Action Committee that Frank joined during the campaign was part of the Congress of Industrial Organizations. Its registration drive, under the slogan "Every worker a voter," was given much of the credit for the large turnout that resulted in the Democrats' election victory. Many Republicans regarded PAC and its Lithuanian-born leader, Sidney Hillman, as red. A limerick submitted to one anti-Roosevelt newspaper included:

> Political pots have a lid,
> Beneath which the cooking is hid.
> But it's easy to tell
> From the Bolshevik smell
> Which stew was concocted by Sid.

In the weeks before the election Frank had become a member of the Independent Voters Committee of the Arts and Sciences for Roosevelt, which later became the Independent Citizens Committee of the Arts, Sciences and Professions (ICCASP). "We should keep an eye on this outfit," FBI director J. Edgar Hoover scrawled on a press clipping about the group, "as the names of some of its members indicate they range from legitimate liberals to fellow travelers and Commies."

Political affiliations aside, Frank was behaving without restraint, as though he could do as he wished with impunity. On election night, while drinking with Orson Welles, he had reportedly declared that he wanted to "beat up" the powerful anti-Roosevelt columnist Westbrook Pegler. Pegler, like Sinatra and Welles, was staying at the Waldorf. One source had it that Frank tried and failed to find Pegler, then trashed Pegler's room instead. Pegler denied that, but said Frank had been "shrieking drunk" and had to be subdued by a policeman. One of the columnist's staff said his boss had needled Frank from inside the room, calling out: "Are you that little Italian boy from Hoboken who sings on the radio?" Frank had then gone back to his own suite, smashed up the furniture, and threw a chair out the window.

Welles said there had been no incident of any kind. Frank admitted having "had a few drinks" and having gone to Pegler's room, but said he departed peacefully on finding he was out. A few nights later, ignoring a warning by Hank Sanicola that Pegler was "too powerful to mess around with," he contrived to keep the columnist out of his show at the Waldorf's Wedgwood Room. Pegler's version of the election night saga had it that Frank had spent time at PAC headquarters, which, he wrote, "were the Communist headquarters too."

Frank had shrugged off warnings that getting involved in politics could damage his career. "The way I saw it," he said, "if you live in a country—if you're a father and you've got kids—if you love your country . . . If I want to have my say as a citizen, and doing it is going to hurt me in show business, then, I said, 'To hell with it!' "

Having his say, along with the way he conducted his personal life, was soon to make Frank dangerous enemies.

10

Citizen of the Community

FRANK'S MIGRATION to Hollywood had been a move not only to glitz and glamour but to a political hornet's nest. There was an unmistakable buzz rising from the studios and many of the grand homes in the surrounding hills, the buzz of liberal and left-of-liberal zeal. "All phases of radical and communistic activities," a congressional investigator had declared in 1938, "are rampant among the studios of Hollywood." By 1947, the House Un-American Activities Committee was beginning its inquisition in earnest, and taking aim at Hollywood.

The committee and the FBI were the right's effective fist. Hoover smelled in Hollywood "the dank air of Communism." Other foes of the left in the world of movies ranged from conservative stars and directors to nervous studio bosses to interfering crackpots. Not yet thirty, outspoken, self-consciously working-class yet fabulously rich, an idol of youth constantly in the public eye, Frank was a prime target. Since the mid-1930s, when Moscow exhorted communists in the West to work with liberals to form a "popular front" against Hitler and fascism, and during the war when America and the Soviet Union were allies, the Communist Party had seemed acceptable to many on the American left. Energetic and committed, Hollywood's couple of hundred card-carrying members exerted an influence disproportionate to their number.

American communists had supported Roosevelt, presenting themselves, as the journalist Ronald Brownstein has written, for all the world "something like very left-wing Democrats." With the war over, though, and the Soviets trying to foment subversion in the United States and steal military secrets, the right was ready to pounce.

Frank's political philosophy was simple, naive even. Roosevelt had spoken up for "the forgotten man at the bottom of the economic pyramid," a concept with which Frank identified. "The thing I like about the President," he had said, "he's pretty fond of the little man. Well, I'm one, even with all my good fortune." Frank repeatedly declared himself "a little guy from Hoboken," one of the "ordinary guys. . . ." "I am not a heavy thinker . . ." "not the kind of guy who does a lot of brain work about why or how I happened to get into something. I get an idea—maybe I get sore about something. And when I get sore enough, I do something about it."

In 1945 and 1946, in between some thirty recording sessions that produced, most memorably, "These Foolish Things," "All of Me," and "Put Your Dreams Away," Frank loudly supported causes that were suspect in the eyes of the right. He was a sponsor of a concert in aid of the Committee for Yugoslav Relief, soon to be on the attorney general's list of subversive organizations. He made a large contribution to a Croatian committee deemed by the FBI to be a "communist front" group. His name was linked to anti-Franco groups, the Action Committee to Free Spain Now and the Veterans of the Abraham Lincoln Brigade.

Delegates to the World Youth Conference in London had said Frank helped pay their expenses, and he had contacts with American Youth for Democracy. Both these groups were also labeled as red by conservatives. When the American Federation of Radio Artists elected him to its board, an informant told the FBI he was "a follower of the left-wing faction" of the association.

In February 1946, Frank was elected vice chairman of ICCASP, and soon after to the same office with HICCASP, the group's Hollywood affiliate. These were pressure groups with their roots in mainstream Democratic election campaigns, boasting former Interior Secretary Harold Ickes as national chairman, FDR's son James as director, and Albert Einstein as a member. By that summer, though, HICCASP was in crisis. "The Commies," one HICCASP member told **Time**, "are boring in like weevils in a biscuit," and the group did indeed include Party members. After a stormy meeting at which members traded epithets—"capitalist scum" and "Fascist" countered by cries of "enemy of the proletariat" and "witch-hunter"—some leery liberals resigned. Frank, though, was still vice chairman when, months later, the organization called for "universal disarmament," the lifting of secrecy on atomic energy research, and opposed the ending of the wartime alliance with the Soviet Union.

Of the more than one thousand pages in the FBI dossier on Sinatra, almost a quarter relate to his left-wing connections. In 1944, a year after the bureau began collecting material on him, it received a report quoting Sam Falcone, a prominent union member in upstate New York. Falcone, a member of the Communist Party, had suggested "Sinatra come to Schenectady to be on a fundraising program, inasmuch as Sinatra was an old member of the Young Communist League and would come for the Communist Party at a nominal rate." Another informant later claimed that Frank "formerly held membership in the American Youth for Democracy organization of New Jersey, but has recently been admitted to the New York branch of the Communist Party."

The government intercepted letters from Frank when monitoring mail received by communists and others deemed to be security risks. His name even cropped up during surveillance of a suspect in one of the great postwar Soviet espionage cases. The FBI was following up on the confessions of Elizabeth Bentley, who for six years had been a courier passing information from high-level Washington sources to superiors in the communist underground. She was working for agents of the NKVD, an arm of Soviet intelligence, which code-named her Clever Girl. Bentley told American interrogators of a contact known in the underground as "Charlie," a "Russian-Jewish" dentist who served as a conduit for "certain material."

FBI agents strongly suspected the traitor was Dr. Abraham Weinstein, a New York dentist of Russian extraction. Weinstein denied being a communist, but did admit to having treated American communist functionaries and a Soviet consular official, and to having contributed to American-Soviet organizations. It did not escape the FBI's notice, meanwhile, that Sinatra—who by 1946 sported a set of very white capped front teeth—was one of Weinstein's patients. Or that he had arranged for Weinstein and his wife to see his show at the Waldorf-Astoria.

There is no credible evidence that Frank was a communist or in any way disloyal. FBI investigators, raking over every detail of his record years later, said as much. In 1946, following right-wing insinuations arising from a HICCASP event to aid war veterans, he reacted with characteristic exasperation. "The Committee was urging passage of legislation to provide houses for veterans," he exploded. "If that was subversive activity, I'm all for it!" Frank was a political greenhorn, who did not understand how apparent allies might seek to exploit his famous name or enemies seek to smear it. The fact that he had chatted with President Roosevelt, and had found himself on a first-name basis with Attorney General Tom Clark, may have gone to his head. Frank was now devoting so much time to speechmaking and entertaining in aid of liberal causes that his income dipped significantly. There he was on national radio, not singing but sounding off on veterans' rights and the Big Four conference in Paris and quoting Thomas Paine.

His closest advisers urged him on. "George Evans and I encouraged this newly developed social conscience," said Jack Keller, "for we could see that it would certainly set Frank aside as 'a citizen of the community' as well as being a star." Evans, who was close to Dr. Weinstein, according to the FBI, saw to it that Frank's thoughts on making a "better world" were distributed to young people. He had also introduced Frank to sixty-two-year-old Jo Davidson, a fellow Roosevelt supporter and an acclaimed sculptor.

Davidson had been chairman of ICCASP since its founding. Frank held him in high esteem and heeded his counsel on political matters. Davidson thought Frank looked like "a younger Lincoln," and was soon at work on a bust of his new friend. He and Frank were spotted sitting in on a session of the fledgling United Nations, listening to Soviet delegate Andrei Gromyko.

To the right, the Davidson connection was further evidence of what one columnist called Frank's "veering to portside." The sculptor, whose parents were Russian, had in his youth been close to Emma Goldman, a prominent anarchist deported from the United States as a "dangerous radical." He would soon be described in **Life** as one of a number of "dupes and fellow travelers" who "dress up communist fronts."

PM magazine, which served as a platform for Frank's ideas before and after the 1944 election, was the organ of the Popular Front in New York. It was unmistakably left-wing, included card-carrying communists on its staff, and was viewed by some as a vehicle for "American communism."

American communists did indeed try to harness liberal Democratic artists to their purposes.

As one observer put it, they were as "earthbound" as the artists were "ethereal." One of the first liberals to realize he and his friends were being manipulated, the screenwriter Philip Dunne, said he and many of his fellows had been "innocents." "We were mostly virgin voices in things political," Jo Davidson said later.

Frank's activist friends also included Orson Welles, under the baleful eye of the FBI since his iconoclastic film **Citizen Kane**, and Gene Kelly, another leading member of HICCASP. Other liberals in his circle or coming into it were Humphrey Bogart, Lauren Bacall, Gregory Peck, Judy Garland, and Ava Gardner. To whatever degree these friends were political innocents, there could be no casual commitment to left-wing causes once the Un-American Activities Committee turned its guns on Hollywood.

In January 1946, the prominent evangelist and racist Gerald Smith called on the committee to investigate Frank. Sinatra, he said, was involved with American Youth for Democracy, "certainly" being used by the Communist Party, and "not a naive dupe." Frank responded bullishly. "If that means agreeing with Jefferson and Tom Paine, [Wendell] Willkie and Franklin Roosevelt, then I'll gladly accept the title," he said. "Let's not just ignore Smith. . . . Let's do what most people do with crackpots—get rid of them."

Frank's aides became more cautious. Months

later, when American Youth for Democracy asked Frank to contribute an article on race problems, his staff pressed for more information about the organization. Frank's "political beliefs," an aide emphasized to the caller, "don't run towards Communism." Yet Frank himself did not readily cave in. "The minute anyone tries to help the little guy, he's called a Communist," he grumbled when a Catholic lay organization assailed him for speaking at a left-wing rally. In early 1947 he published an open letter to Henry Wallace just after the former vice president had called for a softer line toward the Soviet Union.

"Divisionist tactics," Frank wrote, "have been able to invade the minds of people who think of themselves as liberal. . . . It was pretty easy to march with the liberals and the progressives in the years of Roosevelt. We knew he wouldn't let us go wrong. Until another leader we can trust, as we trusted him, takes up the fight we like to think of as ours—the fight for tolerance, which is the basis of any fight for peace—it's going to be tough to be a liberal."

Two months later, again raking up Frank's relations with American Youth for Democracy, then congressman Karl Mundt of the Un-American Activities Committee accused him of conduct "inimical to the best interests of America." Soon, it was reported, Frank was going to be subpoenaed to testify in Washington. He never was, although he was one of the celebrities who formed the Committee for the First Amendment to oppose the Un-American Committee's excesses.

In fall 1947 Frank and others met at the home of lyricist Ira Gershwin to plan protests against the Un-American Activities Committee. Those present included Bogart and Bacall, Rita Hayworth, Groucho Marx, and Gene Kelly—an FBI informant jotted down their license plate numbers as they arrived.

"Once they get the movies throttled," Frank said in a statement, "how long will it be before the Committee goes to work on freedom of the air? How long will it be before we're told what we can and cannot say into a microphone? If you make a pitch on a nationwide network for a square deal for the underdog, will they call you a Commie? . . . Are they gonna scare us into silence? I wonder."

As the right kept up the pressure, many Hollywood liberals backed away from politics, fearing for their careers. Frank began to steer clear of groups that were being labeled communist fronts, ended his noisy protests, and eventually went out of his way to demonstrate his opposition to communism. In 1948 it was announced that he and other prominent Italian-Americans were to record a broadcast appeal to voters in Italy not to vote communist in the forthcoming elections. He responded furiously to continuing innuendo about his left-wing sympathies. "If they don't cut it out," he bridled, "I'll show them how much an American can fight back—even if it's against the state—if that American happens to be right. I'm right, not Left."

In 1950, shortly before the Un-American Activities Committee began a fresh assault on Hollywood, according to the FBI, Frank sent an emissary to bureau headquarters:

> to arrange an appointment to see the Director to offer his services. [EMISSARY'S NAME DELETED] pointed out that Sinatra had first been desirous of offering his services to the CIA, but that he had told Sinatra that the CIA was not the proper organization to approach . . . a friend of his in CIA told him that he should take the matter up with the Bureau . . . Sinatra was sensitive about the allegations that have been made concerning his subversive activities . . . denies any subversive affiliations or interests, but feels that in view of the publicity which he has received, these subversive elements are not sure of his position, and accordingly Sinatra feels that he could be of assistance to the Bureau.

"We want nothing to do with him," J. Edgar Hoover scribbled on the report.

Lingering doubt about Frank's loyalty repeatedly led the U.S. Army to reject him as an entertainer of troops, on the last occasion in 1954 in the aftermath of the war in Korea. According to an army report, General Alfred Kastner told Frank that a "serious question existed" as to his "sympathies with respect to communism, communists and fellow travelers." Frank said he "hated and despised" everything about communism. He was, he insisted, "as communistic as the Pope."

In early 1955, nevertheless, the FBI began a year-long probe into his background that involved nine FBI offices and numerous informants. It was triggered by a request from the State Department, which was querying Frank's most recent application for a passport. The government was at the time refusing passports not only to communists but to anyone whose activity abroad might in its view aid communism or, casting an even wider net, be "contrary to the best interests of the United States." Frank had said under oath that he had never been either a Party member or a member of a communist front organization. Given his background, the State Department wanted to know, had he made a false statement? If so, were there grounds to prosecute? Hoover eventually reported that the only black mark against Frank was that he had been vice chairman of HICCASP. The group had been designated a communist front only by the California Un-American Activities Committee, not by the federal government, and the authorities let the matter drop.

Years later, Frank would still be fulminating about the official pressure that had been brought to bear. In 1966 he dispatched an intermediary to Washington to "determine the identity of the 'S.O.B.' " who years earlier had tagged him a "commie" and led the army to turn him down as an entertainer. Phil Silvers's then-wife, Jo-Carroll Dennison, who often talked politics with Frank in the postwar years, said, "Many of the friends that I had, and have, were literally members of the Communist Party, dedicated to the overthrow of capitalism. But I'm confident that Frank was not like that. He was in my opinion an absolutely true liberal in the best sense of the word. He believed in civil rights, human rights, women's rights, and put himself on the line in that way.

"Frank was ambitious and driven," she said, "and I'm sure he was terrified, crumbling in his stomach, to think his career was in danger during the Un-American Activities Committee business. But I don't think he backed down. Frank was very brave."

"My first recollection of your father was during the time of Roosevelt," former Vice President Hubert Humphrey was to write in a letter to Sinatra's daughter Nancy. "He is a solid, devoted

American liberal in the tradition of Roosevelt and Truman, Kennedy and Johnson. . . . What I recall most about your father is his great concern for the country, and particularly for black Americans who have been so long denied an equal opportunity."

11

"What Is America?"

FRANK MAY HAVE EXAGGERATED his family's early poverty, may have allowed publicists to embroider the facts about his youth, but he certainly had seen prejudice. In his childhood, he told a group of young people in 1945, African-American children had been dismissed as "niggers," Jews as "kikes" and "sheenies." He had been called "little dago" and showered with rocks by other children.

Frank blamed prejudice not on children but on parents, including his own parents. He remembered his mother pestering him about the ethnic origin of boyhood friends, his father "hating" people of different ethnic origins who might take his job away. The Ku Klux Klan had a significant membership in New Jersey during Frank's youth, and its enmity was applied widely.

At seventeen, when Frank spent a year fending

for himself in New York, he had tried to get a job as a messenger on Wall Street. "One of the questions that was on almost every form I had to fill out," he remembered, "read 'religion?' It meant that whether you got a job or not—a matter of life or death with people such as I came from—depended largely on your religion."

Hanging out on 52nd Street, he had seen for himself how deeply racial prejudice was ingrained. At the end of the 1930s, there were still few places outside Harlem where a black band could play in New York. Even when invisible to the audience, on the radio, black musicians could not play with white bands.

Conditions for entertainers reflected those in society at large, as Frank discovered when he traveled around the country. World War II changed little, though black resentment grew. Blacks were allowed to perform in some first-class hotels, but not stay there as guests. The police in Washington, D.C., would tolerate black after-hours clubs, but raided or closed them down if white women were seen entering. After complaints from white guests at a New York hotel, Billie Holiday was ordered to use the service elevator rather than the main one. Duke Ellington could record with Rosemary Clooney, but the record cover could not include a photograph of them together.

Frank detested such rules. To him, Ellington

and Holiday were just two of many African-Americans he admired as colleagues and treated as friends. A 1943 photograph shows him not just sitting and laughing with the black pianist and singer Hazel Scott but, shockingly for the day, holding hands with her. Scott was not only black but an active civil rights campaigner who supported communists.

Frank reacted viscerally on encountering blatant prejudice. "When I was a kid and somebody called me a 'dirty little Guinea,' " he recalled, "there was only one thing to do—break his head. . . . Let anybody yell wop or Jew or nigger around us, we taught him not to do it again." So it was, on numerous occasions, when he became an adult. When he was with the Dorsey band, he knocked a newspaperman out cold at a party for calling another guest a "Jew bastard." Then he had a drink and hit him again as he was being carried out.

Orson Welles witnessed a similar incident. "Sinatra went into a diner for a cup of coffee with some friends of his who were musicians," he recalled, "one of whom happened to be a Negro. The man behind the counter insultingly refused to serve this Negro, and Sinatra knocked him over on his back with a single blow."

On racial matters, however, it dawned on Frank that "you've got to do it through education." He began subtly—though it was noticed soon enough—in his performance of the Jerome Kern classic "Ol' Man River." When Paul Robeson had sung it, in 1927, "darkies" all worked on the Mississippi while the white folk played. Frank's version, from 1943, went: "Here **we** all work while the white folks play." He was to sing it that way, with evident passion, time and again.

In 1944, on one of Frank's visits to the White House, he told President Roosevelt that he intended to start talking to young people "about the need for tolerance and to point out that we mustn't destroy the principles for which our grandfathers founded this country." Roosevelt approved the idea, and Frank kept his word within months. In early 1945, encouraged by George Evans, he went to the Bronx to talk with schoolchildren about juvenile delinquency. In March, at Carnegie Hall, he addressed a World Youth Rally.

Frank made thirty speaking appearances that year alone. "The surprising element was that he came to speak on 'Racial Tolerance' rather than to sing," Grayce Kaneda, a former student, recalled of a visit he made to Philadelphia. "Negroes, Irish, Italians, Chinese, Japanese, Jews, Catholics and Protestants, were all there together."

"The next time you hear anyone say there's no room in this country for foreigners," Frank wrote in an article, "tell him **everybody** in the United States is a foreigner. . . . It would be a fine thing if people chose their associates by the color of their skin! Brothers wouldn't be talking to brothers, and in some families the father and mother wouldn't even talk to each other. Imagine a guy with dark hair like me not talking to blondes. The more you think about all this, the more you realize how important Abraham Lincoln was talking when he said: 'Our fathers brought forth on this continent a new nation conceived in liberty and dedicated to the proposition that all men are created equal.' Get that!"

Though his homilies seem trite today, they were well received. Film director Mervyn LeRoy told Frank, "You could reach a thousand times more people if you'd tell your story on the screen." The pair found an ally in an RKO vice president and got the go-ahead to make a short movie aimed at youngsters likely to be affected by bigotry—and perhaps prepared to listen to advice from a pop singer. The result was a fifteen-minute movie made in just two days, **The House I Live In.**

The film was built around a song that had previously been featured only by a black gospel group and seemed destined for obscurity. Its first three verses:

> What is America to me?
> A name, a map, or a flag I see,

A certain word, democracy
What is America to me?

The house I live in
A plot of earth, a street
The grocer and the butcher
Or the people that I meet.

The children in the playground,
The faces that I see
All races and religions
That's America to me.

Frank made the song powerful populist propaganda. In the movie he played himself, a crooner who emerges from a studio to find a gang of boys abusing a young Jew. "Look, fellas," he admonished them, "religion doesn't make any difference! Except maybe to a Nazi or a dope. . . . God didn't create one people better than another. Your blood is the same as mine, and mine is the same as his. You know what this country is? It's made up of a hundred different kinds of people—and they're all Americans. . . . Let's use our good American brains and not fight each other."

The movie ends with the boys dispersing, tempers calmed, and humming quietly. It was good melting pot stuff and generally well received, as was the news that the proceeds were to go to charity and that Frank had taken no salary. A usually acid columnist, Harriet Van Horne, declared him "a sincere, hard-working young man with a deep sense of his brother's wrong and a social conscience that hasn't been atrophied by money or fame."

"The House I Live In" won Frank and his colleagues on the movie a special Oscar, his first Academy Award and one of which he was especially proud, and he returned to the song time and again over the years. Most recently, in 2001, it was pressed back into service following the terrorist attack on the World Trade Center. Bill Cosby had the lights dimmed a few minutes into one of his shows as the voice of Frank, three years dead, filled the auditorium. Cosby felt the song could help heal America's national trauma. (Others, though, turned the song into a jingoistic anthem.)

In the fall of 1945, Frank went to Benjamin Franklin High in Italian Harlem, where there had been fighting between Italian-American and black students. The saxophone player Sonny Rollins, who was one of them, recalled how "Sinatra came down there and sang in our auditorium . . . after that things got better, and the rioting stopped."

In Gary, Indiana, white students at Froebel High had rioted and gone on strike over a ruling that black students could study alongside whites, use the same library and cafeteria, and swim in the school pool. Many white parents and local businessmen supported the rioters. Frank, who arrived to give a talk, discovered the white students' leader had "three secretaries," and concluded "there must be somebody behind him." On the podium, undeterred by local dignitaries' attempts to interrupt, he accused two prominent local white men of having orchestrated the strike. He then pressed on aggressively until someone brought down the curtain. "I kinda gave 'em hell, didn't I," he said as he was hustled away, and years later he recalled the event as "in a way the most important show I ever gave."

Days later, in Philadelphia, Frank denounced the trouble in Gary as "not spontaneous. It is political. The people behind it are some of the most powerful in the country. It is just staggering." Had he felt any pressure or repercussions since joining the anti-racist struggle? "No, not yet," Frank responded. "But I'm just waiting. I expect it any day." Soon after he made those comments, an FBI informant in Philadelphia alleged he had recently joined the Communist Party. It was just weeks later that Gerald Smith asked the Un-American Activities Committee to investigate him.

Frank came into contact with communists as he campaigned against race hatred. The composer of "The House I Live In," Earl Robinson, was a Party member, as was lyricist Abel Meeropol, who was later to adopt the orphaned children of Julius and Ethel Rosenberg following the couple's execution as Soviet spies. So, at the time, was Albert Maltz, who wrote the movie. All three men were to be denied work during the red-baiting years.

Frank shrugged off the suggestion that he himself "spoke like a Communist." "You know," he said, "they called Shirley Temple a Communist. Me and Shirley both, I guess. . . . The struggle against this race hatred is widespread. I'm only one person trying to do my best in a thing I believe to be the most important thing. Put down the fact that I'm a father and I want my children to grow up in a decent world. . . . This is a fight I intend to stick with. I'm in it for life."

"FRANK DIDN'T CARE if you were purple or green, blue or black," the entertainer Sonny King said. "Every black artist had great respect for this man." Sammy Davis Jr., whom Frank met as a teenager and nurtured from obscurity, said as much to anyone who would listen. He had suffered vile abuse in the army because of his skin color. He had performed at a top-class Las Vegas hotel where he could not stay as a guest or even hail a cab at the entrance; where they drained the pool if a black person had been in the water. "Frank wouldn't go into the Sands or any other place in Vegas," said King, "if Sammy wasn't accepted exactly the same way he was."

Frank applied the same standard in all situations and whatever the status of his companions. "The roof blew off," Frank Jr. recalled, when restaurant staff tried to avoid serving his father's black valet, "and it was Dad who set off the dynamite."

"Billy Eckstine became the first black who ever worked the Copacabana," **Billboard**'s Hal Webman remembered, "when Sinatra got sick in 1950 and he picked Eckstine as his replacement. It was over everyone's dead body, but Sinatra insisted—he had the right to under his contract—and eventually they went along with it." He insisted, too, that his black arranger, Sy Oliver, got to stay at the same "whites only" hotel as he did. The management of the Court Club in Miami Beach forbade Jo Thompson, a black cabaret singer, to sit with white customers when not performing. When Frank came in, he made a point of inviting her to sit at his table. "I think he did it on purpose," said Thompson. "He was one of the white people with a different attitude."

The musicians' unions were long segregated in Hollywood, and Frank fought that. "The film and television industries were very racist," the trombonist Milt Bernhart recalled, "and when Frank had a record date he bent over backwards to try and find black musicians who could play the music." "He insisted on having an integrated orchestra," said guitarist Al Viola; the union barrier was broken after Buddy Collette, a black flautist, was hired for Sinatra dates.

In 1956, when Nat "King" Cole was attacked by racist thugs while on stage in Birmingham, Alabama, Frank phoned from Europe to commiserate. Soon after, in a long article on prejudice for **Ebony** magazine, he described Cole as "a first-rate citizen, a very classy gentleman who honors his profession wherever he appears. I am proud to count him as a friend." There was a stir over the fact that Frank would even write for a black magazine. "His public position on race in the **Ebony** article," an editorial writer declared in **Jet** magazine, "was the most significant stand taken by a famous white person since Mrs. Eleanor Roosevelt gave support to the cause of racial justice and equality when she wrote an article titled 'If I Were a Negro' in **Negro Digest** in 1943." Wilberforce University, one of the first such institutions for black Americans, honored Frank with an honorary doctorate, citing his "practice of true democracy."

His position, Frank had written in **Ebony**, was that "an entertainer's function is to entertain. But he is also a responsible citizen with the same rights and obligations as the next man. . . . I hold certain definite opinions about some of the problems currently dividing our nation and frequently I feel the urge to speak out."

He did so through his craft, too. Fourteen years after **The House I Live In,** he made **Kings Go Forth,** a 1958 film about the white-black issue between the sexes. Produced on a tight budget—movie executives feared it was too "daring"—the film was forgettable except for what Frank called its "great but simple message," that "love can conquer anything, including racial and religious differences." He stood by the precept, controversially, by acting as best man at the marriage of Sammy Davis Jr. and May Britt a few years later.

Frank joined himself to Martin Luther King Jr.'s crusade in the 1960s, raising huge sums by singing at benefits for the National Association for the Advancement of Colored People, the Congress of Racial Equality, and the American Civil Liberties Union. Tears streamed down King's cheeks once as he listened to Frank singing "Ol' Man River." Nancy Sinatra remembered how her father "suffered" on hearing the news that King had been assassinated.

His commitment was sincere, but he had no time for political correctness. He made racist jokes cheerfully and effectively, on the principle that humor broke the silence about bigotry and ridiculed it. The jokes ranged from the playful to the outrageous.

"We'll dedicate the next song to Ben-Gurion," Frank said of the Israeli prime minister during one performance, "and call it 'There Will Never Be Another Jew.' " Most of the jokes were aimed at Sammy Davis, whom he liked to call "Smokey the Bear," sometimes even "jungle bunny": "You'd better wash up 'cos we can't see you in the dark." "Here's a little black boy who will sing for us." When Davis did his take-off of Frank singing "All the Way," Frank commented, "He's just, excuse the expression, a carbon copy." Davis joked back in kind.

In 1974, Frank took things to a gratuitous extreme. "The Polacks are deboning the colored people," he said from a stage in Las Vegas, "and using them for wet suits." That had the power to shock, even in a time when audiences were becoming blasé.

There was an outcry from anti-apartheid groups in 1981 when Frank sang at a resort in Bophuthatswana, a so-called black homeland created by the racist regime in South Africa. Many artists, including Shirley Bassey, Liza Minnelli, Johnny Mathis, Ray Charles, Glen Campbell, the Beach Boys, Cher, Dolly Parton, and Neil Sedaka, also performed in South Africa in the early eighties. Jesse Jackson, however, accused Frank of "trading his birthright for a mess of money." Yet the contract for the concerts had stipulated that anyone, black or white, could attend. "If there's any form of segregation," he said, "I wouldn't play. Because I play to all people, any color, any creed, drunk, sober, anything."

Duke Ellington admired Frank as a "**primo** non-conformist" and more. "I don't know of anyone else," Ellington wrote in his autobiography of Frank's initiatives in the 1940s, "who would have done anything to jeopardize his position so soon after reaching a peak of success, but Francis Sinatra decided to do what is usually considered dangerous and damaging to a budding career. . . . He's an individualist. Nobody tells him what to do or say."

FRANK HELD SIMILARLY STRONG VIEWS on religious freedom—with a generational emphasis on the struggles of the Jews. In 1942, when the first reports of Nazi atrocities reached the United States, Frank had hundreds of medallions made bearing the image of St. Christopher on one side and the Star of David on the other. They went to servicemen overseas, friends, and associates—even policemen who had acted as bodyguards at concerts. "If the war has any blessings at all," Louella Parsons wrote after discussing the medals with Frank, "it is the realization that has come to many people of importance that all religions are good and each one has its part in our world, and we must all respect the other fellow's beliefs."

In Hollywood two years later, Frank sang at a benefit for elderly Jews. For years he had worn a mezuzah, an inscribed scroll in a little metal case, that his Jewish neighbor Mrs. Golden had given him as a child. At the Catholic baptism ceremony for his son, he threatened to walk out when the priest tried to block his choice of Manie Sacks, a Jew, as godfather. The priest backed down. On discovering that some golf clubs excluded Jews, Frank became only the second gentile to join a club with an overwhelmingly Jewish membership.

Where Jews were concerned, his commitment went beyond the fight against religious prejudice. To him, as to many of his contemporaries, establishing a state of Israel seemed a humane response to the horrors of the Holocaust. In September 1947, when the United Nations was moving toward agreement on the establishment of a Jewish state in the Middle East—to the distress and anger of Arabs—he sang at a rally at the Hollywood Bowl attended by twenty thousand supporters of the Zionist cause. The following year, with the U.N. decision made and fighting between Jews and Arabs raging in Palestine, he even did some cloak-and-dagger work for the Jewish underground.

The Copacabana in New York shared a building with the old Hotel Fourteen, which the Haganah, one of the main military arms of Zionism, was using as a headquarters. A key part of the

Haganah mission was to get arms to Jewish fighters in Palestine in defiance of an American embargo on sending arms to the Middle East. In March 1948, in the bar at the Copacabana where Haganah operatives mingled with entertainers, Frank was recruited for a secret operation.

"I had an Irish ship captain sitting in the port of New York with a ship full of munitions destined for Israel," recalled former Jerusalem mayor Teddy Kollek, who in 1948 ran clandestine Haganah operations in the United States. "He had phony bills of lading and was to take the shipment outside the three-mile limit and transfer it on to another ship. But a large sum of money had to be handed over, and I didn't know how to get it to him. If I walked out the door carrying the cash, the Feds would intercept me and wind up confiscating the munitions.

"I went downstairs to the bar and Sinatra came over, and we were talking. I don't know what came over me, but I told him what I was doing in the United States and what my dilemma was. And in the early hours of the following morning I walked out the front door of the building with a satchel, and the Feds followed me. Out the back door went Frank Sinatra, carrying a paper bag filled with cash. He went down to the pier, handed it over, and watched the ship sail."

According to Kollek, the bag Frank carried contained about $1 million ($7 million today). Two

Israeli prime ministers, David Ben-Gurion and Menachem Begin, were one day to thank him privately for what he had done. "It was the beginning of the young nation," Frank told his daughter Nancy. "I wanted to help, I was afraid they might fall down."

Frank remained a champion of Israel, though he did make some effort to be evenhanded. He established the Frank Sinatra International Youth Center in Nazareth to help Arab as well as Jewish children. Nevertheless, Arab League countries for years banned Sinatra records and movies.

Like much else in Frank's life, his commitment to Israel was impulsive, on occasion irrationally so. While in Tel Aviv in 1965 for the shooting of **Cast a Giant Shadow,** a movie about a hero of the conflict that accompanied the founding of the Jewish state, he indulged in an extraordinary outburst. Rock Brynner, whose father, Yul, also starred in the film, remembered it vividly.

"We're in the hotel. It's midnight, and we're drinking," Brynner said. "Suddenly, after only twenty-four hours in Israel, Frank becomes a Jew. He's got to 'get them suckers for the Holocaust deal.' Who could he blame since Hitler's not around? He'd once met Alfried Krupp von Bohlen, the armaments heir, who'd been convicted for using slave labor during World War II. So he picks up the phone after midnight and tells the hotel operator: 'Get me Krupp von Bohlen.'

And she says: 'Where does he live?' And Frank turns to me and says 'Where does von Bohlen live?' And I said Essen, in Germany, and the operator starts trying to explain—this is 1965—that there's no connection during the night. No way.

"But Frank wouldn't listen, and suddenly the operator is a Nazi collaborator disguised as a Jewish phone operator. He's hammering the coffee table with the earpiece of the phone saying: 'I want Krupp von Bohlen in Essen, Germany!' And I go down and try to tell the operator that Mr. Sinatra isn't feeling well. And when I get back Frank has this little ring of plastic in his hand, with a bouquet of wires sticking out of it—all that is left of the phone—still shouting: 'Get me Krupp von Bohlen in Essen, Germany!' "

During the same trip, at the Sinatra Youth Center—and sober—Frank expressed the simpler, worthy goal of his crusade against prejudice. "I don't know what's wrong with the adults and why they act the way they do, but I think I understand kids. If we can get them together when they're young enough, maybe when they get big they'll be smarter than we have been."

As the years proved him wrong, Frank seemed to understand that not all the blame could be laid at the Arabs' door. "He came to the realization," Brad Dexter said, "that Israel was too dominant. He thought the U.S. should show equal support to the Palestinians, because they had a right to a homeland as well." Frank became skeptical about American policy in the region. "We're talking about making peace," he told an interviewer, "and what we're doing is giving them tools of war. We're giving Jordan airplanes, Israel airplanes. It doesn't make any sense to me."

At times of crisis, though, Frank supported Israel. In 1967, on the eve of the Six Day War, he wired President Lyndon Johnson urging him to condemn the "outrageous" actions of Egyptian leader Gamal Abdel Nasser. "I hope they catch that Arafat," he said in 1982 during the Israeli invasion of Lebanon, "and have a proper trial before they execute him."

At positive moments during the long Middle East agony, Frank made hopeful gestures. He performed in the shadow of the Pyramids to raise funds for Egyptian war wounded, lauding President Anwar Sadat as a "great man who's laying the cornerstone of peace for all the Arab nations." Frank raised funds for an International Student Center on the campus of Jerusalem's Hebrew University. This, too, bore his name and was intended for the use of Arabs as well as Jews. A terrorist bomb devastated the center's cafeteria in 2002, killing and maiming Arabs and Jews alike.

The two most infamous Arabs had divergent views on Sinatra's work. According to a former mistress of Saddam Hussein, he liked to dance to "Strangers in the Night" in the privacy of his

Baghdad palace. His liking for the song was known, and owners of fashionable restaurants had it played regularly to ingratiate themselves with the regime. Osama bin Laden, by contrast, was reported in the Iraqi press to "curse the memory of Frank Sinatra every time he hears his songs."

12

The Philanderer

DESPITE HIS hectic political activity in 1945 and 1946, in those two years Frank sang on 160 radio shows, completed thirty-six recording sessions, and made four movies. At one point in 1946, moreover, he was also performing on stage forty-five times a week, singing up to a hundred songs a day. The same year, a new Sinatra record reached the stores every month. Six made the top ten, and total record sales were estimated at 10 million. At one point Frank earned $93,000 ($850,000 today) for just one week on stage.

He was taking care, meanwhile, to work with quality musicians and to break new ground. The advent of the long-playing record was still two years away, but an innovative album set composed of eight 78 rpm Sinatra records appeared that spring. **The Voice of Frank Sinatra,** which included "These Foolish Things" and "Someone to Watch Over Me," offered a cohesive musical mood in one package. It was the first of the "concept albums" that Frank would produce for decades.

Frank had been exploring the musical disciplines. He recorded with a gospel group and with Xavier Cugat, a classical violinist turned rumba bandleader. He listened to some experimental recordings made by Alec Wilder, an eccentric composer whose work floated somewhere between jazz and classical. Wilder could get no one to record them commercially, but Frank said, "I think I can conduct. . . . Using my name, maybe we can do you some good. Let's call Manie."

At Columbia, Manie Sacks thought the notion preposterous, pointing out that Frank could not even read music. Frank insisted, however, and soon a recording date was set, an orchestra assembled. The musicians, who thought Frank a "crooner," were skeptical bordering on hostile. "I've never seen Frank look as frightened as he did that night when he got up to conduct those men," Wilder remembered. "But he admitted his weaknesses right off. 'Gentlemen,' he added, 'I need your help. And I want to help this music.' "

Frank wielded the baton with skill. "Here were all these symphony guys with their goatees and their Stradivarius fiddles," Sacks recalled. "Frank walks in and steps up on a platform just like Koussevitzky, and by the time he's through the musicians are applauding and grabbing and hugging him. I don't know how he did it, but he made the most beautiful records you ever heard."

Frank rejected a first proof of the Wilder record cover because it featured the composer's name in type smaller than his own. Wilder, he insisted, must have at least equal billing. Frank was to conduct on six subsequent albums, little known now except to aficionados.

"Frank had great inner strength," said Jo-Carroll Dennison. "It was always, 'Let's do this. Let's go do that.' Enormous energy and drive. His adrenaline was up all the time. I don't think he was ever still. He had a frenetic personality in those days."

Frenzy had begun to take its toll. In early 1946 Frank had to cancel a performance after his doctor ordered "complete rest." "Hard work and extended play, I mean after hours, never hurt Frank," George Evans said. "But emotional tension absolutely destroyed him. You could always tell when he was troubled. He came down with a bad throat. Germs were never the trouble—unless there are guilt germs."

TO THE PUBLIC, Frank and Nancy still seemed the ideal couple, enjoying their children and their good fortune at the house on Toluca Lake. Frank even preached to young people about decorum and restraint. "Boys will go out with the girls they call 'babes,' " he wrote in an article put out under his name. "But when most men marry they look for girls who will be good wives and mothers. Maybe I'm old-fashioned . . . I owe a lot of the things I have done to Nancy's good orderly mind and to the stabilizing influence she always has been in my life."

Yet Nancy was increasingly unhappy. "I can remember having Christmas dinner with Frank and his family in the late forties," the songwriter Jimmy McHugh said, "and we were all feeling sort of sentimental, and Nancy turned to me and said, 'I'd give anything to be back on the road again with Harry James and making onion sandwiches.' "

Frank, on the other hand, was straining at the leash. One rainy night, as he headed out alone to dinner, Nancy called after him: "Don't forget your galoshes!" That one mundane remark, he told a friend years later, triggered in his mind the thought that the marriage was all but over. Frank had no time now for small domesticities, all too much time for Hollywood glitz, and for other women.

Evans knew about the womanizing. "The relationship between my father and Frank was kind of like father and son," his son Phil said. "My dad felt responsible. I can't tell you how many phone calls there were at two or three o'clock in the morning. It could be Frank on the phone, or—as often—Nancy complaining about Frank's philandering."

The actress Peggy Maley, whom Frank met about that time, fended him off. "He called and asked for a date," she remembered, "but I didn't go out with him. I wasn't about to become a notch in anyone's belt. He was promiscuous, had affairs with practically every woman he ever said 'How d'you do?' to."

According to Jo-Carroll Dennison, Frank was a regular visitor at the apartment Jimmy Van Heusen and Axel Stordahl maintained at the Wilshire Towers. "This was where all the men went during the week for their bachelor orgies. Call girls were in and out of there all the time. . . . They had parties with all kinds of women. And Frank was always there." Friends acting as Frank's proxies were soon to lease another Los Angeles apartment, a "hideaway" for his exclusive use. The FBI began getting information that Frank was using prostitutes.

He was less than discreet about his nightlife, and the gossip columns began running thinly veiled blind items. "What blazing swoon-crooner has been seen night-clubbing with a different starlet every night?" Or: "Wonder if the wonder boy of hit records tells his wife where he goes after dark?"

When he turned fifty, Frank would tell a writers' group, "If I had as many love affairs as you have given me credit for, I would be speaking to you now from a jar at the Harvard Medical School." Yet there is ample evidence that he had a prolific sex life. Shirley Ballard, another actress who met him in Hollywood in the mid-1940s, remembered the "darling, adorable" Frank who took her to bed one night in an apartment overlooking Sunset Strip. "It was like, magic time. I thought, 'I'm going to be seduced by Frank Sinatra. Can this really be happening?' I'd taught myself to sing by listening to his records, so I was prepared to hear his own songs lulling me into his arms. No way! He introduced me to classical music that night, put on something called **Ports of Call** by Jacques Ibert, one of the most outstandingly beautiful pieces of music ever written, just glorious. And up there with him, looking out over the city with, oh-my-God, my idol, was—well—memorable."

They had an on-and-off affair for two or three years. To Ballard, being with Sinatra was like being "in a parallel universe, in orbit with Frank, swept along by an almost electromagnetic energy." As to the sex, she remembers "a pretty considerate lover, not selfish, not hit or miss. . . . There were times like, in the dressing room at NBC where he did his radio show, the little quickies. But they were exciting too."

The romance and the hypnotic quality about

Frank were fresh in her mind more than half a century later. "We were in Palm Springs at the Chi Chi [Club]. . . . It was late, way in the back. And Frank tips back in the chair and eyeballs me and sings, 'I've Got a Crush on You'—to me. Those things you do not forget. . . . Those blue eyes. They nailed you. Nailed you when he was introduced to you, when they were seductive, nailed you when they were angry."

The singer and actress Marilyn Maxwell is most often identified as having been Frank's lover at the time his marriage began to fail. She went way back with Frank as a colleague, and Nancy may have thought she posed no threat. She had begun her career as Marvel Maxwell—her real name—the daughter of a pianist mother. The press focused on her voluptuous looks—"one of the best sweater fillers in the country," was a typical label given her by the press—but she had talent as a dancer and singer and took acting seriously. Colleagues liked her for her intelligence, integrity, and zany humor.

She and Frank had met in 1939 in New York, probably at a radio studio, when he was with Harry James and she was a nineteen-year-old singer with another band. Having encouraged Frank to go out on his own, she had begun to concentrate on acting, dropped Marvel in favor of Marilyn, and moved to Hollywood. She was still there four years later, when he settled in California, and was one of the young women he co-opted as bat girls for his Swooners softball team.

Hired to star in **Wake Up and Live,** a 1944 radio comedy directed by Cecil B. DeMille, Frank insisted that Marilyn play opposite him. Marilyn's character in the play fell for a singer known as "The Phantom Troubadour," played by Frank. The same year, in a movie called **Lost in a Harem,** she performed a song entitled "What Does It Take to Get You?" It contained the line: "I can even get as far as second base with Frank Sinatra." Fictional flirtation was echoed by private passion. Their affair began in 1943 and continued for three years, in spite of the fact that Marilyn, like Frank, was married for at least part of the time. Nick Sevano got the impression they were "crazy about each other."

When the Sinatras threw a party on New Year's Eve 1945, Marilyn showed up wearing a distinctive diamond bracelet—one that Nancy had found by chance days earlier in the glove compartment of one of the family cars. Thinking she had stumbled on a surprise gift for herself, she had left it where it was. Now the bracelet was on another woman's wrist, and she ordered Marilyn out of the house.

Nancy told her daughters of her humiliation years later. When she confronted Frank, she said, he claimed Marilyn meant nothing to him. Six months later, though, while filming in New York, he made plans to escort her to a title fight at Madison Square Garden. George Evans, who knew the press had learned of the affair, dissuaded him. Instead Frank appeared at ringside with Joe DiMaggio and Marlene Dietrich.

Frank and Dietrich also had an involvement. Dietrich was forty-four that year, fourteen years Frank's senior and long since celebrated for her role as the nightclub vamp in **The Blue Angel.** In the movie she had sung—in those husky, hard-soft tones—"Men cluster to me like moths around a flame." In real life, twenty-two movies later, they clustered still. By the time she and Frank got together at Madison Square Garden, he had already joined her collection of male trophies, who included Erich Maria Remarque, Maurice Chevalier, Jean Gabin, Jimmy Stewart, Douglas Fairbanks Jr., Joseph Kennedy, and John Wayne. During the war, while touring European battle zones, Marlene had entertained soldiers in ways beyond the call of USO duty. There were also female lovers, and even a husband back in Germany—who never divorced her in spite of everything.

Marlene's diaries and letters, available since her death in 1992, provide an accurate glimpse of her relationship with Frank. One diary entry suggests they knew each other as early as 1942, and they were evidently close two years later. "I am eating tonight with [Clark] Gable—with the purest intentions," she wrote her daughter in early 1944. "But the choice is difficult—because Sinatra hangs on the phone and he is small and shy. I'll send you his records."

Months later, observing wartime censorship in a letter from Italy, Marlene described entertaining in "Frankie's country." She mentioned being billeted in the northeastern French city of Nancy, which—again to satisfy the censor—she referred to as "Sinatra's wife." The soldiers in her audiences, she recalled, would "swoon and scream, the way bobbysoxers did at Sinatra." "I know they had a thing going," Sammy Cahn said of Frank and Marlene. "She would have been difficult to resist. She had powers as a lover that were spoken of behind people's hands—not least because she was supposedly the champion in the oral sex department."

One night, playing cards with pals at the Wilshire Towers apartment, Frank announced that Marlene was on her way. Cahn thought that if she arrived at all she would walk out when she saw all the men sitting around. "I was wrong," he recalled. "The lady walked in, smiled demurely, allowed Sinatra to take her hand and lead her into the bedroom."

The Dietrich dalliance remained hidden, but in March 1946 Frank featured in coverage of an otherwise obscure New York divorce case. "The day after our marriage," one Sven Ingildsen said in his complaint, his twenty-year-old bride, Josephine, "left me to see Frank Sinatra alone and stayed out until 5 A.M." That story, though, was soon forgotten in a flurry of rumors about Lana Turner.

"KEEP BETTY GRABLE, Lamour and Turner," Frank had sung two years earlier in his first recording of "Nancy," the song about his infant daughter. At twenty-one Lana was already a national celebrity, a classic example of rags to Hollywood riches. Her father, a gambler and bootlegger, had been murdered when she was nine. Her mother, obliged to work, placed her in a series of foster homes. Then, when her daughter was fifteen, she brought her to Los Angeles. Already strikingly beautiful, Lana was rapidly "discovered" and shopped around the studios by a talent agent. She passed muster as an actress and could dance, but her real assets were very evidently physical. Warner Brothers launched her as their "Sweater Girl." More than a dozen movies later, at MGM in 1941, she achieved stardom in **Ziegfeld Girl**, playing alongside Judy Garland and Hedy Lamarr.

By the following year, when she turned twenty-one, Lana had in a matter of months lost her virginity to and been jilted by a Hollywood attorney, had married and divorced the bandleader Artie Shaw, and aborted his child. That summer, after cavorting with innumerable other men, many of them Hollywood "names," she married a nonentity she had known only a few weeks. He had no job, palled around with mobsters and used a bogus name, and, as she later discovered, was still technically married to someone else. By mid-1943, when she gave birth to a baby daughter, that marriage, too, had collapsed.

"The only thing you're interested in," MGM studio boss Louis B. Mayer had told her at a meeting in his office, "is . . ." He pointed at his crotch.

In 1992, in her autobiography, Lana claimed she and Sinatra had never had an affair. "The closest things to dates Frank and I enjoyed," she wrote, "were a few box lunches at MGM." The original manuscript of the book, however, is said to have included a blow-by-blow account of a tempestuous relationship with Frank. It had been deleted, apparently because Lana did not want to "give him the satisfaction."

Ava Gardner, whom Lana called her "good friend," said in an interview for her autobiography that Lana "had a very serious affair with Frank. . . . We met in the ladies' room during a party and she told me her story. She'd been deeply in love with Frank and, so she thought, Frank with her."

According to Joe Bushkin, Frank had met Lana in 1940, while he was in Hollywood with the Dorsey band and at a time when she was hooked on music and musicians. At a club in the San Fernando Valley, she had listened enthralled to the singing of Billie Holiday. Dorsey and Buddy Rich, and Frank, were at the marathon party Lana gave the weekend Pearl Harbor was bombed. In the midst of her other entanglements, she found time to date both Dorsey and Rich, and Manie Sacks. Rich broke his heart over her.

Intimacy with Frank probably came later, after six years of occasional contact. They had been photographed together at MGM, appeared together on Frank's radio show, campaigned together for President Roosevelt. By Lana's account, she and Nancy had become close. "When [Nancy] came back from Hollywood on a visit," her Hoboken friend Marian Brush recalled, "she acted real hoity-toity, saying, 'Oh, we're very close to Lana' and 'We see Lana all the time.' " What transpired in 1946, then, must have hurt Nancy all the more.

Frank and Lana began a dalliance that year at the studio, one they scarcely bothered to hide. "They used to smooch in his car parked on the lot," an MGM executive said. "Kind of funny, considering they both had dressing rooms to go to." The couple had excuses to be in and out of New York that spring, Lana for her new movie, **The Postman Always Rings Twice**, Frank for radio shows and location shooting. There, it seems, they began a full-fledged affair.

Four months later, in October, the troubled

Sinatra marriage became national news. George Evans announced that Frank and Nancy had parted. Reached by a columnist, Nancy said Frank wanted "the freedom of separation without divorce." He had left home and was looking for an apartment. Frank said later that there had been endless squabbling with Nancy "about trivial matters." In fact he had walked out on his wife just twenty-four hours after "dancing many times" with Lana at a Hollywood party—with the press looking on. Soon he was in Palm Springs, where Lana had a place, and was seen with her there at the Chi Chi Club.

In an era when the fan magazines and Hollywood gossip columnists wielded great power, there was good reason to conceal the truth. One in two Americans, it was said, habitually read the gospel handed down by the reigning queens of the craft, Louella Parsons and Hedda Hopper. Both journalists depended on the stars and the studios, and the stars and the studios depended on the columnists. A few words from Parsons or Hopper could make or destroy an actor or a movie.

To have a movie contract in Hollywood, moreover, was to live in a social corset. MGM's standard "morals clause" bound performers to live "with due regard to public conventions and morals," not to "commit any act or thing that will tend to shock, insult or offend the community." At MGM an actor was required to apply to the studio for permission to get married. Were he or she photographed in a nightclub smoking, the studio would try to ensure that the offending cigarette was airbrushed out. This hypocrisy could be enforced as and when the studio chose.

Parsons, who was close to Louis B. Mayer, had long since used her column to enjoin Lana "to behave herself and not go completely berserk." MGM bosses, agonizing over **The Postman Always Rings Twice,** in which she played the adulterous wife, had sought ways to soften the "immoral temptress" nature of the role, to the extent of having her appear on screen wearing virginal white. As for Frank, the studio had cultivated an image of him as a good family man. He and Lana represented a huge financial investment, and it was decided that something had to be done.

That October, MGM troubleshooters descended on Lana and ordered her to start parroting a simple script. "I am not in love with Frank," she was soon saying dutifully with tears in her eyes, "and he is not in love with me. I have never in my life broken up a home. . . . I just can't take these accusations."

While Parsons played up that message, Hedda Hopper castigated Frank in print and warned that he was risking his career. Nancy, she told readers, was a wife so caring that she "refuses to attend any party until she's sure Frank isn't going, for fear it might embarrass him." Hopper even buttonholed Frank at a public function to lecture him on family values. "I warned him that he was public property," she said, "and that part of that public property was Nancy and his children."

Seventeen days after leaving home, Frank was back. His reunion with Nancy, in front of friends, customers, and the press at Slapsie Maxie's, a nightclub on Beverly Boulevard, looked like a publicity gimmick. He and Nancy sat without partners at separate tables, and then owner Max Rosenbloom asked for a song. Frank obliged with "Goin' Home," then Frank walked over to his wife. They kissed and danced and departed, smiling radiantly for a photographer waiting at the door. "It's all over," Frank told a reporter. "I'm home and let's forget it."

It was not all over. Just weeks later in New York, after bringing Nancy east for his opening at the Waldorf, Frank was trysting with Lana again. "I was Frank's beard when he was seeing her one night," George Evans's son Phil remembered. "I remember having to sit around chatting with Lana in one of the lounges while Frank did the show. Then he came back and collected her. I know Lana was his date for the evening."

Frank was "shuttling backward and forward between her bedroom and Nancy's," Ava Gardner recalled Lana telling her, "trying to equate obedience to Catholic doctrines with indulgence in his natural inclinations . . . divorce plans were all set up and wedding plans had been made . . . she felt like she'd been on the verge of marrying Frank." If Frank did encourage Lana to believe that, he let her down. The Sinatras' marriage was to wobble on for four more years.

"I HAVEN'T MUCH TO SAY in my defense," Frank said of that time, "except that I was in a terrible state of mental confusion." He was sick for a while after the Lana furor, and there was newspaper talk of an impending nervous breakdown. A contributory factor must have been overwork. In the seventeen days of the Lana crisis he had done four radio shows, performing a full program of songs on each, spent one day in the studio making a record, two recording for his current movie—**It Happened in Brooklyn**—and one night live on stage. He remembered having been "desperately tired, right on the ragged edges."

MGM production memos for **It Happened in Brooklyn** confirm it: "Sinatra reported he was ill and didn't work," "Sinatra was tired and would not work," "didn't report," "refused calls to come in." Louis B. Mayer sent Frank a telegram complaining of "a long series of violations of your contractual obligations," ensuring that the text got into the newspapers. Frank fired off furious telegrams of his own, including one to Los Angeles **Daily News** drama critic Erskine Johnson: "Just continue to print lies about me, and my temper—not my temperament—will see that you get a belt in your vicious and stupid mouth."

At year's end, the Hollywood Women's Press Club voted him "least cooperative star of 1946," accusing him of turning down hundreds of interview requests. Now began an endless cycle of skirmishing with journalists, bellicose talk, and actual physical violence.

Just before leaving home over Lana, Frank had shocked fellow members of the Screen Actors Guild at a meeting to discuss a current strike. On learning of wild threats by some strikers—there was talk of throwing acid in actors' faces should they cross picket lines—he had responded with an outburst of his own. No one, he was reported as saying, "was going to tell him what to do . . . if anybody got tough with him—why, he knew some tough guys too."

He did indeed, as the nation was about to find out.

13

A Handshake in Havana

On January 30, 1947, Frank took out a license in California to carry a German Walther pistol. Questioned by a reporter at the sheriff's office—someone tipped the press that he was there—he said he needed the weapon for "a personal matter." Carrying a handgun was to become routine for him. He "never left home without it," his valet George Jacobs said of the .38 Smith & Wesson his boss favored in the 1960s. "Always carried the gun in a holster."

In one account Frank claimed the pistol was a souvenir brought home from his postwar USO tour to Italy. He told another reporter that he had "wanted Nancy to have some protection in case of an emergency. So I bought a little gun for the house." Later still, he would say he had needed the weapon "to protect personal funds."

After obtaining the permit, Frank flew to New

York to fulfill a radio commitment, then on to Miami. Before he went south, though, the columnist Earl Wilson got word of his journey, learned who Frank's host in Florida was to be—and was appalled. The host was the mobster Joe Fischetti, and the Miami Beach mansion at which Frank stayed belonged to Joe's older brothers Charles and Rocco, often described as the "heirs to Al Capone." The brothers were just back from attending Capone's funeral in Chicago.

Charles, then forty-six, liked to use the name Dr. Fisher and pose as a wealthy art collector. Friends dubbed him Prince Charlie. In reality, he was a feared extortionist and political fixer. Rocco, three years younger, called himself an antiques dealer. He, too, had come up through the ranks as an enforcer.

Thirty-seven-year-old Joe—his real name was Giuseppe—is described in his FBI file as "the least intelligent and the least aggressive" of the brothers. "I'm the only one in the family who hasn't killed anybody," he once told a visitor, while brandishing the gun he always carried. Joe, too, was linked to extortion. He was an errand boy for his brothers and a front man for an empire based on gambling and, increasingly, show business. The roots of that empire were intertwined with those of gangsters on the East Coast. Rocco had once been arrested while leaving a Mafia gathering with Lucky Luciano. Charlie, for his part, was in regular touch with Willie Moretti.

Frank joined the brothers in Miami at a pivotal moment for organized crime. Luciano was back in circulation. He had been released from prison in New York in early 1946, on condition he go into exile in Italy. Italian police who met his ship escorted him to Sicily, and back to Lercara Friddi. From there Luciano rapidly made his way to Rome, where he was soon ensconced in a fine hotel suite, in contact with American associates and plotting his return to real power. Before leaving the United States Luciano had agreed with one of the most powerful of those associates, Meyer Lansky, as to how to go about it. He would resume control of the empire of crime from Cuba, just ninety miles from the United States mainland.

Luciano arrived in Havana in the late fall of 1946, set up his base of operations with the connivance of Cuban politicians, and began receiving a steady stream of senior American mafiosi. "The guys was coming," he recalled, "not because I asked them to. I ordered it." Rocco and Joe Fischetti flew in on Pan Am from Miami on February 11, 1947. A still frame from newsreel footage shows them walking from the plane, Rocco to the rear, Joe in front with a hand up to his face. Between them, toting a sizable piece of hand baggage, is Frank Sinatra.

Nine days later, American newspapers carried an article with a Havana dateline. "I am frankly puzzled," wrote the columnist Robert Ruark, "as to why Frank Sinatra, the fetish of millions, chooses to spend his vacation in the company of convicted vice operators and assorted hoodlums. . . . He was here for four days last week and his companion in public was Luciano, Luciano's bodyguards, and a rich collection of gamblers. . . . There were considerable speculations of a disgusted nature by observers who saw Frankie, night after night, with Mr. Luciano at the Gran Casino Nacional, the dice emporium and the horse park. . . . Mr. Sinatra, the self-confessed savior of the country's small fry, by virtue of his lectures on clean living and love-thy-neighbor, his movie shorts on tolerance, and his frequent dablings into the do-good department of politics, seems to be setting a most peculiar example."

The article had an explosive effect, and Frank at once denied it all. "Any report that I fraternize with goons and racketeers is a vicious lie," he said. "I go to many places and meet a great many people from all walks of life—editors, scientists, businessmen and, perhaps, unsavory characters."

Frank's accounts of the episode—his association with the Fischettis, the trip to Cuba, and the Luciano encounter—did not remain consistent. He said he had met Joe Fischetti fleetingly while performing in Chicago, but saw little of him. He had just happened to "run into" Fischetti in Miami before the Cuba trip. Questioned later by attorneys for Senator Estes Kefauver's Special Committee to Investigate Organized Crime in Interstate Commerce—the Kefauver Committee—he claimed he had met Charlie and Rocco Fischetti "just to say 'Hello, how are you?' . . . three times at most." He had "not an ounce" of business with any of them.

George Evans told federal agents that his client went to Cuba only at Joe Fischetti's suggestion, because he was being harassed by fans in Miami. Frank told the Kefauver Committee attorneys, however, that he already intended to go to Cuba before mentioning it to Fischetti. Indeed, he said in one interview, he had already been planning the trip when he applied for a gun license before leaving California. Later still, testifying to the Nevada State Gaming Control Board, he said it was pure coincidence that he and the Fischettis flew to Havana on the same plane.

Of the news story reporting his encounter with Luciano, Frank said: "I was brought up to shake a man's hand when I am introduced to him, without first investigating his past." Then, telling "the complete story" in an interview with Hedda Hopper, he said, "I dropped by a casino one night. One of the captains—a sort of host—recognized me and asked if I'd mind meeting a few people. . . . I couldn't refuse. . . . So I went through some routine introductions, scarcely paying attention to the names of the people I was meeting. One happened to be Lucky Luciano. Even if I'd caught his name, I probably wouldn't have associated it with the notorious underworld character. . . . I sat down at a table for about fifteen minutes. Then I got up and went back to the hotel. . . . When such innocent acts are so distorted, you can't win."

In a signed article, Frank came up with another variant. "I was invited to have dinner," he wrote, "and while dining I realized that one of the men in the party was Lucky Luciano. . . . I could think of no way to leave in the middle of dinner without creating a scene. . . . After dinner I toured the nightspots. . . . We finally wound up at the Havana Casino where we passed a table at which were Luciano and several other men. . . . Again, rather than cause a disturbance, I had a quick drink and excused myself."

Frank told the Kefauver Committee attorneys he was introduced to Luciano in Havana by Connie Immerman, whom he described as a "New York restaurateur." In other statements, he said the introduction was made by Nate Gross, a Chicago journalist. The name of America's most notorious mobster, he claimed, had seemed merely "familiar." Only when a dinner companion explained, he said, did he realize who it was he had met. Luciano and the Fischettis were again present, he told Kefauver's staff, when he sat through a show at Sloppy Joe's, a famous nightspot in the Cuban capital.

Finally, questioned as late as 1970 by a New Jersey state body probing organized crime, Frank claimed that he knew no mobsters and remained unaware of Luciano's reputation as a Mafia boss.

In fact, FBI records show, he and the Fischettis had spent a good deal of time together during the months before the Cuba trip. He and Charles Fischetti had spent three hours visiting with the Fischettis' mother at her home in Brooklyn. He had been Rocco's guest at the Vernon Country Club outside Chicago, and in touch with Joe about a meeting in New York. Contrary to Frank's denial of any business relationship with the Fischettis, the brothers told Kefauver Committee attorneys that he was their partner in a car dealership operation. According to an FBI informant, Joe Fischetti had stated on the very eve of the Havana trip that he "had a financial interest in Sinatra."

Both the FBI and the Federal Bureau of Narcotics, which had agents in Havana in 1947, had known Luciano was in town before Frank arrived. After his arrival, two sources on the Narcotics Bureau payroll, an elevator man and a telephone operator at the Hotel Nacional, reported on comings and goings from Luciano's suite on the eighth floor and from Frank's on the floor below. Bureau records and the private papers of journalist Robert Ruark contradict Frank's claim that the meeting with Luciano amounted to one brief handshake.

"While in Havana," bureau supervisor George

White reported to commissioner Harry Anslinger, "Luciano lavishly entertained Frank Costello, Meyer Lansky, Ralph Capone, Rocco and Charlie Fischetti, as well as Frank Sinatra and Bruce Cabot, actors." Willie Moretti was also in Cuba.

Wary of Sinatra's lawyers—Frank would in fact sue over the Havana stories—the executive editor of the **New York World-Telegram** asked Ruark to submit a detailed in-house memorandum on how he had developed his information.

"I was told by Mr. Larry Larrea, [Hotel Nacional] general manager," Ruark responded, "that Frank Sinatra was vacationing in Havana and—to Mr. Larrea's evident horror—was spending most of his waking hours with Lucky Luciano, Mr. Luciano's bodyguard, and an assorted group of gamblers and hoodlums. . . . The caliber of Mr. Sinatra's intimates was so low that Mr. Larrea preferred to stay in his suite rather than run the risk of bumping into Sinatra and his friends in the lobby."

World-Telegram society writer Charles Ventura told Ruark he had seen Frank at the casino with Luciano on two consecutive nights, and that they had also been seen together at the racetrack. Other corroborating witnesses included Connie Immerman, the man Frank said introduced him to Luciano. Immerman, a former manager of the Cotton Club, is referred to in Narcotics Bureau reports as a "Luciano henchman . . . notorious gambler." Immerman characterized Luciano as just "a swell kid . . . just taking it easy and trying to live down his past."

At a second meeting with Larrea, Ruark learned Sinatra was at that very moment upstairs with Luciano. "I wouldn't advise your going up there," the manager warned. "The best you can expect is to get thrown out. They are pretty tough fellows. They've got a lot of women with them, and I don't know how much they've been drinking." The warning, Ruark remembered, included advice "**not** to file my stories concerning Sinatra and Luciano by Western Union . . . it was a practice of the Cuban wireless office to immediately call subject people in stories of the type I intended to write, and that there would be a good chance of the story being lost, badly garbled or distorted. He also said the writer of such a story might be likely to wind up with a 'knot' on his head."

A month after Ruark's scoop, his colleague Ventura told him in a letter that Frank had been involved in an orgy while in Havana. "Emilio Sanchez threw a party at Sinatra's suite when he was here, also attended by Ralph Capone [brother of Al]. . . . Gist of the party was to have too much booze and twelve naked women. Midst of the party a delegation of Cuban Girl Scouts arrived with a mentor to offer some token or other to the Voice. All babes were shooed into the two bedrooms, whilst the Voice came out impeccably garbed in lounge robe and silk scarf. During the ceremony four naked bodies suddenly catapulted into the living room. The Girl Scouts retreated in complete rout."

Years afterward, in a book endorsed by commissioner Anslinger, **Reader's Digest** editor Frederic Sondern told the story as preserved in bureau files. The Girl Scouts, he wrote, had been escorted by a nun and admitted to the suite "through a series of disastrous mistakes by various personnel." They walked into a scene of "ribald chaos. There were bottles on the floor, lingerie hung from wall brackets and a number of people lay sleeping where they had collapsed. The Scouts were marched back into the elevator by their white-faced leader. The sister reported at once to her mother superior, the mother superior to her bishop."

An informant later told the FBI that "a plane-load of call girls" had been sent to Havana courtesy of the Fischetti brothers. They were supplied for "a party at the Hotel Nacional attended by Sinatra."

Four years later, in 1951, Kefauver Committee staff confronted Frank with eight photographs taken in Havana. One, according to committee attorney Joe Nellis, showed him "with his arm around Lucky Luciano on the balcony of the Hotel Nacional . . . another showed Sinatra and Luciano sitting in a nightclub in the Nacional, with lots of bottles, having a hell of a time with some good-looking girls . . . and then there were a couple pictures of him with the Fischetti brothers [and] Luciano." Other shots showed Frank with Santo Trafficante, Johnny Rosselli, and Carlo Gambino, all then rising mafiosi.

A former member of the Hotel Nacional staff, Jorge Jorge, recently provided information suggesting that Frank's involvement went way beyond the supposedly chance handshake with Luciano. Jorge said that for security reasons, Luciano spent most of his time in a set of communicating rooms far from the suite in which he was registered. Luciano and Lansky used two of them, Frank the third.

Jorge, who said he was assigned to serve Luciano because he spoke English, described bringing breakfast to the suite. "We would come with the tables, the tables with the little wheels. And there they'd be, Sinatra, Luciano, and Meyer Lansky. They thought I was going to listen to what they were talking about, so they would change the subject. They waited for me to serve breakfast. . . . Once I had finished, they would look at me as if to say 'Goodbye' and I would leave."

Narcotics Bureau agents learned Luciano was involved in huge casino and resort developments—and, they thought, in narcotics—in Cuba, and for that he needed access to vast sums of money. The bureau's information, later corroborated by the Mafia boss himself, Rocco and Joe Fischetti, and a key associate of Meyer Lansky, was that visiting associates carried huge cash sums to him in Havana.

There were suspicions that Frank and former heavyweight champion Jack Dempsey had acted as couriers during the Cuba episode. Official records suggest the Fischettis contributed as much as $2 million, ($16 million today) and that Frank may have carried the cash into Havana in his hand luggage. After that allegation appeared in the press, Luciano denied it and Frank responded with derision.

"Picture me, skinny Frankie," he said, "lifting $2,000,000 in small bills. For the record, $1,000 in dollar bills weighs three pounds, which makes the load I am supposed to have carried 6,000 pounds. Even assuming the bills were twenties, the bag would still have required a couple of stevedores to carry it." The baggage seen in the film of his airport arrival, Frank said, contained only "my oils, sketching material and personal jewelry." Frank did take up painting and buy art supplies in 1947, but, according to his wife Nancy did so only months after the Havana trip. "If you can find me an attaché case that holds $2,000,000," Frank said in testimony to Nevada's State Gaming Control Board, "I will give you the $2,000,000." Norman Mailer tried it, and discovered that in fact an even larger sum could be packed into an attaché case.

Jerry Lewis said that Frank carried money for the Mafia on more than one occasion. Lewis was born in New Jersey, had been befriended by Dolly Sinatra when he was starting out, met Frank in 1939, and knew some of the same mobsters. In the year of the Cuba episode, he performed at the wedding reception for one of Willie Moretti's daughters. He was on intimate terms with the Fischetti brothers.

In Frank's case, Lewis said, the relationship with the mob "had to do with the morality that a handshake goes before God. Frank, at a cocktail party, told Meyer [Lansky] in no uncertain terms, 'If there is going to be East Coast, West Coast, intercontinental, and foreign—if all that's going to happen, I go all the time, Meyer.' He volunteered to be a messenger for them. And he almost got caught once . . . in New York." Frank was going through Customs, Lewis explained, carrying a briefcase containing "three and a half million in fifties." Customs opened the briefcase, then—because of a crowd of people pushing and shoving behind Frank—aborted the search and let him go on. "We would never have heard of him again," Lewis reflected, had the cash been discovered.

At some point during Frank's stay in Havana, according to Nacional Hotel employee Jorge, Frank performed for the assembled mobsters in the banquet room. "Luciano was very fond of Sinatra's singing," said Lansky's associate Joe Stacher, "but of course our meeting had nothing to do with listening to him sing." Of the various matters on the agenda, one had to do with Bugsy Siegel, the veteran bootlegger, gambling racketeer, and killer operating on the West Coast. Siegel's latest and most grandiose project, the mob-funded Flamingo hotel and casino in Las Vegas, was going badly. Its opening a few weeks earlier had been a fiasco, and the hotel was temporarily closed down. The mafiosi had learned that some of the millions of dollars entrusted to Siegel, including a huge sum contributed by the Fischetti brothers, had been siphoned into private accounts in Switzerland.

The embryonic Las Vegas operation promised to be a fabulous bonanza. Frank, who knew Siegel and other key West Coast mobsters, had himself seen the potential. He had been exploring plans to build a hotel casino of his own in Vegas, one with broadcast facilities. Siegel had complained about the prospect of having Frank as competition, while simultaneously trying to get him to perform at the gala opening of the Flamingo. Frank had not obliged.

At the Mafia gathering in Cuba, Siegel was sentenced to death. He died in a hail of bullets a few months later, his execution approved by Luciano and directed, by one account, by Charles Fischetti. A few days later, said Shirley Ballard, who was still seeing Frank, "We were with a couple of music publishers—probably in Frank's dressing room—and Frank says, 'Okay, we're going to the house where Ben died—he always called Siegel 'Ben'—'and we're going to have a drink for him.'

"So we got in Frank's Cadillac and drove to Beverly Hills, and sat in the living room where Siegel was killed. This was just after he'd been shot. And drank a toast to his memory. It was eerie, like his ghost was still there. Frank and the others got very solemn and raised a glass to him."

In Las Vegas, the syndicate had taken over the Flamingo within hours, and went on to oversee the building of Las Vegas into America's gambling and entertainment mecca, with Frank as star of stars.

AFTER HAVANA, Luciano and Frank sought to minimize their relationship. Luciano denied that Frank "was ever asked to do anything illegal," while Frank insisted in 1952 that the Havana encounter had been the only time they ever met.

The headlines about Frank's adventure in Cuba had proved a boon for the Bureau of Narcotics. Washington put pressure on the Cuban government, and Luciano was once more shipped back to Italy. He would live there for the rest of his life, plotting further crimes and in constant touch with Mafia associates in the United States. The Narcotics Bureau pressured the Italian police to keep him under surveillance and, when a pretext could be found, to conduct searches of his homes.

It was a police search, two years after Frank's Havana trip, that first yielded evidence of the continuing Sinatra connection. "When Italian police raided Lucky's lavish apartment in Rome," New York **Daily Mirror** columnist Jack Lait wrote in transparent code, "they found a sterling silver cigarette case inscribed: 'To My Dear Friend, Charlie Luciano,' over one of the most sought-after American autographs, that of a young star, a known gangster lover." Lait's source was evidently the Narcotics Bureau; a similar passage can be found in a draft manuscript in Anslinger's papers. A later article identified the "star" named in the dedication as "Frank Sinatra."

The story endured, with variants as to whether the gift was gold or silver, and whether it was a cigarette case or a lighter. Frank would claim he made "no gift of any kind, at any time, to Luciano." Speaking of the Cuba trip, Luciano recalled that Frank had given "a few presents to different guys, like a gold cigarette case, a watch, that kind of thing . . . for me, the guy was always Number One OK."

The woman who was Luciano's mistress in the three years prior to his death from a heart attack in 1962, Adriana Rizzo, said recently that she did remember a certain lighter. "I had a gold lighter that he gave me as a present, and he had received it from Sinatra. He had stopped smoking because of the heart ailment." The lighter had been among items removed after Luciano's death by his brother Bartolo, Rizzo said, and she had not seen it since. She remembered, however, that it had been inscribed.

As for a cigarette case, retired General Fulvio Toschi of Italy's Polizia Tributaria, a Treasury enforcement unit, recalled having seen just such a case while searching a Luciano safe deposit box. It was, he said, a "large gold cigarette case with the words, something like, 'To my friend, or pal, Lucky' and the word 'Frank' or 'Frank Sinatra.' "

A document in Anslinger's files indicates that Luciano knew Frank's address a year before the Cuba episode. It records the seizure by Italian police, apparently in early 1946, of Luciano's address book. "Frank Sinatra" was listed in it, along with the California address Frank had by then had for two years.

Back in exile after his foray to Cuba, the mob boss became a familiar figure in the exclusive hotels and restaurants of Rome and Naples. The public came to see him as a sort of Godfather emeritus, a seeming has-been happy to give interviews to journalists and to chat with tourists. Yet Mafia bosses in the United States consulted him regularly in coded telephone calls, and sent couriers with information and money. The Bureau of Narcotics believed he remained a major power, the brains of the burgeoning international drug traffic.

Narcotics Bureau reports indicate that Frank, like Jimmy Durante, George Raft, and other lesser-known show business figures, had repeated contact with the mobster. A Luciano associate since boyhood, Louis Russo, characterized all three entertainers as being the Mafia boss's "close personal friends and great admirers, if not hero-worshippers."

In 1950 and 1960, informants told the FBI that Frank had carried money to Luciano in Italy, as once he allegedly had to Cuba. Reports to the Narcotics Bureau quote Luciano as saying that he expected Frank for Christmas in 1952 and then, when Frank did not make it, that he met him at the Hotel Terminus in Naples the following spring. Frank was in Italy at that time, on a tour that included performances in Naples and Rome.

From time to time, it seems, Luciano made new sorties back across the Atlantic, making his way—more discreetly than in 1947—to Fulgencio Batista's Cuba. Rumor had it, according to a press report, that by 1956 he had surreptitiously entered the United States nine times. Federal agents received information on two Mafia conclaves presided over by the exiled Mafia boss, one in Cuba in 1951, another the following year at the

Plantation Yacht Club on one of the Florida Keys. There were several meetings with Luciano there, according to the wife of the Chicago gangster Murray Humphreys. "We used to meet him at the Plantation Yacht Club," Jeanne Humphreys said. "The boys always threw big 'coming out' bashes for Lucky at the club." According to an FBI report, Sinatra was present at the meeting in 1951.

Frank's valet, George Jacobs, recalled what happened at a Rome hotel a few years later, probably in the summer of 1958. "We walked into the suite," Jacobs said, "and there was Lucky Luciano sitting in the living room. Just sitting there, waiting for us to arrive." When Jacobs saw the infamous face and realized who it was, he was afraid. "I thought maybe this was one of those times when you don't get out of it." Luciano rose from his chair and kissed Frank. "They clearly knew each other well," Jacobs remembered, and the meeting with Luciano struck him as Frank's one "joyous moment" during that trip to Italy.

Soon after Christmas the same year, Frank and Luciano may have got together again twice within weeks, in Cuba and in Florida. Frank and the Mafia boss were both reportedly in Havana in that period, on the eve of the overthrow of the Batista regime. If so, the subject under discussion was likely the building of a new multimillion-dollar casino development. According to an FBI document that cites National City Bank records, Frank and others were investors in the project in association with a mob partner.

According to a firsthand report, Luciano and Frank met again within the month, in Miami. Billy Woodfield, the photographer who often worked with Sinatra, said he saw them there during the shooting of **A Hole in the Head,** a comedy starring Frank and Edward G. Robinson. "The crowd from **Hole in the Head** was there for location shooting," he said. "Frank had me go with him and these guys to the track at Flagler Field. It was funny, they were all wearing short pants and high socks and big Kadiddlehopper hats or fedoras—odd clothes for the races. They were all going into a dining room off the executive area as I was loading film.

"Frank said, 'Billy, take some pictures for me. . . . Make two prints of each picture and give me the negatives. Make no other prints.' One of the guys—he was wearing regular pants—said, 'Whaddya mean, a picture? I'm not supposed to be in the country!' It was Luciano."

Peggy Connelly, a young singer who was Frank's lover in the fifties, knew nothing about organized crime. She could not help but notice, though, that Frank had odd weekend guests and associates about whom he was highly sensitive. "There are some people I've got to say hello to," he said as he took her to a private room in a New York club to meet some hefty fellows in dark suits. "I'll introduce you. I won't say any last names, and don't ask for them."

Once Frank talked with pride of a Mafia meeting he had been allowed to attend. "He told it seriously," Connelly remembered. "He said they were talking about who would be in charge of something, who would be the right man. 'And,' he said, 'they all turned as one and looked at me!' Frank added, of course, that it wasn't really a possibility that he'd be some sort of Godfather—not at all. But he talked as though he could conceive of himself in that light. He was very moved by their sort of appreciation, homage, of him. I could see that his heart went out to this."

Ten years later, when Frank was friendly with President John F. Kennedy, he had become more careful, at least about seeing Luciano. "Sinatra has become somewhat scared off," a source told the Narcotics Bureau in 1961, "and now when in Italy he makes excuses for not visiting Naples and Luciano. However, he always telephones." He also corresponded with Luciano that year, according to another Bureau report.

"Sinatra was a very close friend of Luciano," Adriana Rizzo said. "He certainly was. Sometimes he came to Naples. They met from time to time, at the Excelsior or other leading hotels like the Vesuvio. I was there with Luciano when they spoke on the phone. Always very affectionate phone calls."

The aging mobster had a large collection of Sinatra records. Ensconced in his apartment on Via Tasso in Naples, he listened to them often. "They were very fond of each other," said Rizzo. "And, for Sinatra, Luciano had a lot of respect."

14

Courting Disaster

THE ADVENTURE WITH THE MAFIA in Cuba was "one of the dumbest things I ever did," Frank told Pete Hamill years later. Other follies soon followed, and personal misery.

"Will you be my Valentine?" he had wired Nancy from Havana, suggesting they take a Mexican vacation. Before he left for Havana, she had told him she was pregnant again. She had told him, too, that she was considering having an abortion—illegal then, and an especially radical step for a Catholic. Frank never thought she would go through with it, but she did. When she told him, in Mexico, he was appalled.

Soon after returning to Hollywood, he brought more trouble on himself. On April 8, shortly before midnight, Frank and a male companion arrived at Ciro's, a nightspot on Sunset Boulevard. He drove in through the exit gate, a waiting taxi driver noticed, thus avoiding having his car parked by an attendant. Inside, the columnist Lee Mortimer was finishing dinner with a woman companion. The cab driver, William Taylor, would be the only independent witness to what happened when they came out fifteen minutes later.

"Sinatra came out of Ciro's," investigators later quoted the driver as saying, "walked up behind Mortimer and hit him with his right hand, knocking Mortimer down. After Sinatra had knocked Mortimer down Sinatra backed away. Mortimer got up holding his jaw and said something to the effect 'Why did you hit me?' At this time a man described as 5′11″ or 6′ tall, 200 pounds, black hair, wearing a blue pin-striped suit, grabbed Mortimer and pushed Mortimer down and held him. . . . Sinatra made the statement, 'Let him up, I'll kick his brains in' . . . called Mortimer a 'shit heel' and a 'perverted bastard.' "

Taylor could not see what happened next, because his view was blocked by people rushing out of the club in response to the commotion. Mortimer told investigators Frank hit him several more times, while others held him down. Two other witnesses, his companion and Nat Dallinger, a King Features photographer, also saw others pinioning Mortimer. Dallinger recalled shouting, "Four men against one is too many!" and trying to pull them off.

The melee was quickly over. Bruised but not seriously hurt, Mortimer made his way to the sheriff's office, saw a doctor, and called the press. Frank, who had gone back to the bar and ordered a double brandy, seems at first not to have realized that there would be a price to pay.

The next day, while rehearsing "Oh, What a Beautiful Mornin'!" at a local studio, he was arrested, charged with assault and battery, and released on bail. His license to carry a gun was withdrawn until further notice. The men around Frank at the time of the incident declined to speak with investigating officers "under the advice of their attorney." The heavy fellow identified as having initially held Mortimer down, song plugger Sam Weiss, a longtime friend of Frank, declined to make a statement on the grounds that he was "afraid of policemen." The proprietor of Ciro's and his staff said they had seen nothing.

Frank admitted having hit Mortimer but denied having attacked from behind or that anyone helped him. He had only hit the columnist, he was quoted as saying, because Mortimer insulted him in the restaurant. "He called me a dirty dago sonofabitch, and I wouldn't take that from anyone." The claim earned Frank much sympathy, and he made it so often that many came to believe it. In fact, it had been concocted by one of his PR men. The allegation did not appear in Frank's first conversation with a journalist, held within half an hour of the fracas. He told the columnist Harrison Carroll, who had rushed to Ciro's on receiving a tip, that he and Mortimer had said nothing to each other. Frank attacked Mortimer, he said, because "For two years he has been needling me . . . he gave me a look. I can't describe it. It was one of those 'Who do you amount to?' looks. I followed him outside and I saw red. I hit him. I'm all mixed up. . . . I couldn't help myself."

Mortimer, who specialized in covering show business, had written harsh pieces about Frank. Sinatra fans, to him, were "squealing, shouting neurotic extremists . . . juve delinqs." He had sneered at Frank for waiting "until hostilities were over to take his seven-week joy ride" entertaining troops in Europe. He slammed **The House I Live In** as "class struggle posing as entertainment." Frank, he said, spent "much of his time while in New York with other leftwingers . . . fighting for this and that and almost any goofy cause that comes along." Just weeks earlier, after the Havana episode, he had made a reference to "Frank (Lucky) Sinatra."

The sniping so enraged Frank that he had talked openly of wanting to "belt" the columnist or, according to Sonny King, to "stick his head down into the toilet bowl and flush it." "The next time," Mortimer claimed Frank said at Ciro's, "I'll kill you." It seems possible that he had planned the attack in advance. The district attorney's investigators concluded that "Sinatra, with a gang behind him and with the active assistance of one man, made an unexpected and unprovoked assault."

Yet the case never went to trial. Frank appeared in court, apologized, and agreed to pay Mortimer $9,000 ($72,000 today). The DA then withdrew the charge. Mortimer went on criticizing Frank in his articles and, as he focused increasingly on organized crime, in several books. In **U.S.A. Confidential**, he and coauthor Jack Lait wrote flatly that Frank was "a mob property."

The mob, as well as Frank, had it in for Mortimer. Three years after the attack at Ciro's, the columnist was beaten unconscious by two hoodlums at New Jersey's Riviera club, owned by Willie Moretti. In 1960, FBI surveillance microphones would overhear New Jersey criminals discussing a Mortimer article that excoriated Frank for his links to a mob-run casino in Las Vegas. Someone, one of them predicted, "will shoot or beat up Mortimer sooner or later."

When Mortimer died three years later, of natural causes, Frank took posthumous revenge. "Frank and I were at Jilly [Rizzo]'s club in Manhattan," Brad Dexter remembered. "He said, 'That dirty sonofabitch, I'm glad he's dead.' He told Jilly to get the car—this was 2:30 or 3:00 in the morning, and he was full of whiskey. Mortimer had been buried across the river, and we drove to his grave. Frank unzipped his pants and urinated on the grave.

"Can you imagine how a sick sonofabitch would want to go out there just to piss on the guy's grave? I said: 'What the hell did you want to do that for? D'you think pissing on his grave is going to prove anything?' He said, 'Yeah, this cocksucker made my life miserable. He talked against me, wrote articles, caused me a lot of grief. I got back at him.' Frank always had to even the score."

FRANK HAD BEEN WALKING a tightrope in 1947, courting massive publicity, preaching family values, and espousing controversial political causes while simultaneously philandering, consorting with notorious criminals, and acting like a thug. By physically assaulting and threatening journalists, Frank was inviting retribution.

Most newspapers in the United States were staunchly conservative then, none more so than those of the Hearst chain, with the enormous clout of some fifty newspapers, magazines, radio stations, and film companies. The elderly founder, William Randolph Hearst, was a political kingmaker who thought Franklin Roosevelt had taken the country the way of the Soviet Union. Hollywood's "Reds, Pinks, and Punks," he thought, spread communism.

Frank's whirl of political activity had already made him a target for Hearst's writers. His supportive open letter to former vice president Henry Wallace, an ultraliberal presidential prospect, had been published just weeks before the foolishness in Havana. The man who broke that story, Hearst's Robert Ruark, was soon deriding the news that Frank was to play a priest in his next movie, **The Miracle of the Bells,** as a gimmick designed to "wipe out the picture of Sinatra, the thug's chum." Then came the assault on Mortimer, who was also on the Hearst payroll.

That brief tussle, **Time** noted, got coverage by the Hearst chain "almost fit for an attempted political assassination." Frank received a Thomas Jefferson Award for civil rights work just a few days later, but that was lost in the furor.

Mortimer began digging for new dirt, cultivating sources at the Bureau of Narcotics and the FBI. J. Edgar Hoover had already ordered his staff to collate information on Frank, and now ordered a senior aide to brief Mortimer on Frank's early Mafia backing and the sex charges arrest of a decade earlier. Mortimer passed information on to Hearst's big gun, Westbrook Pegler, a Pulitzer winner for his exposés of union racketeering. Robert Ruark suggested that he and Pegler "hosstrade" information on Sinatra. Pegler wrote a series of anti-Sinatra columns in the fall of 1947, shining more light on the dark side of Frank's life and focusing on the mob connection.

Another Hearst writer, Frank Conniff, issued the single most savage rebuke. "Posing as a do-gooder, lending aid and comfort to Communist-front organizations," he wrote, Frank "openly buddied up to mobsters. . . . No newspaperman would demur if Bing Crosby or Clark Gable or Perry Como occasionally dabbled in transgressions. But be it remembered that these men have never posed as world-changers. . . . The ripe odor of hypocrisy leaks from every pore of Sinatra's recent career."

George Evans could not stop the press onslaught. It took a rare penitent overture by Frank to achieve that. Toward the end of 1947, he got in to see Hearst himself. "I don't know what happened between the two men," Hedda Hopper wrote later, "but I do know that a few hours later an order went out to the Hearst papers to take the heat off Sinatra." Hearst's grandson John, who was present at the encounter, said Frank had been "very contrite." Shortly afterward, he was received as a houseguest at Hearst Sr.'s castle north of Los Angeles.

Frank's career had taken some hits. The makers of Old Gold cigarettes, sponsors of one of his radio shows, dropped him, citing bad publicity and falling ratings. In November, in spite of massive promotion, he drew disappointing audiences during a three-week run at the Capitol Theater in New York. Only four Sinatra singles made the top ten that year. Nevertheless, Frank placed second in an ABC poll to nominate the "most popular living person." Only Bing Crosby was rated more popular. He and Frank ranked ahead of Eleanor Roosevelt, Generals Eisenhower and MacArthur, and Pope Pius XII.

Frank kept up his frenetic pace, focusing above all on his work in the recording studio. He would usually arrive at the studio mid-evening, when he thought his voice was at its best, work through technical routines, then hum along as the orchestra rehearsed. By the time he said "Let's try one!" it was clear he was very much in charge. As Sinatra the man became increasingly erratic, Sinatra the musician was more than ever the committed, innovative professional. When in New York, he returned regularly to his old voice coach John Quinlan. Original session recordings from the period, preserved at Columbia, survive as vivid, audible evidence of a craftsman at work. A November 1947 session—it produced "I'm Glad There Is You" and "Body and Soul"—reflects a Sinatra who involved himself with the musicians, coaxed them into the mood he wanted, became irritated when a cornet player blew a vital passage.

Frank worked on his timing and diction, experimented with syllables, strove for perfection.

When working, he objected to imperfect pronunciation or grammar. "It drives me crazy," he once said, to hear "imagination" rendered as "amagination," "Whom can I turn to?" sung as "Who can I turn to?" Rosemary Clooney, who recorded with him, never forgot Frank's diction. "It was stunningly clear, no matter what he was singing. . . . He dotted the i's and crossed the t's in every word." The singer Julius La Rosa, who collected Frank's old red label Columbia records in his teens, thought he knew the purpose of that honing: "He put a period here, a comma there, to heighten the meaning. It came to be known as phrasing. And all he was doing was telling the story as he believed those words should be spoken. But it was revolutionary and it was what made him Sinatra. Nobody did it before. . . . Sinatra was able to turn a thirty-two-bar song into a three-act play."

Who's Who in America included Frank in its 1948 edition. He appeared as "SINATRA, Frank, baritone," a job description more exact than it would have been a few years earlier. "His voice had a higher pitch when he started out," said guitarist Al Viola, who first heard Frank sing at the Paramount. "Back then, he'd sounded almost like a tenor." His voice took on "darker hues," wrote Charles Granata, recording engineer, producer, and Sinatraphile. "He began to inject some pain into the music, as if he were struggling to extract every nuance of emotion from deep within his soul . . . aching, melancholic."

"The songs that I sing and their lyrics," Frank once insisted, "are never close to me in my own life, despite what some people think." On another occasion, though, he acknowledged that he "felt" a lyric because "I'd been there and back. I **knew** what it was all about."

October 30, 1947, was declared Sinatra Day in Hoboken. At the initiative of the new mayor, an Italian-American Dolly had helped elect, he was to be presented with the key to the city. He accepted the key—an enormous wooden one "from the Hearts of the Citizens of Hoboken"—at City Hall, and made a speech to a shrieking crowd of thousands. Later, as he rode through the streets on a fire engine driven by his father Marty, some reportedly pelted him with garbage.

Behind the scenes, the Sinatras were squabbling. Dolly, who was forever cadging money from relatives and not paying it back, clashed with her wealthy son about finances. For about two years to come, she and Frank would not speak to each other. Months after the visit, his grandfather Francesco died at the age of ninety-one.

Except for one appearance at a local function, Frank did not make another public visit to Hoboken for almost forty years. Toward the end of a flight to New York once, his aide Lee Solters remembered, he "spit at the window" when someone pointed out that the plane was passing over Hoboken.

"Home" had long since been California, though in 1947 and 1948 Frank was often away. Daughter Nancy and Frank Jr. had fond memories of Toluca Lake—fireworks on the Fourth of July, expeditions in their father's big Ford convertible, the arrival of the first television set. For the time being, meanwhile, their mother kept up the pretense that all was well.

The marriage, Nancy told an interviewer, was "as traditional and typically American as a cross-stitch sampler. . . . My job is to watch over Frank's personal needs. . . . It is a wife's chief function." She kept his drawers and closets just so—she approved of his obsession about cleanliness and orderliness—kept him supplied with Argyle socks, went along with his whim that the bedroom should never be without a box of chocolates. Being Mrs. Sinatra, Nancy declared, kept her "deeply satisfied."

The Sinatras got away whenever possible to Palm Springs, the lush oasis in the desert a hundred miles from Los Angeles, still more of a village than a resort, that was to be Frank's principal base in future years. He decided to build a house there, and workmen labored nonstop, even at night under lights, to get the job done. It featured a pool shaped like a grand piano, and a real grand piano was flown in from New York. Frank called the house Twin Palms.

For the children, Palm Springs generated more happy memories—swimming lessons in the pool, bumping around on dirt roads in their father's jeep. For daughter Nancy, though, there were glimpses of her mother's unhappiness—like the day Frank sent the family back to Los Angeles earlier than planned. As they drove away, she noticed that her mother was weeping behind her sunglasses.

News that another baby was on the way, in late 1947, helped dispel rumors of continuing marital trouble. A second daughter, Christina—soon shortened to Tina—arrived the following June. The baby was born on Father's Day, and for the first time Frank was on hand to drive his wife to the hospital. It looked for all the world as though he had mended his ways.

In New York, George Evans had been laboring to rebuild his client's image, to squelch the gossip about womanizing, smother the stories about mobsters. In spite of the Havana revelations, the FBI learned, Frank was still in regular contact with the Fischetti brothers. It was in these months, too, that Joe Fischetti reportedly spoke of the mob's "financial interest in Sinatra." Soon after, Frank's early patron Willie Moretti admitted to bureau agents that he was "associated with Sinatra." It had been reported, moreover, that Frank regularly "kicked in" to Moretti.

While none of that became public, Evans was struggling to control a sordid story linking Frank to the California gangster Mickey Cohen, to mob control of boxing, and to a criminal from Moretti's territory who was operating in Los Angeles. Frank had known the crook in question since his Hoboken days. Moreover, police detectives discovered, Sinatra's name appeared in Cohen's address book. Asked about that, Cohen said, "Why, he's a friend of mine."

FBI agents received information that Frank was a co-investor in the Stables, a Palm Springs nightclub with financing intertwined with a recent fraud case. Palm Springs itself, a California state crime commission would soon report, was a "favorite rendez-vous of many undesirable individuals from throughout the United States." Two of the undesirables named had been prominent during the Havana episode. Another was Allen Smiley, who had been sitting at Bugsy Siegel's side when he was killed. Smiley had an apartment at the Sunset Towers, as did Frank and several friends, and said he knew Frank "quite well." Asked in 1948 to suggest guests for a mob wedding, he included Frank's name.

The dallying with the Mafia in Cuba was part of a lasting pattern. Frank's involvement with criminals was woven into the fabric of his life and career by 1948. "I've known these people all my life," Frank's daughter Nancy said years later. "I've sat with them talking about their families. . . . Then I'd hear their names in the news and I'd say to myself, 'Oh my God. This one's under investigation for tax evasion.' Or, 'That one's just been questioned in a murder.' "

For a long time, Frank was not seriously hurt by what the public learned of his Mafia involvement. The little that got into the papers may even have added to his mystique. Other factors, though, would bring him to his knees.

ONE MIGHT HAVE THOUGHT, as 1949 began, that Frank was riding high in Hollywood. MGM had paid him more than $300,000—over $2 million today—for his movie work over the past twelve months. That was more than Judy Garland and almost as much as the highest paid star of the day, Warner's Bette Davis. Yet Frank's noisy scandals and lack of discipline had pushed the patience of MGM executives to the limits. He had behaved badly, too, when loaned out to RKO for **The Miracle of the Bells,** the movie in which he played a priest, and for **Double Dynamite,** a comedy with Jane Russell and Groucho Marx. He had tried to get out of attending the San Francisco premiere of **Miracle,** and took childish revenge when the producer insisted he show up. At his Fairmont Hotel suite, where he was staying with three associates, he ordered eighty-eight Manhattans (never drunk), took a couple of dozen people out on the town, held an all-night party, then hired a limousine to drive him five hundred miles south to Palm Springs—and charged it all to RKO.

MGM was acutely aware that **It Happened in Brooklyn** had lost money, that **The Kissing Bandit**, a **Zorro**-genre movie Frank would recall as an embarrassment, was a total flop. **Miracle,** in which—the **New York Times** thought—Frank looked "frightened speechless," did poorly. **Double Dynamite** was not released for three years and for all Jane Russell's allure—some said the title was an allusion to her thirty-eight-inch bust—was a box office disaster. Hollywood's investment in Sinatra was not paying off.

The flame of Frank's success as a singer was also flickering. He had only one top ten single, at number seven, in 1948. For the first time in six years, the **Down Beat** poll did not rate him one of America's top three singers. Frank placed fourth, after Billy Eckstine, Frankie Laine, and Bob Crosby, Bing's brother.

Frank had begun complaining about the music industry. He told an interviewer that current popular songs were "decadent . . . bloodless," that Tin Pan Alley was turning out "terrible trash." "We must give people things that move them emotionally," he said. "We're not doing it and there's something wrong someplace." Whatever was or was not wrong with the industry, though, what may have gone wrong for Frank was that he was losing touch with his audience. His bobbysoxers had grown up.

In December 1948, one show business journal ran the headline "Is Sinatra Finished?" A year earlier, it would have seemed ludicrous. Frank told Manie Sacks that he did feel finished, used up. He turned in on himself, headed off on his own to Palm Springs for days on end, Nancy said, and behaved strangely at home. "When we had guests," his wife said, "he would often go off by himself and not feel like talking." Sometimes, one of her sisters recalled, he locked himself in another room to get away from people.

Frank had just turned thirty-three and Nancy was thirty-one. They had a daughter of eight, a son of five, and a new baby. Their tenth wedding anniversary was a month away.

15

Lovers, Eternally

A FEW WEEKS AFTER CHRISTMAS 1948, MGM assembled more than fifty stars for a photograph to mark the studio's silver jubilee. Frank, unsmiling, in gray suit and matching tie, perched on a high tier near the back. Dead center, elegant in royal blue, in pride of place between Clark Gable and Judy Garland, sat an actress on her way up.

Ava Lavinia Gardner came out of Grabtown, North Carolina, a crossroads in tobacco country so insignificant that it did not appear even on local maps. She was born in 1922, the last of the seven children of a struggling farmer and his wife.

She was a tomboy as a child, climbed trees, went barefoot—as she often would in adult life—and learned early to swear. At the age of eight she was smoking behind the barn with the boys. By her mid-teens, however, she had become a shapely dark-haired beauty who painted her nails and longed for dresses she could not afford.

She acted a little at school, was more at ease with dialogue than were her classmates. She sat enraptured at the movies and told a girlfriend she dreamed of being a movie star. She could sing, and talked of singing with one of the big bands, yet expected to wind up as a secretary and marry a local boy. Then a photographer brother-in-law took pictures of Ava, simple, demure shots, and sent them to an MGM talent scout. Not long after, wearing a $16 dress and borrowed high heels, she was doing a screen test. In 1941, at eighteen and with one of her sisters along as chaperone, she found herself on a train to Hollywood.

Ava became just another actress-in-waiting, attending voice and dance classes, posing for cheesecake pictures, and generally doing as she was told. Her first significant movie role would come only after four years of disciplined tedium, true stardom not until the end of the decade. Even then she would make no claim to great talent. "I've never cared enough about acting to put my whole heart into it," she told an interviewer. "I was never an actress—none of us kids at Metro were. We were just good to look at."

Ava's love life, however, soon made news. She always maintained that she had been strictly brought up, was painfully shy, and long resisted men's advances. "I played very hard to get," she said in middle age, "the 'little Southern belle' shit. I think that's better than hopping in the feathers right away and saying 'Golly I'm mad about you.' " Even before leaving for California, though, she had declared her intention of marrying "the biggest movie star in the world."

She began a courtship with the actor they called "King of the Box Office," Mickey Rooney, on her very first day at MGM. The former child star, now twenty-one, was the studio's highest paid performer, its greatest asset. Louis B. Mayer tried to dissuade the couple from marrying. When they insisted, he ensured the wedding took place without fanfare, far from Los Angeles. Ava was just nineteen and had known Rooney for five months. An MGM publicity man stayed near throughout the honeymoon, "damn near," Ava remembered, even "when you went to bed."

"Once he gets into your pants," Mayer had told Ava, "he'll chase after some other broad." According to Ava, Rooney fulfilled the prophecy. Within two months, she said, "I found evidence that he'd had somebody in my bed. I don't know who the hell it was." Rooney said it was Ava who first caused trouble, by paying too much attention to another young actor. The marriage ended in divorce in 1943, after just over a year.

Ava then played the field. Howard Hughes, crazed and obsessive even then, had a thing about big breasts and recently divorced women—"wet decks," he called them—and Ava fit the bill. Ava insisted she never shared his bed, though some believe otherwise. The tycoon, however, was to pursue and spy on her for years to come.

As a youngster in North Carolina, Ava had jitterbugged to the music of Artie Shaw. After war service in the navy, and with hearing problems threatening his career as a musician, Shaw was by his own description now "in a state of dysfunction." At thirty-four he had already gone through four wives—there would eventually be eight—and he was deep into psychoanalysis. Ava thought Shaw "the first intelligent, intellectual male I had ever met." He told her she was "the most perfect woman." They married in 1945, partly to counter the negative publicity generated when it became known they were living together. Once married, Shaw determined to "improve" his perfect woman.

He told Ava to read Freud's **Interpretation of Dreams,** introduced her to a psychiatrist, and hired a Russian grand master to teach her chess. In company, when she spoke up, he told her to shut up. Soon the couple were quarreling constantly, and stopped having sex. They divorced after less than a year. She was twenty-three.

By the late 1940s she had begun to have success as an actress. There were affairs with the singer Mel Tormé, the actors Howard Duff, Robert Taylor, and Robert Mitchum, according to one of his biographers. Tormé's account of his relationship with Ava describes four of her characteristics: her "glorious beauty," her being tipsy, her crudity—she responded to a stranger's well-meaning compliment with "Do you suck?"—and the burst of rage that ended the affair. Duff recalled Ava's inability to relax, mood changes "so fast nobody could keep up with her," the "terrible, terrible quarrels. . . . She could be very violent"—and the drinking.

The British writer Peter Evans, who worked with Gardner on a planned memoir in the 1980s, was driven to distraction by Ava's attempts to "revise her own history, including her own taped interviews with me, to make herself look good. The changes she made, out of a yearning for 'respectability,' distorted her story." The unredacted tapes, however, offer real insights.

"I started to drink seriously when I was with Artie," Ava told Evans. "He'd have a lot of intelligent people around, his so-called intelligent bunch, and I was made to feel a fool. I got drunk because I was insecure." According to Rooney, Ava had demonstrated "a tremendous capacity for liquor" even when she was with him. By the mid-1940s, acquaintances began to notice the actress drinking champagne "like Coca-Cola" and mixing Scotch and beer. Howard Duff remembered her getting him to make an infernal cocktail. "I got the blender and mixed it—vodka, gin, Scotch, brandy, you name it . . . **whammo** . . . we were 'out' on the carpet."

Ava liked to talk of "how much we drank and still carried on. We were never late for work, we always did our job." So "desperately insecure" was she, publicist Ann Straus recalled, that before one theater appearance "she drank several straight bourbons, and even then I had to push her on the stage with the flat of my hand."

She "could change when she drank," said Mearene "Reenie" Jordan, the faithful maid and companion who joined her in the late 1940s, and that contributed to Ava's violent outbursts. "When I lose my temper, honey," Ava acknowledged, "you can't find it anyplace." Rooney recalled how she had once "taken a kitchen knife to every piece of furniture in the house." She is said to have knocked out Howard Hughes with a blow from an ornamental vase. "The quality of rage," Rooney said, "has always been a part of Ava."

Ava could talk and behave like a puritan, or the opposite. She was fascinated by prostitution, so much so that on four well-documented occasions she asked to be taken on guided tours of brothels. "I think fucking's a great sport," she told one writer. "It's all the fucking talk you have to listen to from the man before."

"I want to be married and have children," she had said early in the Rooney relationship. Once wed, though, she told him she never wanted to get pregnant. She claimed she wanted a baby by Artie Shaw, yet still used contraception. "I don't think I genuinely in my heart wanted a baby at all," she told Peter Evans. "Maybe I was playing a part—to make it perfect, the 'perfect wife.' Who the hell knows?"

Ava did get pregnant during the affair with Howard Duff, but had an abortion. According to a woman friend, she went to a quack doctor who "operated on her without an anesthetic, so she would understand the magnitude of what she was doing. He botched the job, not completely removing the fetus. . . . The event so traumatized her that she never fully recovered from the shock."

This was the woman on whom Frank Sinatra became fixated in 1949.

FRANK, TOO, WAS HITTING the bottle. Arriving uninvited and drunk, he caused a scene at a party to mark Mel Tormé's engagement to Candy Toxton, a young actress. When the bride-to-be fled to a bedroom, he harangued her through the locked door. A friend hustled him out of the house as he was about to start a fight with Tormé. Weeks later, at another party, he hit someone over the head with a bottle.

It was at this time, in early 1949, that Frank began his headlong pursuit of Ava Gardner. As she drove to MGM to sit for the studio's group photograph, Ava was overtaken by a speeding car.

The pursuing car slowed down, overtook hers again, slowed again, and then, as the driver doffed his hat, raced on ahead. Frank had gotten her attention.

Ava had long known that he was "a terrible flirt." Years earlier, when she was married to Rooney, Frank had come over to their table at the Hollywood Palladium and joked that he wished he had found her first. He "had eyes for her," too, while she was married to Artie Shaw. Frank had gotten her, like Marilyn Maxwell, to don an "S" for Swooners shirt and act as a bat girl for his softball team.

In 1946, when Ava was out dancing with Howard Hughes and Lana Turner with Frank, the couples had exchanged partners. Later, she had moved into a house overlooked by the Sunset Towers, where Frank and Sammy Cahn had apartments. "Just for mischief," Cahn recalled, "Frank and I would stick our heads out the window and yell her name." She heard "their boozy voices shouting, 'Ava, can you hear me, Ava? Ava Gardner, we know you're down there. Hello, Ava! Hello!' " She claimed she found it less than charming, and she told a friend she thought Frank "conceited, arrogant, overpowering." Even so, there came an evening when they got together and "drank quite a bit." And at some point after that there was another date, one she remembered as special, when "we drank, we talked, and fell in love."

Early in the romance, there came a moment of madness that set the tone for what was to come. One night, according to George Evans's aide Jack Keller, the couple got themselves arrested in a town near Palm Springs. Frank called for help at 3:00 A.M. "I'm in jail," he told Keller. "We thought we'd have a little fun and we shot up a few street lights and store windows with the .38's, that's all. . . . There was this one guy, we creased him a little bit across the stomach. But it's nothing. Just a scratch."

Keller said he chartered a plane, flew in with a stack of money to pay for the damage, buy the silence of the police and everyone else involved, and get Frank and Ava back to Los Angeles. Miraculously, the story was kept out of the newspapers.

On a more sober evening, in Hollywood, Frank told Ava his marriage was effectively over. In late 1949, at the house she had rented in unfashionable, wooded Nichols Canyon, she took him to bed. "We became lovers forever—eternally," she recalled late in life. "Big words. . . . But I truly felt that no matter what happened we would always be in love."

AT THIRTY-FOUR, he was a falling star. At twenty-seven, she was on her way to stardom. Both were outspoken liberals. With Artie Shaw, she had socialized with people some considered reds, even visited the Soviet consulate. She, like Frank, had spoken out on a broadcast protesting the abuses of the House Un-American Activities Committee. She enthused about jazz and socialized with African-American musicians. They had much in common.

Friends and former lovers tried to pry them apart. Lana Turner told Ava that Frank would never leave his wife. Marilyn Maxwell told Frank to "watch it, watch your step." George Evans warned that both their careers were at risk. MGM, he feared, might invoke the morals clause in their contracts.

After months of subterfuge, the couple began to push the limits of propriety. They attended a Broadway premiere together, though with another couple. Ava turned up at Frank's birthday party in New York in December 1949, then joined him when he appeared in Houston, Texas. A photographer there tried to take their picture, Frank threatened him, and the story made news. In California, Nancy at last lost patience.

The day Frank got back from Texas, Valentine's Day, Nancy had her attorney announce that she was seeking a legal separation and property settlement. "My married life," she added, "has become most unhappy and almost unbearable."

Although only nine, daughter Nancy could see that her mother was "terribly hurt." Once, accidentally, she came upon press photographs her mother had hidden away: Frank with Marilyn, Frank with Lana, Frank with Ava.

Frank, too, was increasingly troubled. "The battle I had with myself began to take its toll," he recalled. "I found myself needing pills to sleep, pills to get started in the morning and pills to relax during the day." In New York in March, on the first night of a five-week run at the Copacabana, Frank needed a sedative just to get on stage. It was not only the breakup of his family that was bringing him low. All was not well with Ava.

Both of them were insecure, consumed with jealousy. "If he looked across the room in a restaurant," Mearene Jordan has said, "she would swear, 'Reenie, I saw him, he was winking at a girl. . . . I saw him give her the look.' And the fight would be on." Frank worried obsessively about Howard Hughes, who kept calling Ava, and about the fact that she remained in touch with Artie Shaw.

One night, after one of their quarrels, Ava stomped back to the suite they shared at the Hampshire House and phoned Shaw. She left her address book open to the page bearing his name, where Frank was bound to see it. Shaw, who was living in New York with a new girlfriend, recalled what happened.

"She called at 2:00 A.M. and said she had been with Sinatra and the Fischetti boys. One of the guys had thrown a glass of whiskey in the face of one of her girlfriends, and she had to get away. She said she wanted to see me. I explained that I wasn't alone. But she came anyway, dressed to the nines and saying she wanted to ask me some questions. I asked my girlfriend to go back to bed so Ava and I could talk."

Ava disliked the mobsters around Frank and the way they behaved. What she wanted to talk about now, though, was sex. "When you and I were in bed together," she asked Shaw, "was it okay?" Shaw said the physical side of their marriage had been fine. "Then," according to Shaw, "she heaved a sigh of relief and said, 'Well, then there's nothing wrong with me?' I said, 'No, of course not. What do you mean?' And she said, 'Well, with Frank it's like being in bed with a woman. He's so gentle. It's as though he thinks I'll break, as though I'm a piece of Dresden china and he's gonna hurt me.'

"I said I always thought Frank was a stud, and she said, 'No. . . . I just wanted to know that it's not my fault.' We talked for a while and the phone rang. I picked up the phone—it was now about 3:00 A.M.—and it was Sinatra. He said, 'Is Ava there?' I said, 'Yes,' but Ava was going, 'Oh my God!' and making strange signs. I said, 'I don't think she wants to talk to you. I can't take her by the scruff of the neck and drag her to the phone if she doesn't want to.' He went on yabbering and eventually I just hung up the phone.

"Ava left, but fifteen minutes later the doorbell rang. We had one of those speaker things for the door, and it was Sinatra. Now he said he wanted to talk to **me.** I asked if he was alone and he said yes, so I pressed the button. But he wasn't alone. He came upstairs with a heavyweight fellow. I sat on the couch and Frank stood over me tapping his chest, talking all truculent. I said, 'Frank, are you half as tough as you sound?' He said, 'Yes, I'm that tough.'

"The other guy, the heavyweight, was standing there doing everything but toss the silver dollar, like a George Raft scene. So I said, 'Then what do you need him for?' Frank looked at the guy and snapped his fingers, and the guy left. Like a big mastiff. . . . I said, 'Frank, what's the matter with you? It's four o'clock in the morning and for chrissakes I want to sleep.' In the end he got up and left, a little sheepfaced, a little tail-between-the-legs."

Ava, meanwhile, was back at the Hampshire House, in bed but not asleep. A few nights earlier, worried, she had confided to Kirk Douglas—a fellow guest—that Frank had a gun. Now, with dawn not far off, the phone rang. It was Frank, back from visiting Shaw and calling from a room at the other end of the suite. "I'll never forget his voice," she remembered. "He said, 'I can't stand it any longer. I'm going to kill myself—now!' There was this huge bang in my ear, and I knew it was a revolver shot.

"I threw the phone down and raced across the living room and into Frank's room. . . . And there was a body lying on the bed. Oh, God, was he dead? I threw myself on it saying, 'Frank, Frank . . .' And the face, with a rather pale little smile, turned toward me, and the voice said, 'Oh, hello.' "

Frank had fired his gun into the mattress.

A FEW MONTHS EARLIER, George Evans had made a prediction about Frank: "A year from now you won't hear anything about him. He'll be dead professionally. . . . They're not going to see his pictures. They're not buying his records. . . . The public knows about the trouble with Nancy, and the other dames, and it doesn't like him anymore." Now Evans was gone, dead of a heart attack, and his prophecy seemed to be coming true.

In April 1950, MGM announced that Frank and the studio had decided on a "friendly parting of the ways." In fact, Frank had been fired. Louis B. Mayer had been patient with Frank's past box office failures and had put up with his lack of discipline on the set, but the last straw was an ill-judged Sinatra joke about Mayer's personal life. When he heard about that, the studio boss told Frank to get out and stay out.

Frank had also fallen out with his powerful

agent, Music Corporation of America. "He wanted to be the top guy," an MCA executive said. "He wanted everybody to bow down to him, to kowtow, and not everybody would do it." David "Sonny" Werblin, the agent handling Frank in New York, told an NBC executive that his client "was no good, would not draw flies." Suddenly Frank had no major bookings.

He was run-down, meanwhile, and drinking and smoking too much. "Every single night," Ava recalled, "we would have three or four martinis, big ones in big champagne glasses, then wine with dinner, then go to a nightclub and start drinking Scotch or bourbon. I don't know how we did it." Frank was no longer working very well. As he sang to sparse audiences at the Copacabana, his voice sounded slurred.

Then, in the early hours of May 2, Frank reached for a high note while singing "Bali Ha'i," the theme song from **South Pacific.** He had noticed specks of blood in his mouth for several days, but had done nothing about it. "Like an idiot," he remembered, "I hadn't even gone to the doctor. . . . I went for a note and nothing came out . . . nothing, just dust. . . . Finally I turned to the audience and whispered into the microphone 'Goodnight,' and walked off the floor."

The doctors told Frank he had suffered a hemorrhage of the vocal cords and was not to speak, let alone sing, for several weeks. "I carried a pad and pencil around to write with," he said years later. "After the fortieth day I started to talk again, very quietly, then to do a few vocal exercises."

Frank was not telling the truth. Within ten days, and flouting medical advice, he had headed off to Europe in pursuit of Ava. She was in Spain making **Pandora and the Flying Dutchman,** a movie in which she played a rich expatriate beauty romanced by a matador. A celebrated real-life bull-fighter, thirty-five-year-old Mario Cabré, hand-some, elegant, and charming, played the matador. Ava was spending much of her off-screen time with him, and the papers were saying he had declared his love for her. Eager to minimize her involvement with Frank, a married man, the movie's publicists played up the idea that Ava had a budding romance. From New York, Frank had been bombarding Ava with anxious phone calls. Too often, she was not there when he called.

Now, flying into Barcelona on a three-day visit, he brought Ava an emerald necklace and a barrage of accusations. She denied the Cabré stories and countered with some gibes of her own. In New York, she knew, Frank had been seen with an old flame, Marilyn Maxwell.

On his way home to the States, Frank told a journalist that Cabré meant nothing to Ava. "Nothing!" he shouted over the phone. "Don't you understand?" In Spain, however, Ava was now making a public show of affection for the bull-fighter. When that made the newspapers, people began to mock Frank. "The Ava thing was well known, and also the fact that he was having problems with his voice," said the guitarist Tony Mottola. "I remember being at the races with him, and some hoarse voice called out from the crowd, 'Where's Ava, Frank?' "

In September a weeping Nancy went into Superior Court to describe the miseries of marriage to Frank Sinatra. She made it clear she wanted only a separation, not a divorce. The judge awarded her custody of the children, the family home, a third of her husband's future income up to $150,000 a year—with increments when he earned more—for life. Frank got to keep the house in Palm Springs and "any phonograph records he may desire."

If Ava was straying, so was Frank. Rosemary Clooney described how he seduced her sister Betty at a New York nightclub. He flirted, flashed a "slow, vaguely dangerous" smile, then walked to the bandstand and gave an impromptu performance of "I'll Never Smile Again." Rosemary reminded her sister that Frank was "crazy about Ava Gardner." She was ignored. "When we left the club," she remembered, "we all got into a taxi. Then they dropped me off."

Ava was preoccupied with a new movie project, **Show Boat**, and under pressure from MGM to behave herself. She had been getting hate mail—

"Bitch-Jezebel-Gardner" one writer called her—and now talked of not seeing Frank as long as he remained married. She stayed in California, mostly, while he struggled with his foundering career in New York. "People don't understand the psychology of what happened," said Mitch Miller, the producer who had replaced Manie Sacks at Columbia Records. "It was a different climate in those days. . . . Sinatra, with his public behavior with Ava, and leaving his wife, had the priests saying, 'Don't tell the kids. Don't buy his records.' "

Frank did not have one song on the **Billboard** list of top tunes for 1951. He worked on, but with little reward. He had a TV show on CBS, but it would fold the following year, when sponsors pulled out. His two radio shows had little impact, and one of them went off the air after only seven weeks. Other singers—Frankie Laine, Johnnie Ray, Eddie Fisher—were now more popular. One night in New York Frank walked past the theater where Fisher was singing. Lines of would-be ticket-holders stretched around the block. Some of the Fisher fans jeered at him. He went back to Manie Sacks's apartment, where Sacks later found him. Frank was in the kitchen, lying with his head either on the stovetop or inside the oven itself. The gas was on. He was revived, but friends took the episode seriously.

At a recording session that spring Frank produced two tracks that seemed achingly personal.

One of them incorporated lines he had reworked himself:

> I'm a fool to want you,
> To want a love that can't be true,
> A love that's there for others too . . .
> I know it's wrong, it must be wrong,
> But right or wrong I can't get along
> Without you.

He recorded "I'm a Fool to Want You" in a single take, then rushed from the studio looking distressed. At the same session Frank sang "Love Me"—"Please love, whatever else you do just love me. . . . I'll die if you should tire." The words welled out of him, his early biographer Arnold Shaw thought, "in a voice numb with the fear of losing Ava."

Two months later, Nancy said she would start divorce proceedings. "I am agreeing to give Frank the freedom he has so earnestly requested," she said.

Frank mended fences with his parents and took Ava to Hoboken to see them. She boggled at Dolly Sinatra's immaculate house, and understood the source of Frank's obsessive cleanliness. She saw pictures of Frank as a baby, "sweet little photos that mothers treasure and sons would like to stick up the chimney."

In Hollywood to work on **Meet Danny Wil-**

son—a third-rate movie for Universal in which he played a singer who gets his break thanks to a gangster—Frank was visited on the set by various psychiatrists and a priest from the Catholic Family Counseling Service. Nancy also consulted a psychiatrist. Dr. William Kroger, a pioneer in the psychiatric use of hypnosis, said he "took care of Sinatra's family, took care of Nancy—tried to save the marriage." Ava could not wait to see it dismantled. "We vacillated," she said, "between happiness at our impending wedding and misery as Nancy took longer and longer to actually file for that damn divorce."

Frank accepted a singing engagement at a casino in Nevada, with the primary purpose of fulfilling the residency requirement for a quickie divorce. He was frantic now, "screaming and yelling" at the telephone operators at the Riverside Inn in Reno. He had again been interrogating Ava about Mario Cabré. Had she slept with him? "I tried to evade the question," she said years later, "but Frank suspected and he kept at me." She had been to bed with Cabré, just once, she said in her 1990 memoir, "a single mistake—after one of those romantic, star-filled, dance-filled, booze-filled Spanish nights." In Nevada, she admitted it to Frank. "I told him, and he never forgave me. Ever."

It was still preying on Frank's mind a decade later. "He was drinking pretty good and started to cry on my shoulder," said Brad Dexter, describing a conversation in the early 1960s. "Ava emasculated him, really emasculated him. He suffered."

Late in August the couple had more alcohol-fueled fights while vacationing at Lake Tahoe. Frank railed on about her other men, even as the yacht they were aboard ran aground. A few nights later, after another bitter exchange, Ava drove off through the darkness to Los Angeles. When she got home she learned that Frank had taken an overdose of sleeping pills.

A doctor had been summoned to Frank's hotel room at 4:00 A.M. to find a patient who identified himself as "Henry Sinolo" and said he had swallowed some barbiturates. Asked how many, he replied, "I don't know." The doctor found Frank's vital signs normal, administered a saline solution to induce vomiting and clear the stomach, and departed. Once Ava had rejoined him, Frank told the press he had "just had a bellyache" after taking "two" sleeping pills. "That's all there was to it, honest. . . . Suicide is the farthest thought from my mind."

"I wanted to punch him," Ava remembered, "but instead I forgave him in about twenty-five seconds." To her it had been just another of his "mock suicidal dramas . . . to get me back to his side." It was the third such episode.

When Frank made his first appearance in Las

Vegas, at the Desert Inn a week later, Ava indulged her own insecurity. "Suddenly she got moody," Axel Stordahl recalled. "She thought Frank was looking at a girl in the audience a little longer than was necessary. They ended up throwing books and lamps at each other."

Then Ava spent some time in the hospital for "exhaustion." There were rumors of an abortion. She was a really hot property for MGM now, and to avoid further embarrassments executives decided it was best to get her married to Frank as soon as possible. The studio's attorneys muscled in on the divorce negotiations, and the impasse was finally ended. Nancy obtained her divorce decree in California, and he got his in Nevada. Arrangements were made for Frank and Ava to marry at a supposedly secret East Coast locale.

Still the madness continued. In New York, Ava remembered, she received a letter "from a woman who admitted she was a whore and claimed she had been having an affair with Frank. It was filthy, it gave details that I found convincing, and I felt sick to my stomach. How could I go on with the wedding?"

The ceremony was off. Then, after a long night during which friends shuttled frantically back and forth between Ava's room and Frank's, it was on again. "We had arranged it for weeks," she said in 1989, "nobody knew"—except the nation's press. On November 7, 1951, reporters and photographers gathered at the house near Philadelphia where the marriage was to take place.

"Frank was so angry, poor baby," said Ava. "He spent the whole time at the window upstairs screaming at the press, 'You lousy parasites, fuck off!' at the top of his lungs. He was tempted—we had to hold him—to go out and fight with them. But we finally got him downstairs, got him in front of the preacher. Dick [Jones, an arranger for Tommy Dorsey] played the piano. It was horribly out of tune. I walked down the stairs. I had a lovely little dress that Howard Greer made. Wonderful designer, but you couldn't wear a stitch underneath.

"And we got hitched. I don't remember the ceremony. There was a photograph—Frank kept it in his wallet for years. We were in such a hassle to get out of there, we forgot all our luggage—not a toothbrush between us. We hired a plane and arrived at some little hotel on the beach. In Miami, I guess. . . .

"I had no clothes to wear on the beach. I had Frank's jacket on. I was barefoot, and Frank had his pants rolled up, and we just strolled along the beach. Some fucking photographer got a picture from behind us. Two lonely people holding hands, walking on the beach. It's a sad photograph.

"Frank and I didn't start very good. We went to Havana, in Cuba, and had a fight the first night.

Who knows what we fought about? . . . I remember standing up, pissed drunk, on the balcony of the hotel, on the edge. Standing there, balancing. Frank was afraid to go near me. He thought I was going to jump. . . . God, I was crazy! . . . God Almighty!"

16

Busted

IN FEBRUARY 1952, with just a piano for accompaniment, Frank sang "Bewitched, Bothered and Bewildered"—"this crazy situation has me on the blink"—in a San Francisco club. He told the audience he was singing it for Ava.

Ava was talking of their future, of how they would fix up the house in Palm Springs, of how much she wanted to be a housewife and mother. Yet the fights continued. Within weeks of their marriage they dropped out of a trip to entertain American troops in Europe. "At the last minute in London," Janet Leigh recalled, "Ava and Frank didn't leave on the trip. . . . They'd had a quarrel. Their passion was as stringent as it was romantic . . . hot and cold."

Ava was now addressed as "Mrs. Sinatra," which Frank liked. To humiliate him, though, reporters sometimes addressed him as "Mr. Gardner." "Friends noticed a very different Frank around her," Sammy Cahn's ex-wife Gloria Cahn said. "He was subservient. He bowed to her presence. . . . He was like a little puppy following her, and some people said he'd lost his manliness. And if she wasn't in the mood she would, you know, like, dismiss him."

"Frank didn't have a job," Ava remembered. "Poor baby, his voice had gone. He had got to the point where he literally could not sing because he had lost all confidence. And the worst thing, a proud man as Frank is, who wants to be in control and be the boss, was having to rely on a woman to foot the bills, most of them. His ego, no matter what I did, made it all so much worse.

"He'd done a record with Harry James that was so bad I cried when I listened to it," Ava said. James himself thought it "the worst thing either one of us ever recorded." Frank also did some excellent work in the recording studio, but it was not reflected in sales. Without an agent—MCA took space in the trade papers to announce he was no longer a client—he was a singer nobody seemed to want.

Ava loathed reporters, and Frank railed at the press more than ever. "This is a private affair," he had snarled during a trip to Mexico before the marriage. "I don't have to talk to anyone. It wasn't the press who made me famous. It was my singing and the American public." In Mexico, Frank and his companions damaged a photographer's camera and destroyed his film. One of his bodyguards threatened to shoot the photographer. In an incident at the airport in Los Angeles, Frank appeared to aim his car at a photographer.

When journalists began ignoring him, however, Frank changed his tune. "Most of my troubles with the press were my own fault," he conceded in 1952 in a long signed article in **American Weekly.** "I'll always be grateful to the press for the millions of lines they chose to write which made my name a household word." He promised the Press Photographers Association he would always "be ready in case you ever want to shoot any pictures."

Bob Weitman, who had given Frank his glorious Paramount debut in 1942, gave him another brief run at the Paramount, but the audiences were small. At the Chez Paree in Chicago, a club that could seat 1,500, only 150 customers turned up. "Sinatra had had it," thought the journalist Burt Boyar, who saw him there. "It was sad. From the top to the bottom in one horrible lesson. . . . He was deserted—by his friends, by his public."

He was dropped, too, after nine years, by Columbia Records, where Mitch Miller now said he "couldn't give away" Frank's records. Frank had been clashing not only with Miller but, and this was unusual in his career, with the studio technicians. One of them, Harold Chapman, thought him "one of the meanest men we ever worked for, so we engineers and musicians just sat on our hands and let him go down." The recording session of September 17, 1952, marked the end of a marvelously successful business relationship. "Fuck him," Miller told a fellow executive who asked about Frank. "He's a has-been."

Frank was humiliated even in Hoboken, when he appeared at a firefighters' fund-raiser to oblige his father. The local teenagers of a new generation were unimpressed. "He hit some clinkers," recalled Tony Macagnano, a childhood contemporary. "People booed him and threw fruit and stuff, kidding around. . . . Oh, did he get mad!"

Jule Styne thought Frank "looked like death" when he sang at the French Casino, a downmarket club in a New York hotel basement. The two friends dined together at a restaurant on Mulberry Street, where once Frank had had to leave by the back door to avoid being mobbed. Now no one gave him a second look. "A pigeon on a theater marquee," he said a producer had told him, "would cause more attention than my name."

The screenwriter Budd Schulberg saw Frank perform at "some second-rate joint" in Philadelphia. "The room was less than half-filled," he remembered, "openly hostile because 'The Voice' wasn't there anymore. Yesterday's 'All' was 'Nothing at All,' a pathetic burnout. A heckler told him to shut up and go home. A few other lushes seconded the motion. . . . 'I'm doing one more number,' he threatened, 'and then I'm going to pass among you—with a baseball bat.' " Schulberg thought Frank a classic example of "success in America—the lightning speed with which it strikes and the sudden blackout into which it often disappears."

Sinatra fan clubs were disbanding, above all because of Frank's callous treatment of Nancy and the blatant cavorting with Ava, even if he and Ava were now married. One group of former female admirers mailed Hedda Hopper a record of "Nancy with the Laughing Face" that they had smashed to pieces. They told Hopper their former idol was now "Frankie-Not-So-Hot-Tra."

AT FIRST AVA BLAMED SHOW BUSINESS for the troubles in the marriage. "Today is our seventh anniversary," she told an interviewer in June 1952. "Seven **months.** You want to see your husband, and where is he? Playing the Chez Paree in Chicago! Then he's hitting St. Louis . . . it's rough."

Ava's jealousy and distrust made it rougher, as her nephew Billy Grimes discovered on a visit to New York. After spending an entirely innocent evening together, he and Frank found themselves accused of having visited a whorehouse. "Anything could get me going," Ava said years later. In September, when her husband appeared at the Riviera nightclub, she spotted Marilyn Maxwell in the audience and claimed that Frank was making "cute little gestures" toward her. She stormed out, flew to California, and returned her wedding ring to Frank by mail. He lost it.

Whether or not Frank was guilty of infidelity this early in the marriage, Ava was. "I hate cheating," she told one interviewer years later, "I won't put up with it. I don't do it myself." Yet in the late summer of 1952, while in Utah filming **Ride, Vaquero!**, she had an affair with the movie's director, John Farrow. The source is Farrow's daughter Mia, who would one day become Frank's third wife.

Frank and Ava had an epic fight weeks after shooting ended on **Vaquero!** It took place in October, when the couple got together to make up after the incident at the Riviera. As Ava told it, they started squabbling at home after drinking too much at a restaurant in Los Angeles. Frank yelled, "If you want to know where I am, I'm in Palm Springs fucking Lana Turner." Then he stormed out.

Ava knew that Lana and Benton Cole, the agent she and Turner shared, were staying at Frank's house in Palm Springs. So she set off in hot pursuit in the middle of the night, with one of her sisters for company, in the hope of catching Frank and Lana "in the act." When the two women drove up to the house, they spotted Frank in his car "cruising around as if he was keeping watch." Lana and Cole were indeed at the house, still wide awake according to Ava, though it was around 3:00 A.M. They welcomed Ava and her sister, and the four of them "settled down to have a party." After several drinks, Ava said, "the door bursts open and in storms Frank looking like Al Capone and the Boston Strangler rolled into one." He delivered a stream of abuse, dismissed Lana as a "two-bit whore," claimed the revelers had been "carving him up behind his back," then told all of them to "get the hell out of my house." Ava said it was her house, too, and began grabbing everything she owned. She piled up pictures, books and records, clothes and cosmetics, and Frank hurled them into the driveway.

In her version, Lana said she and Cole fled the fracas, then returned to find "police cars drawn up in front of the house with red lights blinking, radios squawking. The glare of spotlights illuminated the house. . . . Just as we were getting out of the car, the front door opened and Frank and Ava came out, still fighting. The police moved in to separate them."

As Lana put it, a lot of "sick rumors" grew out of that night. One was that Ava arrived to find

Frank, as he had threatened, in bed with Lana. Another story had him bursting in to find Ava and Lana having sex, while another had him walking in on a threesome involving his wife, Lana, and another man. An FBI report released after Frank's death refers to a claim by an unnamed man that he had sex at the house with both Ava and Lana. None of the rumors were supported by facts. That said, the accounts offered by Ava and Lana were not credible.

Having finally thrown everyone out that night, Frank stuffed some clothes into a duffel bag and went to Jimmy Van Heusen's house. Asked by a caller how Frank was, Van Heusen said he was "in the bathroom, throwing up." When Ava changed her phone number, Frank was said to be "close to a breakdown." "You know," he told the Hollywood agent Milt Ebbins, "there isn't a building high enough for me to jump off of." "Sinatra," the columnist Dorothy Kilgallen reported, "is frightening his friends by telephoning in a gloomy voice, 'Please see that the children are taken care of,' and then hanging up." He would call back the following day, Kilgallen wrote, to apologize and explain that he had been drunk.

Deprived of Ava's phone number, Frank asked Earl Wilson to convey his feelings in his column. He now realized, Wilson wrote, that "he loves her more than anything and must do everything to get back together." A man who loathed press intrusion was reduced to using the press to get a message to his wife.

Yet soon, unsurprisingly, the couple were being seen together again, dining at Frascati's, arriving hand in hand at a rally for Democratic presidential candidate Adlai Stevenson. Draped in satin and mink, Ava introduced Frank as "a wonderful, wonderful man" and he sang for the crowd. They went to North Carolina, to visit Ava's family, and then on to Africa. Their destination was Kenya, and the movie location in the bush where John Ford was to direct **Mogambo.** Ava was to play opposite Clark Gable and the young Grace Kelly. Her career was surging at a time when Frank had no work, no prospects, and what in his world passed for no money.

The years of excess, payments to Nancy, and taxes had sucked up his millions. There was "no money, no more glamour," Ava said. "Nobody wanted to hang around him. He couldn't lift the bill, take people out, amuse them. There was nobody but me." Ava had even paid Frank's airfare to Nairobi.

"ARE YOU MARRIED?" British expatriates used to quip. "Or do you live in Kenya?" The upper-class English men and women who held sway in the then British colony led a sybaritic existence. They worked as little as possible, drank too much, and slept around. It was a country a future generation would see through the lens of movies like **White Mischief** and **Out of Africa.**

MGM had decided that **Mogambo** was going to be a "big picture," and were mounting the biggest safari in East African history. On the Kagera River, where three African territories met, the company built an encampment to house 175 whites and several hundred black Africans. A thousand more Africans were on call as extras. There were "dining tents," a hospital tent, an entertainment tent, and—remarkable in 1952—hot and cold running water. Bulldozers had carved out an airstrip.

Africa fascinated and appalled Ava. She raged about the inconveniences, the heat and the flies, and the lions that prowled close by, and she sought refuge in the bottle. Though twenty-three-year-old Grace Kelly would eventually warm to her, she was initially affronted by her co-star's conduct. "Ava is such a mess," Kelly wrote a friend, "it's unbelievable. . . . They are putting up a new tent for her—she didn't like the old one because it was old—her tent is right next to mine, so I can hear all the screaming and yelling."

Ava was dismissive of Frank, location manager Eva Monley said, "treated him like some lost brother coming to bother her. She didn't allow him on the set. I was responsible for allocating accommodation, and Ava would tell me, 'Get him

Records establish that Sinatra's paternal grandfather, Francesco, and his grandmother Rosa Saglimbeni came from the same town and street in Sicily as Mafia boss Lucky Luciano. The church (**background**) where they were baptised and married; their baptism and marriage records (**top and center**); the information on Rosa's U.S. death certificate (**bottom**) that confirms the discovery.

25 LIST OR MANIFEST OF ALIEN IMMIGRANTS FOR THE C[illegible]SIONER OF [illegible]

Required by the regulations of the Secretary of the Treasury of the United States under Act of Congress approved March 3, 1893, to be delivered to the Commissioner of Immigration by the Commanding officer of any vessel having such passengers on board upon arrival at a port in the United States.

S.S. SPARTAN PRINCE sailing from 189 Arriving at Port of 145 189

NAME IN FULL	Age	Sex	Married or Single	Calling or Occupation	Able to Read / Write	Nationality	Last Residence	Seaport for landing in the United States	Final destination in the United States	[illegible]	By whom was passage paid	[illegible]	Whether ever before in the United States	Whether going to join a relative, and if so, what relative, their name and address	[illegible]	Whether a Polygamist	[illegible]	Condition of Health, Mental and Physical	Deformed or Crippled, Nature and Cause
Bianco Antonia	[illegible]			[illegible]		Italian	Cefalù	New York	Baltimore		[illegible]							good	
Brocato Maria [illegible]	16			[illegible]		Italian	Cefalù	New York	Baltimore		[illegible]			my husband Salvatore Brocato [illegible] Baltimore				good	
[illegible]												$30						good	
Sinatra Francesco	43			[illegible]		Italian	Palermo	New York	New York		[illegible]			[illegible]				good	
Romano Salvatore	32			[illegible]		Italian	Palermo	New York	New York		[illegible]			[illegible]				good	

Iavara Giuseppe 49 male

Sinatra Francesco 43 male

Romano Salvatore 32 male

22 [illegible] Rosa 46 M

23 Sinatra Antonino 9 M S

24 Sinatra Giorgio 7 M

25 Sinatra [illegible] 4 M

Francesco Sinatra arrived from Italy in 1900 aboard the S.S. **Spartan Prince,** as recorded (**top**) by U.S. Immigration at Ellis Island. His wife, Rosa, and three of their children, including Frank Sinatra's father Anthony Martin ("Marty"), arrived aboard the S.S. **Citta di Milano** three years later (**bottom**).

Sinatra's parents, Marty and Dolly, married in Jersey City in 1913 (**top left**). Frank (in Little Lord Fauntleroy outfit, **top right**) was an only child, alternately spoiled and intimidated by his feisty mother (with guitar, Frank sitting in front of her, **center**). Frank and Dolly on a trip to the Catskills in 1923 (**right**).

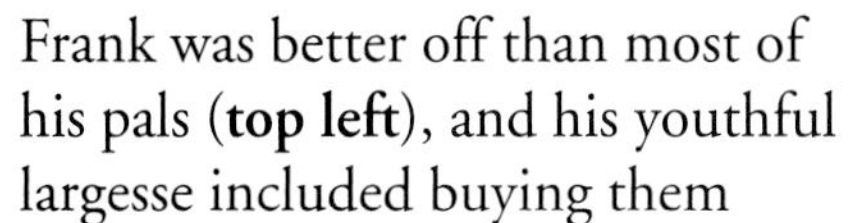

Frank was better off than most of his pals (**top left**), and his youthful largesse included buying them movie tickets and sharing his pass to the swimming pool. He yearned to get out of Hoboken, as the photograph taken on the waterfront (**top right**) suggests.

The first break was a tour with a local singing group—they became the Hoboken Four when he joined. In his youth (**right**) he modeled himself on Bing Crosby, pipe and all.

A singing job at the Rustic Cabin, just across the bridge from Manhattan, was a first step on the ladder. Glenn Miller heard Frank and was unconvinced, but Harry James hired him as "boy singer" for his new band.

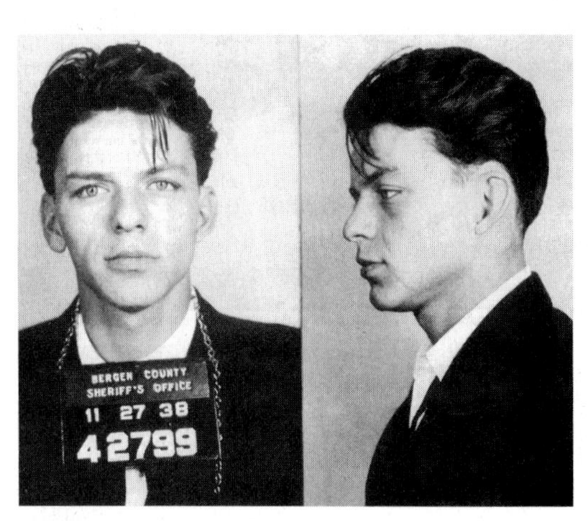

Prisoner no. 42799, charged with "seduction" of a woman he had met at the Cabin. The sequel was a hurried marriage, at age twenty-three, to his first wife, Nancy.

The mob and the Sinatras found each other early. Frank's parents ran a bar during Prohibition, and Marty helped guard booze shipments. They rubbed elbows with bootlegger Waxey Gordon (**top left**), who did business with Lucky Luciano.

The mafioso Angelo "Gyp" De Carlo (**top right**) knew Dolly Sinatra well and was linked to Frank's family by marriage. He answered to Willie Moretti (**right**), a Luciano henchman who got Frank work and remained in touch for years.

Moretti died bloodily, as did other mobsters Frank knew.

By age twenty-one, Frank was taking his music seriously, paying for singing lessons with former Metropolitan Opera singer John Quinlan.

"No one ever heard of him," the trumpeter Harry James said with a laugh, "but he says he's the greatest." Frank's months on the road with James and his band gave him his first real public exposure.

The breakthrough came in 1940, with Tommy Dorsey. "Tommy taught me everything I know," Frank said. Their parting was bitter—the Mafia told Dorsey his children would be kidnapped if he did not release Frank from his contract.

"F-R-A-N-K-I-E-E-E-E-E!" The bobbysoxer mania began at the Paramount. Girls by the thousands mobbed Sinatra and swooned, sometimes because they were paid to do it. At home, they gathered to worship in bedrooms plastered with their idol's picture.

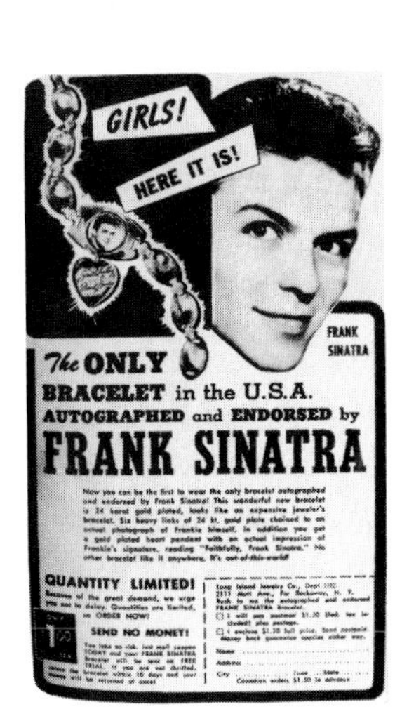

Letter to Director Februa

being set forth below:

" ARMED FORCES INDUCTION STATION
113th Infantry Armory
Sussex Avenue and Jay Street
Newark 4, N.J.

28 December
JN/eak

Subject: Supplementary Information, Frank A. Sinatra.

(c) During the psychiatric interview the patie
that he was 'neurotic, afraid to be in crowds, afraid to go i
makes him feel that he would want to run when surrounded by p
had somatic ideas and headaches and has been very nervous for
five years. Wakens tired in the A.M., is run down and underr
The examining psychiatrist concluded that this selectee suffe
psychoneurosis and was not acceptable material from the psych
viewpoint. Inasmuch as the selectee was to be rejected on an
basis, namely,

(1) Perforation of left tympanum
(2) Chronic mastoiditis, left,

the diagnosis of psychoneurosis, severe was not added to the
Notation of emotional instability was made instead. It was
this would avoid undue unpleasantness for both the selectee a
induction service.

For the Commanding Officer:

s/ JOSEPH
Captain
Chief M

Frank wore a uniform in World War II only to make a movie and (**top left**, wit his press agent George Evans at his side to entertain troops, after the shooting was over. A draft board medical report included a reference to Frank's "psycho-neurosis, severe." Appearances at youth rallies (**bottom**) later fueled claims that he was involved with communists.

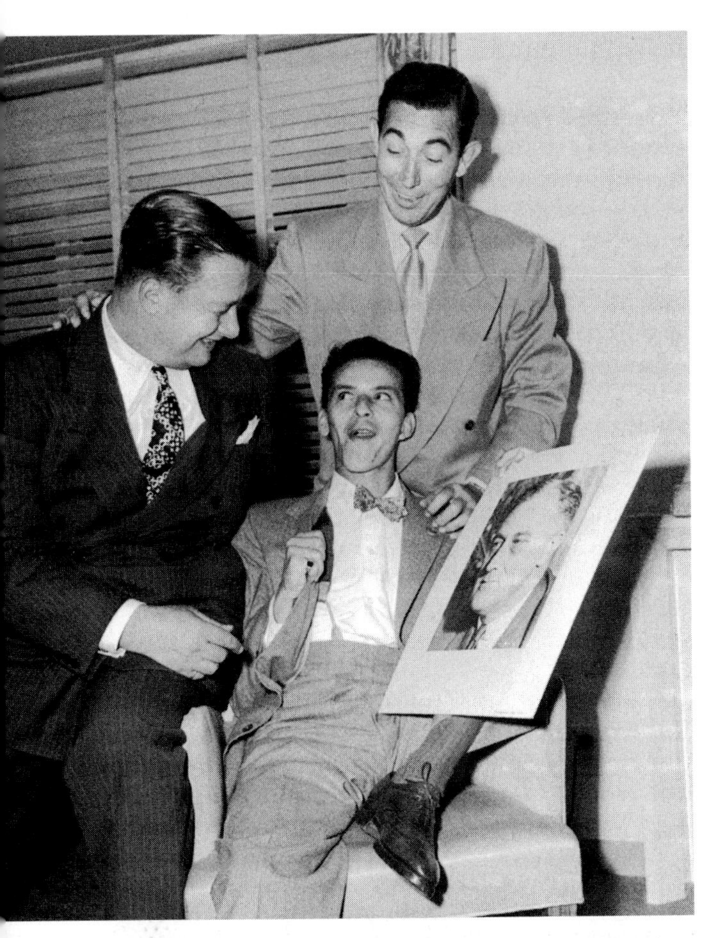

Frank was thrilled when, in 1944, he was invited to join guests at a reception in President Roosevelt's White House (**left**). Another dose of prestige came when he was thirty and the sculptor Jo Davidson immortalized him in bronze (**bottom**). Davidson thought Frank looked like "a younger Lincoln."

Hard evidence of Frank's Mafia involvement—a still frame, taken from 1947 newsreel footage (**above**), as he arrived in Cuba with two Chicago mobsters. The bag in Frank's hand allegedly contained money for Lucky Luciano. The mobsters were Joe Fischetti (foreground, with hand up to face) and his brother Rocco (just visible between Sinatra and man in white shirt). Joe stayed close for years to come. Months after the Cuba episode, Bugsy Siegel was executed by the Mafia (**bottom left**), and Frank visited the scene to toast his memory.

On trial for an "unprovoked assault" (**bottom right**). With others on hand to help him Frank came up behind the columnist Lee Mortimer and beat him up. Years later, when Mortimer died, Sinatra urinated on his grave.

Lucky Luciano (**right**), multiple murderer and the first American godfather. Frank and the Mafia boss shared roots in the same town in Sicily and met in Florida, Cuba, and Italy.

Chico Scimone (**left,** and partying with Luciano years later, **below**) accompanied Frank at his mob "audition." The mafioso's mistress Adriana Rizzo (on far right) said Luciano and Frank were "very close."

Nancy was a loyal wife and mother, but Frank said he had mistaken friendship for love. He thought he could "have every dame" he wanted.

An early dalliance was with Marilyn Maxwell (**above**). She turned up at a Sinatra party wearing a diamond bracelet Nancy thought Frank had bought for **her**.

Lana Turner (**left**) said that she and Frank had "a very serious affair." They pretended to comply with MGM's demand that they break it off but continued to meet in secret.

Frank's obsessive love for Ava Gardner finally destroyed his first marriage and brought him close to ruin. "I don't remember the ceremony," she said of their wedding in 1951. This photograph snatched during the honeymoon (**below**) belied the conflict that followed. Frank pursued Ava until her death in 1990, in spite of their infidelities and compulsive fighting.

Lyricist Sammy Cahn (standing, center) and composer Jule Styne gave Frank hit after hit in the forties. Frank broke with both men, but finally called Cahn to say, "I need some songs." Cahn was still responding to the need more than thirty years later.

"Do yourself a favor. Work with Nelson Riddle," a record executive told Frank in 1953. Together, Riddle and Frank were to produce the albums of Sinatra's golden age. Time has not dimmed **In the Wee Small Hours** or **Only the Lonely**.

"How would you like to work with me, kid?" Frank asked Bill Miller in 1951. The "kid," who was a little older than Sinatra, was to play piano or conduct for him for more than forty years. Frank called him "Suntan Charlie"—because of his facial pallor.

a separate tent, a long way from mine. Don't put it near me.' "

Frank killed time reading, and often took the daily shuttle flight back to civilization. The writer Alan Frank, then a schoolboy on vacation, remembered spotting him at a hotel at Malindi, on Kenya's Indian Ocean coast. He recognized "the figure at the upright piano that stood at the rear of the Eden Roc's spacious verandah lounge. . . . He sat loosely, picking out notes with a single finger and smoking. He was unshaven, clearly far from happy."

In New York, Frank's new agents at William Morris were trying to get him a part in **From Here to Eternity**, the Columbia Pictures adaptation of the James Jones novel about brutality and immorality in the United States Army. They thought their client was a natural for the role of Angelo Maggio, the rebellious, boozing little Italian-American hounded by a bullying sergeant.

Frank felt an affinity for Maggio, thought him a character straight out of the neighborhoods he had known as a boy. "I knew a hundred Maggios," he said, "could have been a Maggio maybe when I was younger. . . . I can act that part better than anybody alive." Before leaving for Africa he had lobbied hard for the role, had even managed to see studio head Harry Cohn himself. Cohn thought he was a singer, not an actor, and a washed-up one at that. "Who in the fuck," he told his aide Jonie

Taps as Frank departed, "would want to see that skinny asshole in a major movie?"

From Africa, Frank had been bombarding Columbia executives with cables signed "Maggio." Ava, who had put in a word for him before they left, reached Cohn by phone and pleaded Frank's cause again. A week after his arrival in Kenya, Frank was summoned home for a screen test.

At the time he left, Ava was pregnant. By some accounts she had suspected it even before leaving home. She had long been telling anyone who would listen how much she wanted to be a mother. "At last I know what I want out of life," she said after marrying Frank, "to be with my husband always and have children with him." Frank had talked of their having "a dozen kids."

Yet now she took a decision that went against everything she had said publicly: "I couldn't go on with it," she said in 1989. "We weren't getting along. We were madly in love, but it was just no time to have a child. So I decided to go to London for an abortion." At the time and in private, she spoke more brutally. "Ava hated Frank so much by this stage," Ford's cameraman Robert Surtees said. "She told my wife, 'I hated Frankie so much. I wanted that baby to go unborn.' "

Ford reminded Ava that abortion was a great sin in the eyes of the Catholic Church and told her she would be hurting Frank terribly. Ava's mind was made up, however. Without consulting her husband, she traveled to London accompanied by a publicist, Paul Mills, and Surtees's wife, Maydell, and had the abortion.

Mills told the British press Ava was being treated for "anemia" brought on by a tropical infection. Recovering at the Savoy Hotel, Ava told **Look**'s William Attwood that the problem was dysentery, brought on by "eating lettuce and drinking tap water." Attwood ended the interview by asking if she would like to have children, and she replied, "Oh my gosh, yes!" Four years later, she would claim she had suffered a miscarriage. "All of my life I had wanted a baby," she said, "and the news that I lost him—I'm sure that it was a boy—was the cruelest blow."

She returned to Africa after the abortion, as did Frank after his screen test. They fought again, and he was depressed by news that six other actors were being considered for the Maggio role. **Mogambo** crew members thought him a miserable, solitary figure, but he won sympathy when Christmas came around. Frank set up a tree, complete with colored lights, in front of Ava's tent, and presented her with a mink and a diamond ring bought during his recent trip back to the States. (He had promised to pay for it later.) Ava was unimpressed, and told colleagues the mink had been paid for with her money.

Frank made Christmas night memorable, walking out of the darkness with African singers bearing huge red candles. The Africans chanted in French as he sang "Noel" in English. Most of those listening sat mesmerized, but not Ava. "She was drinking buckets of alcohol," Eva Monley recalled. "I don't remember who she was with. Then Sinatra came out and started to sing carols. She jeered at him on and off, 'Sing louder!' . . . Then she realized it was too special to laugh. She was stunned into silence."

In January 1953, at a society party in Nairobi, the couple lost all restraint. "He and Ava Gardner got involved in such a slanging match," recalled Lee Harragin, the son of Kenya's then attorney general. "They were shouting and screaming at each other, so much that they had to be literally locked into the host's study to stop them disturbing the rest of the party."

Ava did make her husband happy for a while that month. "I got pregnant again," she said in an interview for her posthumous memoir. "This time Frank did know, and he was delighted. I remember bumping across the African plain with him one day in a jeep, feeling sick as the devil. Right on the spot, for the first and only time in our relationship, Frank decided to sing for me . . . so beautifully, that lovely song 'When You Awake' ":

When you awake the day takes a bow at
your door,

When you awake the sun shines like never
before
Clouds soaked with rain find it hard to
explain to the earth below.
They can't let it rain, for it would stain such
a heavenly show.
You make it so . . .

When Frank flew back to the States to fulfill a singing commitment at a Boston club, Ava flew to London to have another abortion. She again rationalized her action by saying that a woman had no right to have a child unless she and her mate had "a sane, solid lifestyle." Yet she went on saying she wanted a child with Frank, even when their relationship had collapsed beyond repair.

"Pregnancy terrified Ava," said Mickey Rooney. "I don't think she knew why . . . the thought of having a baby filled her with nameless, unreasoning dread." Ava told her friend Spoli Mills decades later that she "thought she'd have been the worst mother in the world."

There is another possibility, one that would surely have led her to insist absolutely on the further abortion.

WHEN FRANK HAD LEARNED that Ava would be doing **Mogambo** with Clark Gable, according to Sonny King, he worried that Ava might stray with her leading man. Gable did have an affair during the shoot, but with Grace Kelly. Ava helped Kelly through the little dramas of the affair, and the two women conspired together in matters of the heart and the bedroom. "We stuck together," she said in one of her last taped interviews, referring to the friendship with Kelly. "We did our **naughty-naughties** [author's italics] on the side. And nobody ever knew." According to Eva Monley, one of Ava's "naughty-naughties" was with a **Mogambo** props man and another with Frank "Bunny" Allen, a professional hunter and notorious Lothario.

Allen was an Englishman with Gypsy blood in his veins, the grandson of a carriage-maker to the British royals, who had followed his brothers to colonial Africa. Everyone called him Bunny, the nickname he earned as a boy snaring rabbits near Windsor Castle. By the early 1950s, when it became fashionable for rich Americans to go on safari in Africa, he was celebrated for his knowledge of big game.

Allen had been the partner of Denys Finch-Hatton, the hunter re-created by Robert Redford in the movie **Out of Africa,** when the future King Edward VIII had come to Kenya to shoot lion and elephant. Allen had had a forearm scarred by a leopard's claws, a hip gored by a buffalo. The ring finger of his left hand was missing. White society in East Africa buzzed for decades about his innumerable conquests, who included the aviatrix Beryl Markham, **Born Free** author Joy Adamson, and a mother who came to Allen's bed to find her daughter already in possession.

Ava ran into Allen continually during the **Mogambo** shoot. He managed all practical aspects of the project and advised on the wild animal scenes. He was riding in the camera truck one day, just behind Ava and Gable, when three charging rhinos shoved it out of control. Allen coolly shot two of the animals dead, and the third ran away. He was, Ava later said, "the kind of man any girl would trust to lead her into the jungle." Later, Allen said of Ava only that she had been "a lovely girl. . . . She will be in my mind and in my heart for the rest of my life."

He never discussed his conquests, but the obituaries that marked his death in 2002 referred to the affair with Ava as fact. "She was running with Bunny Allen," Eva Monley said. "When you're running a camp, which is what I was doing, you know who's going to bed with whom. I went to his tent one day for something. His stepdaughter was there, very upset because she had discovered he was in Ava's tent and not his own. I'm absolutely certain it happened."

"It was common knowledge among certain members of the community that Bunny had a 'walk-out' with Ava Gardner," said Lee Harragin. "Bunny was incredibly discreet. But with someone like Ava Gardner it was a little difficult to conceal—when the husband was making such a fuss"—a reference to the Nairobi party at which Ava and Frank had fought.

Harragin, a retired lawyer, said those present thought the fight "was about the love affair with Bunny. We couldn't think of any other reason why Sinatra should be so frightfully angry. He was a very possessive and jealous man."

The furor at the party occurred shortly before Ava flew to Europe for her second abortion in the three months of the **Mogambo** shoot in Africa. "Bunny didn't know," said Adrian Blomfield, who researched the **London Daily Telegraph**'s obituary of Allen, "whether the child was his." With that doubt in Ava's mind, too, abortion must have seemed essential.

TWO MONTHS after his screen test for **From Here to Eternity**, Frank still did not know if he would get the part. So poor had his chances seemed that producer Buddy Adler had not intended even to watch the test. He did see it eventually, at director Fred Zinnemann's request, and was impressed. Zinnemann and scriptwriter Dan Taradash were interested but not convinced.

"The test was all right but not great," said Taradash. "We'd tested Eli Wallach, and in terms of acting his test was much better. We'd all settled on Wallach." Still, they were struck by Frank's physical appearance. "The scene was one where he was stripped to his shorts and drunk, really wobbly," Taradash said. "Sinatra looked like a plucked chicken. He looked the part of Maggio, whereas Wallach was a well-built guy, muscular. We all finally agreed he probably could do it."

Without the acquiescence of Harry Cohn, who held the power at Columbia, it did not matter what anyone else thought. In the end Cohn was coerced into giving the part to Frank (a subject to which we shall return). He gave in grudgingly, on the condition that Frank be paid a minimal fee.

The news reached Frank in Boston, where he was performing at a club called the Latin Quarter. He shared the good news with Pearl Bailey, who was on the bill along with the Duke Ellington band. "He said, 'Pearl, they've offered me a movie called **From Here to Eternity**,' " Ellington's drummer Louis Bellson recalled. " 'They're paying me $1,000 a week, which is nothing.' Pearl told him, 'Take it, and don't look back.' "

The shooting of **Eternity** began in March 1953, and Frank forged a drunken friendship with Montgomery Clift, the brilliant, doomed alcoholic cast as Maggio's buddy Prewitt. They worked on their parts together, got plastered together. At their hotel in Hawaii, they tossed beer cans from the window and yelled obscenities in the lobby. Burt Lancaster and Deborah Kerr, whose passionate embrace on the beach would soon scandalize and thrill audiences, often had to put Frank and Clift to bed. They drank themselves into oblivion every night, according to Lancaster. "We would get very, very loaded," said James Jones, who often joined the pair. "We talked about the injustice of life and love, and then Monty and I would listen to Frank talk about Ava Gardner."

Seemingly ignorant of Ava's affair with Bunny Allen, Frank was still worrying about his wife and Clark Gable. The **Mogambo** cast were now in Europe, and he called Ava often. When he was drunk, he still talked of killing himself.

He rushed to Europe as soon as filming ended. Ava joined him on a disastrous singing tour of Italy. An audience in Naples, evidently more interested in seeing Ava Gardner than Frank Sinatra, booed Frank off the stage. In a Milan hotel, the couple's high-volume fights disturbed other guests. In Rome Frank sat patiently by as Ava shopped for evening gowns. Then he went off on his own to sing in Scandinavia, Belgium, England, and Scotland.

"I remember exactly the moment when I made the decision to seek a divorce," Ava said in her last interview. "It was the day the phone rang and Frank was on the other end, announcing that he was in bed with another woman. He made it plain that if he was going to be constantly accused of infidelity when he was innocent, there had to come a time when he'd decide he might as well be guilty."

In early October, Ava was still going on to the press about how she and Frank wanted a child "more than anything else in the world." At the end of the month, though, MGM announced that she and Frank had "exhausted every resource to reconcile their differences." They were separating, the statement said, and it was final.

THREE WEEKS LATER in New York, Jimmy Van Heusen returned to his apartment building to find Frank slumped in the elevator bleeding from the left wrist. He paid off the doorman to keep him quiet, got his friend to Mount Sinai Hospital, and put out a statement about an accident with a broken glass.

By November 29, Frank was fit enough to sing on live television. Eddie Fisher, who appeared on the same show, noted the "thin cuts" still visible on his lower arm. It had been Frank's fourth suicide gesture.

Ava was now seeing a psychiatrist. The doctor told the journalist Irv Kupcinet that she had been driven by extreme insecurity to press Frank constantly for proof of his love. He had responded, but never enough for her. He, too, was consulting a psychiatrist.

At thirty-eight, Frank was physically drained and spiritually exhausted. According to the Mount Sinai Hospital record, his weight had dropped to 118 pounds. He was starting to lose his hair. "I was busted," he would say, remembering that low time. "I did lay down for a while and had some large bar bills for about a year. But after that I said, 'Okay, holiday's over, Charlie, let's go back to work.' "

17

An Assist from the Boys

FOR ALL HIS VICISSITUDES, the gamble of casting Frank in **From Here to Eternity** had paid off. The movie had been a hit from the moment it opened in August 1953. Critics who in the past had blasted Frank's acting now praised his portrayal of Maggio. "When the mood is on him," the **Newsweek** reviewer declared, "Sinatra can act." **The New Yorker** hailed him as "a first rate actor."

Suddenly Frank was a crowd-pleaser again, pursued in the street by admirers. "Now," he said, reminding Jule Styne of the time when no one seemed to care who he was, "I'm a star again." Yet he wanted his resurrection endorsed. "Although Mr. S. was one of the least religious men I had ever met," recalled George Jacobs, the valet he had recently hired, "the entire month before the Oscars he'd go down to the Good Shepherd church in Beverly Hills and pray."

The prayers were answered on Oscar night in March 1954, when the Best Supporting Actor award was announced. As the audience broke into tumultuous applause, Frank ran down the aisle to be presented with his statuette, a moment he recalled as having marked the "greatest change" of his life.

"It's funny about that statue. You walk up to the stage like you're in a dream and they hand you that little man before twenty or thirty million people, and you have to fight to keep the tears back. It's a moment. Like your first girl or your first kiss. Like the first time you hit a guy and he went down. . . . I don't think any actor can experience something like that and not change."

At his home a few miles away, the psychiatrist Frank had been seeing had been watching the Oscar ceremony on television. "That's it, then," Dr. Ralph Greenson told his wife with a chuckle. "I won't be seeing him anymore!" He was right. Frank felt secure now, he told an interviewer, fired with new ambition. Things were also looking up on the musical front.

Before the separation from Ava, before the wrist-slashing, he had been taken on by Capitol Records. The songs he began to record came from his nightclub routine. Six months before the Oscar, at the Riviera in New Jersey, Frank had shown that his voice was back in shape. Audiences had been riveted. "Ever see a mammoth opening night crowd stay completely quiet for an hour?" **Metronome**'s George Simon wrote. "Or a huge and pretty corny bunch of dinner gobblers still its cutlery and usual chatter to such a degree that a guy at the very back of a spot as big as the Riviera could catch every soft sound that the performer was making? That's what happened last month when I caught Frank Sinatra on two different occasions." Simon thought the performance that of a singer who was developing into "one of the most knowing showmen of all time."

SOON AFTER FRANK'S STAR began to shine again, two gangsters visited Mario Lanza at his home in Los Angeles. The singer was in financial trouble, and the mobsters offered him $150,000 in cash, tax-free, if he would make movies and record for mob-controlled companies. In their pitch to Lanza, a Bureau of Narcotics report noted, the mobsters pointed out that "Frank Sinatra a few years back had been in a similar financial condition. . . . 'Look,' they said, 'what we have done for him.' "

It is clear enough now what the Mafia did for Frank. In the three years before his professional collapse, Frank had made no nightclub appearances. From early 1950 on, he made many. One of the first, in January 1950, was the Shamrock in Houston, where Allen Smiley wielded influence.

Smiley, who had been Frank's neighbor at the Sunset Towers in Los Angeles, worked closely with associates of Lucky Luciano. He had recently been looking after Willie Moretti, who was spending some time in California.

Three months later Frank opened at the Copacabana in New York, generally believed to be controlled by Frank Costello. Costello's columnist friend John Miller—the mafioso's wife was godmother to Miller's son—remembered a Sinatra that few ever saw. Frank often came to sit at Costello's table during this period, according to Miller, as a supplicant. "He was always asking favors of the old man."

Moretti, back from the West Coast, was at the Copa for Frank's opening. So, too, was Joe Fischetti, and Frank got work at the Chez Paree in Chicago soon after. In September, as his personal crisis deepened, Frank appeared at the Steel Pier in Atlantic City. Months later, and then again as his career began to recover, he returned to Atlantic City to sing at Paul "Skinny" D'Amato's 500 Club. D'Amato had a lifelong association with organized crime. Early on, when D'Amato was starting out in the gambling business, he had been entrusted with the care of Lucky Luciano when the mobster was hiding out from the law.

D'Amato always insisted he was sole owner of the 500 Club. A usually authoritative source, however, states that he fronted for Marco

Reginelli of the Philadelphia mob. Reginelli was a frequent visitor, always treated royally, as was his successor, Angelo Bruno—after whom, by one account, D'Amato named his son.

Frank had known D'Amato since the 1930s, and would be a pallbearer at his funeral. He liked to celebrate his birthday with him and, when his own star was in the ascendant, came to the rescue when business was slack at the 500. It was a friendship cemented at the time Frank had hit bottom.

"Sinatra was down and out," said Roy Gerber, a veteran Atlantic City hotel executive. "He was **out** of show business. He had friends in Atlantic City, though. He could always get work here. . . . Before Sinatra got the part of Maggio in **From Here to Eternity**, that's all there was for him. Places like the 500 Club."

"Before he made the big time again," said Vincent Teresa, the Mafia informer from New England, "he was begging for spots to sing at." Frank did get work in Boston, and according to Teresa borrowed money from Joe "Beans" Palladino, a bookmaker with heavy mob connections. He was beholden to mobsters or mob-related businessmen all over the country.

In 1951, during the breakup of his first marriage, Frank was taken on at the Desert Inn. "At the time you could walk in," Sonny King said, "you could sit in the back of the room for 25 cents and drink Coca-Cola and watch Frank Sinatra—and he was singing to half a house. It broke my heart, because his voice wasn't there."

In spite of the poor performances, Frank was hired again the following year. He got the work thanks to a call from Skinny D'Amato to Moe Dalitz, an alumnus of the old Detroit and Cleveland mobs. Dalitz was the dominant force in the mob's shift to Las Vegas, and the Desert Inn was a key bridgehead. Far more shrewd an operator than Bugsy Siegel, he was to survive into the 1980s and end his days cloaked in respectability.

Dalitz had been present with Luciano and Moretti at the mob conclave that first discussed formation of a national crime syndicate. He had been one of the criminals who saw Luciano off when he went into exile in 1946. To defy Dalitz, according to an intelligence report, was tantamount to defying Luciano.

Frank's relationship with mob figures was such that they readily involved themselves in his personal life. Once, when he was still married to Nancy, Frank had asked Mickey Cohen in Los Angeles to restrain a lesser mobster he suspected of pursuing Ava. Cohen advised Frank to "go on home to Nancy where you belong." Willie Moretti gave Frank the same advice more than once. "When Sinatra was recently separated from his wife," an informant told the FBI in 1948, "a cousin of Sinatra's wife who is related to a key member of the Moretti mob contacted Willie Moretti regarding Sinatra's marriage difficulties . . . as a result Moretti personally instructed Sinatra to go back and live with his wife. Sinatra immediately obeyed."

Two years later, with the news that Frank was involved with Ava and that the Sinatras were separating, Moretti sent Frank a telegram:

> I AM VERY MUCH SURPRISED WHAT I HAVE BEEN READING IN THE NEWSPAPERS BETWEEN YOU AND YOUR DARLING WIFE. REMEMBER YOU HAVE A DECENT WIFE AND CHILDREN. YOU SHOULD BE VERY HAPPY. REGARDS TO ALL. WILLIE

Moretti's admonition was typical of his Italian-American generation, and especially of mafiosi. "The integrity of the family (small 'f') was high on the Mafia's list," wrote Claire Sterling in her study of the Sicilian mob. "A Man of Honor was expected to keep up appearances. . . . Maintaining a mistress was practically compulsory; but a member could be expelled for deserting or divorcing his wife." Costello took the same view. To parade a mistress in public as Frank had Ava, he thought, "showed a lack of respect for the institution of marriage."

In 1953, after Frank's divorce from Nancy and

when his marriage to Ava was collapsing, Luciano met with Frank in Naples. "Luciano was tempted to convince Sinatra to return to his wife Nancy," a Bureau of Narcotics agent in Italy reported. "However, he didn't because he thought it unwise to interfere."

Moretti was dead by that time, executed by fellow gangsters in a New Jersey restaurant. As mob bosses parceled out his business interests, they had debated who should take over his role in the handling of Frank Sinatra. "Because of my dad's Hollywood connections," said the gangster Allen Smiley's daughter, Luellen, "they suggested giving my father a part in managing Sinatra. As it turned out he didn't want it, but that was what was on offer."

Oversight of Frank was entrusted to others. The Mafia had a continuing interest in every aspect of his life and career.

MARIO PUZO'S NOVEL **The Godfather,** and the movie based on it, included a character who could hardly have been modeled on anyone but Frank Sinatra. In the opening chapter of the book, Johnny Fontane, singer protégé of the mob, goes to Mafia boss Don Corleone for help. Fontane had gotten out of his contract with a bandleader called Halley (read Dorsey) thanks to a mob threat to kill Halley. He had then become "the greatest singing sensation in the country" and made money-spinning Hollywood movies. Later, Fontane had "divorced his childhood-sweetheart wife" and left his children to "marry the most glamorous blond star in motion pictures." Only the hair color is wrong. Fontane constantly suspects his new actress wife is unfaithful. He drinks heavily, loses weight, cannot sleep, and takes pills. His voice has gone and he has been dropped by his Hollywood studio, in part because he "used to sing those songs for the liberal organizations." There is a part in a new movie, Fontane tells Corleone, that he is desperate to play.

"The main character is a guy just like me. I wouldn't even have to act, just be myself. I wouldn't even have to sing. I might even win the Academy Award. . . . I'd be big again." The problem, Fontane tells the Don, is that the studio head has refused even to consider him for the part. "He sent the word that if I come and kiss his ass in the studio commissary, maybe he'll think about it."

The studio boss in the novel is Jack Woltz, a New Yorker of Russian extraction who had moved west, invested in the nickelodeon, and risen to become a tyrannical studio head. He is "rapaciously amorous" of women, but over all else loves his thoroughbred horses. Woltz's pride and joy is Khartoum, a fabulously expensive stallion he has purchased. One morning soon after Fontane's meeting with the Don, **Godfather** aficionados know, Woltz wakes to find Khartoum's severed head at the foot of his bed. Message received. Fontane gets the part.

In real life, Harry Cohn was also a New Yorker of Russian parentage. From beginnings in the nickelodeon business, he had risen to become a renowned Hollywood despot. He had a voracious sexual appetite, and was addicted to horse racing. He did not own an Arabian stallion but, as an inveterate gambler, he favored one called Omar Kiam. And, of course, he had resolutely opposed casting Frank in **Eternity.**

"What phony stuff!" Frank was to say of **The Godfather.** "Somebody going to the mob to get a role in a movie!" In private, Frank had long since hinted at a different truth. "Hey," George Jacobs recalled him saying with a Cheshire Cat grin, "I got that part through my own fucking **talent.**" "And then," Jacobs said, "he gave me a wink." Frank admitted to Brad Dexter, as did Ava, that the mob had leaned on Cohn. There is also a first-hand witness.

Martin Jurow, who produced the classic movies **Breakfast at Tiffany's** and **Terms of Endearment,** was the William Morris Agency's man in New York when **Eternity** was being cast. He was forty-one then, an up-and-coming agent who had switched to show business after graduating from Harvard Law School. In 2001, he told how a William Morris colleague, George Wood, brought Frank into his office. Wood explained that Frank was there to discuss his foundering career, and wondered if Jurow had any suggestions. Wood, Jurow knew, was close to the " 'quiet investors' who were willing to pay entertainers large fees for performing in their Las Vegas clubs"—in other words, the mobsters. Wood had been "connected" since Prohibition days, and was close to Frank Costello and Meyer Lansky.

Jurow looked carefully at Frank as he came into the room. Some of the old cockiness remained but he seemed dispirited, almost desperate. When Jurow said finding him a prestigious film role would get him out of the doldrums, Frank said gloomily that there was small chance of that. Jurow, however, knew something Frank did not—that Fred Zinnemann was still looking for the right actor to play Maggio in **Eternity.** Frank looked the part, a loser trying to put on a brave face, and Jurow put his name forward. Zinnemann expressed interest. Cohn, however, reacted with characteristic coarseness. Yelling into the phone, he said he would not have "that bum" Sinatra in his studio.

Hours after being turned down, Jurow went to see Wood at his apartment on Central Park South. There, as he put it fifty years later, "something fantastic occurred." He found Wood, not for the first time, ensconced with a mafioso, "Jimmy Blue Eyes" Alo, a key member of the old Luciano syndicate. Alo had a low profile but a great deal of power. He knew Frank and his family so well, an associate said, that Frank regarded him as "his closest friend in that realm." He was an intimate of Frank's East Coast manager, Henri Giné, though that was something Giné went to great pains to keep quiet. Alo had a stake in the William Morris agency, had known Wood since the 1930s, and visited him almost every day.

That night in New York, Alo was told how Cohn had rebuffed Jurow. Alo knew Cohn, had done him favors in the past. "Harry Cohn, huh?" Jurow recalled Alo responding. "Where is he now? In California? . . . Does he have a private line?" Jurow gave him the number. "Jimmy Blue Eyes then walked over and patted me on the head," Jurow recalled. "He spoke with a finality I have never forgotten: 'He owes us. Expect a call.' Three simple words, but spoken with such ominous certainty." Jurow felt he was "right in the middle of an Edward G. Robinson movie." Cohn did soon telephone—to concede defeat and assure Jurow that Frank would get the part.

Cohn's widow, Joan, acknowledged the mob involvement. The writer Peter Evans, who knew her socially years later, often heard her describe how "two gentlemen from the mob turned up at Columbia Pictures and told Harry Cohn he was **going** to cast Sinatra in **Eternity**." When he passed the word to Zinnemann, as Joan told it, the director said he thought Frank might be right for the part anyway. This gave Cohn a face-saver. He could give the Mafia what it demanded while plausibly maintaining that his decision was based on merit.

According to his biographer, Costello had also been in touch with George Wood at William Morris, and told friends "he was the one who got Sinatra the part." Johnny Rosselli, a key mob emissary on the West Coast—Luciano had authorized his work there—said he delivered the mob threat. He had long been close to Cohn, having produced the cash that gave Cohn control of Columbia Pictures. He advised Cohn on gambling ventures and had been a frequent guest at his home. The two men wore matching rings, rubies set in gold, to attest to their friendship. As in all Mafia relationships, however, the bottom line was fear.

Rosselli "was the one who laid it out," his associate Joe Seide said. "That was serious business. It was in the form of 'Look, you do this for me and maybe we won't do this to you.' " Meredith Harless, the former assistant to Cohn's opposite number at MGM, Louis B. Mayer, said she learned Rosselli delivered a simple ultimatum: "Give Frank the role or I will have you killed."

HAVING HELPED FRANK through a tough period, the Mafia stayed close. In November

1953, when he slashed his wrists in New York, he had been about to leave for a nightclub engagement in St. Louis. When he failed to turn up, it was St. Louis attorney Morris Shenker, the foremost mob lawyer of his day, who let Frank's booking agents know what had happened. Shenker's relations with top gangsters went "far beyond mere legal representation," **Life** reported. The **Sacramento Bee** described him as a "money mover for the mob."

After the wrist-slashing, George Wood was assigned to baby-sit Sinatra. "When Frank ate, I ate," he recalled. "When he slept, I slept, when he felt like walking, I walked with him. When he took a haircut, I took a haircut."

Emotionally unstable though Frank was, the mob had good reason to mollycoddle him. Now, more than ever, he represented an important investment. A fortune in Mafia money was being committed to make Las Vegas the nation's gambling capital, and the way to lure suckers was to provide top-class entertainment. Frank was to be part of a specific new mob enterprise, the Sands Hotel and Casino.

The Sands had opened in late 1952, when Frank had so little money that Ava had had to pay his airfare to Africa. He had been in tax trouble for some time, and the IRS filed a lien for $109,997 ($750,000 today) against him in early 1953. What money Frank had during the down period had come from his club appearances, and the part in **Eternity** had boosted his morale but paid only $10,000. He was still heavily in debt. Then, in August 1953, the **Los Angeles Times** reported that the Nevada Tax Commission had delayed its decision as to whether or not to grant Frank a gambling license "until he has cleared his income tax obligations." The license was necessary, the **Times** explained, if Frank were to hold "a two per cent interest in the Sands Hotel in Las Vegas," an investment of $54,000. Frank got his license a few months later, having told the commissioners he was gradually paying off the tax debt. All of a sudden, evidently, he had access to large sums of money.

One of the secret owners of the Sands was Frank Costello. The building of the complex had been supervised by Jimmy Alo, who was now monitoring progress. The Sands general manager Jack Entratter, a big fellow, had escorted Frank during his initial wild popularity and worked as a bouncer at the Copacabana in New York. Frank was among friends.

In early 1953, during the filming of **From Here to Eternity,** Frank had been seen in Las Vegas cavorting with a New York–based enforcer for a Luciano associate. In October, riding on the wave of his success in the movie, he was back in town for his opening at the Sands. The management installed him in style in the hotel's Presidential

Suite, with its three grand bedrooms and its very own pool. The "quiet investors" were making sure to pamper Frank. He was to sing at the Sands the following year, the year after that, and again and again until the late 1960s. It became, as his daughter Nancy put it, his Las Vegas home. He would reign as "King of Las Vegas," the city's star of stars.

TWO YEARS EARLIER, pressed by Kefauver Committee attorneys to discuss his alleged mob ties, Frank had been in a state of high anxiety. The nation's growing audience of television viewers had been watching as gangster after gangster, compelled to testify in public, ducked and weaved under tough questioning. Desperate to avoid that sort of exposure, Frank agreed to meet investigators at 4:00 A.M. in an office at Rockefeller Center. The attorney who asked the questions, Joe Nellis, vividly remembered how Frank came in looking "like a lost kitten, drawn, frightened to death." He visibly shook as Nellis showed him pictures of Frank in Cuba with Luciano. Frank said the mobsters were "people his mother knew, that his family knew." The Fischettis, he admitted, were "great buddies," "good people, who support the Church." Costello, he said, was just someone with whom he had "once" had a drink.

Nellis thought Frank "an appealing guy with a

very convenient memory . . . an awful liar. He tried desperately to cover up those relationships. If he had appeared in public before the Committee and lied as much as he did, I would have been the first to recommend that he be sent up to the U.S. Attorney on perjury charges." Thus briefed by Nellis, and at a time when the committee was already swamped by publicity, Kefauver let the matter drop. From 1954 on Frank would simply deny his Mafia connection or parry difficult questions with contemptuous replies. He appeared to admire the criminals. "I've always felt Sinatra was frustrated," Broadway press agent Eddie Jaffe said. "He would rather have been a made member of the Mafia than the great singer he was." "Sinatra is a paradoxical cuss," said Bing Crosby. "I think secretly he's always nurtured a childish desire to be a hood." "I remember him saying," Eddie Fisher recalled, " 'I'd rather be a don for the Mafia than President of the United States.' And that's the way he acted."

Frank pursued Mafia roles in movies. In the late 1950s, he lobbied for the part of a Mafia bookkeeper in **The Brothers Rico,** an adaptation of a Georges Simenon novella. Years later, angry though he was about the similarity between himself and the Fontane character in **The Godfather,** he told Francis Ford Coppola he wanted to play Don Corleone. That role went to Brando, of course, but Coppola offered Frank the role of a senior mafioso in **Godfather III.** He turned it down only because he was in his mid-seventies by then and it would have involved a three-month shoot.

Frank came on like a mafioso, saxophonist Don Raffell remembered. "The double doors at Capitol [recording studios] open up and there's Sinatra. He's got on a black hat with a white band, black suit, black shirt, black shoes, white necktie—gangster. He doesn't say anything to anybody, walks into the recording booth and says, 'You've had plenty of time to get the balance on this thing. I don't want any fooling around or it'll be your ass!' . . . He says that like a hoodlum. . . . He was an evil mother!"

Frank liked to talk gangster-style, in a patter that, taken literally, suggested he had the power to order up terrible retribution. One of his favorite lines was: "If anybody hits you, call me." Variations included: "Sometimes I wish someone would really hurt you so I could kill them" and "I could have put him in the hospital, you know." Not everyone was sure Frank was joking.

"When he said to me one day, 'Just let me know if anyone bothers you and I'll take care of it,' " Shirley MacLaine recalled, "an electrical shudder went through me. On the one hand I basked in his protection; on the other—what would he **do** to someone who 'bothered' me? . . . And was it the dangerous mystery of it all that made it attractive?"

"I don't think Frank Sinatra ever murdered anybody," Sonny King said with alarming casualness, "although I think he smacked a few around."

Most of the time, Frank just talked the tough talk.

Others read Frank in much the same way. Earl Wilson noted that Frank's father taught him that "Sicilians were proud and unbeatable fighters . . . unforgiving." "Sinatra," thought his biographer Arnold Shaw, "wanted, like Il Padrone of old, to be a Man of Respect." Gay Talese, who wrote a classic piece on Frank for **Esquire** in the 1960s, saw this in the way he treated his friends. "If they remain loyal, then there is nothing Sinatra will not do in turn. They are wise to remember, however, one thing. He is Sinatra. The boss. Il Padrone." Mario Puzo thought Frank "very obviously modeled his personal behavior on the great Mafia chiefs who lived in Sicily."

If Frank felt an affinity for the mafiosi, by 1953 he also felt indebted. "These are the guys who gave me a job when nobody else would," the Sinatra character says in the 1992 television dramatization of Frank's life, a show for which he provided factual background. "The Boys were the only people who would hire him when his voice gave out," said John Smith, a **Las Vegas Review-Journal** columnist who has often written on organized crime. "They stuck by him, and he was loyal to them after that."

It seems not to have troubled Frank that the **amici** who helped in his resurrection were murderers and extortionists. He had no qualms when Las Vegas bosses plied him with princely payments, kept his name in lights, treated him like royalty. The mobsters were giving Frank his throne back and promising long-term tenure.

From 1951 to 1954, federal agencies received reports that the mobsters were "the owners of Sinatra," that he was "a participating member of the Luciano mob . . . they still 'own' him." "It was a symbiotic relationship," John Smith said. "Las Vegas helped him make his comeback, and he helped to make Las Vegas. Las Vegas is a factory town. The factory is gambling, and you feed the factory by making it sexy.

"Gambling works to the advantage of the house when the house wins and the player loses. If you sit in your seat long enough you will go home penniless. So how do you persuade people to gamble? You have to give customers a reason to come to Las Vegas. Frank Sinatra gave several generations a reason to come to Las Vegas. A guy like that is important to the mob because he's an **earner.**"

It cut both ways. For entertainers, the financial lure was huge. "There's something you have to understand," said Herman Hover, who became an executive at the Frontier Hotel. "Big attractions in those days were not much interested in their salary. What they were interested in was money under the table. . . . Cash, off the books . . . on which they didn't pay an agent's commission or income tax. It was very easy to get money under the table, because [the casinos] had all that gambling money, which they didn't declare anyway."

Frank's drawing power was his bargaining chip, but it did not ensure his safety. Frank's contemporary Jerry Lewis explained his own experience at the Copacabana. "Sunday nights at the Copa at ringside," he recalled, "was the galaxy of the heads of the families . . . and after the show, when you were summoned to the table, you went so that they could introduce you to their children and their wives. Everything was very, very lovely and aboveboard. The next day, the same guy introducing you to his two lovely daughters pumps six shells into some poor sonofabitch in the Bowery, like nothin'."

Lewis felt the danger when he talked back to a heckler one night, only to discover his abuser was Luciano's acolyte Albert Anastasia. "Tell the little bastard he's lucky I've got a sense of humor," Anastasia said afterward.

Balancing his patrons' benevolence with their demands, Lewis discovered, was a delicate game. "The good things these guys did didn't necessarily outweigh the bad things. If you're gonna have them in your life, there's nothing wrong with having them in your life correctly . . . having them incorrectly, it ain't gonna be a long haul. It wouldn't take long."

Max Block, a union boss of the day, knew both the mafiosi and the entertainers they controlled. He saw how apprehensive Lewis was, and sympathized. "Jerry got nervous because of the mob," he recalled. "He didn't want to bow to the big boys, for them to stay on the payroll. Jerry was lucky they didn't shoot him."

Mario Lanza's mob visitors, in 1955, showed their true nature when he resisted their blandishments. "You don't know who you're talking to," said Tommy Lucchese, a close associate of Lucky Luciano. "Keep your big mouth shut or I'll shut it permanently." Later, in Italy, Luciano himself got Lanza to agree to do a concert. Should he renege on his promise, two mob emissaries warned him, he would "never appear in public again." Lanza failed to show up, and died the following day at the age of thirty-eight. Lanza had medical problems and was undergoing weight reduction treatments, but his death was totally unexpected and the precise cause of death was never established. Relevant witnesses vanished soon afterward, according to the singer's widow, Betty, and she believed the Mafia had followed through on its threat. Whatever the truth, the rumors fueled fear of what the Mafia might do to entertainers.

Tommy Lucchese would later be Frank's guest in Atlantic City, and have an interest in a racetrack of which Frank was a director. Questioned about Lucchese by the House Select Committee on Crime, Frank said only that he had met the gangster "once or twice, a long time ago."

Frank took risks. He angered Boston mob bosses by failing to keep a promise to sing in their clubs. They did not take reprisals, but he knew he walked a fine line. After a spat over something trivial with Philadelphia's Angelo Bruno, Bruno's daughter Jean remembered, Frank was in a state of panic for hours.

In the 1970s, he briefly considered collaborating with Pete Hamill on a book about his life. "I told him," Hamill recalled, "I'd have to discuss three subjects with him: his politics, his women, and the mob. He shrugged and said the first two were no problem. 'But if I talk about those other guys, someone might come knocking at my fucking door.' "

Frank more than once crossed the Mafia in ways that could have proved fatal.

"He was always in trouble, you know, with the Boys," said Jimmy Alo. "I had to step in."

18

A Triumph of Talent

ONE EVENING IN EARLY APRIL 1953, well into the **From Here to Eternity** shoot, Frank had begun work at Capitol Records on Melrose Avenue in Hollywood. Stepping up to a studio microphone for the first time in more than six months, he recorded four songs. None would cause any excitement, and for years two would not even be released. Later that month, however, when Frank started working with the arranger Nelson Riddle, his singing career entered a new and brilliant phase.

The Sinatra-Riddle breakthrough came early the following year, with Frank's most successful release in seven years. "Young at Heart"—"Fairytales can come true. It can happen to you"—shot to number two on the **Billboard** singles chart. By March 1954, when Frank picked up his Oscar for **Eternity**, his **Songs for Young Lovers** album was on the charts, and rose to number three. At year's end, a poll of disc jockeys voted Frank top male vocalist. He was **Metronome**'s Singer of the Year, **Down Beat**'s Most Popular Male Vocalist. Because of the success of **Eternity**, he was deluged with film offers.

Dozens of Sinatra singles and sixteen more Sinatra albums were to be hits during Frank's time with Capitol. Three albums would reach number one, and five number two. In late summer 1955, with his fortieth birthday approaching, Frank made the cover of **Time** magazine. The magazine said he was "well away on a second career that promises to be if anything more brilliant than the first." His most glittering period had begun.

It was not easy for Frank to admit how far he had fallen before climbing back. "I was never finished!" he blustered to a friend. In a more honest moment, he admitted to **Los Angeles Times** critic Roger Beck that he had been "absolutely right in putting the knock on my records for a while . . . I stunk. My voice was shot. I knew it and you knew it and everybody knew it." Just as Martin Jurow had seen despair in Sinatra before **Eternity**, so Capitol vice president Alan Livingston recalled the beaten man he met before signing Frank, a man who seemed "meek, a pussycat, humble . . . broke, in debt . . . at the lowest ebb of his life."

Yet Livingston and Dave Dexter, another Capitol executive, thought Frank could make a comeback. For a pittance—the initial payment was reportedly just $1,000—Livingston offered him a contract that tied him to Capitol for seven years. Frank was required to pay his own studio expenses. He signed the deal in a curtained booth at Lucy's Restaurant in Hollywood.

Capitol's salesmen, local managers, and promotion men did not react well when Livingston announced the deal at the company convention. "There must have been a couple of hundred guys there," he remembered, "and the whole room went, 'Unnhhoooo. . . .' The whole staff was so totally underwhelmed that they groaned **en masse.**"

This was the time in America that William Manchester called "the Eisenhower Siesta," an era of national self-confidence to be remembered as an "uncomplicated, golden time . . . cloudless." Yet American society was changing in numerous ways. People were asserting their independence as individuals, not least where sex was concerned. Nude photographs of Marilyn Monroe appeared in a new magazine called **Playboy.** Hemingway was about to win the Nobel Prize for literature. J. D. Salinger's 1951 novel **Catcher in the Rye** had been a sensation and the loner against the world had become a cult figure. In the movies, Bogart had made his mark as the good guy with a cynical edge. The month after Frank won his

Oscar, Bill Haley's "Rock Around the Clock" began its climb to number one. Crucially, though, the time bomb that was rock 'n' roll had yet to explode.

At this cultural turning point, Frank Sinatra reached a new generation. To Barbara Grizzuti, who turned nineteen in 1953, he was a "sweet survivor." "In the fifties, failures, if they were flamboyant enough, endeared themselves to us. . . . He bucked the crowd, as heroes are meant to do. He was the Outsider who fought back and made it. He had no ideology but he was True to Himself. In the fifties, that was good enough."

The writer David Halberstam was also nineteen that year. The Sinatra of the bobbysoxer days, he thought, "had produced music that was quite pleasant to listen to and comfortable to dance to but seemed to hold no mysteries, no genuine emotion." Frank's 1950s sound changed Halberstam's mind. He now sang "so well and so privately that he achieved a musical conversation with his audience. He seemed to understand better than anyone the conundrum of love—how hard it is for two people to be at the same emotional place at the same time.

"In a few years, with the coming of the women's movement, those of us who constituted Sinatra's core audience would be viewed as an empowered male elite who dominated and determined the lives of the women of our generation. But we hardly felt empowered when we were young. More often than not we felt some form of rejection or heartbreak, and certainly a great deal of awkwardness. Sinatra's attraction was that he seemed to feel the same pain.

"His arrival at a particularly poignant moment in his life, his work in the early and mid-fifties constitutes the best—and almost surely the most lasting—shelf ever performed by a popular singer in this country's history."

The literary editor of **The New Republic**, Leon Wieseltier, put it another way. Frank's years at Capitol, he wrote, were a time "when a vocalist became a singer, when an everymanish baritone with a genius for phrasing and an interest in rejection suddenly came forth," producing records that "will forever mark a high point in American music."

If there was genius, it was shared. For its midwife was Nelson Riddle, the one man in the business Frank came to call "Maestro."

RIDDLE HAD BEEN CAPITOL'S in-house arranger for a couple of years. His career choice had been made for him after the war, when a collision with a door destroyed his front teeth and put an end to his potential as a trombonist. He had done arrangements for Bing Crosby's brother Bob, Nat "King" Cole, Mel Tormé, and Billy Eckstine. Even so, and even after giving Cole a hit with "Mona Lisa," he remained, at thirty-one, a fairly obscure figure in the industry.

"Do yourself a favor. Work with Nelson Riddle," Alan Livingston told Frank before the first recording session at Capitol. Frank resisted, preferring Axel Stordahl, with whom he had worked since the glory days began. At the second session, Riddle was waiting on the podium. When Frank asked who he was, a Capitol producer said the arranger was "just conducting the band." Only after he had recorded the exhilarating "I've Got the World on a String," and enthused, was he told the arranger was Riddle.

The Riddle sound was upbeat, a blast of fresh air, and everyone present seemed to sense it. A photographer there that day, Sid Avery, remembered how excited Frank became as he listened to the playback. "Jesus Christ!" Frank exclaimed, "I'm back, baby, I'm back!" There would be other arrangers in the years that followed, but it was Riddle, combining his talents with those of songwriters Cahn and Van Heusen, who provided the magic of the Sinatra renaissance.

The two men had a good deal in common. Riddle had been born in New Jersey only twenty miles from Hoboken. Six years Frank's junior, he, too, grew up in a household where the mother ruled the roost. Though his first marriage lasted far longer than Frank's, it was badly damaged by his philandering. He wound up drinking too much. Riddle's life was suffused with instability, personal disappointment, and emotional loneliness.

The two men's musical pedigrees intersected. Riddle, too, was steeped in the classics. As a teenager he had listened again and again to a record of the pianist Paderewski playing Debussy. He had sat up all night listening to Shostakovich. Riddle had produced some of his early arrangements while playing trombone in the Dorsey band.

Having discovered Riddle's talents, Frank enforced his own musical will. Milt Bernhart, a trombonist who worked for Frank on and off for years, recalled a night early on when Frank called a break, crooked a finger at Riddle, and walked him out of the studio. "I watched them from the hallway," he said. "Nelson was standing frozen, and Frank was doing all the talking . . . but he was not angry. . . . He was gesticulating, his hands going up and down and sideways. . . . He was describing music, and singing."

Frank rejected only about eight of Riddle's arrangements in as many years. He showed himself, as Riddle put it, to be "a perfectionist who drove himself and everybody around him relentlessly. . . ." "He'd have very definite ideas, particularly about the pace of the record and which areas should be soft or loud, happy or sad. He'd sketch out something brief like, 'Start with a bass figure, build up second time through and then fade out at the end.' That's possibly all he would say. Sometimes he'd follow this up with a phone call at three in the morning."

Long before a recording, Frank would tell Riddle what he wanted, and the arranger would take notes. He worked on his arrangements far into the night, sometimes all night. In the studio, Frank might insist on endless takes, working on and on until satisfied he had a song absolutely right.

"If I wasn't conducting the orchestra to his liking," Riddle said, "he'd shove me out of the way and take over. When he'd take over conducting like that I'd feel awful." "That gentle sweet man," said the writer Charles Higham, who used to eat with Riddle at Musso and Frank's on Hollywood Boulevard, "would come to the table shaking after a session with Frank."

Riddle conceded, though, that the shots Frank called were usually the right ones, that doing things his way got the optimum result. "There's no one like him," he would say. "Frank not only encourages you to adventure, but he has such a keen appreciation of achievement that you are compelled to knock yourself out for him. It's not only that his intuitions as to tempi, phrasing, and even configuration are amazingly right, but his taste is so impeccable . . . there is still no one who can approach him."

Frank praised Riddle as "the greatest arranger in the world." He was, he said, "the finest musician" "with the biggest bag of tricks" of any orchestrator he knew.

Nine Sinatra-Riddle albums were produced between 1953 and 1962, some of them with titles that became part of America's cultural language: **Songs for Young Lovers, Swing Easy, In the Wee Small Hours, Songs for Swingin' Lovers, Close to You, A Swingin' Affair, Only the Lonely, Nice 'n' Easy, Sinatra's Swingin' Session.** The period during which Frank produced those albums with Riddle, and later those with Billy May and Gordon Jenkins, was Sinatra's golden age, an extended flow of excellence matched only by the Beatles in the 1960s.

While Frank and Riddle planned the albums together, concept and direction were Frank's alone. "First I decide on the mood, perhaps pick a title," he said. "Or sometimes it might be that I had the title and then picked the mood to fit. . . . Next comes the pacing of the album, which is vitally important; I put the titles of the songs on twelve bits of paper and juggle them around like a jigsaw until the album is telling a complete story lyric-wise. . . . Tommy Dorsey did this with every band show he played. He never told me this; it just suddenly came to me as I sat up on that stand night after night. But this is what I've tried to do with every album I've made."

Sinatra now knew how to get the best out of his musicians. He and Riddle booked the same musicians again and again. The men they hired often marveled at how much Frank knew about their individual backgrounds. Capitol had state-of-the-art equipment, and Frank rapidly learned how to use it to best advantage. David Hanna, a publicist who met him in 1954, listened fascinated to his "lucid, intelligent, and wonderfully knowledgeable forecast of all the revolutions that were coming in the field of sound electronics. The many-syllabled, technical words rippled off his tongue as casually as the lyrics to a Rodgers and Hart song."

Rita Kirwan of **Music** magazine sat in on a late-night recording session to which fans had been admitted. "The ordinary work-a-day atmosphere of the studio becomes charged with excitement. For Frank has the rare ability to establish contact with his audience . . . no matter what the mood he wants to evoke. He breaks the contact constantly when he records, interrupting himself to work over a line, to question the conductor about the arrangement, about tempo or tone or phrasing.

"He breaks the contact when he stops to clown around, to say something in his strange, indistinct diction, so different from the diction of his performances. But even as he draws his spellbound audience up short twenty-seven times in one song, abruptly coming down to earth to correct himself or the orchestra, he can re-establish whatever mood he wishes the instant he begins to sing again.

"From around 8 P.M. to beyond 12 in the morning his recording sessions usually continue. The producer's voice through the mike in the control booth becomes thick with too many cigarettes. . . . After many takes, an array of five minute rests and frequent cups of coffee, Sinatra's exhaustion begins to show in his shoulders. . . .

"Everybody listens to the playback. Sinatra, with his head in his arms, leaning against the glass-paneled control booth, listens harder than anyone. An epidemic of yawns seizes the musicians. Frank looks up. 'Yeah. Yeah, I think that's the one. Whadda you think?' The producer nods . . . Sinatra flops on to one of the chairs, crosses his legs and hums a fragment from one of the songs he's been recording. He waves to the janitor now straightening up the studio and says, 'Jeez. What crazy working hours we've got. We both should've been plumbers, huh?' "

Many of the songs he now recorded were old standards, brought dramatically to new life by Riddle. Frank alternated theme and mood and pace from album to album: from **Swing Easy,** contriving to mix exuberant hope with regret and still swing, to the marvel of melancholia that was **In the Wee Small Hours,** to **Songs for Swingin' Lovers,** a celebration of romance and seduction.

The music reflected Frank's and Riddle's apprenticeship in the big bands, and the jazz that was holy writ to both of them. Above all though, from the carefully designed covers to the delivery, the albums were personal and particular to Frank. This was, critic Henry Pleasants has written, "the moment when swing left the dance floor and moved in behind the singers."

The singer, meanwhile, remade himself. "I changed record companies, changed attorneys, changed accountants, changed picture companies, and changed my clothes," he remembered. The public saw the changed appearance, the fresh image, on the carefully crafted covers of the new albums: the bow ties were gone for good; the narrow face, a little worn now, attractively so; a mischievous smile or a lonesome pose, as required; a suit rendered rakish by a loosened tie and, usually, a cigarette.

Hats, which Frank had long favored, became his jaunty trademark. How he wore them as he sang, pulled well down or tipped back, became "the barometer of his feelings," one observer thought. The headgear covered up his increasing baldness. It was part of George Jacobs's daily duty to "spray hair coloring on the ever-expanding bald spot on the back of Mr. S.'s scalp." Increasingly, Frank wore hairpieces.

All of that was as nothing compared to the way his voice had changed. Frank Jr. had until now thought of his father's singing voice as "romantic, tender, wistful." One day in 1953, though, as he listened to the radio at home, something struck him as different. "Even at the age of nine," he said decades later when he himself had become an accomplished musician, "I noticed that something drastically had changed in my father's approach. . . . Gone was that soft, gentle, dreamy and crooning sound. . . . From that day forward his sound was different. Defiant, assertive, even forceful. And there was something else. . . . In the days of crooning the records he made were merely pleasant musical conversation. But from 'I've Got the World on a String' every record he made was a statement."

"I didn't care for his original voice," Nelson Riddle said. "I thought it was far too syrupy. I prefer to hear the rather angular person come through in his voice. . . . To me his voice only became interesting during the time when I started to work with him." The voice was older now—Frank would turn forty in 1955—and the throat that produced it had been roughened by cigarettes and, increasingly, liquor. Jule Styne, who lived in Frank's apartment for a while early in the Capitol period, recalled him staying "up all night, drinking booze—way, way too much brandy."

Admirers of the new Sinatra, his son pointed out, no longer called him Frankie, as the teenage bobbysoxers once had. He was no mere idol now but a singer, and one who presented himself as a tough sophisticate. This Frank was a cool guy. He occasionally changed the lyrics a little, threw in the odd "man" or "cat" that was not in the original. He replaced a "darling" with "baby" in Cole Porter's "Night and Day." He sang "I've Got You Under My Skin" as "I've got, got, got you," to Porter's annoyance. "Don't sing it," he said, "if you can't keep to the line I composed."

Frank studied the lyrics of songs with immense care. "I've always believed that the written word is first, always first. Not belittling the music behind me, it's really only a curtain. . . . The word actually dictates to you in a song—it really tells you what it needs."

"He could practically have talked the thing for me and it would have been all right," Riddle said. "Frank's personal interpretation of a lyric is like people who read poetry or an actor in a role," the singer Joe Williams said. "With Frank, each song is a vignette for the story." The writer Richard Iaconelli saw Sinatra as conducting a ballet with microphone, cigarette, and outstretched hand, pursuing the concept of "song as miniature stage-play."

Riddle suggested the play was essentially about sex. "Music to me is sex," he said. "It's all tied up somehow. . . . I always have some woman in mind for each song I arrange." Frank, he thought, "points everything he does from a sexual standpoint." Yet the singing on the 1950s albums is something beyond sex, beyond mere performance. David Halberstam thought Frank's delivery "plaintive, almost wounded," the sound of someone who had "lived" his songs. The critic Charles Taylor thought Frank's performances "went beyond luxuriant self-pity and approached luxuriant tragedy." The writer Mikal Gilmore saw "darkness" in Sinatra, "a desperate hunger for the validation that comes from love, a ruinous anger towards anything that challenges that validation."

"He can say 'I love you' with more conviction than anyone I know," said Freddie Karger, who composed some of the music for **From Here to Eternity.** "They're not simply words for him. They convey something he really feels."

Riddle believed he knew exactly what the something was. "It was Ava who did that," he said, "who taught him how to sing a torch song. That's how he learned. She was the greatest love of his life, and he lost her."

From the **Wee Small Hours** album, recorded in early 1955:

I get along without you very well,
Of course I do . . .
I've forgotten you just like I should,
Of course I have,
Except to hear your name,
Or someone's laugh that is the same
But I've forgotten you just like I should.

Yet he had not forgotten Ava, never would.

19

The Lonely Heart

MEN, MARK TWAIN OBSERVED, "will risk fortune, character, reputation, life itself" for sex. Frank had come close to losing all for Ava Gardner, but could not let go of his passion for her. On and off, for more than twenty years, he would talk of their getting together again.

"Frank would call me in Madrid, London, Rome, New York, wherever I happened to be, and say, 'Ava, let's try again,' " she remembered. "I'd say, 'Okay!' and drop everything. . . . And it would be heaven, but it wouldn't last more than twenty-four hours."

Frank tried just months after their formal separation, in December 1953. Ava was in Rome, getting ready to start shooting **The Barefoot Contessa,** when he called to say he was heading for Europe. She told her publicist David Hanna,

"It'll be a mess. Why the hell does he do it? . . . I can't tell him not to come."

He got as far as London, laden with presents, on Christmas Eve, Ava's birthday, only to learn she had left Italy for Spain. Frank chartered a plane to Madrid, and on Christmas night the couple were seen in a restaurant singing carols. They were in Rome, throwing a party, by New Year's Eve.

They wound up that night at a club the American singer Bricktop ran on the Via Veneto. Ava "was sitting half on his lap," Bricktop remembered, "and it seemed to me that she was really trying to get him to enjoy himself. He looked so sad." Frank told colleagues they had been "trying to work things out." Ava, however, told Hanna there was "not a chance" they would make up, in part because she had found herself another lover. She had gone to Madrid to spend Christmas with Luis Miguel Dominguín, the premier matador of Spain, eligible and handsome, a man who counted Picasso and Stravinsky as personal friends. She continued to see him under Frank's nose.

"Tell him I'm at the hairdresser's, tell him anything," Ava urged Betty Wallers, a guest from England, "so long as he doesn't find out about Luis." Frank waited in the house she had rented, alternately forlorn and enraged. George Jacobs thought his boss's Christmas mission a "very masochistic thing" that "added insult to his own injury. . . . Yet he still wanted Ava in his life, whatever the circumstances . . . still hung on to the hope and the dream."

Back in the United States, Frank learned Lauren Bacall was about to travel to Italy to join her husband, Humphrey Bogart, Ava's co-star in **The Barefoot Contessa.** Would she, he asked, mind carrying a coconut cake to Ava? Bacall hand-carried the cake, in a large, awkward box, across the Atlantic and to Ava's dressing room. Ava responded coldly. "She was clearly through with him," Bacall has said, "but it wasn't that way on his side."

"He would call her practically every moment," Reenie Jordan recalled. "He'd call and call her saying 'I need you,' and she'd go to him."

When Ava returned to California between movies, Frank invited her to stay at his place in Palm Springs. She agreed on the condition that he would not be there. Frank duly made himself scarce and dispatched Jacobs to pick Ava up at the airport. She got dead drunk on the ride back, and had to be carried into the house.

The apartment Frank had recently taken, at Wilshire and Beverly Glen in Los Angeles, looked to Jacobs like a shrine to Ava Gardner. "There were pictures of her everywhere, in the bathrooms, in the closet, on the refrigerator." It was the same at the Palm Springs house.

Lonely, Frank got Jule Styne to move into his new place. "I come home at night and enter the living room and it's like a funeral parlor," Styne remembered. "The lights are dim and they just about light up three pictures of Ava. Frank sits in front of them with a bottle of brandy." Sammy Cahn once found Frank in tears, drinking a toast to one of the pictures of Ava.

With adoration came rage. That same night, Frank smashed the framed photograph and tore Ava's image into little pieces. Then, after drinking some more, he tried to put the pieces together again. He became frantic when he could not find the nose. Then it fluttered at last from his sleeve, to be spotted by a delivery man arriving at the door with more liquor. He got the gold watch on Frank's wrist as a reward.

The agent Irving "Swifty" Lazar, who lived in the same complex, once returned to see Frank's light on and his apartment door open. "Frank was hunched down in an easy chair," he said, "shooting a BB gun at three faces of Ava that had been painted by the artist Paul Clemens."

While Frank had been in Rome, Ava had posed for a lifesize nude statue of herself commissioned for a scene in **The Barefoot Contessa.** Frank acquired it, brought it to California, and later—when he moved into a new house on Coldwater Canyon—would install it in the garden.

He did not sleep well now. Styne would hear him pacing up and down, up and down. He would hear him on the phone in the early hours, telling Nancy, the one fixed point in his chaotic personal life, "You're the only one who understands me."

He had eaten dinner with Nancy and the children the night before winning the Oscar for **From Here to Eternity.** Daughter Nancy, by then nearly fourteen, had made a little speech and presented him with a medallion inscribed: "Dad, all our love from here to eternity." For years, Tina recalled, her mother kept some of Frank's shirts in the closet, his monogrammed towels in the bathroom. She hoped, even now, that her husband would come home.

The day he hired Jacobs as his valet, Frank had taken him to meet the family. "Mr. S.," Jacobs recalled, "was like a little boy who had just gotten out of camp, coming home for a home-cooked dinner. Nancy, Big Nancy as she was called . . . was so maternal to Frank, she seemed like his mother rather than his wife, and I could see how the bull-in-a-china-shop boy in him could get tempted by the sirens of the movie business. There was nothing 'bad' about Big Nancy and, alas, that wasn't good. . . . The whole scene was sad."

Frank told Jacobs he would have left Nancy even if he had not met Ava. Years later, though, he told his elder daughter he wished he had stayed. He was torn, and his loneliness was painfully obvious. The night he won the Oscar, he was stopped by a policeman as he wandered, alone and clutching the golden statuette, in Beverly Hills. Earlier, Charlotte Austen, one of several friends who had been celebrating with him at his apartment, had watched him leave. "Frank walked up the path holding that Oscar and looking so alone that it almost broke my heart," she remembered. "Here it was the biggest night of his life, and the only woman he cared about was five thousand miles away in Spain with another man."

AFTER AVA, TINA thought, Frank "would keep a part of himself safe and shut off. As he once told me, 'I will never hurt like that again.' "

During the Gardner saga, Frank had issued what the press dubbed "Sinatra's Law," an edict that his private life was off-limits. Journalists who asked about it, he blustered, would be "through, dead, period." It was a resolve he was to defend to the end of his days, sometimes with his fists. In spite of that, his love life was hardly a secret. To George Jacobs, his boss seemed "the Casanova of modern times." "I got to know all of Mr. S.'s ladies, stars and non-stars," he wrote in his memoir. "I'd pick them up, drive them home, pay them if they were pros, make the candlelit seduction dinner and buy the flowers and chocolates for them if they weren't, then listen to their laments when Mr. S. let them down, which was inevitable."

Frank led some women to believe—and perhaps on occasion believed himself—that he was looking for lasting, fulfilling love. Abundance of opportunity, however, was rarely rewarded by happiness. The fallout for some of the women was disappointment and pain. Even so, an impressive number of them still spoke of him, decades later, with affection.

"It was nightmare time after Ava," said Norma Eberhardt, an actress who played in one of the Dracula movies. "We spent a lot of nights together in Palm Springs trying to chase those nightmares away." The first seduction Jacobs observed involved "a pretty starlet from the studios." The operation was carefully prepared, with roses supplied by Parisian Florist of Hollywood, prosciutto by Monaco's Italian deli, champagne and chocolate from Jurgensen's grocery, and an engraved notebook—the starlet had ambitions to write as well as act. There was also Dinah Shore, whom Frank had known since the 1930s, and with whom he quite often performed. Shore was married, to the actor George Montgomery, but Jacobs said she dallied with Frank over a long period.

In late 1954, Frank made a play for Grace Kelly. Though involved with another man, and in spite of the lasting friendship she had forged with Ava on **Mogambo,** she agreed to see him. Their date reportedly went badly, in part because he was already drunk when he picked her up, in part because he spent a good deal of the evening weeping about Ava. "He held no attraction for her," said Celeste Holm, who later worked with them both on the movie **High Society.** "Grace regarded Frank as a street kid. . . . She was on a different level. She was a princess long before she married Prince Rainier."

Ava, meanwhile, was compounding Frank's emotional confusion. During filming, colleagues noted, her baggage always included a pile of Sinatra records. She had flung a jeweled cross to a toreador in homage, only to beg for its return because it had been a gift from Frank. In the heat of her affair with Dominguín, she returned to the United States to get a divorce—then failed to follow through. The shrine to Ava stayed in place in Frank's apartment, and he kept a photograph of her on the dressing room mirror when filming in Hollywood. He was swinging in the emotional wind.

GEORGE JACOBS thought Frank "craved class" in women. Socially, no one could have been classier than the heiress Gloria Vanderbilt. Thirty-one when she and Frank got together in late 1954, she had come into a fortune—some $27 million in today's dollars—and had for years been married to a man forty-two years her senior, the conductor

Leopold Stokowski. Before that marriage, she had had some chaotic adventures in Hollywood, including an engagement to the actor Van Heflin, an infatuation with Howard Hughes, and a miserable first marriage to a gold-digging agent, Pat De Cicco. She had dabbled in painting, writing poetry, and acting.

When Frank got word to Vanderbilt that he wanted to meet her, she recalled in 1988 in a journal-style memoir, she wanted to tell herself "Stop!"—but didn't. She remembered how years earlier, when they had met after one of her husband's concerts, Frank kept glancing at her. At the time, in the first flush of the marriage to Stokowski, Vanderbilt had barely given it a thought. Now, the idea of being with Sinatra put her in a fever of excitement.

"It was what I had been waiting for," she wrote. "I'm seeing him again tonight. . . . I feel high, like I'm taking deep drafts of some kind of rare oxygen. . . . I am strong because a person of power loves me. . . . In three weeks when he is gone, by then it won't matter, won't matter if I never see him again. He is the bridge, the bridge to set me free."

Vanderbilt stepped out with Frank within days. Then she moved out of the sumptuous home she shared with Stokowski, taking their two small sons with her. After Christmas, having told the press her marriage was over, she arrived for a Broadway premiere on Frank's arm. Interviewed late the same night at the Copacabana, where Frank was opening, she said there was "no romance" between them.

The journalist St. Clair Pugh, who saw them together at Vanderbilt's apartment, thought at once that this was untrue. Vanderbilt's close friend Carol Matthau knew it was not true. Pugh thought the song "It Was a Very Good Year," which Frank was to make famous, included a conscious reference to the fling the poor man's son from Hoboken had enjoyed with a princess of the American aristocracy:

> It was a very good year for blue-blooded girls
> Of independent means. . . .

Vanderbilt would recall midnight suppers with Frank "during which he talked about himself, confiding the split in his mind, like a balance scale, on one side Mafia-dark, on the other side Clark Kent–light, dark and light, up and down, a pull drawing him to the dark." Clark Kent always triumphed in the end, she thought.

She wrote in her journal, "I cannot imagine a long tomorrow with F. and me in it." The doubt was well founded, for their affair lasted only a few weeks. So too did the notion, months later, that the millionairess would star in a movie with Frank. By one account, she had by then been driven to distraction by Frank's obsession with Ava.

The night Frank and Vanderbilt were at the Copacabana, Anita Ekberg, a former Miss Sweden, had been seated nearby. Frank had had a dalliance with the twenty-three-year-old in California, and had flown her to New York. In revenge for a recent slight, though, she turned up at the Copacabana with another man.

Early in January, Jill Corey, a dark-haired nineteen-year-old at the Copacabana with a boyfriend, realized Frank was giving her the eye from the stage. "I noticed," she recalled, "that he was singing love songs kind of in my direction. I remember that my cheeks felt hot. I didn't know why he was doing it, and I kept looking over my shoulder to see if there was a pretty woman sitting behind me."

Corey, who had started life as Norma Jean Speranza, was a coal-miner's daughter from an Italian-American family in Pennsylvania, a friendly girl who had sung contralto in the church choir. Now, with a recording contract and a name change, she had been catapulted into a new and glitzy world. She appeared on television and was featured on the cover of **Life** as a "Small-Town Girl" made good. Then, soon after having been ogled by Frank at the Copacabana, Corey was amazed to get a call from him.

It had been hard to track her down, Frank said. Would she join him at the Copa after his show the following night? In an interview nearly fifty years later, Corey quietly half-sang, half-talked the song she wrote about that first date:

Tonight I've a date with Sinatra,
Oh God, I'm experiencing angst!
In my virginal state, should he kiss me I'd
faint,
And do I call him Frankie or Frank?

. . . On a drive through the park with his
chauffeur,
Dinner, and wine, and a dance.
In the back he holds my hand, sings in my
ear,
It's the beginning of romance . . .

Thus began an intermittent five-year liaison that would last until she met her future husband. There were dates in California, heady encounters with celebrities, and gestures of affection—telegrams, flowers, a teddy bear—when Frank was traveling.

He took pains to hide his affairs from his growing children, not always successfully. The month of the affair with Gloria Vanderbilt, and just days after first romancing Corey, his fourteen-year-old daughter Nancy made an unsettling discovery when he took her along on a tour of Australia—a pair of women's stockings in his hotel bedroom. It upset her a lot.

As Frank ran through woman after woman, the one who ruled his heart remained a chimera. Ava, who for a while had spoken of him coldly as "Sinatra," now spoke of him again as "my old man," even as "the greatest of the great." Her affair with Dominguín had cooled, and for the moment there was no more talk of divorcing Frank. Whenever the two of them got together, though, according to Jacobs, it was clear nothing had changed. "They'd be fighting a lot. He'd come tearing out of the room and she'd come out screaming and cursing." Ava, meanwhile, was talking of moving permanently to Spain.

ACCORDING TO GEORGE JACOBS, Frank would browse movie magazines looking for pictures of young women to "do." Jimmy Van Heusen, who helped recruit them, also knew how to procure the best prostitutes. After a long conversation with a regular girlfriend, Jacobs said, Frank would often hang up the phone and sigh, "Get me a goddamn hooker." Several Los Angeles area prostitutes gossiped about him with a well-known showgirl of the day, Liz Renay. They would giggle about how well endowed Frank was, she said, and say he was a good client.

Renay herself fondly recalled an entirely innocent encounter. One night, when she and her teenage daughter were stranded without transport, Frank told them they could stay with him in his suite. "We had been drinking," she remembered. "Frank said, 'I'm not interested in hanky-panky. Why don't we just lie down like three tin soldiers? We won't even undress.'

"I was afraid he was just saying that, that he'd try to put the make on my daughter. But he just turned away from her towards me, and went to sleep. He joked in the morning, 'Don't tell anybody I slept between two beautiful women and all I did was sleep. . . . It'll ruin my reputation.' "

In the fall of 1955 Frank sought comfort with an old lover. "Sinatra was half in the bag one night," Rosemary Clooney recalled, "and he whispered to me, 'Isn't it interesting that nobody knows about me and Dietrich?' " His return to Marlene Dietrich's diary confirms the liaison. In the same year, at fifty-four, that extraordinary woman was passionately involved with Yul Brynner and "keeping happy"—her euphemism—Adlai Stevenson, the broadcaster Ed Murrow, the playwright William Saroyan, and a long-standing lover whose identity remains unknown.

Dietrich and Frank met again in early September, according to the diary, at a Hollywood dinner party. Frank took her out two days later, followed up with phone calls, then flew with her to Las Vegas. "F drunk but nice," reads the entry for September 9. "To bed at 9 A.M." She stayed on with Frank in Nevada, defying telephoned pleas from Brynner, in Los Angeles, to join him there.

The affair with Frank, Dietrich's daughter Maria Riva thought, was "her private placebo against the loneliness of yearning for Yul." Things soon soured, though. On September 11 Frank was "asleep in chair at 9:30 A.M. . . . Got up without kiss. Bad day . . . did not behave as usual . . . went to his room. He said 'Go to bed'—I was thunderstruck. Left."

Two weeks later, when they met at a party, Dietrich realized Frank was hopelessly drunk, "like a stranger." Then Brynner told her he knew what had been going on with Frank, and said she could do as she pleased. She got together with Frank again soon after, when both were working on **Around the World in 80 Days.** And again the following year, during another upset with Brynner:

December 1st
. . . Home with Frank. Finally, some love.

December 2nd
F called at 9:30 P.M.
Finally some sweetness.
Slept well and long.

In two diary entries referring to nights with Frank, Dietrich wrote of him as having been "sweet and tender." She told her daughter he was "the only really tender man I have ever known. He lets you sleep, he is so grateful—in a nice way, all cozy."

Other women had memories of Frank behaving callously. "He showers a girl with gifts, attention, compliments," said Jacqueline Park, a former Miss Ceylon he dated. "Then all of a sudden he doesn't phone and drops out of her life. . . . He's easily bored." In Vegas with Jill Corey, at a time she thought marriage was in the cards, Frank abruptly abandoned her to go off gambling.

Anita Ekberg had gone home fuming, after a similar experience, only to have Frank come banging on the door at 3:00 A.M. "Open up!" she recalled him yelling. "A woman who goes to dinner with Frank Sinatra must go home with him, even if she has to wait all night." Ekberg did not let him in.

Zsa Zsa Gabor was thirty-eight in 1955, not long divorced—for the third time—and best known professionally for a decorative appearance in the movie **Moulin Rouge.** After a first date with Frank, according to Gabor, he pushed his way into her house and said he wouldn't leave until she had sex with him. When she refused, he claimed he had a terrible headache and said he needed to lie down. Gabor had her maid show him to a guest bedroom and locked herself into her own. Frank then came knocking on her door, to no avail, before retreating to the guest room again. At first light, afraid that her eight-year-old daughter would see Frank, or his Cadillac parked in the driveway, Gabor went to the guest room to ask her unwanted guest to leave. "My begging took nearly an hour," she recalled, "but Frank Sinatra wouldn't leave unless I made love to him. So I did. I made love to Sinatra so that he would leave and from then on I hated him. And Frank knew it."

Other women had bad experiences with Frank. Sandra Giles, a glamour girl trying to break into movies, was in her twenties in 1958. Like Jill Corey, she had recently been the subject of a three-page story in **Life.** One night, while eating with a boyfriend at an Italian restaurant—a place that had phones for communication between tables, a fad at the time in fashionable nightspots—she was amazed to receive a call from a very familiar voice. "This is Frank Sinatra," he told her. "I'd like you to come over to our table and have a drink."

Giles demurred, explaining that she was with a date. Frank persisted, urging her to join him later at a party. When she again declined, he said he might be able to get her work. She agreed to meet him at a television studio, and they began seeing each other. At first she thought Frank merely "nice and sweet . . . not overly romantic." Then came a night after a Grammy Awards ceremony at which he failed to win an award, then proceeded to get drunk. Giles was drinking too and, along with others, wound up going back to his place.

"I sat down on the couch," she recalled, "and someone handed me a Drambuie. I think I'd had four already, and I had just one sip. When I woke up I was in bed—and nude. Frank was in bed with me, and he was nude too. I was shocked. He said, 'Come on, you know we've done it already'—he meant had sex—and I said 'We have? No we haven't.' We talked back and forth, and I got out of bed and went to the bathroom and locked the door. He said, 'What are you doing?' and I said I was calling the police. He said, 'Sandra, come back out. I won't try anything anymore.' . . . He had his chauffeur take me home."

Giles was sure Frank had not had sex with her that night. Pretending that he had, she believed, had been a cynical ploy to have his way with her. She later found a $100 bill stuffed in her purse—a significant sum in those days—and Frank admitted he had put it there. "He said, 'Yeah, that's something for your daughter for a Christmas present.' It was his way of apologizing. He never actually said he was sorry."

Another would-be actress, Shirley Van Dyke, had first become involved with Frank in the mid-1940s, when she was a roller-skating star and he the idol of the bobbysoxers. "She was one of his girls, sexual whatever," said her former husband, Stan Levey, a drummer who worked with Frank, "and he would get her work. If he was doing a picture he would get her work as an extra. There was a bartering system—bartering sex for work."

Van Dyke's son Bob, then a little boy, remembers his mother taking him to a showing of Frank's movie **The Man with the Golden Arm,** which premiered in 1955. "He met us in the aisle and sat us down," he recalled. "He was very nice. My mother had some strong feelings for him, that's for sure. Frank could be generous, but he could also be very hard, from what I understand. I think when Frank called the shots, it was over. She went through a lot of pain about it, never quite got over him."

In early spring of 1957 Van Dyke was taken to the hospital after taking an overdose of sleeping pills. Notes found in her apartment mentioned Tony Curtis, Jerry Lewis—and Frank. "Frank Sinatra, you've done me wrong," read one of them, "you're so big and I'm so small." She recovered, then told the press she had been "sick and tired of being in love with him. . . . I don't know how I ever got so entangled." Frank acknowledged only that he had helped Van Dyke get parts in movies.

A FEW MONTHS LATER, in London, another actress, Eva Bartok, gave birth to a baby girl she named Deana. Bartok, then twenty-eight, was an up-and-coming star who had made films with Burt Lancaster and Dean Martin. The space on the birth certificate for "Father" had been left blank, but twenty years later she told the show business writer Peter Evans that the father was Frank Sinatra. Fearing a lawsuit—Frank was known to be litigious—the newspaper that ran Evans's story hinted at that without making a direct allegation.

In her taped interview with Evans, Bartok told how she met Frank at a Hollywood party at the home of producer Charles Feldman. Rex Harrison, David Niven, and Judy Garland had been there too, but Frank stopped her in her tracks. "Sinatra had meant nothing to me," she told Evans, "but it was like: 'There he is!'—a kind of instant something happening . . . we found ourselves talking as if we had known each other for a very long time. Before I left somehow telephone numbers got exchanged and he asked me to give him a call a little bit later because he was going home."

When she got back to her place, Bartok wondered what in the world she was doing, but phoned Frank anyway. "He said, 'I'm all alone and I can't sleep.' I could easily have thought, 'What an old line!,' but somehow I didn't." Soon, she remembered, "There we were alone in this very nice house at the top of a hill. We sat in front of a fire and talked about books—I remember being surprised by the kind of books I saw on his shelves, more serious than I would have expected. . . . We talked and talked. . . . I remember being surprised when it was suddenly dawn. And he got up and said, 'Well, let's go to bed!'

"There had been none of the usual maneuvering and boudoir strategies. My reaction was astounding. It seemed the most natural thing in the world, the only thing he could really say. It was that simple."

They stayed in touch for a few months. Bartok dined with Frank at Italian restaurants, sat in on recording sessions, spent time with him at home, then returned to Europe. When she learned she was pregnant, she said, she was "1,000 percent" sure that Frank was the father, but did not tell him. "I knew or thought I knew," she said, "that it probably wouldn't have worked out."

A year after the birth she saw Frank when both appeared at a London charity benefit. "He embraced me," she recalled, "and said, 'How are you, angel?' I remember looking at him and seeing those eyes looking back at me, the same eyes I had just left back home in the cot. A woman walked up and asked if I had a picture of the baby. Of course I had. This was the moment. But as I looked down to find the picture in my handbag somebody took Frank away to introduce him to someone else. He would never see his daughter."

In 1973, long after she had told her daughter

who her father was, Bartok managed to reach Frank on the phone. Deana, listening in on another extension, remembered him saying, " 'Hi, Eva! How are you?,' casual and friendly. Mother said, 'I need to talk to you about something.' She didn't want to discuss anything so intimate over the phone. Frank promised, 'I'll call and we'll meet and talk.' "

He did not call. Four years later, when her daughter was almost nineteen, Bartok sent him a letter:

> Dear Frank,
>
> This is a difficult letter to write, so please bear with me. . . . This is about my daughter Deana. I have sometimes wondered during the past eighteen years whether you ever suspected that she is also your daughter. . . . Deana has known this truth since she was three years old. Rightly or wrongly, I have always dissuaded her from contacting you. But now she is virtually a woman, with a mind of her own, and her emotional needs are too strong to be denied any longer. Very simply, she needs that you should know and understand. . . . After all this time, Frank, I don't have to tell you that we have no material needs from you whatsoever. I can only tell you that it is an emotional crisis in her life and quite honestly I can no longer deny

her. . . . I cannot let her continue to be hurt in this way. . . . It would have been so much better to have been able to discuss it with you in person, but you are not the easiest man to meet up with.

Love,
Eva

P.S.: I'm enclosing a recent picture of Deana. She really is very beautiful.

Frank responded through his attorney, but only to say he was "too busy with other family problems" either to acknowledge Bartok's daughter or meet with her. In the early 1990s, at age thirty-six and with children of her own, Deana sent Frank a letter. "My sense of loss at not ever having known you, except at a distance," she wrote, "is breaking my heart. Please respond." He did not.

"NOBODY LOVED FRANK better than Frank," said Jeanne Carmen, who went with him intermittently over a lengthy period starting in the mid-1950s. George Jacobs has described Carmen as an "on-off bedmate" and, less politely, as "a stand-by girl." When she met Frank, she was in her early twenties, a Southern girl with Comanche Indian blood who had already worked as a model, a burlesque artist, a bit-part actress, and a trick-shot golfer. Her stunning looks—she had been **Esquire**'s Calendar Girl in 1952—were to keep her in the girlie magazines throughout the decade.

Carmen took the initiative with Frank by sending him a photograph of herself. The Hollywood furrier Abe Lipsey, whom she knew, then put them together at a Palm Springs dinner party. "We saw each other from then on," she said, "for about seven years." The early phase of the relationship was very soon after Frank's separation from Ava and, Carmen said, he became "Sad Frank" as soon as he was away from company. He would "walk around the house depressed. Sometimes, when he'd let guests out, he'd fall against the door and start crying. He really cried a lot back then. He'd be shaking, and telling me to hold him. He was like a little boy."

For all the excitement of being around Frank, of mixing with his celebrity friends and receiving expensive gifts, Carmen never became deeply involved. In the bedroom, she said, he was no great shakes. "He had the equipment but he didn't know what to do with it. We'd go to bed and he'd say 'Hold me, hold me. . . .' Today he has this reputation of having been a tough guy, but actually I had to mother him—he needed a mother figure. I was just a kid and he was about twenty years older, and I didn't want all that whining, didn't want to be mothering him."

One day, seemingly on sudden impulse, Frank

asked whether Carmen thought they should get married. As swiftly, he turned it into a joke, saying he hoped he could sleep with her friends once they were married. She was not amused, and he dropped the subject. He proposed several times again.

"Frank wanted to get married. That was his bag. He had to be married. I didn't want that. If I was away I kind of missed him. But I just couldn't spend a lot of time with Frank. I would make all kinds of excuses to get out of there before the weekend was up. He was romantic, but in a needy way. He was so needy."

Once Carmen answered the telephone and found herself talking with Ava Gardner. "She knew about me," Carmen recalled. "She said, 'Hi, Jeanne, are you taking care of my Frankie?' I said, 'Apparently not as well as you did, Ava, because he's whining and crying all the time.' She let out such a laugh. . . . She said I was a sort of pale imitation of her."

"There was a 'Frank woman,' " Brad Dexter said. "The 'Frank woman' was Ava, who personified to him the perfect woman—figure, face, everything. It was the image he sought all the time in women. He kept looking for her all the time."

He may have thought, for a while, that he had found her.

20

Peggy

PEGGY CONNELLY was a dark-haired Southern beauty in her early twenties, a band singer starting to break into the business, when she met Frank in early 1955. He was thirty-nine. Her mother, like Ava's, had allowed her to head west only on condition that an older sister watch over her. She was living at the Hollywood Studio Club for Girls, which had rules designed to protect young ladies from predators.

Peggy had no special interest in Frank Sinatra until a close girlfriend who did came up with a madcap scheme. Her idol was in town, she said, and spending a lot of time at one of the in places, the Villa Capri. She wanted to go there in case Frank might show up and notice her, and asked Peggy to tag along. The restaurant was almost empty when they got there, and Peggy was embarrassed.

"I didn't want to be there," she recalled. "I was naive, from the South, had freckles. She was from California, a stunning girl. But Frank was there as she had hoped! We had hardly sat down when suddenly his friend Jimmy Van Heusen came leering over to our booth and said, 'Look, could Mr. Sinatra and I come over for coffee when you've finished your dinner?'

"They came over. I just smiled a lot, but my friend came on too strong. It drove Frank mad. And after ten minutes he stood up and he said to **me**—not to my friend—'Miss Connelly, would you like to have dinner with me next Thursday?' He liked to be formal. And I said yes, and Jimmy took my phone number. And so it began."

Peggy was entering a strange and exotic world and beginning a testing emotional experience, a three-year affair that would bring two Sinatra marriage proposals and a confrontation with Ava Gardner. She would see him singing in his prime, making his mark as an actor once and for all, and—now that he was on top again—exercising Sinatran power.

Between early 1955 and the fall of 1957 Peggy would go with Frank to the studio and hear him record in the period that made him a legend, the years of "You Make Me Feel So Young," "Mind If I Make Love to You?," "It Happened in Monterey," and "I've Got You Under My Skin." "I can still hear him biting off the words," she said in 2003, "his perfect diction and rhythm. I wasn't a connoisseur then. I was too young, and I didn't have the experience. But his technique and timbre, his sense of swing, plus the taste and the intelligence to put it all together—that rates legendary."

Peggy was there when Frank, convinced that Capitol executives were not really listening to his work, decided to prove his point by playing a trick on them. "He had Nelson Riddle write a romantic arrangement for a Jimmy Van Heusen song—'There's a Flaw in My Flue'—that was intended as comedy, pure spoof, with lines like 'Smoke gets in my nose.' Then he recorded it straight, in an absolutely serious way." Capitol approved the album containing the song without demur. Had Frank not then brought the ludicrous song to the attention of the studio, it would have reached the stores as a track on the album **Close to You.**

Frank was in demand again as an actor after his success in **From Here To Eternity.** He took Peggy along for the filming of **Guys and Dolls,** the poor imitation of the hit musical in which he co-starred with Marlon Brando. A year or so earlier, according to his valet, he had "half destroyed" his own living room because Brando had been preferred over him to play the lead in **On the Waterfront.** That the movie was filmed in Hoboken had been salt in the wound.

During the filming of **Guys and Dolls,** the two

men carried on a childish war. They refused to say "Good morning" to each other, and Frank deprecated Brando as "the most overrated actor in the world," called him "Mumbles," and disparaged his Method Acting techniques. He would come out of his dressing room, he told director Joseph Mankiewicz, only "when Mumbles is through rehearsing." He once walked off the set in a rage.

A couple of months later, again with Peggy close by, Frank behaved better and performed better as the smooth-talking bachelor in **The Tender Trap.** His recording of the title song made the charts. Peggy was around, too, when, cast as the sort of gossip column journalist he so abhorred, he made **High Society** with Bing Crosby and Grace Kelly. In contrast to the super-relaxed Crosby, known on the set as "Nembutal" after the much used sleeping pill of the day, the restless Frank was dubbed "Dexedrine."

"I have to **go,**" Frank once complained to the movie director Vincente Minnelli. "No one seems to be able to help with it—doctors, no one. I have to **move.**" Frank "was always on his way somewhere else in his mind," Peggy thought, "even while he was looking you in the eye. Someone once said he had no 'now.' He was never satisfied to be where he was. That's why I used to love it when we would go down to Palm Springs alone, when there were no others around."

It had been a while before Peggy would agree to go away with Frank. "I had had one boyfriend back home," she said, "and that was the extent of my carnal knowledge. He knew that. He had the Italian Madonna/whore complex, so I was the Madonna. I remember the first time he made a real attempt to carry me upstairs at his apartment. I fought my way out and said, 'Take me home,' and he said glumly, 'Get your coat.'

"He had a Cadillac convertible, and it started raining, and he pushed the button for the roof to go up and it wouldn't. I told my girlfriend that it had rained on the famous Frank Sinatra hat! All because I wouldn't stay with him. . . . But we went out now and then after that, and in the end I thought I had said no long enough. I went to bed with him only when everything was clear in advance. He was really delicate about it, and he took me to Palm Springs and we were totally alone."

In bed, Peggy said, Frank was "energetic and interested, but it was more about himself. Being that way doesn't make a man the perfect lover." They had become a couple however, so far as she was concerned, and she remained faithful as long as the affair lasted. She chose not to ask if Frank was too.

"When we'd be apart for two or three weeks at a time," Peggy said, "I figured I didn't want to know. I thought he needed freedom. I've wondered, though, if he found a way to keep an eye on me. When I went off singing somewhere, the phone would mysteriously ring—always at sort of three in the morning. He'd found out where I was, and I'd hear this deep voice on the phone, 'Baby, how're you doing?' . . .

"An older woman friend of mine had told me right away, when I first met him: 'He's played games with the best. Don't ever try to play games with him, because you don't know how. If it doesn't work by you being yourself, it wouldn't have worked anyway.' And that's the way I played it. . . . I did my very best, and always looked for the best in him."

Peggy was rubbing shoulders with Ella Fitzgerald, Judy Garland, Cole Porter, Edward G. Robinson, Joe DiMaggio. "Being with him was like being with a fairy godfather, like having Daddy Warbucks on your side. He gave me a mink stole when we'd hardly known each other a couple of months. He had asked me to say whether I wanted a mink or a car, and I said, 'Neither, you don't have to buy me anything.'

"But he came to pick me up one evening, and got in the front seat of his car and he put his hand over the back and opened a box and put a mink stole over my shoulders. I remember putting it on and saying, 'No, no, no!' But it was the most delicious thing I'd ever touched. . . .

"Life went along like a dream. Wherever I went

when he wasn't with me, he smoothed my way. Things appeared as if by magic. People took care of me. I never handled money, never signed hotel registers. I didn't stop at the concierge's desk, even in places like the Waldorf Towers. No bills were ever presented—to me. I ate in his friends' restaurants in New York as their honored guest, and I brought as many friends with me as I chose. When I told him Edith Piaf was in town and I wouldn't be able to see her, he got me smuggled in to see her rehearse."

Early on, Frank asked Peggy to live with him. She had her own apartment by then, and was not prepared to give it up. The many days and nights she did spend with her lover, though, left her with unique, intimate memories.

Frank was "lucky with his skin. He had that kind of skin that only needed a little while in the sun to turn a lovely golden tan. But not your hirsute Italian—I don't recall any chest hair, perhaps almost none. He was lean of course, then, and he had unusual hands, rounded and padded, strong-looking, not like the rest of him." Peggy, unlike others, never saw Frank use makeup to hide the scars he had been left with after his difficult birth. He had back pain, and rarely exercised. When he did it was to swim lengths in his pool, "to help his lung capacity, although he was smoking—a lot."

She had noticed, that first weekend at Palm Springs—at the new home he had built outside the city—that everything Frank possessed was "the cleanest, the best, fresh-smelling. The sheets, the towels, the whole house, smelled good. Everything around him was immaculate, in perfect order, his home, his dressing room and his bedroom, his closets, his drawers.

"There were two perfumes he used. Yardley's English Lavender for his drawers, shirts, and things. And Jungle Gardenia, which had been Ava Gardner's fragrance. He kept her perfume in his bathroom, and you could smell it on his things."

Out of the public eye, Peggy noted, Frank wore "beautiful cashmere sweaters in orange and olive gradations. He favored peach, and he had beautiful gold sweaters and cotton shirts. I remember the accent on the color orange in the house and in the furnishings."

As early as 1945 a reporter had noticed that Frank had orange lawn furniture. By the 1950s he favored orange shirts, sweaters, blazers, and handkerchiefs, though not orange ties. He would eventually have an apartment at the Waldorf with orange decor, an airplane that sported orange inside and out, and an orange phone. "He hated orange on women," though, said George Jacobs. "Orange was for him and him alone."

Frank never talked about his music or sang at home, in Peggy's experience. When guests came he mostly played classical music. During Peggy's time with him he was enthusing especially about the Italian soprano Renata Tebaldi, who had recently made her American debut in **Aida.**

Peggy said Frank seemed "embarrassed about his lack of formal education. He wasn't a fool. He was very intelligent, intuitive. But when he wrote on a typewriter he used no punctuation and no capitals. Rather than make mistakes, I think, he just wouldn't punctuate at all.

"He read. He always had these big books, whatever was out at the time. Even when we hadn't been together that long, we'd sit in bed with pillows behind us. He would read one of his books, or his script for the next day's shooting. I remember reading **Zen in the Art of Archery.** Sinatra the great lover lying in bed with his studious girlfriend reading Zen books. Even then it struck me as amusing."

In their private moments, Frank was a man of few words. "He wasn't a gabber. He wasn't cold, but reserved, self-contained. He stored things up. He wasn't shy, but he was extremely inhibited. I could never get him to dance with me—except once, when we were alone at a club and I got him to dance half a song. I remember, too, a time on a plane going down to Palm Springs when the plane lurched and he spilled coffee all over himself. He said, 'I'll just clean this off,' and got up and went to the bathroom. And didn't come out again until the plane landed.

"I never saw him careless or vague, dreamy. And

he never exposed his feelings, not ever. He wasn't an openly emotive person. It was important to him to be in command of himself. . . .

"I discovered what you can do if you have enough money and power. Once, when he was smoking and drinking too much, and he had a recording session the next day, I kept saying, 'Don't have that cigarette, don't take that drink,' but of course he did. Then, when we got to Hollywood, he couldn't sing. He tried a couple of songs, and couldn't make it. You know what those sessions involve, and the cost of it all, when musicians and studios are booked. But he just rescheduled it, and did it later when he felt like it."

Frank talked with Peggy about heavy drinking he had done years earlier. He told her that "when he was younger, but already a star, he and a bunch of his friends, the guys around New York and New Jersey, used to take a hotel room for a weekend and just drink and drink and drink. He said, 'I woke up one morning and found myself wrapped around a mailbox in the street. My doctor told me it was time I straightened up and took care of myself, or I wouldn't make it. I wouldn't last.' "

In the mid-1950s, Frank's alcohol use worried his girlfriend. "He amazed me early on, in Palm Springs. The times that he drank it would be late and in private, alone or with close friends. He'd have only Jimmy Van Heusen or one or two of his intimate Italian friends there. They knew how to handle him. I used to look at the bottles in the kitchen in the morning. It never was the stumbling around sort of thing—he just got quieter and quieter. I saw a willful man who wanted instant gratification, and when he didn't have it he got bored. I'd just keep out of the way."

Frank sometimes exploded with rage, though not often in front of Peggy. "If he got angry," she said, "it went from zero to ten. There wasn't much in between. I was with him once in Italy, and the paparazzi had spoiled everything. You can't imagine what it's like. You can't go shopping, go out to eat, do anything. At the Rome airport, when we were leaving, he finally had had enough. We were seated on the plane, seatbelts fastened, and the buzzards were outside the door still. Suddenly he excused himself and got up and disappeared out the door. He came back only slightly ruffled, and sat down again. I only discovered later that he had punched out one of them."

Frank could not bear to be touched. When an elderly politician placed a friendly hand on his shoulder in 1956, according to a story in **Look** magazine, he was rebuffed with a growl of: "Take the hand off the suit, creep." Frank denied the claim.

"In bars or nightclubs where he was singing," Peggy recalled, "people would get pally, say 'Have a drink' or something, and touch him on the shoulder. He would freeze, look down at that hand on his arm and stare, and not move until the hand was taken off. . . . If someone displeased him, he would indicate it with a facial expression, or just say: 'I'm gonna buy back my introduction,' or refer to people as 'rat bastards.' He used that a lot. It could be used seriously or jokingly."

There was nothing funny about what occurred one night in Palm Springs. "We'd been out in town for dinner, and Jimmy Van Heusen picked up two girls and brought them back to the house. I preceded them into the living room and almost immediately there was a ruckus behind me. One of the girls had 'encroached' on Frank and, according to Jimmy, Frank had made a characteristic movement—as if to repel her—with his arm. And somehow she fell and hit her head. I didn't see it myself. And she was cut and bleeding profusely. An ambulance was called and she was gone.

"Frank went and closed himself up in his bedroom, and wouldn't come out. He was so ashamed and sorry. Finally I went in and he was sitting in the dark on the edge of the bed with his head bent, really abject. He called himself a 'monster.' 'Mommy' had to say, 'No, no, no! You're not a monster. . . .' But that was small comfort to him."

Peggy was also at Frank's side in early 1956, when he suffered a sharp professional disappointment. In the late summer and fall of the previous year he had given his all—a phrase that could not accurately be applied to many of his fifty-six movies—to the making of **The Man with the Golden Arm.** He had enthused about playing the protagonist, Frankie Machine, from the moment he read the novel. Winner of the very first National Book Award, Nelson Algren's **The Man with the Golden Arm** was the story of a card dealer struggling to overcome drug addiction and build a new life—a little man fighting back, a character Frank could understand.

He had lobbied for the part, won it over Brando, and worked assiduously to get it right. He consulted with medical specialists, sat behind a peephole to watch a real-life addict going through heroin withdrawal. He cooperated with the director, Otto Preminger, usually behaved well on the set, and turned in a remarkable, moving performance. The result was a box office hit.

If ever Frank had earned an Academy Award, the film critic Daniel O'Brien wrote in 1998, it had been for **The Man with the Golden Arm.** He received a nomination for Best Actor, and in April 1956 attended the Oscar ceremony with high hopes of winning. Instead, Ernest Borgnine won, for his performance in **Marty.** Peggy Connelly, who was with Frank that evening, recalled how distressed he was. "I had wanted to go on to the parties they held afterwards," Peggy recalled, "but we walked out, got in the car, and went home. He went into his bedroom, didn't turn the light on, just sat down on the bed. I finally decided to go in.

"I kneeled down on the floor and put my arms around him. It's embarrassing now to remember what I said to him, 'It's terrible. Ernie Borgnine is fat and ugly. He needs it for his career, but you're Frank Sinatra and you don't need it.' But he had wanted that Oscar like he wanted his last breath, and I was trying not to let him sink. . . . In a few minutes, he got up and walked out."

"Being an 18-karat manic-depressive," Frank would tell an interviewer just a few years later, "and having lived a life of violent emotional contradictions, I have an over-acute capacity for sadness as well as emotion." Also, evidently, a capacity for swift recovery. "The next day, the next week," Peggy noted, "the matter of not having got the award for **The Man with the Golden Arm** was not brought up anymore. He never missed a step. He had plenty to do."

Connelly, who has lived in France for many years, saw parallels between the characters of Frank and the actor Alain Delon. "The charm of both of them," she concluded, "was all wrapped up in the mythology of what the French call the **caïd.** It's an old Arab word, used in France to describe a man who is powerfully attractive but outside the law. Such a man is flamboyant, commanding, cocky, swaggering, big with the ladies—like a Mafia figure. He dominates people. Delon played the **caïd**, Frank lived the part."

Peggy closed her mind to Frank's Mafia connection while she was with him. "I used to get so angry at people who'd say, 'You knew him well. He was Mafia, wasn't he?' I used to say, 'Well, I saw him on the set and in recording sessions, and I never saw him with a machine gun in his hands.' Funny. But they looked, and I never did." Later, she admitted to herself that the Mafia factor had been there all the time. There was the story he told her about having attended a high-level Mafia meeting. There was the night in New York when he introduced her to a mysterious group of men, and warned her not to ask for their names. There were the weekend guests about whom he seemed highly sensitive.

Years before she knew Frank, as a teenager, Peggy had seen a movie called **The Enforcer** and been scared. "I was so frightened," she recalled, "by the idea that you can be walking down the street and shot by someone who doesn't even know you. I remember thinking, 'Please God, protect me from ever coming near to anything like that.' Yet, while I was with Frank, I found myself in it.

"We'd be going to Palm Springs and Frank would say, 'There's gonna be somebody there this weekend. I hate it, but there's nothing I can do about it.' It would be Joe Fischetti. He never went out to dinner with us, as I recall. He was just there. He would be there overnight, and then he'd be gone. . . .

"Frank's bedroom had a little bathroom that I never used because it had saloon doors—doors, you know, that don't come right down to the floor. The adjoining room was the guest bathroom—off the guest bedroom. One weekend, in the middle of the night, I got up to go to the guest bathroom. And as I stepped through, Joe Fischetti stepped out. Both of us stark naked. . . . I'd walked through the door nude, in front of a mafioso. . . . I shrieked and backed out the door, and so did he."

Frank, Peggy thought, was going through "a period when he didn't want to be associated with those people, didn't want to talk about it, was trying to climb up socially. . . . But he used to say he had to play host to various people. . . . He always winced painfully and said, 'I've got to do this. I can't get out of it.' "

At the same time, she realized, "Frank was fascinated by them. You just don't throw that off. . . . You do it, and you grit your teeth."

MORE THAN A YEAR into his relationship with Peggy, Frank remained so close-mouthed on personal matters that she assumed his father was dead. As for his mother, she said, he was "avoiding her like the plague. . . . I remember asking him why he had a valet and not a housekeeper, and he said, 'I don't want another dame around. It took me long enough to get rid of my mother.' " Frank never spoke of Nancy around Peggy, and rarely of his children, though he once brought his twelve-year-old son to Thanksgiving dinner.

Nor did he share his thoughts about Ava Gardner, who by early 1956 had left the United States and set up house in Spain. As fate would have it, however, Spain was the couple's destination when, within days of the Oscar ceremony, they flew out of Los Angeles. Frank was there for location work on **The Pride and the Passion**, a movie epic based on a C. S. Forester novel about the struggle between Spanish peasant fighters and the French in the nineteenth century. He played the Spanish guerrilla leader, co-starring with Cary Grant and Sophia Loren, and insisted on doing all the things usually left to a double, clambering up mountains, running through explosions and fires. He put in a good performance, but his contrariness surpassed even his own bad reputation.

He refused the location accommodations and insisted on driving three hours each night to a suite at the Castellano Hilton in Madrid. He complained about poor communications and about the length of the shooting schedule. "Sixteen weeks!" he complained to the director, Stanley Kramer. "I can't stay in one place sixteen weeks. I'll kill myself."

"Tension," Kramer said of Frank, "walks in beside him." He would be in his dressing room in a "black, angry mood," sitting for half an hour with his head bowed, pulling on his lower lip. He was preoccupied about his thinning hair, which was compensated for in the movie by an improbable hairpiece. When phoned by a crew member he would sometimes pretend to be someone else, just to put off going to the set. Once, frustrated by the time a night shoot was taking, he said he would urinate on Kramer if they were not finished by 11:30. Peggy, meanwhile, noticed that Frank was drinking far too much Spanish Fundador brandy. Being so close to Ava was hard for him to bear.

Ava had looked forward to his arrival in Madrid. She had earlier arranged a special viewing of **The Man with the Golden Arm** for herself and followed through with a congratulatory telegram. She was roaring around in a new sports car, a present from Frank, and playing his records constantly. When he arrived, she played the brokenhearted wife.

"We and our crowd used to go to one restaurant every night," Peggy said. "Ava would come in too. If she were there when we arrived, she would get up and rush out. Sometimes in tears. Or we would be there first, and she would come in, and zip out when she spied us. . . . A friend of mine had told me, 'Take care. Ava can get physical, she's capable of throwing a bottle.' But it was always she who would run out crying, and I knew there would be some kind of denouement. I'm not a fool, and I knew Frank would see her if he got the chance."

The denouement came when Peggy returned to the suite at the Hilton after a brief trip out of the country. "His timing was bad. The first thing I saw was the unmade bed and the mess in the bedroom, and knew something had been going on. Then I caught a glimpse of Ava through the living room door. But I went in anyway to pick up my mail. She was sitting on the couch, curled up and reading the newspaper and wearing Frank's bathrobe.

"I had no doubt at all that Ava had spent the night there. I said something like, 'This is an uncomfortable situation, isn't it?' She didn't reply, just looked daggers, and I picked up my mail and left. I went to the location to see Frank for lunch. He couldn't have been cooler. A kiss, then he asked me, 'How were things at the hotel?,' a completely inane remark unless there was something wrong at the hotel. I said, just as cool, 'Crowded.' And he said, 'Oh, was she still there?' There was no drama. From the way he spoke Ava could have been any girl he'd left at the hotel, a prostitute even."

Yet Frank could not wait to get out of Spain. In

late July, weeks before his scenes were completed and over the director's protests, he flew back to the States. As he landed in New York, Ava announced that their long-awaited divorce was nearing completion. She hinted that she might marry her latest suitor, Italian comedian Walter Chiari.

Frank was reported to have reacted "like a wild man" to the stories about Chiari, to have cringed "like a whipped dog" when Ava spoke ill of him in an interview. She took to calling him "Mr. Sinada," a play on his name and the Spanish word for "nothing."

Frank compensated with extravagant gestures of affection for others. He gave Peggy a white Thunderbird—the same model he had recently helped Ellie Graham, an occasional lover who had recently aborted his baby, to purchase. At Lipsey's in Beverly Hills just before Christmas, he bought Peggy a mink coat, another for Nancy, and a third for his secretary. He also proposed to Peggy.

"It was kind of: 'Don't you think we ought to get married?' " Peggy remembered. "My ego kept me from saying 'Oh darling, yes,' because I knew vaguely about his shadowy goings-on with other women. I thought, 'I'm going to need something more serious than this before I accept.' "

The affair with Peggy would last for much of 1957. Frank even proposed again, but she again declined. The encounter with Ava aside, she could no longer ignore the whispers about other women, about Frank's use of whores; she knew she could never live with that. She wanted to pursue her singing career, moreover, and he did not want her to work. One weekend at Palm Springs, Peggy fabricated an excuse to leave. She never went back, and soon afterward married Dick Martin, who was then an up-and-coming comedian.

In May of that year Frank recorded a new, drawn-out version of "I'm a Fool to Want You," on an LP entitled **Where Are You?** Ava was in Mexico, working on her new movie, **The Sun Also Rises,** and behaving badly. She saw a number of men and drank heavily. She corralled a group of itinerant musicians, took them to her hotel, then phoned Frank in Hollywood so that he could hear their plaintive Spanish love songs. The writer Peter Viertel, whom she begged to sleep at her side one night, thought her in the grip of "almost panicky loneliness."

Then, before leaving Mexico, she at last sued Frank for divorce—on the grounds of desertion. The decree was issued in early July, a milestone **Newsweek** summarized as follows:

> **Divorced:** Film actress AVA GARDNER, 34, from singer and actor FRANK SINATRA, 39, after nearly four years of separation.

Frank was in fact almost forty-two. He and his PR people had long been putting it about that he was a year or two younger than he was.

Frank was increasingly lonely. "My father," Tina Sinatra would say years later, "was a deeply feeling man who could not attain a meaningful intimate relationship."

EARLY IN 1956, Peggy remembered, Frank had become involved in a musical project based on verses by Norman Sickel, a little-known poet. Sickel had written a series of twelve interconnected poems, each dedicated to a color. Frank commissioned a group of composers to produce music to suit the poems' mood, and he conducted the resulting orchestration himself. He called the album **Tone Poems of Color,** and it was issued with the poems printed on the cover.

Gilbert Gigliotti, a professor of English who teaches a course on Sinatra at Central Connecticut State University and has written a book on the singer, devoted an entire chapter to the poems and the album. The verses that so interested Frank, he wrote, "haunt the reader with their darkness . . . depict a tortured universe in which greed, haughtiness, violence and intrigue overpower laughter, love and innocence." For Gigliotti, **Tone Poems** reflects a Sinatra who, having once been primarily the idol of female fans, now spoke increasingly to disillusioned American men. The poems, he thought, convey a sense of a man left "bloodied and alone" by love, a man more interested now in controlling women than in romancing them.

Frank once said he favored the color orange above all others because it was "happiest." The orange of the poems, however, is more about cynicism than happiness:

> Orange is the gay
> deceiver
> and I do deceive
> but nicely. . . .
> My shade is correct
> and stylish,
> but never will it pierce
> my skin
> to affect my soul . . .

As arranged by Frank, the sequence of colors started positively enough with "bridal veil white" and green, an evocation of fulfilling love. As the poems moved across the palette, though, melancholy predominated. Blue, near the end, was for "the dreamer" who had "made a friend of sadness." Red, the final color, was "violent," consuming, going faster and faster "not knowing where I go or why."

Frank did seem to be in an emotional void.

When a woman fell for him, or became special, he tended to dump her. For years to come there was to be more whoring than loving. With the exception of a few old cronies, he now placed less trust in friendship. During his brief professional collapse, he said, he "lost a great deal of faith in human nature. . . . A lot of my so-called friends disappeared." They had been "like my shadow, only there when the sun shines."

An occasional refuge was the home of Nancy and the three children, who lived in Holmby Hills. As often as not, when he visited, Frank would wind up fast asleep on the couch. From time to time, Tina has hinted, Nancy even allowed him into her bed. As for the children, Frank tried to make up for long absences with lavish presents; one Christmas, when she was only fifteen, daughter Nancy found a gift-wrapped Chevrolet convertible sitting in the driveway.

Even the children, however, saw the other side of their father. "One night," said Doug Prestine, a neighbor's son friendly with thirteen-year-old Frank Jr., "the two of us were watching television in the library of the Sinatra house when Big Frank crashed through the gate in his Eldorado Cadillac. . . . He was real drunk and wearing a white dinner jacket that was torn and dirty. . . . He slurred his words and said, 'What are you two doing?' . . . I'd never seen a grown-up drunk before but Frankie wasn't surprised at all.

"He very matter-of-factly went outside, got his dad out of the car, and carried him into the house, where we tried to wash him up and poured some coffee down him. Then Big Frank passed out on the couch, and we went back to watching TV. Frankie acted like it happened all the time."

Bing Crosby, in Las Vegas to see Frank during a break in shooting **High Society**, was told that he was on the verge of collapse, caused by "no sleep or rest, and a great deal of sauce." At a Friars Club dinner for comedian Jack Benny, Frank downed most of a bottle of whiskey.

Liquor fueled his rage against people he considered enemies. After years of gushing about Frank, Dorothy Kilgallen offended him in 1956 with a series of caustic articles that led off by calling him a "Jekyll and Hyde dressed in sharpie clothes." Frank raged about her at first in private, among friends. One of them, Armand Deutsch, recalled him hurling darts at a board that featured "ghastly likenesses" of three female columnists, Kilgallen, Louella Parsons, and Hedda Hopper. He later resorted to abusing Kilgallen in public, and would still be inveighing against her on stage in Las Vegas, while obviously drunk, long after she was dead.

Frank emerged from a Sunset Strip club one night in the mid-1950s, glass in hand, and got into a brawl with a waiting journalist, Bill Byron. Each accused the other of starting it, but Maxwell

House heir Bob Neal, who was present, said later that Frank "pushed the journalist into a phone booth, then closed the booth." When he emerged, Byron said, Frank "swung at me and kicked me in the shins."

When Bill Davidson of **Look** magazine reported this and other follies, Frank sued the publisher. Davidson's widow said that later, during an encounter at a hotel, "Bill was sitting in the restaurant and Sinatra was a table or so away with his henchmen. . . . They got up and the guys came over and tried to work him over." Davidson, a former athlete, gave as good as he got.

The bully-boy bluster aside, Frank's loneliness in the late 1950s showed as much in his work as in his private life. He recorded the album **Only the Lonely**, a collection of haunting ballads—saloon songs, he called them—about sadness and loss. It was so melancholic, Frank Jr. once said, that it "should be available in drugstores by prescription only."

Frank's favorite track on the album was "Angel Eyes." "Angel" had been his nickname for Ava, when things were going well between them. In the 1970s, he would close his "retirement" concert with the song:

> . . . have fun, you happy people
> The drink and the laugh's on me.

Not long before the divorce from Ava and the breakup with Peggy Connelly, Frank had moved into a new house high up in Coldwater Canyon, in Beverly Hills. It was deliberately isolated, at the end of a long driveway closed off by an electronically controlled gate. A sign at the entrance read: "If You Haven't Been Invited You Better Have a Damn Good Reason for Ringing the Bell!"

Many nights, those living further down the mountain heard classical music coming from the house, played hour after hour. The lights often burned all night and sometimes neighbors could see the silhouette of a solitary figure far above them hunched over a telescope, staring at the stars.

At other times, Frank gathered glittering company around him. "I drove here this morning to stay with Frankie," the English playwright Noël Coward wrote in his diary after spending New Year's at the Palm Springs house. "People of all shapes and sizes swirling through this very small house like the relentless waves of the sea. . . . Bogie pushed Irving Lazar into the pool and Irving Lazar pushed Bogie into the pool. . . . The prevailing chaos is dominated by Frankie who contrives, apparently without effort, to be cheerful and unflagging. . . . His is a remarkable personality—tough, vulnerable and somehow touching."

As Humphrey Bogart and Lauren Bacall left that night, Frank asked them to stay. He looked "forlorn," Bacall thought and told her husband they should have stayed. "No," said Bogart. "It's too bad if he's lonely, but that's his choice. . . . He chose to live the way he's living—alone."

21

Betty

FRANK HAD KNOWN THE BOGARTS since just after the war, when they had appeared on radio together. He had sailed on Bogart's yacht, gone drinking with him and Henry Fonda. Lauren Bacall remembered that from 1954, when Frank was at a low ebb after separating from Ava, he "practically lived at our house . . . five or six days a week."

Bogart, Brad Dexter thought, was "the one guy Frank hero-worshipped"—like no other man at any point in his life. Bacall—"Betty" to intimates—thought he seemed "in awe of Bogie." On the surface there were similarities between the two men. Both had reached the pinnacle of stardom at about the same time. Both had won Oscars—Bogart for Best Actor in **The African Queen.** Both were little men with receding hair—Bogart wore toupees too—yet legions of women found them attractive. Both had tough guy images, and both were drinkers. Both had opposed the House Un-American Activities Committee and were perceived as liberals.

In reality they were very different. Bogart, the son of a prominent New York surgeon, had a privileged childhood. He had been sent to a private school in the expectation that he would go on to an Ivy League college, and had served briefly in the Navy at the end of World War I. He was fifty-four to Frank's thirty-eight when their friendship began.

Bogart had been happily married to Bacall for nine years. Like Sinatra he often got into angry confrontations, but avoided actual fighting. He had moderated his drinking. Though not a paragon of marital fidelity, he was not a casual womanizer. His self-control where women were concerned, Bacall thought, puzzled and fascinated Frank. "He just didn't understand how a man could be not only talented but so intelligent, and also have a family and not fuck around. He just didn't understand how anyone could do that, because all **he** did was fuck around."

Bogart was exceptionally well read, articulate on a vast range of subjects, and Frank saw him as a mentor. He rued his own lack of education more with each passing year, and often asked Bogart what books he should read. "I think we're parent substitutes for him or something," Bogart once told the writer Richard Gehman. He saw Frank as not being "adult emotionally," as a man who should "stay away from broads" and concentrate on acting. Nevertheless, Bacall said, he liked Frank and "enjoyed his 'fighting windmills.' "

Being around the Bogarts brought Frank good cheer in a time of personal gloom. The couple's home on Mapleton Drive in Holmby Hills was described by a friend as "a kind of endless open house." When the light over the front door was on, friends knew, they were welcome to come in for drinks.

Frank had become part of a coterie that included Judy Garland, John Huston, David Niven, "Prince" Mike Romanoff of Romanoff's restaurant, the screenwriter Nunnally Johnson, and Swifty Lazar. Other friends included Spencer Tracy and Katharine Hepburn, the young Richard Burton, and Adlai Stevenson. A party at the Bogarts', Rosemary Clooney recalled, was "a whirl of music and laughter."

There were also exotic weekends afloat, for Bogart was an avid sailor. "We dropped anchor in Cherry Cove," Niven wrote of one such trip, "and Frank Sinatra moored alongside us in a chartered motor cruiser with several beautiful girls and a small piano. After dinner, with Jimmy

Van Heusen accompanying him, Sinatra began to sing. He sang all night . . . his monumental talent and exquisite phrasing undimmed by a bottle of Jack Daniel's on top of the piano. . . . He sang till the moon and the stars paled in the predawn sky."

Burton, who was also there, remembered it differently. "Frankie did sing all through the night," he noted in his diary after reading the Niven account, "but Bogie and I went out lobster-potting and Frankie got really pissed off with Bogie . . . nobody could stop Francis from going on and on. . . . Bogie and Frank nearly came to blows next day about the singing the night before, and I drove Betty home because she was so angry about Bogie's cracks about Frank's singing. . . . Bogie was unnecessarily cruel."

Bogart could only take so much of Frank's extravagant style, exemplified in June 1955 when he flew friends to celebrate Noël Coward's debut in Las Vegas. Frank splurged on "four days and nights of concentrated self-indulgence," Niven remembered, "individual apartments for everyone . . . food and drink twenty-four hours a day . . . a big bag of silver dollars presented to each girl in the party to gamble with." The entire party had then been flown to Frank's home in Palm Springs for the weekend.

That degree of flamboyance soon palled on Bogart. As much as anyone, though, he enjoyed the razzmatazz of the rambunctious little group they formed.

THE ORIGINAL RAT PACK was born of a night of drinking at Romanoff's, according to Joe Hyams, a journalist who knew most of those involved. The in crowd, he learned, had decided to form "an organization with a platform of iconoclasm . . . against everything and everyone, including themselves." Hyams interviewed Bogart, then wrote a story that appeared in the **New York Herald Tribune** on December 15, 1955:

"The Holmby Hills Rat Pack held its first annual meeting last night at Romanoff's restaurant in Beverly Hills and elected officers for the coming year. Named to executive positions were: Frank Sinatra, pack master; Judy Garland, first vice-president; Lauren Bacall, den mother . . . Humphrey Bogart, rat-in-charge-of public relations; Irving Lazar, recording secretary and treasurer."

The founding members, readers were told, had approved a coat of arms designed by Rat Pack historian Nathaniel Benchley, Bogart's friend and the son of Robert Benchley, a renowned wit and a member of the Algonquin Round Table. It featured a rat gnawing on a human hand, and the legend "Never rat on a rat." Members would soon be sporting lapel pins in the shape of rat's heads, with rubies for eyes. The organization, Bogart told Hyams, had no function other than "the relief of boredom and the perpetuation of independence. We admire ourselves and don't care for anyone else."

According to Niven, the group got its name when Bacall told the hungover survivors of the recent bacchanal in Las Vegas that they looked like "a goddamned rat pack." Sands Hotel executive Jack Entratter then sent each member of the party a white rat—gift-wrapped. According to Hyams, it was in Beverly Hills, at Romanoff's, that Bacall had welcomed her friends—"adults who acted much of the time like overprivileged delinquents"—with the crack, "I see the rat pack is all here." Bogart said the name derived from the name he used for the English racing cars he and his pals owned, the Beverly Hills Rat Traps.

"Rats," Bogart told another reporter, "are for staying up late and drinking lots of booze. We're against squares and being bored and for lots of fun." Members had to be "against the PTA," his wife quipped, "stay up late and drink and laugh a lot and not care what anybody said about you or thought about you."

Louella Parsons was not amused. She knew, she wrote in her column, "that you and your good pals meet only for social events or gay weekend expeditions to Sinatra's house in Palm Springs. . . . It would all be very funny if it weren't for the fact that so many teenagers take everything done by movie stars with dead seriousness." "People have worked for years to lend dignity to our profession," said William Holden. "It might sound stuffy and dull, but it is quite possible for people to have social intercourse without resorting to a rat pack."

Hollywood had seen similar cliques before. John Barrymore, and after him Errol Flynn, had presided over their own circles of dedicated drinkers. His little group, Bogart insisted, was only a joke. Two months after his Rat Pack announcement, though, the laughter faded. During a weekend at Frank's home in Palm Springs, friends learned that Bogart had cancer of the throat.

Frank was a constant support as his friend's health declined. When in California, he visited Bogart at home almost every day. In the summer of 1956, when he was in Spain making **The Pride and the Passion,** he phoned or sent telegrams. "He cheered Bogie up when he was with him," Bacall remembered, "kept the ring-a-ding act in high gear. . . ." As Bogart wasted away, he cracked jokes about his lean friend Frank. "I've slimmed down so much," the sick man told the writer Charles Hamblett, "it's got Sinatra worried. He was here yesterday afternoon, and he got quite jealous of my waistline."

In January 1957, in his last hours of full consciousness, Bogart watched Frank's 1945 movie **Anchors Aweigh** on television. When he died, thirty-six hours later, Frank was in New York playing the Copacabana. He canceled performances and locked himself in his room, avoiding calls from everyone except Bacall. Then, after telling her he planned to fly back for the funeral, he asked Peggy Connelly to attend in his place.

Frank did not sound especially emotional when he called about the funeral. "He **never** exposed his feelings," Peggy said.

THE MARRIAGE OF "BOGIE AND BACALL" is usually depicted as the show business romance of their day, Bogart's death as its tragic last act. Yet all was not perfect.

Bogart's hairdresser and personal assistant, Verita Thompson, said years later that she had a long, sporadic affair with him that continued until 1954, nine years into the marriage to Bacall. The director Nicholas Ray, who knew Bogart well and directed two of his movies, claimed Bacall was no paragon of fidelity either.

Bacall had found fame in 1944 after playing opposite Bogart in **To Have and Have Not.** She had been nineteen then, twenty-five years younger than the man she was soon to marry. By the 1950s, she acknowledged in her memoirs, she was occasionally tempted to stray. She had an "infatuation" for Adlai Stevenson, whom she first got to know during the 1952 presidential campaign. "His flirtatiousness encouraged me," she wrote, and she saw him when she could. The following year she had been "very attracted" to the composer Leonard Bernstein. "If Lenny and I had been on the loose," she said, "God knows what madness would have taken over."

By her account, no madness ever did take over. "I never dared. . . . I knew that Bogie—however much he loved me—would put up with flirtation, but if I ever really did anything he would leave me."

Peggy Connelly suspected that Frank and Bacall began an affair before Bogart died. "Frank loved Bogart," she said, "but his woman was . . . just something else." "It was no secret to any of us," the playwright Ketti Frings said. "Everybody knew about Betty and Frank. We just hoped Bogie wouldn't find out. That would have been more killing than the cancer." Bogart did not know about his wife's "real relationship" with Frank, Verita Thompson said. The actor William Campbell, however, thought Bogart had been uneasy on that score. "That's the way I picked it up. . . . Because there was some relationship there, more on her part than his. And I think Bogart was aware of it."

Bogart was still worrying about it only months before he died. When Frank arranged a birthday party for Bacall in Las Vegas, in September 1956, her husband stayed away. He was "edgy and resentful" when she got home, and she soon found out why. "He was somewhat jealous of Frank," Bacall remembered, ". . . partly because he thought Frank was in love with me, partly because our physical life together, which had always ranked high, had less than flourished with his illness."

By contrast, she said, Frank "represented physical health. . . ." He was "wildly attractive, electrifying . . . there must have always been a special feeling alive between Frank and me."

In the weeks after Bogart's death, the special feeling intensified. By spring 1957 Frank and Bacall were going out together. On July 5, the day Frank's divorce from Ava became final, he and Bacall were cruising off the coast of California aboard a rented yacht. "After that weekend," she said, "the relationship just grew." Frank was "very attentive, very caring, very lovely, and sweet with the kids."

Yet, looking back, Bacall could see that things had never been quite right even then. Frank had become inexplicably "remote—polite but remote," before the boat trip. The cruise had been off, then suddenly on again. During the trip, she remembered wearily, Frank "got drunk and got into a fight with a waiter . . . he always did."

In September, nevertheless, she sold the home

on Mapleton Drive she had shared with Bogart, because she felt "Frank would feel better if I moved." She rented another house, having first had her clivia plants dug up and transferred to Frank's garden because "they were his favorite color, orange."

At Christmas, just months after his most recent proposal to Peggy Connelly, Frank asked Bacall to marry him. How she responded is not clear, but two days into the new year he got drunk and behaved "like a maniac." "He's really acting peculiarly," Bacall told Jack Entratter, a fellow guest at Palm Springs. "I think I should get out of here." For more than a month the couple had no contact at all.

In March, in Los Angeles, Frank came to see her. He seemed contrite, and proposed again. "I said, 'Oh, well—what changed?' " Bacall remembered, but, "he was very convincing . . . all my barriers fell . . . I said, 'Okay.' "

When they ate at a Japanese restaurant that evening, a fellow diner came over to ask for autographs. Frank urged her: "Put down your new name," and she scribbled "Betty Sinatra" on a napkin. By the time he left a few days later, to sing at the Fontainebleau in Miami Beach, Bacall felt blissfully happy. "The children would have a father, I would have a husband, we'd have a home again."

Just days later, on March 12, newspapers trumpeted: "Sinatra to Wed Lauren Bacall." " 'Oh, Frankie!' Sighs Lauren . . . He Popped the Question over Sukiyaki." "Nuptials Maybe, in Oscar Time."

The story had been leaked either by the agent Swifty Lazar, with whom the couple had shared their news from the start, or by Bacall herself. According to one journalist, she said Frank had proposed and that she intended to marry him. Another quoted her as having said, "I don't know nothing. Call Miami."

The reporters did call Miami, and an interview with a press spokesman led to a very different headline: "Sinatra Won't Say if He'll Marry Bacall." When a reporter got to Frank to ask if the marriage was on, he got a brutal reply. "What for? Just so I'd have to come home earlier every night? Nuts!"

Bacall had phoned Frank as soon as the story broke, and he had not seemed angry. Then, a few days later, Frank called accusing her of having leaked the proposal to the press. Then he simply cut off all contact. A month later, when the two of them dined at the home of mutual friends, he totally ignored her. He did the same when they bumped into each other after a concert in Palm Springs. "My humiliation was indescribable," Bacall remembered. Frank had behaved "like a complete shit." For years to come, they did not speak at all.

It occurred to her later that the marriage would have been doomed anyway. He would soon have been unfaithful, "because that's what he did. That's the Swingin' Guy." When she had been Bogart's wife, by contrast, she had been "married to a grown-up." She saw Frank as having been "incredibly juvenile and insecure." Had she married Frank, Bacall told the director Peter Bogdanovich in 2002, she "couldn't have lived with that fucking mercurial personality."

Swifty Lazar, who was close to both Sinatra and Bacall, thought Frank "a cross between the most generous man on earth and an absolute shit heel."

22

Leader of the Pack

As Frank Sinatra stood again at the pinnacle of popular music, rock 'n' roll was exploding around him. In June 1956, **Time** magazine had noted a seismic upheaval: "An electric guitar turned up so loud that its sound shatters and splits . . . a vocal group that shudders and exercises violently to the beat while roughly chanting either a near-nonsense phrase or a moronic lyric in hillbilly idiom."

The children of Sinatra's bobbysoxers, themselves teenagers, cared little what **Time** thought. They now bought almost half the records sold in the United States and had their own idols. The first rock 'n' roll hit, a song called "Sh-Boom" by a group called the Crew Cuts, had gone to number one as early as 1954. The following year, Bill Haley's "Rock Around the Clock" had made number one. In 1956 "Heartbreak Hotel,"

"Hound Dog," and "Don't Be Cruel," pumped out by a former truck driver named Elvis Presley, changed pop music history.

With his pouting lips and bucking hips, Presley in performance was to some lechery personified, so much so that for a while television would not show his gyrations below the waist. He was an affront to middle-class America, which was part of what brought him teenage adulation.

Ironically, Presley was introduced to the nation on television, during a CBS variety show, by Tommy Dorsey. Fifty by then, the man who had been instrumental in Frank's phenomenal rise looked worn and outdated beside twenty-one-year-old Presley. Dorsey died soon after, choking to death in his sleep after eating a huge dinner followed by sleeping pills. After a further TV appearance on Ed Sullivan's show, Presley records were reported to be bringing in $75,000 a day ($500,000 today).

As Presley triumphed, Frank watched, listened, and brooded. An era had died with Dorsey, as he put it in a letter, and he felt threatened. He "hated Elvis so much," George Jacobs recalled, "that he'd sit in the den by himself at the music console and listen to every new track over and over. . . . He was trying to figure out just what the hell this new stuff was, both artistically (though he'd never concede it was art) and culturally (though he'd never concede it was culture). Why was the public digging this stuff? What did it have? . . . These questions got the better of Mr. S."

In a 1957 magazine article Frank declared rock 'n' roll "the most brutal, ugly, degenerate, vicious form of expression it has been my displeasure to hear. . . . It fosters almost totally negative and destructive reactions in young people. It smells phony and false. It is sung, played and written for the most part by cretinous goons and by means of its almost imbecilic reiterations and sly, lewd—in plain fact dirty—lyrics."

Frank worried that the rock 'n' roll craze would ruin the market for his music. For a while, anxious about his income, he compromised and recorded some songs that rocked a little. It was doing what he did best, though, in new and spellbinding ways, that won him fabulous new success.

In 1957 and 1958 came the release of "All the Way," "I Couldn't Sleep a Wink Last Night," "Come Fly with Me," "Let's Get Away from It All," "It's Nice to Go Trav'ling," "Moonlight in Vermont," "Only the Lonely," "Angel Eyes," and "One for My Baby." The album **Only the Lonely** went to number one and stayed on the charts for two and a half years. **Only the Lonely** and **Come Fly with Me** were the two best-selling albums of 1958. Nineteen-fifty-nine saw the release of more songs of lasting resonance: "Come Dance with

Me," "Dancing in the Dark," "Cheek to Cheek," "Baubles, Bangles and Beads," "When No One Cares," "I Can't Get Started," and "A Cottage for Sale."

In those three years Frank recorded 124 songs, the majority of them for the first time, in thirty-seven recording sessions. He appeared on television more than forty times and performed in Texas, Utah, California, Washington state, Canada, London, Monaco, and Australia. He made eleven charity appearances. He starred in six movies, as a Spanish freedom fighter in **The Pride and the Passion,** nightclub comic in **The Joker Is Wild,** hustler and womanizer in **Pal Joey,** World War II soldier in **Kings Go Forth,** would-be writer in **Some Came Running,** and failed businessman in **A Hole in the Head.** All but one of the movies succeeded.

To the editor of **Metronome,** Frank was "the most fantastic symbol of American maleness yet discovered." To the **New York Post**'s Sidney Skolsky he was "the love voice of America." He was deemed cool—the word was "in" by now—but his private life was increasingly defined by unhappiness. There was a brief relationship with Lady Adelle Beatty, a sometime model from Oklahoma recently divorced from a British war hero. This was "a very important relationship," Shirley MacLaine recalled Frank telling her, "but he didn't know how to deal with her jealousy." With the exception of a relationship with Juliet Prowse that began during the shooting of **Can-Can**, Frank's sex life for years to come seems to have consisted of one-night stands and assignations with hookers.

In the emotional wings, as always, was Ava. Frank performed in 1959 in Australia, she said, only because she was working there at the time. "We wanted to talk," she recalled, "to look at each other, to be together." They had two nights together, then parted. A few months later, Ava remembered, Frank beseeched her to "Come home again." He sent her a gold key inscribed: "For when you want to come home." "I'd fall for it," Ava said. "I'd go back, and it would last twenty-four hours. Then I'd piss off again."

"One for My Baby," the lament of a drunk who has loved and lost and has no one to talk to but the barman, was rapidly becoming Frank's signature song.

> It's quarter to three, there's no one in the
>   place
> Except you and me.
> So set 'em up Joe, I got a little story
> I think you ought to know . . .
> . . . this torch that I found, it's gotta be
>   drowned
> Or it's gonna explode.

Make it one for my baby,
And one more for the road.

The song was especially meaningful for him, Frank was to say, because "I've experienced just that scene many times." He was fond of a story circulating at that time about a group of lonesome drinkers talking with each other as his "One for My Baby" played on the jukebox. "I wonder," one of them slurred, "who **he** listens to."

Frank's public profile continued to camouflage the private unhappiness. The annual **Down Beat** polls showed he had firmly reclaimed the position of Top Male Singer. Any concerns Frank had had about money were a thing of the past. A 1957 TV deal alone, sponsored by Chesterfield cigarettes and Bulova watches, was said to have guaranteed him $7 million ($46 million today) over three years. Movie deals brought still more. His gross income over the same three years, it was predicted, would amount to $4 million a year. The Hollywood correspondent of the **New York Times** figured Frank had become "the highest-paid performer in the history of show business." By early 1959 **Down Beat** would rate him "the hottest property in the business." Bing Crosby said he thought Frank would come to be seen as "the world's greatest entertainer."

As rock 'n' roll mounted its frontal assault on the old values, Frank had become a Pied Piper for "cool" grown-ups, bewitching millions. He was also creating a new Rat Pack, the one that would be remembered.

IN FEBRUARY 1957, just a month after Humphrey Bogart's death, Frank had performed in Los Angeles alongside a suave, seemingly imperturbable singer and comic named Dean Martin. They appeared together again three times that year. In January 1958 a diminutive black dancer named Sammy Davis Jr. was featured on Frank's TV show. Others now linked increasingly with Frank were Joey Bishop, a forty-year-old nightclub veteran with a dour humor, and Peter Lawford, thirty-four, an English actor who could dance a little. Soon, too, there would be Shirley MacLaine, just twenty-four, already a talented actress and dancer. These were the five members of Sinatra's pack.

Martin was a mystery even to those closest to him. As his second wife, Jeanne, said: "There is something in him that is unreachable." The Italian journalist Oriana Fallaci came away from an interview declaring Martin a walking "dilemma." Americans who thought him "simple, easy . . . a very fine person touched by a few glamorous faults," she wrote, were mistaken.

Eighteen months Frank's junior, Martin was the son of an Italian immigrant barber in Steubenville, Ohio. His real name was Dino Crocetti and he spoke nothing but Italian, a regional dialect at that, until he was five. Steubenville was a tough steel town, and Martin grew up rough-cut. He quit high school, and his early jobs included shining shoes and pumping gas. He did a little prizefighting, which left him with a somewhat battered face, then worked as a mill hand. Illegal gambling thrived in Steubenville—Las Vegas and Atlantic City would one day teem with dealers who had learned their trade there—and Martin dabbled in gambling even as a schoolboy. In 1936, at nineteen, he was dealing blackjack and working a craps table. "Your son's gonna be a gangster," he remembered relatives warning his parents. "He's gonna die in the electric chair."

Martin and the Mafia were no strangers to each other. As a teenager he helped run bootleg whiskey across the state border to Pennsylvania. As a dealer he met the local Mafia boss. His record remained clean, though, and his singing ability offered an escape route from Steubenville. He took voice lessons from the mayor's wife, listened to Bing Crosby at the movies, and began performing with a band. Nights, after finishing work as a dealer, he sang at a local bar.

He became Dino Martini, singing for a while at joints run by the mob, and eventually Dean Martin. When war came, his double hernia saved him from the draft. In 1944, at twenty-six, he was asked to fill in in New York for a singer who had canceled at the Riobamba—Frank Sinatra. Martin became "The Tall, Dark and Handsome Voice," was even compared to Frank, but the big time still eluded him. Then, at a nightspot called the Glass Hat, he met Jerry Lewis.

Lewis, billed at the time for his "Satirical Impressions in Pantomimicry," teamed up with Martin—described as "a mike-romanticist"—and for a decade they would be one of the most successful acts in show business history. Lewis, playing the lovable dope, was paired with Martin, the indulgent straight man who could sing. They performed across the nation, made funny movies, and commanded huge fees.

"I'm no singer," Martin told **Variety,** "but we crooners get by because we're fairly painless." His records "That's Amore" and "Memories Are Made of This" each sold more than a million copies in the 1950s. He took a risk by breaking with Lewis in 1956, but flourished. His first venture into serious acting, as a draft-dodging playboy in the war movie **The Young Lions,** was much praised. Martin thought movies were fun, not real work.

Frank had first met Martin in the late 1940s at the Copacabana. Both were Italians from humble beginnings, school dropouts who had made it. They had intersecting Mafia connections. Martin knew the Fischetti brothers, and he had performed with Lewis at the wedding of one of Willie

Moretti's daughters. Unlike Frank, Martin was careful not to flaunt these associations.

Both men had sown more than their share of wild oats, but Martin now exercised self-control. He rarely lost his temper. He had previously been a heavy drinker and would play the drunk on stage, but he had moderated his drinking. As the 1950s ended, his marriage was surviving. Unlike Frank, who came alive at night and slept late, Martin preferred to get to bed before midnight and rise early to play golf.

Though not part of the Bogart Rat Pack, Martin had been welcomed to Bogart's social circle and had become Frank's friend, too; he was "Uncle Dean" to Frank's children. It was not Martin's way, however, to permit real closeness.

"Theirs was an uneven relationship," his second wife, Jeanne, said. "Dean loved to play with Frank—I say 'play,' because they were like children—though later Dean would eventually grow up and stop playing. He had great admiration for Frank as a singer, but didn't respect him as a man."

FRANK'S RELATIONS with Sammy Davis Jr. seemed simple enough—a story of generosity rewarded by undying gratitude. "Those who entered Sinatra's private circle," wrote Wil Haygood, author of a recent Davis biography, "were either the dazzlingly talented or those whose ridiculous fawning he simply tolerated. Sammy was rare: he met both requirements."

Ten years Frank's junior, Davis was the son of a black from the South who had fled to New York fearing a racist attack, and then become lead dancer in a traveling vaudeville revue. Davis's mother, a chorus girl with Cuban blood, went back on the road soon after giving birth. His paternal grandmother in Harlem cared for him until he was three, and then his father took him on the road.

The child watched from the wings, mimicked the performers, even walked on stage and capered around. During the Depression, while still a child, he became part of a trio with his father and his partner, vaudevillian Will Mastin. At seven he won the title role in a movie about a black boy who dreamed of becoming president. By his midteens he was already a dancer, singer, and drummer. He did a stint in the army toward the end of World War II, then rejoined his father and Mastin on the stage. He specialized, now, in doing brilliant impersonations of the famous—Frank Sinatra included.

The two men had met before America entered the war. Later, when Davis greeted him outside a radio studio in Hollywood, Frank made sure he got tickets to the show. In 1947, when Frank was arranging an appearance at a New York theater, he asked that the trio join him on the bill. At his insistence, they were paid more than three times their usual pay.

As Davis said: "All the great things happened after that." Many months of struggle later, he began to be accepted at the Hollywood clubs that white stars patronized. Frank stayed in touch, sent supportive telegrams, continued to urge Davis to break down the race barrier. "Sammy might never have made it if it wasn't for him," said Marilyn Sinatra, a cousin whose father worked as a gofer for Frank on the West Coast. "Later, when he and Frank were together, they wouldn't let Sammy into some hotel. Frank said, 'If he doesn't come in, I don't,' and that was the end of that."

In 1954, after a car crash that nearly killed Davis and destroyed his left eye, Frank visited him at the hospital. He had Davis stay at his Palm Springs home to recuperate, took him to his parents' home in New Jersey for Christmas, found him a new place to live, and encouraged him to perform again. From then on, Peggy Connelly thought, Davis's feeling for Frank verged on idolatry.

Davis began imitating Sinatra off stage as well as on. When Frank started sporting white raincoats, so did Davis. He wore hats similar to Frank's, even affected Frank's gait, and took endless photographs of his hero. Frank, meanwhile, spoke publicly of Davis's "staggering talents," and emulated aspects of Davis's performing style—clipping notes, snapping his fingers.

There seemed no limit to Davis's devotion. Peggy King, a band singer who was for a while his girlfriend, witnessed one moment of camaraderie. "Frank just beat up a couple of hookers," Davis exclaimed one night after taking a phone call. "I have to go."

As a highly visible black man, Davis was forever attracting controversy. He did so when he began wearing a Star of David on a necklace and declared he was embracing Judaism. Like Frank he was hugely promiscuous, and attracted attention by constantly pursuing white women. This was a virtual obsession, and it put him in harm's way. Harry Cohn became apoplectic when, in 1957, Davis became involved with Columbia's rising star Kim Novak. The studio boss saw the potential scandal as a threat to the bottom line, and called in the mob to frighten Davis off. Davis's press agent, Jess Rand, recalled arriving at a hotel room in Chicago to find his client confronting a hoodlum with a gun. The gunman was threatening to put out Davis's remaining eye.

Then suddenly, as rumors of his trouble surfaced in the press, Davis astonished everyone by marrying Loray White, an obscure black singer with whom he was not involved at all. It was a phony union, and would be dissolved a year later.

Long afterward, Davis revealed that an unnamed "well-connected friend" had warned him in frightening detail that the Mafia threat was serious. The friend, he said, passed on the warning in a Las Vegas dressing room. He told too of contacts with a Chicago Mafia boss that ended, once it was known he was going to marry White, with the message: "Relax . . . the pressure's off."

The photographer Billy Woodfield, who knew Davis and traveled extensively with Frank, offered a firsthand insight. He recalled Davis arriving, highly agitated, at Frank's dressing room in Las Vegas. "Sammy said, 'Is Frank here?' and I said 'Not yet.' About that moment Frank walked in and took a look at him and said 'What's wrong?' Sammy said, 'I gotta talk to you,' and Frank gave me a little nod. I went and sat outside. There was some yelling and screaming and then Sammy came out and paced around. I heard Frank saying 'Get me Fischetti.' "

Frank spoke on the phone—almost certainly to Joe Fischetti—then talked with Davis again. Davis left looking "really distraught." On the train between Los Angeles and Las Vegas, Woodfield said, quoting Frank, Davis had been accosted by two gangsters. They had told him: "You're now a one-eyed nigger Jew. You ever see this blonde again, you're gonna be a blind nigger Jew. You're getting married this weekend—go figure out who you're marrying." Chicago, Frank told Woodfield, had returned a favor to Harry Cohn. Frank was being used as intermediary, to ensure Davis understood what he needed to do.

For all the talk of Davis's devotion and Frank's steadfast support, theirs was a fragile relationship. Two years earlier, when a scandal magazine hinted that Davis had dallied with Ava Gardner, Frank had been furious until Ava assured him that the story was baseless. Once, shown a photograph of himself seated beside another of Frank's women, Cindy Bitterman, Davis tore the print in half to obliterate Bitterman's face. He was afraid of what Frank might do if he saw the photograph.

"Talent," Davis would say in a 1959 radio interview, "is not an excuse for bad manners. I love Frank but there are many things he does that there is no excuse for. I don't care if you are the most talented person in the world. It does not give you the right to step on people and treat them rotten. This is what he does occasionally. . . . I think it's inexcusable."

Frank retaliated by severing relations with Davis and ensuring that he was dropped from a forthcoming movie. Months later, after Davis apologized publicly during a charity performance, he and Frank embraced in front of the audience in a display that Dean Martin thought "disgusting." Davis was restored to the status of "Charley," the

Sinatra set's catch-all name for a pal, and remained close to Frank for years to come.

PETER LAWFORD, "Charley the Seal" to Frank until they fell out, once described himself as "a halfway decent-looking English boy who looked nice in a drawing-room standing by a piano." He had been born in 1928 into London "society," and brought to the United States as a teenager. His father, a retired British lieutenant general, had been knighted for heroism in World War I. His mother, the daughter of landed gentry, was an unhappy woman who considered the birth of her son "an awful accident."

If she had to have a child, Lady Lawford said, she would have preferred a daughter. Like Frank's mother, she dressed her son in girl's clothing in infancy, and continued to do so until he was eleven. He was educated by governesses, one of whom sexually abused him at the age of ten. Early on, he announced to his parents that he did not want to follow in his father's footsteps and go to military college. He wanted to become an actor, a notion his mother encouraged.

In England, where he appeared in a movie at the age of eight, a newspaper declared Lawford "Britain's Jackie Coogan." When his mother took him to Hollywood, in his early teens, his English accent and good looks landed him a role alongside

Mickey Rooney. Then after several difficult years—his parents' finances collapsed—came a bit part as a young English flier in **Mrs. Miniver,** the hit movie about London in the Blitz. Another war movie appearance won him a contract at MGM.

Lawford, now described as a "well-hewn god . . . six-foot . . . devilish blue eyes," spent as much time as he could at the beach. He socialized with the stars, including some of the women in Sinatra's constellation—Marilyn Maxwell, Lana Turner, with whom he had an affair, and even Ava Gardner.

Lawford first met Frank at an MGM party in 1944, when he was twenty-one and Frank and Nancy had just moved to Hollywood. He went to parties at their home, good-humoredly took part in skits that played up his lack of money compared to the wealth of other guests.

Two years later, when cast with Frank in **It Happened in Brooklyn**—Lawford played an English aristocrat—he spoke in an interview of Sinatra's "singular temper." The anger could last for a long time, as he soon discovered. In 1954, after Frank's breakup with Ava, the press reported that she and Lawford had met for a "date." It had been no more than a get-together with friends, according to the actor and his manager, who was present, but Frank would have none of it.

"I was in bed at three in the morning," Lawford recalled, "and the telephone rings. Then comes a voice at the other end of the telephone. . . . 'What's this about you and Ava? Listen, creep. You wanna stay healthy? I'll have your legs broken, you bum. If I hear anything more about this, with Ava, you've had it.' "

Three years passed before Frank spoke with or saw Lawford or appeared in public with him. Then in 1957, sometime after Lawford had married Patricia Kennedy, a sister of Senator John F. Kennedy, they met at a dinner party and resumed the relationship as though there had never been a rift. Frank and Lawford would soon be doing a song-and-dance routine on Dinah Shore's TV show, then go on to appear together in movies, and even become partners in the restaurant business. They caroused together on trips to England, Monaco, and Italy. When they were drunk together in a hotel suite in Rome, Frank did something uncharacteristic. "He looked up," Lawford remembered, "and said: 'Charley, I'm . . . ah . . . sorry.' Frank was finally apologizing for that tantrum over the Ava business."

Lawford began enthusing about Frank to anyone who would listen. Like Sammy Davis Jr. before him, some thought, he even aped Frank's style and mannerisms. "This is such an **enormous** talent," he told a reporter. Frank had "some kind of magic that a lot of us wish we had. . . . I consider it a privilege to live in the same era Frank's in. I **do.** I think he's a giant; a fantastic human being."

THE IMPROBABLE BIRTHPLACE of the Sinatra Rat Pack was Madison, Indiana, population: 10,500, a "typical American town" according to the World War II Office of War Information. It had once been a boomtown, but the days of prosperity were long gone in August 1958, when Frank roared into town. He was there to make the movie **Some Came Running,** based on a new James Jones novel.

The movie tells the story of a whiskey-swilling army veteran and would-be writer, Frank's character, who returns to his hometown after a long absence. Dean Martin co-stars as another heavy drinker, a professional gambler. Shirley MacLaine plays a sweet but simple floozie who falls for the army veteran and dies tragically in the last reel. The misbegotten trio contrast sharply with the dull, decent people of the little town in which the story is set. So it was, in real life. Frank and his entourage brought to the people of Madison not only excitement and a welcome cascade of dollars, but also insulting, boorish behavior—most of it ascribed to Frank.

He mocked locals, believing no one who cared was listening: "Hiya, you ugly old bag. . . . Hello there, hillbilly. . . . Drop dead, ya fink." He imported "pleasure girls" and drank heavily. He ripped a telephone out of the wall because he thought the operator was listening in on his calls. He was said to have smashed a TV screen with a beer bottle. Worst of all, he physically assaulted John Byam, a sixty-seven-year-old hotel clerk, after someone in Frank's party complained about slow service. "Mr. Sinatra grabbed me by the shirt front and began shoving me around the room . . . yelling at me. . . . He finally let me go and I sat down at my desk and began crying." The clerk stayed away from work for several days.

MacLaine, for whom the movie was a marvelous break, had regular access to the house Frank and Martin rented during the shoot. "I was the mascot," she said. "I would clean up the house, make them cappuccinos, and answer the door . . . they wouldn't let any other woman in the house." She watched, fascinated, as the pair splashed on cologne, primped to go out in their fine suits, selected smart ties, and donned wide-brimmed hats right out of the racetrack number from **Guys and Dolls.** She looked on wide-eyed as they slipped $100 tips to bellboys.

Frank and Martin separately came knocking at MacLaine's hotel room door, but she felt they were just going through the motions. "Neither of them ever put the make on me. It was acknowledged that I was not going to do that, and if anyone else tried, he was toast. I was the 'little girl'/'mother,' and they did not cross those lines." Later, as she watched their involvements with women, she wondered whether either man saw women as "real beings with needs and intelligence. Did they ever communicate on a fulfilling level?"

Frank and Martin, MacLaine noticed, "could dislike people because of small things that personally offended them. They couldn't overcome their judgment of a person's teeth or smell. They'd make jokes under their breath . . . cast someone out of their lives because his jockstrap showed under his shorts."

She saw these grown men stuff crackers in each other's beds, throw spaghetti over a man's tuxedo, give an admirer an ice cube and tell him to skate on it. Though MacLaine came to like much about them, even eventually took a shine to Martin, she thought them "primitive children." Although Frank treated her well, she noticed how rude, cruel even, he could be to others. He seemed never to weigh the consequences of his actions, never to her knowledge admitted he was wrong, and "demanded total loyalty without deviation." He "had to live in a world he created in order to control it," MacLaine thought, "and his talent and street-smart shrewdness enabled him to get away with it."

Frank's behavior during the making of **Some Came Running** attracted national attention. "A

Life magazine reporter came down to interview us," MacLaine remembered. "We wouldn't talk to him—and because we were never apart he dubbed us The Clan."

For a while, that was the name that stuck. They were not yet the Rat Pack, but the **Life** story gave the group an identity in the public mind: "Non-conformity is now the key to social importance," Paul O'Neil wrote in the magazine. "That Angry Middle-aged Man, Frank Sinatra, is its prophet—and the reigning social monarch. . . . But only the clan (composed of those on whom Frank smiles) REALLY MATTERS. . . . Today there is no Frank but Frank. . . . As paramount chieftain and head witch doctor of the clan Frank personifies its non-conformist attitude: a public and aggressive indifference. . . . He is known, variously, among the faithful as The Pope, The General or The Dago."

Frank's close associates, O'Neil noted, were mostly forty or older. They lived or hoped to live in homes that cost $250,000, a sizable sum then. They bought seersucker jackets from a classy tailor who supplied, for $125, what New Yorkers could buy elsewhere for $29. Several of them drove Dual-Ghias, racy Italian automobiles powered by Dodge engines. They gave each other pricey gifts ranging from inscribed silverware to personalized bedroom slippers. Frank's secretary, readers were told, often summoned the Clan's "appointed ones" to his house on short notice.

There they would sing, play their own music to each other, view movies, and play poker.

Sammy Davis was the only member of the group quoted in **Life**, and some suspected he was the magazine's principal source. Later, he said the cult of personality, Frank's personality, had been paramount. "He was our leader," Davis recalled. "Nobody did it like Frank. Nobody dared."

The group's members eventually disowned the label Clan, not least because it sounded too much like Klan. They became instead the Rat Pack, once described by Davis as "just a group of clean, wholesome, ordinary guys who meet once a year to take over the world." To that end, they had their own lingo and their own jokey patter.

Pressed by the humorist Art Buchwald, Frank offered these definitions of Ratpackspeak:

gas: a good situation, as in "a gas of a week-end."

clyde: a catch-all for whatever you want it to mean. As in "Pass the clyde" when you want the salt, "I have to go to the clyde" when you mean "party," or "I don't like her clyde" when you mean "voice."

bunter: the opposite of a gasser . . . a nowhere.

cool: expression of admiration or approval.

crazy: similar to "cool."

Harvey: a square. A Harvey, or Harv, is the

> typical tourist who goes into a French restaurant and says, "What's ready?"

Many of the other words in the Rat Pack lexicon focused on sex: "bird"—for the genitals, male or female, but more often the former; "quim"—dated English slang for vagina, probably a Lawford contribution; "charlies"—when not applied to a pal, could do double duty and refer to a fine pair of breasts. "Mother," as in "motherfucker," was used often. "I'm not a prude," the singer Keely Smith once said, alluding to an affair she had with Frank during those years, "but that's one of the reasons I never married Frank, because of the language in that group. . . . I knew I couldn't raise my kids around that."

The way the Rat Pack performed in public in early 1960, though, endowed Frank and his gang, almost overnight, with the status of national icons.

THE SHOWS THEY STAGED that year at the Sands in Las Vegas were billed as "The Summit," a name casino boss Jack Entratter took from the press shorthand for the meeting of American, Soviet, British, and French leaders planned for the spring. Entratter had sent off a series of spoof telegrams of which one, signed "Khrushchev" and addressed to the Sinatra group, read: "You come to my summit meeting and I'll come to yours."

In just four weeks, some 34,000 people came to the Sands to see the Rat Pack's shows. People offered $100 for tickets priced at $3. The Pack, Robert Legare wrote in **Playboy**, embodied "a wild iconoclasm that millions envy secretly or even unconsciously—which makes them, in the public eye, the innest in-group in the world." More recently, having watched an old kinescope of the Sinatra group at work, the journalist James Wolcott described the Rat Pack as "the Mount Rushmore of men having fun."

The pack's show consisted of singing and dancing—mostly Davis's—and slapstick humor. In one running joke, the man in the spotlight would be interrupted by one of those waiting in the wings. "Hey, where the hell's the toilet back here?" Dean Martin would say off stage. "I gotta go real bad." Soon, on stage, Joey Bishop would ask, "Dean, close the bathroom door." Two Rat Pack members would march into view, in their undershorts but wearing tuxedo shirts and jackets and with their pants over their arms. Thousands of people found this funny.

Being drunk, and making cracks about being drunk, was supposed to be hilarious. "Here they are, folks," Joey Bishop would say as Martin entered with Frank, "Haig and Vague." "Breakfast," Martin mumbled, as Frank rolled on stage a portable bar laden with booze. Martin, playing the drunk as always, would feign swilling Scotch from an ice bucket and exhort the audience to "buy a copy of my new book, 'The Power of Positive Drinking.' "

Davis was to call Martin "the only cold-sober lush in show business," and say he rarely consumed real alcohol on stage. However, Ed Walters, a Sands pit boss, said, "They were all really drinking on stage, except Joey." The shows, one columnist cheerfully observed, were "a glorification of the American alcoholic." "Drinking a great deal was a prerequisite for being a Clan member," Davis said.

As the civil rights movement gathered momentum, the Rat Pack joked about race. Davis was ridiculed and ridiculed himself, to positive effect. "**You** wanna dance with **me**?" Davis would ask Lawford. "Do you realize I happen to be one of the greatest Jewish Mau Mau dancers?" To which Lawford replied, "I'm not prejudiced." Davis: "I know your kind. You'll dance with me. But you won't go to school with me."

Sometimes the humor crossed a line. "I'll dance wit' ya," Martin told Davis, "I'll sing wit' ya, I'll swim wit' ya, I'll cut the lawn wit' ya, I'll go to bar mitzvahs wit' ya but"—this as the black man put a friendly hand on his shoulder—"don't touch me." Such cracks could be hurtful, Davis admitted years later. He went along with them because the Pack was a rainbow group—two Italian-Americans, a black man, a Jew (Bishop), and a sometime Englishman (Lawford)—and they were making a point.

Frank and Martin slipped in myriad sex jokes, sometimes by mangling the lyrics of familiar songs. "You made me love you, I didn't wanna do it, I didn't wanna do it" became, "You made me love you, You woke me up to do it." A line in "Chattanooga Choo Choo," "Nothing could be finer than to have your ham an' eggs in Carolina" might come out as, "Nothing could be finer than to shack up with a minor."

During the day, the five men worked on location shooting the movie **Ocean's 11**, the story of a group of war veterans who plot simultaneous robberies of five Las Vegas casinos. Afternoons, they repaired to what became known as their "Clubhouse," the steam room and health club next to the pool at the Sands. There they lolled in white robes monogrammed either with their initials—FAS for Frank—or their nicknames: DAG, as in Dago, for Martin, and SON OF A GUN for Bishop, because that was one of his trademark phrases. Frank once arranged for Davis to be issued a brown robe, brown towels, and brown soap.

Women were on tap in the Clubhouse. "I went, took off my clothes, and walked in," Kirk Douglas recalled. "Sitting next to me in the mist was a beautiful naked girl. We chatted for about ten minutes. When I came out the 'boys' were watching me. . . . I said, 'That's a real nice guy in there.' "

Paul Anka never forgot an early experience in Vegas. "I was like eighteen or nineteen—they wouldn't even let me in the casino. . . . I meet Sinatra and the guys, and they hang out. The greatest times I ever had were in that steam room. Everything went on in there that you could imagine. . . . The women who were around all the time! Not only were they good-looking but they knew what they were doing. . . . If you wanted to get laid—and really get laid—that's where you could get laid."

"The place was crawling with the most gorgeous girls," said Henry Silva, who played a gangster in **Ocean's 11** and attended all "The Summit" shows. "These women . . . would stick their key in your pocket and say, 'Come on up to Room whatever, I'll be there, I'll be bathed, I'll take care of you, make love to you like you've never been made love to before.' You could have two or three girls at the same time."

"There were poker games in the massage room," said Count Guido Deiro, a casino dealer. "A big table with five, six guys with towels around them, and women under the table giving oral sex."

"When Dean came to town," pit boss Ed Walters said, "the cocktail waitresses fought to see who would give him a blowjob." Entratter sometimes sent the best of the new showgirls to Frank's suite, George Jacobs said, as an "on-the-house nightcap."

"Women were treated like chattels," Deiro said, "and Sinatra was probably the first real star to have groupies. Some women threw their room keys onto the stage. But most of the women he fooled around with were professionals—hookers."

DURING "THE SUMMIT" SHOWS, the sybarites at the Sands were to play host to a distinguished visitor from Washington, Senator John F. Kennedy, Peter Lawford's brother-in-law. With hindsight, Frank's 1957 reconciliation with Brother-in-Lawford, as he took to calling him, had been so swift and total as to seem peculiar. The Lawfords had begun weekending at Frank's Palm Springs home so often that they kept clothes there. So warmly had Frank acted toward Patricia Kennedy Lawford that Frank's valet Jacobs thought he planned to seduce her. The Lawfords named the daughter born to them in late 1958 Victoria Frances—Victoria in honor of her Uncle Jack's reelection to the Senate, Frances for Francis Sinatra.

Looking back, however, Lawford would reflect on the fact that Frank had made up with him at the very time his brother-in-law was being talked up as the hot candidate for the 1960 Democratic nomination. "I think we were very attractive to Frank," he said later, "because of Jack. . . . Frank could see a bandwagon coming."

23

The Guest from Chicago

JOHN F. KENNEDY appeared to bring to his presidential candidacy much more than his keen intellect and a record of bravery in World War II. As he entered his forties he seemed youthful, robust, a family man with a stylish wife and baby. The image was to woo millions of voters, but it was in large part bogus.

Kennedy was suffering from a chronic, painful illness that would have destroyed his candidacy had it been made public at the time. He had been hospitalized time and again for intestinal ailments, back trouble, and Addison's disease, a condition of the adrenal glands that reduces the body's ability to resist infection. The extent of the health problems became, in the words of the scholar Robert Dallek, who had access to medical records at the Kennedy Library in 2002, "one of the best-kept secrets of recent U.S. history." Only intimates learned of Kennedy's profligate use of drugs, some prescribed by his doctors, some—amphetamines—provided by a celebrity quack to help Kennedy cope with pain and stress, some purely recreational.

"Peter Lawford and the future president did lines of cocaine" at Palm Springs on several occasions, according to George Jacobs. Kennedy said the cocaine was "for his back," then followed up with a "bad-boy wink."

Where sex was concerned Kennedy behaved, as future secretary to the Cabinet Fred Dutton put it, "like God, fucking anybody he wants to anytime he feels like it." "I once asked him why," said the writer Priscilla Johnson, who worked for Kennedy in the 1950s, "why he was taking a chance on getting caught in a scandal at the same time he was trying to make his career take off. . . . Finally he shrugged and said, 'I don't know really. I guess I just can't help it.' " "Where sex was concerned," Kennedy's friend Senator George Smathers once said, "he felt he could walk on water." The same applied to his—and his father's—involvement with the Mafia.

Joe Kennedy had been deeply involved in bootlegging, and that had led to dealings with some of Lucky Luciano's closest associates. Frank Costello said he and Kennedy were "partners" in the illegal liquor business. According to Richard Mahoney, who has written on the history of the Kennedy family, they still had business links in the mid-1950s; they fell out, then, over a Manhattan property deal. Other criminals, Joe Stacher, Moe Dalitz, and Owney Madden, all spoke of Kennedy's Prohibition era activity. "I discussed the Kennedy partnership with him many times," Madden's attorney Q. Byrum Hurst said. "Owney controlled all the nightclubs in New York . . . and Joe wanted the outlets for his liquor." John Kohlert, a musician Al Capone took under his wing for a while, recalled being present in 1926 at a meeting at which Joe and Capone discussed a bootleg liquor deal. In Canadian customs documents for the same year, Kennedy's name appears along with those of Capone and mobster Jake Guzik, listed with them as an "importer" of whiskey to the United States.

Joe's close friend Mike McLaney, whose name has been linked to syndicate operations, said in a 1994 interview that he knew Kennedy used routes "controlled by Lucky Luciano" to bring in bootleg liquor. Kennedy features in two bootleggers' stories of liquor truck hijackings, in one of which, in southern New England, eleven men were shot dead. Dolly Sinatra, her granddaughter Tina recalled, spoke of Joe as a "rum-running son-of-a-bitch."

After Prohibition, Joe Kennedy added to his fortune by importing liquor legally. As his glittering public career proceeded—as chairman of the Securities and Exchange Commission and the

Maritime Commission, and as United States ambassador to Britain—he continued to deal with mobsters. The Kefauver Committee heard testimony that a lawyer Kennedy picked to represent his liquor company, Tom Cassara, was a Mafia front man. In 1946, when Cassara was gunned down in Chicago, Kennedy promptly sold the company and its inventory of Scotch to two former bootleggers for $8 million ($74 million today). One of the purchasers was a longtime associate of Willie Moretti.

Joe got out of the liquor business just as his son John was getting into politics, and that was probably no coincidence. The whiskey trade, as Joe's biographer Richard Whalen put it, had become "vaguely embarrassing" now that he was focused on putting a Kennedy in the White House. Joe's abysmal performance as ambassador to London, the diplomatic blunders and opposition to U.S. involvement in the war against Nazi Germany that had culminated in his resignation, had long since put paid to his own presidential prospects. He was now pinning his hopes on his son Jack.

John Kennedy was at first ambivalent about entering politics but, his father recalled, "I told him he had to." Winning at any cost was an overriding imperative for the Kennedy children, and Joe brought all his resources to bear when it came to winning in politics. "Everything Joe got he bought and paid for," said a close aide, "and politics is like war. It takes three things to win. The first is money and the second is money and the third is money." Kennedy cash flowed at an unprecedented rate during John's congressional campaign of 1946, much of it distributed covertly.

With his election to the House and then the Senate, John Kennedy showed that he had the potential to fulfill his father's hopes. "I will work out the plans to elect you President," Joe was heard by a Kennedy staffer to say as early as 1952 during his son's run for the Senate, as though winning the White House were already a fait accompli. Those plans were to involve the Mafia.

According to Bill Bonanno, son of Mafia boss Joe Bonanno, Joe Kennedy visited his father at his Arizona retreat in 1954, long before the start of overt campaigning for the presidency, and again in 1956. Joe Bonanno, who had originally come to power in New York as a Luciano ally, was a member of the "Commission" that arbitrated relations between the Mafia families. He was a longtime friend of Frank Costello, whom he admired, he said, for his "skill at cultivating friendships among politicians and public officials." Decades earlier, Bonanno's illegal arrival in the United States had been facilitated by Willie Moretti.

"No Democrat in New York got elected," Bill Bonanno has said, without a go-ahead from the city's key Mafia families. His father was not only head of one of those families, but also influenced politics in the Southwest. Before the 1956 election, according to Bill, "Kennedy told my father that he wanted to get his son on the national ticket—if only to prepare the way for a real run at the presidency in 1960. . . . My father—and his allies in New York and in the Arizona Democratic establishment—agreed." West Coast mobsters duly produced money for the Kennedy campaign chest.

In 1958, FBI agents reported, John F. Kennedy attended mass in Tucson with Joe Bonanno's best friend, Gus Battaglia, a senior official of the Arizona state Democratic Party. According to Bonanno, he himself met with Kennedy at Battaglia's ranch. He was also in touch with Frank Sinatra, whom he invited to sing at a family wedding, and, according to FBI reports, would be a guest of Frank at a gathering in Atlantic City in 1959.

In the end, though, it was not Bonanno who served as the Kennedys' principal mob connection during the race for the White House.

SAM GIANCANA was one of the most powerful criminals of the mid-twentieth century. Born Salvatore Giangana in 1908, the son of poor Sicilian immigrants, he left school at eleven, was jailed for auto theft at seventeen, and arrested for murder at eighteen—a charge dropped when a prosecution witness was killed. By that time he had become Sam "Mooney" Giancana, a thin-featured youth with a sadistic streak and a growing reputation in Chicago as a getaway driver. He was soon jailed again, for armed robbery.

After World War II, he was often seen at the side of Al Capone's heir, Tony "The Big Tuna" Accardo. By the 1950s, the Chicago crime empire controlled myriad clubs, jukebox rackets, elements of the movie industry, gambling in Las Vegas, and enterprises in Cuba. And in 1957, when Accardo stepped aside, the power passed to Giancana.

He lived to all appearances like a respectable middle-class family man. Home was a yellow-brick house in a leafy suburb, spacious but not ostentatious, shared with a loyal, industrious wife. Their three daughters attended private Catholic schools, and Giancana played golf at a country club. He gave to worthy charities, collected paintings and antique porcelain. When his wife died young, he was seen on his knees in church, weeping.

Giancana dressed, one of his daughters thought, "like someone in a **Fortune 500** executive photograph . . . could have been mistaken for the president of General Motors." The tailored suit, white shirt, and tie might have passed muster, though the solid gold cuff links, with the initials in diamonds, were over the top.

Some thought Giancana charming. Eddie Fisher saw him as "a warm, vital, funny man, who just happened to have these big, burly guys hanging around him all the time." "He's such great fun," said Joe Shimon, a former Washington police inspector, who welcomed Giancana to his home more than once: "My wife thinks he's lovable."

Others disagreed. Yul Brynner's son Rock Brynner remembered him as "scary, so profoundly ugly it was hard to look at him. His ugliness, unlike most people's, seemed to reflect his soul." "He was as serious as death and taxes," said Michael Corbitt, a gas station owner who got sucked into crime by Giancana, "very moody. He could give you a look that was second to none. A killer look." The Mafia boss beat one of his daughters, and had to be restrained from causing her serious injury. He once shot a television to pieces when it did not work properly. An FBI report characterized him as "ruthless, without human feeling."

Giancana lived by the gun, the instrument used in crimes in which he was implicated, the robbing and killing of a barber in 1926, in another murder two years later, in a kidnapping in 1946, that Giancana ordered to be used to kill a banker in

1948, then to finish off a "friend of the family" involved in the same case. That victim, the forensic evidence indicated, had been tied hand and foot, forced to kneel, then strangled and left riddled with bullets.

Frank Sinatra would one day insist, in sworn testimony to the Nevada gaming authorities, that he had not met Giancana until about 1960. In 1959 he told the FBI that he did not even know how to reach Giancana, months after the bureau had established that the mobster had **Frank's** home and business numbers. The connection between the two men had in fact been forged years earlier, as a mass of information confirms.

They had first been introduced, an FBI document suggests, by the New Jersey mafioso Angelo De Carlo, who had hired Frank when he was starting out. In the early 1950s, when Frank's career stalled, Giancana found him work. "That hoodlum," Frank told Ava Gardner, "is responsible for giving me a job."

Giancana's daughter Antoinette recalled Frank having sung at a charity performance her mother organized in 1953. Her father and Frank embraced and seemed "very affectionate," she said, when they met privately the following year. Often, though by no means always, they were discreet about meeting. "My father would be the go-between," said Marilyn Sinatra, daughter of the Sinatra cousin who worked for Frank in California. "Sam would come to our house with his men. Or my dad would take them to meet Frank wherever Frank said it was possible to meet."

George Jacobs recalled an occasion in 1956, when Giancana came to stay at Frank's Palm Springs house. He was clearly a "special guest," and Frank was "nervous about everything being just so, the linens, the soap, the caviar." When the mobster showed up, accompanied by fellow gangsters, Frank seemed "thrilled." He followed Giancana around, Jacobs said, always "on perfect behavior, like a little altar boy." "What he and Giancana talked about," Jacobs recalled, "was business, the business of running casinos. The numbers I heard them throw around made my head reel. . . . Sinatra owned a piece of the Sands, in return for his making it his exclusive venue in Vegas, and he loved the notion of being a capitalist, a proprietor. He wanted to own even more. Sam Giancana was his mentor in these ambitions. . . . Mr. S. insisted the man was a wizard, a business mastermind."

In early 1958, when Frank performed at the Sands, he and the Mafia boss were seen together at another casino, El Rancho Vegas. In the summer, when Frank was in Indiana making **Some Came Running,** Giancana was there too. One of Giancana's men, who served him as bodyguard, driver, and chef, cooked for Frank, as he would on location for other movies. Shirley MacLaine, who met

Giancana during the filming, did not at first know who he was and one night, when the mobster kept beating her at gin rummy, jokingly pointed a water pistol at him. He responded by pulling a very real .38 pistol on her.

The same month, when Frank arrived in Chicago, Joe Fischetti picked him up at the airport. The following day, accompanied by Dean Martin, he was driven to the residence of Giancana's predecessor, Tony Accardo. There, the FBI was told, the pair gave a private "command performance." Frank and Martin also sang for Giancana and "a closed group of individuals" in 1959, according to FBI files, at the Armory Lounge, the former speakeasy Giancana used as his headquarters.

Records indicate that in July, when Giancana threw an elaborate wedding for his daughter Bonnie at the Fontainebleau, Frank flew from California to attend. The same month, while playing the 500 Club in Atlantic City, Frank rented the entire first floor of the Claridge Hotel for a "private party" that included both Giancana and Joe Bonanno.

Giancana enjoyed having entertainers around him, and liked to manipulate them. It was to him that Sammy Davis Jr. had turned when threatened by the mob because of his affair with Kim Novak, and it was he who, after Davis married a black girl, told him the threat had been lifted.

According to information the FBI later received, Giancana was the secret owner of the Worldwide Actors Agency, which numbered among its clients Jimmy Durante, Sonny King—and Frank. He was distracted too by the glitz and glamour of show business. He had been "in heat" since his wife's death, as his biographer William Brashler put it, and that gave him and Frank a common interest. FBI reports reflect Frank having introduced the mobster to a woman, and vice versa. Keely Smith also became close to Giancana.

Frank went out of his way to please the Mafia boss. When he learned that Giancana liked a particular Cuban cigar, he arranged for a supply to be flown in. More significantly, he presented the Mafia boss with a star sapphire pinkie ring. Giancana, who admired Frank's work, obtained a print of **From Here to Eternity** and viewed it time and again. He referred to Frank as a "skinny little runt," but in tones that for him, his daughter Antoinette thought, denoted a measure of affection. She did not, however, think her father had much respect for entertainers. He merely used them, she said, "to further his own interests."

Politicians ranked even lower in Giancana's estimation. "They're all rats," Antoinette recalled her father saying, "lower than a snake's belly . . . low-life individuals." Politicians did, however, like entertainers, have their uses.

24

The Candidate and the Courtesan

JOHN F. KENNEDY and Frank had first met in 1955, when Frank addressed a Democratic Party rally. Some people, Frank had told the audience, thought entertainers should stay out of politics because political involvement could ruin a career. So deeply did Sinatra believe in the cause that brought him to the rally, Senator Alan Cranston recalled him saying, that "if it meant the end of the entertaining phase of his life, then so be it."

Frank had long been a registered Democrat, had campaigned for Roosevelt, Truman, and Adlai Stevenson, and would support Stevenson again in 1956. At the Democratic convention that year, he sang his personal civil rights anthem, "The House I Live In." He was sitting with Kennedy's supporters when, after Stevenson had been selected as his party's candidate, Kennedy failed in his bid for the vice presidential slot.

Frank heard Stevenson praise Kennedy as "the real hero of the hour" for the way he conducted himself at the convention, and he heard the Kennedy side's reaction. They were enthusing, already, about the 1960 campaign.

Frank had enthused over earlier leaders because of their policies. He and John Kennedy, however, were drawn together by other factors. They were of the same generation, wealthy to an extent that made money an irrelevance, and both basked in an aura of glamour. On trips to the East Coast in the mid-1950s, Frank began visiting Kennedy at Washington's Mayflower Hotel. The senator kept a hideaway there, a room where he gave dinner parties for celebrity guests, and Frank was now one of them.

Kennedy probably first visited Frank at Palm Springs in the summer of 1958. Called upon to give Kennedy back rubs, George Jacobs found himself peppered with prurient questions. "Does Shirley MacLaine have a red pussy?" Kennedy wanted to know. Were her legs as good as Cyd Charisse's? If MacLaine was not going with Frank, how come she had been cast in **Some Came Running**?

Kennedy loved gossip about Hollywood women, and Frank provided it—as well as the real thing. "I know that when Jack Kennedy was running for President and stayed with Sinatra," Richard Burton noted in his journal, "the place was like a whorehouse, with Kennedy as chief customer." That sort of thing, of course, was spoken of only in whispers. The cascade of positive publicity about the senator was the envy of more experienced politicians.

In late 1958, after Kennedy won reelection to the Senate, Frank let it be known for the first time that they were close. "Senator Kennedy," he told reporters, "is a friend of mine."

To the dancer Juliet Prowse, who began an affair with Frank months later, he and Kennedy appeared to be bosom pals. "It was a mutual admiration thing," she said. "Of course, Frank loves the power of politics, the power of those things that make things happen."

JOE KENNEDY REMAINED INVOLVED, though behind the scenes, and he, too, visited Frank in Palm Springs. According to Jacobs he bad-mouthed the help with racist comments, and burned one of the prostitutes Frank provided with his cigar. "Mr. S.," the valet recalled, "said he'd 'earned the right.' . . . Sinatra respected his arrogance."

"We're going to sell Jack like soap flakes," Joe told a friend, and he did just that. He manipulated the press, ensuring that his son's face was on the cover of magazines with influence, and he supplied seemingly limitless amounts of money. When there was criticism, John Kennedy laughed it off. "I have just received the following wire from my generous daddy," he announced at the annual Gridiron Club dinner, a lighthearted press affair in Washington. " 'Dear Jack—Don't buy a single vote more than is necessary—I'll be damned if I'm going to pay for a landslide.' "

Sprawled on the floor with a map of the United States, Joe had amazed a companion with his encyclopedic knowledge of key contacts across the nation. He knew "who the bosses were behind the scenes," said Democratic congressman Eugene Keogh. "He was in contact with them by phone, presenting Jack's case." He also kept open a line of communication to the Mafia.

In the winter of 1959, he sent an intermediary to talk with a representative of Joe Bonanno. "Joe Kennedy had been involved with us from the beginning," Bill Bonanno said. "He asked for a favor and it was granted." The meeting, he added, led to fund-raising and systematic consultation with other national crime figures.

The old Mafia order was in a state of flux and bloody upheaval. Top men in the old Luciano network were dead or in decline. In New York there had been a failed attempt to kill Frank Costello, and a successful one to assassinate Albert Anastasia. In Italy, there had been two attempts on the life of Luciano himself. Luciano then met in Sicily with American mafiosi, including Joe Bonanno, to discuss the way forward.

For all the divisions, the criminal empire was flourishing. In Havana and Las Vegas, gambling thrived. Narcotics trafficking was on the increase. The mob was diversifying, penetrating the legitimate business world as never before. As the Mafia prospered, though, there was growing congressional pressure to curb its power. To counter it, just as some politicians sought support from criminals, shrewd criminals eyed potentially compliant politicians.

Bill Bonanno is the only mob source to have talked of the early phase of the Kennedys' dalliance with the mafiosi. "I was instructed to go back [from Tucson] to New York and sound out other leaders about a concerted effort to back JFK," he recalled. "The divisions over Kennedy were deep. Joe Profaci [a New York mob boss], for example, said he just didn't trust Kennedy. Midwestern leaders—in Cleveland and Michigan—had let it be known that we should get behind someone who was more rooted in the unions, where we had more influence."

Younger mob leaders were divided, according to Bill Bonanno. Santo Trafficante, from Tampa, was hesitant about backing Kennedy. Carlos Marcello of New Orleans was vehemently opposed. Giancana, on the other hand, appeared to be in favor, and Joe Kennedy needed a way to reach out to him.

The elder Bonanno was of little use in that

regard because he had recently suffered a heart attack and because he and Giancana did not get along. Joe Kennedy turned instead to "Jimmy Blue Eyes" Alo. "Joe came to me early," Alo said. "Kennedy and I had a mutual friend, Phil Regan, the actor and singer from Brooklyn. I got a call from an old friend I'd known since Detroit, from the casino. He said, 'Phil Regan's in town, he wants to talk with you.' . . . Joe Kennedy had sent Phil to see me."

Regan, a former New York City policeman who had become an entertainer, acknowledged in an interview that he had known the Kennedy family since the early 1930s. He said, too, "Back in '59 I worked for Jack's father. . . . I traveled with Jack all through 1959." He was also close to New Jersey mobsters, and would eventually go to prison in California for trying to bribe a county official.

Alo recalled the approach by Regan. "We met in Bal Harbor, Florida, and we talked. He said, 'Well, you know Jack Kennedy's going for the nomination for president? The old man has delegated me to see you, because he's got everything figured out. . . .' He said, 'Do you know Sam Giancana?' . . .

"I said, 'Oh yeah.' He said, 'Would you talk with him?' . . . Joe Kennedy wanted me to talk to him about helping Jack in Chicago. . . . I said, 'Leave me alone with these politicians! . . . Phil, don't mix me up with politics 'cause I don't want no part of it.' . . . I turned him down. . . . The next thing I hear is that they went to Sinatra."

Politicians and crime bosses had long been using and abusing the democratic process. Two decades earlier, according to Lucky Luciano, he and Costello had met secretly with the 1928 Democratic presidential candidate, Al Smith, to trade support for the promise of future favors. Four years later, when Smith fought Roosevelt for the nomination, the mob covered their bets. Luciano shared a hotel suite at the Democratic convention with a key Smith supporter, while Costello huddled with a top Roosevelt aide in another. Roosevelt proved no patron, but the Mafia bosses continued to believe they could influence politics.

Llewella Humphreys, daughter of Giancana's associate Murray "The Camel" Humphreys, said she was received at the White House by President Harry Truman. She claimed, too, to have met Dwight Eisenhower at a syndicate meeting in Chicago convened to "decide who would be the next president of the United States." "Father," she said, "didn't have a great respect for politicians . . . he knew he could control them."

As an apprentice gangster in Chicago, Giancana had been a "floater" during the Republican primary of 1928, one of dozens of hoodlums who rushed from precinct to precinct casting phony votes. When gangsters committed the ultimate electoral abuse that year—they shot dead one candidate to ensure the election of another—he had been one of those questioned.

By the end of the 1950s, as head of the Chicago mob, Giancana had two congressmen, several state representatives, and numerous ward committeemen in his pocket. Mayor Richard Daley rarely opposed his will. Now, the stakes were about to be raised.

Organized crime has always sought ways to corrupt public officials by compromising them, by exploiting their weakness, and John Kennedy had made it easy for the mobsters to identify his Achilles' heel. On a junket to Havana in the 1950s, as a senator, Meyer Lansky's widow said, Kennedy had asked her husband's advice on where to find the best girls. "Throw him a broad," Giancana said in 1959, "and he'll do anything."

Giancana was especially well placed to have such knowledge. One summer night in 1958 the FBI learned that Pat and Peter Lawford were out socializing at the Mocambo with Bea Korshak. Mrs. Korshak's husband, Sidney, was a powerful mob attorney close to Giancana—and to Frank—with proven expertise in compromising his foes. He had avoided having to testify to the Kefauver Committee by obtaining compromising photographs of Senator Kefauver in a hotel bedroom with two women, then confronting Kefauver with them.

Frank, as Peter Lawford put it long afterward, was currently "Jack's pimp." He could both effect introductions to desirable women in Hollywood and arrange assignations with hookers. There were what the FBI called "indiscreet parties in Palm Springs, Las Vegas, and New York City" involving Kennedy, Lawford, Frank, and prostitutes. There was also what William Safire has called "the most startling dual relationship in the history of crime and politics."

FOR A COUPLE OF NIGHTS in the first week of November 1959, after a fund-raiser in Los Angeles, Kennedy and his aide Dave Powers were Frank's guests at his house in Palm Springs. Powers remembered how each morning "music filled the house, even the bathrooms." Frank took pride in the visit, christened the quarters Kennedy had used the "Kennedy Room," and eventually had a plaque reading "JOHN F. KENNEDY SLEPT HERE" mounted on the door. The decision to stay over, which had been made at the last minute, was evidently considered a good one. "We had a great time," Powers said.

Before Frank and Kennedy left Los Angeles for Palm Springs, they had dined at Puccini's restaurant in Beverly Hills. Nick Sevano, who was there that evening, remembered that Kennedy and Frank took a great interest in two women seated at another table—the actress Angie Dickinson and a dark-haired beauty named Judith Campbell. "Frank sent a note to me saying 'Bring the broads over,' " Sevano said. "I brought them over, and we wound up at Frank's house until three in the morning, watching movies. [The girls] didn't stay there—just watched the movies."

Judith Campbell—best known now by her later married name, Judith Exner—was the daughter of a well-to-do architect and a former Bonwit's model. She had grown up in New Jersey and Southern California and in her teens had socialized on the fringes of Hollywood society. She had briefly dated Robert Wagner, married an actor, William Campbell, when she was eighteen, and then divorced him—after a two-year separation—in early 1959, when she was twenty-five. She first met Frank "at parties," she said, just months before the encounter at Puccini's.

Campbell was to remain unknown to the public until, sixteen years later, a Senate committee turned up evidence that during the Kennedy presidency she had been in regular contact not only with Kennedy but also with Giancana and Johnny Rosselli. The relevant passage of the committee's report established nothing about the nature of those relationships, and did not mention Sinatra. Campbell's memoir, **My Story**, published in 1977, said nothing about Kennedy having been present at Puccini's, or about the foursome having gone from the restaurant to Frank's house.

By her account Frank had sent Sevano over to ask if she would "like to go out with him." She had agreed, and Frank followed up by phoning and then buttonholing her, again at Puccini's, for a conversation. Soon after, as best one can calculate while Kennedy was staying with him at Palm Springs, he called to ask Campbell to join him on a trip to Honolulu. She flew out two days later, on November 9, and found Frank ensconced in the penthouse of the Surfrider Hotel with Peter and Pat Lawford and others.

There was heavy drinking, inconsequential talk, and a shopping expedition. Campbell made a point, she said, of paying for her purchases herself. She went to bed with Frank that night, an experience she described as "idyllic." The romantic mood was broken on the third day, however, when Frank and Lawford went off to a bedroom with two Japanese women for a "massage." Lawford later made a play for Campbell, which she said she rebuffed. On two successive nights, Frank sank into an ugly mood and pursued another woman.

Karen Dynan, a tourist who was vacationing in Hawaii that week, recalled Frank, in an orange bathing suit, having flirted with **her.** She saw Campbell taking leave of Sinatra, and it looked to Dynan as though she were being dismissed. "We were having drinks, and this woman walked out, a beautiful dark-haired woman, dressed in a suit and ready to travel, fully made-up. Lawford said, 'Well goodbye Judy.' Sinatra didn't look at her or say anything. We thought she must have been some kind of hooker or something."

When Campbell got back to Los Angeles, a local gossip columnist asked whether she and Frank had been dating in Hawaii. "Hardly," she responded. Frank, however, got back in touch at once, eager to pursue the relationship. They saw each other again two weeks before Christmas at his house in Palm Springs. Peter and Pat Lawford were again present, along with Jack Entratter and Johnny Formosa, a close associate of Giancana. Campbell, who gathered that Formosa had "some connection with the Chicago underworld," thought Frank "walked very carefully around him."

The conversation at dinner was dominated by politics. Frank seemed "subdued" during the discussion, and in bed that night talked on and on about Kennedy. "I'll bet even money," he told Campbell, "Jack gets the nomination. . . . He's my friend. I know how to help my friends."

The following month, Frank went into a studio to record a special version of "High Hopes," a song he had recorded the previous year for the movie **A Hole in the Head.** The new version, with

Nelson Riddle conducting and special lyrics by Sammy Cahn, was called "High Hopes with Jack Kennedy":

> Everyone wants to back Jack
> Jack is on the right track.

It was to be the campaign theme song, blared from loudspeakers as the candidate made his way from city to city and town to town in the months that followed. "I'm Jack Kennedy," he would say as he shook another hand. Then: "I come from a thousand miles from here. I am not your neighbor, but I don't think that has anything to do with it. What counts is the quality of a man and his good judgment."

Frank was to have more impact on the Kennedy campaign than any entertainer has had on any presidential campaign before or since. Frank is said to have shown guests framed notes he claimed Kennedy had sent him during the campaign. "Frank," one of them read, "what can we count on the boys from Vegas for?"

In January 1960, Kennedy began working the primary states aboard the **Caroline**, the airplane his family had acquired months earlier. Frank, meanwhile, shuttled between Los Angeles, Palm Springs, and Las Vegas, where he was making **Ocean's 11** and performing at the Sands in the

Rat Pack shows. It was then, at the Sands, according to Judith Campbell, that she met Kennedy.

KENNEDY FLEW INTO LAS VEGAS on Sunday, February 7, 1960. "There was no goddamn reason for stopping there," said Blair Clark, a CBS reporter traveling aboard the **Caroline,** "except fun and games. We all figured, 'How bad can it be to catch Sinatra at the Sands?' " As Kennedy watched the shows that weekend, he became part of the entertainment.

"Ladies and gentlemen," Frank announced that first night, "Senator John F. Kennedy, from the great state of Massachusetts. . . . The next president of the United States!" Kennedy rose, bowed, and got a standing ovation. "You son of a gun," cried Bishop. "You've got the Jewish vote!" "What," Dean Martin asked, "did you say his name was? Frank, if he gets in, you'll be ambassador to Italy."

Cradling Sammy Davis in his arms, Frank voiced thanks for the "trophy" that had "arrived from the National Association for the Advancement of Colored People." It was a gag they often used, but on this occasion Frank walked over and dropped Davis in Kennedy's lap. "It's perfectly all right with me," Davis told him, "as long as I'm not being donated to [prominent segregationists] George Wallace or James Eastland."

Kennedy was the center of attention that night and the next when, in the wee hours, he reboarded the **Caroline** to resume campaigning. After the shows, Davis recalled in his memoirs, everyone sat up talking about politics and how to rally show business support. Within weeks of the Kennedy visit, though, the FBI heard that Kennedy, Sinatra, and Lawford had been "involved in some sort of indiscreet party." The owner of El Rancho Vegas, an informant claimed, had told of "showgirls" running in and out of Kennedy's suite. The candidate's campaign manager had "bewailed Kennedy's association with Sinatra" and "certain sex activities by Kennedy that he hopes never are publicized."

Blair Clark, who had been a classmate of Kennedy at Harvard, sat at Sinatra's table in the lounge of the Sands and was invited to join the senator in Frank's suite upstairs. There had been "bimbos and showgirls" around the table, Clark remembered, and two women present in the suite. He and Mary McGrory of the **Washington Star** had excused themselves, Clark said, "because we sensed that Jack and Frank and a couple of the girls were about to have a party." A former senior IRS investigator learned from an actress working on **Ocean's 11** that Kennedy was provided with women and "sampled the goodies."

Sands pit boss Ed Walters heard from fellow hotel staff, including those involved in cleaning the senator's rooms, not only about Kennedy's womanizing but also that he was using cocaine. Campaign workers even tried to buy cocaine on his behalf. Others in the Kennedy camp, however, were concerned. "With the old-style PBX system we had," Walters said, "the phone operators knew who was calling who and heard things. Kennedy's family back east worried about him, about it getting out that he was being seduced by Sinatra and the girls, and about his medical problems—he had a doctor with him when he came. We wondered, if he was running for president, about how close he was getting to Sinatra."

When Clark and McGrory decided it was prudent to leave Sinatra's suite, Clark recalled, one of the women with Frank and Kennedy had been Judith Campbell.

"I WAS AT A TABLE at the Sands with Peter and Pat and Jack," Lawford's agent Milt Ebbins said years afterward. "The lights were low but I sensed a lady come and sit down beside me—maybe it was her perfume. And she said, 'I'm Judith Campbell, I'm a guest of Mr. Sinatra's. He asked me to sit at this table.' "

When the show ended, Ebbins said, he introduced her around the table. She subsequently went "upstairs" with Kennedy. "I went to Peter later and said, 'Who is this girl?' And Peter said, 'She's a hooker. Frank gave her $200 to stop at our table . . . to go to bed with Jack." Sands dealer Count Deiro said Campbell was one of three such women around Kennedy that weekend.

Campbell's memoir offered a more romantic version of the story. Kennedy "looked so handsome in his pin-striped suit," as he sat at Frank's table, she wrote. "Those strong white teeth and smiling Irish eyes. . . . I was tremendously impressed by his poise and wit and charm." It was Edward Kennedy, she said, who pursued her the first night: she had to fend him off when he saw her to her door. Then John phoned, inviting her to lunch with him the next day on Frank's patio. They met for three hours and, she said, spent most of that time discussing religion. They were both Catholics, and Kennedy's religion was a campaign issue. That second night, in Jack Entratter's booth, they watched the Rat Pack perform. Kennedy made no moves that weekend, she claimed, but called soon afterward asking to see her again. They had sex for the first time a month later, according to Campbell, at the Plaza Hotel in New York. There followed what she characterized as "a long and intimate relationship" that lasted into the second year of the Kennedy presidency.

In her memoir, Campbell told how, two days after having sex with Kennedy, at Sinatra's urging, she flew to Miami to see the Rat Pack perform at the Fontainebleau. When she arrived, she said, Frank introduced her to Joe Fischetti, then—at a social gathering—to Giancana.

"Come here, Judy," Campbell recalled Frank saying. "I want you to meet a good friend of mine, Sam Flood." Giancana was using one of his aliases. As she moved around the room, Campbell said, "Flood's eyes never left me. . . . There was a little smile on his face." Next day, she was seated next to Giancana at dinner. When she checked out, she discovered he had paid her hotel bill.

Campbell's life would now be dominated by her sexual relationship with John F. Kennedy and parallel contacts with Giancana. Controversially, she claimed before her death that Kennedy used her as a sort of courier, to carry envelopes to Giancana. She carried money during the election campaign, she said, and, early in the presidency, papers relating to plans to assassinate Fidel Castro. She also claimed to have witnessed secret meetings between Kennedy and Giancana.

When she began speaking out, in 1975, keepers of the Kennedy flame denied or derided Campbell's claims. "The only Campbell I know," Dave Powers sneered, "is chunky vegetable soup." Frank issued a press release when Campbell announced she was going to write a book. "Hell hath no fury," it read, "like a hustler with a literary agent."

Yet much of what Campbell claimed is credible. A good deal of it is supported by phone records, White House logs, and other documentation. Interestingly, some of her more controversial claims, suspect because she did not make them publicly until many years had passed, were first made contemporaneously as **private** confidences. It seems, nevertheless, that Campbell was far from candid. She was not, as she portrayed herself, a somewhat reserved young woman swept off her feet by glamorous men.

Frank's acid 1976 press statement on Campbell had been edited by his attorney. In Frank's draft, he had called her not a hustler but a "hooker." Campbell always vigorously denied she took money for sex, and began a libel action when a book made that claim. Yet an FBI agent who investigated her, William Carter, said that he and colleagues "definitely thought she was selling her favors." He had considered Campbell a "high-class whore."

Carter's statement buttresses those of Karen Dynan, who thought Campbell was a hooker when she saw her in Hawaii, and of Lawford's agent Milt Ebbins. According to George Jacobs, Campbell was a sort of "call girl" who turned "discreet tricks." If not exactly a prostitute, "she would date anybody. . . . She was the perfect Eisenhower era pinup of the girl next door. That she charged for her wholesomeness was beside the point. . . . If one of Sinatra's friends came to town and wanted to get laid, he'd send Judy over . . . she stopped charging Frank, as a commission for the introductions. She made thousands. They got good money in those days. . . . All the pit bosses, the hotel bosses knew her."

"Campbell was notorious to us in the hotel," Sands dealer Count Guido Deiro said. "In those days we pimped out people from the pit all of the time. It was part of the complimentary package of delights that was offered to players. Her number may have been on the list, I'm not sure. . . . She was notorious in the sense that we knew who she was and that we considered her a high-class girl that could be bought."

Just as there are doubts about Campbell's denials that she took money for sex, there is reason to doubt what she said of her relations with mobsters. In the memoir, she wrote as though the world of the mob was unknown territory to her. Count Deiro said she was especially familiar to Sands staff "because she was a girlfriend of Johnny Rosselli." At the time Campbell met Kennedy, Rosselli was operating in Las Vegas on behalf of Giancana. He also had a long-standing connection to Joe Kennedy—they were occasional golf partners and played cards together. Campbell told the Senate Intelligence Committee that she met Rosselli for the first time "possibly in 1960." Until that year, she claimed in an interview, she had known no mobsters. In her memoir, however, she said she had met him "once briefly years before."

Rosselli said in 1975 that he had known Campbell since 1951, when she was seventeen, that he met her later during her short-lived marriage, then dated her once she was divorced. Patricia Breen, widow of one of Rosselli's Hollywood associates, said Rosselli saw Campbell "frequently." Brad Dexter, who knew all the individuals involved, said Rosselli and Campbell had a sexual relationship. He also dismissed Campbell's claim not to have met Giancana until **after** the start of her involvement with Kennedy, saying he was sure she had met Giancana earlier, through Rosselli. Rosselli himself said he saw Campbell with Giancana before 1960. These assertions, indicating that the woman with whom Kennedy became involved was already associating with a Mafia boss at the time she met him, put a new, more ominous cast on the entire shabby episode.

"When Sam wanted a girl," George Jacobs said, "Sinatra sent her to him." The order in which Campbell connected with the key men involved, Jacobs added, was not—as she claimed—Sinatra, followed by Kennedy, followed by Giancana. It was, rather: Sinatra, followed by Giancana, and then John Kennedy.

After Campbell's memoir was published, Peter Lawford began compiling notes about the Judith Campbell affair. In a surviving fragment, retrieved after his death, he wrote: "Judy was a mob moll."

CAMPBELL WENT TO LAS VEGAS the weekend she got together with Kennedy, she claimed, only because Sinatra asked her to. A **Newsweek** story published in 1975, when the Campbell-Kennedy story first broke, suggests another scenario. An unnamed source in that story—now identifiable as Sammy Davis Jr.—was much involved that weekend. He put his car and chauffeur at Kennedy's disposal, and socialized with Frank and Kennedy in Sinatra's suite. It had been assumed in advance, Davis told **Newsweek**, that Kennedy would want female company because "We all knew he was a swinger." Accordingly, he said, female company was arranged. It was done, **Newsweek** reported Davis as explaining, "discreetly: rather than find somebody local . . . they decided on an 'outside girl'—and someone asked Giancana to put in a call to Los Angeles."

Giancana may have been close by when Campbell and Kennedy met. Sammy Cahn's wife Gloria was in Sinatra's party that weekend. She knew who Giancana was and, striving to remember when interviewed in 2002, said she thought the

Mafia boss had been present in the hotel. She recalled people saying, at some point, "How can Frank possibly have those people around when he's got the Senator and other wonderful people?"

Frank may have had little concern about that. For in those heady days, and even during the presidency, Kennedy himself behaved as though he could get away with anything, including a relationship with Giancana. "I met Jack Kennedy when he was a senator," said Nick Sevano, "and we had dinner with Sam [Giancana] and a few others. Jack was very respectful to Giancana." The society columnist Taki Theodoracopulos, who mixed with the people around the Kennedys in the early 1960s, recalled a night out in New York with Peter Lawford and Giancana, who was introduced by his nickname Sam Mooney. "They talked about all the girls that Mooney used to produce for the Kennedys," Theodoracopulos said, "reminiscing about the girls that JFK had through Mooney. Mooney was very proud of his Kennedy connection. Always dropping, 'When JFK said this, when he said that, when he sent his plane. . . .' You could tell that they'd met together."

"I don't think it takes a great deal of imagination," Judith Campbell said years afterward, "to think there is a possibility I was used." "They deliberately fed her to Jack," Brad Dexter said before his death in 2002, "and Frank was part of it. Very serious."

THE SENATE INTELLIGENCE COMMITTEE stumbled on the Kennedy-Campbell affair in the mid-1970s while investigating whether, while president, Kennedy knew of plots to murder foreign leaders. The committee could not question Giancana because he was shot to death the day Senate staff arrived to arrange his testimony.

Rosselli did testify, but repeatedly refused to answer questions as to what he knew about Campbell's first meeting with Kennedy. "I will not answer that question," he said. Asked whether he ever saw her with Kennedy, he replied, "I think I will stop. I could answer some of these questions, but I do not think I want to get into it." He never would answer those key questions, for he in turn was killed a few months later.

Campbell was questioned, but not under oath. She was allotted just one paragraph in the committee's interim report, which referred to her only as an unnamed "close friend" of the president. The committee did not interview Frank, a striking omission never satisfactorily explained. William Safire fulminated about the omission in several columns, listing more than a dozen questions Frank should have been asked. Among them:

- When did you introduce Sam Giancana to Judith Campbell, if you did, and at whose request?
- Did the mobsters ask you to introduce her or anyone else to the Kennedys?
- Did you ever see Campbell and Kennedy together, or Giancana-Rosselli and Campbell together?
- To your knowledge, were any recordings ever made of any meetings between Miss Campbell and John Kennedy, or were any pictures taken of them that could have been used by organized crime for blackmail purposes?
- Were you aware of any communications between the President and men hired to kill Castro through the woman you introduced to both?

It was unacceptable, Safire wrote, for the committee chairman to "slam the lid of Pandora's box now that he has glimpsed the evil that lurks therein. As that great matchmaker of Mafia hoodlums, good-looking women, and a president of the United States used to croon: 'All—or nothing at all.' "

In March 1960, the week Campbell said she first dined with Giancana, in Florida, an FBI report quoted an informant as having said that Frank was "being made available to assist Senator

Kennedy's campaign whereby Joe Fischetti and other hoodlums will have an entrée to Senator Kennedy." The mobsters, moreover, were "financially supporting and actively endeavoring to secure [Kennedy's] nomination."

Sinatra and Joe Kennedy were also in Miami at that time, and Frank asked Sammy Cahn to do him a favor. "Frank," Cahn said, "asked me, 'Sammy, take Papa Joe down the hall and introduce him to Mr. Fischetti.' So there I was, walking through the hotel, taking the father of the soon-to-be Democratic nominee down the hall to meet Mr. Fischetti. I mean, one of the best-known criminals in the United States!" Cahn did as he was told, though it occurred to him, even then, that these men were playing "a dangerous game."

25

The Go-Between

"It's not the Pope I'm afraid of, it's the Pop," former president Harry Truman said of the prospect that John Kennedy, a Catholic, might win the White House. "Old Joe Kennedy is as big a crook as we've got anywhere in this country." As the campaign heated up, Joe courted the Mafia more assiduously than ever. The month before the Miami episode, he invited Giancana and Rosselli and other mob leaders to join him for lunch at Felix Young's restaurant in New York. Giancana listened to Joe make his case, but did not commit to helping his son win the presidency. Giancana's adviser Murray Humphreys, who remembered the quarrels with Joe Kennedy during Prohibition, was leery of his blandishments. Giancana knew, too, that the would-be president's brother Robert was a zealous foe of organized crime—during his work for the Senate Subcommittee on

Investigations he had targeted and personally interrogated the Mafia boss. Giancana wondered if he might fare better with Richard Nixon in the White House.

Joe Kennedy needed to bring Giancana on board because the mob's hold on Illinois politics was so strong and Illinois was a key election state. Nearly three decades later, when his daughter Tina was preparing the TV movie of her father's life, Frank revealed what happened next. Over lunch at the Kennedy compound in Hyannis Port, he said, Joe Kennedy told him what he wanted. As rendered in the film, the conversation ran as follows:

JOE KENNEDY: Frank, we're cut from the same cloth, came from the same world, worked our way up. We know the same people. And I know you know the people I mean.

FRANK: Sure, I know.

KENNEDY: We need a boost from our friends in Chicago who control the unions. They can win this race for us. But you understand, Frank, I can't go to those people. It might come back to Jack. The White House can't owe them any favors. The best thing you can do for Jack is to ask for the help as a personal favor to you.

FRANK: I understand.

Frank agreed to be an intermediary. His first mission, though, involved not Illinois, but a vital primary campaign. In real life, and in the movie, he broached the subject with Giancana during a golf game. "My friend Jack Kennedy," Frank told the mafioso, "needs some help with the West Virginia primary."

West Virginia had looked like a sure thing until Hubert Humphrey, a Protestant, entered the race. The population of West Virginia was more than 95 percent Protestant, and had never elected a Catholic to any important office. Yet Kennedy trounced Humphrey in the primary, a victory clouded by allegations of corruption ever since.

"I knew Joe Kennedy well," Bob Neal said. "He made a deal with Giancana, and the first part of it was West Virginia." Giancana had finally been won over at secret one-to-one meetings with Kennedy that Frank arranged. The mobster's associate Murray Humphreys, who had remained skeptical even after having been "talked up" by Frank, lost the argument. Humphreys concluded, his wife Jeanne said years later, that Giancana agreed "to get that Joe Kennedy's kid elected president" in part "to impress Sinatra."

In West Virginia, Frank's friend Skinny D'Amato was soon spreading money around like manure. "We got them in," D'Amato said, acknowledging that he talked with "the Old Man," one of the Kennedy brothers, or one of their close aides, every day throughout the campaign. A contemporary photograph shows him in conversation with John Kennedy. Also visible in the photograph is Angelo Malandra, a mob lawyer who, an FBI agent said, was "one of the people who, with Sinatra, had the mob's money in West Virginia."

A former Democratic county chairman in West Virginia, John Chernenko, said he received a message in 1960 from a known racketeer. "Frank Sinatra," the contact said, "was interested in knowing if there was any money needed."

Money for West Virginia, D'Amato was overheard saying on an FBI wiretap, had come from Las Vegas. Back in February, as Kennedy relaxed in Frank's suite at the Sands, Peter Lawford had taken Sammy Davis aside. "If you want to see what a million dollars in cash looks like," he whispered, "go into the next room. There's a brown leather satchel in the closet. Open it. It's a gift from the hotel owners for Jack's campaign."

After an evening out with Frank that year, Brad Dexter had a similar experience. "We got back," Dexter said, "and he said there was a valise in his car, and to go get it for him. I brought it in, and he said 'Open it.' The goddamn valise was chock-full of hundred-dollar bills, wrapped in packages. There had to have been a hundred, two hundred thousand dollars in there.

"I said 'Jesus Christ, Frank, we've been out all night. Any of the parking attendants could have taken the valise out of the car and swung with all this fuckin' money.' He says, 'Don't worry about it, Brad. There's more where that came from.' " Frank explained that the money in the bag came from "the Boys"—the mob. Frank's secretary Gloria Lovell, Dexter said, "used to take messages and money back and forth for him, to Chicago, to Sam Giancana, for Jack Kennedy, to distribute for payoffs." Giancana would say that Frank had been merely "our errand boy."

In July, at the Democratic convention in Los Angeles, the errand boy was busy. With Davis and Lawford—Dean Martin in those days cared little for politics—Frank entertained three thousand Democratic faithful at the convention eve banquet. He sat beside Kennedy on the dais, talking animatedly.

Los Angeles police later learned that both men were supplied with prostitutes "just prior to the opening day of the convention." On the opening day itself, according to Judith Campbell, Kennedy tried to get her to do something Frank had tried months earlier, to have sex with him and another woman.

The convention opened with Frank and twenty other stars singing the national anthem to a noticeably jazzy rhythm. All 4,509 delegates and alternates had been handed Frank's campaign record on arrival—his special version of "High Hopes" on one side, "All the Way" on the other.

Frank roamed the convention floor all week, drumming up support for his man. Mindful of the television cameras, he had the bald patch on the crown of his head covered with black makeup. Bob Neal, who was at his side much of the time, thought Frank "really loved politics. He was just in the middle of everything, loved to be part of it. Macho, just great."

Gore Vidal, who was at the convention as a delegate, saw Frank as (an improbably slender) Falstaff to Kennedy's Prince Hal. At a party thrown by Tony Curtis and Janet Leigh after Kennedy had been nominated, the author observed Frank closely. "I was placed, along with Sinatra, at the table where Kennedy would sit. We waited. And waited. Sinatra looked edgy; started to drink heavily. Dinner began. Then one of the toothy sisters of the nominee said, casually, 'Oh, Jack's sorry. He can't come. He's gone to the movies.' Opposite me, Falstaff deflated and spoke no more that evening."

Frank did see Kennedy the following day, at the Lawfords' house, and Peter Lawford witnessed an interesting exchange. The guests he planned to bring to the week's final reception, Frank said, might include “some friends from Chicago.” “Well, Frank,” Kennedy replied with mock solemnity, “just make sure they leave their shades in the car.”

On the eve of the convention, Murray Humphreys had labored to nail down support for Kennedy. Holed up in a Chicago hotel suite, he worked the phones and huddled with politicians and union officials.

Important mobsters were also in Los Angeles during the convention, according to Bill Bonanno. For some of them, he said, Kennedy remained a “hard, almost impossible sell. . . . More people in our world were behind Lyndon Johnson than Kennedy.” Tommy Lucchese, the old Luciano hand from New York, paid a quiet visit to Joe Kennedy and, according to Bonanno, made a deal. Those under Mafia control at the convention were now told to throw their weight behind his son John.

Giancana met with Humphreys the following month. They talked over dinner about “what politicians had to be ‘turned around,’ ” Jeanne Humphreys remembered, which “union heads had to be convinced. . . . Mooney [Giancana] was exuberant. . . . There was a lot of ‘Frank said this’ and ‘Frank said that’ and ‘It’ll all pay off.’ ” In jest, Jeanne said, she told Giancana that someone ought to put her on the campaign payroll. The

Mafia boss responded, "We'll all get our payoff in the end."

IN CALIFORNIA and across the country, Frank had embarked on a marathon of campaign activity. Rosalind Wyman, a key Democratic campaign organizer on the West Coast, thought him "the one who really made a difference." He was hugely effective as a fund-raiser. People paid $50 a head to hear him sing from the diving board by the pool at Tony Curtis's house in Beverly Hills. "He'd get on the phone to somebody," said Milt Ebbins, "and before you knew it he'd be saying, 'Gotcha down for ten thousand.' . . . Frank snapped his fingers and people fell into line."

"If he asked people to go somewhere, they'd go," said Wyman. "Sammy Davis, Jr., Nat King Cole, Ella Fitzgerald, Milton Berle, Bobby Darin, Steve Allen and Jayne Meadows. Frank got them all to do events for us." When transport was needed, Frank supplied the plane.

"We'd spread out," Davis remembered. "I'd do rallies in L.A., San Diego, and up the coast to San Francisco, then we'd meet back at Frank's. 'How'd it go? What happened?' . . . There were always groups huddling, planning activities, and it was exciting to be there, everybody knew you and you knew everybody and you were all giving yourselves to something in which you deeply believed."

"Just a simple call," said Joseph Cerrell, who was a political consultant during the campaign, "and [Frank] takes care of the whole thing. There aren't any bills for the orchestra. . . . People don't say no to him."

Frank's energy and enthusiasm were boundless. He lent his name to a book, **Many Happy Returns,** that featured recipes recommended by Democrats Eleanor Roosevelt, Dinah Shore, Bette Davis, and Lauren Bacall. He made time for politics even when working, barnstorming around the Hawaiian islands by private plane during location work for **The Devil at 4 O'Clock,** a forgettable adventure movie. "I wish I had Sinatra's stamina," said Robert Kennedy, who was himself known for his staying power.

In mid-October, when Frank appeared at a rally in New Jersey, the crowd's welcome seemed more for him than for the politicians on the podium. Thousands surged forward shouting "We want Sinatra!" and he had to cut short his remarks. Two days later, he took part in a radio program with Eleanor Roosevelt.

The offices of two of Kennedy's doctors were burgled during the campaign, probably Republican efforts to get information on his health problems. With similar intent, undercover operatives for Joe Kennedy had been trying to confirm rumors that Nixon had for some time consulted Dr. Arnold Hutschnecker, a New York psychotherapist. They succeeded, Kennedy confided later, in getting hold of "a whole dossier." Milt Ebbins confirmed this. "The one thing they stole," he said, "was a report on Nixon, a detailed report about four to six typed pages. I remember the word 'paranoid.' . . . The doctor's recommendation was that Nixon should go to some place and get treatment."

On November 6, less than forty-eight hours before the election, Dr. Hutschnecker was startled to receive a call from an Associated Press reporter. Would the doctor care to comment, the reporter wanted to know, on his patient Richard Nixon? Hutschnecker would not comment, and the information stayed out of the news until well into the future. The man who had leaked the story to the press, according to a later **Washington Post** report, was Frank Sinatra.

Frank was at Tony Curtis's house to watch the returns on election night. At midnight, eight miles away at the Ambassador Hotel, Nixon was saying privately that Kennedy was going to win. In front of the cameras, however, Kennedy's opponent would not concede. "Frank was drunk," Janet Leigh recalled, "and he yelled at the TV screen, 'Concede, you son-of-a-bitch! Concede!' Frank called the hotel where Nixon was and tried to get him and told someone to tell him to concede. It was a heavy night."

The world learned the following morning that

Kennedy had won the popular vote with a majority of just 113,057 votes out of nearly 69 million cast. He would have lost in the electoral college, the crucial part of the process, had 28,000 voters in Texas and 4,500 in Illinois cast their votes differently. Suspicions of fraud focused above all on Illinois.

Frank had kept a line open to Chicago throughout election day, checking tallies every half hour on the half hour with Democratic ward boss Jake Arvey, who was close to Giancana. During the cliff-hanger evening hours, before going to Janet Leigh's house, Frank spoke time and again with Giancana himself, turning to friends repeatedly to forecast, "It's gonna turn, it's gonna turn."

John Kennedy had made a call of his own, from Hyannis Port, to Chicago's Mayor Richard Daley. Daley had assured him, Kennedy told aides, that "we're going to make it with the help of a few close friends."

In his office at the Armory Lounge, Giancana had presided over his own bank of phones. With Johnny Rosselli, he monitored local returns as they came in. Orders had been issued, and field operatives bent the voting process as required.

"Votes weren't bought," said Murray Humphreys's wife, so much as "commanded, demanded and in a few cases cajoled." According to Giancana's brother Chuck, "guys stood menacingly alongside the voting booths, where they made clear to prospective voters that all ballots were to be cast for Kennedy . . . more than a few arms and legs were broken."

Big players in the know had placed big bets. "I know for a fact that Joe Kennedy put down $22,000, to win, on his boy," said former bookmaker Harry Hall. "Frank Sinatra and Dean Martin made big bets also."

The votes that put Kennedy over the top in Illinois had been "stolen—let me repeat that—stolen," Notre Dame professor Robert Blakey, an organized crime specialist, has said. FBI wiretaps alone, he said, show that mob money and muscle made a difference. The Mafia does nothing for nothing, however, and Blakey was sure Giancana thought "the Kennedys would do something for them" in return.

According to Jeanne Humphreys, Joe Kennedy had assured Giancana that a Kennedy administration would "lay off the mob." Former FBI agent William Roemer, who orchestrated FBI surveillance in Chicago, recalled the import of bugged Mafia conversations, some of them in Sicilian dialect, before and after the elections. "Eventually," Roemer wrote, Giancana had a conversation in which he "indicated that Frank Sinatra had made a commitment to Giancana in 1960. . . . The agreement was that if Giancana used his influence in Chicago with the 'West Side Bloc' and other public officials on Kennedy's behalf,

Sinatra felt he could get Kennedy to back off from the FBI investigation of Giancana."

Even Lucky Luciano was harboring hopes of a return from exile. In the late 1950s, he recalled, he had been visited by an American senator "with a yen to be in the White House"—not Kennedy—who "talked about trying to fix up a way for me to come back." Nothing came of it. During the 1960 campaign, however, for reasons Luciano did not reveal, his hopes rose.

"We were playing gin rummy on the veranda and talking," said Sal Vizzini, a Bureau of Narcotics undercover man who got close to Luciano at that time, "and I got a feeling that Costello and Lansky were promising him an opportunity to come back if Kennedy won. He wasn't supposed to do anything himself because they could do it for him. . . . He inferred that he would get a crack at going back to the States."

Luciano's associate Joe Adonis, who had been deported to Italy in 1956, was a multiple murderer, another of those gangsters whom Frank claimed to know only on a "hello and goodbye" basis, though FBI records suggest otherwise. He may have had special reason for optimism about returning to America. According to an intimate of Skinny D'Amato, Michael Hellerman, Joe Kennedy had promised to "do what he could," should his son become president, to see that Adonis was allowed back.

"Joe Adonis expects to be allowed to return from Italian exile in the spring," Walter Winchell wrote within weeks of the election. "Christmas cards from Lucky Luciano arriving in New York. . . . Frank Costello should be sprung before the snow melts."

On the matter of the Mafia, though, the Kennedy family was at odds with itself.

FOUR YEARS EARLIER, as chief counsel of the Senate Subcommittee on Investigations, Bobby Kennedy had resolved to expose the penetration of the labor unions by organized crime. His father had thought the idea "dangerous . . . not the sort of thing or the sort of people to mess around with," and they had argued bitterly. Bobby held firm, and by 1959 he was pursuing Sam Giancana. He personally interrogated Giancana in a public session, grilled him about the disposal of cadavers, taunted him for giggling like a girl in response to questions. Giancana had taken the Fifth Amendment thirty-three times.

Frank, who watched the hearing on television, had exploded with rage as Kennedy questioned his friend. "Can you believe this little weasel?" he exclaimed. "Can you believe how crazy this goddamn Mick is!" Giancana himself, said his daughter Antoinette, "really hated Bobby Kennedy . . .

Bobby was 'the rat of the family,' while Jack was different."

The month after the election, John Kennedy announced Bobby's appointment as attorney general. Mobsters across the country were amazed and appalled that their nemesis had become the nation's senior law enforcement officer. Speaking from the steps of the Department of Justice, Bobby made it clear that he intended to wage war on organized crime.

FBI files show that Giancana's name was placed close to the top of the list of those selected for "concentrated intensified action." He was already under electronic surveillance, and FBI agents were soon to plant a bug in his headquarters. He would eventually be subjected to "lockstep" physical surveillance, designed to keep him off balance. Where he drove, agents drove. When he played golf, golfing FBI agents followed one hole behind.

As the FBI wiretaps and other evidence show, Giancana simmered with rage. He had been double-crossed, as he saw it, and Frank was at least partly to blame.

ENTERTAINERS HAD NEVER BEEN immune to violent retribution, and least of all from Giancana. It had been a young Giancana, some have claimed, who knifed Joe E. Lewis in the late

1920s. He had been involved in the mob threat to Sammy Davis in 1957. It would be he, according to a fellow mobster, who in 1961 would issue an order to kill Desi Arnaz—later rescinded—because he was making **The Untouchables,** a TV series that depicted mobsters as ruthless killers.

Early that same year, just as it was becoming clear that the Kennedy administration was not going to be soft on organized crime, Frank experienced a moment of sheer terror. Melville Shavelson, an Oscar-nominated screenwriter later to become president of the Writers Guild, learned what had happened at the time. He and his partner, Jack Rose, had worked on the Kennedy inaugural gala, with the assurance that Frank would be helpful should they need a favor. Holding him to the promise, they asked Frank if he would star in a movie that was in the works at Paramount. Frank said he might be interested, and asked the writers to meet him at the Fontainebleau in Miami Beach. Shavelson and Rose flew there, arrived at the hotel, and took the elevator to Frank's penthouse suite. "We went into the living room," Shavelson said, "and there was a bunch of his henchmen sitting around. And one of them asked what we wanted. And I said, 'Frank told us to come down to talk about a movie.' He said, 'You don't tell it to him today.' I said, 'Why not?' And he replied, 'Because he ain't going to come out of his room.'

" 'Why not?' I asked again. And Frank's guy told me, 'He ordered room service last night, and they brought it up to him on a silver tray with a platter covered with a silver dome.' I don't know if Frank lifted it or one of them lifted the dome, but under it, they told us, was the skinned head of a lamb. . . . Frank got up, went into his room, and didn't come out. He didn't show at all the next day."

Dead animals have indeed been used by the Mafia to deliver warnings and threats. Though a fiction, the horse's head in **The Godfather** was in the authentic Mafia tradition. A "sheep with its throat cut" left outside a man's door, wrote Herner Hess in his study of the Sicilian Mafia, is one of a range of threats used against nonmembers.

Far into the future, according to a member of Frank's staff, he could not abide the smell of roast lamb. Whether as affectation or in caution, he preferred to sit in restaurants with his back to the wall. Frank had gone to Giancana on the Kennedys' behalf, his daughter Tina has said, expecting nothing back. "What he did **not** expect was to be set up like a blindsided innocent, like a fool to take the fall."

26

Friends Fall Out

IN JANUARY 1961, two nights before John Kennedy's inauguration, Frank had spent the evening at Robert Kennedy's grand house outside Washington. The Kennedy children behaved as if he were "a god who had dropped out of the sky," fellow guest Joan Braden thought. After endless requests that he sing, he finally leaned back in his chair, removed his toupee—an astonishing departure—and sang for them. Then he rose and said, "That's enough of Frank Sinatra. Bobby, get me a drink."

The previous night, at another Kennedy party, Frank had sat beside the president-elect. A month after his forty-fifth birthday, it seemed, he not only had fame and fortune but entrée at the pinnacle of political power. The inauguration gala he produced, featuring a plethora of stars, was rated a huge success. Though only three thousand people made it to the show—there was a blizzard—all twelve thousand seats had been sold in advance at prices ranging from $100 to $1,500, with boxes costing as much as $10,000. The gala reduced the party's debt by $1.5 million.

In return Frank was honored. Jacqueline Kennedy, who did not approve of the Rat Pack's antics, walked to the presidential box on his arm. John Kennedy took the microphone to declare himself "indebted to a great friend, Frank Sinatra. . . . You cannot imagine the work that he has done. . . . I thank him on behalf of all of you."

The next day, however, when Kennedy stood in the cold in front of the Capitol to take the oath of office, Frank was not among the six hundred men and women seated in the area set aside for the president's friends. Instead he was in his suite at the Statler Hilton, watching on television. The composer Leonard Gershe, who watched with him, said "Frank didn't want to go—it was something like twelve degrees below zero." According to the **New York Daily News,** Frank had turned up drunk before the ceremony. "There was a stand that had assigned seats, and Frank was not on the list," said Bob Neal. "He climbed up and said 'I'm Frank Sinatra,' and a guy said 'We don't care if you're the Pope. You're not on the list.' And the cops threw him out. That's what I heard."

At the Hilton that night, when Frank gave a dinner for his fellow entertainers, there was caviar and champagne and, for each person present, the gift of an inscribed silver cigarette box. Frank had commissioned the boxes in bulk from Ruser's of Beverly Hills at a cost of thousands of dollars. This was Frank's sumptuous inauguration sideshow, and the president had promised to drop in.

Gloria Cahn remembered how Frank sat "very much on edge, waiting, watching, wondering when Kennedy was going to get there." Then came a message that the president was in the hotel and wanted the stars to come downstairs to shake his hand. "Tell him," Frank said, "that we're eating." He slipped away after a while, though, and persuaded Kennedy to come up to talk with the stars.

The following day, when it was time for a select group of celebrities to fly to Palm Beach to visit the president's father, Frank was not among them. Janet Leigh was surprised to find him still in his suite with his current girlfriend, Juliet Prowse. "Tony [Curtis] and I went into the living room and he and Juliet were having breakfast. I said, 'Oh! You're not dressed yet.' He said, 'We're not going. I have to go back to Hollywood.' Everything had seemed friendly and cozy the previous night, and Poppa Kennedy had gotten houses for Frank and the rest of us. Then it was just, pftt, he didn't come.

"At the time I didn't know what happened. But

later we were told—I think by Peter Lawford—that something had been said after the ball, or that morning. Frank was not in a happy mood. . . . Something had happened." The relationship between Frank and the Kennedys had in fact had been coming apart for some time.

In March 1960, there had been a flap when Frank announced he was hiring Albert Maltz to write the screenplay for a planned movie. Fifteen years earlier, Maltz had worked on **The House I Live In,** but he had subsequently been exposed as a communist and sent to prison for defying the House Un-American Activities Committee. The selection of Maltz, the conservative press suggested, tainted not only Frank but his friend John Kennedy. Frank fought back for a while, then dropped Maltz—under pressure from Joe and Robert Kennedy. Frank was enraged, according to George Jacobs. He got drunk for three days, tore up scripts, threw furniture around, and swore he would get out of show business.

Frank had again drawn conservative fire when the Rat Pack began to be dubbed the "Jack Pack." There were fears in the Democratic camp, once again, that the association with Frank would hurt Kennedy. "It is hoped," wrote an aide, "that Sinatra would . . . keep his distance from the Senator." Jacqueline Kennedy let it be known that she thought the same. Word was passed to Frank, and he obliged by making himself less visible.

What really galled him was Kennedy's backsliding on the race issue. Sammy Davis had been booed by Southerners at the Democratic convention, not merely because he was black but because he had announced plans to marry a white woman, the Swedish actress May Britt. A month before the election, with the wedding imminent, the press suggested that Davis's links to the Democratic campaign would cost Kennedy votes. Joe Kennedy applied pressure again, and again Frank obliged him. He asked Davis to postpone the marriage until after the election, and Davis agreed. Their reward was an outrageous snub.

Three days before the inauguration, Davis received a call from John Kennedy's secretary, Evelyn Lincoln. The president-elect, she told him, had asked her to say that "he does not want you to be present at his inauguration. . . . He very much hopes you will understand." Minutes later Peter Lawford called with the same message. Davis canceled his trip to Washington.

Frank was appalled, quarreled furiously with Lawford on the eve of the inauguration gala, and had to be dissuaded from abandoning the whole thing. Days afterward, when Frank sang at a benefit for Martin Luther King Jr. in New York, he was drinking hard. Peter Levinson, a publicist admitted to his dressing room, saw Frank down twelve shots of bourbon before walking on stage to sing.

Despite it all, Kennedy phoned Frank occasionally, and came on the line when Frank called on his birthday. "Happy Birthday, Prez!" was his precise greeting. Frank visited Kennedy in the White House, though only once on his own. Yet his hope of sustaining the friendship alternated with rage over continuing slights.

Joe Kennedy ordered footage of Frank removed from the film of the inaugural gala, then grudgingly had it put back in again, then failed to invite Frank to a viewing. Joe told Frank he was welcome to join him on vacation on the Côte d'Azur and then, responding to fresh barbs in the press, let it be known that there was, after all, "no room" for Frank at his villa.

In the fall of 1961, the Kennedys received Frank at the family compound in Massachusetts. The alcohol flowed and, Joe's chauffeur recalled, women who "looked like whores" arrived. One, seen being pawed by Joe Kennedy in the evening, was wrapped around one of Frank's friends the next morning. Frank was "loud and obnoxious," and White House press secretary Pierre Salinger went out of his way to say he had been the guest not of the president but of Peter Lawford.

Frank was received at the White House that month, but as part of a group and only by mischance. "Frank Sinatra is also coming," the president's secretary noted in a memo. "Tish [Baldrige, Jacqueline's social secretary] said there was no way she could keep from asking him as he was in Peter Lawford's room when she called." Princess Helen Chavchavadze, who was present when he came to the White House, remembered Frank as "showing off, being quite objectionable." Lounging on a balcony with a Bloody Mary, Frank seemed oblivious to the disapproval. "All the work I did for Jack," he said to Dave Powers. "Sitting here makes it all worthwhile."

In early 1962, however, Frank dropped the pretense that all was well. "He was in a snit," arranger Billy May recalled of a recording session on March 6. "We had done 'The Boys' Night Out,' and all during the recording Frank just glared. . . . Then it came time to do the second song, 'Cathy,' which was a pretty song—a waltz. Frank did a rehearsal, and then looked over at Van Heusen and said, 'Tell you what, Chester. Why don't you get Jack Kennedy to record this fucking song, and then see how many records it sells?' "

Two days later, Frank's office announced that he would not be flying to Florida to sing at a dinner for the president's friend George Smathers. Though Frank's voice had seemed fine in the studio that week, his spokesman claimed that he had a bad throat. He was backing away from a commitment he had made to Kennedy personally, almost certainly because he knew outright humiliation was imminent.

Even before the president took office, Frank

had ordered extensive construction work at his Palm Springs house. "He spent thousands," Peter Lawford recalled, "put in guest quarters, extra telephones, even a helipad. All to accommodate the President. Sinatra had it in his head that his house would become sort of the Western White House."

With Kennedy due to spend a weekend in Palm Springs in late March, Frank had made frantic preparations. Parties were planned, guest lists drawn up. Then Frank was told the president would not be staying with him, would not even be dropping in. He would instead be staying at Bing Crosby's Silver Spur Ranch.

Peter Lawford delivered the bad news, initially by telephone, and Frank exploded. He tore a phone from the wall, then tried unsuccessfully to get through to the White House. Lawford then arrived in person, and Sonny King witnessed what happened. "Frank grabbed him by the neck. He didn't hit him but he threw him down some stairs, told him he never wanted to see his face again. . . . Frank went into a rage like one of those maniacal kings in the movies."

According to King and George Jacobs, Frank kicked at a door, smashed photographs of the Kennedys, and pounded the concrete helipad with a sledgehammer. This time the rupture with Lawford was final.

Frank laid the blame on Robert Kennedy. "He

was madder than hell that Bobby wouldn't let the president stay at his house," Shirley MacLaine remembered. "But he adored JFK." Frank spoke fondly of John Kennedy to the end of his days. He cherished mementos of their friendship—a telegram, an inauguration-issue book of matches, even the red phone he had installed for the visit that never took place.

Yet the president had agreed with the decision not to stay at Sinatra's house. Months earlier, during a previous presidential visit to California, Marilyn Monroe had been present as the Kennedy brothers discussed Frank. She told the journalist Sidney Skolsky, a confidant, how the conversation had gone. "Jack," she quoted Bobby Kennedy as having said, "you can't have him coming in the front door or the side door of the White House. You can't stay at his house, can't pal around with him." The president's friend Red Fay recalled Bobby having used almost identical words: "Johnny, you just can't associate with this guy." According to Myer Feldman, a special assistant at the White House, the president concurred.

"It meant nothing to him," said Richard Goodwin, another special assistant. "If Kennedy thought about it in any way, if he thought it would in the slightest way wound his presidency, of course he would cut it off. He would cut off people a lot closer than Sinatra if he had to."

"I don't know if Frank got it," said MacLaine,

"but he had met his match in terms of theatrical manipulation . . . in terms of the code of 'This is what I want, this is what I'm gonna do.' It was up for grabs who was going to be the most cruel."

The message Lawford delivered had included a specific explanation. "Peter told him," said Sonny King, "that JFK couldn't come because of his association with the guys I prefer to call 'the gentlemen of notoriety,' because of the situation between Frank and Sam Giancana." Myer Feldman insisted, "It was a question of whether or not it might damage the nation. The personal damage to him never concerned him so much."

Yet Frank's entanglement with Giancana was inseparable from the involvements of the Kennedys themselves.

27

Paying the Price

As John Kennedy settled in for the weekend at the Crosby estate, Bobby had been announcing victories in his very personal war on organized crime. New laws and specialized intelligence, Bobby told a crime prevention conference, had top gangsters on the run. Three hundred and fifty mobsters were indicted that year alone, 138 of them convicted. Some mobsters were fleeing the United States rather than face justice.

Luciano and Adonis were still in exile. Frank's friend Skinny D'Amato reminded Joe Kennedy that D'Amato's help in the election had been against a promise of intervention on Adonis's behalf. Robert Kennedy, however, had no intention of allowing Adonis to return, and D'Amato himself was indicted on tax charges. The attorney general also pressed for the deportation of any other mafiosi who could be shown to be aliens.

There were new efforts to expel Costello and Rosselli. Early on, New Orleans Mafia boss Carlos Marcello had been bundled into a plane, flown out of the country, and dumped in Guatemala.

Giancana could not be deported, for he had been born in the United States, but he, too, was vigorously pursued. On a visit to Chicago, Bobby surprised FBI agents by how much he knew about the Mafia boss. Messages from Washington urged "all-out" pressure against him, and soon it was reported that Giancana was becoming "highly concerned."

Some mafiosi turned to Frank in the belief that he had the ear of the president. Frank's attorney Milton "Mickey" Rudin, characterized by a senior officer in the Los Angeles police intelligence division as a "hoodlum lawyer," interceded on D'Amato's behalf. To indict him on tax charges, he said, was "unfair . . . a political act." On "instructions" from the Mafia, a senior FBI agent reported, Frank tried to help Costello in his fight against deportation. The transcript of an FBI surveillance tape indicates that Frank spoke on Marcello's behalf with both the president and his brother. All to no avail.

Giancana and Rosselli hoped for special treatment, because both had been involved in CIA plots to assassinate Fidel Castro and, as Giancana put it, considered they were "working for the government." Giancana felt, too, that he had an assurance of leniency because of his help during the campaign. He asked Frank to intercede.

Los Angeles boss Mickey Cohen said, "Sinatra went to President Kennedy. . . . John says to him, 'Go talk to Bobby. . . .' But Bobby was really insulting to Frank and very unreceptive. So Frank went back to John Kennedy. . . . John told Frank, 'Why don't you go see Dad, go talk to Father about that.' "

Frank claimed he went to both Bobby and Joe Kennedy, according to a conversation picked up by an FBI bug in December 1961. Giancana's Las Vegas operative Johnny Formosa reported back that Frank had described how he lobbied the attorney general and his father, taking pains to avoid electronic surveillance. As Formosa relayed it:

> [Frank said] "Johnny, I took Sam's name and wrote it down, and told Bobby Kennedy, 'This is my buddy. . . . This is what I want you to know, Bob.' " . . . [and] Frank saw Joe Kennedy three different times. . . . Joe Kennedy called Frank three different times.

Formosa said Frank was "starting to see the light," to realize that the Kennedys were "not faithful to him." Giancana groused that his "donation" had been in vain, that "if I even get a speeding ticket, none of these [obscenity deleted in FBI transcript] would know me . . . they just worry about themselves, keep themselves clean, take the heat off of them."

Giancana himself no longer believed a word Frank said, he told Formosa:

> One minute he tells me this and then he tells me that. The last time I talked to him was at the hotel in Florida. . . . And he said, 'If I can't talk to the old man I'll talk to The Man [the President].' One minute he says he talked to Robert, and the next minute he says he hasn't talked to him. . . . So, he never did talk to him. It's a lot of [obscenity deleted]. Forget about it. Why lie to me? I haven't got that coming. . . . I don't think that [obscenity] did a [obscenity] thing.

Giancana ordered Formosa to book Frank and Dean Martin for a two-week run of performances at a mob-controlled venue, and added a threat. If either star should fail to comply, he said, "We'll give them a little headache. . . . All they know is the arm. . . . If you ever hit that guy you'll break his jaw. Then he can't sing."

Two weeks later, Rosselli reported to Giancana that Frank seemed to be avoiding his calls. He promised to "punch the [obscenity] out of him in Palm Springs if I don't like the way he talks." Even junior White House officials had no time for Frank, Rosselli told Giancana. "They don't want him. They treat him like you'd treat a whore. You [obscenity] them, you pay them, and they're through. You got the right idea, Moe [familiar name for Giancana]. Go the other way. [Obscenity] everybody. . . . They only know one way. Now let them see the other side of you."

Giancana was furious. "Lying [obscenity]!" he exclaimed to another associate. "If I ever listen to that [obscenity] again. . . . I figured with this guy [Sinatra], maybe we'll be all right. I might have known, this guy'd [obscenity] me. . . . When a guy lies to you . . ."

Any hope Frank may still have had of deflecting the gangsters' rage by getting Joe Kennedy to intervene had just been extinguished. Shortly before Christmas 1961, the president's father had suffered a cerebral thrombosis that left him crippled and unable to speak. "Why, oh why," George Jacobs heard Frank exclaim, "did Joe get that fucking stroke?"

"PEEL THE BANANA," Robert Kennedy had told his organized crime team, "attack the 'respectable' associates of the Mafia." Early in 1962 one of Kennedy's young lawyers, Dougald McMillan, kept coming across Frank's name as he worked on a case involving Joe Fischetti. "Sinatra's affiliation with the mob was so blatant," he recalled, "you couldn't miss it." He began building a file on him.

Soon McMillan's superior, Edwyn Silberling, recommended to Bobby that Frank's tax affairs be thoroughly investigated. He was turned down. Later, during a staff meeting, McMillan drew Kennedy's attention to the FBI's discovery that Judith Campbell was in touch with both the president and Giancana. He thought Campbell should be given immunity and compelled to testify before a grand jury. The proposal was rejected.

Later, when Frank tried to avoid appearing before a grand jury—he asked a White House staffer to intervene—McMillan threatened to resign. When Frank did testify, but evasively, McMillan requested that he be called back for a second appearance. The request was refused. Frank had by then hired a lawyer who also represented Giancana.

William Hundley, who became head of the Organized Crime Section of the Justice Department at the time, had said his team "considered Sinatra very bad news . . . a tool of these people." Even so, Bobby never gave the go-ahead to pursue Frank. "I believe there was an enormously compelling reason beyond his authority that prevented him from saying yes," McMillan said. "It was fear that deterred him from approving an investigation of Sinatra. Fear of exposure. . . . It would have been politically devastating to JFK." Bobby, McMillan thought, was "between a rock and a hard place," between his commitment to crush the Mafia and the fact that his own family was hopelessly compromised.

EVEN AFTER THE TROUBLE it had brought him, Frank continued to keep company with Chicago-based gangsters. In Florida, FBI agents and informants saw him with Joe Fischetti time and again. One Miami Beach source said simply, "Fischetti is Sinatra." Whatever his motivation, and in spite of his anger at Frank over the failed intercession with the Kennedys, Giancana himself also stayed close. Frank was seen with the Mafia boss in Atlantic City, "in a private dining room on Sinatra's floor of the Claridge Hotel." In September, Giancana was at Palm Springs, phoning "the unlisted number of Frank Sinatra" and visiting "Frank Sinatra's residence." In November, with Dean Martin and Sammy Davis, Frank sang to capacity crowds at Giancana's Villa Venice supper club outside Chicago, a command performance.

Frank spent Christmas of 1962 in Acapulco with Giancana and a group that included the Maharani of Jaipur, the French industrialist Paul-Louis Weiller, the Anglo-Irish businessman Loel Guinness and his wife, Gloria, the Dominican playboy Porfirio Rubirosa, and Yul Brynner, who had brought his son Rock along. "I think Giancana introduced himself as 'Dr. Moody,' " Rock said. "I turned sixteen that Christmas, so it became legal for me to drive, and I was recruited to drive 'Dr. Moody' around the watering holes of Acapulco. There I was, roaring around in a pink-and-white-striped jeep with this scary guy." Brynner thought Giancana and Frank seemed to "trust each other, but there wasn't the feeling that they were very close, or part of anything together."

In February 1963, Giancana and Sinatra dined in New York. In March they were seen together in Palm Springs, and in May in Hawaii (Giancana called himself "J. J. Bracket" there). By June, when he and Frank spoke on the phone, he had become "James Perno." Frank also brought Giancana home to New Jersey that month, to sample his mother's cooking.

Contrary to Rock Brynner's notion, Frank and Giancana had long since secretly been part of something together. They were both involved in the Cal-Neva Lodge and Casino, a cluster of mock rustic buildings overlooking Lake Tahoe, on California's border with Nevada. There, too, there was a Kennedy connection.

JOE KENNEDY had frequented the Cal-Neva for decades, since the days when it had been merely a refuge for hunters and fishermen. He liked it so much that in the mid-1950s, using an old business contact as a front, he bought into it—whether in part or outright is not clear. Then, during the 1960 campaign, Frank and several others purchased a 49.5 percent interest in the lodge.

The true owner of Frank's share in the Cal-Neva was almost certainly Giancana. According to FBI documents, the Mafia boss admitted as much. The irony is striking: Giancana effectively co-owned a gambling casino with the father of an attorney general dedicated to destroying everything the mafioso stood for.

By the summer of 1963, revamped and known now as Sinatra's Cal-Neva, the resort was into its third season of gambling and top-flight entertainment. A prostitution operation was being run from the front desk. Skinny D'Amato had been brought in from Atlantic City, and Rosselli and Johnny Formosa were seen at the Lodge. Formosa appeared to have a management role. Nevada Gaming Control Board investigators suspected irregularities, but could prove nothing. In 2003, however, the co-pilot of Frank's private plane remembered flying what the crew knew as "the skim run." "They'd call up and tell us we were going to Truckee-Tahoe, and from there to the Sands and on to Burbank, which meant they were going on a money run," Dan Arney said. "I remember once there were three briefcases, and I got to go back during the flight and see inside one of them. The cash was in $10,000 stacks."

Money also flowed in from Giancana in Chicago. Giancana's associate Joe Pignatello told a friend, Tony Montana, about a courier mission he performed. "Giancana gave Joe a package filled with money," said Montana. "He said, 'Take this to Tahoe and give it to Skinny D'Amato. If anyone takes it from you, the only thing that's going to save you is if you have a hole in your head. In other words, the only way you give up the money is if you're dead.' Skinny happened to be away in San Francisco, so Joe had to stay in a room for two days with the money chained to his arm."

Giancana made at least one appearance at the Cal-Neva in the summer of 1962, when Marilyn Monroe was there. She was just days away from death, agonizing over her relationships with John and Robert Kennedy. People who saw her at the Lodge thought she was in a miserable state, visibly either drunk or drugged. Billy Woodfield recalled how, sometime afterward, Frank asked him to process and print a roll of photographs he had taken at the Cal-Neva. "I developed the film," Woodfield recalled, "and some of the pictures, about nine frames, showed Marilyn, on all fours. She looked sick. Astride her, either riding her like a horse or trying to help her up—I couldn't make out which—was Sam Giancana."

Monroe appeared in the photographs to be in distress, and Woodfield wondered what Frank had been thinking of to use his camera at all. "Frank asked me what I thought he should do with the pictures," Woodfield said. "I said I'd burn them.

He took out his lighter, burned them, and that was the end of it."

Though both Monroe and Giancana were fully clothed in the photographs, the mafioso told several people he and the actress had sex at the Cal-Neva. Monroe said so, too, according to Jeanne Carmen, who was her friend. Giancana mocked her poor performance, and she spoke of the episode with disgust.

These goings-on would have been of great interest to officials of the Nevada Gaming Control Board, because Giancana should not have been at the Cal-Neva in the first place. As one of the notorious mobsters listed in the board's Black Book, he was not allowed to set foot in any casino in the state. In fact, as Nick Sevano recalled, "He'd sneak in to see Sinatra, by helicopter, would you believe. Money was spread around with the police, so no one checked. Sinatra had a separate place in Cal-Neva that nobody knew about. They used to sneak in there to have dinner. I was there."

In late July 1963, word reached the authorities that Giancana had been at the lodge with his lover, the singer Phyllis McGuire, and had gotten into a noisy fistfight involving McGuire's road manager, Frank, and George Jacobs. Afterward, Giancana had left for Palm Springs. The police had been called, however, and Gaming Control Board officials investigated. Frank denied there had been a fight. D'Amato and the maître d' obstructed the board's agents. Then, on Labor

Day weekend, Frank brought serious trouble on himself when he called board chairman Ed Olsen.

Olsen's chief investigator and the Gaming Commission secretary listened in on extensions as Frank subjected their boss to a long tirade. It was peppered with so much foul language that Olsen's memorandum for the record bore the label "OBSCENE OBSCENE." Frank opened by telling Olsen he was "acting like a fucking cop." Could they not, he asked, talk off the record?

Olsen declined, saying he would subpoena Frank if he wanted a formal interview. "You just try and find me," said Frank. "And if you do, you can look for a big fat surprise . . . a big, fat, fucking surprise. You remember that. Now listen to me, Ed. . . . Don't fuck with me. Don't fuck with me. Just don't fuck with me."

Olsen asked if this was a threat, and Frank replied very deliberately—as vividly indicated in the original text of Olsen's memo: "No . . . j u s t d o n ' t f u c k w i t h m e . . . . And you can tell that to your fucking Board and that fucking Commission, too." Later, when board agents arrived at the Cal-Neva for a prearranged inspection, Frank had them ejected. The following day, when they showed up again, D'Amato tried to bribe them with hundred-dollar bills.

Olsen briefed the gaming authorities and the governor of Nevada. The board issued a formal complaint, noting that Frank's corporation had broken the law by knowingly hosting Giancana even though he was banned from Nevada casinos, had defied the authorities by saying he would continue the association, by having an employee refuse to testify, and by attempting to "intimidate and coerce" the authorities.

Frank was cornered, and he knew it. He announced a month later that he would not fight the charges but divest himself of his interests in Nevada, at the Sands and at the Cal-Neva. Coming as it did after his problems with the Kennedys, this was a huge financial and psychological blow.

Frank had felt let down, abandoned, for more than a year, ever since the president decided not to stay at his house. "If he would only pick up the phone and call me and say it was politically difficult to have me around," Angie Dickinson recalled Frank saying, "I would understand. I don't want to hurt him. But he has never called me."

John Kennedy had not abandoned him entirely. On a trip to Las Vegas during the Cal-Neva debacle, the president put in a word on his behalf. "What are you guys doing to my friend Frank Sinatra?" he asked Governor Grant Sawyer as they drove together in an open limousine. The governor replied, he recalled in his memoirs, "Well, Mr. President, I'll try to take care of things here in Nevada, and I wish you luck on the national level." Though Sawyer did not mention the fact in his book, he told his friend Ralph Denton that

Kennedy had in fact gone a little further. "Is there anything you can do for Frank?" he had asked. Sawyer replied, "No."

It is unlikely Frank knew of this. Eddie Fisher thought the break with the Kennedys "devastated" him. "It was hurt beyond hurt," said Leonora Hornblow, another friend. "With Ava, one of the great pains of his life."

At a key moment in the Cal-Neva fiasco, Frank had flown Giancana to Palm Springs aboard his private plane. The FBI knew that, as it now knew virtually every move the mobster made. So intensive was the surveillance, Giancana said, it was as if he were living under a communist dictatorship. Worse, FBI eavesdroppers heard Giancana complain, many of his usual sources of funds were being cut off. He told a friend that the Cal-Neva mess had cost the Chicago mob $470,000. There were rumors he might be ousted from the leadership. An October surveillance report noted that Giancana, stymied at every turn, was cursing the government.

The Nevada gambling authorities formally stripped Frank of his licenses on October 22. In early November Giancana was again reported staying with Frank in Palm Springs.

THE WEEKEND BEFORE JOHN KENNEDY'S TRIP to Dallas, the president watched the movie

Tom Jones at his father's home in Florida. After dinner, close aides remembered later, he launched into "September Song," the melancholy Kurt Weill number Frank had recorded early in the presidency:

> . . . the days dwindle down to a precious few
> September, November . . .

In California that week, Judith Campbell was feeling distraught and confused. She had not dated either the president or Giancana for months—though Giancana stayed in occasional touch by phone—and the FBI, aware of her involvements from telephone surveillance, was constantly on her heels. Once, when Campbell was at the Key Club in Palm Springs, Giancana and Frank had studiedly behaved as though they did not know her.

Nevertheless, phone records reflect sixty calls between Campbell and the Mafia boss in the summer of 1963, and sixteen to Frank while he was at the Cal-Neva. The calls were guarded, for all three knew the FBI was watching and listening. She said she felt "like I was in a giant maze . . . sick of the intrigue, of not knowing what was going on." On November 20, Johnny Rosselli installed Campbell in a hotel room in Beverly Hills.

On November 22, in Texas, President Kennedy was assassinated. Frank was on location that day, playing a mobster in **Robin and the 7 Hoods**, a parody of the Robin Hood legend set in 1920s Chicago. They were shooting a scene in a Los Angeles cemetery, and there had been laughter earlier when someone spotted an old gravestone inscribed "John F. Kennedy."

When the news from Dallas came, Frank walked off among the graves. Then he made a call to Washington, finished the cemetery scene, and left for Palm Springs. He stayed there for several days, George Jacobs said, living on sandwiches and "vast amounts" of Jack Daniel's. Frank was not invited to the president's funeral, but sent flowers.

The following week he seemed uneasy, distant, during Thanksgiving dinner. Eight days later, Frank Jr., now nearly twenty and starting out on a singing career of his own, was kidnapped at a Lake Tahoe lodge. Two gunmen gained access to his room on the pretext of making a delivery, forced him into a car during a blizzard, drove him to a house near Los Angeles, and made ransom demands.

Frank spent two days and three nights flying to and from Nevada by rented airplane, fielding calls from the kidnappers, and arranging for the delivery of $240,000 ($1.5 million today). His son was released, the money recovered, and the kidnappers caught and jailed. They turned out to be a trio of apparent amateurs, one of whom had gone to school with the Sinatras' elder daughter. Testifying in court during their trial, though, Frank Jr. said he had heard his kidnappers talking as though they "were only executing a plan concocted by higher-ups . . . higher-ups in organized crime."

During the ordeal, Tina Sinatra has said, her father was haunted by the notion that the kidnapping was a message from the mob, a warning to him to stay silent about anything he might know that implicated the Mafia in the president's assassination.

At the time, such a notion would have seemed bizarre. The public was told that the president had been shot by a lone gunman. The doubts raised when Lee Harvey Oswald was killed by Jack Ruby were dispelled when the Warren Commission depicted Jack Ruby as a misguided loner. Any suggestion of conspiracy focused more on the Soviet Union and Cuba. Today, however, many of those who believe there was a conspiracy think the Mafia was involved. The chief counsel of the House Select Committee on Assassinations, Robert Blakey, has said flatly that "the Mob did it."

Those who share this view focus on three Mafia bosses in particular—Carlos Marcello, Santo Trafficante, and Sam Giancana. Within hours of his brother's death, Bobby Kennedy had asked Julius Draznin, a rackets specialist with the National Labor Relations Board, to look for mob leads in Chicago. "He meant," said Draznin, "Sam Giancana."

For five days after the assassination, Judith Campbell shut herself up in the hotel room in which Rosselli had left her, refusing even to speak on the telephone. Rosselli then took her to Palm Springs and there, at the Canyon Country Club, she encountered Frank. He looked straight through her, and they never spoke again. Giancana and Rosselli abandoned her soon thereafter.

In the days after the assassination, according to George Jacobs, "Sinatra wondered aloud (though not too loud) if Mr. Sam [Giancana], who knew Jack Ruby from the strip-club circuit in which he had a hand, could have had something to do with it."

It was not until sixteen years later, when the Assassinations Committee's report was published, that the extent of Ruby's organized crime connections became generally known. He had grown up in Chicago and become a petty criminal in cahoots with Chicago mafiosi. His eventual move to Dallas, he said, had been on mob instructions. When Giancana associates convened in Dallas to discuss bookmaking operations, a few months before the assassination, they met at Ruby's Carousel Club.

The assassination saga touched in an odd way on Reprise, the recording company Frank had founded in 1960. In November 1963, when discussing the promotion of a rock 'n' roll record with a musician in Dallas, Ruby had claimed "connections" with the company. He had made several calls in recent months to the various phone numbers of Mike Shore, an adviser and publicist for Frank who had an office at Reprise. Shore testified later that the calls had related to problems Ruby was having with a then mob-dominated union, the American Guild of Variety Artists. The same day as one of the calls to Shore, four weeks before the assassination, Ruby also phoned a man named Irwin Weiner in Chicago. Weiner, an underworld figure who was an associate of Giancana, had grown up with Earl Ruby, Jack's brother, and with Mike Shore. Weiner was to claim in a 1978 interview that Ruby's call to him had not been about the union problem. A few months later, testifying under oath to the House Assassinations Committee, he said it was.

After Ruby murdered Oswald, Shore said, he responded to a call from Ruby's brother by helping to find Oswald's killer a defense attorney and to raise funds to cover legal fees. Plans were made for photojournalist Billy Woodfield to interview Ruby in jail, with the lion's share of the anticipated income going to Ruby. **My Story,** by Jack Ruby and Woodfield, was published in serial form and appeared in newspapers around the world. Shore said he never discussed the Ruby matter with Sinatra.

Tony Oppedisano, a producer who was to become Frank's closest male intimate in his declining years, said the president's murder was something on which Frank said "things in confidence that I wouldn't divulge. . . . He had his own opinion as to the scenario that led up to it."

SAM GIANCANA NEVER DID FORGIVE Frank for his role in the failed relationship with the Kennedys or for the loss of the Cal-Neva. According to a member of the mobster's family, only the intercession of East Coast associates persuaded Giancana not to have Frank killed in 1963. "That motherfucker," he said when Frank arrived unexpectedly at the Armory Lounge, "is lucky to be alive."

In the years that followed, the Mafia boss alternately socialized with Frank and terrorized him. Once, when Frank was performing in Las Vegas, Giancana sent word that he wanted to see him. Then he said he did not want to see him. Then he sent abuse. Frank cut short his performance and left. Giancana continued to speak from time to time of having Frank killed.

On June 19, 1975, after the Mafia boss was found shot dead at his home in Chicago, investigators noted that the execution bullet had been fired into the back of his head and six others into his mouth and throat. The six additional shots, it was said, were to indicate that the Mafia knew Giancana could no longer be trusted to remain silent, and to warn others not to make the same mistake. As noted earlier, Senate Intelligence Committee staff members had that very day arrived in Chicago to make arrangements for Giancana to testify.

A few months later, when it became clear that the committee was not going to interrogate Sinatra, William Safire published the long list of questions that he felt Frank should have been asked. The final question, the columnist wrote, should have been: "Before or after the Kennedy assassination, did Giancana or Rosselli ever mention the name of Jack Ruby to you?" Sinatra, Safire wrote, "might emerge from such an interrogation with honor bright. Perhaps he can put the lie to any sinister insinuations. But we can put our dreams away for another day. . . . We are left to ponder what might have been learned if only 'Old Blue Eyes' had been required to sing."

The allusion was to the melancholy song Frank had made his theme song in the 1940s. His last recording of it had been released three months before the assassination:

> Put your dreams away for another day
> . . . it's time to make a new start.

28

The Lonely Millionaire

THE NEW START ALMOST ENDED before it began. In May 1964, while wading in the surf on the Hawaiian island of Kauai, Frank went to the aid of a woman friend who was being pulled out to sea by the undertow—only to be swept away himself. Both came very close to death. "He looked like a goner," recalled Brad Dexter, who played a key role in the rescue. "They were both suffering from hypoxia—which occurs when you lose all the oxygen in your head, and you're blind. Frank said 'I can hear you, but I can't see you! . . . Save her, and leave me . . . I'm going to die.'

"I said, 'Frank, for Christ's sake! Be a man, and let's fight this through.' But he couldn't, he just didn't have the physical strength. When I'd grabbed him, there was no musculature at all. He was not a strong man. . . . Then came these two Hawaiians with giant surfboards, and they took them in. They were both unconscious . . . and when I got to the shore I gave them artificial respiration. . . . The water poured out of Frank's lungs."

A little later, when Dexter went to see how Frank was doing, he found him sitting with his daughter Nancy. "He said, 'My family thanks you,' " Dexter remembered, "not just 'Thank you.' He never, ever thanked me for saving his life."

Frank kept Dexter close by for several years afterward, and sent film work his way. When they eventually fell out, however, Frank claimed privately that Dexter "didn't really save my life. It was an old guy on a surfboard." "If Brad hadn't been there," said Ruth Koch, the widow of producer Howard W. Koch and the woman who shared Frank's ordeal that day, "I don't think Mr. Sinatra would have survived."

"Frank and I had a great relationship," Dexter said later. "He loved me, and I loved him—as friends. But he couldn't stand the fact that I'd saved his life. I never let him feel he was beholden to me. But he would have preferred to have saved **my** life, because then **I** would have been beholden to **him.**"

Joey Bishop had sent Frank a telegram after the near-drowning. "Did you forget yourself?" he asked. "You could have walked on the waves." In an article entitled "The Enigma of Frank Sinatra," Richard Gehman wrote of Frank's need to sustain the notion that he had power over events and over his fellow human beings. He pointed out that Frank had in fact become an "immensely powerful force—a law unto himself . . . as he has grown bigger and more powerful he has grown more demandingly arrogant."

His power, Gehman reported, was both personal and financial. He could demand a share of the profits in any movie in which he starred, could dictate which songs were plugged. He also made himself so inaccessible that meaningful reporting about him was almost impossible.

"Sinatra has become the most feared man in Hollywood," Gehman wrote. "A veteran Hollywood reporter told me recently, 'No one will talk about him. He's an untouchable.' " While preparing his article, Gehman noted, he himself received a threatening call in the middle of the night. "If you know what's good for you," the voice on the phone told him, "lay off Frank."

"It would be disturbing," wrote the editors of **Good Housekeeping,** which published Gehman's article, "if this enormous power were in the hands of a completely stable and predictable human being. When it is in the hands of a man torn by emotions that he apparently either cannot or does not care to control, it is something to view with alarm."

Gehman thought that was going too far. He later reminded readers of the compassionate Sinatra, the Sinatra who responded, when a club owner's widow found herself in financial difficulty, by showing up with a twenty-one-piece orchestra and performing for free. Above all, Gehman thought, Frank's sheer talent ought to be given more weight than the dark side of his personality. "It does not matter how powerful, or corrupt, he is or may become. We can forgive him so long as he continues to enchant us solely by existing." For all his flaws, Frank never lost that seductive power.

ONE DAY IN MARCH 1962, Frank had gone into the recording booth to sing "I Gotta Right to Sing the Blues." On that track, radio host and Sinatra devotee Jonathan Schwartz has said, Frank sounded "as if he stood before the microphone reading a sports section and chewing gum." At a previous session, he had ripped up his sheet music rather than do another take. He had been in a foul mood because, after months of festering resentment, he was making his last recording for Capitol Records.

Frank had wanted more creative control, and the company had not given it to him. "Fuck you! Fuck your company!" he had yelled when Capitol's Alan Livingston tried to find a way through the impasse. Though Capitol had been his label through the glory years of his recording career, the break had become inevitable. "I helped build that," he had told a colleague as they walked along Vine Street past Capitol's trademark circular headquarters. "Now let's build one of our own." He had established Reprise Records—"Reprise," Frank explained, because he intended to make records "to play and play again." He pronounced the word, however, not as "repreese" but as in "reprisal." Some dubbed the new company Revenge Records.

Promotional copy said the new company brought the world "a new, happier emancipated Sinatra . . . untrammelled, unfettered, unconfined." The aspiration was to bring Frank and the artists he contracted more creative freedom and more money. He produced ten albums in the first three years, recording his versions of "Ring-A-Ding-Ding," "In the Still of the Night," "Call Me Irresponsible," "The Second Time Around," and new takes on old Sinatra favorites. Indulging his interest in jazz, Frank also made an album with Count Basie. In the same period he performed in eleven foreign countries, appeared on television, and kept up a hectic pace on other fronts—all this amidst his personal turmoil during the Kennedy presidency.

Frank had said when he launched Reprise that he saw his future "not so much as an entertainer but as a high-level executive. . . . I've been getting fascinated with finances." Billy Woodfield photographed him in a grand office, shirtsleeved, cigarette in hand, presiding over a meeting of twelve executives. There was a UPI news ticker to one side of him, a picture of President Kennedy on the sideboard. Another photograph showed Frank standing below a huge tabulated blowup crammed with numbers and headed "Comparative Gross Receipts."

Though more publicity gimmick than a reflection of how he really spent his time, the pictures evoked an image of Frank as The Chairman of the Board, a nickname that was to stick. (It had been coined, ironically, by the disc jockey William B. Williams, when searching for a sobriquet that spoke to his musical authority.) Yet Frank had chosen an inauspicious moment to start the new company, and Reprise got off to a shaky start.

The big moneymaking singles were increasingly being sung by young men and women for a young market. Frank was in his late forties, the fans who had made him only slightly younger. No Sinatra single had made the top ten since 1956; it had become difficult for him even to get into the top forty. Capitol was taking its commercial revenge, undercutting Frank's company by reissuing Sinatra albums that it controlled at discounted prices. Reprise was in trouble.

Then, in August 1963, at a time when everything seemed to be going wrong for him, Frank was suddenly going about showing friends a certified check for a million dollars ($6 million today). So delighted with it was he that he did not deposit the check for days. Frank had sold two-thirds of Reprise to Warner Brothers Records, and the million dollars was only the downpayment. The deal was driven by the fact that Frank owed the company money, a Warner Brothers source told the FBI. Warner soon after acquired a major slice of Frank's movie projects, guaranteeing him $250,000 a picture plus 15 percent of the gross. It made him the highest-paid actor-entertainer in Hollywood.

Nine Sinatra movies were churned out from 1961 to 1965, five of them involving members of the Rat Pack. After 1961, however, there were no more films that could really be described as Rat Pack movies. Frank liked to work with Dean Martin and Sammy Davis, but he had come to loathe the name Rat Pack. Movies made by Sinatra and friends, moreover, no longer attracted large audiences.

There was also a disaster movie, **The Devil at 4 O'Clock,** which was indeed a disaster, and two war movies that earned good reviews and good box office. **None but the Brave,** about the ordeal of American servicemen stranded on an island in the Pacific, did respectably at the box office; **Von Ryan's Express,** about a mass escape by Allied prisoners from an Italian prison camp, was a major hit. There had also been **The Manchurian**

Candidate, the fine film about American soldiers brainwashed in Korea, which culminates in a plot to assassinate a presidential candidate. It was at the same time a complex political satire on the United States of the McCarthy period. Frank gave a superb performance as the army major, himself a shattered veteran, who thwarts the murder of the presidential nominee. The movie attracted meager audiences, though, and was soon withdrawn. Frank thought it "without doubt the finest picture I have ever made." He had a queen of diamonds, the "control key" for the brainwashed assassin of the movie, imprinted on the bottom of his Palm Springs pool.

In the deal with Warner, Frank became "special assistant" to Jack Warner himself, a prestigious title in a mighty empire. He operated from an office of appropriate grandeur, decked out in orange of course, with inscribed photographs of Democratic presidents on display. In the anteroom stood the bust of himself that Jo Davidson had cast two decades earlier.

By 1965 Frank was presiding over Reprise Records; two movie companies, Artanis—"Sinatra" spelled backward—Productions and Park Lake Enterprises; Cal Jet Airway, an airplane charter business; and Titanium Metal Forming, which made parts for aircraft and missiles. The air charter company boasted two jets—an eight-seater Lear and a three-seater Morane-Saulnier—and a helicopter. Often Frank would leave Palm Springs about noon, early for him, make the seventeen-minute commute to Burbank aboard the Lear, then drive to the Warner Brothers lot in his black Dual-Ghia. The Lear was also handy for whisking houseguests to and from Palm Springs or to Las Vegas.

Frank's enterprises employed seventy-five people full-time, including secretaries answering fan mail, his pilots, and, ubiquitous now, a posse of bodyguards. The Palm Springs house had recently been enlarged and boasted a saltwater pool—in the middle of the desert. He rented a five-bedroom apartment on East River Drive in Manhattan and a ten-room house in Beverly Hills. Though he had lost his Nevada gambling licenses, he still owned the buildings that made up the Cal-Neva Lodge on Lake Tahoe. **Look** magazine calculated his annual income in 1965 at $3.5 million ($20 million today) before taxes.

Money gushed out as fast as it poured in. He "lives like royalty," said his producer friend William Goetz. When Frank went on a sea cruise, he chartered not only a yacht but a seaplane to follow it. He once had a barber flown from New York to Miami to give him a haircut. For all the millions Frank spent on self-indulgent excess, though, a constant flow went to help others. He had been performing at benefits since the 1940s, raising vast sums for children's hospitals, the aged, refugees, mental health, the blind, for the fight against cancer, and many other health-related charities. In 1962, declaring that as an "over-privileged adult" he should do something for underprivileged children, he had undertaken a World Tour for Children that took in ten countries and raised, in today's dollars, nearly $6 million. He himself paid the expenses, which were about half that sum.

He sent Jule Styne's mother, whom he did not know, four dozen roses a day when she was sick in a New York hospital. He pulled Phil Silvers out of a dire professional hole by performing alongside him. He cheered up the singer Joey Napoli by sending him a hundred canes when he suffered severe injuries in a car accident. When his pianist Bill Miller's home was destroyed in a mudslide in which his wife died, Frank paid the hospital bills not covered by insurance, found Miller a new home, and completely furnished it.

He paid the hospital bills when serious illness felled Buddy Rich, Joe Louis—whom he had flown to Texas for top-flight treatment following a stroke—Lee J. Cobb, Claudette Colbert's husband Joel Pressman, and later Peggy Lee. He looked after the bills for Mabel Mercer when she was old, ailing, and penniless.

Horrified to hear that Billie Holiday was dying a miserable death in the psychiatric ward of a New York hospital, Frank pulled strings to get her transferred to a private hospital. Her death had a deep effect on him and he later recorded the song "Lady Day" as a tribute to her:

> So many shadows in her eye
> . . . Lady Day has too much pain.

Frank arranged medical care for the husband of his maid at a hotel. He gave $1,000 to a bootblack at another hotel when he learned he was a former champion boxer fallen on hard times. A girl's leg was saved when Frank rushed specialists to the scene of an accident on an escalator at Bonwit Teller's. He sent an attorney to represent an elderly immigrant couple threatened with eviction. He helped a child burned in a household accident. He arranged for a truckload of food and goods to be sent to the children of a dying woman in Long Beach.

Tina Sinatra was with her father one day when, after seeing a television news report about a poor family whose home had been destroyed in a Christmas tree fire, he ordered his business manager to "send them a nickel." When he referred to a nickel in that context, she explained, he meant $5,000.

Frank asked Whitey Littlefield, a business associate, to buy a bus for delivery to a school in Ohio. "The one condition," Littlefield said, "was that no one was ever to know where the bus came from."

Frank's generosity was most often driven by nothing other than heartfelt goodwill. So much of the giving was triggered by random chance, by a press or radio report of some small human misery. At the same time, there may have been something of the Sicilian **padrone** about him, of a compulsion to garner authority and respect by dispensing help to the needy. "In a certain way," said the bandleader Peter Duchin, "he was very emotional . . . very Italian."

IN EARLY NOVEMBER 1965, a month before Frank's fiftieth birthday, the writer Gay Talese flew to Los Angeles to interview him. Talese had been assured by his editor at **Esquire** magazine that the interview was "all set up." Instead he was fobbed off by a publicist with a string of lame excuses. Limited to only a very brief exchange with Sinatra, he spent five weeks watching Frank and talking to those around him.

The article Talese wrote is still acclaimed as the most closely observed piece ever written on Sinatra. He studied Frank in the studio, in a Las Vegas casino, on a movie set, and drinking late at night in a private club. **Esquire** readers learned of Frank's arrogance, of his compulsion to control others, and of the anxiety he instilled in those around him. Yet, Talese wrote, "In an age when the very young seem to be taking over . . . Frank

Sinatra survives as a national phenomenon, one of the few pre-war products to stand the test of time. . . . He does not feel old, he makes old men feel young, makes them feel that if Frank Sinatra can do it, it can be done."

Yet Frank was feeling the passage of time. Three years earlier he had said, "As a singer I'll only have a few more years to go—as an actor maybe a few more than that, but not many . . . and frankly I'm getting a bit tired."

As Frank reached fifty, he performed on an hour-long NBC show to mark the occasion. He also agreed to be filmed for **Sinatra: An American Original**, a CBS News documentary to be narrated by Walter Cronkite—even though, his publicist told Talese, he feared the network would "try to nail him with the Mafia." **Billboard** ran an eighty-nine-page tribute, and there were major stories in **Life, Look,** and **Newsweek.**

Frank also recorded a musical milestone, the album **September of My Years.** The voice was lower now, that of an older man, a man, moreover, who had smoked many thousands of unfiltered Camels. "The silken baritone of 1943," the writer Arnold Shaw thought, was now "like torn velvet." Wistful, haunting, the songs on the album proclaimed that Frank was now well into middle age: "How Old Am I?," "Last Night When We Were Young," "It Was a Very Good Year," "Hello, Young Lovers," and "This Is All I Ask":

And let the music play as long as there's a
song to sing
Then I will stay younger than spring.

At the birthday party first wife Nancy threw for him, a glittering black-tie affair at the Beverly Wilshire Hotel, daughter Nancy teased Frank about his baldness. Now about to achieve prominence as a singer herself, she sang to the tune of "Tit Willow":

The rug he once cut he now wears on his
head
My Daddy, my Daddy, my Daddy. . . .

Frank's hair was so sparse now that he had in his retinue a woman whose sole duty was to care for his sixty toupees. He would soon consult a hair transplant surgeon in New York. When he pulled out his gold lighter to light a woman's cigarette, Talese noticed, his fingers were "nubby and raw . . . so stiff with arthritis that he could hardly bend them."

Frank was very much set in his ways. In his dressing room at the Royal Festival Hall in London, the broadcaster David Jacobs had witnessed an astonishing ritual. "I was ushered into the presence and there was Frank Sinatra sitting in his dress shirt and his silk socks, bow tie and his underpants. It occurred to Mr. George Jacobs, the black valet, that it was time the master got dressed.

"So he jumped up on the table, which I thought was very strange, and Mr. Jacobs went to the cupboard and got out Sinatra's trousers, which were hanging on one of those old-fashioned kind of trouser hangers that you clip at the very bottom. And he unclipped them, did a most wonderful movement like a magician, and held them for Sinatra, who was still standing on the table.

"And Sinatra put one stiff leg in one leg of the trousers, and ditto the other, and stepped onto a chair. And when he got to the chair Mr. Jacobs held him under the armpits and lifted him down. Mr. Jacobs zipped up Sinatra's fly. Then he got the jacket out and Sinatra put one stiff arm into the jacket, and then the other, and he was buttoned up.

"And I said to him, 'Forgive me, but would you mind telling me why you dress in this extraordinary fashion?' He looked at me and said, 'Well, when I go out onto the stage I don't want to stand there in a crumpled suit—like yours is.' He then walked out to tumultuous applause in a spotlight, and as soon as he got to the center of the stage he jumped up on a stool and cocked his legs and crossed his arms—and you couldn't see his suit anyway."

"I'm a symmetrical man almost to a fault," Frank acknowledged as his fiftieth birthday approached. "I demand everything in its place."

The spirit of 1965, however, was not about symmetry. That year, in a poem later published in his anthology **The Fall of America,** Allen Ginsberg wrote of: "Frank Sinatra lamenting distant years, old sad voic'd September'd recordings, and Beatles crying Help! their voices woodling for tenderness." The Beatles had made their assault on American culture the previous year. They had been greeted at Kennedy Airport by some five thousand screaming teenagers, and seventy-three million people had seen their appearance on **The Ed Sullivan Show.**

Jule Styne had declared in 1962 that Frank had "defeated rock 'n' roll." Two months after the Beatles' arrival, though, they had the top **five** singles on the **Billboard** chart, and the top two albums. Frank had no single and just one album on the charts, at number ten. As fate would have it, the Beatles had not only signed with Capitol Records, but had been brought on board by Alan Livingston, with whom Frank had fallen out.

"We came out of nowhere," Paul McCartney said later, "with funny hair, looking like marionettes or something. . . . I think that was really one of the big things that broke us—the hairdo more than the music originally. A lot of people's fathers had wanted to turn us off."

Frank was such a father. "Long hair," said George Jacobs, "drove him batty. . . . He didn't care how good the new music was . . . to him it was all one big excuse to take drugs." Frank would later smash a car radio with the heel of his shoe because every station seemed to be playing the Doors' "Light My Fire." "He genuinely hated rock 'n' roll, hated the Beatles," Rock Brynner remembered. "It was generational. He had nothing but contempt for all of that." The new sound repelled Frank, his son said.

The latest rock 'n' roll groups, Frank was to say, "miss the point because they don't stop to think what lyrics mean: they listen to themselves too much. Some shout the whole damn night, like singing the Declaration of Independence in every note. Don't they know shadow, nuance, color? That offends me."

John Lennon, for his part, had no time for Frank's music. "Peggy Lee I could listen to all day," he said. "Ella Fitzgerald is great." But: "Sinatra's not for me; it just doesn't do it, you know?" McCartney, characteristically, took the broader view. As a teenager in the mid-1950s, he said, he had realized that "if anyone wanted to go into show business . . . you were looking at a Sinatra-type person as the most rockin' you were gonna get." When he wrote "When I'm Sixty-Four," at the age of about sixteen, McCartney remembered, "I thought I was writing a song for Sinatra."

To most teenagers of the mid-1960s, Frank and his music were old hat, and he knew it. In public he began to make accommodating noises, conceding that, "We must stop and think that twenty-five years ago we made the music of our era. . . . Kids want identity."

A few years later, Frank would record a birthday song for Ringo Starr's wife, make his jet available to Paul McCartney, and welcome George Harrison as a houseguest. He would record both Harrison's "Something" and Lennon and McCartney's "Yesterday" and praise them as the best love songs written in decades. Frank could recognize talent, even in rock 'n' rollers. In the end, it turned out, the new music and the Sinatra sound would coexist.

Even in 1965, many young people responded when Frank did what he did best. When "In the Wee Small Hours" was played in a Beverly Hills club, Talese noticed, "it inspired many young people who had been sitting, tired of twisting, to get up and move slowly around the dance floor, holding one another very close. . . . It was, like so many of his classics, a song that evoked loneliness and sensuality . . . a kind of airy aphrodisiac. Undoubtedly the words from this song, and others like it, had put millions in the mood, it was music to make love by, and doubtless much love had been made to it all over America."

Lovemaking to the Sinatra sound, Talese wrote, had been enjoyed by couples rich and poor, "in cars, while the batteries burned down, in cottages by the lake, in secluded parks and exclusive penthouses and furnished rooms . . . in all places where Sinatra's songs could be heard were these words that warmed women, wooed and won them, snipped the final thread of inhibition and gratified the male egos of ungrateful lovers."

As he mused at that Beverly Hills club, Talese watched Frank standing in a dark corner, a glass of bourbon in one hand and a cigarette in the other. Sinatra was staring out into the room beyond the bar, where the young people were clustered. He had been in a "mood of sullen silence" all week. On either side of him was an attractive blonde, each of whom appeared to be waiting in vain for him to say something.

Again and again in the weeks that followed, in recording studios and in the casino at the Sands, on a movie set and in the street, Talese watched women around Frank. They swayed to his music, smiled smiles of adulation in his direction. None, so far as Talese could tell, got anywhere. "He needs a great deal of love," the writer quoted Hank Sanicola as saying. "He wants it twenty-four hours a day." In 1965, however, Frank found lasting love with a woman as unattainable as ever.

Emotionally, he was still bound to Ava.

29

The Child Bride

IF AVA GARDNER COULD NOT LIVE WITH FRANK, it seemed she was unable to live without him. In 1961 she had turned up for a Sinatra opening in Las Vegas, discovered that the first Mrs. Sinatra and her children had arrived ahead of her, and left town. A year later, she and Frank were seen out together in Los Angeles. Then, during his World Tour for Children, he made a detour to see her in Madrid.

It was not a happy visit. She had lived there for six years now, and had become known as a beautiful, pathetic drunk. The co-pilot of Frank's plane, Dan Arney, witnessed a furious fight between them during the visit. "They went to dinner and got into a pissing match. Every time they got together they got into a pissing match. . . . She'd say, 'I'll never talk to that wop son of a bitch again.' "

Ava dragged Arney and the other pilot off to "a place that was really like a whorehouse, a motel with a lot of broads around. We go into this room with a big dance floor, and Ava orders up some flamenco dancers. . . . At 5:30 in the morning we said we gotta go, and she started cursing people out. . . . We saw her flat-assed drunk more than once."

When Ava came to the States, Frank put his plane at her disposal. It ferried her to and from Palm Springs and Las Vegas and, to dry out, to the Elizabeth Arden spa in Arizona. "Can you imagine?" Frank said to Sonny King. "The way I used to chase Ava! And now she's my patient." Yet he still was chasing her.

He also constantly pursued other women. Frank would simply issue a summons, often with a message sent across a crowded room to a woman who caught his eye. His approach could involve effrontery. One evening in the 1960s, he sent a crony to another table in a New York restaurant to tell D'Amato's friend Michael Hellerman that he would like to "take out" his date. "I brought the girl over to meet Frank," said Hellerman. "Her eyes were glowing like two diamonds. She forgot I even existed. When she went out with Frank, she got so nervous that she threw up. He had to put her in a cab to get her home."

Frank might date a celebrity, or a hatcheck girl, or pay for sex with a whore. The liaisons were usually brief, and left the nonprofessionals puzzled.

"First, there were the incessant calls," a young actress told Richard Gehman. "Funny calls, jokey, kookie calls. . . . Then there were the flowers and champagne and presents . . . then the nights at his favorite restaurant." Then "all of a sudden he just stopped . . . just didn't call." Another woman said: "I don't understand him. He takes me out, then seems to spend most of the evening talking to the guys."

"I'm supposed to have a Ph.D. on the subject of women," Frank told **Life** in the course of an otherwise vacuous interview in 1965, "but the truth is I've flunked more often than not. . . ."

He had flunked, laboriously and over many months, with the dancer Juliet Prowse. They had met on the set of **Can-Can** in 1959. She had been twenty-three to his forty-four, a tall, intelligent, brilliant dancer who, had it not been for her height, would probably have become a ballerina. "He was singing a love song to her," said her friend Shirley MacLaine, who introduced them, "and he fell in love with the person to whom he was singing, and she fell in love with his voice and the fact that he was Frank. Is that love?" The song Frank had sung to Prowse in **Can-Can** had been "It's All Right with Me":

> It's not her face, but such a charming face
> That it's all right with me.

Juliet was no easy conquest, and perhaps that worked in her favor. The child of a British colonial family, raised in South Africa, she had been a dancing prodigy from early childhood. She was impressed when Frank made advances, but not bowled over. They went out together for four months before the affair became sexual, she said in her only in-depth interview about the relationship.

Frank seemed "amazingly kind and gentle. Maybe it was because I was close to his daughter's age. Maybe he respected that more. I wasn't a woman who had run around a lot. . . . I remember him saying—he said that many times—that this was the most comfortable he ever felt in a relationship with anybody." There were times, Juliet said, when they sat quietly by the pool while she knitted socks for him. She tended the garden and he painted—a hobby he had taken up in the 1940s but for which he had little time. "She smothers me, and I love that," Frank told MacLaine.

Frank proposed to Juliet. He flew to South Africa to meet her family and made her parents welcome when they flew to Los Angeles in late 1960. She resisted, however, and continued to do so even after five proposals. Though Frank was good to her, she did not like what happened when he got drunk. He tore into good friends for no reason, or would "throw things on the floor if the service was not as he wanted it to be." He blatantly lied, saying he had "never ever quarreled or had a hard word" with the women in his life. He said a future wife of his ought to stop working, and that rankled with Juliet. Dancing was her passion and vocation. Frank would carry on, too, about Ava, "the big love in his life . . . the only one he ever spoke about." Juliet put up with that, but his possessiveness was another matter.

Frank allowed her no life of her own, she said. He would stand on a street corner, watch her drive by, then nag her about driving too fast, rage at her for doing a dancer's cartwheels in public in a fit of exuberance. He was, she said later, "really like a father figure." When it came to other men, he was unfairly jealous.

"I knew he was seeing other girls," Juliet said, "that he wasn't just dating me. So I saw no reason why I shouldn't also go out with this dancer, Nick Nevara. Well, he found out about it and came to my apartment at three o'clock in the morning, banging on my door. And I wouldn't answer the door because I had Nick with me inside. He then disappeared, screaming and yelling. . . . I got mad, thinking, 'How dare he do this to my life?' . . . I just read him the riot act, said I never wanted to see him again and he shouldn't try to get hold of me." For six months, from the summer of 1961, they did not see each other. Frank did, however, see Marilyn Monroe.

SINATRA AND MONROE. Here were stars who shone with equal brilliance. They had met in 1954, when she was married to Joe DiMaggio and working on **The Seven Year Itch.** Frank and DiMaggio were pals then, and that year they collaborated in a bizarre episode involving Marilyn.

James Bacon, then a young journalist, saw them together at the Villa Capri on the evening of November 5. "It looked like a Sons of Italy meeting," he recalled. "Sinatra, DiMaggio, and a few other **paisanos.** . . . I could see that DiMaggio was in a terrible mood." At about midnight, Sinatra and DiMaggio joined private detectives, whom Frank had hired, outside a West Hollywood apartment building. The detectives had been watching the building in the belief that Marilyn was inside with a lover. Moments later, some of the men broke down an apartment door and rushed into the bedroom of a sleeping female resident—who was not Marilyn. They had raided the wrong apartment.

Frank would deny having gone inside the building but admit to having been present outside. One of the detectives involved, however, said Sinatra had been one of the intruders. DiMaggio's friendship with Frank did not last. By 1960, long divorced from Marilyn but still obsessing about her, DiMaggio came to believe she was sleeping with Frank.

It seems clear that there was some sort of an affair, at a time when Marilyn was an emotional basket case. Frank had become solicitous during the collapse of her marriage to Arthur Miller. He presented her with a white poodle that she christened Maf, as in Mafia. In February 1961, when she was released after a spell in New York's Payne Whitney Psychiatric Clinic, Frank allowed her to use his house in Coldwater Canyon. One of Monroe's press aides, Rupert Allan, thought Frank was merely acting as a good friend. Sonny King felt that he was her "big protector," she his "favorite little friend."

Marilyn was at the Sands, in a pitiful state, when Frank performed there in early June. "As physically beautiful as she was," Eddie Fisher recalled, "the drinking and the pills made her ugly. . . . I don't know whether Marilyn was drunk or stoned, but she was slobbering all over herself. When Frank started singing she started banging on the stage floor. I saw Frank make a simple gesture toward her, and guards appeared almost immediately and practically dragged Marilyn out of the room."

The actress was still in bad shape in August when she joined Frank and friends for a weekend on his yacht. "I remember going up to Frank's house before we got on the boat," said Dean Martin's wife, Jeanne, "and he said, 'Will you please go in and get Marilyn dressed, so we can get in the limo and go.' She couldn't get herself organized."

Marilyn shared Frank's cabin. A photograph taken during the trip shows Frank lying on his back beside the actress, reading a magazine. Marilyn tried to socialize, others on board recalled, but seemed disoriented. "She was taking sleeping pills," said Mike Romanoff's wife, Gloria, "so she'd disappear at ten o'clock at night and not be awake till eleven or twelve the next day. We kidded Frank, saying, 'Some romance this is!' " Jeanne Martin remembered Marilyn "wandering around the deck, pitifully trying to find more pills. She'd be unable to sleep and go lurching about half-dressed, trying to find someone who could give her 'reds' at three o'clock in the morning." When the yacht pulled into harbor, and as the rest of the party got ready for a further gathering on shore, Marilyn walked off and disappeared.

Weeks later she had her New York maid, Lena Pepitone, fly to Los Angeles with a special dress. She was wearing it, looking her glittering best, when Frank arrived to take her out for the evening. "He pulled a box out of his pocket," Pepitone said, "and clipped two gorgeous emerald earrings on Marilyn's ears. They kissed so passionately that I was embarrassed to be standing by."

That summer, according to Pepitone, the

actress was talking of marrying Frank. Soon after New Year's 1962, however, as Marilyn sat with the screenwriter Nunnally Johnson, she read a newspaper report that, Johnson recalled, gave her "the vapors": Frank had gotten engaged to Juliet Prowse.

In the seven months remaining to Marilyn, she would be rejected by the Kennedy brothers and see a good deal of Frank. It was in late July that he photographed her in a state of distress at the Cal-Neva Lodge in the company of Sam Giancana. Days later, at thirty-six, Marilyn would be dead.

Frank told the press he was "deeply saddened" by the news, that he would miss Marilyn very much. George Jacobs thought he was "in shock." Barred from the funeral ceremony, he tried in vain to bribe his way in. He probably now regretted his throwaway line of a few weeks earlier, when a reporter had asked how well he knew Marilyn. "Who?" he had replied sarcastically. "Miss Monroe reminds me of a saintly young girl I went to high school with, who later became a nun. This is a recording."

Told of this exchange, Marilyn had responded, "Tell him to look in **Who's Who.**"

AFTER SIX MONTHS during which Frank and Juliet Prowse had not even spoken, he had met her at Los Angeles Airport, produced a diamond ring, and popped the question yet again. Juliet had said yes, but they called it off a little over a month later.

Frank's insistence that Juliet should give up her work had contributed to the final break. So had his adamant refusal to fly to South Africa again, to discuss the marriage plans with his future in-laws. "He was the master of control, and he saw that as Juliet wanting to get her parents' approval," Shirley MacLaine remembered. "He wouldn't even discuss it, wouldn't even call her. He walked away, and Juliet didn't pursue it anymore—because it was all so insane."

During the brief engagement, Ava had sent Frank a telegram of congratulations. That anguished connection persisted, as the author Stephen Birmingham realized in 1963 in Mexico during the shooting of **The Night of the Iguana.** She and Frank, he learned, "stayed very, very close. Every time I'd be with her, he would call at least once . . . she would go up into her bedroom, close the door, and talk for half an hour."

Even now, their occasional meetings were ruined by jealousy. "If a pretty girl came up and spoke to him," Birmingham noted, "Ava would get furious. And Ava's eyes liked to travel around the room; she'd fix on this one and that one, and the next thing you'd know the person would be over at the table and Frank would get furious."

In 1964 they were both in Italy, where Ava was

making **The Bible** with George C. Scott and Frank was shooting **Von Ryan's Express.** She was involved with Scott. "Frank and I were living in a villa on the Via Appia," Brad Dexter recalled. "The three of us would have dinner together, and she'd get drunk and stagger off upstairs. It was really sad. Frank turned to me one night and said, 'She's the only woman I've ever been in love with in my whole life, and look at her. She's turned into a falling-down drunk.' "

Ava was forty-two. In October, while in Los Angeles shooting interior scenes for **Von Ryan's Express,** Frank took up with a nineteen-year-old.

MIA FARROW'S PARENTS, writer-director John Farrow and the actress Maureen O'Sullivan, had moved into separate bedrooms when she was eight, because her father was having an affair with Ava Gardner. When she was eleven, she had been introduced to Frank while out dining with her father. When Frank had said what a pretty little girl she was, her father responded, "You stay away from her."

She next met Frank in 1964 at Twentieth Century-Fox, when she was nineteen and playing the lovelorn daughter in the TV version of the novel **Peyton Place.** Mia was familiar with the ways of Hollywood. Her parents were the product of it; her godmother was gossip queen Louella

Parsons, her godfather the director George Cukor. According to the press, however, she was then "a wide-eyed sprite," a "waif" with the "heartbreaking innocence, the defenselessness of a child." She has described herself as having been an "impossibly naive teenager . . . afraid of men." The only time she had been in bed with a man, she recalled, had been when required to fake a lovemaking scene during filming.

Mia looked the part of the innocent waif. She was just over five feet five inches tall, and gave her measurements as 20-20-20. She wore falsies, and once refused to do a nude scene because she felt the audience might be disappointed. Chaste though she may have been, the nineteen-year-old Mia was not entirely innocent in the ways of the world. While living in New York, she had been taken by Salvador Dalí to a Greenwich Village party at which she had seen other guests engaging in group sex. Frank's friend Edie Goetz, Louis B. Mayer's daughter, thought her "a very clever young lady . . . she knew exactly what she was about and what she wanted." Liza Minnelli, a friend from childhood, said Mia was "stronger than all of us."

Frank took the initiative when they met at Fox, Mia wrote in her 1997 autobiography. According to her, he struck up a conversation when she visited a neighboring soundstage where he was working on **Von Ryan's Express.** He invited her to a private screening of one of his movies, she wrote, held her hand when the lights went down, and asked her to fly with him—"that very evening"—to Palm Springs. Brad Dexter remembered the encounter differently. Mia made "googly eyes" at Frank on the set, he said, and badgered him to let her come down to Palm Springs.

Frank did send his jet for Mia, not right after the screening but the next day, and she duly arrived at his house—with her cat. Though there were photographs of Ava all over the place, she remained unfazed. Frank took her in his arms while showing her to her room and, in her words, "the cat slept alone that night."

Soon the couple were spending every weekend together. Frank painted, and she sketched, beside the pool. They labored over crossword puzzles together, and he introduced her to Vaughan Williams symphonies. At Christmas, when Mia was hoping for a puppy, Frank gave her "a diamond koala bear." He also gave her a gold cigarette case and a yellow Thunderbird, to "match your hair."

Mia called Frank "Charlie Brown." He called her "Angel Face" or "Baby Face." From their first meeting, she thought "what a beautiful face he had, full of pain." "They don't really know him," she recalled thinking. "They can't see the wounding tenderness that even he can't bear to acknowledge."

The song "The Impossible Dream," from **Man of La Mancha,** reminded Mia of Frank, whose aftershave lotion, she noticed, was the same as her father's. "I think of him," she said of Frank early on, "as a man covered with scars who still fights to reach the unreachable star." She suggested Frank record the song, and he did.

Frank kept Mia very much to himself for the best part of a year. He did not introduce her to his children, and she was not at his fiftieth birthday party. "Frank was really plastered that night," Sonny King remembered. "He slipped on the stairs, fell down. . . . His former wife Nancy helped him up and put his head on her shoulder. Then some of us got in the car—without Nancy and feeling no pain—and went to a hilltop retreat in the Hollywood Hills. When we walked in, there by the fireplace was Mia Farrow.

"That was my first meeting with her. She looked like a little elf, and I liked her. But she didn't fit. . . . She was like a hippie at the corner of Haight-Ashbury. Frank was hip in his own way, but not a hippie. . . . She had her own thoughts and he had his elderly thoughts. They just didn't mix."

Though not optimistic, Frank's young daughters befriended Mia. At the same time, oddly, their father went out of his way to cultivate people his own age or older.

"Frank had decided that it was time for him to

enter middle age," an unnamed associate told **Life.** "He switched tailors. He started wearing double-breasted bankers' clothes. . . . He took up with the old-time Hollywood establishment and began partying with the actresses Rosalind Russell, Claudette Colbert and Merle Oberon and their husbands. It seemed all his women friends were past fifty and all the men past sixty. He pulled Mia into this group and forced her on them, and neither she nor they liked each other."

Mia found herself in a set that also included Billy Wilder and Kirk Douglas; William Paley, the chairman of CBS; Random House president Bennett Cerf; the Irish businessman Loel Guinness; producer Arthur Hornblow; Twentieth Century-Fox production head William Goetz; Sears, Roebuck heir Armand Deutsch; and their respective wives. On occasion, Mia recalled, she encountered the children of such guests—all of them older than she. They would dine at what she termed the "kids' table" while she sat with "the grown-ups." After dinner at the Goetzes', priceless Picassos would be mechanically raised and replaced by a movie screen, for the after-dinner movie.

Life with Frank, Mia came to think, was comprised of three separate compartments. The first was their private time together, the second their highfalutin social whirl, the third Frank's disconcerting "other world" in Las Vegas and New York. Being around the casino fraternity could be challenging for Mia. "She would call me up," Sonny King recalled, "and say, 'Sonny, could you come over and teach me how to say some words in Italian so I can answer Frank's friends.' She wanted to be in with them."

Mia would watch Frank gamble, throw money around, and drink. She discovered that he was capable of consuming an entire bottle of Jack Daniel's at one sitting. During what Mia remembered as the "interminable Vegas nights," the men mostly talked with the men, the women with the women. In the predawn hours, she often found herself making conversation with painted women in slinky dresses, some of them hookers. (Soon after Frank and Mia met, according to George Jacobs, Frank had sent out for whores who bore a resemblance to Mia.)

Press speculation about the couple had begun less than a year into the relationship, when Frank took Mia and a group of his older friends on a yacht cruise along the eastern seaboard. She bristled when people made cracks about their age difference—Dean Martin's was that he had a bottle of Scotch older than Mia. The yacht trip was a magnet for the press, made more so when Frank went ashore at Hyannis Port to visit Joe Kennedy, still wheelchair-bound four years after his stroke. **Time** thought the voyage "probably the most closely watched since Cleopatra floated down the Nile to meet Mark Antony."

Frank and Mia were tumbling around, as she put it, in a "chasm of insecurities." She went off traveling with a much younger man. Frank had an affair with forty-one-year-old Sheila MacRae, the entertainer and estranged wife of the actor Gordon MacRae. In the same period, in Miami, according to an FBI report, he took delivery of a "beautiful brunette" brought to his room by Joe Fischetti.

They reconciled in the summer of 1966, after Frank had called Mia from Las Vegas in the middle of the night. Soon he asked her to marry him, and she accepted. He bought an $85,000 diamond engagement ring and presented it to her—in a cake box—during a transcontinental flight.

"Marry Mia?" her fifty-four-year-old mother Maureen O'Sullivan had said of Frank earlier. "It would make better sense if he married **me**." She thought her daughter not "emotionally prepared for marriage." Dolly Sinatra dismissed the idea, saying, "My son is just helping this girl become a star."

Frank himself had doubts. At dinner with Juliet Prowse, he confessed that he "couldn't seem to make up his mind." He told Shirley MacLaine that he wanted her to meet Mia, to "pass judgment on her. He asked what I thought, and I think I said something like, 'What do you say about someone who looks like a twelve-year-old boy?' "

Ava, in New York for a premiere, was asked about Mia by the critic Rex Reed. "The Ava eyes brighten to a soft clubhouse green," he wrote later. "The answer comes like so many cats lapping so many saucers of cream. 'Hah! I always knew Frank would end up in bed with a boy.' "

Frank continued to see Ava whenever they were in the same city at the same time. One evening in New York, Skinny D'Amato's friend Michael Hellerman witnessed a disquieting moment. "I went up to Sinatra's apartment," he recalled. "He was as happy a guy as I've ever seen. We were all sitting there on the couch talking, when the doorbell rang. Suddenly Ava walked out of another room all dressed, carrying a suitcase, and headed straight for the door. She opened it, turned, gave a little wave, saying goodbye to Frank. . . . The guy at the door was a Spanish airline pilot. We were so embarrassed for Frank."

He saw her again in London, even so, when he was there starting work on a new movie, a bad thriller called **The Naked Runner.** Ava, who was tiring of life in Spain, was spending a good deal of her time in England. George Jacobs thought Frank still hoped to win her back. "I guess," the valet remembered his boss saying after seeing Ava and being rejected yet again, "I got nowhere to run."

What he did was to run pell-mell into marriage to Mia, earlier than planned and in a rage. "The thing that triggered it," said Brad Dexter, who was producing **Naked Runner,** "was when I told him that instead of marrying Mia he should go to see a psychiatrist. There was a renowned man in London, and I said it would be a good idea to visit him. He knew there was something wrong, but he looked at me and said, 'What? Do you think I'm crazy?' Then Frank went ape. He picked up the phone and called Las Vegas and got Jack Entratter and said, 'I'm flying in. You get in touch with Mia and get her ass up there. . . . I want to get married.' He left the next morning."

In New York on his way to Las Vegas, Frank dined with Peggy Connelly and visited Sheila MacRae. He rambled on to MacRae about how he could help extract her from her twenty-five-year marriage. Then he quieted down, stared out the window, and said, "I want to be married." According to Jacobs he then returned to his apartment and had a prostitute come over, before heading off to Las Vegas.

He and Mia were married the following day, July 19, 1966, in a four-minute ceremony at the Sands. The hotel had been given just a few hours to arrange the wedding license, a judge to officiate—not too hard a task in Nevada—and the cake and the champagne. Frank had not told his family what he was about to do, but just before the ceremony instructed Jacobs to "call Miss G.," so that she would not hear the news first from someone else.

Frank referred to Mia as "my child bride" during the honeymoon, sat her on a stool and sang "September Song" to her in front of fellow houseguests. It all felt, Mia has said, "a little bit like an adoption." Frank's daughter Nancy, who saw them as "the Swinger and the Flower Child," thought the contrast romantic. Tina, who was eighteen at the time, thought it "cute" when Frank showed up with Mia at the Daisy, a trendy Beverly Hills club, wearing a Nehru jacket and love beads. Sonny King, though, thought people were put off "when Frank walked in with one of those guru suits, and the chains that looked like chestnuts."

Frank's former girlfriend Sandra Giles also saw the couple at the Daisy. "Mia Farrow was dancing with all the men," she said. "He looked very lonely. And he came up to my table and said, 'Sandra, would you mind if I sit with you guys?' " Along with the incongruities, there were deeper differences. Mia wanted children; Frank did not. Mia supported the anti–Vietnam War movement; Frank, who had begun to move to the right politically, did not.

When they were away from each other making movies, in early 1967, it was evident the marriage was in trouble. The actress Tiffany Bolling said she had a dalliance with Frank while on location with him in Florida for **Tony Rome**, a detective movie. He seemed to her to be sad and lonesome, and he was drinking too much. Mia, meanwhile, was working on **Dandy in Aspic**, which involved location shooting in England and Germany. During that period, according to a published report, she sent her co-star Laurence Harvey a golden bird in a golden cage—with a note saying she felt much like the bird.

As it had been with Juliet Prowse, the terminal rift was over Mia's career. She insisted on honoring her commitment to finish her work on **Rosemary's Baby**, rather than join her husband to work on another movie. "To lose Frank was unthinkable," she said, "but I didn't think he would leave me."

One afternoon in November of that year, without prior warning, Frank's principal attorney, Mickey Rudin, showed up on the set of **Rosemary's Baby** with separation documents drawn up and ready for signature. Mia signed where required and set off soon after for India, there to engage in meditation with the fashionable Maharishi Mahesh Yogi. She was joined there by the Beatles. Mia was now in tune with the rock 'n' roll aristocracy of her generation, and utterly out of tune with Frank. He had her flown to Mexico a few months later for the divorce. They had been married just over two years.

THERE HAD BEEN RUMORS toward the end that Frank had been physically abusing Mia. The producer David Susskind said she once "showed up for work with black welts all over her body . . . bruised from head to foot, with mean red gashes and marks all over her arms and shoulders and throat, as though she'd been badly beaten." Mia has repeatedly said Frank did not inflict these injuries. "If there's one guy I don't tolerate, it's a guy who mistreats women," Frank once said. Yet there are troubling questions about his treatment of women.

As mentioned earlier, Zsa Zsa Gabor told of how, in the mid-fifties, Frank badgered her for hours until she had sex with him, just to get him out of her house. Now, more than a decade later, there was another incident.

"I accepted an invitation to go to a screening at his house on Mulholland," Gabor has written. "He was married to Mia Farrow, whom I knew and liked. . . . We all had drinks, then they began screening the film. In the middle, I went to the powder room. And Frank followed me and pushed his way in, persisting, 'My darling . . . I want to make love to you again.' With that, Frank began to undo the buttons on my black silk blouse. . . . Summoning all my strength, I pushed past him and out of the powder room, turning only to threaten, 'Frank—I am leaving. Don't you ever, ever try to touch me again.'"

Susan Murphy's allegation is far more serious. In the late 1960s as now, Murphy was just another resident of Palm Springs. In late February or early March 1969, when she met Frank, she was just twenty and he fifty-three. He had been divorced from Mia for six months.

The encounter began with Frank's routine approach. One night when Murphy was on a date at a Palm Springs restaurant, he sent someone to her table with a note asking her to come and join him. She thought it "quite rude," because she was obviously with another man, and she stayed with her date. Soon after, however, another male friend asked her to go with him to a party at Frank's Palm Springs home. She went, she remembered nearly four decades later, wearing a "beautiful high-necked silk dress I'd bought at Bullock's. It had sequins around the neck, and I wore silver shoes."

The first hint of trouble from Frank, though she failed to recognize it as such at the time, came early on. "What happened," she said with some embarrassment, "was that I went to the bathroom and hadn't securely locked the door. Sinatra walked in on me. He just opened the door. I had the feeling he knew I was in there, had followed me. He didn't say 'Excuse me' and then close the door. He just looked at me, stared. It was like he had set out to do it. Then he turned around and walked away. I walked out and didn't mention the incident to anyone."

As the evening wore on, Murphy's date left.

"The next thing I knew the idea came up that a few of us, Danny Schwartz [a wealthy industrialist friend of Frank] and his wife, and Sinatra and myself—and the pilot of course—should fly to Las Vegas. I thought 'What the heck? That'll be kind of fun.' So we went to Vegas on his plane, to a casino. He drew a lot of attention. He acted like everybody was supposed to completely stop when he walked in the room.

"I didn't even know how to gamble, and Sinatra walked over and handed me a hundred-dollar bill and told Mrs. Schwartz to help me out. She told me to change the hundred, and was kind of teaching me how to play blackjack. Sinatra walked across and totally insulted me because I'd broken up the money. I was supposed to place it all on one bet. Everyone stared. At that point I thought, 'I can't wait to get home.' And after not very much longer we got back on the jet. We flew to Palm Springs and the two of us were taken back to the house. It was one or two in the morning by then.

"So I'm thinking to myself, 'Well, I'm getting my stuff together. I'm going to leave.' But he said he wanted to show me the rest of the house. At the beginning of the evening I'd seen only the main building, and I said 'Well, all right.' There were all these individual bungalows. So we walked into one, and I said something like 'Really lovely. Well, I must go now.' And he said, 'No you don't.'

"He threw me on the bed. I said, 'God, no!' But

he threw me where my back hit the bed, and just pulled my dress up, pulled down my panties, and did what he wanted to do. I knew I couldn't overpower him. He was forceful, and it was over very quickly. I do remember—I found out without caring to—that he was quite large in that department. And that was that. Afterward I was crying, and in no condition to drive or anything. I felt kind of halfway dead. So I just lay there and kind of went to sleep. He stayed, too, but he never said a word.

"When I got up he asked me—I guess he was feeling some kind of compunction—if I couldn't stay. I couldn't believe the gall of that. I said, 'Oh my God, definitely not!' I was devastated. I had mascara and everything all over, and he wanted me to **stay** there! He said, 'My friends call me Francis.' I thought, 'This is unbelievable, after what he did to me, saying that I'm his friend.' I said I had to go, and I gathered my things and went. He got a driver for me. I never saw him again."

Murphy gave away the silk dress she had worn that night, and threw her underclothes in the trash. She told no one what had happened until long afterward. "I was frightened to bring it up. I wanted to go to the police, but I thought, 'Me against Frank Sinatra? . . . No one's going to believe this. So just keep your mouth shut.' I was very scared because he knew a lot of people and had a lot of connections. I wasn't anybody important, so I could be overlooked very easily. It frightens me even now, telling anyone about this."

Asked if she thought Frank was drunk when he assaulted her, Murphy replied, "I would say that he was, but it was not like he was staggering or falling down at all. He was in control." At the party, hours before the assault, Murphy's impression had been that Frank "needed, just demanded, the limelight. Egotistical. He acted like he was God."

30

Out of Control

A STAR IS A SPECIAL THING," the social scientist Leo Rosten said on the Walter Cronkite program to mark Frank's fiftieth birthday. "A Picasso. Frank Lloyd Wright. Frank Sinatra. We shower them with special license, like the royalty of an earlier time. We say, 'Gratify your desires. Satisfy every whim. Don't resist temptation. Live for us. Live as we would live if we were beautiful or brilliant or lucky and very, very rich.'

"Mr. Sinatra generates excitement. He tantalizes the public and defies it with his private escapades. He's a complicated man. . . . He has an animal tension. A suggestion of violence, even of danger."

The public forgave Frank his flaws and "shenanigans," Rosten thought. At the time, though, people did not know the full extent of the simmering violence in the man, nor how often it manifested itself.

Emerging from the tough culture of 1930s Hoboken, swept along on a wave of success, the youthful Sinatra had applied no brake to his temper. For a while in the 1950s, chastened perhaps by the publicity and the court case that followed his attack on Lee Mortimer, he lost control less often. He no longer sent telegrams warning of a "belt in your vicious mouth," as he had to newspaperman Erskine Johnson. The press remained a bête noire, however, especially if it defied his edict that everything to do with his personal life was off-limits.

The menaces were not reserved for the media. There was the 3:00 A.M. call to Peter Lawford telling him "I'll have your legs broken," should he see Ava again. Talk of leg-breaking did not mean legs would be broken, but no one could be sure of that. "Let me tell you something," Frank snapped at the producer Sam Spiegel in a restaurant. "The day you don't speak to me is the day you get your fucking teeth knocked in." Then he turned to Spiegel's wife, Betty: "Look, doll. You got a pretty puss. You want to keep it that way, and shut up." Spiegel's offense that evening, a friend of the producer said, had been to greet Sinatra with a mere "Hello there" instead of addressing him by name.

Juliet Prowse's first breakup with Frank was

provoked in part by a warning call from his secretary. "You'd better get out of there," the secretary told Prowse as she sat in her apartment. "Frank's arranged to blow up your building." Though nothing happened, she took the threat seriously. She knew Frank was close to gangsters and, she said, she "knew he had used them before."

Tiffany Bolling, a female distraction for Frank at a low point in the marriage to Mia, remembered an evening when he threw a chair at someone who insulted him in a restaurant, then left in a rage. When his bodyguards spoke of returning to beat the man, Bolling said, she was so upset that she went home. Frank later told her he had restrained his men.

David Susskind received a warning call after crossing Frank during the marriage to Mia. "It's Sinatra," a woman close to Jimmy Alo told him. "He's put the word out to get you. . . . He's mad and he's going to get other gangsters to do it for him. My guy says that no one touches anyone in the East without his okay, and that if anyone touches you, he won't be alive the next day. But he says that you're not to go to Las Vegas or Miami. He can't control what happens there." Susskind avoided those cities for a while.

Frank made light of stories that he attacked reporters. "In some segments of the press," he said in 1965 at a dinner for James Bacon, a friendly journalist, "I am known as the Eichmann of song. . . . These are lies, vicious rumors started by a few disgruntled reporters I happened to run down with my own car."

According to a report in the **New York Journal-American,** Frank had done exactly that while leaving a New York City nightclub in 1958. It began, according to reporter Dan Vandergrift, when Frank angrily objected to being addressed as "Frank." Much as he had in his outburst at Spiegel, he insisted that Vandergrift address him as "Mr. Sinatra." Then, photographer Mel Finkelstein said, Frank's chauffeured limousine struck him a glancing blow as it was driven away. Finkelstein filed a complaint with the police, and there was widespread press coverage. The limousine driver admitted that the photographer "might" have been hooked by the rear bumper. From his suite at the Waldorf Towers, Frank issued a statement dismissing the story as "wild imagination."

The same year, on a trip to Monaco, Frank threatened to throw a **Time** magazine journalist off a terrace. He was restrained and dissuaded by Billy Woodfield, who was traveling with him. In 1962, in San Francisco, Frank wrestled a photographer to the floor and insisted that he surrender his film. In 1964, following a clash with reporters in Spain, he was charged with disturbing the peace and fined. He claimed the journalists involved in these last two incidents had been trying to set him up by photographing him with women he did not know.

That same year, in Paris, he tossed cherry bombs at photographers, first in the street and then in a restaurant. **Time** quoted Frank as having threatened to "smash in" a female journalist's face, and said he and his party routed French journalists "with drawn knives, a gin bottle, and a couple of clubs." Frank scoffed at claims that two photographers had been injured, saying that if there were any injuries they were "self-inflicted."

Rock Brynner, who was with Frank on the trip, remembered it as the "catastrophic assault on Europe." "As the paparazzi's cars would gather around ours," he said, "Frank would ask the driver to find a cul-de-sac. There were cars in front of us as well as behind. So we would signal, and the car in front would turn down the cul-de-sac. He and his companion would pitch cherry bombs, doing very serious damage. Those cars would crash. There were people hurt. We'd trap the paparazzi, and I saw Frank's companion drag one guy out by the collar and throw him down and mash his heel into the guy's hand, just crushing the bones in the photographer's hand. I remember that vividly."

Cherry bombs had become Frank's weapon of choice against photographers. He stuffed his pockets with them, Mia remembered, when setting out for the evening during their honeymoon. Frank also knocked **New York Post** photographer Jerry Engels to the ground during the trip, smashing his camera. The paparazzi can be unacceptably intrusive, but Sinatra's acts of violence were indefensible.

Philip Irwin, one of the private detectives involved in the botched apartment raid designed to catch Marilyn Monroe with a lover, believed he was one of Frank's victims. He had been beaten up by thugs, he told a state investigating committee under oath, after reporting to the California Bureau of Private Investigators and Adjusters that Frank had played a leading role in the raid. Irwin had no hard evidence as to who was behind the attack, but said he was "very much afraid" of Frank. Now that he had testified in public, he said, he was "afraid of being beaten up again."

The agent, Milt Ebbins, said he heard of two alleged assaults by Frank himself. One, involving a hatcheck girl at Hollywood's Florentine Gardens restaurant, had echoes of the sexual violence alleged by Susan Murphy. "Frank took the girl to his house," Ebbins said. "As I understood it, she wouldn't cooperate sexually and got into an altercation with him. He pushed her through a plate-glass window, and she was severely injured. Many stitches . . . Frank settled for a large sum of money."

The second incident involved a parking attendant at Romanoff's restaurant. When Frank abused him verbally for not fetching his car fast enough, the attendant slapped him in the face. "Frank didn't do anything then," Ebbins said. "He never did unless he had a heavyweight behind him. He left, but then he got ahold of Hank Sanicola, who was good with his fists. He and Sanicola later followed the guy as far as Mulholland, and they cut the car off and stopped it. Frank called the kid every name under the sun, and Sanicola beat the shit out of him."

While Ebbins's stories are hearsay, another parking lot fracas is well documented. It occurred when, Frank claimed, a car driven by a parking attendant missed him by inches. Of three attendants involved in the ensuing skirmish, one had his shirt ripped off by Frank. Another was pushed around. A third, who wound up at Hollywood Receiving Hospital with cuts and bruises, said he had been beaten by "Sinatra and a bodyguard." The heavy, one of Sammy Davis's employees, was sentenced to ten days in jail and probation. Frank was sued for assault and battery, and settled out of court.

In 1964, during the Bing Crosby golf tournament at Pebble Beach, California, Frank turned up in the lobby of the Del Monte Lodge at 1:00 A.M. demanding something to eat. Told the kitchen was closed, he grabbed the phone and insisted on speaking to the hotel's owner. When the owner arrived, carrying a bottle of champagne by way of apology for the lack of food, he was rewarded with a punch in the eye.

In Israel, in 1965, Frank went out looking for trouble. "Whenever Frank had too much time on his hands," Rock Brynner said, "mischief was bound to follow. One evening, bored to death in the hotel, he said, 'C'mon Rock, let's go for a walk.' Well, that meant trouble. We didn't have security or anything, and he was really going out to provoke a fight. There were paparazzi, and also ardent fans rushing to get near him. He waited until the crowd was really close and tight and then he said, 'Come on, let's get outta here.' A melee ensued, and we punched our way out to get back to the hotel. . . . It was always perfectly foreseeable."

Over dinner at the Bistro in Los Angeles one evening in 1965, a drunken Sinatra abused the writer Dominick Dunne behind his back, then turned on his wife. Frank also spat venom at Lauren Bacall, Maureen O'Sullivan, and Swifty Lazar, who were also present. By way of finale, he tore the tablecloth from under the plates, glasses, and silverware, threw food over Lazar, and stormed out.

Dunne never did find out why Frank loathed him, though he may have borne a grudge over a TV show on which the writer had worked years earlier. An even worse incident took place the following year. "It was at the Daisy after a friend's wedding," Dunne recalled. "My wife and I were with a small group, and Frank was at the next table with Mia and Nancy and Tina. There was a captain at the Daisy, a wonderful guy, Italian, and he came and tapped me on the shoulder.

"I turned around to look up at him, and he said, 'Oh, Mr. Dunne, I'm so sorry.' Then he hauled off and punched me. The punch landed on my head, and the crowded restaurant went silent. I looked across at Frank, and he was looking back at me with kind of a smile on his face. It was as though I was his entertainment. I felt hate for him, because I knew this guy who had hit me as a decent, decent man. We got up and left. And as we were standing outside, waiting for the boy to bring my car, the captain ran out. He was sobbing and he said again, 'I'm sorry, so sorry. Mr. Sinatra made me do it.'

"He said Sinatra had paid him $50, which back then was something like $300 is today. It was the social talk of the town. Horrible, and it showed the kind of power Sinatra had, to make a decent man do an indecent act."

AS OFTEN AS NOT, Frank's rages were triggered by alcohol, as they had been since the late 1940s. By the 1960s, he was openly flaunting his use of hard liquor. A flag emblazoned with a Jack

Daniel's bottle flew outside his house on occasion—as did another, spelling out Alka-Seltzer, for the mornings after. "Jackie Daniels," Frank said, was his friend.

A bottle of the stuff was a required item in his dressing room, and he sported a blazer with the Jack Daniel's crest on the breast pocket. Frank was a walking commercial for the brand, so much so that the distillers named him—with Elizabeth Taylor, Paul Newman, and J. Edgar Hoover—a member of the Tennessee Squires, people formally allotted a spot of land at Jack Daniel's headquarters in recognition of their proven devotion. Instead of the nominal square foot granted to other Squires, Frank was awarded an entire acre.

Frank joked about his alcohol use, and routinely appeared on stage carrying a glass that appeared to contain liquor—and often did. He claimed at one point that whiskey was good for his voice, and saw it as social fuel, "gasoline." He ate a lot of chocolate, he said, because it absorbed the booze.

Frank used liquor as a stage prop to evoke both sadness and fun: sadness when he was the singing drunk in a bar, asking the barman for just one more for the road; fun as in a line quoted from his friend Joe E. Lewis: "You're not drunk if you can lay on the floor without holding on." Or in the inscription on a photograph of himself, with bottle, given to a friend: "Drink, Dickie! It's good for your bird."

In the 1970s, Frank would reminisce about sitting up until dawn with Yul Brynner getting "bombed, absolutely bombed, and playing Wagner as loud as anyone could play it." A club owner in Hawaii recalled him coming in with a party of eight, ordering a bottle of Jack Daniel's, then insisting on changing the order to "a bottle each for everyone." All the bottles were emptied.

"I feel sorry for people who don't drink," Frank said. "When they wake up in the morning, that's as good as they're going to feel all day." And later, in Las Vegas, on a rare occasion when he was obviously drunk on stage: "I don't trust anybody who doesn't drink. There's something wrong with him."

Frank usually quit drinking and smoking in the weeks before a performance, some who knew him have said. He knew excess was folly for a singer. Once, during a taping, the comedy writer Sheldon Keller saw him slumped in a chair reproaching himself: "Drink, drink, drink. Smoke, smoke, smoke. Schmuck, schmuck, schmuck!"

Some people got the impression that he was not really a big drinker. "More times than not," Rosalind Russell said, "he talks more about drinking than he actually imbibes." "In all the long years I knew him I only saw him really drunk once," Leonora Hornblow said. "He had an enormous capacity for drink." Where drinking is concerned, though, appearances can deceive.

The role of Maggio, the rebellious private in **From Here to Eternity** (**left**), was tailor-made for Frank. He fought to get the part and won the Oscar for Best Supporting Actor in 1953, and his failing career soon recovered.

lis performance as a drug addict in **The lan with the Golden Arm** (**right**) earned a est Actor nomination but not the Oscar. rank thought the 1962 movie **The Man-hurian Candidate** "the finest picture I have ver made" (**bottom right**), but audience ırnout was poor. He often found filming ·dious—as a photograph taken on the set of **)irty Dingus Magee** (**bottom left**) suggests.

"What phony stuff!" Frank said of **The Godfather** episode about the Maf helping a singer to get a part in a movie. Yet the mob did get him his role **From Here to Eternity**. Agent George Wood (**top left**) called in the mafio Jimmy Alo (**top right**) and Frank Costello (**bottom left**), who pressured Colun bia's Harry Cohn (**center**). When Johnny Rosselli (**bottom right**) threatened h life, Cohn gave Frank the part.

Frank's valet thought him "the Casanova of modern times." After Ava, there was a fling with Gloria Vanderbilt in 1954 (**left**), a romance with nineteen-year-old singer Jill Corey (**center right**), trysts with Marlene Dietrich (**bottom left**), a drunken night with would-be actress Sandra Giles (**center**), and a relationship with glamorous "stand-by girl" Jeanne Carmen (**bottom right**).

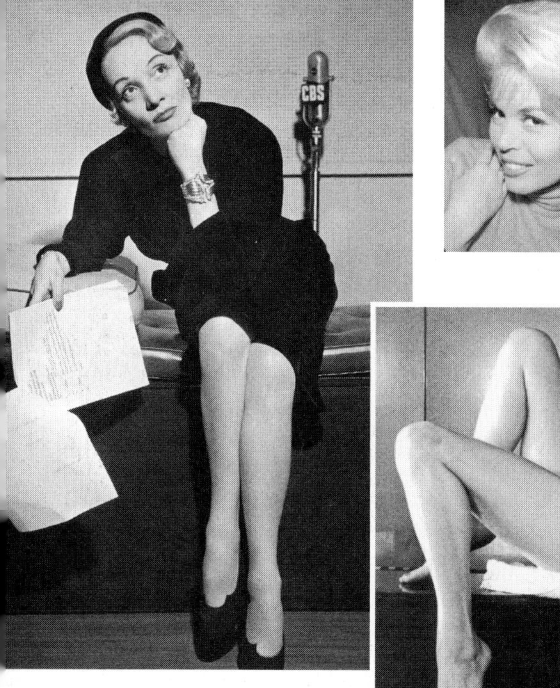

Peggy Connelly (**left and above**) gained rare insights into Frank's personality. Frank gave her minks and a white Thunderbird, and proposed twice. He also asked Lauren Bacall (**bottom left**) to marry him, then dropped her in a fit of pique. Eva Bartok (**bottom right**) had a baby that she said was his, but Frank was "too busy" to meet with her.

The Rat Pack was "just a group of clean, wholesome, ordinary guys who meet once a year to take over the world," Sammy Davis Jr. said. When they took over Las Vegas in early 1960, 34,000 people came to their shows in just four weeks. The jokes were mostly about drinking and sex. Women were on tap in the Rat Pack's Clubhouse, the steam room and health club at the Sands.

Joe Kennedy (**left**) said he would "sell Jack like soap flakes." Frank was part of the sell, publicly and in ways that long remained secret. A campaign photograph (**top right**) shows Skinny D'Amato of the 500 Club leaning in to speak with John F. Kennedy. Looking on at the top left of the picture is Angelo Malandra, a mob lawyer said to be one of those who "with Sinatra, had the mob's money in West Virginia."

Both John F. Kennedy and Sinatra dallied with Marilyn Monroe during the presidency. On a 1961 yacht trip with Frank, she was guzzling pills and disoriented. She was in a similar state while with Frank and mob boss Sam Giancana days before her death the following year.

When he took office, the new president was to describe Frank as "a great friend." He and his brother then distanced themselves from him because of his Mafia connections. Robert Kennedy blocked calls to investigate Sinatra, however, because he knew a probe could destroy the presidency.

The president's relationship with Judith Campbell was more dangerous than previously understood. New information suggests the "affair" was a Mafia setup. Frank was involved at all stages, but the Senate Intelligence Committee failed to call him to testify.

Frank had once obliged Chicago gangster Murray Humphreys (**top left**) by singing at the high school graduation (**right**) of Humphreys's daughter Llewella. He liaised with Humphreys over mob support for Kennedy in 1960.

Frank played go-between to secure the help of Sam Giancana (**left**), the murderer who headed the Chicago mob, to get Kennedy elected. When law enforcement pressure continued, Giancana blamed Frank and spoke of having him killed. Even after the mobster was himself murdered in 1975 (**below**), Frank continued to lie about their relationship.

The rebuffs and defeats of the Kennedy years were a setback. Frank had said when he launched his own record company that he saw his future "not so much as an entertainer but as a high-level executive." He encouraged the notion that he was "Chairman of the Board"(**below**), but the company was soon in trouble.

Frank met Mia Farrow on a film set in 1964. She was thirty years his junior.

After their Las Vegas wedding (**below left**) he spoke of Mia as "my child bride." She thought the marriage "a little bit like an adoption." It lasted just over two years.

Frank sexually assaulted twenty-year-old Susan Murphy (**below**), she has claimed, soon after his divorce from Mia. "He acted like he was God," Murphy said.

Frank joked that alcohol was his "gasoline," but the drunken Frank, a friend said, could be "the meanest son of a bitch that God ever put on earth." Drink was usually a factor when he resorted to violence.

Frank's presence in a casino attracted customers—and sometimes trouble. At the Sands in 1967, and at Caesars Palace in 1970, he went on rampages and fought with senior executives.

Frank usually had heavies to protect him. They prudently stood aside, though, when he confronted Carl Cohen, the Sands's powerful vice president. Cohen knocked out two of his front teeth.

Hubert Humphrey, for whom Frank campaigned in 1968, called him a "solid, devoted American liberal." Frank continued to insist he was a lifelong Democrat, even though he later began supporting Republican candidates. The lineup in 1971 (**below**), when his mother opened a medical facility named in memory of her husband, Marty, tells the story. Frank was now backing Ronald Reagan, whom he had earlier dismissed as "a bozo," and was accepting overtures from Vice President Spiro Agnew.

"Nixon scares me," Frank had said. Yet he supported Nixon in 1972 and sang at a White House state dinner for the prime minister of Italy. Frank's comment on Watergate: "Nobody's perfect."

Mafia boss Joe Colombo (**right**) put out a contract on Frank's life when he failed to perform at a rally for Italian-American rights. Frank did perform at the next one. Jilly Rizzo, Frank's closest confidant, (**above**) was deeply involved with the Mafia. Frank cheerfully posed for a photograph (**below**) with Mafia boss Carlo Gambino and seven other men associated with organized crime. He later claimed that he had known nothing about their backgrounds.

You're Scrumptious
Much Love,
Francis

The man who sang of love long found love elusive. The actress Lois Nettleton (**above**) still has the notes Frank wrote to her. He asked her to marry him, then promptly ruined it all with an angry tirade. He married former Las Vegas showgirl Barbara Marx (**right**) in 1976, and they stayed together until he died.

In 1988, at seventy-two, Frank persuaded Dean Martin and Sammy Davis Jr. to join him on a "Together Again" tour (**above**). Martin quit before it was over, and Davis died in 1990, but Frank sang on and on until he was almost eighty. His son Frank Jr. (**below**), who conducted for him in his dotage, thought he would become "a dribbling madman" were he to retire. Frank's voice was gone and his memory was in tatters, but he could still stir deep emotions.

THE BEST IS YET TO COME
FRANCIS ALBERT SINATRA
1915 † 1998
BELOVED HUSBAND & FATHER

There is some evidence that heavy drinking ran in the family. Frank once spoke of his father as having been a "drinking man." His mother drank "a case of beer a day" in middle age, according to Frank's cousin Marilyn Sinatra. Frank's own drinking had a long history. He confided to Peggy Connelly that a doctor had warned him when he was still in his twenties that continued alcohol abuse could kill him. Gloria Cahn remembered Frank drinking hard with Jimmy Van Heusen soon after he moved to the West Coast in the mid-1940s. The comedian Pat Cooper, who warmed up audiences for Frank in the mid-1960s, thought it miraculous that "someone who would smoke and drink and drink and smoke the way he did" could survive, as would Frank, into old age. Holmes Hendricksen, the former entertainment director of Harrah's, on Lake Tahoe, where Frank performed in the 1970s and early 1980s, recalled consuming "an awful lot of whiskey" with him both at home and on the road. Armand Deutsch, a regular weekend guest at the Palm Springs house, said Frank drank an entire bottle of whiskey every day over a long period. Frank admitted as much to his doctor. "He needed it," Hornblow thought. "It became the pattern of his life."

Rock Brynner, an alcoholic who achieved sobriety, remembered Frank as having been one of his "better professors" in the matter of drink. He thought Frank had suffered from "the outrageous, tragic effect of the disease of alcohol. I certainly saw him close to falling-down drunk, though more so at home. That isn't to say that he couldn't show some restraint. In public he was vertical at least. . . . It could be such a pleasure to be in his company. There was a great moment when the chemistry was great. Add two hours, and more Jack Daniel's, and it was sickness. When you talk about Frank's behavior, his mercurial shifts, a lot of it was just sick, fucked-up behavior—crazy alcoholic shit."

The writer and radio host Jonathan Schwartz has said flatly that Frank was an alcoholic. Schwartz, who himself once sought treatment for alcoholism, thought Sinatra "a textbook case, who presented drinking as an act of manliness to millions of innocent drinking citizens the world over. . . . I didn't catch on until late in the game because he was so gifted at covering it up with a bravado that authorized it, did it proud."

The information on Frank's drinking in this book was shared with two specialists in the field of alcoholism. Dr. Robert Morse, chairman of the Medical/Scientific Committee of the National Council on Alcoholism and Drug Dependence, said: "There is little doubt that Sinatra had a serious 'drinking problem.' He had several of the symptoms associated with alcoholism, but not necessarily diagnostic of that condition. To have had such a high tolerance—I see references to consumption of a bottle a day of Jack Daniel's—is the most specific symptom. One can have this kind of tolerance only by becoming alcoholic. Much of what we know about Sinatra's drinking is consistent with alcoholism." The same information led James Graham, an authority on alcoholism in celebrities, to conclude that "Sinatra was an alcoholic."

Symptoms of alcoholism, Dr. Morse noted, include "personality change while drinking, going from pleasant to nasty," and "repetitive violent episodes." "Sinatra would get angry with drink, especially after shows," said Dean Martin's agent, Mort Viner. "Something would set him off," Bob Neal said. "He had a trigger you wouldn't believe." "The trick," Swifty Lazar thought, was "to see him between mood swings. You can do it, but it's a lot easier if he's not on the booze. When he was sober, Frank had the potential to be a pussycat; when he was drunk, he was the meanest son of a bitch that God ever put on earth. It was Jekyll-and-Hyde time. . . . Jimmy Van Heusen once gave me some good advice on how to handle Frank if he's drunk: Disappear!"

"It was predictable if you got to know him," Brynner said. "You could see the turn coming. But he had an enormous temper, and when he got into a temper it had to pretty much burn itself out. He had no off switch."

AN HOUR OR SO AFTER MIDNIGHT on June 7, 1966, the month before he married Mia Farrow, Frank arrived at the Beverly Hills Hotel with Dean Martin and eight other people to celebrate Martin's birthday. They settled noisily in a booth in the Polo Lounge, too noisily for one customer seated nearby. The millionaire businessman and art collector Frederick Weisman objected to the obscenities that were flying around and asked Frank to get his group to pipe down. Moments later, he was down, seriously injured. Frank and Martin were gone by the time the police arrived.

Weisman had sustained a fracture to the skull and been rushed by ambulance to Beverly Hills Emergency Hospital, where he lapsed into a coma. He began to recover consciousness only three days later, after brain surgery lasting two and a half hours. He suffered from amnesia for some time, and told detectives he could remember nothing after having arrived at the Polo Lounge and having noticed Frank Sinatra.

Frank did not make himself available for questioning at first, and the Beverly Hills police chief said he was "in hiding." "We all drove down to Palm Springs that night," George Jacobs recalled, "to lie low." Frank did eventually speak with the police by phone. Jack Entratter's wife, Corinne, who was staying at Frank's house, remembered the aftermath of the incident as "the only time I think I ever saw that man scared. . . . We just didn't go anywhere. We just waited it out. Nobody knew how it would come out." Three weeks later, the Beverly Hills district attorney announced that there was "no evidence of a crime," and the case was closed.

Newspaper readers of the day were left only with the accounts Frank and Martin had given the police. "The guy was cursing me and using four-letter words," Frank had said initially. "I told him, 'I don't think you ought to be sitting there with your glasses on making that kind of conversation.' The guy got up and lunged at me. I defended myself, naturally." Later, however, he said, "I at no point saw anyone hit him—and I certainly did not."

Though no independent witness saw the injury, the **Los Angeles Times** reported that Frank's right eye was "discolored." Frank was quoted as saying Weisman had hit him with either his fists or an ashtray. Martin, who had gone to Lake Tahoe after the incident, told police that "some man struck Mr. Sinatra. Another man jumped between the two of them and our party walked out. As I looked back I saw a man lying on the ground. But I saw no one strike this man."

The friend who had been with Weisman at the

Polo Lounge, Franklin Fox, said Frank had indeed told Weisman it was a mistake to sit there with his glasses on. According to Fox, though, Frank then came up "to vent his anger." He tried to keep Frank away from Weisman, but then: "I was standing in front of Fred when Sinatra **threw the telephone** [authors' italics]. . . . Dean Martin was trying to get him out of there, and the next thing I knew Fred was lying on the floor."

Weisman never spoke publicly about the fracas, but discussed it with his cousin Carol Weisman Wilson. She recalled him saying, when his memory returned, that the end of the confrontation had come in the valet parking area outside the restaurant. There, she said, "they just beat him up."

The following year, Martin changed his version of events. "We were a little loud," he said. "When we were goin' out the door, there is a couple of guys, and one of them says: 'There goes the two loud Dagos.' Well, Frank got there one split second ahead of me, and he hit one guy, I hit the other, picked 'em up and threw 'em up against the wall. The cops came. We said we didn't know who did it and walked out. But we did, yeah." Asked in a recent interview whether Frank struck Weisman, Martin's former wife Jeanne nodded emphatically.

Weisman never fully recovered from his injury,

according to Carol Weisman Wilson: "He never was exactly the same personality after that."

THE MONTH AFTER THE WEISMAN INCIDENT, in London, Frank became enraged when Brad Dexter advised him against marrying Mia Farrow. "He went crazy," Dexter said, "went ape, began to tear up the apartment on Grosvenor Square, busted lamps, turned the table over."

A few months later, his new wife at his side, Frank caused a scene in Las Vegas. As the comedian Jackie Mason was doing his act at the Aladdin, Frank began abusing him from the audience. Mason responded by calling Frank "a middle-aged juvenile delinquent . . . a nut case."

Soon after, someone phoned the comedian warning him not to repeat his remarks about Frank. Three shots were later fired through the window of his hotel room. Mason was unhurt, and went on cracking jokes about Frank. Three months later, when he and Frank were both working in Miami, there were more warnings and a physical assault. "I was in the car with a girl," Mason remembered, "and we were a few blocks from the hotel that I was playing. I'm sitting there with her talking. And all of a sudden the door opens and a fist comes in, right into my nose and busted me—a fist with some kind of a ring on it that's supposed to cut your face open." Mason's nose had been broken, and he required plastic surgery.

Mason's woman companion vividly recalled the assault. Later—she had jumped out of the car and fled during the incident—Mason told her what the assailant said before running off. "Like, 'This is not the worst that can happen if you don't keep your mouth shut about Frank Sinatra'. . . . Something like that." Mason could prove nothing, and the police investigation was dropped.

Frank spent several weeks in early 1967 in Miami with Joe Fischetti. In Mia's absence, according to the FBI agents monitoring Fischetti, the mobster fixed him up with women. Stories spread that Frank had smashed up furniture and thrown a television set out the window of his suite at the Fontainebleau. Drinking hard, like Frank, was another comedian, Shecky Greene.

"As bad shape as I was in emotionally," Greene recalled, "I used to feel that if I needed four psychiatrists, he needed five. There was a show on television once called **Sybil**, about this woman with multiple personalities. It could have been about Frank."

Greene fought with Frank, not least because he, too, made acid remarks about Frank during his act. He told how one night, in the lobby of the Fontainebleau, "things got a little bloody." His head was split open, he said, by one of Frank's bodyguards and by Fischetti, who was wielding a blackjack. Greene appeared in Frank's movie **Tony Rome** with his head bandaged, a detail explained in the film as an injury from a car crash. In reality, according to Greene, "the bandage over my head is from the beating."

"Frank had so many people sucking around him then," Greene has said. "Those bodyguards would attack on command. Even if he doesn't order the beatings, he allows the violence to happen by having those guys around." Frank also used his own fists. That spring in Miami, according to an FBI source, he became enraged with an employee at the Eden Roc Hotel who answered the phone and refused to believe he was talking to Frank Sinatra. "Feeling no pain as he had consumed plenty of Jack Daniel's," according to the bureau report, Frank rushed to the Eden Roc and beat up the offender. The FBI was told that he then returned to the Fontainebleau, "laughing and feeling happy about the whole incident."

On the night of Friday, September 8, in Las Vegas, Frank entered the casino at the Sands with a group of visiting Apollo astronauts. When he asked for credit, which he had long been able to do as a matter of course, it was refused. The Sands had recently been purchased by Howard Hughes, Frank's hated rival because of their mutual interest in Ava. Frank owed the house money, and had been heard to say he had no intention of paying off the debt. In response, Hughes's manager had now cut off his credit.

Frank restrained his anger in front of the astronauts. He left the casino, but returned in the early-morning hours in a rage. Paul Anka recalled how he "got up on that table and started yelling and screaming right in the middle of the casino." Frank told one of the pit bosses he was "gonna break both your legs." He told graveyard shift supervisor Dave Silverman that "were he not an old man he would bury him." "I built this hotel from a sandpile," Frank shouted, "and before I'm through that's what it will be again." Then he left, only to return at 10:15 A.M.

Mia recalled riding with Frank on a golf cart as they at last headed, as she imagined, to bed. Her husband was wearing a shoe box on his head, to shield his eyes from the morning sun. Suddenly, to Mia's horror, Frank speeded up, swerved, and smashed into a plate-glass window. He then strode into the casino, heaped up chairs, and tried unsuccessfully to set them on fire with his gold lighter.

Frank flew home to Palm Springs, slept a while, and began drinking his way through the weekend. Sometime on Sunday night he ordered up his plane, returned to Vegas, and apologized to the pit bosses for his behavior of two nights earlier. By dawn on Monday, though, he was roaring around demanding to speak with either Jack Entratter or

Sands vice president Carl Cohen. Both were sleeping, but Frank told the hotel operator that if they were not roused he would "tear up this goddamn fucking place" and rip out every wire in the telephone room. Three frightened female telephone operators cowered in their office as Frank kicked and pounded on the door. When an armed security guard tried to restrain him, Frank said he would take his gun and "shove it up his ass."

Shortly before 6:00 A.M., having been woken, Cohen joined Frank at a table in the restaurant. Frank called him a "son-of-a-bitch," "motherfucker," "rat fink," and "cock sucker," and said "I'll get a guy to bury you." Then he turned the table over on Cohen.

At that point, according to the report filed by the county sheriff's investigators, Cohen "reached out with his right fist, striking Frank Sinatra in the upper lip, resulting in the loss of two front teeth." Cohen stood over six feet tall and weighed about 250 pounds. Frank was knocked to the floor, but got back on his feet and screamed "You broke my teeth. I will kill you"—along with a new stream of invective. He again tried to hit Cohen and bashed a security man over the head with a chair when he intervened, opening a cut that required stitches. Then he left, having again threatened to have the casino boss killed. He phoned Mia sounding, she recalled, "bewildered and upset," his speech "unclear." Cohen had demolished much of the expensive dentistry on his front teeth.

Two of the usual heavies had been at Frank's side during the fracas, and at one point, according to Sonny King, Frank ordered them to "get" Cohen. Cohen responded, "You make one move and they won't know which part of the desert to find you," and the heavies backed off. "In that town," pit boss Ed Walters has said, referring to the confrontation, "there were some people no entertainer better fuck with." Cohen was one of them.

The county sheriff's investigators spoke with more than a dozen members of the Sands staff, but could not contact Frank, who had again left town. Years later, when testifying before the Nevada State Gaming Control Board, Frank dismissed the episode as having been "just an argument between two fellows" that he would "rather not discuss."

A couple of days before the Cohen incident, when his credit was cut off, Frank had phoned New York and protested to Jimmy Alo. Alo wielded great influence at the Sands, but he told Frank to drop the matter. Now, having had his teeth knocked out, Frank appealed to Alo again. Ken Roberts, then a New York–based concert promoter, was sitting with Alo and Henri Giné, Frank's East Coast representative, when Frank phoned. "Jimmy was sitting there with a hat on, even in the heat," Roberts remembered. "Sinatra kept calling, and Jimmy was so angry at him because of what he'd done. Instead of talking to Frank he spoke loud, so that Frank could hear him. Jimmy said, 'Henri, tell him. He needed me Friday. I spoke to him Friday. I told him what to do. I told him to go home and forget about it, and he didn't do it. I don't need to talk to him.'" Alo felt Frank had it coming.

Even before the incident, Frank had been in discussions about taking his talent elsewhere. Now that Howard Hughes owned the Sands, he had no wish to stay. Now, a contract with Caesars Palace was announced even before his New York dentist arrived to fix his teeth.

Frank was adrift. His latest marriage had failed, the long-standing business tie with the Sands had been severed, and he was an emotional mess. Watching him at work in a recording studio in 1967, the music critic Gene Lees thought how lonely he looked.

"All his jokes, all his small pleasantries," Lees wrote in **High Fidelity** magazine, "have drawn laughs from the control booth. But gradually I realize that it is more laughter than they deserve, and at this latest remark, everyone cracks up as if this were one of Fred Allen's most pungent witticisms. It's as if they have to, all these surrounding people. What's odd about it is that they're separated from him by a double window; he can't hear them, has no way of knowing who laughed hardest at his joke. But they do it anyway.

"This is the one hint of the staggering power that inheres in this contradictory man, whose tangled and obviously lonely life is a strange amalgam of elegance and ugliness, of profound failure and dizzying success, of adamant loyalties and equally adamant dislikes, of kindness and courtesies and rudeness. . . . Somewhere within him, Frank Sinatra aches. Fine. That's the way it's always been; the audience's pleasure derives from the artist's pain."

31

Looking for an Exit

FRANK'S RECORDING CAREER SURGED during his time of turmoil in the mid-1960s. "Strangers in the Night" in 1966 and "My Way" in 1968 became his new musical signature, Sinatra songs for a new generation.

Frank did not like either song. "I don't want to sing this," he told his longtime aide Irving Weiss when he brought him the sheet music for "Strangers in the Night," "it's a piece of shit." Soon after the song became a hit, when he was at a Las Vegas casino, he promised to "stick that violin bow up where the sun don't shine" if the orchestra leader played the tune just one more time.

Once, as he finished singing "Strangers," an open microphone picked him up saying, "That's the worst fucking song I ever heard." "If you like that song," he told an audience, "you must be crazy about pineapple yoghurt." "You **still** like it?" he would mutter, after applause, then shake his head in disbelief. Al Viola, Frank's favorite guitarist, recalled how he liked to mangle the lyrics. It amused Frank to have the stranger

Wond'ring in the night
Just where my pants is. . . .

There were critics who called "Strangers" "dreck," a "lounge lizard song," and scoffed at the doo-be-doo-be-doo-ing at the end as "bad scatting . . . as if Alistair Cooke were talking jive." Frank might have agreed, but he was a realist. "He'd make fun of that song," Armand Deutsch said, "but he'd say, 'It's helped keep me in pizza'—it put a lot of money in his pocket."

"Strangers" became Frank's first number one single in eleven years, and stayed in that position for fifteen weeks. It won four Grammy Awards, including Record of the Year and Best Male Vocal Performance. (The Beatles' "Michelle" took the Grammy for Song of the Year.)

Viola liked to stay on after a recording session to listen to the playbacks. It was a habit that, late on December 30, 1968, made him the first person ever to listen to "My Way." "I was thrilled and shocked," Viola recalled. "Shocked because it was so good. It was history. The man was singing about his life."

One day, tongue in cheek, Frank would dub "My Way" his "national anthem." The song as he sang it—of a life lived hard, through laughter and tears and love and loss, without apology—came over as defiant autobiography. It had already been a hit in France when Paul Anka wrote English lyrics for it and brought it to Frank in Las Vegas. Frank thought it "kooky," and had to be talked into recording it. He did, though, within forty-eight hours.

"My Way" "really had nothing to do with my life whatsoever," Frank would claim later. Yet Anka thought the song was "all him," and Frank Sinatra Jr. said the "five words of plain English" of the refrain—"I did it my way"—summed up his father exactly.

The Atlantic Monthly's critic, Stephen Holden, dismissed the song as a "surly roar of self-satisfaction." To Peter Silverton of the London **Observer** it was "something Hitler might have sung as he marched into Paris." For Sarah Vowell, writing for **Salon** in 1997, it evoked "the temper tantrums of two-year-olds or perhaps the last words spoken to Eva Braun. . . . Can't you imagine Oliver North defacing the Constitution with graffiti like 'I faced it all. And I stood tall . . .'? Who wants to be remembered for blind rigidity?"

"Every time I get up to sing that song I grit my teeth," Frank said for public consumption, "because no matter what the image may seem to be, I hate boastfulness in others." He told one audience that he only wished the "little Arab"—Anka is of Lebanese ancestry—would write a hit for him more often. His "embarrassment," Anka said, was voiced only after "My Way" had been "overplayed and oversung."

"My Way" did not go to the top of the charts in the United States but, like "Strangers in the Night," it established that Frank was still a major player. Yet he was as unsettled musically as he was in his personal life. The album **My Way**—the song was simply tacked onto the front of the next collection due to go on the market—misfired as an attempt to echo contemporary style. "For Once in My Life" belonged to Tony Bennett, and Frank's version sounded like trespassing. He sounded not cool but plain silly when he tortured the words of "Mrs. Robinson" with bawdy Rat Pack—era slang—"How's your bird, Mrs. Robinson?"

To try to make "Some Enchanted Evening" swing, as Frank did in this same period, was a bizarre misjudgment. It was folly, too, to imagine as he did that he could play the comedian and have a successful record simply by reciting Rudyard Kipling's poem "Gunga Din," with only bugle blasts and battlefield sound effects for accompaniment. Recorded just two days after the beating of Frederick Weisman, it sounded merely gauche. It was never released.

There was much experimentation in the ten Sinatra albums released between 1967 and 1971. Two collections of work done with the Brazilian musician Antonio Carlos Jobim, creator of "The Girl from Ipanema," included some brilliant performances, but were not for Frank's traditional audience. The good moments in a collaboration with the pop poet Rod McKuen, on an album entitled **A Man Alone,** were obscured by descents into dross. **Watertown,** the soliloquy of a man whose wife has left him, was a protracted mix of narration and song. One critic thought it just "one more entry in a long era of unimportance."

In May 1969, earthbound millions watched as the Apollo 10 astronauts circled the moon—the spacecraft was the first to send back live color pictures—and saw a cassette being loaded into a tape recorder. Across space came the voice of astronaut Gene Cernan addressing Mission Control: "This is just so that you guys don't get too excited about the TV and forget what your job is down there." Then viewers heard a familiar voice singing:

> Fly me to the moon, let me swing among the stars,
> Let me see what spring is like on Jupiter and Mars . . .

To a global audience, a Frank Sinatra song remained a synonym for love and romance. Yet as the 1960s ended, Frank was a man alone.

FRANK'S FATHER, MARTY, suffered from emphysema, and died in 1969 at seventy-four. His son had flown him to Texas for last-ditch heart surgery in vain. Hundreds turned out when Marty was brought home to New Jersey for burial. Dolly tried to throw herself into the grave.

Frank took the loss hard. He arranged for his father's remains to be disinterred and reburied in Palm Springs. He also raised funds for a modern medical training facility in the city, the Martin Anthony Sinatra Medical Education Center, which still operates today.

Dolly moved from New Jersey to live next door to Frank, though she loathed California. A constant physical presence now, she continued to pick fights with her son. While her father "adored" his mother and gave her anything she wanted, Tina Sinatra thought, "she drove him crazy."

Tina was twenty-one as the 1970s began, emerging from a bumpy adolescence. While reproaching her father for his absences during her childhood, she has also praised him as the family's "rock" in times of trouble. Frank Jr., by then in his mid-twenties and making his way as a singer, had felt shut out since being sent off to boarding school in his early teens. From that point on, he said, he was "away from the inner family circle."

As a professional musician, Frank Jr. was trapped in his father's aura. "Is it genuine talent," a writer asked, "or the warm remembrance of the golden Sinatra era that has catapulted Frankie's boy into the limelight?" Frank Jr. said bitterly that he had "just one simple dream—to say or do something, anything, any damn thing at all, that was mine, 100 percent mine. . . . I couldn't even walk across a room without someone remarking, 'He walks just like his old man.' Often I would ask myself, 'Who am I? As Frank Sinatra Jr., am I cursed or blessed?' "

Daughter Nancy had made it as a popular singer. "These Boots Are Made for Walkin' " and "Somethin' Stupid," a duet with her father, had been huge hits. She was nudging thirty, embarking on a second marriage, and starting work on a book about her father to be entitled, she said, **A Very Gentle Man.** Two decades after their divorce, Nancy, his first wife, remained a quiet presence in Frank's life, and evidently never seriously considered remarrying.

Frank was still pursuing women, but halfheartedly. He had dalliances after his marriage to Mia collapsed, but none went anywhere. He had used his old ploy, a summons to his table at a restaurant, to pick up the actress Patty Duke. She went to bed with him that night, she said, but they did not have sex: "Nothing happened. . . . I spent a few weeks with him off and on. . . . We slept in the same bed, but never was there any sex."

Ava held his affection, even now, though she could be unnecessarily cruel. As a husband, she told a journalist, Frank had been "a sacred monster . . . convinced there was nobody in the world except him." Soon after that was published, Pete Hamill sat drinking with Frank and friends at P. J. Clarke's saloon in New York. In the early hours, as the whiskey flowed, someone played "I'm a Fool to Want You" on the jukebox. "A song out of Sinatra's past," Hamill realized. "Out of 1951 and Ava Gardner and the most terrible time of his life. Everybody at the table knew the story. Sinatra stared for a moment at the bourbon in his glass. Then he shook his head. 'Time to go,' he said. We all rose, and went to the side door and followed Frank Sinatra into the night."

In his mid-fifties now, Frank was increasingly alone in other ways. His concept of loyalty, a concept he held sacrosanct, had led him to destroy key relationships. "My son is like me," Dolly once said. "You cross him, he never forgets." His concept of loyalty, Orson Welles thought, involved an element of "ferocity."

Long before, Hank Sanicola had warned Frank that his involvement with Sam Giancana would lead to financial disaster, and Frank had rejected the advice. His twenty-five-year partnership with

Sanicola had ended in one explosive argument. Frank had cut Jack Entratter out of his life after the fight at the Sands, and never spoke to him again. They, too, had been associates for a quarter of a century. The singer Phyllis McGuire thought it the action of a man "capable of being generous and gentle yet so cruel, a great friend yet a man who cut off friends." Frank had broken with Brad Dexter by having him fired by a gofer.

George Jacobs, too, had been dumped. On the eve of Frank's divorce from Mia, when the valet met her by chance at a Beverly Hills disco, she had asked him to dance with her. He obliged, and Frank heard about it. When Jacobs got back to Palm Springs, his key no longer fit the front gate. He was handed an attorney's letter banning him from the premises, given no chance to explain, and—after fifteen years service—received no severance pay.

Four people who had been fixtures in Frank's world died in just a few months in 1971: Entratter, dead at fifty-seven; Joe E. Lewis, finally killed by alcohol; Louis Armstrong, with whom Frank had starred repeatedly over the years; Michael Romanoff, a stalwart companion. Marilyn Maxwell, with whom he had stayed in touch, would die at the age of forty-nine. Hank Sanicola would also soon die.

"To be Frank's friend," Rosalind Russell said, "is like one of his songs, 'All or Nothing at All.' It is a total, unconditional commitment, a never-fraying security blanket." Frank now received the required loyalty from a heavyset, one-eyed New Yorker named Jilly Rizzo. Born Ermenigildo Rizzo to Italian immigrant parents on the lower West Side, he had once dreamed of becoming a professional fighter. He looked the part—Frank joked that he had once mistaken him for a rhinoceros. After a four-year hitch in the army and a series of bartending jobs, Rizzo had bought his own nightspot, Jilly's, on 52nd Street in Manhattan. It became Frank's favorite watering hole.

With a flashing sign proclaiming it "Home of the King" and photographs of Frank adorning the walls, Jilly's became a Sinatra shrine. Frank held court there when he was in town, enthroned in his personal blue wooden chair at the table that was always reserved for him. Rizzo sat beside him in an identical chair. When Frank wanted privacy, other customers were evicted.

Rizzo had been at hand in crisis after crisis—the brush with death in Hawaii, the kidnapping of Frank Jr., the breakup with Mia, and the death of Marty Sinatra. Frank's mother called Rizzo "fuckface," as a term of affection. Tina said Rizzo came to be part of the family. His services ranged from fixing Frank up with hookers to traveling with him to meet with grand personages: Queen Elizabeth II, American presidents, Jackie Kennedy Onassis. As Frank put it, Rizzo could "clean up real good." The pair sometimes sported matching orange jackets embroidered on the back with the slogan "Living well is the best revenge, F.T.A." "F.T.A." stood for "Fuck them all!" To be close to Frank, Rizzo relocated to Palm Springs.

Rizzo said he loved Frank "like a goddamn father . . . the greatest human being around." He recalled having told his hero, "Frank, you purify the goddamn room." Frank reciprocated by giving Rizzo small parts in three of his movies, and appointed him to a post with his movie company, Artanis Productions. He inserted the line "Jilly loves you more than you can know" in his rendering of the song "Mrs. Robinson." He rated Jilly a "poet," for his silver tongue and what Frank saw as his "old-world wisdom."

Rizzo had been arrested twice for assault before meeting Frank, a grounding perhaps for his bodyguard role, one he preferred to disown. A comic joked that Rizzo was Frank's "tractor," for the way he forged a path through the crowds. Often, what he did for Frank was not a joking matter.

In 1964 in Paris, according to Rock Brynner, it was Rizzo who had stomped on the hand of a French photographer, breaking bones. In 1972, at a Monte Carlo nightclub, Rizzo "pulverized" a young student suspected of snapping photographs. He was then spirited to the airport, to avoid arrest, and flown out on Frank's private jet. At Las Vegas, Rizzo punished an abusive drunk by hauling him to a quiet spot and exploding cherry bombs in his pocket, so many of them that his hip was shattered.

In 1973, Rizzo took the fall after a guest was beaten up at a Palm Springs hotel. The guest sued, claiming that men in Frank's party had surrounded him in the restroom chanting "Respect the Man! Respect the Man!" Then, on an order and a snap of the fingers from Frank, they had hit him in the head and body. Rizzo, who admitted having been one of the assailants, was found guilty of assault and ordered to pay the plaintiff $101,000.

Rizzo was deeply involved with the Mafia, though his FBI dossier contains conflicting reports as to whether he was actually a "made man." One document categorizes him as an "LCN"—La Cosa Nostra—"associate." Others connect him to Sam Giancana, Joe Fischetti, and the New York families. His best mobster friend was Dave Iacovetti of the Gambino crime family, with whom he and Frank socialized. He was on intimate terms with the family of another senior Gambino operative, Thomas Bilotti. Bilotti's brother Jimmy acted as mentor to one of Rizzo's sons and, after Dolly's death, Bilotti's mother would lavish affection on Frank as though he were her own child. With Carlo Gambino, according to an allegation in a 1971 report, Frank and Rizzo put up $100,000—nearly half a million at today's rates—that was used in a failed stock scam.

Rizzo's mob connections were to catch up with him in 1990, when he and several accomplices were convicted of a fraud that drained $8 million from a savings and loan association. He was spared jail on account of his age and poor health, and ordered to work a thousand hours of community service. Rizzo would be buried near Frank in the Sinatra family plot.

THE AMERICAN-ITALIAN ANTI-DEFAMATION LEAGUE (AID), a new pressure group, was founded in 1967 with the stated aim of rebutting what it claimed were false allegations in books, movies, and the media that "taint unfairly 22,000,000 American-Italians as people of sinister character." Frank, the most celebrated Italian-American of them all, agreed to be the group's chairman. Eighteen thousand people jammed Madison Square Garden in October to hear him, resplendent in tuxedo and red pocket handkerchief, sing and rally people to the cause.

Taking on the chairmanship brought immediate negative publicity. A retired organized crime specialist with the New York Police Department, Ralph Salerno, told the **New York Times** that Frank's involvement with mafiosi "hardly matches the image the League is seeking to project." What was needed, Salerno said, was for the "fine decent people" who made up the vast majority of the Italian-

American population to disassociate themselves from "about 10,000 wrongdoers," the criminal community that included so many of Frank's friends.

On AID's board of directors, it soon emerged, were at least seven men who had Mafia membership or associations. Frank resigned and, though the board was cleaned up, the group faded from sight—only to be replaced in 1970 by the Italian-American Civil Rights League (IACRL). Again in the name of eradicating prejudice, the new organization drew huge attendance at rallies, raised thousands of dollars, and received national attention. Thanks to the group's efforts, broadcasters and the Justice Department agreed not to use the words "Mafia" and "Cosa Nostra" in programs and official documents. This second league, however, was even more a creature of organized crime than its predecessor. Its founder and vociferous leading light was Joe Colombo, head of one of New York's five crime families.

Leery now, Frank turned down a request from Colombo to perform at an IACRL rally. "Colombo was furious that Sinatra had pulled a no-show," said Hector Saldana, a journalist to whom Jimmy Alo described what happened. "He let Sinatra know that if he came east of the Mississippi he would pay with his life. Alo checked and learned that a contract had indeed been put out.

Sinatra was very frightened. 'He called me every day crying,' Alo said. 'He was a crybaby.' "

Alo negotiated a compromise with Colombo. The hit would be called off if Frank would agree to perform at the league's next big event, a concert at Madison Square Garden. He did perform, but skipped accompanying functions. "As far as can be ascertained," an FBI report noted, "Sinatra no longer wants to be associated with the hoodlum element."

During the first phase of the Italian-American protests, when Frank had been keen to help, he had been rebuked in print by Mario Puzo, then a little-known Italian-American writer. Puzo's 1969 novel **The Godfather,** just the kind of book the league did not want published, sold a million copies in hardcover and eight million in paperback. The movie that followed, the first of three **Godfather** movies, made Francis Ford Coppola's name and became one of the most lucrative films in the history of cinema. The film generated massive publicity, not least because, as mentioned earlier, the singer and Mafia protégé of the story was unmistakably based on Sinatra.

Frank got wind of it before the book came out—the movie rights had been optioned well in advance—and had his attorneys demand to see the manuscript. When that failed, he fought to get the Sinatra character written out of the movie.

To placate him, and to avoid litigation, the producers cut back the role of the mobbed-up singer.

"Sinatra still wasn't happy, and tried to have me muscled out of the part," said Al Martino, who played the singer in the film. "But I had muscle of my own." According to Martino, Frank was told to back off by Sam Giancana. During a chance encounter at Chasen's restaurant in Beverly Hills, Puzo recalled, Frank abused him in a "frenzied, high-pitched" voice, accused him of being a "pimp," and threatened to "beat hell" out of him.

The Godfather furor was just one element in a barrage of bad press. In 1969, from New Jersey, came revelations obtained by FBI bugs planted in the office of Angelo De Carlo, Frank's earliest Mafia patron. De Carlo had repeatedly been overheard discussing Frank—raising the possibility that Frank would contribute funds for a casino, telling how he had fixed Frank up with a woman, and talking about their quite recent contacts.

That summer, while aboard a yacht at Highlands, New Jersey, and thus within the state's jurisdiction, Frank was served with a subpoena to appear before a commission investigating Mafia activity. He fought for months to avoid testifying, caving in only when the U.S. Supreme Court ruled that he would be subject to a three-year jail term should he fail to comply. When he appeared, Frank solemnly told his questioners he was unaware that top gangsters he knew or had known were mafiosi. Were Lucky Luciano, Willie Moretti, Sam Giancana, and Joe Fischetti Mafia members? Not so far as Frank knew. He did not know a single person, he said under oath, who could be described as belonging to organized crime.

As often as he was asked to testify about Mafia matters, Frank struggled to avoid doing so. In 1968 he used spurious excuses to put off appearing in a Miami court in connection with a libel case involving the Fontainebleau Hotel and the **Miami Herald**, then left Florida when ordered by a circuit judge to show up or go to jail. The matter became moot soon afterward, when the suit was dropped.

Four years later, having initially let it be known that he was prepared to appear before the House Select Committee on Crime, Frank left for England. When the committee voted to take steps to force him to appear, he vanished from London's Savoy Hotel and laid low for a while in Europe. Six weeks later, when he did deign to appear on Capitol Hill, he was in a belligerent mood.

"Let's dispense with that kind of questioning," Frank said, when asked about his acquaintance with Tommy Lucchese, the Luciano ally who before his death had gone on to become a mob boss in his own right. Was there such a thing as the Mafia? "From the standpoint of reading," Frank said, "I suppose you might say it exists. But I really couldn't put my finger on it and say it does exist, because I don't know about it." After testifying, he sounded off in the **New York Times** with an innocent citizen's outrage that he had been summoned to appear at all.

Frank had roared into Washington "like Lear denouncing the wind," wrote **Life**'s Thomas Thompson. In his appearances before both the New Jersey commission and the House committee, Frank had echoed Joe Colombo's claim that he was being persecuted solely because of his ethnic identity. "If a man cries 'Foul' and 'Innocent' long enough and loud enough," Thompson wrote, "it becomes easier and easier to believe him."

ON THE NIGHT OF JUNE 13, 1971, Thompson sat talking with Frank in a dressing room at the Los Angeles Music Center. Frank was smoking, wearing a shirt and tuxedo pants, and had one black patent-leather boot hooked over a knee. He called for hot tea, then changed the order to vodka. Then, as Al Viola strummed a melody, he quietly began to sing:

> When a woman loves a man . . . try a little
> tenderness. . . .

Thompson thought the voice sounded "whispery, from far away, but gleaming, burnished like a gold coin kept in a velvet box."

The five thousand people who would hear Frank

sing that night included the vice president of the United States, the national security adviser, the governor of California, Her Serene Highness Princess Grace of Monaco (Grace Kelly), Cary Grant, Bob Hope, Jimmy Stewart, Jimmy Durante, Rock Hudson, David Niven, Jack Benny, Pearl Bailey, Barbra Streisand, Edward G. Robinson, Steve Allen, Carol Burnett, Diahann Carroll, Natalie Wood, Ali MacGraw, Clint Eastwood, Robert Wagner, and Frank's family. They were there because Frank had announced that this would be the last performance of his show business career.

Two months earlier, Tina had come upon her father busy with pen and paper beside the pool at Palm Springs. He was drafting a statement, to be published by the columnist Suzy (Aileen Mehle) a week or so later, announcing his "retirement from the entertainment world and public life." Frank had never had much opportunity, the statement said, for "reflection, reading, self-examination." Now he looked forward to having time with his family, doing some writing, perhaps even teaching. His decision, he said, was final.

The press sought a deeper explanation. Was he sick? Frank told Thompson that night at the Music Center that his health was "spectacular." Was he quitting because his record sales had dipped and his most recent movie, the spoof western **Dirty Dingus Magee**, had flopped? Over the vodka with Thompson, Frank merely said, "I've had enough.

Maybe the public's had enough, too." He had recorded more than nine hundred songs, many of them more than once, produced eighty-seven albums, and made forty-three movies.

In part, Frank said later, he decided to quit because "Being a public figure got to me. People were always spiritually peeking in my windows." He excoriated certain reporters as "slobs" and "garbage collectors," a category in which he would certainly have included the prize-winning journalist Nicholas Gage. Gage had written a groundbreaking story in 1968 in **The Wall Street Journal** that for the first time publicly exposed details of Frank's Mafia contacts.

The retirement announcement, moreover, came a few months after another violent confrontation between Frank and a casino official, this time at Caesars Palace. The mob had again failed to back him up. Giancana, who mostly lived abroad following a spell in prison, was a spent force. Angelo De Carlo and Jimmy Alo were in jail. Joe Fischetti soon would be.

Frank worried about his personal security. Two women he dated in 1971 said that he still carried a gun. He went out of his way to show it to one of them when she visited his home at Palm Springs. The other was stunned to see that he carried a gun in a leather shoulder holster.

Peggy Connelly saw Frank at about this time. "He was not the him I'd known," she said. "He had lost something. He had always been so vital, and now he had lost his charm. He seemed dead, in a way." "All of us have our areas of despair if we are sensitive," Burt Lancaster said the year Frank retired. "I think one of the reasons Frank is retiring while he is still a vital person is that he is seeking his own way to his own peace."

After midnight on the night of the retirement appearance, as Streisand finished a rocking rendition of "Oh, Happy Day," Frank slipped on his tuxedo jacket and walked on stage. He said, "Here's how it started," and launched into "All or Nothing at All." As he sang, many in the audience wept. Frank closed with "Angel Eyes," uttered the last melancholy line, "Excuse me while I disappear" in the halo of a single spotlight, and walked off into the darkness.

He returned to acknowledge a standing ovation, but declined to do an encore. "I'm tired," Frank told Thomas Thompson in the limousine that swept him away from the Music Center. "It's been a helluva thirty-five years."

As a Mexican lament played on the limousine's radio, Frank improvised some lyrics, sang a few bars, then stopped. "That, ladies and gentlemen," he told his companions, "is the last time Frank Sinatra will open his mouth."

Everybody laughed.

32

“Let Me Try Again”

FRANK INSISTED HIS CAREER WAS OVER. “I’m finished, really finished. . . . I don’t want to put any more makeup on. I don’t want to perform anymore. I’m not going to stop living. . . . Maybe I’m going to start living. . . . Like the first thing is not to do anything at all for eight months.” He would have time now for painting, he said—he had done numerous competent landscapes over the years, and was now experimenting with abstracts. He planned, too, to take photographs of cacti and hang them in the hospital wing dedicated to his father. He would “read Plato and grow petunias.”

For months to come, Frank did not sing. “I wouldn’t even hum for anybody. Not a sound did I make. . . . I played a lot of music—I get a big buzz out of the opera and of classics.” He was spotted in art galleries pursuing his interest in modern American painters—and in Picasso, whom he revered. He worked a little on his golf score or, he said, did "absolutely zero."

He was stupendously rich, and laden with honors. In early 1971 he had received a special Oscar, his third, in recognition of his charitable work. He had sat listening in the gallery of the Senate as members marked his retirement with extravagant tributes. Senator John Tunney of California declared him "the greatest entertainer" in American history. The city of Palm Springs held a Frank Sinatra Day, and renamed the road he lived on—in the community today known as Rancho Mirage—Frank Sinatra Drive.

Yet, Tina thought, Frank was the loneliest man in the world. He was finding it as hard as ever to sustain a relationship with a woman. Marianna Case, a twice-married dancer in her late twenties, was working part-time as a **Playboy** bunny when Frank noticed her in a bra commercial. He got a mutual friend to call and say Frank Sinatra hoped she would join him for dinner.

On their first date, Frank sat Marianna next to him at a crowded restaurant table. She thought he was at once gentlemanly, loud, and nervous. He asked her out again, and there were more raucous evenings with his assorted male pals. Frank cooked for her at his place. She saw him when he had drunk too much, and when, as Jilly Rizzo explained one night, he was "having another mood swing"; when he raged, "face contorted in frustration," after losing at the tables in Las Vegas. She was once summoned because, Rizzo told her, Frank was "acting really crazy, and I think if you came over he'd calm down. He always seems to lighten up when you're around." She arrived to find Frank having a temper tantrum, and watched silently as he screamed obscenities and hurled tapes around.

She came to think she was an "entertainment" for Frank, though not in the bedroom. Once she asked if she could just "lay with him" for the night, but he said he did not want to "spoil anything." The closest the couple came to having sex was "a kiss and a hug." Marianna admired the side of Frank that put women, some women, "on pedestals." Barbara Walters, then on the threshold of national celebrity, put him on her list of ten favorite men in 1971 "because of his old-fashioned courtliness. . . . He treats women as if they were made of glass. He's as concerned with their comfort and dignity as a Victorian."

Frank deplored the recent excesses in women's behavior and dress. What he looked for in a woman, he said, was intelligence, a degree of reserve, and elegance. He wanted "women to be women."

The actress Lois Nettleton, whom he began dating early in 1971, seemed in many ways to fit the bill. She was a lovely, vivacious woman fifteen years his junior, divorced and unencumbered by children. She was highly intelligent and articulate, with an established track record on Broadway, in films, and on television. After their first date, a symphony concert, Lois and Frank began a relationship that was to last almost a year.

They became lovers, and as a regular houseguest she saw the private Sinatra, the man with a compulsion about neatness and order, who liked to lavish gifts on intimates. She cruised with Frank on his yacht, slept with him in his red, white, and blue stateroom, still has a jacket inscribed "Aboard the Christina." They "went cycling together on quiet roads near his house in Palm Springs," Lois remembered. "He gave me a bicycle with a beautifully woven basket on the front, and the day he gave it to me he'd had the basket filled with daisies—my favorite flowers. . . . He'd send me notes signed 'Francis'—he preferred those who knew him to use 'Francis' rather than 'Frank.' One I've kept just says: 'You're scrumptious.' "

Frank opened up a good deal, described what he knew of his difficult birth, talked of how much he had always loved trains—how as a little boy he had yearned to be given a model locomotive. He had told Marianna a few months earlier that he sometimes still felt as though he were a little boy. Now he showed Lois the sailor costume he had worn more than a quarter of a century ago for **Anchors Aweigh,** and reflected ruefully on the fact that it no longer fit.

Since the 1940s, when he had first taken up painting, Frank had been drawing or painting pictures of clowns. One of the first of them had been a clown's head with flour-white cheeks and a bright red mouth, with a ruffle at the neck. He hung a sad-faced clown face over his desk in his Warner Brothers office, dressed up as a clown when he went to a costume party. Special friends and intimates received clown pictures as gifts. Peggy Connelly had one he drew on a toothbrush glass, with the scrawled message, "Good morning, darling." Lois got a clown painting.

Frank's interest in clowns, he said, derived from his admiration for Emmett Kelly, the famous clown of the 1940s and 1950s. Kelly, creator of the hobo character Weary Willie, described himself as a "sad and ragged little guy who is very serious about everything he attempts—no matter how futile or how foolish it appears to be." According to Tina, some of Frank's clowns were self-portraits.

With her, Lois said, Frank was almost always "tender, romantic." His first compliment had been to tell Lois she was "such a lady." "I realized that was especially important to him at that time. It was like he was going into another stage of his life. His idea of retirement was somehow to become part of really high-class life. He was very involved in the finer things in life, art, politics, social issues.

"He gathered wonderful people around him, very elegant people, even among the performers. . . . We went to Gregory and Veronique Peck's house for tea, to one of Phyllis Cerf's [Bennett's wife's] parties . . . Candice Bergen and her mom came to dinner. My picture of Francis, definitely, is of him being the distinguished artist in an elegant world. He would sit at the head of the table, with me on his right. I had the sense that he was proud of me, wanted everyone to see him with me. I wasn't flashy or 'Hollywood,' and I didn't have hysterical fits. I was raised to be ladylike, tried always to be socially graceful and do the right thing. I think that mattered to him.

"It's like he was the king who points to the lady and says, 'It's you . . .' I was one of the many women in his life, but I was chosen from amongst the court. It was lovely for a year or so." Lois got the impression Frank had cut back on his drinking, and there was no coarse behavior while she was with him, no brutality. "With me, he was always a knight in shining armor. Yet there was an edgy side to him. He didn't like to be challenged. He needed to be in control, and he had a quicksilver temperament. I was always a little frightened that he would change." One night in late 1971, in the space of a couple of hours, he did.

"He had a party at a Beverly Hills restaurant.

We got there a little early, ahead of the other people. We were having a glass of wine and he said, 'What do you think about us getting married?' I was breathless, swept away. I only remember the happiness, but I probably said something like, 'That'd be lovely.' People were starting to arrive, and then we all sat down to dinner. After the meal I went to the ladies' room to put on lipstick and fix my hair. Something had spilled on my dress and I was cleaning it off. A couple of my fans came in and I got talking to them. Then Tina, I think, came in and said, 'Lois, what're you doing? We're leaving.' Though I didn't realize it at the time, everyone else had started to leave just after I'd got up to go to the ladies' room. I guess Francis had figured he'd pick me up at the door. But I wasn't there. . . .

"When I caught up with him, on the sidewalk, he turned on me and screamed at me at the top of his lungs. He screamed in my face and called me names—because I'd been away so long. I'd left him hanging about, and he was so **furious.** The way he saw it, I realized, I'd humiliated him. I got into a car and I did go back to the house. Jilly Rizzo was there, and he sat me down in a bedroom and said, 'He'll calm down, he'll come back.' I thought 'Well, okay,' and it seemed as though I sat there forever. I had a gift for Francis with me, for either his birthday or Christmas, a little Sagittarius medallion on a chain.

"I sat there in a fog holding that Sagittarius. We'd just been talking of getting married, and then he had screamed and left me stranded! I could hear them talking and laughing and drinking in the living room, and eventually I asked Jilly to get someone to drive me home. And that, really, was the end of it."

Frank asked Lois after a while to see him again, and they did meet a few times. The damage he had done, though, was irreparable.

DURING THEIR AFFAIR, Lois had once found herself seated at Frank's side as he played host to President Richard Nixon's national security adviser, Henry Kissinger, and his deputy, Alexander Haig. A few years earlier, they would not have been his guests. "Long after he has ceased to sing," John Kennedy had said of Frank in 1961, "he's going to be standing up for the Democratic Party."

Frank would continue to proclaim that he was "a lifelong Democrat." Yet there he was, entertaining the opposition. When he dedicated the hospital wing in memory of his father, Vice President Spiro Agnew and California governor Ronald Reagan were his guests of honor. Agnew had hurried away from Tricia Nixon's wedding, in Washington, to attend the Sinatra retirement concert in California. Frank's earlier views on Nixon and

Reagan had been savage. In 1960, asked to think of something that made him laugh, he had replied derisively by saying, "Nixon!" Shirley MacLaine recalled that he "hated Nixon with deep vitriol." Frank had long despised Reagan for having appeared as a "friendly witness" before the House Un-American Activities Committee. He dismissed him as "a bozo, or **Bonzo**"—after the chimpanzee that Reagan appeared with in one of his movies—as a "stupid bore" who had gone into politics only because his acting career had stalled. He thought Nancy Reagan, whom he had met during her acting days, "a dumb broad with fat ankles." In 1966, when Reagan was elected governor, Frank declared that he might "leave the country . . . certainly ought to get out of this state." He took to altering the chorus of "The Lady Is a Tramp" to:

> She dislikes California, it's Reagan and
> damp . . .
> That's why the lady is a tramp.

Yet in 1970, when Reagan was running for reelection, Frank campaigned for him. "I support the man, not the party anymore," Frank said. "If people don't like that, screw 'em." Suddenly he was praising Reagan as "the outstanding candidate . . . a very honest guy" who "believes what he does."

Though Frank never said as much, the Democrats had upset Frank. He had for some time remained loyal, in spite of the rebuffs of the Kennedy years. He had supported Hubert Humphrey in 1968. He was received with contempt, however, when Humphrey brought him to the White House in the spring to see President Johnson. Johnson at first ignored him, then sent him off with a souvenir booklet and a lipstick bearing the White House seal. He said of the lipstick, "It'll make a big man of you with your women."

Frank continued to support Humphrey, even so, and did so yet more energetically once Robert Kennedy declared his candidacy. "Bobby," he said, "is just not qualified to be President." He shed no tears when Kennedy was assassinated. To Frank, his Reprise publicist Mike Shore recalled, Bobby had been " 'that fuckin' cop.' . . . The worst thing he could think of was to call somebody a cop!"

Two months after Bobby's assassination, Frank's mob connection had the effect on the Humphrey camp that it had once had on John Kennedy. In May 1968, there was a press report that Frank had been dining with aides to jailed Teamsters leader Jimmy Hoffa. Then, in August, came **The Wall Street Journal**'s story on his links to the Mafia. Humphrey's senior aide Joe Nellis, who as an attorney for the Kefauver Committee had once interrogated Frank about his mob links, sent Humphrey a warning memo. Soon thereafter, Frank faded from public view as a prominent Humphrey supporter.

All the same, well into the first Nixon presidency, Frank was still talking like a Democrat where national politics were concerned. "Nixon scares me," he told the **Los Angeles Times** in July 1970. "He's running the country into the ground. . . . The Democrats have got to get together and beat Nixon in '72." Then, as Thanksgiving approached, an internal White House memo shows, Nixon's political strategist Charles Colson raised the idea of wooing Frank to the Republican cause.

Vice President Agnew was at work on the project within days. As he later recalled it, he and Frank happened to meet at a Palm Springs country club, got together over the holiday, and hit it off. As a Greek-American, he said, his Mediterranean ancestry gave him a good deal in common with Frank. It helped, too, that he was hooked on the music of the 1940s, could play the piano, and liked to sing.

Agnew became a regular houseguest at Frank's place, and made eighteen visits in the months that followed. The two men played golf together, dined out, talked through the night in Frank's den, and on one occasion watched the porn movie **Deep Throat** together. Frank's guest quarters, once remodeled for John F. Kennedy, were eventually renamed "Agnew House."

By early 1971 an Agnew aide was able to tell the White House in a memo that "Sinatra is ready to be invited aboard." Nixon's chief of staff, H. R. Haldeman, was told that Frank had "the muscle to bring along a lot of the younger lights . . . he should very shortly be invited to the White House to entertain." There was some hesitation—the FBI had alerted the president's office to Frank's mob connections—but it gradually evaporated.

"While Sinatra has been controversial," presidential counsel Dick Moore wrote in November, "he seems to have settled down since his retirement." Within two days Nixon himself sent Frank congratulations on a California state award, and Frank gave Attorney General John Mitchell's wife, Martha, a ride in his private jet. When the House Select Crime Committee tried to force Frank to testify, Agnew attempted to delay the service of a subpoena. When he did testify, in July 1972, the president himself phoned to praise him for his defiant performance.

"He's aboard now," Haldeman wrote in his journal the following month, and it was soon clear the Republican courtship had worked. Frank supported Nixon in his successful reelection campaign in 1972. After the Republican victory, Frank rented a house in Washington with Agnew's aide Peter Malatesta. He continued to enjoy the favor of the Nixon White House, however badly he behaved.

On the eve of the 1973 inauguration, in the lobby of Washington's Fairfax Hotel, Frank spotted the columnist Maxine Cheshire, who had months earlier asked him whether his mob ties might embarrass Agnew. On encountering her now, he abused her as "nothing but a cunt," a two-dollar whore. For public consumption, Nixon was said to be "livid." In private, a White House tape transcript reveals, he said Cheshire was worth "two bits, not two dollars." Two weeks after the inauguration, Nixon asked Frank to sing at a White House reception for the Italian prime minister.

The lure of performing at a state occasion induced Frank to interrupt his retirement. He had never been so honored, even by Kennedy. At the reception in April 1973 he sang ten songs, mostly old favorites, and at Nixon's personal request closed with "The House I Live In." The president told the audience Frank was as an entertainer "what the Washington Monument is to Washington . . . the top."

The Nixon administration embraced Frank so thoroughly that, wherever he might be in the world, accredited callers could reach him through the White House switchboard. He even acquired a Secret Service code name—"Napoleon." Nixon and his men were already enmeshed in the Watergate affair when Frank performed at the White House, but he remained undeterred.

In October, accused of taking kickbacks, Agnew pled no contest to tax evasion charges and resigned. Frank had given him refuge in his home while the pressure was on, had urged him to cling to office, and made a massive contribution to his legal costs. After Nixon's resignation, he was one of the first to offer comfort when the former president emerged from seclusion.

Watergate troubled Frank little. His only known comment, in a conversation with Tina, was a shrugged "Nobody's perfect." It did look as though he might be wavering in his loyalties when, three months after Nixon's resignation, Frank appeared at a state fund-raiser for New York Democrats. His course, however, was set. From Gerald Ford to Reagan—Frank kept a lower profile during the Jimmy Carter presidency—and then from Reagan to George H. W. Bush, he was to bask in the Republican sunshine.

Frank's new affiliation did not really change him, according to Tina, who said he remained a supporter of liberal causes—of a woman's right to opt for an abortion, of handgun reform. He moved, she said, "to his own beat."

As early as the Kennedy administration, according to one of his closest friends, Frank had imagined he might be honored with an ambassadorship. "He worked his head off for John

Kennedy in hopes this would come about," Sonny King recalled. "Then the same thing happened with Ronald Reagan, and still it never came to pass. He became bitter about politics, and sad." It was a ludicrous aspiration. The questioning of Sinatra at a confirmation hearing would have been an unthinkable embarrassment to any administration.

Gore Vidal, a liberal Democrat, thought Frank "a neutered creature of the American right . . . an Italo-American Faust" whose deal with the Republican devil got him nowhere. Joseph Cerrell, a political consultant who worked with Frank before the defection, was more to the point. "I think Sinatra would fall into the category of doing it for his ego . . . he likes the attention. I think he's still a little kid from Hoboken who likes to be stroked by presidents."

Another factor may have contributed to Frank's abandoning the Democrats in favor of the Republicans. Shirley MacLaine was told at the time he made the switch, she said, that he did so under pressure from the mob. The Mafia, she was given to understand, had decided that for them the grass had become greener on the Republican side of the political divide.

AFTER THE MOST OVERT OF THE STROKING, at the White House reception in 1973, Nixon made a suggestion. "You must get out of retirement," he told Frank. The president was preaching to the converted.

"I didn't think he would stay retired," recalled Bill Miller, Frank's pianist for nearly forty years. "I was on a retainer at the time, not a salary, and I stayed on that retainer for a year and a half. So I knew. Why would he keep me on?"

"A great artist is a great artist," said Reprise executive Bob Regehr. "How many times did Judy Garland retire? And each time she came back. Singers retire, actors retire, bullfighters retire, but they all come back."

Frank himself would claim he had never said he was quitting, that he had merely wanted a rest. The notion that he had even spoken of "retirement," he lied, was just "a figment of somebody's imagination." Pressure to return, he said, had come from his children and in thirty thousand letters from "people who wanted to hear me sing." More candidly, he admitted that he simply "missed the crazy world of show business."

The radical change of lifestyle, from a frenzied schedule to puttering around at home, had not worked. Rosalind Russell said Frank simply got bored. "He couldn't stand it," said his longtime music copyist, Vern Yocum. "He had lived with that adulation, that spontaneous reaction from people that was almost like food to him. He couldn't live without it."

The comeback began in the guise of "private" appearances at public events. In February 1972, just seven months into the "retirement," Frank had sung at a Palm Springs police show. In the spring, he had performed at a Salute to Ted Agnew Night in Baltimore. In April the following year, three days after the White House concert for Nixon, it was announced that Frank would star in an hour-long television special. Discussions had begun on a return to Las Vegas, and he was working on a new album, **Ol' Blue Eyes Is Back.** Frank had never been called "Ol' Blue Eyes"—that was invented by the art director at Reprise—but the tag rapidly became common parlance around the world.

The televised concert marking Frank's "official" return began the way the retirement show had ended, with his face illuminated by a single spotlight. The audience gave him a rapturous welcome, though the ratings and reviews were less encouraging. The new album did well, but it was not a smash.

The previous year, when Frank had sung for Agnew, his voice had sounded a little "cracked," the **Washington Post**'s Sally Quinn wrote. He had apologized to the audience on that occasion, then vocalized for months to get the voice back in shape. It still sounded "rusty," though, to Dwight Whitney, reporting for **TV Guide** on the taping of the concert. Frank's lip trembled as he began singing, and he blew one of the lyrics. Cecil Smith of the **Los Angeles Times** noted that the face in the spotlight was "puffier, rounder in the jaw" now, and Frank had a paunch. He was nearly fifty-eight, had punished his body throughout his adult life, and it showed.

That night, and dozens of times in the year that followed—in Las Vegas, Miami, Los Angeles, Boston, Buffalo, Philadelphia, Pittsburgh, New York, Japan, and Australia—he sang a song that, like "My Way," was a French original with English lyrics co-written by Paul Anka:

> I know I said that I was leaving
> But I just couldn't say good-bye
> It was only self-deceiving
> . . . Let me try again.

When he sang "Let Me Try Again" in late 1974, at Madison Square Garden, twenty thousand people roared approval. "Ah, Frankie everlovin'," former bobbysoxer Martha Lear wrote in the arts section of the **New York Times,** "here we are at the Garden dancing cheek to cheek, and the lights are low and it's oh so sweet. . . . It's Ol' Blue Eyes now, with the paunch and the jowl and the wig, and the hell with them. The blue eyes still burn, the cuffs are still incomparably shot, the style, the **style,** is still all there, and what's left of the voice still gets to me like no other voice, and it always will." A concert around the same time at Carnegie Hall was described in **Newsweek** as an "oldsters' Woodstock."

Others agreed about Frank's voice, but saw little else to praise. "That style he set was big enough and broad enough to carry the careers of half a dozen others," Ralph Gleason wrote in **Rolling Stone,** remembering 1941, "but Ol' Blue Eyes is a drag that Frankie never was. . . . It is simply weird now to see him all glossed up like a wax dummy, with that rug on his head looking silly, and the onstage movement, which used to be panther-tense, now a self-conscious hoodlum bustle.

"His possible appearance is the occasion for bodyguards and hush-hush phone calls and big security plans and a blanket of secrecy. . . . I don't think anyone but those clowns on his payroll really think any of this panoply of power is necessary. . . . For Frank Sinatra, whose voice made him the friend of millions of Americans, to carry on like a Caribbean dictator holding back history with bodyguards and a secret police is simply obscene. . . . I think he went somewhere that makes him alien now to me in a way he never was before."

Thomas Thompson catalogued the more recent sordid episodes—the abuse of female journalists (Maxine Cheshire had not been Frank's only target), the beating of the hotel guest in a restroom at Palm Springs, the support for the corrupt

Agnew—and expressed exasperation. "Frank is back onstage," Thompson noted, "a scowl darkening his blue eyes like a storm in the late afternoon, starring this time in a continuing drama with scenes so ugly and unpleasant that you want your money back. . . . I cannot begin to understand this man—indeed I doubt that he understands himself."

George Frazier, the legendary **Boston Globe** critic, addressed Frank directly: "All your life you wanted to be a big man, but the wrong kind of big man. . . . You're a sad case, Frankie. I think you're the best male vocalist that ever lived, but I also think you're a miserable failure as a human being."

"Don't worry about me," Frank had once reassured Tina after the death of a close friend. "I will never get old." He turned fifty-nine, though, as 1974 ended, and he was still alone.

33

Barbara

FOUR YEARS EARLIER, when Marianna Case was seeing Frank, she had become aware of an older woman named Barbara Marx who sometimes turned up at the Palm Springs house. Once, when Marianna sat to Frank's right at dinner, he placed Marx to his left. She stared at Marianna, made her feel "uncomfortable." Later, Lois Nettleton also met Marx. The bold way she spoke to Frank, Lois thought, suggested they knew each other well. "She was trying to urge Francis to go back, to come out of retirement. She was kind of really at him about it. And finally he said 'Stop it!' or something to that effect. They seemed close, but I never thought of it as a romantic thing." At a later meeting, however, Lois's feminine radar did pick something up. Marx now seemed oddly possessive toward Frank. Eventually, she would have the right to be.

Barbara Marx was the wife of Zeppo, the youngest of the Marx brothers and, though Frank would long date other women and keep Marx on a string, she was to become the fourth Mrs. Sinatra.

She was born Barbara Blakeley in 1927 in Missouri, the daughter of a small-town butcher who fell on hard times, relocated, and eventually settled with his family in Long Beach, California. According to a fragment of a ghostwritten memoir she commissioned and then aborted, she grew up promising herself that she would "pursue a life of excitement."

In her teens Barbara was tall, "long-stemmed," and blond. She entered beauty contests, tried modeling, appeared at auto shows and in department stores, and found work in New York for a while. She married a young would-be singer and gave birth to a baby boy. Back in Long Beach, when the marriage failed, she ran a School of Modeling Arts for a while. That proved either insufficiently rewarding or not exciting enough. Barbara's "secret yearning," she said, was to live in Las Vegas.

She moved there with her young son when she was in her late twenties, and became a showgirl at the Riviera. The hotel, Mafia-run like so many others in Las Vegas, boasted a casino, 250 rooms, and a gigantic open-air pool. The showgirls and dancers, fluttering about in silk and sequins, were one of the principal attractions. Their on-stage job, said Ed Becker, who was the Riviera's entertainment director at the time, was to be "beautiful objects." Off stage, after the midnight show, they "had to spend an hour or two in the lobby cocktail lounge, to be sort of reachable to high rollers." The hotel was billed as the "meeting place for celebrities," and Barbara hooked a minor one.

Zeppo Marx was a casino regular. He would come in night after night, Becker recalled, "with his tongue hanging out, panting over Barbara." Zeppo and Barbara became a couple, and married in 1959. He was fifty-eight, she thirty-two. She moved into his Palm Springs home and became a decorative figure in local society. Barbara's life became one long round of mornings on the golf course or the tennis court, lunches at the Racquet Club, and dinners out.

One day, probably less than a year later, Ava Gardner arrived in Palm Springs on one of her occasional visits to see Frank. As she was waiting for him, she recalled, she decided she would like a tennis game. "I called the Racquet Club and asked for somebody to come over and play with me. A pro came over, and he said, 'Mrs. Sinatra, Barbara Marx lives just across the fairway and she loves tennis. Why don't you invite her over? We can play some doubles.'

"We played tennis that afternoon, and we were sitting inside having Coca-Cola when Frank arrived. I introduced him to Barbara and the others. He was livid. . . . He had been looking forward to this homecoming, and there in his house were a bunch of strangers. That was the first time they met. I introduced him to that cow!"

Barbara turned up often at the house during the 1960s, George Jacobs remembered. "Zeppo was in his sixties and sick all the time, and often at night when he'd gone to sleep Barbara would sneak out and visit Mr. S. . . . she lived across the golf course from us. And he'd say, 'Who the fuck asked her to come over?' He hated her at first. Wouldn't date her, and everywhere we'd go she'd show up. He said, 'Who keeps inviting her around?' " As late as the summer of 1971, eleven years after their first meeting, the relationship with Barbara seemed to be going nowhere. Tina thought Barbara was merely "a stopgap, a one-night stand with an extended visa."

She was wrong. By 1974, Barbara was divorced from Marx and being seen constantly with Frank. He did not give her an easy time. Though Barbara liked a drink herself, she often sat in silence as Frank caroused with his rougher cronies. She preferred him to "hang out with the elite," Jilly Rizzo's friend Joey Villa said. Frank saw other women, and Barbara objected to that. Yet she never gave up.

In the spring of 1976, sixteen years after their first meeting, Frank asked Barbara to marry him.

He arrived unexpectedly at a family gathering with the bride-to-be on his arm wearing, as Tina remembered it, a ring "with a diamond the size of a quail's egg." He had not told his daughters he was getting engaged. Dolly Sinatra had not taken to Barbara. "I don't want no whore coming into this family," she had said. Rather than confront his mother, Frank sent his attorney to tell her he was getting married again.

The marriage, on July 11, was a grandiose affair at the home of former ambassador Walter Annenberg. The more than a hundred guests included Ronald Reagan—he interrupted his presidential campaign to attend—Spiro Agnew, Gregory Peck and Kirk Douglas and their wives, and the heart surgeon Michael DeBakey, who had treated Frank's father during his last illness. The bride's matron of honor was Bea Korshak, wife of the attorney and mob associate Sidney Korshak. Frank's daughters attended, but Frank Jr. did not. For all her misgivings, his mother was present.

The couple took their vows, the **Ladies' Home Journal** reported, "before a black marble fireplace banked with gardenia trees and two cloisonné cranes holding more white flowers delicately in their beaks." When the judge asked Barbara whether she took Frank "for richer or for poorer," Frank answered for her. "Richer, richer!" he joked. His wedding gift to her was a peacock-blue Rolls-Royce. She gave him a green Jaguar. At the reception after the ceremony, Sidney Korshak quietly handed Tina a cheap pen. He urged her to keep it as a souvenir because, he said, it had saved her a great deal of money. Frank and Barbara had used the pen, he explained, to sign a prenuptial agreement. According to Tina, in her book **My Father's Daughter,** the agreement stipulated that Frank's existing assets, as well as his future earnings, would not go to Barbara. It did, however, provide her with a generous monthly allowance. Barbara had balked at signing it, Tina wrote, until the last possible moment.

Frank had had his doubts about marrying Barbara as he had before marrying Mia. A year or so earlier, he had been joined at Lake Tahoe by his first wife, Nancy, who later called one of her daughters to confide that she was about to take a vacation with her former husband. They spent several days together and then, Tina recalled, had a "romantic interlude" at the Palm Springs house. Later, and just minutes before marrying Barbara, Frank told his daughters that he had been hoping to reconcile with Nancy—a quarter century after their divorce.

He had also been clinging, as ever, to the fantasy that he and Ava could make a fresh start. Pete Hamill had recently encountered a tipsy Ava in Frank's New York apartment. "Frank would ring her in London," her friend Spoli Mills said, "and pour out his heart."

Even when the marriage to Barbara was set, Ava's companion Reenie Jordan said, Frank "called her several times and asked if she would come back. . . . I asked her why she told him no, and she said, 'Reenie, Frank's getting old and he needs someone who's going to be there. You know I'm not going to take his shit and stay there, with all his friends. But Barbara will stay with him. He'll have somebody with him.' . . . The last call before he got married again, Ava told him to marry Barbara."

"Not too much news," Ava scrawled in a letter to Mills, "Frank and his gal finally tied the knot yesterday—That wedding sure fucked up our invitation to Palm Springs house. . . . I need a vacation. . . . I've got a monumental hangover."

Being married, Frank said nine months later, gave him a "kind of wonderful tranquillity." It also seemed to have renewed his appetite for work. He made ninety-two concert appearances in those nine months alone. There would be well over a thousand live performances between 1976 and 1990.

"I'm sixty-one years old," he said in 1977. "I'll continue what I'm doing for another five or six years and then get the hell out before becoming a bore. . . . I'll pick up my Social Security and go home when the time comes." He told another interviewer, more accurately as things turned out, that he would not give up until "I just cannot work anymore."

Frank now spent far less time in the recording studio. His three new albums in the fourteen years to 1990 would make the charts, but only one, **Trilogy**, would be a major success. One single, "New York, New York," was a blockbuster song, his last, and became an indelible part of his legend:

> . . . if I can make it there, I can make it anywhere,
> It's up to you, New York, New York.

Frank first sang the song in public in October 1978, during a charity event at the Waldorf-Astoria. The previous year, when it had been the theme song for the eponymous movie, it had not really taken off. Performed live by Frank, it became a show-stopper. It was in 1979, in Los Angeles, that he made the recording that endures today. It came over as a new, defiant personal statement as much as a paean to a city.

In June 1980, in a fever of anticipation, New Yorkers thronged to hear Frank at Carnegie Hall. San Diego **Union-Leader** columnist Don Freeman recalled how on hearing the first tentative sounds of the song the audience "erupted into a thunderclap of loving recognition. Sinatra the wise showman allowed the applause and the cheers to reach a high-decibel peak, and descend into a deliciously tense, expectant silence. Sinatra the artist would bring the audience along to the heights again, but on his terms. He puffed on a cigarette, sipped from a glass of wine. And then he sang 'New York, New York.' . . . Unforgettable."

Millions around the globe were to hear Frank perform the song live—he usually made it his finale—as he sang on and on. He made his long last stand as he had begun, on stage. There were international performances that made news: before royalty and assorted glitterati at London's Royal Albert Hall—wags said it should be renamed the Francis Albert Hall; in the Egyptian desert at night under the nose of the Sphinx—"the biggest room I ever played," Frank said; and before some 175,000 people at Rio de Janeiro's Maracaña Stadium—at the time, according to the **Guinness Book of Records,** the largest audience ever drawn by a solo performer.

It was a rare month when Frank was not on the road somewhere, from the big venues in Las Vegas, New York, and Los Angeles to smaller cities like Saratoga, New York, Devon, Pennsylvania, Clarkston, Michigan, and San Carlos, California. Americans may have seen more of him in his last two decades than in his entire previous career.

MANY HEARD FRANK PERFORM a song entitled "Barbara":

> . . . the song I'm singing my whole life long.
> There's no one just like her, like Barbara. . . .

Frank had commissioned the song in honor of his new wife. The music writer Will Friedwald, who called it "disappointingly subpar," was being polite. Barbara traveled with Frank almost everywhere he went, and he described her as "the sunshine of my life."

Barbara greatly changed the Palm Springs compound, and her husband's old coterie no longer had the same access. Yul Brynner, a friend of twenty years' standing, no longer felt welcome. Eventually even Jilly Rizzo would become persona non grata. With the help of her friend Bea Korshak, interior designer to the smart set, Barbara had given the property a new look. She remodeled the main house, installing a many-mirrored suite for her personal use. She got rid of much of Frank's all-pervasive orange—the orange furniture, carpeting, drapes, towels, the orange refrigerator. Buildings and rooms were purged of the names Frank had given them. "Most of those friends weren't living anymore," Barbara pointed out, and she and Korshak renamed them after his songs. The main building became "The House I Live In," the projection theater "Send in the Clowns," two of the guest houses "High Hopes" and "Young at Heart," and another—the quarters John Kennedy had once used—"The Tender Trap." Frank's office became "My Way," a separate bedroom he maintained "I Sing the Songs." In a corner of the bedroom, according to **Architec-**

tural Digest, stood a statuette of St. Francis. Barbara's bedroom was christened "True Love."

"All she wants is to make Frank happy," Barbara's mother, Irene, said, "that's her one goal in life." No one talked now of Frank having extramarital affairs. Frank was reported to have moderated his drinking, to be sleeping better, to have calmed down. "He seemed to have nothing like the level of nervous energy one had come to expect," the author Charles Higham recalled of a meeting in 1982. "He was quietly courteous."

Here at last was a woman who could challenge Frank's authority and, much of the time, get away with it. "Barbara began sorting out whom Frank could and could not see," Leonora Hornblow remembered. Yet Barbara did not always have things her own way. One summer she tried to get her husband to vacation at the tony end of Long Island. "Can you picture me in the fucking Hamptons?" Frank asked Larry King off-camera. "Sinatra in the Hamptons! . . . The only thing they do that I like to do is drink."

If Barbara thought Frank was being overly generous, she intervened. Over dinner one night, when Merv Griffin admired Frank's exquisite gold lighter, Frank characteristically told him to keep it. By the time the meal ended, however, Barbara had gotten it back. "Frank," she said, "isn't always right."

Nancy and their daughters were outraged to

learn that he was planning a legal adoption of Barbara's twenty-six-year-old son, Bobby. He abandoned the idea, but upset the family even more when he obtained an annulment of his Roman Catholic marriage to Nancy. The first they knew of it of was when they read it in the newspapers. Nancy felt "betrayed," Tina said, "by both the man she loved and the church she'd believed in." However the annulment was dressed up in church verbiage and formal legitimacy, it mocked most Catholics' concept of marriage.

Barbara, meanwhile, had converted to Catholicism, making it possible to marry Frank in church. For the rest of the family, the ceremony added insult to injury. The marriage endured, though not without serious problems and a brief separation. Tina, who had been made an executor of her father's will, began to worry that "Dad's legacy" would be dissipated. It was the start of an ugly, protracted feud.

Dolly Sinatra, meanwhile, had died at the age of eighty. Six months after Frank's marriage to Barbara, her chartered jet had smashed into Mount San Gorgonio, near Palm Springs. She had been on her way to Las Vegas to see her son perform, and her death left him grief-stricken. For some time afterward he would sit for hours at a time looking hopeless, saying nothing. "They'd fought through his childhood and continued to do so to her dying day," his daughter Nancy has written. "But I believe that to counter her steel will he'd developed his own. . . . Now there was a gap. A vast void of love."

"He was a different man after Dolly passed on," Sonny King said. "Frank was not a churchgoing man. But two weeks after she died I was at church in Vegas—the Guardian Angel Cathedral—and I felt a tap on my shoulder and turned around and there were Frank and Barbara. I grabbed his hand and he grabbed mine. He was crying. . . . Though he got out of his shell after a little while, that's how devastated he was."

34

The Photograph

Early in 1976 a guest at a Palm Springs hotel, a concert promoter named Tommy Marson, asked to use the telephone at poolside. The employee who brought him the phone then overheard one end of an odd conversation. Marson sounded irate, peremptory.

"He dials the number," the employee said, "and then I hear him say, 'Frank, I need you at the Westchester [Premier] Theater'—he specified exactly when he needed him—'Frank, I don't give a fuck what you got to do. You be there.' And he slams down the phone. It was not a request. It was an order."

The theater was in Tarrytown, New York, and Frank performed there as demanded on ten nights in April 1976, nine nights in September and October, and eight nights in May of the following year. Soon, though, in spite of his appearances and those of other stars, the brand-new theater folded. It had been a Mafia operation funded with Mafia money, and the protracted investigation that followed led to a series of trials involving stock fraud, racketeering, and profit-skimming offenses. Eleven defendants eventually went to jail or paid hefty fines.

Though not charged, Frank and two close associates came under suspicion. United States Attorney Nathaniel Akerman said he had testimony that Jilly Rizzo had received a share of the skim, and "tape-recorded evidence" that Frank's attorney, Mickey Rudin, received $5,000. Information gleaned from the wiretapping of one of Frank's secretaries, according to documents related to the first of the trials, showed she had been "knowledgeable about one aspect of the ticket skimming. . . ." In a legal brief, Akerman wrote that another person, "one of the accomplice witnesses," had stated that "Sinatra had received $50,000 in cash under the table for the first series of concerts."

Another wiretap recorded a conversation between two of the men who were later jailed, mafioso Gregory DePalma and theater president Eliot Weisman, who was to become Frank's manager after serving his time. DePalma told Weisman:

> You should've seen the nice time I had with [Sinatra] last night. . . . Him, Barbara and

> Jilly. . . . I was talking to Frank all about the joint. . . . If we could get some financing. About seven and half million dollars. He says, "We'll talk a little bit. Me and you. . . . I got the gist of it in the dressing room." He says, "You must be responsible for ninety percent of the money here." I says, "Oh, yeah, easy, believe me." . . . I could jockey this guy into position.

Exhibit 181, produced by the prosecution at a pretrial hearing in November 1978, was a photograph of Frank, in open-necked shirt, and eight other men wearing suits. Frank was smiling broadly, as were almost all the others, and his arms were draped around the shoulders of the two men closest to him.

Third from the right, in the back row, was New York Mafia boss Carlo Gambino. At the far left was his chosen successor, Paul Castellano, and seated in the foreground was his nephew Joseph Gambino. Also in the photograph were Jimmy "The Weasel" Fratianno, a senior Mafia figure from California who later turned FBI informant, and Salvatore Spatola, described at the time as a "reputed member of organized crime" and later identified by the FBI as a Gambino soldier. Kneeling beside him was Richard "Nerves" Fusco, who managed ticketing at Westchester and would go to prison for his role in the scam.

The men Frank had his arms around were DePalma, the Gambino man who ran concessions at the theater, and Tommy Marson. Three of the men in the photograph were defendants in the case, and no one disputed the fact that the picture had been taken in Frank's dressing room at the Westchester. The negative of the photograph had been destroyed by the time the FBI obtained the picture from an informant. The man who had taken it, the United States attorney recalled, was "scared shitless" when subpoenaed by the prosecution.

Frank had no comment when the picture was made public. His publicist, Lee Solters, responded to a reporter's question by saying, "I didn't hear a word you said," then, when pressed, said, "I can't say anything." Two years later, when the Nevada Gaming Control Board asked about the picture, Frank said he was forever being asked to pose for photographs with people. Someone would say, "Would you take a photograph with three Chinamen from Hong Kong," he said, "and I say, 'Fine.' So, they take a picture. I wouldn't know their reputation. I am not about to ask for a sputum test, because it would embarrass everybody."

Frank offered the board his version of how the Westchester photograph came to be taken. "I was asked by one of the members of the theater—who he was doesn't come to me—he told me Mr. Gambino had arrived with his granddaughter, whose name happened to be Sinatra. Her daddy is a doctor in New York, not related at all . . . and they'd like to take a picture. I said 'Fine.'

"They came in and I took a picture with the little girl, and before I realized what happened there were eight or nine men standing around me, and several other snapshots were made. That is the whole incident."

Frank said he had known nothing at the time about the backgrounds of the men in the photograph, and still did not. He had never met Carlo Gambino. Frank acknowledged that he knew Marson and that he had met Fratianno—whom he claimed he knew only as "Jimmy"—just once, at Marson's house. He had been entirely unaware of the crooked goings-on at the theater, he said.

Fratianno was to say that Frank had welcomed Carlo Gambino to his dressing room "with a kiss and hug" on the night the photograph was taken. Gambino's son-in-law meanwhile, the New York doctor Frank mentioned, should have been familiar to him—he had been on the board of the American-Italian Anti-Defamation League. Fratianno said he had seen more of Frank than Frank admitted. They had first met, the mobster said, not in the late 1970s but in the early 1950s. DePalma and Frank, FBI wiretap evidence indicates, had substantive conversations at least twice.

The prosecutors were especially interested in a defendant **not** in the photograph. This was Louis "Louie Dome" Pacella, a New York restaurateur jailed for evading taxes on $50,000 skimmed from the Westchester proceeds. Pacella, the prosecutor said in a court brief, had knowledge of the "involvement of Frank Sinatra, Mickey Rudin, and Jilly Rizzo in the skimming of receipts." Pacella, however, refused to answer the grand jury's questions about Frank, and his silence led to a contempt charge and additional time in jail.

Asked about Pacella by the Nevada Gaming Control Board, Frank admitted that he was a good friend. He had become fond of the man, he said, during visits to Pacella's Manhattan restaurant. Pacella's attorney put it more strongly. "You will find," he told the court, "that Frank Sinatra and Louis Pacella were very, very, very close and dear friends. In fact, the evidence will show to you that they were brothers, not because they shared the same mother and father but because they shared love, admiration and friendship for many, many years."

Pacella was reportedly a capo in the Genovese crime family and, according to the Drug Enforcement Administration, a heroin dealer. He had inherited a special assignment. "After Sam Giancana was murdered," said Philip Leonetti, a high-ranking mafioso who later turned FBI informant, Pacella "took over control of Frank Sinatra."

In January 1981, on the eve of his inauguration, President-elect Reagan was asked what he thought about Frank and the Westchester case. "We've heard those things about Frank for years," the **Philadelphia Inquirer** quoted Reagan as saying, "and we just hope none of them are true." It was not a ringing statement of belief in Frank's innocence. Already, however, Reagan had asked Frank to stage his inaugural gala.

All had been harmony between the two men since 1970, when Frank backed Reagan for reelection as governor. Reagan had gone out of his way to demonstrate friendship for the man who had once excoriated him as a buffoon. He attended both Frank's wedding to Barbara and Dolly Sinatra's funeral.

In the presidential campaign the previous year, Frank had derided Jimmy Carter, the Democratic incumbent, as "our President the tooth fairy," otherwise known as "Mickey Mouse," while raking in large sums for the Republicans by appearing at fund-raisers. "It isn't every candidate," said Reagan, undeterred by the headlines about Frank and the Mafia, "who has a king in his corner."

Frank was "jubilant," the columnist James Bacon reported, about being asked to produce the gala. Though dismissed as "a trashy Las Vegas floor show" by the critic Rex Reed, and as a "Grecian Formula homecoming" by the columnist Rex Winston, the show raised $5.5 million for the Republican Party. Frank doled out engraved cigarette boxes to fellow participants, just as he had after the concert for Kennedy in 1961, and went home happy.

Months earlier, Frank had applied to the Nevada gambling authority for a new license, and the pivotal hearing before the Gaming Control Board took place only three weeks after the Reagan inaugural. The board's chairman declared as he opened the meeting that "the burden of proof is on the applicant to prove suitability." Yet Frank was given the easiest possible ride. Asked about mob-related episodes, he responded time and again with denials or bland "don't knows." No one challenged him. Gregory Peck and Kirk Douglas said what a good fellow he was and praised Frank's work for charity and his generosity. Not a single specialist on organized crime was called to testify. One board member declared himself "satisfied" by all this, another voiced the hope that Frank had "changed some." The chairman said that "in the gaming business we aren't necessarily going to have a group of choirboys." The board awarded Frank his license and wished him good luck. Those present clapped. Robert Lindsey of the **New York Times** reported that the board's fact-finding "appeared to have been naively superficial." Frank, Lindsey thought, had been treated with "a kind of awe."

Reagan's attorney general-designate, William

French Smith, who weeks earlier had attended Frank's sixty-fifth birthday celebration, had said shortly before the hearing that he was "totally unaware of any allegations about Frank Sinatra's background." This after more than two years of publicity about the Westchester case.

When applying for the license, Frank had listed Reagan as a reference. That, a Reagan aide said at the time, had no more significance than the use of a man's name in an application for a Sears, Roebuck card. Then, on the morning of the gambling authority's decision, the papers reported that Reagan had told the board through his attorney that Frank was "an honorable person—completely honest and loyal."

The Reagan-Sinatra relationship continued to flourish. The month after the granting of the license, when the president was shot and wounded, Frank canceled his run at Caesars Palace and flew to Washington to comfort Nancy Reagan. Later, during an awards ceremony for the National Sclerosis Society, of which Frank was campaign chairman, he presented the president with a sculpture of a bucking bronco inscribed: "To the American in the White House, our President, who has straddled courage and rides it hard." Frank was put in charge of the inaugural gala for Reagan's second term. In the spring of 1985, Reagan awarded him the nation's highest civilian award, the Medal of Freedom, praising

Frank as "one of our most remarkable and distinguished Americans."

FRANK CELEBRATED HIS SEVENTIETH BIRTHDAY that year with little fanfare. When he had turned sixty-five, Barbara had thrown a party for more than two hundred guests. The year before that, he had celebrated his birthday and his fortieth anniversary in show business with a thousand guests at Caesars Palace. Two specially commissioned Sinatra portraits, measuring eighty by forty-five feet, had graced the hotel's facade.

More of the landmark people in his life were gone now: Bing Crosby; Harry James; Skinny D'Amato, his patron in Atlantic City; Nelson Riddle, Yul Brynner, and Orson Welles had died within four days of one another two months before Frank's seventieth birthday.

In 1977, after his mother's death, Frank had said he was working on his autobiography. He embarked on the project, writing in longhand and talking into a tape recorder, but after a while let it drop. Then, in 1983, he said he might be "forced to write a book . . . to defend accusations. Everybody now is planning to write a book."

Just one independent author, in fact, had such plans. Kitty Kelley, already known for unvarnished biographies of Jacqueline Kennedy Onassis and Elizabeth Taylor, had been digging into Frank's life for the past year. She had repeatedly written to him requesting an interview, but he had not replied—except to sue her before she had written a word. He sought $2 million in punitive damages for, Kelley recalled, "presuming to write without his authorization. He claimed that he alone, or someone he anointed, could write his life story. . . . He further claimed that I was misrepresenting myself as his official biographer to get 'inside knowledge of the private aspects or events of his life.' Asserting that I was misappropriating his name and likeness for commercial purposes, he asked the court to issue an injunction."

The suit came to nothing. Frank's months of legal jousting achieved little, except perhaps to deter some potential interviewees. Some, Kelley said, were "so terrified that they refused to talk to me for fear of physical reprisals." More than eight hundred others did agree to talk. Kelley's book **His Way**, published in the fall of 1986, went to the top of the **New York Times** bestseller list and broke sales records for biography in several countries. Frank's attempts to stop the book had backfired and instead guaranteed the author and her publishers massive publicity. Though her book was overly negative, Kelley had done some pioneering work. She had opened doors Frank had long kept sealed.

"I never read it," he insisted months after the book appeared. "I don't even talk about it." Two years later, on television, he railed about "pimps and prostitutes . . . parasites" who wrote "a lot of crap" for money. It was the closest he would come in public to discussing Kelley. It was taboo, he told his family, even to mention her name.

Daughter Nancy has said the Sinatras "nearly strangled on our pain and anger." In 2004 she publicly reviled Kelley as "the big C-word. . . . I hate her. . . . If I ever met her, I don't know what I'd do. She's just scum." Tina said the book made her father ill and, coincidence or not, the year **His Way** was published marked the beginning of a decline.

Frank's throat had given him trouble in recent years. In the summer of 1986 polyps were removed from his colon—not necessarily a serious matter. He was said to have cut back on cigarettes and, though there were lapses, on his drinking. He resumed a hectic schedule within ten days of the polyp procedure, flying off to Atlantic City, Honolulu, Los Angeles, Chicago, Madrid, Milan, Dallas, Las Vegas, and Atlantic City again. Then severe pain forced him back into the hospital.

An abscess on the large intestine required major surgery and a temporary colostomy. "If I hadn't come back from the trip I was on," Frank said later, "I would have bought it. They would have had flowers and a big band behind the casket. . . . It was a seven-and-a-half-hour operation." Yet he was back on the road, astonishingly, within two weeks—to Las Vegas, Carnegie Hall, Los Angeles,

Las Vegas again, Honolulu, Chicago, Genoa—sixty-eight concerts all told in 1987.

A week or so before Christmas that year, dressed in tuxedos at a morning press conference, Frank, Dean Martin, and Sammy Davis announced that they were soon to embark on a twenty-nine-city "Together Again" tour. "As if replaying a lounge act," Dennis McDougal noted in the **Los Angeles Times,** the three of them "grounded their ad libs and answers in death-defying talk about cigarettes, alcohol and carousing until the wee hours."

For Martin, in his seventy-first year, the drinking that had once been an act was now his refuge. He mixed alcohol with prescription painkillers and suffered from ulcers and kidney trouble. He had been shattered, earlier that year, by the death in a flying accident of one of his sons, Dean Paul, a pilot in the Air National Guard. Davis, now sixty-two, had abused alcohol and drugs for years. He had liver trouble and was soon to undergo a hip operation.

They began the tour in March 1988, playing to 14,500 people at the Coliseum Arena in Oakland, California. Frank's "I've Got the World on a String" brought the crowd to its feet. Davis overcame his hip pain to dance to "The Girl from Ipanema" and do a Michael Jackson impersonation. "Every time you drink it rains bourbon from heaven," Martin sang. He forgot the words to familiar songs, though, and had lost his edge.

Frank had had to cajole Martin into doing the tour in the first place, and now they were bickering. Martin had fallen down on stage at Oakland, had flicked a lighted cigarette into the crowd, and Frank had berated him. Frank wanted to party into the night, but his colleagues did not. "They weren't in shape for it," said Hank Cattaneo, Frank's concert production manager. "After a half-hour Dean would say, 'I gotta go to bed,' and then Sammy would say, 'Please, let me go too.' But the old man loved to hang, to talk and tell stories."

After the fourth show, in Chicago, angry shouts were heard from the dressing room. Two nights later, after Frank had again harassed Martin over not wanting to party into the night, Martin chartered a plane and flew to California. He had his manager tell the press he was sick, and even checked into a hospital—a charade, according to his son Ricci. "He loved Frank and he wasn't vengeful," Ricci said. "He just couldn't endure Frank's routine anymore."

Martin was replaced by Liza Minnelli, and the tour continued. That year and the next, Davis performed with Frank frequently. A "scratchy throat" during the "Together Again" tour, however, had been an early sign of cancer. Davis died in May 1990, having refused surgery that might have saved his life but risked destroying his voice. Coming as it did on the heels of the death earlier in the year of Jimmy Van Heusen, Tina said, Davis's death left Frank "in little pieces." He had visited Davis repeatedly in his last months, had sobbed as he left afterward. Davis was laid to rest, as he had instructed, wearing on his wrist the gold watch Sinatra had given him after their last tour together.

IN 1986, nearing the end of her own cigarette and alcohol marathon, Ava Gardner had suffered a stroke while in the hospital with pneumonia. It left her with some facial paralysis, difficulty walking, and an arm that was all but useless. She retreated to her London apartment, went on smoking and drinking, and worked with the writer Peter Evans on an autobiography. She told Evans much about Frank that was fond. Asked whether he had been the love of her life, though, she said, "I can't say really, no. No." She said she had loved all three of her husbands equally. In a conversation with her actress friend Arlene Dahl, however, she said she had loved Frank more than any other man.

Every year since they had split up, Frank had sent Ava a huge bouquet on her birthday. And for the twelve months until the next bouquet arrived, her sister remembered, the long-dead flowers remained on Ava's dresser. About the time of her stroke, Frank had sent her a photograph of their wedding that he had kept in his wallet for thirty-five years.

As Ava's condition worsened, Frank sent a plane to bring her to California for treatment. Each day during Ava's stay, he had a limousine take her to the hospital for physiotherapy.

On January 25, 1990, a month after her sixty-seventh birthday, Ava was found dead in bed at her London apartment. Frank broke down when he heard the news. Ava had been sick again recently, and he reproached himself for not having flown to London to be with her. When she was brought home to North Carolina for burial, however, he was not among the three thousand mourners who filed by the coffin. Instead he sent a wreath. The card with it read, "With my love, Francis."

The following day, a crowd of eighteen thousand saw Frank perform at the Knickerbocker Arena in Albany, New York. He walked around the stage with a bottle of Jack Daniel's in his hand, and appeared to drink more than half of it.

"Sinatra seemed confused, distraught, at times," an onlooker remembered. "As he was walking around the stage and started doing 'One for My Baby,' the ghost of Ava Gardner was there on the stage with him."

Make it one for my baby,
and one more, for the road.

35

To the End of the Road

IN 1991, AT SEVENTY-FIVE, Frank embarked on a world tour. There would be eighty concerts that year, eighty-seven the next, ninety-seven the next, and sixty in 1994.

The future movie **Heist** would include the following exchange:

GENE HACKMAN (IN THE ROLE OF A ROBBER): "Nobody lives forever."
REBECCA PIDGEON (PLAYING HIS WIFE): "Frank Sinatra gave it a shot."

The television special to mark Frank's seventy-fifth birthday was entitled **The Best Is Yet to Come,** and the **New York Times** marked the occasion by publishing a story both warm and melancholy. "Physically," it said, "Mr. Sinatra is no Dorian Gray. In concert nowadays he often wears the puffy look of a veteran barroom pugilist who has staggered to his feet for one more round.

"Even when he reads his lyrics from television TelePrompTers at the front of the stage, there is no guarantee that he will deliver a complete set of words. Increasingly—inevitably—the voice cracks, and notes that are strained after are never reached."

In 1984, in London, a critic had said Frank's sixty-eight-year-old voice was "cracked . . . jerks about like a wayward needle on one of his LP's." Four years later, a critic in Los Angeles thought the voice "shook and fuzzed." By 1991, when Frank appeared in Milan, "La Voce" was said to sound "opaque and toneless." The Sinatra sound, a London **Times** critic said, was now "in a state of grand deterioration."

So, increasingly, was the body. Frank's hearing and eyesight were failing. He was struggling with a hearing aid and—though not at every performance—was indeed reading from TelePrompTers. "He was using one or two monitors as early as 1984," said the trumpeter Frank Fighera, who played for Frank in the final years. "By the 1990s there would be five or six. Each succeeding year the print got larger and larger, and even then he loused up." A cataract operation helped but did not solve the problem.

There was a greater worry. A reviewer had noted as early as 1978 that Frank "forgot lyrics to some songs." It had happened again in 1980, in front of that audience of 175,000 people in Brazil. As Frank himself recalled: "I was in the midst of singing a song I know as well as my hand when I lost the lyric. Just blew it. Nothing. I had been singing 'Strangers in the Night' and when I stopped and couldn't remember how it went, the whole stadium started to sing it for me—in **English.** I was touched."

There had been a similar incident a year later, in Boston. "We were doing 'These Foolish Things,' " guitarist Tony Mottola said, "and when I played the chord to go into the release of the song, he drew a blank. He turned to me and said, 'What's the next word?' and I said, 'I don't know, but the next chord is C sharp minor 7.' Then someone in the audience gave him the next word, and he continued on."

In 1984, at a concert in Canada, Frank's memory failed him so badly that he walked off the stage. By the late 1980s the press was reporting that he had been "incoherently rambling" on stage, saying words in the wrong order. Most assumed he had been drinking, and he did not disabuse them. "What the hell is this?" he exclaimed on one occasion when he got muddled up. "I should never have had Coca-Cola before dinner."

"The sickness could come overnight," Fighera said. "In New York State once, when he'd finished the show, he told two jokes, introduced the band, introduced his wife, and then sang. When he had sung, he said, 'Thank you, ladies and gentlemen, and went on to do the same two jokes, introduce the band and his wife, and do the same song, all over again.

"Sometime after that, when we did a gig, I would look at him and he looked like a robot. His eyes were glazed. He would fumble to find the microphone, and they'd say, 'It's his medication.' "

Daughter Nancy, on a visit to Palm Springs, found a smorgasbord of pill bottles on her father's breakfast table. They included diuretics, sleeping pills, a barbiturate for migraine, and an antidepressant called Elavil. Told that the drug could have upsetting side effects, including disorientation, she and her sister voiced concern. Barbara Sinatra, however, insisted that the Elavil was working wonders for Frank's mood swings, making him calmer.

Tina had always admired her father's keen intellect and remarkable memory. By the late 1980s, however, he was very much changed. At Bally's, in Reno, she thought Frank sounded "unsure . . . tentative in demeanor, unsteady of voice" on stage. Later, when he asked her to come up to his suite, she found him "pale and hyperventilating," and was told he had inadvertently taken twice the prescribed dose of Elavil.

The arranger Buddy Bregman, who had known Frank for years, recalled a disquieting encounter at Hillcrest Country Club. When Bregman asked "How are you?" Frank gave him a blank look and said, "Where's the fuckin' bar?" Bregman tried again, but Frank just hurried off. Once Frank failed to recognize Liza Minnelli, whom he knew well and who had recently performed with him.

Darrien Iacocca, wife of the Chrysler boss, recalled sitting beside Frank at the White House during the first Bush presidency. "He was either drunk or just not coherent. He chatted on and on about nothing, except the pasta sauce he used to make. He seemed out of it. In the ladies' room, Barbara told me, 'I never leave his side, not for a moment.' " Darrien may have been seeing the side effects of medication, or of drink and medication combined. She wondered, though, as did others at that time, whether she was seeing the onset of Alzheimer's. Frank's Los Angeles physician, Rex Kennamer, said his patient "definitely had some degree of dementia."

"If I were a pitcher," Frank said in the late 1980s, "they'd have taken me out after six and a third innings." When he decided to stay in for the full nine, Jonathan Schwartz wrote at the time, he could "no longer sustain a line of lyric; he must chop it up and while doing so throw in, by repetition of a word or a phrase, or a fallback to his own legendary slang, bits and pieces of deflective magic." And yet: "People will look away from the rubble with their ears to enjoy the sideshow."

Frank was still a riveting performer, Stephen Holden wrote in **The New Yorker** in 1990, because of "the spontaneity of phrasing and intonation he brings to almost everything he sings, no matter how many hundreds of times he has sung the songs. Even while reading lyrics from a prompter at the front of the stage, Mr. Sinatra still seemed compelled to experiment, trying out little tricks of phrasing, indulging in impromptu scoops and dives and interpolations that worked."

"My guess," Daniel Okrent predicted in **Esquire,** "is that when his voice can finally no longer traverse an octave, he will passionately perform songs that require less than an octave." Like Mabel Mercer, Okrent thought, Frank would go on until he was simply speaking the lyrics to a musical accompaniment.

The producer Tony Oppedisano gained an inkling of the mind-set that drove Frank to go on. Though a much younger man—Oppedisano was then in his late thirties—he had known Frank for years and, Rizzo aside, had become his closest male companion. He attended functions with Frank, often traveled with him, and spent time with him in private. Sometimes Oppedisano was close by at night when Frank settled down in bed, closed his eyes, and offered up a prayer. Frank prayed aloud, and a typical prayer was, "God, give me my health. Let me provide for Barbara and Nancy and Frankie and Tina, and for A.J. and Amanda. . . . But God, I don't want to make a ton of money. Just make me a dollar more than I need."

A.J.—Angela Jennifer—and Amanda, Frank's daughter Nancy's children, were in their teens by the early 1990s. Tina had been twice married and divorced. Frank Jr., though unmarried, had a son, Michael; he had been named Sinatra because of Frank's desire for a grandson to carry on the family name.

Frank's anxiety about being able to provide for his family may not have been as outlandish as it seems. Over the years, his lavish expenditure had stretched even his fabulous income. Before the sale of Reprise to Warner Brothers in 1963, executives at the record company said, he had been forced to borrow on his life insurance. In the early 1970s, after a period of relative stability, he had vastly overspent—at one point to the tune of some $500,000 a **month** after taxes. He had emerged from his brief retirement in the early 1970s at least in part at the urging of his financial advisers.

There were acrimonious family exchanges about money, according to Tina, during the period of her father's decline. Frank's prenuptial agreement with

Barbara had been superseded in late 1987 by an "Agreement to Rescind Pre-Marital Agreement." It stipulated, Tina wrote, that Barbara, whom she cast as the wicked stepmother, was to receive 50 percent of everything Frank had earned during the marriage, and of any future income. Again according to Tina, a new will Frank signed in 1991 ensured that his wife would receive more money on his death than had a previous version signed only days earlier. As Tina saw it, Barbara had married her father for his money.

Tina claimed, too, that Barbara would "ridicule Dad, even call him a has-been," that—though caring toward her husband when visitors were present—she was "openly dismissive" toward him when only family were present. Once, said Tina, Frank had phoned her mother to say he wished he had never left her.

The book Tina wrote after her father's death is the only published account of Sinatra's final years, and for that alone deserves serious attention. Because the book is in large part a chronicle of bitter strife with Barbara, however, it should be treated with caution. More detached observers have depicted Barbara as the loving mainstay of Frank's old age. Sonny King thought her "the greatest thing that happened to him in his later years." Armand Deutsch said she was "the best thing in his life." Dr. Kennamer described her as "wonderful."

Frank's home life now revolved around reading the papers, with growing difficulty, listening to classical music, and watching television. He also retained a boyish enthusiasm for his collection of model trains. The Palm Springs compound housed five of them, capable of running on independent loops on three levels, based around a realistic model of a train station. Frank liked to have children in to see, as he put it, "all the trains going 90 mph around the rail . . . lots of crashes and collisions." Barbara said her husband had "an engineer's hat and a whistle and everything."

In the summer of 1991, the violist Ann Barak dined at a Los Angeles restaurant with Frank, Barbara, and Frank Jr., who now conducted at almost all of his father's concerts. After dinner, Barak remembered, "He asked for a cigarette, and when I said I had some he said, 'Come on, let's go,' and marched me out of the restaurant and into the street. The cigarettes I had were filtered but he said 'No problem,' and broke off the filter. We stood there on the corner at night smoking like two naughty children. Then he said, 'Have you got any spare that I can take home for my stash?' I gave him a bunch of cigarettes, and he stuffed them in his pockets. I said I hoped he wouldn't get caught, and he said, 'Nah, don't worry. I know what to do.' He put his arms around me and hugged me and said, 'Thank you! I've had a ball.' . . . The next time I saw him was the following week, when we played the next concert. Back on the road."

Frank surely sang on not just because of any money worries he may have had but because he craved what Paul Anka has called "the strongest drug in the world, the needle in the arm called show business." Frank had said it himself years earlier—"It gives me a high." Frank Jr. thought his father would become "a dribbling madman" were he to retire. Tina believed singing was "his life force."

When it was reported that George Michael, a singer some fifty years his junior, was quitting to "reduce the strain of celebrity," Frank wrote a letter to the **Los Angeles Times.** The young star should be grateful for his fame, he wrote, "until the day that no one shows up and you're singing to the cleaning lady in some empty joint."

FRANK WORKED ON even when weighed down by personal loss. He sank to his knees in despair, Oppedisano said, on hearing in the spring of 1992 that Jilly Rizzo had been killed in a car accident. Soon after, he was off on a concert tour that took him to England, Spain, Portugal, and Greece. At London's Albert Hall, with the British prime minister in the audience, he had to be helped out onto the stage.

In the fall, Frank performed in nine American cities on a tour that included eight nights at Radio City Music Hall in New York. Shirley MacLaine, the sole surviving Rat Pack member still performing, toured with him. It would be "a ring ding time," he had promised, except that he might forget his lyrics. He did have trouble with them, and once forgot MacLaine's name when introducing her. MacLaine groped for a way to make the show work. "When he began to sing 'You Make Me Feel So Young,' " she recalled, "I stared at him. When he sang 'And even when I'm old and gray,' I said 'You **are** old and gray.' " Frank laughed, and so did the audience.

Late at night, in city after city, Frank took MacLaine along to meals in Italian restaurants hosted by aging local mob bosses. She sat mesmerized, watching "the subtle power plays that ebbed and flowed between him and the gangsters." As dinner began, Frank would seem "deferential." Then, emboldened by a second martini, he would behave as though he, not the mafiosi, were in control.

MacLaine marveled at Frank's capacity to outlast his companions. He would still be there at the hotel bar, spinning yarns to strangers, long after weary colleagues had retreated to bed. "They would sit with him because of who he was," she thought. "They knew he was lonely." In California, in November 1992, Frank and Oppedisano sat up late to see Bill Clinton elected. "He and I completely devoured a bottle of Jack Daniel's," Oppedisano recalled, "and I don't remember seeing him stagger."

Frank staggered, in every sense, through the winter and into the spring of 1993—Nevada, Florida, New York, New Jersey, Illinois, Scandinavia, Germany, New York, Vegas. Meanwhile, something special was brewing.

That year, the record producer Phil Ramone was urging Frank to return to the recording studio to perform "duets" with a galaxy of other big names—Barbra Streisand, Bono, Aretha Franklin, Carly Simon, Tony Bennett, Julio Iglesias, Luther Vandross, and others—without meeting them. Frank's partners would do their recording only after he had done his, and their work would be transmitted from distant cities by a fiber optic system, over telephone lines, eventually to be mixed into the final discs.

Frank thought it a bizarre concept, but Ramone lured him by pointing out that Laurence Olivier, who had done Shakespeare in his twenties, had had something different and splendid to offer in his seventies. Frank came around, then balked when asked to perform in a specially designed booth. "I'm singing out there with the band," he insisted, and Ramone's technicians found a way to accommodate him. Frank then recorded old favorite after old favorite for four solid hours.

Later, when he heard how the synthetic "duets" sounded—the first one played back to him was "The Lady Is a Tramp" with the mixed-in voice of Vandross—the revelation of what technology could achieve reduced him to tears.

When the **Duets** album was released in October 1993, there were those who did not approve. Bono performing with Sinatra on "I've Got You Under My Skin," one aficionado complained in a letter to **GQ** magazine, was "like Andy Warhol collaborating with Michelangelo on the Sistine Chapel." The public had no such quibbles. **Duets** went to number two on the **Billboard** chart and sold two million copies within weeks, three million eventually. It became Frank's largest selling album ever.

On hearing that news, said daughter Nancy, Frank reacted "like a little kid." There were some other wonderful moments. In New Jersey, couples half a century his junior danced in the aisles as Frank sang "Summer Wind." The words were freighted now with a special poignancy:

> The autumn wind, and the winter wind,
> have come and gone,
> And still the days, those lonely days, go on
> and on. . . .

More often than not, though, he had to confront harsh reality. He lost his way entirely while performing before the Queen of Sweden that year. At a concert in New York he shouted in desperation, "What the hell are the words?" Wherever Frank appeared, aides stood by with an oxygen tank.

A show at Aurora, Illinois, misfired badly. "Frank Sinatra is old tonight," Tom Junod wrote in **GQ.** "He's supposed to be singing 'Guess I'll Hang My Tears Out to Dry,' and that's what the orchestra keep playing as the Old Man stands out there alone. The lights are still on him, and the TelePrompTers are spelling out the lyrics . . . but the Old Man cries out with scary desperation, 'I can't see! I can't hear!' "

In Las Vegas, Frank shuffled off stage miserable about his memory loss, shouting that the audience should be given its money back. Murray Kempton, writing in **Newsday,** thought the slide went deeper than shattered synapses. The electronic tricks of **Duets** had not fooled Kempton.

"He well remembers the bounce of these songs," Kempton wrote sadly, "but he has forgotten how they feel. The voice still drives as of old, but it can never again breathe the loneliness of the heart. Sinatra's supreme gift was to make us glad to be unhappy. He can't do that any longer . . . to see him now is just to be unhappy."

EARLY IN MARCH 1994, orange handkerchief in tuxedo buttonhole, wearing a steel-gray toupee like a cap, Frank stepped onto a New York stage not to sing but to receive a Grammy "Legend" Award. On hand to present it was a modern musical hero, U2's Bono.

Reading from a prepared script, Bono characterized Frank as "a man heavier than the Empire State, more connected than the Twin Towers, as recognizable as the Statue of Liberty." Frank responded emotionally, blew kisses to Barbara in the audience, said he loved her, and complained genially that no arrangements had been made for him to sing. The ceremony was being broadcast live, but Frank suddenly vanished from the screen. He had been cut off, on the instructions of someone who feared he might babble on out of control.

Five days later, while singing "My Way" at a concert in Richmond, Virginia, Frank collapsed. Oppedisano, who rushed to his side, found that he was drenched in sweat "right through to the outer shell of his jacket." Frank came to, was lifted into a wheelchair, and waved feebly as he was taken from the stage. The audience applauded.

Doctors at a local hospital concluded that Frank was dehydrated. He had been drinking heavily the night before, Oppedisano said. Ignoring advice that he should stay overnight for observation, Frank flew back to California. Days later, when **Time** magazine asked why he still lived so fast and hard, Frank replied by fax: "You write for a magazine. I tour. It's what I do." He appeared in Oklahoma less than three weeks after the collapse.

A month later, at Radio City Music Hall, he became tearful. "This," Frank said, "may be the last time we will be together." It was indeed his last New York appearance. In the months that followed he gave his last shows in Las Vegas, Chicago, and Atlantic City, and ranged as far afield as the Philippines and Japan.

The Tokyo performances survive on videotape. They show a frail old man, rheumy-eyed, puffy in the jowls, waddling rather than walking, making awkward hand movements as he croaked through his repertoire. Some of his musicians found it painful to watch, and thought it would have been better had Frank not appeared. Watching the tape today, though, every song has poignancy. Frank's last rendition of "One for My Baby," with final amendments to the original lyric, takes on special meaning:

"We're drinking, my friend, to the end of a brief episode . . . when I'm gloomy, please listen to me before it's all passed away. . . . I hope you didn't mind my bendin' your ear . . . that long . . . that long . . . it's a very long, long road."

Natalie Cole, who starred with Frank in Tokyo, flew home with him on his private jet. "Even before the wheels left the runway," she remembered, "he was knocking back the Jack Daniel's one after the other. . . . We had been in the air about an hour or so when Frank suddenly looked around at all of us in the cabin and bellowed, 'Who the hell are all these people?' "

He "stood and started going around, confronting everyone in turn, getting close up in each face and demanding to know, 'Who the hell are **you**?' . . . He started with his housekeeper, who'd been with him some fifty years. His personal valet was next. . . . I ducked out and slept until we landed in Honolulu to refuel. At that point Frank suddenly had a moment of clarity. He was lucid, but he had no idea why he was on the plane."

Frank appeared as a performer just once more, at a Palm Springs resort hotel, at the close of the annual golf tournament that was and still is named after him. According to Oppedisano, he performed bravely and well.

Frank's eightieth birthday, in December 1995, was marked by grand public gestures. The Empire State Building glowed blue, and gigantic billboards along Fifth Avenue served as a nation's birthday cards. Frank appeared on television for the very last time, in a two-hour special. Many stars paid homage.

Bruce Springsteen called him the "Patron Saint of New Jersey." Bob Dylan sang a new song, with lyrics in a vein not unlike those of "My Way." The proceedings closed with "New York, New York," and Frank sang along with his fellow stars, managing somehow to hold on to the last note longer than anyone else.

For years now, Frank had been ending his shows with a toast to long life, his version of the old Italian "**cent'anni!**"—"to a hundred years!" "May you live to be a hundred," he had told audiences all over the world, "and may the last voice you hear be mine."

36

Exit

"YOU GOTTA LOVE LIVING," Frank liked to say in those last years, "because dyin's a pain in the ass."

His world was shrinking rapidly. At one of his last concerts, he had choked up as he embarked on "Guess I'll Hang My Tears Out to Dry," a Sammy Cahn and Jule Styne song he had been singing for years. Cahn had died the previous year, Styne just a week before the concert. Swifty Lazar was gone, too. Frank did not like to say friends had died. He preferred to say they had "gone to the mountains."

Dean Martin had gone to the mountains on Christmas Day 1995 at the age of seventy-eight, his lungs ruined by cigarettes, his liver and kidneys by alcohol. Frank had a statement put out describing Martin as his "brother." The relationship had never been the same, though, since Martin abandoned the "Together Again" tour. "There was a wall between them," Oppedisano said. Frank did not attend Martin's funeral.

The Sands, cradle of Frank's Las Vegas career, was about to close forever. Its roulette and blackjack tables, its thousand slot machines, would be sold at auction. The glittering casino in which Frank had walked like a prince, the luxury suites in which he had partied, would be razed. "Frank took it as a personal affront," Jerry Lewis recalled. "He asked 'How could they do that?' "

Frank had been uprooted, too, from the place he had called home for almost forty years, the compound near Palm Springs that bore his name. The house and its contents had long been more than the material proof of fabulous success. It was the haven to which Frank had always been able to retreat, a place of comfort imbued with memories. There was the art collection: ranging from Fabergé treasures from old Russia to paintings by modern American artists including Grandma Moses, Guy Wiggins, Andrew Wyeth, and William Merritt Chase. One of the works by Wiggins was an oil painting of Fifth Avenue in the snow, probably the one Frank had long ago bought for first wife Nancy. Here were the gifts from departed friends: a silver-and-gold cigarette case from Cahn and Styne; a gold dressing table box set with diamonds from Mike Romanoff; a watch from Sammy Davis inscribed: "To

Charley Shoulders Thanks Smokey the 'B.' "
Here was Frank's Bösendorfer grand piano—he could play a little—his two 1930s vintage radios, his mounted busts of John F. Kennedy. Here were Frank's trains: the precisely tooled working models, an actual old caboose he had named **Chicago** and converted into a massage room, train sculptures in wood and copper, train collages, train photographs.

Within a year of Frank's final performance, most of these items and other possessions were auctioned off at Christie's for $2 million. The house itself had been sold earlier for almost $5 million. It had been decided that the Sinatras should leave Palm Springs for Los Angeles. Frank had owned the house for forty years, had first built a home in the area half a century earlier. Yet Barbara thought it was time for a change because "everybody is in the L.A. area now." Frank would be closer to his children, and to the widest possible range of medical care.

He seemed at first to accept the prospect of moving, but he was devastated when the time came, "grieving as though someone had died," according to Tina. The sympathetic new owner, a Canadian businessman, allowed the Sinatras to stay on for a few more weeks. When the dread day of departure came, the twenty-six members of Frank's household staff lined up on each side of the driveway. Some were moved to tears when

Frank emerged, clambered into a town car, and left.

The Sinatras owned two fine houses in the Los Angeles area, one in Beverly Hills, another on the beach at Malibu. The Beverly Hills spread, hidden in an orange grove and sealed off behind high security gates, was a place of Gatsby-style opulence. The place at Malibu, on Broad Beach, was more modest but nonetheless fit for a star. Neighbors included Dinah Shore, Steven Spielberg, and Jack Lemmon. The Beverly Hills house seemed sterile to Frank, oversized; it reminded him of a hotel. "They must be doing lousy business in this joint," he joked gloomily one day as he sat drinking in his own bar with Oppedisano. He liked the house at the beach better because, he said, just being by the ocean reminded him of growing up near the New Jersey shore.

Frank sorely missed the desert. One night Oppedisano heard him ask Barbara, "When are we going home?" When she replied that they were home, he said, "This is **your** home. When are we going to **my** home?" At times he was utterly disoriented. On another night at Malibu, as he sat outside under the stars, he turned to others present in sudden alarm. "Where am I?" he wanted to know.

In July 1996, to mark twenty years of marriage, Frank and Barbara went to Our Lady of Malibu church to renew their wedding vows. Daughters

Nancy and Tina were invited but did not attend. Tension between them and their stepmother had not eased.

In November, a month short of his eighty-first birthday, Frank was admitted to Cedars-Sinai Hospital for treatment of what his publicist described as "a pinched nerve." In fact he had suffered a heart attack, complicated by pneumonia and cancer of the ureter. The cancer was not life-threatening. The heart and lung trouble was very serious. Brain scans had now firmly identified dementia.

George Jacobs got to see Frank about this time. "He didn't know who he was," Jacobs remembered. "He said hello, and then 'Sinatra will be here any minute now.' I left crying." The confusion remained intermittent, but Frank's medical team now included a geriatric psychiatrist. A nurse was on hand at all times.

On one of his good days, in April 1997, Frank watched on television as the House of Representatives voted to award him the Congressional Gold Medal. It is the highest tribute the Congress can pay, and past recipients have included George Washington, Ulysses S. Grant, Sir Winston Churchill, and, from the world of show business, George and Ira Gershwin, Marian Anderson, John Wayne, and Bob Hope.

Frank had long since said there was one sort of tribute he could do without. He had begged Tina not to let him "wind up on a coffee mug." The use of his name and likeness on a pasta sauce and silk ties had passed muster. In the fall of 1997, however, **The Wall Street Journal** ran a piece headlined "Sinatra's Wife and Kids Battle Over Frank Inc. While His Health Slips." "Family members have clashed repeatedly," the story said, "over arguably tacky merchandise, such as a 'singing' Franklin Mint souvenir plate with Mr. Sinatra on vocals via computer chip. Sinatra cigars are being readied. . . . The licensing barrage has largely been the doing of Tina Sinatra."

On December 12, the great classical violinist Isaac Stern called Frank and played "Happy Birthday" over the telephone. Frank was eighty-two.

Some of his best moments, now, were spent sitting quietly with Oppedisano. They talked, sipped drinks into the night, and watched television. Frank was amused, in early 1998, when the Monica Lewinsky scandal broke. He and Bill Clinton had dined together early in the presidency, and had got on well.

Frank tended to tell old jokes again and again, and the Lewinsky affair prompted him to trot out one about the 1991 furor over Supreme Court nominee Clarence Thomas and his alleged sexual harassment of Anita Hill. "Obviously," Frank would say, "that guy hadn't read the Bible. It's right in there: 'Thou shalt not discuss thy rod with thy staff!' "

As he grew less and less mobile, the television was at once an umbilical to the outside world and a constant irritation. "I sat with him in his study," Don Rickles recalled, "and we watched television and he kept telling me to change the channel. He'd sit there and say, 'Turn that off, that's not good . . . turn that off . . . turn that off.' One time we came across him singing, and he said 'Turn **that** off!' "

Old friends still came around to play poker. On Sunday, May 10, Jack Lemmon, singer Jerry Vale, screenwriter Larry Gelbart, and the comic Tom Dreesen arrived for a game. Frank did not join them. "I went to his room to say hi," recalled Dreesen, who had long worked as Frank's warm-up man, "and he was in his pajamas, resting." Frank roused himself enough to express affection in his time-worn way. "If anybody ever hits you," he told Dreesen, "call me."

The following day, Oppedisano remembered, "Barbara had gone out, and I gave him a nonalcoholic beer. And, at least in his mind, he thought he was looped, that he was bombed. He and I had a great laugh."

A little earlier, when his daughter Tina had come to visit, Frank had asked how long it was until the millennium. He had once promised that he would see in the year 2000 by throwing the ultimate birthday party, in the Roman Colosseum perhaps, or in downtown Manhattan. Now, told by Tina that the millennium was less than two years off, he responded, "Oh, I can do that. Nothin' to it."

On Tuesday May 12 and the following day, however, Frank seemed dispirited, more miserable than usual about being an invalid. "This is not me," he told Oppedisano. "I don't want to go on this way."

Ever since his mother's death, Frank had given more serious thought to the Roman Catholic faith in which he had been raised. He had discussed the possibility of an afterlife with Shirley MacLaine. "We had a talk about reincarnation," she remembered, "and he was extremely open to it. Because he was old enough then, and so many memories, déjà vus, were coming to him. He used me a lot to look into those areas, would call me when something drastic happened in his life, looking for spiritual sustenance. This was not wacky to him at all."

Oppedisano, too, was aware of Frank's belief in the spirit world. During the final series of concerts, in Manila, Frank had told him he believed they had met before in a previous life. In his final months, he would say that Jilly Rizzo, dead since 1992, had been visiting him. Once he asked Oppedisano in a whisper to, "get my mother out of here." He insisted that Dolly was sitting "right over there in the chair."

Frank had a notion of what constituted an

admirable death. Sir Winston Churchill, he said, had "closed his eyes at ninety-one, sitting in a rocker with a good cigar in one hand, a snifter of brandy in the other. That's my kind of cat." Sir Winston, however, did not die like that. He died sick and helpless in his bed, after weeks in a virtual coma.

On the evening of Thursday, May 14, 1998, while Barbara was out dining with friends, Frank complained to his nurse of chest pain and difficulty in breathing. Sometime after that he sat up and screamed, then fell back on the bed. His lips had turned blue. Fire Department paramedics, responding to an emergency call, rushed him the short distance to Cedars-Sinai.

Dr. Kennamer was alerted, and hurried to the hospital. The housekeeper reached both Barbara and Oppedisano by telephone, and they arrived to find the doctor still working on Frank. He was alive, but barely, after suffering another heart attack.

Accounts differ as to his condition in the brief time that remained to him. Oppedisano said Frank was "still very much aware when I arrived. I held his hand." Barbara said her husband told her he was "very tired." She responded, she said, with, "Fight, darling, you must fight." According to a statement put out by the family, Frank's last words were, "I'm losing it." Dr. Kennamer, however, said he was "beyond talking. . . . We worked on him for about an hour and a half. We gave him a lot of intravenous medication. . . . But basically he was dead."

Frank was formally pronounced dead at 10:50 P.M. His daughters arrived—they had not been called immediately—to find their father lying on a gurney, his eyes closed, his hands on his chest.

As the news got out, newspaper editors stopped the presses, changed front pages, began preparing special editions. Broadcasters dug out archive footage, rushed programs onto the air. In New York, the top of the Empire State Building was lit in blue once again. In Hollywood, the top of the Capitol Records tower was draped in black.

In Las Vegas the following night, the casinos along the Strip turned off their lights for a few minutes. The traffic stopped, and thousands gathered on the sidewalk holding flickering candles. When the lights at Caesars Palace came back on again, they revealed a giant illuminated likeness of Sinatra. At the Cal-Neva Lodge on Lake Tahoe, they played Sinatra music nonstop and served a blue cocktail dreamed up for the occasion. On the grand piano, which remained unplayed, they laid a solitary red rose.

In Hoboken, there was standing room only at a memorial mass held in St. Francis Church, where Frank had been baptized. A large portrait of him in his prime, trademark cigarette in hand, stood propped on the altar among the candles.

Some in the congregation wept, then all rose as one to sing "My Way," which was played as the recessional. As they finished, the Italian-American singer chimed in with, "Frankie took the blows, but he did it his way." Some then made the pilgrimage to the plaque that marked Frank's birthplace at 415 Monroe Street—the house itself was long since gone—to leave loaves of Italian bread and bottles of Jack Daniel's on the sidewalk.

In a Beverly Hills church, with far greater pomp and circumstance, Cardinal Roger Mahony presided over a vigil and a funeral mass. At the vigil, Frank's pianist Bill Miller played "In the Wee Small Hours of the Morning" and "All the Way." The family followed the casket into a church packed with the aristocracy of show business. Those at the mass the following morning included Gregory Peck, Kirk Douglas, Tony Bennett, Sophia Loren, Liza Minnelli, Tony Curtis, Paul Anka, Anthony Quinn, Milton Berle, Diahann Carroll, Dionne Warwick, Debbie Reynolds, Peggy Lee, Jack Nicholson, Gene Autry, Sidney Poitier, Janet Leigh, Faye Dunaway, and Bruce Springsteen. Nancy Reagan and former New York governor Hugh Carey were there, as were Larry King and Phil Donahue, Joey Bishop, Dean Martin's former wife Jeanne, and Sammy Davis's widow, Altovise. Frank's two surviving former wives, Nancy Sinatra and Mia Farrow, sat behind the immediate family. The air was permeated with the fragrance of gardenias, from the flowers that blanketed Frank's coffin.

After "Ave Maria," from the choir, Frank's voice filled the church. "Put your dreams away for another day . . ." he sang, and the tears flowed.

The invited mourners emerged into the sunlight, where some five hundred people were gathered. Photographers jostled to grab pictures of famous faces. Overhead, a skywriting plane traced the initials "F.S." in the air, then embraced them with the shape of a heart.

FRANK SINATRA'S REMAINS were flown that afternoon to Palm Springs, then taken to Desert Memorial Park for burial. A priest, from another church named after St. Francis, conducted a last ceremony.

A Marine Corps major general presented a folded Stars and Stripes to Barbara Sinatra "on behalf of a grateful nation." President Clinton had approved this final honor in response to an initiative by Frank's daughter Nancy, even though her father had never served in the armed forces. The Medal of Freedom and the Congressional Gold Medal were deemed justification enough.

Screened off from view for privacy, the casket was lowered into the bronze-lined burial vault that contained Frank's parents. Frank's grave marker is flanked by those of his parents and Jilly

Rizzo. It is small, flush with the well-groomed turf, and bears only his name, dates of birth and death, and the hopeful epitaph, "The Best Is Yet to Come."

Frank had included that song in his last big concert. "The best is yet to come," he had sung, and then with emphasis, not quite according to the original lyric, "Babe, it's gonna be fine."

He knew it had not all been fine. He had decided never to write his autobiography, he had said, "because I'm not proud of too many things I've done." What he wished to be remembered for, he told an interviewer, was "to have succeeded in making popular music an art form—to have reached people. . . ." He had also once said: "Whatever else has been said about me is unimportant. When I sing, I believe."

Acknowledgments

PEOPLE ARE THE LIFEBLOOD of biography, often more important than the paper record. This one was born thanks to that publishing veteran Jim Silberman, who had the best of ideas—a simple one. He realized that there was no substantial, rounded, book on the life of Frank Sinatra, a book that sought out the truth about the artist whose shimmering talent and goodwill was accompanied by decadence and delinquency. That was our brief. Knopf chairman Sonny Mehta, a champion of quality publishing in difficult times, had confidence in us and funded the project over a tough four years. We thank him especially, as we do Jonathan Segal, a king among editors in an era when cutbacks make that profession a vanishing breed, and Leyla Aker, our guide on the last lap to publication.

We owe a special debt of gratitude to Ric Ross, in Los Angeles, who is rightly credited—not least by Sinatra's daughter Nancy, whose book on her father benefited from his scholarship—as a walking encyclopedia on the singer's life. He is a stickler for accuracy, and the manuscript benefited from his careful reading. It gained, too, from the eagle eyes of Knopf associate general counsel Jon Fine and of copy editor Fred Chase.

Our lead researcher was Kelly Dinardo, who for three years found the unfindable for us with industry and good cheer. Bob Lamb, Catherine Valeriote, and April Lubold made valuable contributions. In Rome, Livia Borghese brought her sharp intellect to the matter of the Sinatra family's origins and the involvement with Lucky Luciano. In Sicily, supposedly a place that rebuffs nosy foreigners, we were greeted with good cheer by everyone—from historians to citizens in humble villages. Special thanks to Nicolò Sangiorgio, the fount of all knowledge on Lercara Friddi, who honored his promise to keep a confidence; to the historian Salvatore Lupo and Umberto Santino of the Centro Siciliano de Documentazione, both brave voices against the Mafia; to Maria Gerardi, archives director at Agrigento and Mariella Marguglio at the Biblioteca Centrale in Palermo; Dottore Virginio Alberelli and officer Vera Fichera at the police headquarters in Palermo; and Kathy Kirkpatrick of GenTracer, a professional genealogist specializing in Sicily, who conducted research crucial to clinching our discovery that the Sinatras and the Luciano family shared the same town of origin.

We asked Sinatra's first wife, Nancy, and her three children for interviews—and in the case of daughters Nancy and Tina pressed the requests after receiving no initial response. Tina replied through an attorney, saying that the Sinatras were not prepared to participate. We also asked Sinatra's fourth wife, Barbara, for an interview, in vain. The immediate family's silence contrasted with the cooperation received from first cousins Frank Monaco, Rose Sinatra Paldino, Rose Ellman Sinatra, Morris Esposito, and second cousins Marilyn Sinatra and Maryann Paldino Flannery. Eva Bartok's daughter Deana, who claims Sinatra was her father and has taken his name, shared her poignant story. In Hoboken, Anthony and James Petrozelli and Rose Tamburro, relatives of two of the Hoboken Four singers, as well as Lucille Kirk Buccini, who sang with Sinatra at the Rustic Cabin, were generous with information. Bandleader Frank Mane's widow, Mary Mane, and her attorney Robert Mandelbaum, kindly allowed us to hear Sinatra's first recording, and Sinatra devotee Ed Shirak was helpful with photographs of the young Sinatra in Hoboken.

Of the more than five hundred people who spoke with us, we are especially grateful to Sammy Cahn's first wife, Gloria Cahn Franks, and his widow, Tita; George Evans's son Phil; the late

Janet Leigh; Jerry Lewis; Shirley MacLaine; Jeanne Martin; Harry James's first wife, Louise Tobin; agents Milt Ebbins and the late Mort Viner; Lee Solters, Sinatra's longtime publicist; and producer George Schlatter. Fellow singers Buddy Greco, Connie Haines, Jo Stafford, and the comedian Joey Villa shared memories with us, as did musicians Joe Bushkin and Tony Mottola, both sadly now deceased, Frank Fighera, Al Porcino, and Al Viola. Violist Ann Barak and violinist Tony Posk were especially generous with their time—Ann also joined us on the difficult quest in Sicily. Vernise Yocum Pelzel, daughter of copyist Vern Yocum, shared recollections her late father had compiled.

One of the most sensitive tasks for a biographer, especially when the subject is a major celebrity, is the subject's love life. Only those personally involved can really describe a relationship. Sinatra and Ava Gardner are both gone, but we had the great fortune to have access to extended taped interviews, never published, that she gave to the author Peter Evans, and to which he holds the copyright. Warm thanks to Evans, a fine professional and a good friend. Mearene "Reenie" Jordan, who was on intimate terms with Gardner for more than forty years, talked with us in California, as did Spoli Mills, the actress's best friend in London, and Gardner's first husband, the late Artie Shaw. The singer Peggy Connelly and the actress Lois Nettleton, who both had lengthy affairs with Sinatra, were compassionate where they might have been unkind—and patient with intrusive questions. So were Jeanne Carmen, Marianna Case, Jill Corey, Carole Lynley, and Sandra Giles. Humphrey Bogart's lover Verita Thompson, and former showgirl Liz Renay had insights. Susan Murphy described a distressing sexual experience, and did not refuse our probing. The journalist St. Clair Pugh had a personal memory of the affair with Gloria Vanderbilt, as did Peter Duchin of his evening with Sinatra and with Jackie Kennedy Onassis.

Of the singer's friends and acquaintances, we especially appreciate the contributions of Nick Sevano and Sonny King—who knew Sinatra almost all his life—and of Rock Brynner, the late Brad Dexter, Leonora Hornblow, Bob Neal, and Tony Oppedisano. Armand Deutsch, Matty Jordan's widow, Jackie, and Abbe Lane also made time to talk. Phyllis McGuire, who was close to Sinatra's Mafia associate Sam Giancana, contrived to say little but communicate a good deal. Dr. Rex Kennamer, family physician and friend, said as much as he could without betraying his professional trust. The writer Pete Hamill, in whom Sinatra placed unusual confidence, expanded on his admirable memoir **Why Sinatra Matters.** George Jacobs, the valet, whom author Summers first interviewed twenty years ago, talked loyally but openly about the man he served so long. Johnnie Spotts, one of Sinatra's pilots, spoke carefully. Another pilot, Dan Arney, was more trenchant. Dominick Dunne remembered the abusive, violent Sinatra.

We strove to get to the heart of the matter everyone has wondered about, the singer's involvement with the Mafia. The late Joe Nellis, who questioned Sinatra for the Kefauver Committee; Nick Akerman, former Assistant United States Attorney for the southern district of New York; the late Ralph Salerno, the prominent organized crime consultant; and Sal Vizzini, a former courageous undercover agent for the Federal Bureau of Narcotics, were open and forthright. So was Dougald McMillan, who was an attorney in the Organized Crime Section of the Kennedy Justice Department, who in the past was very close-mouthed. Still enviably fit at the age of ninety-one, in Taormina, Sicily, the pianist Chico Scimone recalled playing for Sinatra at his mob "audition." Angela Marrocco, Willie Moretti's daughter, spoke with us, briefly but usefully. "Jimmy Blue Eyes" Alo's niece Carole Russo and his friend, former concert promoter Ken Roberts, were forthcoming, as were Luellen Smiley, Allen Smiley's daughter, and Joseph Sullivan, Angelo De Carlo's grandson. Joe Shimon's daughter Toni augmented the authors' earlier interviews of her late father with memories of what he said about

Sinatra, Sam Giancana, and Johnny Rosselli. Billy Woodfield, who died while the book was being prepared, vividly described experiences with Sinatra that featured Luciano and Giancana, and his widow, Lili, provided some superb Woodfield photographs. Tommy Dorsey's children, Tommy Dorsey III and the late Patricia Dorsey Hooker, were helpful on the mob threat to their father. Her husband being incapacitated, Martin Jurow's wife, Erin Jo, complemented her husband's published account of the Mafia role in securing Sinatra a part in **From Here to Eternity.** The late Dan Taradash knew nothing of that, but described what he learned of the casting process as screenwriter. The distinguished screenwriter and director Mel Shavelson recalled how a lamb's head on a platter led Sinatra to cancel a meeting. Invaluable information on Sinatra in Las Vegas was provided by Count Guido Deiro and Ed Walters, once dealer and pit boss respectively at the Sands in Las Vegas; Eve Quillin, cosmetologist and columnist; Ed Becker, author and former entertainment director at the Riviera; Ralph Denton, attorney and close confidant of Nevada governor Grant Sawyer; and John Smith, the **Las Vegas Review-Journal**'s authoritative writer on the city's darker history. We much respect the work of early Sinatra biographer Arnold Shaw, whose widow Ghita kindly gave us access to his papers.

More general help came from too many people

to thank them all here. Ed O'Brien, who has written extensively on Sinatra, talked and corresponded over many months. Rick Apt, who runs Ric Apt's Collectibles at www.blue-eyes.com, opened up his remarkable video archive to us. Nevada state senator Bob Coffin, who can be reached at bcoffin@vegas.infi.net, supplied books and photographs from his collection in Las Vegas. Thanks, too, to Mary Ann Mastrodonato, Josephine Collins in Los Angeles—she has an astonishing fund of unpublished phone numbers—and Artie Shaw's assistant Pattie Porter.

Two authors of books on Sinatra, Donald Clarke and Michael Freedland, helped generously with guidance. Our friend Sally Denton, coauthor of **The Money and the Power,** the seminal book on Las Vegas, let us roam in her files. Gus Russo, fresh from writing **The Outfit,** his authoritative book on the Chicago mob, swapped informational gold once again. So did the eclectic author Dick Russell, a colleague on whom we can always rely, and Douglas Valentine, who shared Mafia morsels picked up while writing his history of the Federal Bureau of Narcotics, **The Strength of the Wolf.** Murray Dubin, a journalist with expertise on the Philadelphia mob, led us to Angelo Bruno's daughter. In the midst of preparations for the movie **The Aviator,** which draws on his work, Charles Higham made time to discuss the background to his biography of Ava Gardner.

Robert Lacey, always collegiate, helped us leapfrog from material in his book **Little Man,** on Meyer Lansky, to living sources on the old mobsters. Peter J. Levinson, author of authoritative books on Harry James and Nelson Riddle, told us of his encounters with Sinatra. In London, Gavin MacFadyen and Michael Gillard shared the files they built while preparing their two Sinatra programs for Hart Ryan Productions, shown by ITVMeridian Broadcasting in the UK in 2000. John J. Binder, author of **The Chicago Outfit,** provided us with photographs from his extensive collection. Alf Batchelder sent us material on Sinatra's visits to Australia. Sylvia Schmitt gave us welcome help in Palm Springs.

Librarians, essential to all biographers, too often remain faceless. We thank especially the energetic staff of the Margaret Herrick Library at the Academy of Motion Picture Arts and Sciences, David Schwartz and Joyce Marshall at the University of Nevada at Las Vegas, James Hastings and Fred Romanski of the Textual Reference Branch at the National Archives, Sharon Kelly at the John F. Kennedy Library, Tim Noakes at the Department of Special Collections at Stanford, the Palm Springs Historical Society, and Frank Prain, library manager at the **Melbourne Age,** in Melbourne, Australia. Jim Lesar, our attorney for Freedom of Information Act requests, again moved the immovable. The talented team at Paladin InVision, in London, fought and won the effort to make a major TV documentary arising from our work, at a time when funding is excruciatingly hard to raise. It should air on A&E, the BBC, and other networks, coincidental with publication of this book.

We thank our agents, Sterling Lord and his assistant Robert Guinsler in New York, and Jonathan Lloyd, who heads Curtis Brown in London. Also in London, Patrick Janson-Smith and Marianne Velmans, and the team at Transworld, gave us new heart when they came on board. We have enormous admiration for the Knopf team who wrestled the book to publication, publicity director Paul Bogaards, Victoria Gerken, and Lydia Buechler.

Four good friends, especially, helped. The hospitality of Henry Ehrlich and Tamara Glenny in New York, and Robert Dorff and Padrick Peper in Los Angeles, made it possible to avoid some devastating hotel expenses. In Iowa, for the third time, Sondra Feldstein applied her scholarly mind to reading and annotating some of the more than five hundred books consulted. Here in Ireland, no fewer than fifteen people contributed one way or the other. Murphy Media, in Waterford, performed wonders with photographs. Pauline Lombard, Ciara Guiry, and Sally and Sam Brittain kept order in a system of 1,500 files, tapes, and a monster chronology. Jeanette Woods and Angela

Daly logged taped interviews, and Ger Killalea kept the machines going. James Ronayne once again drove thousands of miles for us, and Jenny Barlow and Ann Dalton managed our brood of children.

Our personal assistants, first Michele Sheehan and then Sinéad Sweeney, were key to the project. Sinéad brought to the job her keen intelligence and commitment, and we owe her special thanks.

Our love and gratitude to our neglected children, who when they grow up will know better than to be nonfiction authors. On the other hand, they may have noticed that—however challenging the work—we think ourselves lucky in our chosen profession.

Anthony Summers and
Robbyn Swan
Ireland, 2005

Notes and Sources

Full citations for books mentioned in the Notes and Sources appear in the Bibliography.

ABBREVIATIONS USED IN NOTES AND SOURCES

BN	Record Group 170, Federal Bureau of Narcotics files, National Archives
corr.	correspondence with authors
ELSUR	FBI transcripts of electronic surveillance tapes
FOIA	Freedom of Information Act
FS	Frank Sinatra
FSFBI	FBI headquarters file on Sinatra, FBI 62-83219
HSCA	Select Committee on Assassinations, U.S. House of Representatives, 95th Cong., 2nd sess., 1979
int.	interview conducted by the authors
JFK	documents related to the assassination of President Kennedy gathered during the work of the Assassination Records Review Board and held at the National Archives
LAT	**Los Angeles Times**
LAHE	**Los Angeles Herald-Examiner**
LLBN	Lucky Luciano File, Record Group 170, Federal Bureau of Narcotics Files, National Archives
M/G int.	interview conducted for the 2000 ITV (U.K.) television documentary **Sinatra: Good Guy, Bad Guy,** supplied to the authors by journalists Michael Gillard and Gavin MacFadyen
MHL	material held at Margaret Herrick Library, Academy of Motion Picture Arts and Sciences
NA	National Archives, Washington, D.C.

NYT	**New York Times**
PITV	interview conducted for the Paladin InVision documentary for BBC1 (U.K.) and A&E (U.S.) made in collaboration with the authors
WP	**Washington Post**

Chapter 1: Debut

4–5 **"May I sing?"/first studio recording:** ints. Mary Mane, widow of Frank Mane, Mrs. Mane's attorney, Robert Mandelbaum; Charles Granata, **Sessions with Sinatra,** Chicago: A Cappella (Chicago Review Press), 1999, 2–, Will Friedwald, **Sinatra! The Song Is You,** New York: Da Capo Press, 1997, 65; **("Our Love")** words and music by Larry Clinton, Buddy Bernier, and Bob Emmerich, New York: Chappell, 1939; **(technology)** ints. Alan Graves, of the Audio Lathe; **(label)** photo and corr. Robert Mandelbaum, Jan. 4, 2004; **(thousand and more)** Granata, xiv.

5 **"best singer":** Sammy Cahn, **I Should Care,** New York: Arbor House, 1974, 132.

Chapter 2: A Family from Sicily

6 **I am Sicilian/"I don't think":** FS comments during Italian tour, 1987, RAI UNO (Italian TV), videotape in authors' collection.

7 **fire and paradox:** Donald Ordway, **Sicily: Island of Fire,** New York: National Travel Club, 1930, 2–.

7 **"ungovernable":** Luigi Barzini, **From Caesar to the Mafia,** New York: Library Press, 1971, 68.

7 **crime rate:** Will Monroe, **The Spell of Sicily,** Boston: Page, 1909, 123.

8 **Mafia characterization: ("mafia"/"Mafia")** Luigi Barzini, **The Italians,** New York: Atheneum, 1964, 253–. The authors also studied **A Family Business,** the study of kinship in organized crime by Francis Ianni and Elizabeth Reuss-Ianni (New York: Russell Sage Foundation, 1972); **(marriage/divorce)** Charlotte Chapman, **Milocca: A Sicilian Village,** Cambridge, MA: Schenkman, 1971, 88–; ***(padrone)*** Donna Gabaccia, **From Sicily to Elizabeth Street,** Albany, NY: State University of New York Press, 1984, 5–, Gay Talese, "Frank Sinatra Has a Cold," Esquire, Apr. 1966; ***(uomini rispettati)*** ibid., Barzini, **Italians,**

256–, Claire Sterling, **The Mafia,** London: Hamish Hamilton, 1990, 49, 72–.

8 **corruption/rigging elections:** M. I. Finley, Denis Mack Smith, and Christopher Duggan, **A History of Sicily,** New York: Elisabeth Sifton-Viking, 1987, 183, 197–, Sterling, 47, Barzini, **Italians,** 256.

9 **"not a dish for the timid":** Ordway, 7.

9 **paternal grandfather: (obituary) NYT,** Apr. 10, 1948; **(death certificate)** "Frank" Sinatra, no. 226, Apr. 12, 1948, NJ Department of Health—Bureau of Vital Statistics; **(1964/Catania) Il Giornale,** Dec. 20, 1997, corr. Office of the Mayor, Comune di Lumarzo, Genoa, Dec. 2002; **(1987)** FS comments during 1987 Italian tour, RAI UNO; **(Agrigento)** int. Ann Barak Stutch; **(Nancy's books)** Nancy Sinatra, **Frank Sinatra: An American Legend,** New York: Reader's Digest, 1998, 15, and see Nancy Sinatra, **Frank Sinatra: My Father,** New York: Pocket, 1985, 2–.

10 **Sicilian and U.S. records:** To establish the correct names, birthplace, and birthdates of Sinatra's paternal grandparents, the authors relied above all on information supplied by the grandparents themselves during their lifetimes, and by their granddaughter Rose Paldino. The facts as to their origins were collated with the assistance of Kathy Kirkpatrick, a genealogist specializing in the study of Sicilian records. Kirkpatrick is in accord with the authors' findings.

Critical bits of information were the maiden names of Sinatra's paternal grandmother, Rosa Saglimbeni, and her mother, Angela Lo Forte, which are noted on Rosa's death certificate. Using her maiden name—married women in Italy were identified by their maiden names—Rosa Saglimbeni Sinatra entered the United States at Ellis Island with three young children—including Sinatra's father, Antonino—in 1903. Further research in Ellis Island records established the earlier arrival of Sinatra's grandfather Francesco, in 1900, and his uncle Salvatore, in 1902.

The information supplied to U.S. immigration officials by Rosa and Francesco, along with data they later supplied for the U.S. Census, established their true ages, Francesco's occupation (shoemaker), and their port of departure from Sicily—Palermo. A search of civil birth records for the Palermo suburb of Brancaccio yielded the birth certificate of Antonino Sinatra, dated May 4, 1894—the known birthdate of Sinatra's father—to Rosa

Saglimbeni and Francesco Sinatra. Subsequent research in the records of the Brancaccio parish church uncovered Antonino's baptismal record.

The vague recollections of an octogenarian priest led the authors to the village of Lercara Friddi. Registries in Lercara's church of Maria S.S. della Neve include Sinatra's grandparents' baptismal and marriage records, firmly identifiable thanks to the inclusion of **their** parents' names, which match data in U.S. official records (death certificates—for Frank [Francesco] Sinatra, Apr. 12, 1948, no. 226—listing father's name as Isidor, and for Rosa Sinatra, Feb. 28, 1925, no. 20—listing parents' names as Salvatori Saglimbene [sic] and Angela Lo Forte, NJ Department of Health—Bureau of Vital Statistics; Ellis Island records—see sourcing for emigration to United States later in this chapter; U.S. Census—Frank and Rose Sinatra responses for U.S. Census, 1920; Palermo records—Antonino Sinatra entry, May 4, 1894, civil birth records, Palermo, microfilm FHL 1963806, Genealogical Society of Utah, and baptism certificate dated May 8, 1894, reflecting May 4 birth, in Parrochia S.S. Salvatore, Palermo—certificate shows one godparent bore Rosa's mother's maiden name, Lo Forte; priest—Don Antonino Scianna, cited in **La Repubblica,** Jun. 13, 1987; Lercara Friddi—marriage register, Jan. 2, 1881, entry for Francesco Sinatra, son of Isidor Sinatra and Dorotea Siragusa, to Rosa Saglimbeni, daughter of Salvatore Saglimbeni and Angela Lo Forte, reflecting marriage on Dec. 30, 1880, Libro dei Matrimonia no. XV, 1881–1889, baptismal certificates for Francesco, Feb. 24, 1857, and for Rosa, Sep. 9, 1857, Libro dei Battesimi, Archivio Parrocchiale Maria S.S. della Neve, Lercara Friddi).

10–11 **Lercara Friddi: (background)** Finley et al., 160–, 192–, Nicolò Sangiorgio, **Lercara Friddi,** Palermo, Sicily: Edizioni Kefagrafica, 1991, 143–, Giuseppe Mavaro, **Dialogo tra un maestro ed i suoi alunni sulla storia di Lercara Friddi,** Lercara Friddi, Sicily: Biblioteca Comunale, 2002, corr. Nicolò Sangiorgio, int. Salvatore Lupo; **("core territory")** Alberto Consiglio, **Lucky Luciano,** Milan: Editrice A and G Marco, 1972, 11–, int. Salvatore Lupo; **(Corleone/mafiosi)** ibid., and Carl Sifakis, **The Mafia File,** Wellingborough (U.K.): Thorsons, 1987, 89, 223; **(Prizzi/stronghold)** Salvatore Lupo, **Storia della Mafia,** Rome: Donzelli, 1996, refs.; **(Luciano born)** Lupo, 29, Consiglio, 11–; **("without**

doubt") Sifakis, 200; **("head")** Virgil Peterson, **The Mob,** Ottawa, IL: Green Hill, 1983, 181; **("founder")** George Wolf with Joseph DiMona, **Frank Costello: Prime Minister of the Underworld,** New York: William Morrow, 1974, 95– and flap.

11 **Sinatras and Lucanias: (marriage/baptismal registers)** entries for the marriage of Francesco Sinatra and Rosa Saglimbeni and for Antonio Lucania and Rosalia Cafarelli/Capanelli, Apr. 1883, Libro dei Matrimonia no. XV, 1881–1889, entries for baptisms of Isidor (1884) and Salvatore (1887) Sinatra, Bartholomey (1891) and Salvatore (1897) Lucania, Libro dei Battesimi, Archivio Parrocchiale Maria S.S. della Neve, Lercara Friddi; **(lived same short street)** Sangiorgio to authors, Dec. 21, 2002, and Jan. 12, 2003, citing birth records of Salvatore Lucania and Isidoro Sinatra.

11–12 **address book/Saglimbeni:** "Agenda Personale di Lucania Salvatore," attachment to Cusack to Giordano, Jun. 20, 1962, LLBN. Antonino Saglimbeni and Rosa Saglimbeni, whom Francesco Sinatra was to marry, were second cousins, twice removed. Though in modern society in the urban United States and Europe this would be regarded as a distant relationship—and thus usually insignificant—in rural Sicily such relatives interact with each other regularly. In his book **From Caesar to the Mafia,** Luigi Barzini wrote: "Power has many sources. The first and nearest source is one's family. In Sicily the family includes relatives as far as the third, fourth, or fifth degree" (cousins—civil birth and marriage records for Lercara Friddi, 1719–1920, Genealogical Society of Utah—Antonino and Rosa were descendants of Salvatore Saglimbeni, corr. genealogist Katharine Kirkpatrick; "Power has"—Barzini, **Caesar,** 69); **(Francesco after wife's death) Photoplay,** Sep. 1956; **(age of ninety-one)** death certificate—other official data shows he was ninety-one at death, not sixty-four as reported in the press; **(Sinatra himself indicated)** FS int. by Sid Mark, Apr. 19, 1983, WPHT (Philadelphia, PA), **Photoplay,** Aug. 1945; **("very close") Photoplay,** Sep. 1956, citing Lee Bartletta Amorino; **("check back")** FS commentary during 1987 Italian tour, RAI UNO.

13 **Francesco: (could not read)** response in passenger manifest for S.S. **Spartan Prince,** Jul. 6, 1900, Ellis Island Foundation; **(shoemaker)** ibid., corr. Nicolò Sangiorgio, citing civil birth records of Isidor and Salvatore Sinatra, int. Rose Paldino, and see Sinatra,

My Father, 2—Francesco's son Marty (FS's father) was nicknamed "Tony the Shoemaker"; **(two sons)** baptismal records for Isidor and Salvatore Sinatra, corr. Nicolò Sangiorgio.

13 **desperate times: (going hungry)** Monroe, 107, 121–; **(riots/crime)** Sterling, 47, 133, Monroe, 123.

13 **Mafia's power: (western Sicily)** Monroe, 141, Barzini, **Italians,** 254, Nicholas Gage, **The Mafia Is Not an Equal Opportunity Employer,** New York: Dell, 1972, 34, Sterling, 44; **(Don Vito [Vito Cascioferro])** Barzini, **Italians,** 263, Sterling, 48, Peterson, **The Mob,** 482–, **Life,** Mar. 1985—but see Richard Gambino, **Blood of My Blood,** New York: Anchor Books, 1974, 277; **(Don Carlo [Calogero Vizzini])** Barzini, **Italians,** 268, Sterling, 52, 63; **(Accardo)** William Roemer, **Accardo,** New York: Donald Fine, 1995, 17; **(Gambino)** Ed Reid, **The Grim Reapers,** New York: Bantam, 1969, 287–; **(Giancana)** William Brashler, **The Don,** New York: Ballantine, 1977, 12–; **(Trafficante)** File Update, "Santo Trafficante, Jr.," Case 1-139, Aug. 24, 1977, Dade County Public Safety Department, Organized Crime Division.

13 **Palermo move:** "Last Residence" entry in S.S. **Spartan Prince** manifest.

13–14 **two sons born—die in cholera epidemic?:** A registry in the parish church in Brancaccio, Palermo, records the birth and baptism in 1889 of a boy named Giuseppe. Civil records show that another son, Antonino, was born in 1892. There is no record of his having been baptized, an indication that he may have died at birth or very soon thereafter. The authors located no further record of either of these children. The genealogist who specializes in Sicily states that it was customary, when a child bearing a traditional family name died, to give the next child the same name. This is almost certainly why Sinatra's father, born in 1894, was also named Antonino.

Study of the family genealogy establishes that the Sinatras' first child had been a daughter, Dorotea, born in Lercara Friddi in 1881. It seems that, like the two boys who died in Palermo, she, too, did not survive. The Sinatras also named their last child, a daughter, Dorotea, at her birth in 1899 (Giuseppe—baptism certificate, Dec. 8, 1889, Parrochia S.S. Salvatore, Palermo; Antonino—entry, civil birth records, Palermo, FHL 135000814, Genealogical Society of Utah, corr. Kathy Kirkpatrick; Dorotea—civil birth records, Dorotea Sinatra, Oct. 13, 1881,

Lercara Friddi, Palermo, Italia, FHL 1965252, Genealogical Society of Utah; cholera epidemic—int. Fr. Alerio Montalbano [priest], Parrochia S.S. Salvatore, Brancaccio, Palermo, a plaque on church commemorates cholera epidemic of early 1890s).

14 **emigration: (exodus)** Finley et al., 202, Nick Tosches, **Dino, Living High in the Dirty Business of Dreams,** New York: Delta, 1992, 6.

14 **Francesco journey/arrival:** S.S. **Spartan Prince** manifest.

14 **surviving Sinatra children:** At the time of his emigration to America, Francesco Sinatra and his wife, Rosa, had five living children. The eldest, Isidor, had been born in 1884, followed by Salvatore in 1887, Antonino (FS's father) in 1894, Angelina in 1896, and Dorotea in 1899 (baptism records for Isidor [Feb. 6, 1884] and Salvatore [Jan. 19, 1887], Libro dei Battesimi; immigration records for Antonino, Angelina, and Dorotea, passenger manifest, **Citta di Milano,** arriving Dec. 21, 1903, Ellis Island Foundation, which list ages at time of arrival in the United States).

14 **Isidor joined Francesco:** The authors did not locate a record of Isidor's arrival at Ellis Island, but he did join the family in the United States at some point. The Hoboken city directory for 1915 lists an Isidor Sinatra living at Francesco's address. According to Francesco's granddaughter Rose Paldino, he died young from diabetes.

14 **Salvatore/Rosa/children:** passenger manifests, S.S. **Marco Minghetti,** arriving Ellis Island on Jun. 2, 1902, and for **Citta di Milano,** Ellis Island Foundation, ints. Rose Sinatra Paldino, Hoboken city directories 1909–1930.

14–15 **Statue smiled:** FS address, **100th Birthday Tribute to the Statue of Liberty,** Jul. 3, 1986, videotape in authors' collection.

15 **hostility: (dirty)** David Evanier, **Making the Wiseguys Weep,** New York: Farrar, Straus and Giroux, 1998, 19; **(criminal)** Donald Clarke, **All or Nothing at All,** New York: Fromm, 2000, 3; **(epithets)** Evanier, 23, Pete Hamill, **Why Sinatra Matters,** Boston: Little, Brown, 1998, 38; **("not even white"/Sicily especially)** "Italians in America" (TV documentary), Greystones Communications for A&E, on History Channel, 1998, Gambino, 84–; **(Klan)** ibid., and **New Yorker,** Nov. 9, 1946; **(churches)** Michael Freedland, **All the Way,** London: Orion, 1998, 6.

15 **criminality: (fugitives)** Sterling, 49–; **(Don Vito)** ibid., and passenger manifest, S.S. **Champagne,** for arrival on Sep. 30, 1901; **(protection)** Sterling, 50, Barzini, **Italians,** 272–, John Cummings and Ernest Volkman, **Goombata,** Boston: Little, Brown, 1990, 23–, Gage, 44; **(Alo) Miami Herald,** Apr. 8, 2001.

16 **Luciano arrived:** The Lucania family's date of arrival has previously been reported variously as having been in either 1904, 1906, or 1907. U.S. Census data indicate that, like the Sinatras, they arrived in several stages. Lucanio's father arrived in 1906 and his wife and two of his children—including his son Salvatore, today remembered as "Lucky"—the following year (U.S. Census, 1920).

16 **"We was surrounded":** Martin Gosch and Richard Hammer, **The Last Testament of Lucky Luciano,** Boston: Little, Brown, 1975, 8, and see Tony Sciacca, **Luciano,** New York: Pinnacle Books, 1975, 16.

16 **Francesco/Rosa jobs: (shoemakers)** Hamill, 40; **(boilermaker/factory/grocery)** Sinatra, **Legend,** 15—Francesco is listed in the 1920 U.S. Census as grocery "proprietor."

16 **$11/$200 today:** Modern equivalents for dollar sums at earlier dates have been calculated according to data provided by Professor Robert Sahr of the Oregon State University Political Science Department and available on the **Columbia Journalism Review** website, www.cjr.org/tools/inflation.

16–17 **Hoboken: (resort)** Clarke, 4, "The Abridged History of Hoboken," hobokenmuseum.org; **(grubby industrial town)** Arnold Shaw, **Sinatra, Twentieth Century Romantic,** New York: Holt, Rhinehart and Winston, 1968, 9; **(Irish ran)** Freedland, 8; **(Italian territory)** Barzini, **Italians,** 272–, Chapman, 151; **(attack)** FS int. in **Sinatra: An American Original,** CBS News special, 1965; **(battle) NYT,** May 6, 1909.

18 **Isidor/grocery:** Hoboken city directory, 1915, 1918.

18 **Salvatore/baker:** int. daughter, Rose Paldino.

18–19 **Marty: (dropped out)** FS int. by Sidney Zion at seminar, Yale University, Apr. 15, 1986, videotape in authors' collection; **(illiterate)** ibid., Sinatra, **Legend,** 22, Tina Sinatra with Jeff Coplon, **My Father's Daughter,** New York: Simon and Schuster, 2000, 63, int. Rose Paldino; **("mushroom")** Kitty Kelley, **His Way,** New York: Bantam, 1986, 96; **(tattoos)** ibid., 9, **Esquire,** Apr. 1966; **(asthma)** Sinatra, **My Father,** 6, **Look,** May 14, 1957;

(gentle) Sinatra, **My Father,** 3, 5; **(silences)** Hamill, 71, and see Freedland, 16–; **(explosive temper)** Earl Wilson, **Sinatra: An Unauthorized Biography,** New York: Signet, 1977, 17; **(drink)** Robin Douglas-Home, **Sinatra,** London: Michael Joseph, 1962, 51; **(shoemaker)** Sinatra, **My Father,** 2; **("chauffeur")** FS birth certificate, Dec. 17, 1915, New Jersey Bureau of Vital Statistics; **(accident) Jersey Journal,** May 8, 1918; **(stolen goods)** Kelley, 1; **(boxer)** Sinatra, **Legend,** 15; **(Italian boxers)** Hickman Powell, **Lucky Luciano,** Secaucus, NJ: Arno, 1975, 70fn; **(sponsor)** FS int. by Zion.

19 **Natalina "Dolly" Garaventa:** birth certificate, Natalina Garaventa, Dec. 26, 1896, Comune di Lumarzo, Genoa, **Oggi,** Jul. 1987, ints. Julianna Casagranda, nephew Frank Monaco. As cited on her birth certificate, Dolly's full name was Natalina Maria Vittoria Garaventa. Her maiden name has been rendered variously over the years. On two official documents Dolly spelled it Garavanti. Her granddaughter Nancy used Garavente in her books about her father. The authors have used the spelling on Dolly's Italian birth certificate, Garaventa (FS birth certificate, pictured at Sinatra, **Legend,** 17, Natalie Sinatra, Social Security application, 151-32-9978, Nov. 1958).

19 **father a peasant:** data supplied by mayor's office, Comune di Lumarzo, Dec. 2002. Dolly's father has previously been referred to as having been a lithographer or a stonecutter for a lithographer before leaving Italy. The authors used the information supplied in Italy (int. Frank Monaco, Sinatra, **Legend,** 15, **[Rochester, NY] Democrat & Chronicle,** Jan. 8, 1977, Wilson, 16).

19–20 **Garaventa brothers: (Dominick) Jersey Journal,** Apr. 15, 1931, and see Bill Davidson to Asst. Dir. Louis Nichols, and Jones to Nichols, Jan. 23, 1957, FSFBI rereviewed for authors, 2004, int. Rose Paldino; **(Lawrence) Jersey Journal,** Apr. 15, 1931, Aug. 17, 19, 1946, Dec. 14, 1948, Jan. 15, 1949, **Jersey Observer,** Mar. 13, 1919, **NYT,** Feb. 1, 3, 4, 1922, ints. Frank Monaco, Anthony Petrozelli, James Petrozelli Jr., Rose Paldino, Nick Sevano, and see Kelley, 15, citing **Jersey Observer; (Gustavo)** Kelley, 527, 222, 1.

20 **Dolly described: (eyes and hair)** M/G int. of Nick Sevano, Ed Shirak, **Our Way,** Hoboken, NJ: Lepore's Publishing, 1995, 102, Shaw, 8, Tony Sciacca, **Sinatra,** New York: Pinnacle, 1976, 94;

(height) Sinatra, **Legend,** 16; **(dressed as boy)** ibid., 15, **Congressional Record,** Jun. 30, 1971, 22893; **(talked tough)** ints. Rose Paldino, Frank Monaco; **(never forgot)** Shaw, 10; **(English/dialects)** Hamill, 78; **(good organizer)** FS in **New York Daily News,** Jan. 17, 1982; **(singing)** Sciacca, **Sinatra,** 103, **Chicago's American,** Sep. 25, 1966; **(Clam Broth House)** Shirak, 102.

20–21 **Marty and Dolly: (met)** Hamill, 57; **(serenading)** "Frank Sinatra's Own Hit Parade," unpub. FS int. by Dorothy O'Leary, Mar. 24, 1948, MHL; **(brainier/bossy)** ints. Rose Paldino, Phyllis McGuire, Brad Dexter, Kelley, 24, **Sound Track,** undated c. 1976; **(ran away)** Sinatra, **Legend,** 15; **(Charlie)** int. Rose Paldino; **(slum?) Motion Picture,** Jun. 16, 1947, **American Weekly,** Jul. 20, 1952, int. Rose Paldino, Freedland, 7, Sciacca, **Sinatra,** 92; **(house described)** int. Rose Paldino; **(Dominick)** Sciacca, **Sinatra,** 92.

22 **Victrolas:** Hamill, 52, and "Recording Industry History," http://acusd.edu/gen/recording/notes.

Chapter 3: The Only Child

23 **"We were married": Look,** May 28, 1957.

23–24 **birth: (wintry)** FS in CBS News special; **(snow) NYT,** Dec. 12, 1915; **(table/ninety pounds)** FS in CBS News special; **(birth)** ibid., Sinatra, **Legend,** 16, **Look,** May 28, 1957, Wilson, 14; **(women)** int. Frank Monaco, Shirak, 103—neighbor was Margaret Fiore; **("I don't think")** Sciacca, **Sinatra,** 93; **(unable to bear more children)** FS int. by Zion, **Goldmine,** Mar. 22, 1991; **(scars)** Sinatra, **Legend,** 17, ints. Peggy Connelly, Tony Oppedisano; **(makeup) Look,** May 14, 1957, ints. Peter Levinson, George Jacobs and William Stadiem, **Mr. S: My Life with Frank Sinatra,** New York: Harper, 2003, 56; **(gratitude)** FS in CBS News special; **(tried to attack)** Sinatra, **My Father,** 282, J. Randy Taraborrelli, **Sinatra: A Complete Life,** New York: Birch Lane, 1997, 12; **("They weren't thinking")** int. Peggy Connelly.

24–25 **birth certificate/"Francis A.":** Sinatra, **Legend,** 17. Nancy Sinatra's book **Legend** states flatly that Frank Sinatra was named after his godfather, Frank Garrick. Other sources suggest he was named Frank purely by accident, his parents having decided to call the baby Martin. Far more likely is that the name was selected to honor his paternal grandfather, Francesco, as was the Italian custom.

The invitations to Sinatra's first wedding include the middle initial "A.," as does his 1943 draft card and a reregistration of his birth filed in 1945. In 1976, in yet another reregistration, it was formally specified that the singer's second name was Albert. Sinatra himself reportedly said as late as 1947 that he had no middle name (Garrick—Sinatra, **Legend,** 16; by accident—Taraborrelli, 7; custom—corr. Kathy Kirkpatrick, int. cousin Rose Paldino, whose eldest brother was also named Frank in honor of their grandfather Sinatra; middle name—Sinatra, **Legend,** 17, Freedland, 5, Don Dwiggins, **Frankie,** New York: Paperback Library, 1961, 92, "Frank Albert Sinatra," Selective Service registration card, #2615).

25 **"God loves you":** Wilson, 14–.

25 **baby photographs:** Sinatra, **Legend,** 16—not available for use in this book.

25 **Josie:** Sciacca, **Sinatra,** 93.

25 **"I didn't care"/Francesco/grandmother: Look,** May 28, Jun. 11, 1957, **Photoplay,** Sep. 1956.

26 **"bit of a sissy":** Kelley, 20, citing Kathryn Buhan.

26 **draft:** Draft Registration Records, Hoboken, NJ, 1917–18, microfilms 1712108/09/10.

26 **Dolly: (volunteered) Star,** citing Hoboken Library FS exhibit, undat., 1986, and see **The Worker,** Nov. 25, 1945; **(chained)** Sinatra with Coplon, 11; **("I was asked") Look,** May 28, 1957, **Photoplay,** Sep. 1956; **(influence)** Freedland, 11–, **Time,** Aug. 25, 1965, Gerry Romero, **Sinatra's Women,** New York: Manor, 1976, 22, **Woman's Home Companion,** May 1956, Sciacca, **Sinatra,** 94, int. Nick Sevano; **("godmother")** int. Anthony Petrozelli.

27 **Dolly and politicians/mayors:** Hoboken Historical Museum **Newsletter,** Mar./Apr. 1987, **Hoboken History,** iss. 17, 1997, Warren Strickle, **New Jersey Democracy and the Urban Coalition, 1919–1932,** Washington, D.C.: Georgetown University, unpub. doc. diss., May 1971, eds. Edward Foster and Geoffrey Clark, **Hoboken,** New York: Irvington, 1976, 63–, "General Crime Survey: Newark Field Division," May 13, 1944, FBI 62-75147-31-2. The mayors were Bernard McFeeley (Hoboken) and Frank Hague (Jersey City); **("buying votes")** Sinatra with

Coplon, 11; **("Marty wasn't smart enough")** int. Rose Paldino; **(tease)** Sinatra, **Legend,** 18.

27 **FS carrying placards: Chicago's American,** Sep. 25, 1966, and Seymour Hersh, **The Dark Side of Camelot,** Boston: Little, Brown, 1997, 139. Though Tina Sinatra said her father carried placards for the Democrats before he could read the words on them, FS himself said his first campaigning was when he took part in a parade for Al Smith at the age of twelve. That would have been in 1928, when Smith, having been four times elected governor of New York, ran for the presidency. Given Dolly Sinatra's affiliation to corrupt local politicians, and the Sinatra links to Lucky Luciano, it is interesting that Smith reportedly solicited Luciano's help during the campaign. According to Luciano's associate Frank Costello, Smith again met with Luciano during the 1932 presidential contest. If the adult Sinatra became aware of such contacts as the years passed, the Kennedy involvement with the Mafia years later—in which Sinatra played go-between—may not have seemed out of the ordinary ("I marched"—Sinatra, **Legend,** 149, and see **Chicago's American,** Sep. 25, 1966; Smith/Luciano—Gosch and Hammer, 98–, Wolf with DiMona, 97–, Sciacca, **Luciano,** 108–).

27 **Dolly midwife: (directory)** Hoboken city directory, 1925–26, 126; **(Kelley)** Kelley, 25–, 32; **(arrested)** Jones to Nichols, Jan. 23, 1957, and Bill Davidson to Lou Nichols, Jan. 23, 1957, FSFBI, Taraborrelli, 26–, and see family acknowledgment at Friedwald, 62; **("Hatpin Dolly") Star,** undat. 1986; **(FS barred)** Clarke, 19, Friedwald, 62; **(other memories)** ints. Anthony Petrozelli, Nick Sevano, James and Angela Petrozelli, Ed Shirak, Joe Spaccavento, Rose Ellman Sinatra, Al Certo, cited in Evanier, 47.

28 **farmed out:** Sinatra, **Legend,** 17–, Sinatra, **My Father,** 4, George Carpozi, **Frank Sinatra: Is This Man Mafia?** New York: Manor, 1979, 10.

28 **Mrs. Golden: Look,** May 28, 1957, **Woman's Home Companion,** May 1956, **Good Housekeeping,** Jun. 1964, Wilson, 17, 360. Mrs. Golden's name is also variously rendered as Goldman and Goldberg, but Golden predominates; **(Rose)** Sciacca, **Sinatra,** 94, 97, Clarke, 17.

28 **FS and Yiddish/Italian:** Friedwald, 61–, 62n1. Two Italian-American friends, entertainer Sonny King and singer Dean Martin, have commented on Sinatra's grasp of the language. King said

he picked up a few words in childhood, and occasionally came out with an Italian catchphrase. Dean Martin recalled speaking Italian with Sinatra, Vic Damone, and Nick Conte, "'cause we didn't want others to listen to what we were talking about." Sinatra told an audience: "I don't know enough Italian to speak to you in Italian." Though he had little Italian, it is not accurate to say that he "never spoke a word" of the language, as Ava Gardner was to suggest (int. Sonny King, Dean Martin cited in Oriana Fallaci, **The Egotists,** Chicago: Regnery, 1968, 163, FS commentary on 1987 Italian tour, RAI UNO, Ava Gardner, **My Story,** New York: Bantam, 1990, 151).

28–29 **Dolly/material things: (bikes)** Time, Aug. 19, 1955; **(toys/Catskills)** LAHE, Sciacca, **Sinatra,** 98, Carpozi, 10, Alan Frank, **Sinatra,** New York: Leon Amiel, 1978, 13; **(clothes)** ibid., Freedland, 13, int. Nick Sevano; **("velvet pants")** Sinatra, **My Father,** 5; **(Geismar's) New Jersey Monthly,** Feb. 1982; **(Tredy)** Sinatra, **My Father,** 7; **(solitary figure)** Kelley, 16, Clarke, 11.

29 **ashtray/cleanliness: (Dolly) Woman's Home Companion,** May 1956; **(FS) Look,** May 14, 1957; **("Lady Macbeth")** Shaw, 10; **("fanatic")** int. Tony Oppedisano; **(money/"I can't") Look,** May 14, 1957, draft for **Movieland,** Jun. 11, 1945, MHL; **(glasses)** int. Peter Levinson.

30 **"We were on the beach":** draft for **Movieland,** Oct. 1945, MHL.

30 **"always expected":** Nancy Barbato Sinatra, cited in "Sinatra's Song," **Sinatra Music Society,** 2000, www.sinatra-ms.com.

30 **"Dad took it out": Photoplay,** Aug. 1945. This beating by his father was apparently an exception. Elsewhere, FS said his father never laid a hand on him (Sinatra, **My Father,** 5).

30 **Dolly beatings: (grown stout)** photo in Sinatra, **Legend,** 18; **(falling down stairs)** Sinatra, **My Father,** 4; **(Tina's version)** Sinatra with Coplon, 54; **("She used to beat")** ints. Rose Paldino, Rose Ellman Sinatra; **("give me a rap")** Hamill, 84; **("When she came close")** "The Two Sinatras," usnews.com, May 25, 1998.

31 **Dolly/adult FS: ("Yes, mama") Look,** Jun. 11, 1957; **("Okay, mom")** int. Peter Levinson; **("avoiding")** int. Peggy Connelly; **("She was a pisser")** Shirley MacLaine, **My Lucky Stars,** New York: Bantam, 1995, 85; **(devastated)** Sinatra, **Legend,** 252–, int. Rock Brynner; **(only children)** Robert Needham, MD,

"Only Children," Benjamin Spock, MD, "Spoiling, Why We Do It," www.drspock.com.

32 **World War I/Hoboken: (troopships)** Freedland, 8, **The Official Record of the United States Part in the Great War,** U.S. Government, chap. 3, 35–; **("Heaven, Hell")** "The Abridged History of Hoboken," Hoboken Museum; **(bars closed)** Kelley, 13; **(bars sprang up)** M/G int. of Nick Sevano, **Hoboken History,** iss. 17, 1997, Hoboken Vigilance Committee to President Herbert Hoover, Jul. 1, 1929, Larson Papers, Box 21, Bk. 151, New Jersey State Archives.

32–33 **Marty's bar: (money borrowed) New York,** Apr. 28, 1980, Carpozi, 9; **("bar and grill")** FS int. by Zion, Hamill, 77; **(bounce drunks)** M/G int. of Nick Sevano, int. John Marotta, Hamill, 84; **(Marty/horse)** Sinatra, **My Father,** 3, int. Rose Paldino; **("a quiet, gentle guy")** int. Tony Oppedisano.

33 **Prohibition/Sinatras: ("new ball game")** Wolf with DiMona, 33; **(key transit point)** Sciacca, **Sinatra,** 93, **Hoboken History,** iss. 17, 1997, Wolf with DiMona, 48, Shaw, 9.

33–34 **"He aided":** FS int. by Zion. The timing of this incident is unclear. In his Yale interview, Sinatra indicated that it preceded the opening of his father's bar, but the Sinatras are said to have opened the bar "before Prohibition." That could mean before Prohibition came to New Jersey in 1917, or before national Prohibition, which began in January 1920.

34 **Marty/Waxey Gordon: ("one of the tough guys")** FS int. by Zion; **("rub elbows")** Sinatra, **Legend,** 22; **(Luciano)** Sciacca, **Luciano,** 65–, Sifakis, 143, Jonathan Van Meter, **The Last Good Time,** New York: Crown, 2003, 48, **(Bologna, Italy) Il Resto del Carlino,** Nov. 20, 1954; **("a regular")** Hamill, 80.

34 **FS in bar: (homework)** int. Tony Oppedisano; **(sing)** Hamill, 87, and FS cited on cbsnews.com, May 19, 1998.

35 **Dominick/Lawrence:** see chapter 2; **(Dolly close)** ints. Frank Monaco, Rose Paldino; **(Lawrence selling liquor) Jersey Observer,** Mar. 13, 1919.

35 **American Express murder:** NYT, Feb. 1, 1922. Pete Hamill, at p. 73, and Kitty Kelley, at p. 14–, wrote that this incident involved a "Railway Express" driver. According to the **New York Times** of Feb. 1, 1922, it was an American Express messenger who was killed; **(other holdups/murder)** ibid.; **(policeman shot)** NYT, Feb. 4, 1922; **(killer named) Jersey Journal,** Jan. 31,

1922—the Gordon associate was Carl Rettich, ibid., and **Providence Sunday Journal**, Apr. 28, 1935, **Providence Journal**, Feb. 14, 1950; **(trial)** Hamill, 73, Kelley, 14–.

35 **Lawrence after prison: (lived with Sinatras)** int. Frank Monaco; **(FS adored) Jersey City Chronicle**, Jul. 22, 1978, **Star**, Nov. 27, 1979; **(shootout) Jersey Journal**, Apr. 15, 1931—car was found at 415 Madison Street, while the Monaco family home was at 417/418 Madison; **(FS/Josie) Look**, May 28, 1957; **(father-in-law/liquor violations case)** int. Frank Monaco, **Hudson Observer**, Feb. 20, 1919; **(gangster gunned down)** Sinatra, **Legend**, 22—the gangster was Joe Miotta, **Look**, May 28, 1957; **(Schultz used Italians)** Jack Lait and Lee Mortimer, **Chicago Confidential**, New York: Crown, 1950, 169; **(Luciano)** Sciacca, **Luciano**, 113, Leonard Katz, **Uncle Frank**, London: W. H. Allen, 1974, 95—though eventually, in 1935, he was a prime suspect in Schultz's murder.

36 **other gangsters: ("My dad grew up")** Hersh, 138; **(Fischettis)** ints. Matthew Donohue, Bob Buccino, Hoboken city directories 1915–62, U.S. Census, 1920 and 1930, int. and corr. Rocco Fischetti, "Joseph John Fischetti," memo, Jul. 24, 1972, FBI 92-3024, 15, "Misc. Information Crime Survey," Sep. 26, 1946, FBI 62-8861-531; **(close to FS)** int. Anthony Petrozelli; **(Fischettis in touch)** ints. David Fagen, Jack Clarke, "Biographical Summary," Jul. 16, 1957, "Joseph John Fischetti," memo, Jul. 24, 1972, FBI 92-3024, 15, Rocco Fischetti File, FBI 63-HQ-599-10, Chicago Field Office Report, Rocco Fischetti, Dec. 23, 1967, FBI 92-2915—1, Apr. 24, 1964, FBI 92-2915-48, Virgil Peterson, **Barbarians in Our Midst**, Boston: Little, Brown, 1952, 158; **(Joe "Stingy")** Lait and Mortimer, 183; **("top hoodlum")** "Correlation Summary," Feb. 25, 1969, FSFBI; **(entertainment industry)** Assistant Attorney General Herbert Miller to William Hundley, Jan. 22, 1964, Department of Justice, Organized Crime Division, 70A-3642-71; **(close companion) Wall Street Journal**, Aug. 19, 1968, ints. Peggy Connelly, Peggy Maley; **("youngsters")** "Joseph John Fischetti" memo, Feb. 28, 1963, citing interview of Fischetti, FBI 92-3024-58, p. 15; **(Alo) Miami Herald**, Apr. 8, 2001, int. Ken Roberts.

37 **Sinatras moved up: (apartment)** Sinatra, **My Father**, 5.

37–38 **firefighter:** "Sinatra Tour," Hoboken Historical Museum, Freedland, 6, Fire Department records, Hoboken Fire Department

Museum, (Newark, NJ) **Sunday Star Ledger,** Jan. 26, 1969, **Esquire,** Apr. 1966, **New Yorker,** Nov. 9, 1946. Marty Sinatra was promoted to captain at the Hoboken Fire Department in 1944; **(joke) Hoboken History,** issue 17, 1997.

38 **kept Marty O'Brien's going:** "Sinatra Tour," Hoboken Historical Museum, Sinatra, **My Father,** 35–.

38 **FS childhood from age twelve: ("grand piano") Photoplay,** Sep. 1956; **("blending saxophones")** George Simon, **The Big Bands,** London: Collier-Macmillan, 1967, vii; **(Marty's mother)** int. Rose Paldino, Rose Sinatra death certificate—the powerful earthquake was the same day, Feb. 28, 1925; **(Francesco) Photoplay,** Sep. 1956; **("sweet old gent"/exhortations)** ibid., Aug. 1945; **("Pops's whole life") Photoplay,** Sep. 1956; **(clothes)** Freedland, 13, **Time,** Aug. 29, 1955, Carpozi, 11; **(gifts to friends)** Shaw, 10, Shirak, 81, **Look,** May 28, 1957; **(Silvers)** ibid.; **(car)** Carpozi, 15, Wilson, 20, Kelley, 27; **("prince")** M/G int. Nick Sevano.

39–40 **schooling: (trouble)** Shirak, 9; **(cousin Sam)** Sinatra, **My Father,** 5, int. Rose Ellman Sinatra; **(certificate)** Sinatra, **Legend,** 21; **("lazy"/"No talent")** Kelley, 27; **(record card) Look,** May 28, 1957; **("School was very uninteresting")** American Weekly, Jul. 27, 1952; **(cut classes)** Freedland, 15–; **(Hudson Burlesque)** int. Frank Monaco.

40 **dropped out?/expelled?:** NYT, Jun. 30, 1981, **Photoplay,** Sep. 1956, **American Weekly,** Jul. 27, 1952. Hoboken had a junior and senior high school system in those days. Students attended junior high school through the end of ninth grade. Sinatra began at Demarest High School in the tenth grade—apparently in February 1931 (NYT, Jun. 30, 1981, Shaw, 7, int. Frank Monaco).

40–41 **FS trouble in youth: ("Angles"/pigeons/cat) Time,** Aug. 29, 1955; **(firecrackers)** Shirak, 103; **(cherry bombs)** ints. Rock Brynner, George Jacobs, **Star,** Feb. 17, 1976, citing Peter Lawford; **("a bunch of us") Photoplay,** Aug. 1945; **(other stories)** American Weekly, Jul. 27, 1952; **("All I knew"/"The kids")** **Cosmopolitan,** May 1956, **American Weekly,** Jul. 27, 1952.

42–44 **violence/fighting: (Klan) Photoplay,** Oct. 1945; **("I would hear")** Hamill, 38; **("I skirted")** FS int. in CBS News special; **("A big kid")** Wilson, 17; **("bitter, bloody") Ebony,** Jul. 1958; **("everyone carried")** Freedland, 9; **("Sometimes")** Hamill, 49; **(buck teeth)** draft for **Movieland,** Aug. 15, 1946, MHL; **("a**

Coke bottle") ibid.—another version of this story suggests it was a milk bottle, Don Dwiggins, 5; **(bicycle chain?) Cosmopolitan,** May 1956; **("I was hit")** draft for **Movieland,** Aug. 15, 1946, MHL; **(Dominick)** Sciacca, **Sinatra,** 102; **("used to show")** Hamill, 58; **("I was five") Jersey Journal,** Apr. 25, 1983; **("My favorite exercise")** draft for **Movieland,** Jun. 11, 1945, MHL; **(publicity photos) New Jersey Monthly,** Feb. 1982; **(worked out/gyms)** Shaw, 57; **("ownership" of heavyweights)** draft **Movieland,** Jun. 11, 1945, draft for **Blue Ribbon,** undated 1943, MHL; **("Anybody hits you")** FS to Sammy Cahn, Oct. 29, 1991, courtesy of Tita Cahn; **("gang fights"/"plainclothesmen") American Weekly,** Jul. 27, 1952, **Cosmopolitan,** May 1956; **("Many of the kids") Parade,** Jan. 12, 1964; **("Everyone in my")** Kelley, 142; **(reform school/jail) Photoplay,** Aug. 1945; **(Sevano)** M/G int. of Nick Sevano; **("no gang fights")** Sciacca, **Sinatra,** 12.

44 **"never had a fight":** Westbrook Pegler column in **New York Journal-American,** Sep. 13, 1960—Pegler misidentified the speaker as "Frank Garavanti [sic]." According to Frank Monaco, who was present during the conversation, he was in fact Lawrence "Buddy" Garaventa, Sinatra's cousin; **("That stuff") Look,** May 28, 1957.

45–46 **parents' career hopes: ("Her way"/"terribly upset")** int. Rose Paldino. Sinatra's daughter Nancy, in her book **Legend,** ascribes a different response to Dolly. According to her, Dolly had wanted her son to become the family's first college graduate. The authors, however, have accepted the account of Rose Paldino, Sinatra's contemporary. In 1985, when Sinatra was almost seventy, he would receive an honorary doctorate in engineering from the Stevens Institute. Many undergraduates signed a petition objecting to the honor, noting that he had no distinction in the field of engineering and alluding to his recent run-in with the New Jersey Casino Control Commission (Dolly—Sinatra, **Legend,** 20; honorary doctorate—**Jersey Journal,** May 10, 1985); **(drawing/father hoped) Star,** May 6, 1986, draft for **Movieland,** Sep. 11, 1954, MHL, intro. by Tina Sinatra, **A Man and His Art: Frank Sinatra,** New York: Random House, 1991, viii; **(FS had encouraged)** Sinatra, **Legend,** 20–; **("I didn't want")** ibid., 22, 21; **("If I had the chance")** ed. Guy Yarwood, **Sinatra in His Own Words,** London: Omnibus, 1982, 14, and see ints. Nick Sevano, Tony Oppedisano, Rock Brynner; **("cellophane")** int. Frank Sinatra Jr., undated, Arnold Shaw Collection, University of Nevada, Las Vegas; **("He craved")** int. Brad Dexter; **("that there was only") Photoplay,** Aug. 1945.

46 **first jobs: (Casey Jones School) New Jersey Monthly,** Feb. 1982; **(Drake)** Shaw, 7, **Goldmine,** Mar. 22, 1991; **(*Jersey Observer*) New Yorker,** Nov. 9, 1946, **Metronome,** May 1943, Sinatra's Diamond Jubilee World Tour program, **Look,** May 28, 1957 (citing Mrs. Charles Brody, editor's widow), Kelley, 28, 500, and see FS entry in **Who's Who in America, 1948.**

47 **desirable part of town:** "Sinatra Tour," Hoboken Historical Museum, author's visit, int. Frank Monaco, Sarah Vowell, **Take the Cannoli,** New York: Simon and Schuster, 2000, 74—the address was 841 Garden Street.

47 **FS yearnings: ("Be proud")** Wilson, 17; **(resented) Photoplay,** Aug. 1945; **(*la via vecchia*)** Gambino, 3–, and see excellent analysis at Hamill, 50; **("shoemakers") Newsweek,** Jul. 23, 1945; **("an affinity")** int. Tony Oppedisano; **("mudhole") Philadelphia Inquirer,** May 6, 1984; **("sewer")** Vowell, 73; **("just wanted")** Hamill, 51; **(trains as child) A Man and His Art,** x, Taraborrelli, 489, **USA Weekend,** Dec. 18, 1988; **(train room)** int. Jackie Jordan, **Architectural Digest,** Dec. 1998, Jacobs and Stadiem, 247; **(ferries)** transcript, FS int. for **Larry King Live,** CNN, May 19, 1998, rerun of 1988 program; **(photograph)** Shirak, first picture section.

49 **FS meets Nancy Barbato:** FS twice said early on that "the year I met Nancy" was "the summer I was fifteen," which would date their meeting as summer 1931. Passages in his daughter Nancy's book **Frank Sinatra: An American Legend** have placed the meeting later. This quotes her mother as saying she and FS had dated for four and a half years before their marriage in 1939, a reference perhaps to when the relationship became serious rather than to their initial meeting. We have used Sinatra's own early recollection as to their meeting (draft for **Movieland,** Oct. 1945, MHL, **Photoplay,** Sep. 1945, Sinatra, **Legend,** 22, 33).

49–50 **Nancy Barbato: (dance)** Kelley, 27; **(fourteen)** Nancy was born Mar. 25, 1917; **(Long Branch)** int. Frank Monaco, **Photoplay,** Sep. 1945; **("The first time")** ibid.; **("That summer")** draft for **Movieland,** Oct. 1945, MHL; **(snow) Redbook,** Oct. 1951; **(background)** U.S. Census, Jersey City, NJ, 1915, 1920, and 1930; **(Barbatos' welcome)** Sinatra with Coplon, 18, **Redbook,** Oct. 1951, Sinatra, **Legend,** 24; **("I was a poor")** **American Weekly,** Jul. 20, 1952.

Chapter 4: "I'm Going to Be a Singer"

52–53 **music in childhood: ("Sometimes I think")** Hamill, 98; **(parents' bar)** FS address, Zion Lecture Series; **(family and music)** Sciacca, **Sinatra,** 103, int. Rose Paldino; **(Dolly/guitar)** Frank, 13; **(cousin)** Sinatra, **My Father,** 17—cousin was Fred Tredy, int. Frank Monaco; **(Ray Sinatra) Variety,** Nov. 7, 1980; **(St. Francis's)** Freedland, 15, int. Rose Paldino, **Metronome,** May 1943, **Chicago's American,** Sep. 25, 1966; **("at some hotel") Life,** Jun. 25, 1971; **(Lawrence) Jersey Dispatch,** Jun. 23, 1977; **(Dominick/ukulele)** Sciacca, **Sinatra,** 103, and see **Variety,** Jan. 27, 1989, int. Tony Oppedisano; **("He was the only")** Carpozi, 22; **(serenaded Nancy)** Dwiggins, 9, Sinatra, **Legend,** 22; **("The cheers kept") Chicago's American,** Sep. 25, 1966; **(baby grand/phone)** Sinatra, **Legend,** 21; **(society page)** Kelley, 31; **(a few jobs)** Sinatra, **Legend,** 21–.

53–54 **first appearances: ("In exchange")** Kelley, 33–, and see draft for **Movieland,** Jun. 11, 1945, MHL; **(Marty allowed)** M/G int. of Nick Sevano; **(Madison Street) Chicago's American,** Sep. 25, 1966; Sciacca, **Sinatra,** 104; **(social clubs/women's groups)** Dwiggins, 7, **Wall Street Journal,** May 19, 1998, **New Jersey Monthly,** Feb. 1982, **Look,** May 28, 1957; **(parties/meetings)** "Old Blue Eyes at 75!" Starlog Communications, 1990; **Chicago's American,** Sep. 25, 1966; **("I performed")** Sinatra's Diamond Jubilee World Tour program; **(Fabian's Follies)** "Sinatra Tour," Hoboken Historical Museum; **(Cockeyed Henny's) New Jersey Monthly,** Feb. 1982; **("Frankie would sneak in")** int. and corr. Rocco Fischetti; **(Catholic Union)** Michael Immerso, **Newark's Little Italy,** New Brunswick, NJ: Rutgers University Press; 1997, 118; **("People began")** FS int. by Zion; **("monologist") Life,** Apr. 23, 1965.

55–56 **Bing Crosby: ("A short time")** Sciacca, **Sinatra,** 104. Sinatra's Aunt Josie, who said she remembered it "like it was yesterday," placed the Crosby concert as having occurred at the Paramount in New York City, "in the summer he was seventeen"—which was 1933. The singer's early biographer, Arnold

Shaw, dated the Crosby appearance to March 1933. An article drawing on a 1943 interview of FS suggests it took place in 1935, as did a later quotation of his wife Nancy. E. J. Kahn of the **New Yorker,** writing in 1946, suggested it was in 1936. Several sources place the concert in a Jersey City vaudeville house, while FS, in a 1948 interview, referred to having made the decision after seeing a Crosby movie (Josie—Sciacca, **Sinatra,** 104; Shaw—Shaw, Sinatra, 13; 1943 interview—**Blue Ribbon;** Nancy—Sinatra, **Legend,** 25; Kahn—**New Yorker,** Nov. 9, 1946, and see **Cosmopolitan,** May 1956; Crosby movie?—**Silver Screen,** Mar. 24, 1948); **(Most people") Saturday Evening Post,** Aug. 24, 1946; **("Someday")** Sinatra, **Legend,** 25; **(FS recalled)** Murray Frymer article, Sinatra Society of Las Vegas, undat., Feb. 1980, corr. George Giacomini, University of Santa Clara; **("From the time"/"Will Rogers") Chicago's American,** Sep. 25, 1966, **Billboard,** Nov. 20, 1965; **(songs to make love to)** Sheilah Graham, **My Hollywood,** London: Michael Joseph, 1984, 44; **("the biggest thing"/"Bing was my first")** Hamill, 100, unid. clip, ?Variety, Aug. 1943, MHL; **("standing on street corners")** Freedland, 16, and see Sciacca, **Sinatra,** 105; **("My father said")** int. James Petrozelli; **(publicity photo—1938) Star,** May 6, 1986; **(rehearsals)** E. J. Kahn, **The Voice: The Story of an American Phenomenon,** New York: Harper, 1946, 11; **("sang so easily"/"He was so relaxed") Blue Ribbon,** ca. 1943, MHL, Hamill, 88.

57 **parents' reaction: ("threw a shoe")** Carpozi, 18; **("obsessed")** M/G int. of Nick Sevano; **("I remember") A Conversation with Frank Sinatra,** Bill Boggs, Metromedia TV, 1975, and see **LAHE,** Sep. 27, 1975; **("He didn't speak")** FS int. by Zion.

57 **FS left home:** Douglas-Home, 21. In her book **Legend,** Sinatra's daughter Nancy dates her father's eviction to early 1932, when he was sixteen. In an earlier interview, however, Sinatra himself recalled having left home when he was seventeen—which means the very last days of 1932, or in 1933 (Sinatra, **Legend,** 21–, Douglas-Home, 21); **("They call me") New York Post,** Apr. 11, 1947; **(sound system) Redbook,** Oct. 1951, Carpozi, 18, Shaw, 14.

58 **megaphones/microphones: (Vallee)** Simon, 501; **("like it was part")** Freedland, 22, citing John Marotta; **("Guys would throw")** Bill Boggs int.; **(Crosby/microphone)** Steve Schoen-

herr, "Recording Technology History," http://history.acusd.edu; **("I discovered very early")** Hamill, 97–; **("tightly gripping")** Kahn, 14; **(left the stage)** Granata, x; **(secret weapon)** ed. Leonard Mustazza, **Frank Sinatra and Popular Culture,** Westport, CT: Praeger, 1998, 119; **("speech-level singing")** Gene Lees, **Singers and the Song II,** New York: Oxford University Press, 1998, 97; **("with great economy"/"black one")** ed. Yarwood, 37; **(With a microphone/Vidal)** cbsnews.com, May 15, 1998; **("To Sinatra")** John Lahr, **Sinatra: The Artist and the Man,** New York: Random House, 1997, 14; **(room in NYC)** Sinatra, **Legend,** 21; **("I went around")** Douglas-Home, 21; **(Macy's)** Larry King int.; **(Roseland)** FS int. by Arlene Francis, Sep. 25, 1981, WOR (NY).

60 **52nd Street: (described)** Arnold Shaw, **52nd Street: The Street of Jazz,** Cambridge, MA: Da Capo, 1977—first published as **The Street That Never Slept; (Crosby)** Shaw, **Sinatra,** 6, ed. Ethlie Ann Vare, **Legend: Frank Sinatra and the American Dream,** New York: Boulevard, 1995, 154; **("jazzmen") Ebony,** Jul. 1958; **("Talent")** ibid.; **(heard Holiday/When he first/accolade)** ibid., FS cited in **Melody Maker,** Oct. 18, 1958; **("shading") New York,** Apr. 28, 1980, Donald Clarke, **Wishing on the Moon,** New York: Viking, 1994, 225; **("lived inside")** Hamill, 115; **(female Sinatra)** Freedland, 66; **(Goodman/Onyx/Dorsey)** Shaw, **52nd Street,** 19, 61, 68–; **(speakeasies)** ibid., x; **(gangsters' penetration)** int. NJ State Organized Crime Division investigator Bob Buccino, Clarke, **Wishing on the Moon,** 93; **(nightspots/Luciano)** Gosch and Hammer, 153—he favored Dave's Blue Room, and see Shaw, **52nd Street,** references to Dave's Blue Room; **(Costello)** Irving Lazar with Annette Tapert, **Swifty,** New York: Simon and Schuster, 1995, 49, Wolf with DiMona, 97, and see **Collier's,** Apr. 12, 1947; **(Moretti)** Evanier, 45, Gosch and Hammer, 48–, Richard Hammer, **The Illustrated History of Organized Crime,** Philadelphia, PA: Courage Books, 1989, 86; **(Schultz)** int. Marie Marcus, Lazar with Tapert, 48, "Marie Marcus Biography," www.reostudios.com, Peterson, **Barbarians,** 216, Gosch and Hammer, 187.

62 **"a kind of ":** FS int. by Zion.

62 **efforts to get work: (sheet music)** Shaw, **Sinatra,** 14, Kelley, 34; **(stage fright/"I swear") New Yorker,** Nov. 9, 1946, Larry King

int. of FS, May 19, 1998 (rerun); **(amateur contests)** Shaw, 13–, Dwiggins, 14; **(WAAT)** Sciacca, **Sinatra,** 105, Friedwald, 63.

63–64 **Three Flashes/audition: (frequented bar)** Sinatra, **My Father,** 14; **("Frank hung around")** Sciacca, **Sinatra,** 105, **New Jersey Monthly,** Feb. 1982; **(Dolly role)** ints. Anthony Petrozelli, James Jr. and Angela Petrozelli, Rose Tamburro, Rose Paldino, **Look,** May 28, 1957, citing James Petrozelli Sr.—the latter later reversed himself and said there was no pressure from Dolly (Sciacca, **Sinatra,** 106); **(now four/"Shine")** corr. Ric Ross, **New Jersey Monthly,** Feb. 1982; **(solo lines)** Friedwald, 64; **("Night and Day") Silver Screen,** Mar. 24, 1948.

64 **Hoboken Four: ("fools") New Jersey Monthly,** Feb. 1982; **(applause)** Romero, 27; **($75)** Sinatra, **My Father,** 15, but $50 according to Sinatra, **Legend,** 25; **(tour route)** Freedland, 31–, Sciacca, **Sinatra,** 106; **(without rehearsal)** ibid., 107; **("He got so good")** ibid., 109–; **("Frank stood out")** ibid., 107; **("He could get")** Carpozi, 206; **(beatings)** Sciacca, **Sinatra,** 107–, Evanier, 48, int. James Petrozelli Jr.; **(unconscious) New Jersey Monthly,** Feb. 1982; **("got homesick") Silver Screen,** Mar. 24, 1948, Sinatra, **Legend,** 25; **(Three Flashes later) New Jersey Monthly,** Feb. 1982, int. Rose Tamburro; **("made me stick") Silver Screen,** Mar. 24, 1948.

67–68 **further search for work: ("panic period")** Simon, viii; **(Comfort's)** corr. Bill Kelly; **(Union Club)** Shaw, **Sinatra,** 15, Fred Dellar, **Sinatra, His Life and Times,** London: Omnibus Press, 1995, "Sinatra Tour," Hoboken Historical Museum; **("Minstrel Show")** program, Dec. 11–12, 1936, kindly supplied to authors by Ric Ross; **(Rich/WNEW/WOR/WAAT)** Shaw, **Sinatra,** 15, Freedland, 34, ints. Tony Mottola, John Marotta, **Metro Newark,** Apr. 1981; **(Ray Sinatra)** Dwiggins, 11–, Taraborrelli, 25; **("cream cheese") New York Post,** Apr. 11, 1947; **("one basic theory")** Douglas-Home, 21.

68–69 **Sevano/Sanicola: (meeting Sanicola)** M/G int. of Nick Sevano, int. Lucille Kirk Buccini, **Billboard,** Nov. 20, 1965, ed. Yarwood, 124; **(banged away) Modern Screen,** Jul. 17, 1947, Shaw, **Sinatra,** 28; **("strong arm") Look,** Jun. 11, 1957; **(slipping money)** Douglas-Home, 21.

69 **Van Heusen: Billboard,** Nov. 20, 1965, **LAT,** Feb. 8, 1990, ints. Gloria Cahn Franks, Tita Cahn.

69 **"kolo": Billboard,** Nov. 20, 1965.

70 **Hickory House:** Shaw, **52nd Street,** 150.

70 **Billie Holiday: (on 52nd)** ibid., 21, 84–, 110–, 246, Billie Holiday with William Dufty, **Lady Sings the Blues,** London: Abacus, 1975, 94–; **(studied)** int. Tony Oppedisano, Arlene Francis int. of FS, WOR (NY), Oct. 1, 1977, audiotape in authors' collection; **(FS temper)** Romero, 65.

70 **Ethel Waters: (FS "touched") Ebony,** Jul. 1958. Sinatra also greatly admired Ella Fitzgerald and Sylvia Syms. He came to think of Fitzgerald as "the greatest of all contemporary jazz singers." In 1983 he made an album with Syms. Sinatra and Syms were friends; he nicknamed her his "little Buddha." Neither, however, was a regular on 52nd Street in the mid- to late 1930s (Fitzgerald—**Ebony,** Jul. 1958, Friedwald, 86; Syms, friends—"Sinatra and Syms," album liner notes by Sidney Zion, 1983, **Philadelphia Daily News,** Apr. 5, 1962, ed. Mustazza, 241; "Buddha"—**Star,** May 26, 1992).

70 **Mabel Mercer: (FS listens)** Wilson, 22, Bill Boggs int., Arlene Francis int. of FS, WOR (NY); **(background)** Shaw, **52nd Street,** 175–, Romero, 63; **(Jaffe)** M/G int. of Eddie Jaffe.

70–71 **opera: (People in the business) New York Daily News,** Jan. 17, 1982; **(opera was played)** Sinatra, **My Father,** 35; **(*I Pagliacci*)** **LAT,** Aug. 12, 1943; **("greatest baritone")** Bill Boggs int.; **(Merrill/Pavarotti)** Geoffrey Giuliano, **Sinatra: A Tribute,** New York: Bantam Doubleday Dell Audio, 1998, Sinatra's Diamond Jubilee World Tour program, **New York Daily News,** Jan. 17, 1982, int. Tony Oppedisano, **Philadelphia Enquirer,** May 17, 1998.

71 **voice coaches: (Tamburro)** Kelley, 41; **(Sevano)** M/G int. of Nick Sevano, confirmed by FS, **Metro Newark,** Apr. 1981; **(Quinlan) Metronome,** Oct. 1948, FS int. by Zion, Kelley, 41, Frank Sinatra and John Quinlan, **Tips on Popular Singing,** London: Maurice Music Co., 1941.

72 **business card: New Jersey Monthly,** Feb. 1982.

72 **"I wasn't": New York Post,** Apr. 11, 1947.

Chapter 5: "Did I Know Those Guys?"

73 **sobbing/"I suppose":** Dwiggins, 15–.

73–74 **Rustic Cabin: (described)** Caye and Russ Jehn, **The History of Englewood Cliffs, 1964–1994,** Englewood Cliffs, NJ: Centennial Committee, 1995, 111, 113, Simon, ix, Friedwald, 44, ints.

Rose Paldino, Mary Mane, Lucille Kirk Buccini; **("sneak joint")** Charles Pignone, **The Sinatra Treasures,** New York: Bulfinch, 2004, 29; **(link) New York Journal-American,** Feb. 27, 1956, Shaw, **Sinatra,** 15, John Rockwell, **Sinatra,** New York: Rolling Stone Press, 1984, 32, Evanier, 48.

74 **"Working with a good band":** Simon, viii.

74 **scouts:** Shaw, **Sinatra,** 18.

74–75 **Cabin job: (described)** Gary L. Doctor, **The Sinatra Scrapbook,** New York: Carol, 1991, 16, Granata, 3, "A Mother Flipping Cockroach," broadwaytovegas.com, Jun. 21, 1999, int. John Marotta, **American Weekly,** Jul. 20, 1952; **(Arden)** Dwiggins, 15.

75 **Harry Steeper:** Dwiggins, 16, Carpozi, 26, **Look,** May 28, 1957, int. Ethel Steeper Bolz, **NYT,** Sep., 26, 1943. Steeper was close to James Petrillo, who became president of the American Federation of Musicians in 1940. The union had long been penetrated by organized crime, and Petrillo—nicknamed "Little Caesar"—was known for "sending the goons in" when nightclubs or musicians failed to cooperate.

Dolly's version aside, it is clear Sinatra also pushed fellow musicians at the Cabin to help get him the work. He said so himself years later, and Lucille Kirk Buccini—widow of the trumpeter who played there—said "he bugged my husband constantly" (Steeper background—"A Brief History of the AFM," afm.org, "The Struggle for an Integrated Musicians Union," jazzinstituteofchicago.org, "The Genesis of Organized Crime in Chicago," ipsn.org., Dan Moldea, **Dark Victory: Ronald Reagan, MCA and the Mob,** New York: Penguin, 1986, 22–, 28; FS "bugged"—Sinatra, **Legend,** 31, int. Lucille Kirk Buccini).

75 **mob: (Some believed) Look,** May 28, 1957, Dwiggins, 95–; **(Mortimer) New American Mercury,** Aug. 1951; **("Did I know?") New York,** Apr. 28, 1980.

75–76 **usage of "Mafia":** Strictly speaking, "Mafia" refers to the crime network that originated in Sicily. American organized crime rapidly came to include individuals of other ethnic origins, and has been given different names at different times—Cosa Nostra, the Outfit, the Syndicate, the mob, and so on. The authors are aware of the specialist distinctions between the various titles, and that Italian-American mafiosi are said to have stopped using the term "Mafia" as of the 1930s. "Mafia," however, has become common parlance to describe organized crime—hence its use in that general context in these pages.

76 **CBS interview: NYT,** Nov. 28, **Newsweek,** Nov. 29, 1965, Don Hewitt, **Tell Me a Story,** New York: Public Affairs, 2001, 94–, Walter Cronkite, **A Reporter's Life,** New York: Knopf, 1996, 329–, CBS News special. When shooting resumed, Sinatra described "accusations that I was consorting with mobsters" as "ridiculous" (CBS News special); **(evasive)** e.g., exchange with Kefauver Committee attorney Joseph Nellis, cited in Hank Messick with Joseph Nellis, **The Private Lives of Public Enemies,** New York: Dell, 1974, 236.

77 **"I've met": American Weekly,** Jul. 27, 1952.

77 **Caruso/gangsters:** Henry Greenfeld, **Caruso,** New York: Putnam, 1983, 153–, 238.

77 **Crosby/money demands:** Gus Russo, **The Outfit,** New York: Bloomsbury, 2001, 123–, "Bing Crosby's Secret Life," americanmafia.com, Dec. 22, 1999, Donald Shepherd and Robert Slatzer, **Bing Crosby,** New York: Pinnacle, 1981, 100–.

77 **Lanza and underworld:** Raymond Strait and Terry Robinson, **Lanza,** Englewood Cliffs, NJ: Prentice-Hall, 1980, 162–, 145–, **Parade,** Jan. 12, 1964, "Memorandum Report," Bureau of Narcotics, District 17, Nov. 12, 1957, and "In re Thomas Lucchese," Nov. 27, 1956, Harry Anslinger Papers, Box 4, File 13, University of Pennsylvania Special Collections. In a 1957 interview with the Federal Bureau of Narcotics, Lanza said that over the years he had been approached by Frank Costello, one of the Fischetti brothers, and Chicago Mafia boss Tony Accardo. Tommy Lucchese, a longtime associate of Lucky Luciano, had threatened him in 1955. The latter threat, and an exchange in 1959 with Luciano himself, will be covered in detail in chapter 17 (Bureau of Narcotics, District 17, Nov. 12, 1957, and "In re Thomas Lucchese," Nov. 26, 1956, Harry Anslinger Papers, Box 4, File 13, University of Pennsylvania Special Collections).

77 **Martino deal:** "About Al Martino," almartino.com, **Mean,** Sep. 2001.

78 **Tormé:** Mel Tormé, **It Wasn't All Velvet,** New York: Viking, 1988, 118–.

78 **entertainers close to FS manipulated:** Sinatra was an admirer, personal friend—and reportedly at one point a business partner—of Durante, who dubbed him "Moonlight Sinatra."

Raft, too, became a family friend and went gambling with Sinatra. He told reporters Sinatra offered to do "anything in the world to help" at the time of his tax trial—and sent him a blank check. Lewis went to Sinatra family celebrations, traveled abroad with Sinatra, shared a hotel suite with him, and drank with him in the company of mob chieftain Santo Trafficante. Sinatra performed in Lewis's place when he was sick, cared for him personally, and paid his medical bills. He had portrayed Lewis in **The Joker Is Wild,** the 1957 movie based on the comic's life ("Moonlight"—"The Best of Person to Person," Edward R. Murrow int. of FS, Sep. 14, 1956; Durante—Sinatra with Coplon, 94, Memo to File, Mar. 1, 1955, "Summary Memo on Frank Sinatra," FBI 100-41713-4, int. Tony Oppedisano; Raft—Sinatra with Coplon, 131, **Billboard,** Nov. 1965, Director, FBI, to Attorney General, Feb. 10, 1961, FSFBI, radio int. of Paul "Skinny" D'Amato, University of Nevada, Las Vegas, audiotape in authors' collection, **Look,** Nov. 30, 1965, Hank Messick, **The Mob in Show Business,** New York: Pyramid, 1973 220; Lewis—Sinatra with Coplon, 94, 135–, **LAHE,** Jul. 6, 1964, **Life,** Apr. 23, 1965, Frank Ragano and Selwyn Raab, **Mob Lawyer,** New York: Scribner's, 1994, 215, Art Cohn, **The Joker Is Wild,** New York: Random House, 1955, 249, **JazzTimes,** May 1998, Irv Kupcinet with Paul Neimark, **Kup,** Chicago: Bonus, 1988, 208).

78 **Durante/gangsters:** Lewis Yablonsky, **George Raft,** New York: McGraw-Hill, 1974, 31–, Stephen Fox, **Blood and Power,** New York: William Morrow, 1989, 82–, Dean Jennings, **We Only Kill Each Other,** New York: Penguin, 1992, 20, Frank Rose, **The Agency,** New York: HarperBusiness, 1995, 93, 108, 146, 230, 241, Russo, 126, 171, 294, Antoinette Giancana and Thomas Renner, **Mafia Princess,** New York: William Morrow, 1984, 94–.

78 **Raft/mobsters: (Siegel)** Jennings, 20, Ed Reid and Ovid Demaris, **The Green Felt Jungle,** New York, Trident, 1963, 20; **(booze trucks)** Gage, 80–, Yablonsky, 37, 246–; **(Capri)** Vincent Teresa with Thomas C. Renner, **My Life in the Mafia,** London: Grafton, 1974, 223–, Legal Attaché Havana to Director, Jan. 14, 1958, FBI 62-75147-210-109, "Supplemental Correlation Summary," Feb. 25, 1969, "Subject: Frank Sinatra," FSFBI; **(IRS/shot)** Hank Messick, **The Mob in Show Business,** New York: Pyramid, 1973, 216–; **(Vegas)** Dennis Eisenberg, Uri Dan,

and Eli Landau, **Meyer Lansky,** New York: Paddington, 1979, 267; **(barred)** House Assassinations Committee review of FBI files, obtained by author, Gage, 81.

78–79 **Lewis/gangsters: (tenor)** Art Cohn, **The Joker Is Wild,** New York: Random House, 1955, 30, 41; **(slashed)** ibid., 3–, 35–; **("sandpaper")** NYT, Jun. 5, 1971; **(continued)** Messick, **The Mob in Show Business,** 53, "Title of Case: Samuel M. Giancana," Chicago Field Office Report, Jul. 27, 1964, FBI 92-3171-1447.

79–80 **mob and entertainers: (King)** ints. Sonny King; **(Teresa)** Teresa with Renner, 123–, 121–; **(jukeboxes)** Steve Schoenherr, "Recording Technology History," www.history.acusd.edu., Russo, 187–, Dwiggins, 11, Robert F. Kennedy, **The Enemy Within,** New York: Harper and Row, 1960, 247–, Messick, **Show Business,** 162, M/G int. of Ed Jaffee; **("We're gonna")** M/G int. of Artie Shaw.

80–81 **Luciano background: (shoplifting)** Sifakis, 200; **(narcotics/revolver, etc.)** "Memorandum re Charles Luciano" (with aliases), Aug. 28, 1935, FBI 39-2141-3, "Agent Benjamin Fitzgerald Report on Luciano," Jun. 13, 1951, Lucky Luciano Files, LLBN, Sciacca, **Luciano,** 23, Harry Anslinger and Will Oursler, **The Murderers,** New York: Farrar, Straus and Cudahy, 1962, 102–, Rodney Campbell, **The Luciano Project,** New York: McGraw-Hill, 1977, 71–; **(twenty murders)** Sciacca, **Luciano,** 14; **("sadistic")** Wolf with DiMona, 9; **("wily")** Campbell, 3; **(distanced)** Sciacca, **Luciano,** 47, 50, Katz, 57, 89.

81 **Luciano emerged:** Fred Cook, **The Secret Rulers,** New York: Duell, Sloan and Pearce, 1966, 99; Luciano was apparently present at the murder scene after Arnold "the Brain" Rothstein was shot dead in 1928, was certainly present when New York Mafia boss Joe Masseria was killed three years later, and was reportedly one of those who, the same year, organized the murder of the first and only "Boss of Bosses," Salvatore Maranzano (Rothstein—Katz, 79; Masseria—ibid., 83, Sciacca, **Luciano,** 97–; Maranzano—ibid., 101, Katz, 87); **(Waldorf Towers)** Sciacca, **Luciano,** 121, Martin Gosch and Richard Hammer, **The Last Testament of Lucky Luciano,** Boston: Little, Brown, 1974, 148; **(Durante/Lewis/Raft)** ibid., 152, **Parade,** Jan. 12, 1964, Cohn, 339, Yablonsky, 246, Cusack to Anslinger, Mar. 2, 1961—Jimmy Durante's name appears repeatedly in Luciano's address books,

examined by Italian police and supplied to the U.S. Bureau of Narcotics in 1949 and 1951, LLBN; **(musicals)** Sciacca, **Luciano,** 51; **(stage employees' union)** Russo, 135, 140.

82 **Luciano imprisonment: (Public Enemy)** Sciacca, **Luciano,** 126; **("brilliant criminal executives")** Alfred McCoy, **The Politics of Heroin,** New York: Lawrence Hill, 1991, 28, Cook, 99, **Time,** Mar. 12, 1951.

82 **Costello/Moretti: (visits)** (NY) **Daily Mirror,** Apr. 7, 1954, Sciacca, **Luciano,** 166, 170, 182; **(Moretti "idolized"/loyal)** "Summary Report on Thomas Eboli," Jul. 13, 1962, LLBN, SAC New York to Director, May 1, 1950, FBI 62-75147-34-106; **(Costello/Moretti/Luciano)** Gosch and Hammer, 24–, 51–, 94, Wolf with DiMona, 193, Katz, 43, 138–, 193; **(Moretti record)** Cook, 152, Gosch and Hammer, 51, **Time,** Dec. 25, 1950, Jack Lait and Lee Mortimer, **Washington Confidential,** New York: Crown, 1951, 303, "Willie Moretti aka Willie Moore," Willie Moretti File, Alpha Names File, Kefauver Committee Papers, NA; **(Moretti family man) Life,** Dec. 25, 1950, Katz, 194; **(murderer)** Peterson, **The Mob,** 387, Sifakis, 225, Gosch and Hammer, 49, Cook, 153–; **(Costello record)** Wolf with DiMona, 31–, Katz, 39–, Sifakis, 91–; **(Costello adviser)** Cook, 101–; **(killer)** Wolf with DiMona, 93, 95, Sifakis, 92; **(Moretti controlled)** Sifakis, 225; **(Riviera)** ibid., Cook, 172, "General Crime Survey," May 13, 1944, FBI 62-75147-31-2, Tosches, 149, Rose, 162, int. Joe Nellis; **(Sinatra stop by)** Bill Boggs int.

83 **Costello and Copacabana: Parade,** Jan. 12, 1964, Katz, 132, Sifakis, 300, Fisher with Fisher, 30–. Costello had been subpoenaed during a 1944 probe into the Copacabana's links to mobsters. He refused to testify. The club management, meanwhile, stated that it would sever any connection "it may now have or have had" with the mobster. In fact, things continued as before under a new city administration (Tosches, 158); **(Stork) Collier's,** Apr. 12, 1947; **(Tropicana)** Pete Earley, **Super Casino,** New York: Bantam, 2000, 46, Wallace Turner, **Gamblers' Money,** Boston: Houghton Mifflin, 1965, 21; **(Lewis)** Katz, 251, Cohn, 295; **(Lanza)** "Memorandum Report," Bureau of Narcotics, District 17, Nov. 12, 1957, Harry Anslinger Papers, Box 4, File 13, University of Pennsylvania Special Collections; **(Cohn/Warner)** Rose, 92, Katz, 140, 225.

83 **Sinatra and Luciano: (chance encounter)** New York Daily News, Apr. 11, 1947, **American Weekly,** Jul. 27, 1952; **("Even if I'd caught")** "Hedda Hopper's Hollywood," Apr. 9, 1947.

83 **Sinatra and Costello: ("Hello")** transcript, FS questioning by Kefauver Committee investigators, **Gallery,** Sep. 1978, Messick with Nellis, 235, **American Weekly,** Jul. 27, 1952; **("those guys")** int. Nick Sevano; **("Sinatra and Frank C.")** Kelley, 194, 526—Miller was indeed close to Costello, see Katz, refs.

84 **Sinatra and Moretti: (FS versions) American Weekly,** Jul. 27, 1952, FS testimony, Nevada State Gaming Control Board, Feb. 11, 1981, and see excerpt, Feb. 17, 1970, FS testimony to New Jersey State Investigation Commission, Kelley, 393.

84 **"Our backyards":** int. Angela Marrocco. The Sinatras owned a home at 220 Lawrence Avenue in Hasbrouck Heights, New Jersey, in 1943 and 1944. Moretti appears to have used two different houses in Hasbrouck Heights during the 1940s. One of them, at 201 Bell Avenue, was only a few hundred yards from the Sinatra home. The other, at 301 Roosevelt, is a little over a mile from the Sinatras' house. Since Sinatra himself described Moretti as a "neighbor," it is likely the mobster was using the closer—Bell Avenue—address at the relevant time (Lawrence Avenue—Sinatra, **My Father,** 46, 56, Dwiggins, 54, property records for 220 Lawrence Avenue, Block 84, Parcel no. 45-47, 1944, Hasbrouck Heights, NJ; Moretti houses—**Paterson** (NJ) **Call,** Sep. 22, 1947, "Guarino W. Moretti," background memo, Willie Moretti File, Alpha Names File, Kefauver Committee, NA Newark to Director, Jul. 31, 1943, FBI 100-215961-2; property records for 201 Bell Avenue, Block 84, Parcel no. 32-35, 1944, Hasbrouck Heights, NJ, and ints. Office of Tax Assessor); **(at Copacabana)** handwritten notes of George Evans int., Sep. 10, 1947, Pegler Papers, Kelley, 146; **(Pignatello) Las Vegas Review-Journal,** Dec. 14, 1995, Aug. 11, 2001, int. John Smith—Pignatello was the chef of Chicago's Sam Giancana; **("all his life")** Sinatra with Coplon, 73.

85 **De Carlo: ("laid-back")** Evanier, 67; **(background)** "Petition for Commutation of Sentence," Apr. 4, 1972, "Application for Executive Clemency of Angelo De Carlo," Jul. 7, 1972, J. Keith to Mr. Cleveland, Apr. 2, 1973, Angelo De Carlo Cross References, FBI, Cook, 207, Evanier, 67, **Mountainside** (NJ) **Echo,** Oct. 25, 1973, **Elizabeth** (NJ) **Daily Journal,** Oct. 22, 1973,

NYT, Sep. 16, 1924, int. Jack Clarke; **("executioner")** David Scheim, **Contract on America,** New York: Shapolsky, 1988, 231, 304–, **Life,** Sep. 1, 1967, Jonathan Kwitny, **Vicious Circles,** New York: Norton, 1979, 60, Evanier, 75–; **(Luciano/in touch)** White to Anslinger, Feb. 5, 1951, "Agenda Personale di Lucania Salvatore" attachment to Cusack to Giordano, Jun. 20, 1962, LLBN; **("My grandfather")** int. Joseph Sullivan; **(De Carlo/Moretti)** "General Crime Survey," Oct. 19, 1948, FBI 94-419-84, "General Crime Survey," May 13, 1944, FBI 62-75147-31-2, "CAPGA: Crime Survey," Aug. 8, 1946, FBI 62-8861-153; **(De Carlo and Dolly)** int. Joseph Sullivan—De Carlo's grandson.

85 **Sam Sinatra:** Sinatra's cousin Sam, with whom he grew up (see p. 23 **supra.**), married Loretta Riley in 1939. Loretta's sister Agnes was already married to Angelo De Carlo by that time. According to Sam Sinatra's last wife, Rose, her husband was "very close" to his De Carlo relatives—he treated the gangster's daughter and grandchildren "like they were his own" (ints. Rose Ellman Sinatra, Rose Paldino, Joseph Sullivan, U.S. Census 1930, "Certificate of Marriage," Sam Sinatra and Loretta Riley, Nov. 4, 1939, "Supplemental Correlation Summary," Feb. 25, 1969, "Subject: Francis Albert Sinatra, Sr.," 20, FBI 62-83219, "File Review and Summary Checks," Mar. 26, 1970, "Subject: Francis Albert Sinatra," 50, FBI LA 100-41413, SA Wilcus to SAC Newark, Apr. 22, 1964, FBI 137-3514-588); **("He used to check")** int. Joseph Sullivan.

85–86 **De Carlo and entertainers: (proprietary interest)** ints. Jimmy Roselli, Anthony Petrozelli, Bob Buccino, Evanier, 69–, Scheim, 359, Gerald Zelmanowitz testimony, Subcommittee on Investigations of Committee on Government Operations, U.S. Senate, 92nd Cong., 1st sess., Jul. 13, 1973; **("He loved")** int. Anthony Petrozelli; **("Gyp had a lot")** int. James Petrozelli; **(Sam's widow Rose)** int. Rose Ellman Sinatra; **("Sinatra was nowhere")** int. Robert Phillips, and, re "duke-in," see Sal Vizzini with Oscar Fraley and Marshall Smith, **Vizzini,** London: Futura, 1974, 55.

86 **Luciano and Sinatra: (maintained/"investments")** Sciacca, **Luciano,** 170–, Gosch and Hammer, 48, 232, 240.

87 **"When I was":** Gosch and Hammer, 312. Doubts have been raised as to the credibility of **The Last Testament of Lucky**

Luciano, by Martin Gosch and Richard Hammer, published in 1975. Over the years, critics have pointed out historical errors in the text. Having looked into the controversy, and having studied relevant police files in Italy, we conclude that—while the book does contain inaccuracies—Luciano did indeed give lengthy interviews to author Gosch. It is likely that the mobster spoke inexactly about events in his distant past, and that the book suffered from the fact that neither Luciano nor coauthor Gosch could review the manuscript—both died before publication. We interviewed surviving coauthor Richard Hammer, a former **New York Times** reporter and National Book Award nominee, who acknowledged that he gave a "voice" to Luciano based on Gosch's extensive notes. Specific inaccuracies aside, our research suggests there is no reason to doubt the overall veracity of the recollections attributed to Luciano (int. Richard Hammer, **NYT,** Dec. 17, 20, 23, 1974, Mar. 14, 1975, Sciacca, **Luciano,** 230, "Interrogation of Martin Arnold Gosch," Jan. 27, 1962, 10th Legion of the Guardia di Finanza, Rome, Allan May, "The Last Testament of Lucky Luciano," pts. 1 and 2, americanmafia.com, Aug./Sep. 2002, Jack Anderson, "The Last Days of Lucky Luciano," **WP,** Jun. 26, 1962).

87 **Lascari:** Virgil Peterson, **The Jukebox Racket,** confidential report for law enforcement, Chicago: Chicago Crime Commission, Sep. 1954, 135, Russo, 188–, Katz, 146, Peterson, **The Mob,** 247. Lascari, who by his account got into the jukebox business in 1937, was a Luciano intimate of long standing—at one point he lived with the Luciano family. His name appears in a Luciano address book, and in Luciano's phone records (Petersen, **The Jukebox Racket,** 135, Anslinger to Kefauver, Luciano address book extract attachment, Feb. 8, 1951, "Memorandum for File," "Charles Luciano," Jul. 10, 1947, and J. Ray Olivera to Garland Williams, Mar. 21, 1947, LLBN).

87 **mobsters' role at start of FS career: ("discovered")** 1951 Bureau of Narcotics document, cited in "Correlation Summary," Jun. 8, 1964, "Subject: Francis Albert Sinatra," FSFBI; **(" 'brought up' ")** "Supplemental Correlation Summary," Feb. 25, 1969, FSFBI; **(Moretti "financial interest")** "General Crime Survey," May 13, 1944, by Capt. Matthew Donohue, cited in "Summary Memorandum re Francis Albert Sinatra," Sep. 29, 1950, FSFBI; **("admitted his association")** "General Crime Sur-

vey," Apr. 15, 1948, cited in "Summary Memorandum re Francis Albert Sinatra," Sep. 29, 1950, FSFBI; **(Donohue)** int. Matthew Donohue Jr.—Donohue Sr. was under-sheriff of Bergen County, New Jersey, from 1936 to 1939 and went on to become chief of police.

88–89 **Scimone: (story and background)** ints. Chico Scimone, "Processo Verbale di Interrogatorio, Francesco Scimone," and multiple references cited in **Commisione Parliamentare d'Inchiesta Sul Fenomeno Della Mafia in Sicilia,** vol. 4, 205–, 210–, 280–, 465, 557–, 773–, 818–; **(Vitaliti)** refs. in files "Processo Verbale di Interrogatorio, Adrianna Rizzo," 10th Legione Guardia di Finanza, Jan. 1962, **Commisione Parlimentare D'inchiesta Sul Fenomeno Della Mafia in Sicilia,** vol. 4, 557–, and see Gosch and Hammer, multiple refs.; **(Vitaliti/Luciano)** ibid., and "Agenda Personale di Lucania Salvatore" attachment to Cusack to Giordano, Jun. 20, 1962, LLBN.

89 **"Night and Day":** " 'Night and Day' was my best number," Sinatra said in 1948, "so I used it for almost every audition." He had used it when the Hoboken Four auditioned for Major Bowes (**Silver Screen,** Mar. 24, 1948).

90 **"The Boys":** int. Sonny King.

90 **"had nothing to do":** FS testimony, Nevada State Gaming Control Board, Feb. 11, 1981.

90 **"made some band dates":** transcript, FS questioning by Kefauver Committee investigators, **Gallery,** Sept. 1978.

Chapter 6: All, or Nothing at All

91 **stint at Cabin: ("Frank hated")** "A Mother Flipping Cockroach," www.broadwaytovegas.com, Jun. 21, 1999—the Travalena quoted is the father of comedian Fred Travalena; **("bow to the boss")** Doctor, 16; **("half piano")** Sinatra, **Legend,** 31; **("was the boy singer")** M/G int. Lucille Buccini (**nee** Kirk).

92 **youthful attraction to women: (rarely shared thoughts)** Trivial details aside, it seems to be a fact that Sinatra did not talk in any depth—for public consumption, at least—about relationships between men and women. This may be not least because he thought marriage "a personal arrangement between two beings [that] should properly concern no one else" (**Ebony,** Jul. 1958, ed. Yarwood, 69); **(flirt) Bergen** (NJ) **Record,** May 17, 1998;

("We're animals"/"He was a skinny") Taraborrelli, 28; **("I'm just looking")** ibid., 31; **("You got something")** Dwiggins, 20; **("His voice")** ibid.; **("He had sex")** Taraborrelli, 29–.

93 **penis size: ("There's only ten pounds")** Charles Higham, **Ava,** New York: Delacorte, 1974, 133. D'Orazio described Sinatra as "hung like a horse," while Anthony Petrozelli said he "hung pretty heavy." The actress Jeanne Carmen described the penis as "a biggie"—"a watermelon on the end of a toothpick." Lena Samuels, a sometime lover of both Sinatra and Sammy Davis, said Sinatra was pleased when she assured him that his was bigger than Davis's. In contrast to this smorgasbord of prurience, Sinatra's daughter Tina has said that—when she and her siblings took showers with their father—"He looked normal to me" (D'Orazio—Taraborrelli, 30; Petrozelli—int. Anthony Petrozelli; Carmen—int. Jeanne Carmen, C. David Heymann, **RFK,** New York: Dutton, 1998, 314n; Samuels—Taraborrelli, 218; "He looked"—**New York Daily News,** Jun. 12, 2003; **(" 'Big Frankie' ")** Taraborrelli, 31; **("bundle of bones")** Freedland, 20; **("cuddler"/"C'mon, God")** Taraborrelli, 29–.

94–96 **Della Penta: (main episode)** Kelley, 1–, Taraborrelli, 32–, "A Mother Flipping Cockroach," M/G int. of Lucille Kirk Buccini, ints. Matthew Donohue Jr., Criminal Judicial District Court of the County of Bergen, Docket 15228, Nov. 26, 1938, and 15307, Dec. 21, 1938, Box 72, Pegler Papers, Jones to Nichols, Jan. 23, 1957, FSFBI, undat. clips re Nov. 26 arrest and Della Penta re Dolly fracas, Jersey City Library—the woman's full name was Antoinette Della Penta Francke. Her age is taken from the U.S. Census of 1930. More than twenty years later, when he was being vetted for a Nevada gaming license, Sinatra said through his attorney that a medical examination had established that Della Penta was not pregnant. In Sinatra's view, she was a "crank" ("Sands Hotel," Jan. 21, 1963, FBI 92-6314-2); **FS "called up someone")** Taraborrelli, 34.

96–97 **Nancy marriage: ("What Nancy don't know")** Taraborrelli, 32; **("Nancy was crushed")** ibid., 33; **(never happen again)** Sinatra, **Legend,** 32; **(invitations)** ibid.; **("I was quite taken"/ shower)** Kelley, 43, int. Adeline Biondy Yacenda; **(FS borrowed) Modern Screen,** Jul. 17, 1947.

97 **wedding dress:** The authors have used the reference to the dress that appears in daughter Nancy Sinatra's book, **Legend.** Nancy

said in a 1947 interview, however, that she wore a dress she designed and made herself (Sinatra, **Legend,** 33, Peterson draft); **("awfully nice")** "My Life with Frank Sinatra," Marva Peterson draft, Jul. 21, 1947, MHL; **(tears)** Kelley, 44; **(" 'gone' ")** Peterson draft; **("saddest")** Kelley, 44.

98 **"cheerful little apartment"/"too busy":** Peterson draft. While Nancy said in 1947 that the couple had no honeymoon, Sinatra said in 1943 that they had a "three-day honeymoon." Elsewhere, it has been said they had a four-day honeymoon, which included driving to North Carolina and back (Nancy—Peterson draft; FS—**Metronome,** May 1943; North Carolina?—**Jersey Journal,** Feb. 13, 1939, Kelley, 45; **(curtains)** Dwiggins, 20; **("Frank doesn't believe")** Peterson draft; **(Nancy secretary) American Weekly,** Jul. 20, 1952; **($25)** Peterson draft; **("Our marriage started") American Weekly,** Jul. 20, 1952; **(Sevano)** ints. Nick Sevano, M/G int. of Nick Sevano; **("I'm going") Look,** Jun. 11, 1957; **("What I had mistaken") American Weekly,** Jul. 20, 1952; **("Poor Nancy") Modern Screen,** Jul. 17, 1947.

100 **other jobs: ("I was running")** Simon, viii, and see **Billboard,** Nov. 20, 1965.

100 **"Our Love":** Sinatra's daughter Nancy has written that her father gave "Our Love" to her mother as a wedding gift on February 4, 1939, having recorded it the previous day. This seems to be wrong—the date of the recording, typed on the label, was March 18, 1939 (Sinatra, **Legend,** 32); **("I was segueing")** Friedwald, 68, and see **Life,** Jun. 25, 1971.

100–101 **Miller/Dorsey: ("I walked up")** Friedwald, 68; **("a god")** Douglas-Home, 23; **(Dorsey persuaded) Crescendo & Jazz Music,** Oct./Nov. 1992—spotter was Dorsey saxophonist Vince Carbone; **(Nola Studios)** FS liner notes at http://radio.cbc.ca/inperformance.

101 **Chester: Metronome,** May 1943, **Goldmine,** Mar. 22, 1991, **Billboard,** Nov. 20, 1965, Friedwald, 68. For a while in early 1939, FS rehearsed regularly with the Bob Chester band in the mornings and with another band in the afternoons. According to former Chester trumpeter Alec Fila, he also sang with Chester at the New Yorker hotel (Simon, ix, **Metronome,** May 1943, **Billboard,** Nov. 20, 1965, Friedwald, 68); **("When he saw us") Screen Star,** Jun. 28, 1955.

101 **Charlie's Grill:** int. Matthew Donohue, "General Crime Survey," May 13, 1944, FBI—62-75147-31-2, SAC NY to Director, Apr. 15, 1954, FBI 62-78122-17. Accounts of the first Dorsey encounter are various and inconsistent. Sinatra himself described it much as did Dorsey, but said they met "a few years" before he joined the Dorsey band in 1940. That would place the episode in 1937 or—more likely—1938. The singer's daughter Nancy has offered two different accounts in her books on her father. In **Frank Sinatra, My Father,** she wrote that Dorsey heard Sinatra sing sometime in 1939 in New York when he was with Harry James. In **Legend** she places the episode in December 1939 just before Sinatra left James, but at the Rustic Cabin, on a night her father returned to make a guest appearance. The reported appearance at Charlie's Grill, supplied to the authors by former police investigator Matthew Donohue Jr., reflects the fact that Sinatra was singing where and whenever he could. Others have recalled him singing at other New Jersey venues (various accounts—Douglas-Home, 23, Sinatra, **My Father,** 24, Sinatra, **Legend,** 38–; other venues—Friedwald, 65, Kelley, 42).

101 **"I dedicated": Star,** May 6, 1986, **LAT,** Oct. 31, 1993, Friedwald, 44.

102 **Harry James: (De Carlo)** int. Joseph Sullivan; **("I was packing")** int. Louise Tobin; **("I asked the manager") Billboard,** Nov. 20, 1965; **(mere chance) Movieland,** Jun. 11, 1945; **("Oh, yeah")** int. Lucille Kirk Buccini; **(photograph)** Sinatra, **Legend,** 34; **("he took off his apron")** Kelley, 48, and see Peter Levinson, **Trumpet Blues: The Life of Harry James,** New York: Oxford University Press, 1999, 67; **("Begin the Beguine")** Helen Hover int. of FS, unid. clip, 1944, MHL; **("was destined")** Levinson, 67.

103 **FS offered job/$75:** Helen Hover int. of FS. Elsewhere FS said $65, Granata, 8. James's biographer reports that the contract was for only one year, while two sources indicate it was for two years. It has been suggested, too, that James's interest in Sinatra was prompted by recording industry executive Manie Sacks, who was at that time in the talent agency business. The agent Swifty Lazar, meanwhile, said James told him about Sinatra before going out to see him at the Rustic Cabin. The authors have accepted what James's then wife has told them (one year—Levinson, 68, 80; two years—George Evans press release, 1942, MHL, Dwiggins, 21;

Sacks—**Woman's Home Companion,** May 1956, Richard Gehman, **Sinatra and His Rat Pack,** New York: Belmont, 1961, 191; Lazar—Lazar with Tapert, 153); **(to be let go)** ibid.; **("I nearly broke")** Friedwald, 67; **("I called Nancy")** Dwiggins, 21; **(James background)** Levinson, 3–, 19–, 26, 112–; **("I loved Harry James") Philadelphia Inquirer,** Jul. 8, 1983; **(poor bookings)** Levinson, 65–; **("We were struggling")** int. Louise Tobin; **(at the Paramount) Billboard,** Nov. 20, 1965.

104 **Frankie Satin:** Levinson, 68, Hamill, 71, 38. Earlier, at the Rustic Cabin, Sinatra had called himself "Frankie Trent." His mother objected vociferously and it lasted only a couple of weeks (**Life,** Oct. 1995).

104 **James tour: (Connie Haines)** Levinson, 66, 69, Dwiggins, 21.

104 **Baltimore appearance:** Shaw, **Sinatra,** 19. Most sources place Sinatra's first performance with the James band in Baltimore. Jack Palmer, a James trumpeter, thought Sinatra first joined at New Haven, Connecticut (Granata, 4–); **(Steel Pier)** ed. Mustazza, 85, 224; **("He sounded somewhat"/"the very pleasing") Billboard,** Nov. 20, 1965; **("He was always") Goldmine,** Mar. 22, 1991, with correction May 3, 1991; **(breath control) Philadelphia Inquirer,** Jul. 8, 1983, Levinson, 70; **(recordings)** Granata, 5–, Shaw, **Sinatra,** 21; **($50)** Levinson, 69–; **("It was new")** Granata, 7.

106 **"All or Nothing at All":** Sinatra recorded "All or Nothing at All" with Harry James in August 1939. Release of the song was delayed until June the following year because the American Society of Composers, Authors and Publishers (ASCAP), which published the song, was in a dispute with broadcasters. A second union action, a strike by the American Federation of Musicians, prevented union musicians from recording between 1942 and 1944. Then, with broadcasters hungry for "new" material, the Sinatra-James recording of "All or Nothing at All" was rereleased and became a hit (Clarke, **All or Nothing,** 33–, Levinson, 72–, Shaw, **Sinatra,** 21, Friedwald, 75, 132–, Adam Woog, **The Importance of Frank Sinatra,** San Diego, CA: Lucent Books, 2001, 40); **(Miller)** Friedwald, 37; **(four times)** Granata, 6–; **("That guy sings")** LAHE, Dec. 7, 1979; **("I went over")** Clarke, **Wishing on the Moon,** 225–; **("The male singer")** autograph description, sothebys.com, Jan. 10, 2003; **("Not so loud")** Shaw, **Sinatra,** 20; **(ballroom burned/Victor Hugo/**

broke) ibid., **American Weekly,** Nov. 26, 1950, Dwiggins, 22; **("The place was so small") Chicago's American,** Sep. 25, 1966; **("A number of times")** Sciacca, **Sinatra,** 111; **(Count Basie)** Granata, 168, Simon, 82.

109 **Tommy Dorsey: (hopes)** ed. Yarwood, 17, Sinatra, **Legend,** 39, **Life,** Apr. 23, 1965.

109 **Dorsey had heard/meeting:** Dwiggins, 24, Friedwald, 82, Sciacca, **Sinatra,** 38–, **Billboard,** Nov. 20, 1965, **Screen Star,** Jun. 28, 1955, M/G int. of Nick Sevano, Herb Sanford, **Tommy and Jimmy,** New Rochelle, NY: Da Capo Press, 1972, 182–, "Artanis Knarf," unid. article by Bobby Burns. Dorsey would have heard the song on the radio rather than on a record, because the recording Sinatra had made had not yet been released. It has been said that Dorsey's current singer, Jack Leonard, had become temperamental, and there were rumors he was going to go out on his own. It seems more likely, though, that he and Dorsey were simply communicating badly, and that Dorsey jumped to conclusions (not released—Friedwald, 82–; Leonard—Wilson, 28, Dwiggins, 26, Sanford, 182, Simon, 165); **(another singer)** Wilson, 28.

109 **Dorsey contract:** The authors have relied on Sinatra's statement that Dorsey paid him $100 a week. Dorsey, though, said the pay was $150. Other sources offer both $125 and $110 (Dorsey—Dwiggins, 28; $125—Douglas-Home, 22, Levinson, 78; $110—**Time,** Aug. 28, 1955); **("if we don't do any better")** Levinson, 79, and see **Chicago Daily News,** May 10, 1976; **(friend/mentor)** Friedwald, 69; **("made it all possible")** Sinatra, **Legend,** 38.

109–110 **Christmas: (Nancy pregnant)** Dwiggins, 22; **Redbook,** Oct. 1951; **(pneumonia/gloves)** Dwiggins, 29, "The Sinatra Story," unid. clip, 1951, MHL.

110 **leaving James: (Shea Theatre)** Levinson, 79. James and Sinatra did work together later, on a government film promoting war bonds in 1944, and briefly recorded together in 1951. They also made some nightclub appearances over the years, and performed on a John Denver television special in 1976. In 1979 James joined in the televised tribute commemorating Sinatra's fortieth year in show business. They remained close until James's death (Daniel O'Brien, **Frank Sinatra Film Guide,** London: Butler and Tanner, 1998, 209, Levinson, 80, 242–, Friedwald, 75–, int.

Louise Tobin); **("The bus pulled out")** Douglas-Home, 22–; **(home in New Jersey)** Sinatra, **Legend,** 42, Freedland, 54.

110 **"Roses of Picardy": (NJ) Star Ledger,** Jan. 23, 25, 2000, **Hudson Reporter,** undat., 2000. The "Roses of Picardy" disc bears no identification except the title, which is scratched onto the record. Experts have accepted that it was recorded after 1935 but have been unable to date it more precisely. Costello's sister Rita Scalzo, however, has said the recording was made between Sinatra's stint with James and his start with Dorsey, and the authors have accepted her account. Sinatra recorded "Roses of Picardy" again in 1962.

111 **"It's a lot farther": New Yorker,** May 25, 1998.

Chapter 7: "Let Him Go"

112 **poll: Metronome,** Jan. 1940.

113–114 **Dorsey background: ("No. 1")** FS int. by Tom Jones, Melbourne, Australia, 1955, supplied to author by Alf Batcheldor; **("General Motors")** Peter Levinson, **September in the Rain: The Life of Nelson Riddle,** New York: Billboard, 2001, 44; **("most beautiful")** Levinson, **September,** 46; **("the Starmaker")** int. Connie Haines; **(childhood/early career)** Simon, 142, Levinson, **September,** 46–, **Current Biography,** New York, H. W. Wilson, 1942, 16–, "The Great American Big Bands" Big Bands Database; **("If you could put up")** Levinson, **September,** 46; **(fined)** Douglas-Home, 24; **(singer fired)** Simon, 165—the singer was Jack Leonard; **(arrangers)** Levinson, **September,** 50; **(chased/hit drummer)** ibid., 46; **(drove like a maniac)** Simon, 145; **(swore)** Levinson, **September,** 46; **(womanizer)** Cahn, 131; **(drank)** Simon, 145, Mel Tormé, **Traps, the Drum Wonder: The Life of Buddy Rich,** Alma, MI: Rebeats Publications, 1991, 68, **Palm Springs Life,** Feb. 2002; **("I do")** Wilson, **Sinatra,** 32; **("Why don't")** Simon, 146; **("Well, shit heel")** Levinson, **September,** 47.

114 **first sang in Indianapolis:** The first Sinatra performance with Dorsey is variously said to have been in Sheboygan, Wisconsin, Indianapolis, Minneapolis, Milwaukee, or Baltimore (Friedwald, 83, **Goldmine,** Mar. 22, 1991).

114 **talk of altering/"will never":** Freedland, 52.

114–115 **Dorsey/FS start: ("Romantic Virtuoso")** Sanford, 269; **("We knew")** Freedland, 52; **("Out came"/"I just thought")**

Freedland, 52, Dwiggins, 33, Hamill, 109, int. Jo Stafford; **(Boy, this) Palm Springs Life,** Feb. 2002; **("broke it up")** Simon, 166; **("actually looked") New Yorker,** Nov. 9, 1946; **("in awe") Palm Springs Life,** Feb. 2002; **(intruder)** Douglas-Home, 23; **("He just moved") Billboard,** Nov. 20, 1965; **(band routine)** Frank, 30–, Dwiggins, 33; **(groomed)** Frank, 30, **New Yorker,** Nov. 9, 1946; **(Sevano joined)** int. Nick Sevano; **(extravagant) New Yorker,** Nov. 9, 1946; **("broke")** "Artanis Knarf," unid. Bobby Burns article, MHL.

116–117 **FS/Dorsey relations: (dinner)** Douglas-Home, 24; **(Patsy's) Newsday,** Jul. 24, 2002; **("One time")** Douglas-Home, 24; **("At first everyone")** "Artanis Knarf," unid. Bobby Burns article, MHL; **("the old man") Screen Star,** Jun. 28, 1955; **("like a father")** Friedwald, 88; **("I'd sit up")** Douglas-Home, 24; **(education)** Simon, 170; **(Dorsey mother)** Wilson, 34; **(pranks)** ibid., 35, Earl Wilson, **The Show Business Nobody Knows,** New York: Bantam, 1973, 155–; **(cologne/toothpaste) Palm Springs Life,** Feb. 2002; **(trains)** Simon, 171; **(perfection)** int. Peter Levinson.

118–119 **breath control: ("sang a song") Screen Star,** Jun. 28, 1955; **(barely any coaching) Life,** Apr. 23, 1965; **("Tommy taught me")** Shaw, **Sinatra,** 33; **(elocution)** ed. Yarwood, 63; **("I used to watch"/"I'd swear"/"He showed")** Bill Boggs int., and see FS int. by Zion, **LAHE,** Jun. 6, 1981; **(invitation)** ibid.

119 **FS and classical music:** George Evans press release, 1940, MHL, **LAT,** Aug. 12, 1943. The huge record collection Sinatra would amass once he became wealthy, while largely devoted to jazz, would include more than two hundred classical albums (**Metronome,** May 1943, **Movie Show,** Jul. 31, 1947); **(Debussy) Movieland,** Jun. 11, 1945; **(Brahms) Silver Screen,** Mar. 24, 1948; **(Heifetz) McCall's,** Jul. 1968; Sinatra Diamond Jubilee Tour program, FS int. by Arlene Francis, Oct. 1, 1977, WOR (NY), Joy Williams, "Frank Sinatra," www.artistwd.com; **("Every time"/"You never"/"I thought")** FS int. by Zion, **Life,** Apr. 23, 1965, and see Freedland, 65–, Friedwald, 87; **("I did lots")** FS int. by Zion, and see Bill Boggs int.; **(increase range)** int. Joey Bushkin; **("Frank can hold")** Cahn, 130–; **("calisthenics"/vocalize)** FS int. by Zion, Freedland, 55; **(rehearsed)** Friedwald, 88.

120 ***bel canto:*** **(waiter said) New York Daily News,** Jan. 17, 1982.

120 **"something different": Life**, Apr. 23, 1965—Sinatra suggested in this article that his work on **bel canto** began in the mid-1930s, yet goes on to indicate that his work in this area was later, from about 1940. This makes more sense; **("never-never-land stuff ") Opera News**, Nov. 1996; **(Pavarotti)** Sinatra, **Legend**, 289; **("moaning")** Henry Pleasants, **The Great American Popular Singers**, New York: Simon and Schuster, 1974, 187, and see **Stereo Review**, Nov. 1971; **("I didn't know")** int. Connie Haines.

121 **"We were all sure":** Friedwald, 84–.

121 **Astor: (location) NYT**, Dec. 29, 2002; **(reopening/FS performance)** Friedwald, 90–, int. Joe Bushkin; **(jam-packed)** Tormé, 61.

122 **records: (anxious)** Wilson, **Sinatra**, 29, **Goldmine**, Mar. 22, 1991; **("three hard-thrill")** Shaw, **Sinatra**, 192; **(Eighty-four songs) Billboard**, Nov. 20, 1945; **(forty in the first year)** John Ridgway, **The Sinatra File, Part 2**, Birmingham, UK: John Ridgway Books, 1978, 14.

122–123 **"Never Smile":** Shaw, **Sinatra**, 27, Sanford, 176, Friedwald, 93, ints. Joe Bushkin, Jo Stafford. Sources have disagreed on the genesis of the song. The initial version was that songwriter Ruth Lowe wrote it following the death of her music publicist husband during an operation. This account was later questioned, as was the process by which the song reached Dorsey (Wilson, **Sinatra**, 29, Dwiggins, 34–, "Composers and Lyricists Database," http:info.net/.CAL/t16.html, FS int. WOR (NY), Sep. 25, 1981, **Goldmine**, Mar. 22, 1991); **("real easy")** Dwiggins, 34; **(twelve weeks)** Ed O'Brien with Robert Wilson, **Sinatra 101**, New York: Boulevard Books, 1996, 3, "Sinatra on the Wireless," Sinatra Music Society, 2000—author John Rockwell notes that "Never Smile" stayed on the charts for four months, Rockwell, 72; **(endless play)** Sciacca, **Sinatra**, 40; **(bonus)** Wilson, **Sinatra**, 30; **(milestone)** FS in **Silver Screen**, Mar. 24, 1948.

124 **war mood: ("until, in God's good time")** Harold Evans, **The American Century**, London: Jonathan Cape, 1998, 301; **(draft)** Address to the Registrants under the Selective Service Law, Oct. 16, 1940, Mt. Holyoke Library; **(questionnaire)** SAC Newark to Director, Feb. 10, 1944, FBI 25-244122-3; **("Young man") As I Remember It**, Frank Sinatra Jr. commentary, Angel Records, 1996.

124 ***Las Vegas Nights:*** **(Palladium)** Tormé, 64–, Simon, 169; **("Never Smile"/fee)** O'Brien, 204, int. A. C. Lyles; **("lying in that warm")** "Artanis Knarf," unid. Bobby Burns article, MHL; **(suite)** int. Connie Haines.

125 **affairs/state of marriage: (Gooding)** int. Nick Sevano, Kelley, 56–; **(excited by news) Modern Screen,** Jul. 17, 1947, Sinatra, **Legend,** 43; **("Miss Moonbeams")** Freedland, 55; **("Nancy")** Friedwald, 142–, Sinatra, **My Father,** 69–; **("Frank would tap")** int. Joe Bushkin; **("I used to stand")** David Hanna, **Sinatra,** New York: Gramercy Books, 1990, 16; **("I looked up")** Liz Smith, **Natural Blonde,** New York: Hyperion, 2000, 306; **("There was this thin")** int. Peggy Maley; **("the way he caressed")** ed. Vare, 43; **("I can have")** Taraborrelli, 46; **(Cahn)** Cahn, 132; **("A short time after") American Weekly,** Jul. 20, 1952; **("because of ")** Sinatra with Coplon, 15.

127 **"This Love of Mine":** Friedwald, 106, Shaw, **Sinatra,** 29—Sol Parker, a shirt salesman, also contributed to the song. Although eight songs have been attributed to Sinatra, the music writer Will Friedwald commits himself only to Sinatra's authorship of "This Love of Mine" and "I'm a Fool to Want You" ("Sinatra the Songwriter," at www.members.aol.com/artanis103/sinatra.html).

127 **"Nothing meant":** Levinson, **September,** 114.

127 **Dorsey had said repeatedly: Cosmopolitan,** May 1956.

128 **FS remembered: Life,** Apr. 23, 1965.

128 **Crosby and FS:** ed. Yarwood, 116, Hamill, 24–. Don Dwiggins, author of **Frankie,** wrote that Sinatra and Crosby met briefly during the shooting of **Las Vegas Nights.** Other sources indicate they did not meet until 1941 or 1943 (Dwiggins, 35, but see Friedwald, 92, **Saturday Evening Post,** Aug. 24, 1946, and Louella Parsons in **Los Angeles Examiner,** Jan. 7, 1962).

128 **"This Sinatra":** "Artanis Knarf," unid. Bobby Burns article, MHL.

128 **survey/magazines:** Shaw, **Sinatra,** 28–, **Goldmine,** Mar. 22, 1991, Sciacca, **Sinatra,** 40, **Palm Springs Life,** Feb. 2002.

128 **arrogance/violence: ("cocky") Metronome,** Sep. 1943; **("best singer")** Cahn, 132; **(Wilson)** Wilson, **Sinatra,** 30–; **("He didn't like me"/"He called me 'cornball' ") Palm Springs Life,** Feb. 2002, int. Connie Haines, and see Connie Haines, **For Once in My Life,** New York: Warner, 1976, 39–; **("sulk") Screen Star,** Jun. 28, 1955; **("I was changing")** int. Lucille Kirk Buccini,

M/G int. of Buccini; **(Hawkins)** Levinson, **Blues,** 70; **(drunk)** Sanford, 184; **("flew off")** Shaw, **Sinatra,** 26; **("The trouble")** Milton Berle, **Milton Berle,** New York: Delacorte, 1974, 212.

129–131 **Rich: (egos)** Simon, 169; **(tempers)** Levinson, **Blues,** 209, Tormé, **Traps,** 62; **(rooming)** Douglas-Home, 23; **(bus)** photo—Sinatra, **Legend,** 45; **(little chance)** Tormé, **Traps,** 60–; **(billing) Palm Springs Life,** Feb. 2002; **(irritate) Billboard,** Nov. 20, 1965, Dwiggins, 34, ints. Joe Bushkin, Jo Stafford, Freedland, 61; **(pitcher incident) Palm Springs Life,** Feb. 2002, ints. Jo Stafford, Joe Bushkin, Connie Haines, Tormé, **Traps,** 62; **(Rich beaten up) Down Beat,** Sep. 1, 1940; **("coldly"/"he had asked")** Tormé, **Traps,** 62–; **(Frank lent) New Jersey Monthly,** Feb. 1982, Dwiggins, 34; **(performed together) JazzTimes,** May 1998, Golden Nugget poster; **(helped when ill)** (Ireland) **Sunday Independent,** Apr. 15, 2001; **("He's the most")** Kelley, 64.

131–133 **FS/Dorsey rift: (short fuse)** Simon, 170, int. Tommy Dorsey III, **Palm Springs Life,** Feb. 2002; **(FS sent home)** Tormé, **Traps,** 63; **(fired FS)** int. Connie Haines; **("all they wanted") Billboard,** Nov. 20, 1965, **New Yorker,** Nov. 9, 1946; **("This boy's going")** Wilson, **Sinatra,** 31—the reporter was Earl Wilson; **(Dorsey and uniforms)** Simon, 171; **("go and comb") Palm Springs Life,** Feb. 2002; **("We were like puppets") Life,** May 3, 1943, and see Hamill, 110; **(year's notice)** Douglas-Home, 25, Friedwald, 111, but see doubt as to whether he gave notice at Levinson, **September,** 114; **($250)** ed. Vare, 34; **("strike"?)** Wilson, **Sinatra,** 33; **(rehearsed)** Friedwald, 108; **("It was a real")** Dwiggins, 40; **("Frank sat")** Haines, 41; **(well received)** Shaw, **Sinatra,** 31; **(polls) New Yorker,** Nov. 9, 1946, **Redbook,** Oct. 1951, Freedland, 59, Taraborrelli, 50; **(encores)** Shaw, **Sinatra,** 32.

133 **raise to $400:** While Dorsey biographer Peter Levinson refers to a raise to $400, Sinatra asserted later that he was earning only $150 a week at this time (**Palm Springs Life,** Feb. 2002, **American Weekly,** Jul. 27, 1952).

133–134 **FS leaves Dorsey: ("He started talking")** Kelley, 60–; **(FS felt had to leave)** Douglas-Home, 25, FS int. by Zion, Shaw, **Sinatra,** 32; **(Dorsey reaction)** FS int. by Zion, **New York Daily News,** Jan. 23, 1978, Kelley, 61, Sinatra, **Legend,** 50; **(two more years?)** FS in **American Weekly,** Jul. 27, 1952—FS referred to "one more year with options" while Nick Sevano has spoken of the full contract having been for five years; M/G int. of Sevano; **(late/walking out)** M/G int. of Nick Sevano; **(schedule)** Sinatra, **Legend,** 48–; **("Let him go")** Wilson, **Sinatra,** 35.

134 **sang with Dorsey last time:** Sinatra himself, and a contemporary report by **Metronome**'s George Simon, indicate that the last performance with Dorsey was on September 10 (**Billboard,** Nov. 20, 1965, **Metronome,** May 1943).

134 **"was literally crying": Cosmopolitan,** May 1956.

134 **"You're not gonna leave":** FS int. by Zion.

134 **severance deal: (terms)** "Assignment of Wages," Sep. 3, 1942, supplied to authors by Tommy Dorsey III, FS in **American Weekly,** Jul. 27, 1952, **Saturday Evening Post,** Aug. 24, 1946, Freedland, 69. One music magazine was to calculate that Sinatra was committed to pay over 93 percent of his earnings to others. Another waggish theory had it that he had managed to sell more than 100 percent of himself. Sinatra's predecessor Jack Leonard had been released only under basically the same conditions. Connie Haines had a similar contract, although Dorsey did not hold her to it (percentages—Shaw, **Sinatra,** 62; Leonard/Haines—Sciacca, **Sinatra,** 39, int. Connie Haines, Haines, 58); **(unlimited)** ibid., int. Tommy Dorsey III, and see "Assignment of Wages."

135 **FS/Dorsey dispute: ("wrong for anybody")** Shaw, **Sinatra,** 62, **New York Journal-American,** Aug. 25, 1943; **("ratty")** Sinatra, **Legend,** 49; **(suit) New York Journal-American,** Aug. 25, 1943, **Chicago's American,** Sep. 26, 1966.

135–136 **"I hired": American Weekly,** Jul. 27, 1952. References to the amount of the severance deal have varied. The authors here cite Sinatra's 1952 version, but Nancy Sinatra's two books on her father refer to a total sum of $75,000. It has generally been said that Sinatra's contribution to the deal was ponied up by Columbia Records, as an advance against future royalties. Columbia was reportedly persuaded to pay on Sinatra's behalf by its senior executive Manie Sacks, who believed in Sinatra's potential. Another theory, propounded by author Michael Freedland, is that Dorsey made the arrangement possible for Sinatra by agreeing to wait until he could find the money ($60,000—**American Weekly,** Jul. 27, 1952, and see **Down Beat,** Aug. 1998 reprinting article of Sep. 15, 1953; $75,000—Sinatra, **My Father,** 40, Sinatra, **Legend,** 50; Columbia—**Saturday Evening Post,** Aug. 24, 1946, **Billboard,** Nov. 20, 1965; Freedland—Freedland, 72); **("No!**

No! No!") FS int. by Zion; **(Jaffe/Dorsey exchange)** drawn from FS int. by Zion, and Sinatra, **My Father,** 40.

136 **physical threat to Dorsey: (article) New American Mercury,** Aug. 1951—the article was by the hostile journalist Lee Mortimer; **("Tommy told me")** int. Ed Becker; **(FS insisted) American Weekly,** Jul. 27, 1952, Sinatra, **My Father,** 39, FS int. by Zion, and see FS testimony, Nevada State Gaming Control Board, Feb. 11, 1981; **(attorney/aide)** Kelley, 63–; **(Dexter)** ints. Brad Dexter.

136–137 **Dorsey children and threat:** ints. Tommy Dorsey III, Patricia Dorsey Hooker. As reported in Randy Taraborrelli's biography of Sinatra, quoting Sinatra's friend Joey D'Orazio, Dorsey was threatened not by "real underworld characters but just some frightening fellows" known to Sinatra and Hank Sanicola. D'Orazio knew this, he is quoted as saying, because he himself had been asked to fly to Los Angeles with the men involved. He refused to take part, but learned about the threat to Dorsey afterward. He said Sanicola "didn't want Sinatra to know any of the details . . . he always wanted Sinatra to be able to claim that he didn't know nuttin' about nuttin'." Taraborrelli also quoted Bea Wilken, a friend of Dorsey's then wife Pat Dane, as saying that Sinatra "sent his fellows to hurt Tommy" (Taraborrelli, 65).

137–138 **Moretti involvement?: ("I was visited") Parade,** Jan. 12, 1964; **("The Italians")** Eisenberg, Dan, and Landau, 233; **("when some dough")** Gosch and Hammer, 312; **(Bureau of Narcotics document)** "File Review and Summary Check," Frank Sinatra, Sep. 19, 1960, FBI 100-41413-121, and see "Correlation Summary," Frank Sinatra, Jun. 8, 1964, FSFBI, **Wall Street Journal,** Aug. 19, 1968, Gage, 81–, int. Ralph Salerno; **("assigned")** int. Sonny King; **("friends with the Boys") Las Vegas Review-Journal,** May 17, 1998; **("You don't know Italians")** Lees, 91, ints. Gene Lees, Gene DiNovi.

Chapter 8: "F-R-A-N-K-I-E-E-E-E-E!"

139 **Dorsey on FS leaving: ("I hope you fall")** Sinatra, **Legend,** 50; **(did not think)** Lawrence Quirk and William Schoell, **The Rat Pack,** Dallas: Taylor, 1998, 25.

139 **Sacks recognized: Saturday Evening Post,** Aug. 24, 1946.

139 **industry paralyzed: Goldmine,** Mar. 22, 1991, Simon, 54. Sacks had known Sinatra since his days at the Rustic Cabin, twice heard him sing with Dorsey, and assured him of recording work as a soloist "anytime you're free." He reportedly persuaded Columbia to contribute $25,000 to help Sinatra get out of his Dorsey contract (see chapter 7, page 74 **supra.**). Sacks and Sinatra signed an initial agreement in 1942, and Columbia found ways around the union dispute. In May 1943 the company rereleased "All or Nothing at All," which had been recorded with Harry James in 1939, and it now became a million-copy best seller. The following month Sinatra cut the first of nine solo songs sung a capella, accompanied only by voices because of the ban on using musicians. Normal recording did not resume until November 1944, by which time Sinatra had shot to the top by other routes (Sacks—**Woman's Home Companion,** May 1956, **Saturday Evening Post,** Aug. 24, 1946, **Billboard,** Nov. 20, 1965; first agreement—Friedwald, 122; "All or Nothing at All"/a capella—Ridgway, pt. 2, 21, 26–).

139–140 **no sure thing: (*Reveille*)** O'Brien, 204; **(NBC) Billboard,** Nov. 20, 1965, Shaw, 38; **(Burns)** George Burns, **Dr. Burns' Prescription for Happiness,** New York: Putnam, 1984, 151; **(Babs)** Music Web Encyclopedia of Popular Music, www.musicweb.uk.net; **(CBS) Saturday Evening Post,** Aug. 24, 1946, Friedwald, 121–; **(theaters)** FS int. by Zion, FS int. by Arlene Francis, Oct. 1, 1977, WOR (NY).

140 **Romm/Weitman/Mosque: (got the attention) Saturday Evening Post,** Aug. 24, 1946, **Chicago's American,** Sep. 26, 1966; **(half full) Woman's Home Companion,** May 1956; **("He rang me")** FS int. by Zion.

141 **Paramount: (described)** "Paramount Building Timeline," Tobin Parnes Design Enterprises, http://tobinparnes.com, "The Paramount Building," www.greatgridlock.net, Wilson, **Sinatra,** 25; **(At dawn)** FS int. by Zion.

141–142 **"EXTRA" at Paramount:** photo in Doctor, 26. Sources have varied as to whether the Paramount opening was on December 30 or 31, 1942. A contemporary advertisement in **Metronome** established that it was on December 30 (30th—entry, **Where or When?** CD compiled by Giuseppe Marcucci, Dick Schwarz, and Ed Vanhellemonk, privately published, Jan. 2002, Shaw, **Sinatra,** 40, Dwiggins, 45; 31st—Friedwald, 123, FS int. by Zion; advertisement—Doctor, 25–). **("Who's he")** Shaw, **Sinatra,** 40; **("Benny"/"I thought")** Sinatra, My Father, 44; **("F-R-A-N-K-I-E-E-E-E-E")** ibid., 45; **("absolutely deafening"/Goodman could not imagine)** Dwiggins, 45, Kelley, 66; **("For Me and My Gal")** Dwiggins, 45; **("Black Magic") Silver Screen,** Mar. 24, 1948; **("The devout") New Republic,** Nov. 6, 1944; **(a hundred songs)** Wilson, **Sinatra,** 40; **(nine shows) Life,** Aug. 23, 1965—but see "10 shows," **Life,** Jun. 25, 1971; **("One Saturday")** Larry King int. of FS, May 19, 1998 (rerun); **(family to theater) New York Daily News,** Apr. 2, 1944, Kelley, 95–; **(Marty/Francesco)** Freedland, 80, **NYT,** May 17, 1990, FS int. on **Suzy Visits; (appearance extended) Life,** May 3, 1943, **Saturday Evening Post,** Aug. 24, 1946, **Newsweek,** Mar. 22, 1943, **Metronome,** May 1943.

143–144 **bobbysoxers: (typically dressed)** Taraborrelli, 54fn; **(bobbysoxers) New Republic,** Nov. 6, 1944; **("The squealing")** Armand Deutsch, **Me and Bogie,** New York: Putnam, 1991, 103, int. Armand Deutsch; **(settled in) New Yorker,** Nov. 2, 1946, int. Al Viola, Alan Dale, **The Spider and the Marionettes,** New York: Lyle Stuart, 1965, 53; **(urinated) Hi Fidelity,** Aug. 1971, Shaw, **Sinatra,** 42; **("They would scream")** int. Al Viola; **("hushed")** Kahn, 51; **(to knees/billboards)** Freedland, 78, Wilson, **Sinatra,** 40, Kahn, 54; **(trimmings) Liberty,** Feb. 12, 1944, Kahn, 55, Wilson, **Sinatra,** 56; **(handkerchief)** Wilson, **Sinatra,** 54; **(in front of his car)** Kahn, 55, int. Jo Carroll Dennison; **(flowers, etc.)** Kahn, 66; **(underwear thrown)** int. Nick Sevano; **(brassieres/opened coat)** Dwiggins, 37; **("He was my idol")** int. Marie Caruba; **("Groups of little girls") All or Nothing at All,** BBC radio documentary, undated, audiotape in authors' collection, **NYT,** Oct. 13, 1974—Lear appears to have seen FS at the Paramount and in Boston, and see Friedwald, 124, Kahn, 63, Dwiggins, 48; **("poor") New Republic,** Nov. 6, 1944; **("plain")** Kahn, 46; **("unkempt") Cosmopolitan,** May 1956.

146–147 **Riobamba: ("for kids")** Wilson, Sinatra, 43; **(business down) Newsday,** Nov. 15, 1991; **(Jarwood changed mind)** Wilson, **Sinatra,** 43; **(FS fretted)** Shaw, **Sinatra,** 43; **(packed them in) New York Journal-American,** Feb. 27, 1956, Wilson, **Sinatra,** 42; **("We could hardly")** ibid. 46; **(critic drunk?) Saturday Evening Post,** Aug. 24, 1946; **("wondrous")** Wilson, **Sinatra,** 44–; **("most cosmopolitan")** Cahn, 132; **("Three**

times") Life, May 3, 1943; **(Barrett and O'Keefe dropped)** **New York Journal-American,** Feb. 27, 1956; **("When I came")** **Saturday Evening Post,** Aug. 24, 1946.

147–148 **progress 1943/1944: (back to Paramount)** Metronome, May 1943, Dwiggins, 46; **(orchestras)** Shaw, **Sinatra,** 55, NYT, Aug. 4, 1943, **Life,** Aug. 23, 1943, Dwiggins, 58–, Wilson, **Sinatra,** 52, Kahn, 61, "Special Concert for the Benefit of the National Symphony," program, Jul. 25, 1943; **(Los Angeles)** LAT, Aug. 1, 4, 12, 16, **Metronome,** Sep. 1943, **Movie Stars,** Jul. 1966; **("swing-shift Caruso")** Dwiggins, 59; **(*Higher and Higher*)** O'Brien, 12–, Ridgway, pt. 3, 4—the successor movie would be **Step Lively; (Waldorf)** Wilson, **Sinatra,** 49, 53–, **Billboard,** Nov. 20, 1965.

148 ***Your Hit Parade:*** Shaw, **Sinatra,** 87–, Kahn, 111–, Friedwald, 127–. Sinatra's first appearance on **Your Hit Parade** was on February 27, 1943. While working on **Hit Parade,** Sinatra began his first radio series, **The Broadway Bandbox.** Other radio shows to feature Sinatra in this period were **The Frank Sinatra Program, The Frank Sinatra Show, Songs by Sinatra** (Ridgway, pt. 1, 6–).

148 ***Anchors Aweigh:*** **(described)** O'Brien, 20–; **("I couldn't walk")** eds. Sheila and J. P. Cantillon, **Sinatra: His Life and Loves Decade by Decade,** collector's edition, Los Angeles: LFP, 1990, 50;

149–150 **October 11 opening: (general)** Shaw, **Sinatra,** 45–, NYT, Oct. 13, **New Republic,** Nov. 6, 1944, **Motion Picture Herald,** Oct. 21, 1944; **("I ventured down")** Wilson, **Sinatra,** 59–; **(until nightfall)** Sinatra, **Legend,** 54; **(Chicago, etc.)** Shaw, **Sinatra,** 47.

150–152 **swooners: (reportedly)** Wilson, **Show Business Nobody Knows,** 325, **Time,** Aug. 29, 1955, Kahn, 63, 103; **("A girl in the twelfth row")** William Manchester, **The Glory and the Dream,** Boston: Little, Brown, 1973, 307; **("appeared at the theater")** Dwiggins, 46–; **("These dames")** **Chicago's American,** Sep. 25, 1966; **("slump")** **New Republic,** Nov. 6, 1944; **("I fell")** Kahn, 50; **("We loved")** NYT, Oct. 13, 1974; **("The whole sobbing business")** int. Celeste Holm, BBC Radio, **All or Nothing at All; (Rubin)** Dwiggins, 45–, Wilson, **Sinatra,** 47.

152 **Evans: (represented)** Shaw, **Sinatra,** 54, int. Phil Evans, Quirk and Schoell, 77–, Tosches, 149; **("certain things"/$5,000)** Kahn, 67, and see **Liberty,** Feb. 12, 1944; **("I like to keep")** **Time,** Jul. 5, 1943; Gehman, 194, Dwiggins, 46; **(lipstick)**

Shaw, **Sinatra,** 54; **(basement)** Wilson, **Sinatra,** 41; **("had someone throw")** M/G int. of Nick Sevano; **(clothes torn) New Yorker,** Oct. 26, 1946, Deutsch, 103; **("breakaway suits")** Shaw, **Sinatra,** 55.

153 **"hired to scream":** John Lahr, "Sinatra's Song," www.sinatra-ms.com, **LAHE,** May 15, 1975. Keller became a celebrated press agent in his own right. Jerry Lewis, who would soon become his client, described him as having "an astonishing intellect . . . as close a friend as I would ever hope to have." He was in at the inception of Lewis's campaign to help those suffering from muscular dystrophy (Jerry Lewis with Herb Gluck, **Jerry Lewis, in Person,** London: Robson, 1983, 161, 214, and see **LAHE,** May 15, 1975); **("98% synthetic") Chicago's American,** Sep. 26, 1966; **("It was kind of comical")** Quirk and Schoell, 26.

153 **FS and fans: (surprise?) Life,** Apr. 23, 1965, FS int. by Zion, Suzy Visits; **(disliked shrieking)** Friedwald, 134; **("I was the boy") NYT,** May 16, 1998; **(stare/tongue/"I never saw")** Kahn, 51, 77.

153–154 **reason for hysteria?: (general)** Kahn, 48–, Manchester, 309, **New Republic,** Nov. 6, 1944; **("a sort of melodic") New Republic,** Nov. 6, 1944; **("To femmes of fifteen")** Freedland, 88; **("The young Sinatra")** Atlantic Monthly, Sep. 1998; **("The sex element") Down Beat,** May 12, 1960; **("What yo-yos!")** NYT, Oct. 13, 1974; **("What is it?") Movieland,** Aug. 15, 1946.

154–155 **FS made a star: (rushed into a studio) Billboard,** Nov. 20, 1965; **(Seventeen songs)** Ridgway, pt. 2, 27–; **($20,000) New Republic,** Nov. 6, 1944, and see **Saturday Evening Post,** Aug. 24, 1946.

155 **$1.5 million income:** Kahn, 2, **Movieland,** Aug. 15, 1946. These extraordinary figures are those that were accepted at the time by reputable sources. George Evans was quoted in 1944 as saying that his client was making about $1 million a year, most of which went in taxes. In her 1995 book **Legend,** Sinatra's daughter Nancy suggested her father was paid as much as $25,000 a week as of early 1943, which does not square with other accounts (**Stars and Stripes,** Jul. 5, 1944, Sinatra, **Legend,** 51–); **("I couldn't believe")** Louella Parsons, **Tell It to Louella,** New York: Putnam, 1961, 150—the remark was made to Parsons, probably in 1945; **("I now own") New Yorker,** Nov. 9, 1946; **(Barton Music)** int. Joe Bushkin, Kahn, 41, **Chicago's American,** Sep.

26, 1966, Shaw, **Sinatra,** 57–; **(office building) Billboard,** Nov. 20, 1965; **(booking agent) New Yorker,** Nov. 9, 1946.

155–156 **Stordahl and FS:** Douglas-Home, 25–, FS int. by Tom Jones, Melbourne, Australia, 1955, audiotape in authors' collection supplied by Alf Batchelder. Stordahl's musical partnership with Sinatra would essentially last from the time of the break with Dorsey to the end of his tenure with Columbia Records in 1953. They also worked together at the start and end of Sinatra's time at Capitol Records, which followed. The two men were long close personally, to the extent that Stordahl was best man at Sinatra's wedding to Ava Gardner. His career was cut short, however, by his death at fifty in 1963 (Shaw, **Sinatra,** 153).

156 **Cahn/Styne and FS:** Cahn, 133–, FS int. by Arlene Francis, Oct. 1, 1977, WOR (NY), Theodore Taylor, **Jule,** New York: Random House, 1979, 4–, 95–, **Modern Screen,** Jul. 17, 1947. Sinatra's relations with Cahn and Styne did not run smoothly. Relations with Cahn were to improve, after a rift. With Styne, however, there was a lasting chill (Cahn, 141–, int. Tita Cahn, Taylor, 125); **(Sanicola)** Douglas-Home, 25–, int. of FS by Helen Hover, undat. clip, MHL, Cahn, 141; **(sonofabitch who "would go down")** Wilson, **Sinatra,** 36; **(fired Sevano)** int. Nick Sevano, Kelley, 80–.

156 **FS pugnacious image: (cousin Frank)** ints. Marilyn Sinatra—daughter, Rose Paldino, Rose Ellman Sinatra, **National Enquirer,** May 22, 1979; **(Sanicola bodyguard) Look,** Jun. 11, 1957; **("I'd like to see") NYT,** Dec. 18, 1943; **(Tamburro)** see earlier references, int. Rose Tamburro; **(work out/Silvani) Newsweek,** Mar. 22, 1943, **Life,** May 3, 1943, **NYT,** Oct. 20, 1984; **Billboard,** Nov. 20, 1965, **Sports Illustrated,** Feb. 14, 1972; **(Silvani bodyguard)** int. Gloria Cahn Franks; **("I was intimidated")** Granata, 32.

157 **"He was my special nurse":** Peggy Lee, **Miss Peggy Lee,** New York: Donald Fine, 1989, 20.

157 **FS largesse: (Anthony)** Dwiggins, 32; **(musician/snowstorm) Modern Screen,** undat. article, 1946?, by George Evans, MHL; **(three hundred lighters/cuff links/key chain/Navy crew)** Kahn, 23–, **New Yorker,** Oct. 26, 1946; **(Styne)** Taylor, 95; **(Ragland)** Shaw, **Sinatra,** 100; **(FS glittered) New Yorker,** Oct. 26, 1946, Helen Hover int. of FS, undat. clip, MHL, **Newsweek,** Mar. 22, 1943.

158 **FS clothes: (general)** Wilson, 49, **Life,** May 3, 1943, Kahn, 26–, **Movie Stars Parade,** Jun. 4, 1947; **(shirts)** M/G int. of Nick Sevano, Wilson, **Sinatra,** 47; **(fifty suits, etc.)** Kahn, 25.

158 **Hasbrouck Heights: Newsweek,** Mar. 22, 1943, Dwiggins, 54.

158–159 **Toluca Lake: (MGM contract) American Weekly,** Jul. 20, 1952; **(described) Movieland,** Jun. 11, 1945, Eleanor Harris, "If You Were a House Guest of the Frank Sinatras," undat. 1945? MHL, Shaw, **Sinatra,** 71; **(Lakeside Country Club) Woman's Home Companion,** Jun. 1956, Cahn, 119, and see Sinatra, **Legend,** 63; **(Warm Valley)** Dwiggins, 83; **(Lanza) LAT,** Jun. 4, 1951, Strait and Robinson, 14–; **(home entertainment)** Taylor, 111; **(the Swooners)** Rockwell, 69, Sinatra, **Legend,** 81–, photo following Cahn, 91, but see **Hollywood Citizen-News,** Aug. 20, 1945—re team called "Cleffs"; **(cards on raft)** Sinatra, **Legend,** 61; **(gin rummy)** int. Gloria Cahn Franks, Cahn, 119.

160–161 **state of marriage: (Evans anxious)** Gehman, 199, Wilson, **Sinatra,** 80, **Redbook,** Oct. 1951; **(schmaltzy stories)** "If You Were a House Guest of the Frank Sinatras," **Photoplay,** Sep. 1945, Helen Hover int. of FS, **Movieland,** Aug. 15, 1946, **New York Journal-American,** Feb. 27, 1956, **Junior Miss,** Sep. 1944, ed. Yarwood, 119; **(Frank Jr. birth) Jersey Observer,** Jan. 11, 1944, int. Adeline Biondy Yacenda; **(naming)** Sinatra, **My Father,** 53; **(cement?/"Little by little") American Weekly,** Jul. 20, 1952; **(fan mail) Chicago's American,** Sep. 26, 1966, Sinatra, **Legend,** 52; **(handle the money)** Wilson, **Sinatra,** 48; **(siege) New Republic,** Nov. 6, 1944, **Bergen** (NJ) **Record,** May 16, 1998, **Los Angeles Examiner,** Aug. 5, 1945, **Woman's Home Companion,** May 1956; **(Frank's boxers) Bergen** (NJ) **Record,** May 17, 1998, Wilson, **Sinatra,** 78; **(kidnap?) Los Angeles Evening Herald Express,** Jun. 13, 1944, **Los Angeles Examiner,** Aug. 5, 1945, and see memo to file, March 1, 1955, FBI 100-41713-4; **("People tried")** int. Gloria Cahn Franks, Shaw, **Sinatra,** 71; **(Nancy's family) Look,** May 14, 1957, Gehman, 199; Sinatra, **My Father,** 58; **("I was on edge") American Weekly,** Jul. 20, 1952; **(parties on his own) Cosmopolitan,** May 1956; **(drink) Woman's Home Companion,** Jun. 1956, int. Brad Dexter; **("I began to drink")** FS int., unid. French article supplied to authors by Peggy Connelly.

161 **list of women:** Shaw, **Sinatra,** 73. Sources differ as to whether the supposed list was on the door during shooting of **Anchors**

Aweigh or earlier, during **Higher and Higher** (Shaw, **Sinatra,** 71, Sciacca, **Sinatra,** 123); **(Bau)** int. Bau by Robert Slatzer, supplied to authors.

Chapter 9: Rejected for Service

163–164 **Sinatra singing in war: ("When the Yanks")** int. Joe Bushkin, **Billboard,** Nov. 20, 1965, Friedwald, 136, Ridgway, pt. 2, 258—the song was written by FS's former Dorsey colleague, Joe Bushkin; **(V-Discs)** ibid., 257–; **(The Voice painted/ Shivarg)** Derek Jewell, **Frank Sinatra: A Celebration,** New York: Applause, 1999, 6, int. Alexander Shivarg; **(Tokyo Rose)** "Tokyo Rose" bio, www.fbi.gov, Freedland, 122; **("Some women")** Hamill, 128; **("said for the boys")** Lees, 93.

165–166 **FS war support: ("As we listened")** Lana Turner, **Lana: The Lady, the Legend, the Truth,** New York: Dutton, 1982, 75, int. Joe Bushkin; ***(Command Performance)*** "AFRTS and Hollywood," American Forces Radio and Television Service website; **(rallies/shows) Movie Stars Parade,** Jun. 4, 1947, **Blue Ribbon,** undat., 1943, **Billboard,** Nov. 20, 1965, ed. Leonard Mustazza, **Sinatra: An Annotated Bibliography,** Westport, CT: Greenwood Press, 1999, 216, "Frank Sinatra: The Columbia Years; The V-Discs," Sep. 1994 press release, www.legacyrecordings.com, Kelley, 83, Sinatra, **Legend,** 55, 57, 59; **(WAVES)** Freedland, 90; **(donate clothing)** NYT, Apr. 6, 1945; **(loan drive)** Dwiggins, 63.

166–167 **entertainers who served:** int. Joe Bushkin, Simon, 173, 363–, 422, Kelley, 74, Levinson, **September,** 54, "Artanis Knarf," undat. article by Bobby Burns, MHL, Shaw, **Sinatra,** 65, Sanford, 206, Dwiggins, 27, int. Jimmy Roselli, "The Stars Go to War," http://history.sandiego.edu, "Celebrities in Uniform," USAF Museum, "USO Recruits Support Troops," www.defenselink.mil/news, Clive Hirschhorn, **Gene Kelly,** New York: St. Martin's, 1974, 101, 107, 124–.

167–169 **FS and military service: (flagpole/patriotism)** Sinatra with Coplon, 144, Sinatra, **My Father,** 364; **(controversy)** "Classification History: Frank Albert Sinatra, Serial Number 2615, Order Number 204," released to authors 2003, ints. and corr. Alyce Burton, Office of Public and Congressional Affairs, Selective Service System; **("first duty")** "Address to the Registrants under the Selective Service Law," Oct. 16, 1940, Mt. Holyoke

Library; **(Italian-Americans) The Italians in America,** TV documentary, **supra.; ("a bunch of") WP,** Dec. 7, 2001; **(coast guard)** fingerprint record, FBI 3-734-610 in NY 166-3211, Sect. 1; **(Evans/publicity)** Dwiggins, 62–, **NYT,** Nov. 6, 1943, Shaw, **Sinatra,** 65, Wilson, **Sinatra,** 56; **(physical)** Memo to the Director, Feb. 10, 1944, "Frank Albert Sinatra," FBI 25-244122; **(height)** ibid., "Registrar's Report," Oct. 16, 1940—supplied to authors by Selective Service Administration, "Biography of Frank Sinatra," Solters & Roskin Public Relations, circa 1979; **(rejected) NYT,** Dec. 10, 1943, Dwiggins, 57, Shaw, **Sinatra,** 65; **("Sinatra has no more")** letter to Walter Winchell, Dec. 30, 1943, FBI 25-244122; **("How do you get")** Wilson, **Sinatra,** 57; **("draft dodger")** Hamill, 27; **("There's a lot")** Dwiggins, 66, Shaw, **Sinatra,** 91, "Artanis Knarf," unid. article by Bobby Burns, MHL; **(egg) LAT,** Oct. 15, **Los Angeles Examiner,** Oct. 16, 1944; **(tomatoes)** ibid., eds. Tom and Phil Kuntz, **The Sinatra Files,** New York: Three Rivers, 2000, photo section; **(booed)** "What Is Frank Sinatra Really Like?" unid. article by Jack Holland, 1943, MHL; **("It is not too much")** Manchester, 309.

169 **2-A(F) classification:** The Selective Service record released to the authors states that the 2-A(F) reclassification applied as of May 9, 1944. Confused contemporary press reports suggested this designation applied only as of the start of March 1945. In fact, early March marked the restoration of his 4-F status (**New York Sun,** Mar. 3, 1945, **Jersey Observer,** Mar. 5, 1945, Kelley, 102); **("Is crooning?")** Freedland, 95; **(summoned back) Washington Times-Herald,** Feb. 2, **New York Sun,** Jan. 30, **LAT,** Feb. 4, 1945; **(fans/Fort Jay) New York Sun,** Feb. 8, 10, 13, 1945, Dwiggins, 63–, Shaw, **Sinatra,** 89–; **("for review") New York Sun,** Mar. 3, 1945; **("Frail Finch") Jersey Observer,** Mar. 5, 1945.

170 **4-F again:** At the time, both an initial official statement and press reports suggested that Sinatra was to remain 2-A(F) until September 1945, stating that this meant he was doing essential civilian work. The official Selective Service record, however, reflects the restoration of 4-F status, as Sinatra's press agent George Evans made clear in an announcement (**New York Sun,** Mar. 3, **Jersey Observer,** Mar. 5, **Los Angeles Herald Express,** Mar. 6, 1945, Kelley, 101, Wilson, **Sinatra,** 58).

170–171 **controversy over FS and draft: ("Can you tell me?")** New York **Sun,** Mar. 1, 1945; **(Sokolsky)** ibid.; **(Mortimer)** (NY) **Sunday Mirror,** Jul. 15, 1945; **(Pegler) Washington Times-Herald,** Jan. 24, 1948; **("glad to serve"/"gunnery")** NYT, Nov. 6, 1943; **(marines?)** Wilson, **Sinatra,** 57; **("desperate")** Sinatra, **Legend,** 48, and see Kelley, 76, **Los Angeles Examiner,** Aug. 20, 1960, **Modern Screen,** undat. 1946, MHL; **("singing night and day")** **Modern Screen,** May 1947; **(seven-week tour)** Newsweek, Jul. 23, 1945, **Billboard,** Nov. 20, 1965, Kahn, 115; **("soldiers in greasepaint") B.G. News,** Feb. 5, 2003; **(Jolson/Brown/Oberon)** "The Great Entertainers," www.dinesp.fsnet.co.uk, "The Friendly Log Cabin," USO exhibit, University of Alaska, www.lib.uaa.alaska.edu, "1st Fighter Group History, 1944," www.1stfighter.org; **(Bing)** "Bing Crosby Internet Museum," www.kcmetro.cc.mo.us, Hamill, 26; **(Hope)** "The Stars Go to War," http://history.sandiego.edu; **(Dietrich)** Kahn, 115.

171 **"the FBI denied":** Sinatra, **My Father,** 67, Freedland, 96. Press agent George Evans reportedly made a claim similar to Nancy's (Freedland, 96); **(Wayne)** Garry Wills, **John Wayne's America,** New York: Simon and Schuster, 1997, 107–, 331n13; **(Martin)** William Schoell, **Martini Man,** Dallas: Taylor, 1999, 17, Michael Freedland, **Dino: The Dean Martin Story,** London: Comet, 1984, 22; **(Lewis)** Lewis with Gluck, 102–; **("another punctured")** NYT, Dec. 10, 1943.

172 **ear ailment issue: (bribe?)** letter to Walter Winchell, Dec. 30, 1943, FBI 25-244122.

172–173 **FBI/Weintrob/Povalski/questionnaires:** S. K. McKee Memos to the Director, "Frank Albert Sinatra, Selective Service," Feb. 10, 17, 24, 1944, Weintrob to Surgeon General, Dec. 27, 1943, Weintrob to Commanding General, Dec. 28, 1943, Callan to Ladd, Feb. 26, 1944, FBI 25-244122, int. Beverly Weintrob. There is a reference to a mastoid operation in Kitty Kelley's book **His Way.** And according to Al Certo, a former Hoboken tailor who knew him in the early days, he "had an operation for an abscess on the inner ear" in childhood. As mentioned earlier, another account has it that the eardrum was damaged when Sinatra was hit with a bicycle chain during a boyhood fight (Kelley, 17, Evanier, 49, **Cosmopolitan,** May 1956).

173–174 **FS "psychiatric interview":** Weintrob to Commanding General, Dec. 28, 1943, FBI 25-244122-7. The FBI, which had a copy of the doctor's report, secretly leaked the gist of the information in 1947, but it remained unpublished until after Sinatra's death, when his FBI file was released. The full text related to his psychiatric condition is published here for the first time (Ruark to Pegler, Mar. 14, 1947, Box 72, Pegler Papers, Herbert Hoover Library, Memo to Tolson, May 12, 1947, FSFBI); **("should have gone")** int. Bob Neal.

174 **just like any other: New York Sun,** Jan. 30, 1945.

174–175 **FS and politics in early 1940s: ("indoctrinated")** Giuliano audiotape; **(election rally)** Kahn, 30; **("some kind of public") PM,** undat. 1945, MHL; **(reading into night)** Clarke, 43; **("He always had")** int. Peggy Connelly; **(trains/four titles) PM,** undat. 1945, MHL; **(postwar interviewer) Movie Show,** Jul. 31, 1947.

175 **FS admiration for FDR: (FDR alienated)** Gambino, 326; **(Dolly)** Kelley, 93; **("almost amounted")** Shaw, **Sinatra,** 91; **(auction) Billboard,** Nov. 20, 1965.

176 **FDR photographs:** Shaw, **Sinatra,** 91. Years later, he would proudly show Edward R. Murrow an autographed drawing of Roosevelt he had been given after the president's death. It was, he told Murrow, "one of the last times [FDR] ever signed his signature to anything" (**Edward R. Murrow: The Best of Person to Person,** CBS News video, Beverly Hills, CA: FoxVideo, 1992); **(voted Democrat)** Kelley, 93.

176–178 **FS and 1944 campaign: (political George Evans)** int. Phil Evans, Friedwald, 323; **(offered his services) PM,** undat. 1945, MHL; **("Mr. President") PM,** Oct. 2, 1944; **(visit to White House)** "Tea at the White House" guest list, Sep. 28, 1944, Frank Sinatra file, Franklin D. Roosevelt Library, Kahn, 31, Shaw, **Sinatra,** 77, **WP,** Sep. 29, **New York Herald Tribune,** Sep. 29, 1944, **New York Journal-American,** Sep. 12, 1947; **("When I neared him") Movieland,** Jun. 11, 1945; **("Imagine this guy")** Patricia Seaton Lawford with Ted Schwarz, **The Peter Lawford Story,** New York: Carroll and Graf, 1988, 72; **(other occasion)** Sinatra, **My Father,** 53, and see **Movie Stars' Parade,** Jun. 4, 1947; **(columnists)** Kelley, 93–; **(parody)** Dwiggins, 71; **($7,500) New Republic,** Nov. 6, 1944, Kahn, 32; **(Dewey) New Republic,** Nov. 6, 1944, **Time,** Aug. 29, 1955; **(buttons) New Yorker,** Nov. 2, 1946; **(flyer)** "Correlation Summary," Jun. 8, 1964, FSFBI; **(Show business people) LAT,** Oct. 3, 1944,

Ronald Brownstein, **The Power and the Glitter,** New York: Pantheon, 1990, 93–, David Thomson, **Rosebud,** London: Little, Brown, 1996, 209, 257–; **(Robinson)** Ted Morgan, **FDR: A Biography,** New York: Simon and Schuster, 1985, 726; **(FS broadcasts) PM,** Oct. 2, **NYT,** Oct. 28, Nov. 4, 1944; **(Carnegie Hall)** ed. Vare, 116, Kelley, 94; **(Madison Square Garden) PM,** undat. 1945, MHL.

179 **broadcasts in Italian: PM,** Nov. 5, 1944, **NYT,** Oct. 28, Nov. 4, 1944, "Administrative Page," FBI 100-26603—C72 and 100-26603-3485. It is not clear whether these were broadcasts for Italian Americans in the United States who spoke no English, or propaganda for transmission to Italy at this point of the war. Sinatra reportedly did make broadcasts for Italy on behalf of the government, but after the war, in 1948 (**Los Angeles Examiner,** Apr. 5, 1948); **(Astor rally)** Dwiggins, 71; **(drinking with Welles) New York Post,** Feb. 5, 1945; **(hoisting FS)** Sinatra, **Legend,** 64.

179 **"When I go": PM,** undat. 1945, MHL.

179–180 **FDR inauguration/death: (not able to attend) Modern Screen,** Jul. 17, 1947, and see guest list for Jan. 19, 1945, luncheon, Frank Sinatra file, Franklin D. Roosevelt Library; **(FS reaction to death)** Wilson, **Show Business,** vii; **(memorial service)** corr. Raymond Teichman to authors, Apr. 17, 30, 2003—Teichman is archivist of Roosevelt Presidential Library, **NYT,** Apr. 12, 1946, Shaw, **Sinatra,** 91; **(cheered FDR's passing)** Morgan, 765.

180–181 **criticism of FS politics: ("third of the nation")** "Fireside Chat on Reorganization of the Judiciary," Mar. 9, 1937, Franklin D. Roosevelt Library; **("Poverty") PM,** undat. 1945, MHL; **(admired Wallace)** Kelley, 110, and see **New Republic,** Jan. 6, 1947; **(Wallace "communist")** e.g., Morgan, 76, **Atlantic Monthly,** Aug. 1948; **(PAC)** Morgan, 738–, 740, "Labor Wants Out of the Limelight after Glare of Probes," cnn.com, Mar. 31, 1998; **(limerick)** cited at http://historymatters.gmu.edu; **(ICCASP)** Kahn, 32; **("We should keep")** "Summary Memorandum re Francis Albert Sinatra," Sep. 29, 1950, FSFBI, referring to scrawl on **Washington Daily News,** Mar. 11, 1946.

181–182 **election night incident: (Welles drinking)** Simon Callow, **Orson Welles,** London: Vintage, 1996, 283–; **("beat up") New Yorker,** Oct. 26, 1946, referring to Drew Pearson report,

Nov. 1944; **(Pegler denied) Washington Times-Herald,** Jan. 30, 1945; **("shrieking drunk") New York Journal-American,** Dec. 10, 1947; **("Are you that?") Look,** May 28, 1957; **(Welles said) New York Post,** Feb. 5, 1945; **(Frank admitted/ignoring warning)** Kelley, 99; **(at PAC headquarters) Washington Times-Herald,** Jan. 30, 1945, **New York Journal-American,** Dec. 10, 1947; **("The way I saw it") PM,** undat. 1945, MHL.

Chapter 10: Citizen of the Community

184 **liberal Hollywood: ("All phases")** Brownstein, 67; **("the dank air")** Kenneth O'Reilly, **Hoover and the Un-Americans,** Philadelphia: Temple, 1983, 91.

185 **"popular front":** In 1935, from the Soviet Union, Stalin called on the world communist movement to join with liberals of all stripes in a "popular front" to fight fascism. In the United States, "Popular Front" became the umbrella title used to describe both the periods of such cooperation and the many Left organizations involved (Brownstein, 49–, Denning, refs., **Columbia Encyclopedia,** 6th ed., cited at www.bartleby.com); **(card-carrying members)** Brownstein, 53, Larry Ceplair and Steven Englund, **The Inquisition in Hollywood,** Garden City, NY: Anchor Press, 1980, 145; **("something like")** Brownstein, 65; 515–.

185 **FS political philosophy: ("the forgotten man")** Morgan, 346; **("The thing I like") PM,** Oct. 2, 1944; **("a little guy")** Shaw, **Sinatra,** 80; **("ordinary guys") PM,** undat. 1945, MHL; **("heavy thinker") New Yorker,** Oct. 26, 1946; **("not the kind of guy") PM,** undat. 1945, MHL.

186 **FS causes: (Yugoslav Relief)** "Memorandum re Frank Albert Sinatra," Jul. 6, 1950, and "Correlation Summary," Jun. 8, 1964, FSFBI, "File Review and Summary Check," Mar. 1, 1955, FBI 100-41713-4; **(Croatian committee)** Rosen to Director, Feb. 26, 1947, and "Summary Memorandum," Sep. 29, 1950, FSFBI; **(anti-Franco)** "Summary Memorandum," Sep. 29, 1950, FSFBI, "Subversive References, Francis Albert Sinatra," Mar. 28, 1955, FBI 100-80275, Shaw, **Sinatra,** 99; **(World Youth Conference)** "Memorandum re Frank Albert Sinatra," Feb. 26, 1947, FBI O & C File 125, "Summary Memorandum," Sep. 29, 1950, and SAC Washington to Director, May 23, 1955, FSFBI.

186 **AYD:** "Summary Memorandum," Sep. 29, 1950, SAC Detroit to Director, Apr. 8, 1955, SAC New York to Director, Jul. 21, 1955, "Francis Albert Sinatra, Security Matter—C," Nov. 8, 1955, SAC Philadelphia to Director, Mar. 31, 1955, and SAC Washington to Director, May 23, 1955, FSFBI, **New York Journal-American**, Apr. 16, 1947, David Caute, **The Great Fear,** New York: Simon and Schuster, 1978, 172. In 1947, after allegations against him to the House Un-American Activities Committee, Frank would say he "knew nothing" of the AYD and that if the group had listed him as a sponsor it was without his consent (Gerald L. K. Smith testimony, Jan. 30, 1946, 17, Hearings, Committee on Un-American Activities, U.S. House of Representatives, 79th Cong., 2nd sess., **New York Post,** Apr. 10, 1947); **(Radio Artists)** "Summary Memorandum," Sep. 29, 1950, FSFBI; **(ICCASP/HICCASP)** Ceplair and Englund, 225–, 393; **(FS and ICCASP/HICCASP)** "Summary Memorandum," Sep. 29, 1950, FSFBI, "Summary Memo on Frank Sinatra," Mar. 1, 1955, FBI LA 100-41413.

187 **"The Commies are boring in":** Steven Vaughn, **Ronald Reagan in Hollywood,** New York: Cambridge University Press, 1994, 122–. Future president Ronald Reagan was a member, and would soon become an FBI confidential informant—code number T-10—phoning in reports on HICCASP from the pay phone at the Nutburger stand on Sunset Boulevard (FBI 100-382196, 100-338892, 62-56921, 100-15732, Athan Theoharis and John S. Cox, **The Boss,** Philadelphia: Temple University Press, 1988, 255, Garry Wills, **Reagan's America,** Garden City, NY: Doubleday, 1987, 246); **(liberals resigned)** ibid., 123; **(FS still vice chairman)** SAC Washington to Director, May 23, 1955, FSFBI; **(a quarter of FBI file)** Gerald Meyer, "Frank Sinatra: The Popular Front and an American Icon," **Science & Society,** Fall 2002. The total file consists of 1,275 pages.

187 **Falcone:** SAC Philadelphia to Director, Mar. 31, 1955, FSFBI. Falcone was chairman of Local 301 of the Electrical, Radio and Machine Workers of America ("Summary Memorandum," Sep. 29, 1950, SAC Philadelphia to Director, Dec. 12, 1945, SAC Los Angeles to Director, Oct. 11, 1955, FSFBI, SAC Los Angeles to Director, Apr. 21, 1955, FBI LA 100-41413).

188 **intercepted letters:** "Correlation Summary," Jun. 8, 1964, and "Memorandum re Francis Albert Sinatra," Feb. 26, 1947, FSFBI.

188–189 **Weinstein: (Bentley case)** Nigel West, **Venona,** London: HarperCollins, 1999, 219–, Allen Weinstein and Alexander Vassiliev, **The Haunted Wood,** New York: Random House, 1999, 87–, John E. Haynes and Harvey Klehr, **Venona,** New Haven: Yale University Press, 1999, 97–, 153–; **(Clever Girl)** West, 227—but also perhaps Mirna and Good Girl, Christopher Andrew and Vasili Mitrokin, **The Mitrokhin Archive,** London: Penguin, 1999, 145; **(FBI/FS and Weinstein)** "Re Abraham Benedict Weinstein," Dec. 15, 1945, FBI 65-56402-36, "Gregory-Espionage," Jan. 28, 1947, Jun. 7, 1947, FBI 65-56402, "Subversive References, Francis Albert Sinatra," Mar. 28, 1955, FBI 100-80275, SAC New York to Director, Jul. 21, 1955, FSFBI; **(FS capped teeth)** Kahn, 37; **(no credible evidence/investigation)** "Summary Memorandum," Sep. 29, 1950, and "Francis Albert Sinatra—Security Matter—C," Nov. 8, 1955, FSFBI.

189–190 **FS liberal attitudes and associates: ("The Committee was") Daily Worker,** May 21, 1946; **(Tom Clark)** FS/Clark corr., Nov. 11, 14, 1947, Aug. 4, 1949, Tom C. Clark Papers, Harry S. Truman Library; **(income dipped/radio/Paine) New Yorker,** Oct. 26, 1946; **("George Evans and I")** Kelley, 106–, the quote comes from Keller's oral history tapes, and see int. Phil Evans; **(Evans/Weinstein)** "Summary Memorandum," Sep. 29, 1950, FSFBI; **("better world")** Taraborrelli, 78.

190 **Davidson: (Evans introduced)** Kelley, 106, and see int. Phil Evans; **(background)** int. Jacques Davidson, **NYT,** Jan. 3, 1952, Jo Davidson, **Between Sittings,** New York: Dial, 1951, refs., Davidson bio, Hofstra Museum of Art; **(ICCASP chairman)** Vaughn, 123, **Science & Society; (FS esteem)** FS int. on **Suzy Visits; (counsel) Cosmopolitan,** May 1956; **(FS bust) New Yorker,** Oct. 26, 1946, **Hollywood Reporter,** Oct. 10, 1946; **(at United Nations) Newsweek,** Apr. 22, 1946; **("veering") Los Angeles Examiner,** Apr. 10, 1947, citing Lee Mortimer; **(Goldman)** Emma Goldman, **Living My Life,** New York: Knopf, 1931, chap. 31, Anthony Summers, **Official & Confidential,** New York: Putnam, 1993, 38.

190 **Davidson one of "dupes": Life,** Apr. 5, 1949. Davidson's son Jacques told the authors that he could vouch for the fact that his late father was "not a Communist, card-carrying or otherwise" (corr. Jacques Davidson, 2003).

190 ***PM*/left-wing:** Michael Denning, **The Cultural Front,** London: Verso, 1998, 16, 146, 95, 158.

190–191 **communists/liberal artists: ("earthbound")** Brownstein, 98; **("innocents")** ibid., 114; **("We were mostly")** ibid., 98.

191–192 **FS/friends and right: (Welles)** Callow, 557, ed. Mark Estrin, **Orson Welles: Interviews,** Jackson, MS: University Press of Mississippi, 2002, vxi–, Orson Welles and Peter Bogdanovich, **This Is Orson Welles,** New York: Da Capo Press, 1998, 364; **(Kelly)** "Summary Memo on Frank Sinatra," Mar. 1, 1955, FBI LA 100-41413; **(Bogart/Bacall)** Denning, 62, Vaughn, 146, Paul Buhle and Dave Wagner, **Radical Hollywood,** New York: New Press, 2002, 437; **(Peck)** Gerard Molyneaux, **Gregory Peck,** Westport, CT: Greenwood, 1995, 24–, **Variety,** Dec. 14, 1995; **(Garland)** Vaughn, 124, Buhle and Wagner, 437; **(Gardner)** ibid., 438, and copyrighted int. of Ava Gardner by Peter Evans by permission; **(Smith)** David Margolis, "Gerald L. K. Smith Revisited," www.davidmargolis.com, Gerald L. K. Smith testimony, 17, 47; **("If that means agreeing")** "Summary Memo on Frank Sinatra," Mar. 1, 1955, FSFBI; **("political beliefs don't")** "Summary Memorandum," Sep. 29, 1950, FSFBI; **("The minute anyone") Daily Worker,** May 21, 1946; **(letter to Wallace) New Republic,** Jan. 6, 1947—Wallace was then the magazine's editor, **Science & Society; (Wallace call for softer line)** Robert Vexler, **The Vice Presidents and Cabinet Members,** vol. 2, Dobbs Ferry, NY: Oceana, 1975, 589; **("inimical")** "Bills to Curb or Outlaw the Communist Party of the US," Mar. 24–28, 1947, Hearings, Committee on Un-American Activities, U.S. House of Representatives, 80th Cong., 1st sess., 299.

193 **FS to be called to testify by HUAC:** (NY) **Daily Mirror, New York Journal-American,** Apr. 13, 1947, Shaw, **Sinatra,** 113. One can only surmise why Sinatra was never subpoenaed by the Un-American Activities Committee, nor blacklisted in Hollywood. It has been noted that the committee never did corral a major movie star—and also that it tended to target Jews (**Science & Society**); **(FS and others met) Science & Society; ("Once they get the movies throttled")** "Francis Albert Sinatra—Security Matter—C," Nov. 8, 1955, FSFBI; **(liberals backed away)** Ceplair and Englund, 290–; **(FS began to steer) Washington Times-Herald,** Nov. 14, 1947.

193 **appeal to voters in Italy: Los Angeles Examiner,** Apr. 5, 1948, **Science & Society.** Details of the project remain unclear. Some reports said Sinatra organized it, and one suggested he came up with the idea in the first place. Official records indicate that a proposal by him and others that there should be a tour—rather than a radio broadcast—was turned down. U.S. intelligence almost certainly played a role in arranging the broadcast, but there is no evidence that the celebrities involved were aware of that (FS organized?—Kupcinet with Neimark, 213; tour—**Diplomatic History,** Winter 1983; U.S. intelligence—Christopher Simpson, **Blowback,** New York: Collier, 1989, 91fn); **("If they don't") NYT,** Jun. 9, 1949.

194 **FS emissary to FBI:** "Summary Memorandum," Sep. 29, 1950, FSFBI.

195 **Kastner/FS discussion:** "Memorandum for the Record," Sep. 17, 1954, FSFBI.

195 **FBI probe: (investigation)** see 1954–55 corr. at FBI 62-83219-28 through 62-83219-37X15; **(nine offices) Science & Society; (FS passport application)** "Francis Albert Sinatra—Security Matter—C," Nov. 8, 1955, FSFBI—application was apparently for Australia tour, Sinatra, **Legend,** 120; **(refusing passports)** Ceplair and Englund, 403; **(intermediary)** Brennan to Sullivan, Mar. 31, 1966, FSFBI.

196 **"Many of the friends":** int. Jo Carroll Dennison.

196 **"My first recollection":** Hubert Humphrey to Nancy Sinatra, Dec. 10, 1969, Interim files, Misc. Corr., Sf-S1, 148.A.9.4F, Minnesota Historical Society.

Chapter 11: "What Is America?"

198–199 **FS experience of prejudice: ("niggers," etc.) Science & Society,** and **Los Angeles Examiner,** Sep. 30, 1945, Dwiggins, 2; **(mother pestering)** Sinatra, My Father, 7–; **(father "hating") Motion Picture,** Jun. 16, 1947; **(Klan)** Kahn, 87, Hamill, 72; **("One of the questions") Motion Picture,** Jun. 16, 1947; **(52nd Street)** Shaw, **52nd Street,** 16, 20, 110, 254, 258; **(black resentment grew)** ibid., 265–; **(clubs)** Robert Parker, **Capitol Hill in Black and White,** New York: Dodd, Mead: 1986, 17; **(hotels/Holiday/Ellington)** Rosemary Clooney with Joan Barthel, **Girl Singer,** New York: Random House, 1999, 191; **(Ellington friend)** Friedwald, 301.

200 **FS and Hazel Scott:** Scott's career was promoted by New York nightclub owner Barney Josephson, a left-winger who featured in the FBI investigation of Abraham Weinstein, the Sinatra dentist and espionage suspect mentioned in chapter 10. After testifying to the Un-American Activities Committee in the early 1950s, Scott would be blacklisted (**New York Post,** Apr. 6, 1943, Denning, 325, 335, 338–, 347, Bill Reed, "The Smokin' Life of Hazel Scott," for msnbc.com); **("When I was a kid"/"Let anybody")** ed. Yarwood, 80, **PM,** Oct. 2, 1944; **(numerous occasions)** ints. Lee Solters, Tony Mottola, Bricktop with James Haskins, **Bricktop,** New York: Atheneum, 1983, 215–.

200 **"Jew bastard": Down Beat,** Oct. 1, 1941, Dwiggins, 30–. A contemporary newspaper account indicated the remark was directed at Benny Goodman's brother Harry, a bassist. The Goodmans were Jewish. Author Don Dwiggins's version, which suggests the insult was aimed at Tommy Dorsey himself, is almost certainly in error (**Down Beat,** Oct. 1, 1941, Dwiggins, 30–); **("Sinatra went") New York Post,** Feb. 5, 1945; **("you've got to")** ed. Yarwood, 80.

201 **"Ol' Man River":** The word "darkies" occurs on only two Sinatra recordings, according to Sinatra scholar Will Friedwald, the August 14, 1943, performance of "Ol' Man River" at the Hollywood Bowl, and in "Without a Song," recorded in 1941 (Friedwald, 317–, 23, **New Yorker,** Oct. 26, 1946, FS retirement concert, Jun. 13, 1971, videotape in authors' collection).

201 **FS action re prejudice: (told FDR) Photoplay,** Oct. 1945; **(Bronx)** Friedwald, 323–; **(World Youth Rally) Science & Society, PM,** undat. 1945, MHL; **(thirty speaking appearances) Science & Society,** Friedwald, 323, Dwiggins, 73; **("The surprising element") Minidoka (WS) Irrigator,** May 19, 1945; **("The next time") Scholastic,** Sep. 17, 1945.

202 ***The House I Live In:*** **("You could reach") Movie Land,** Jun. 11, 1945, Dwiggins, 75.

202–204 **"House" background:** Friedwald, 322–. Written in 1942, the song was performed by the black gospel group Golden Gate Quartet in the movie **Follow the Boys.** Sinatra recorded gospel songs with another black group, the Charioteers, in 1945 (Friedwald, 323, Howlett, 36, and see Earl Robinson with Eric Gordon, **Ballad of an American,** Lanham, MD: Scarecrow Press, 1998, 151–); **("Look, fellas")** O'Brien, 209, Dwiggins, 76;

("Let's use"/humming) "Summary Memo on Frank Sinatra," Mar. 1, 1955, FBI 100-41713-4; **(well received/"a sincere")** Shaw, **Sinatra,** 86–.

204 **FS Oscar:** The award was shared with director LeRoy, screenwriter Albert Maltz, and producer Frank Ross (www.oscars.org); **(proud)** Edward R. Murrow video.

204 **"House" and Cosby/others: Hartford Courant,** Sep. 8, 2002. The song Sinatra audiences heard never did contain all the lyrics its writer Abel Meeropol had intended. The second verse, which was meant to include the line "My neighbors white and black," was dropped from the movie, as was a line about "the worker and the farmer." Apparently such wording was considered too explicit and populist for a general audience, and the omission enraged Meeropol. "House" had certainly lost its original cast by 1991 when Sinatra—by then long since perceived as being more right than left—sang it in support of U.S. troops engaged in the first Iraq conflict (**Science & Society**).

204 **Benjamin Franklin High: NYT,** Sep. 29, 30, Oct. 1, 2, 9, 1945, **Daily Worker,** Oct. 27, 1945, **Science & Society, New York,** Aug. 10, 1998, eds. Jennifer Guglielmo and Salvatore Salerno, **Are Italians White?** New York: Routledge, 2003, 161–. Nat "King" Cole also visited the school.

204–205 **Gary: (FS arrived) Life,** Nov. 12, 1945, Kelley, 107–, "Summary Memorandum," Sep. 29, 1950, FSFBI, (**Gary, IN**) **Post-Tribune,** undat., www.post-trib.com; **("three secretaries") The Worker,** Nov. 25, 1945; **("I kinda gave")** Dwiggins, 1–; **("in a way") Ebony,** Jul. 1958; **("not spontaneous") The Worker,** Nov. 25, 1945.

205 **communist contacts/insinuations: (Robinson, Meeropol) Science & Society,** (**San Jose, CA**) **Mercury News,** Apr. 7, 2003, **Hartford Courant,** Sep. 8, 2002. Meeropol, who wrote under the pen name Lewis Allan, was also the author of the anti-lynching song "Strange Fruit," sung most memorably by Billie Holiday (Michael Denning, **The Cultural Front,** New York: Verso, 1998, 327).

206 **Maltz:** Buhle and Wagner, 381–, Vaughn, 145–. Maltz would be the focus of fierce controversy involving Sinatra in 1960. As reported in a later chapter, political pressure was to force Sinatra to drop him as screenwriter on the movie **The Execution of Private Slovik.** The project was abandoned. The screenwriter on

three other Sinatra movies of the forties, Isobel Lennart, was a Sinatra friend and also a member of the Communist Party. Lennart, the writer on **Anchors Aweigh, It Happened in Brooklyn,** and **The Kissing Bandit,** was pressured into testifying to the House Un-American Activities Committee (Lennart—O'Brien, 22, Hedda Hopper int. of FS, **Chicago Tribune–NY News** syndicate, undat. 1947 draft, MHL, "Isobel Lennart" entry at www.spartacus.schoolnet.co.uk); **("spoke like")** The Worker, Nov. 25, 1945.

206–209 **FS and black entertainers: ("Frank didn't care")** M/G int. of Sonny King and see M/G int. of Freddie Bell; **(Davis nurtured)** Gerald Early, **The Sammy Davis, Jr., Reader,** New York: Farrar, Straus and Giroux, 2001, 25, Shaw, **Sinatra,** 118, **Down Beat,** Aug. 1956; **(abuse in army)** Sammy Davis Jr., Jane Boyar, and Burt Boyar, **Yes, I Can,** New York: Farrar, Straus and Giroux, 1965, 51–; **(hotel)** ibid., 89–, 92, 198; **(drained the pool)** ed. Early, 398, Rosemary Clooney with Joan Barthel, **Girl Singer,** New York: Random House, 1999, 190–; **("The roof blew") Good Housekeeping,** Jun. 1964; **("Billy Eckstine became")** int. Hal Webman; **(Sy Oliver)** Sinatra with Coplon, 95; **(Jo Thompson) Philadelphia Inquirer,** May 17, 1998; **(unions/ Bernhart/Viola/Collette)** Granata, 108–; **(Cole) Look,** May 14, 1957, ed. Yarwood, 79; ***(Ebony)*** **Ebony,** Jul. 1958; **("His public position") Jet,** Oct. 13, 1986; **(doctorate)** ibid.; ***(Kings Go Forth)*** O'Brien, 105–, **Ebony,** Jul. 1958, Sinatra, **My Father,** 331; **(FS best man)** Davis, Boyar, and Boyar, 558, 583; **(King's crusade)** Taylor Branch, **Parting the Waters,** New York: Simon and Schuster, 1988, 574, Sinatra, **Legend,** 190, **Hollywood Reporter,** Nov. 1, 1963, **Valley Times Today,** Oct. 9, 1963, int. Mort Viner; **(King listened)** Frank Sinatra Jr., **As I Remember It; ("suffered")** McCall's, Jul. 1968.

209–210 **racist jokes: ("We'll dedicate")** ed. Yarwood, 52; **("Smokey")** Wilson, **Sinatra,** 5; **("jungle bunny") Variety Clubs All Star Tribute to Skinny D'Amato,** Nov. 20, 1983, videotape in authors' collection; **("You'd better")** "Sinatra, Inc.," CNN **Impact,** circa 1998, videotape in authors' collection; **("Here's a little")** Deutsch, 117; **("He's just, excuse")** Taraborrelli, 214; **("The Polacks") New York,** Apr. 28, 1980.

210 **Bophuthatswana:** "Register of Entertainers, Actors, and Others Who Have Performed in Apartheid South Africa," U.N. Centre

Against Apartheid, Oct. 1983, UNST/PSCA (05) N911; **Chicago Tribune,** Oct. 27, 1983, **People,** Aug. 10, 1981, int. Lee Solters.

210 **Jackson:** Kelley, 488.

210–211 **"If there's any form":** Giuliano audiotape.

211 **FS "*primo* non-conformist"/"I don't know":** Jet, Oct. 13, 1986. Awards for charity activity aside, Sinatra won honors from civil rights organizations. They included, as early as 1946, the Thomas Jefferson Award from the Council Against Intolerance, and a Life Achievement award from the NAACP in 1987—well after the furor about the concert in Bophuthatswana. He received a commendation from the National Conference of Christians and Jews in 1946, and in 1980 became a fellow of the Simon Wiesenthal Center. In 1972 he received Israel's Medallion of Valor in recognition of the millions of dollars he had raised. In 1980 Jerusalem mayor Teddy Kollek presented him with an award from the Jerusalem Foundation (awards—Sinatra, **My Father,** 300–; **Jet,** Mar. 23, Jun. 1, 1987, **Philadelphia Daily News,** Jan. 18, 1982; medallion—**LAHE,** Nov. 2, 1972; Kollek—**New York Post,** Jun. 16, 1980).

211 **FS and Jews: (medallions/"If the war")** Sinatra, **Legend,** 48, **Los Angeles Examiner,** Sep. 30, 1945, **Liberty,** Feb. 12, 1944; **(benefit for elderly)** Sinatra, **Legend,** 59; **(mezuzah) Look,** May 28, 1957, and see p. 17.

212 **Frank Jr. baptism:** The authors have accepted daughter Nancy Sinatra's account of the christening. Another account has it that Sinatra did storm out and Sacks was named godfather "elsewhere" (Sinatra, **My Father,** xviii, Bill Zehme, **The Way You Wear Your Hat,** New York: HarperCollins, 1997, 210); **(golf clubs)** Sinatra, **Legend,** 63—the club he did join was Hillcrest Country Club.

212 **rally at Hollywood Bowl: People's World,** Sep. 27, 1947.

213 **"I had an Irish"/Teddy Kollek:** Sinatra's role as money courier has been variously described in Kollek's memoir **For Jerusalem,** Nancy Sinatra's **Legend,** Michael Freedland's **All The Way,** and most recently in the authors' interview with **Las Vegas Sun** editor Brian Greenspun in 2002. The quotations used here are taken from all four sources. Kollek's accounts, both in his memoir and as recalled by Greenspun, suggest Sinatra was performing at the Copacabana at the time of the Haganah contact. The record does

not reflect such performances, but does show that he was in New York in March 1948 and at the club for an interview on the 24th (Hotel Fourteen—Clooney with Barthel, 87; FS visit—eds. Giuseppe Marcucci, Dick Schwarz, and Ed Vanhellemont, **Where or When?**, CD-ROM, privately published, Jan. 2002; carrying money—ints. Brian Greenspun, George Schlatter, Teddy Kollek with Amos Kollek, **For Jerusalem,** New York: Random House, 1978, 237, Freedland, 148–, Sinatra, **Legend,** 83; thanked—ibid., 247, Kollek, 237).

214 **"It was the beginning":** Sinatra, **Legend,** 83.

214–217 **FS and Israel: (established Youth Center) Hollywood Reporter,** Apr. 11, 1962, **(London) Daily Mail,** May 8, 1962; **(Arab League)** Freedland, 297, **LAHE,** Sep. 25, 1962, **Variety,** Sep. 26, Oct. 15, 1962; **(outburst)** int. Rock Brynner; **("I don't know")** int. Melville Shavelson, Melville Shavelson, **How to Make a Jewish Movie,** Englewood Cliffs, NJ: Prentice-Hall, 1971, 175–; **("He came to the realization")** int. Brad Dexter; **("We're talking")** Bill Boggs int. of FS; **(support 1967/wired LBJ)** FS to LBJ, Jun. 4, 1967, White House Central Files, Name File, "Frank Sinatra," Box 320, Lyndon Baines Johnson Library, SAC Los Angeles to Director, Jun. 21, 1967, FBI 105-53922-692, Sinatra, **Legend,** 202; **("I hope they catch") Jewish Week,** May 22, 1998; **(performed/a "great man")** int. Frank Sinatra on ABC's **20/20,** 1979, videotape in authors' collection, **Ladies' Home Journal,** Oct. 1979; **(Student Center) Jewish Week,** May 22, 1998; Sinatra, **My Father,** 261; **(bomb) AP,** Jul. 31, **Irish Times,** Aug. 1, 2002; **(Saddam) New York Post,** Sep. 8, www.abcnews.com, Sep. 12, 2002, **(London) Sunday Times,** Jan. 4, 2004; **("curse the memory") New York Post,** Sep. 5, 2002.

Chapter 12: The Philanderer

218–219 **FS work 1945/1946: (radio/recording/movies)** Where or When?—ten of the recording sessions were for movies; **(forty-five shows/one hundred songs)** Shaw, **Sinatra,** 99; **(Six made the top ten/10 million)** Sayers and O'Brien, 264, Kahn, 7–; **($93,000)** Shaw, **Sinatra,** 99, but see Friedwald, 160—the stage appearances were in Chicago; **(album)** Granata, 47–, Doctor, 33; **(gospel/Cugat)** Shaw, **Sinatra,** 94.

219–220 **Alec Wilder episode:** Granata, 49, **New Yorker,** Oct. 26, 1946, **Billboard,** Nov. 20, 1965, liner notes to **Frank Sinatra Conducts Music of Alec Wilder,** Columbia Records, ML 4271. The albums featuring Sinatra as conductor are **Tone Poems of Color** (1956), for Peggy Lee on **The Man I Love** (1957), for Dean Martin on **Sleep Warm** (1959), **Sinatra Conducts Music from Pictures and Plays** (1962), for Sylvia Syms on **Syms by Sinatra** (1982), and for the trumpeter Charles Turner on **What's New** (1983).

220 **FS overwork: ("Frank had great")** int. Jo-Carroll Dennison; **(had to cancel)** LAT, Jan. 7, 1946; **("Hard work")** Shaw, **Sinatra,** 100.

220–221 **status of marriage: ("Boys will") Photoplay,** Sep. 1945; **("I can remember") Billboard,** Nov. 20, 1965; **("Don't forget")** Hamill, 147.

222 **FS womanizing: ("The relationship")** int. Phil Evans; **("He called")** int. Peggy Maley—later one of Ava Gardner's closest friends; **("This was where")** int. Jo Carroll Dennison, Kelley, 112; **("They had parties")** int. Jo-Carroll Dennison; **("hideaway")** Bill Davidson, **The Real and the Unreal,** New York: Lancer, 1962; **(prostitutes)** Rosen to Tamm, Apr. 17, 1947, Belmont to Ladd, Sep. 29, 1950, FSFBI, 37; **("What blazing"/ "Wonder if ")** Parsons, 151.

222–223 **"If I had":** The photographer Phil Stern responded by creating a gag picture of a specimen jar with Sinatra bottled up inside. A delighted Sinatra promptly requested a dozen copies (**Newsweek,** Apr. 19, 1965; int. Phil Stern on CNN **Impact;** May 1998).

223 **"darling, adorable"/Ballard affair:** int. Shirley Ballard.

224–225 **Marilyn Maxwell: (background)** Laura Wagner, "Marilyn Maxwell: The Other MM," www.classicimages.com, Feb. 2000; **("sweater fillers")** Earl Wilson quote, Maxwell file, MHL, **LAHE,** Aug. 25, 1972; **(Colleagues liked)** undat. **Photoplay,** 1972; **(met FS)** unid. clip by Babs Carter, 1945, Maxwell Collection, Nodaway Valley (IA) Historical Society, **(Clarinda, IA) Herald Journal,** Apr. 17, 1939, Jack Holland, "What Is Frank Sinatra Really Like?" undat. MHL, **LAT,** Oct. 23, 1946—Maxwell was singing with Ted Weems's band; **(encouraged FS)** unid. clip by Babs Carter; **(bat girls)** Sinatra, **Legend,** 81–, Kelley, 91; **(FS insisted)** "Wake Up and Live," Lux Radio Theater, Feb. 21, 1944, **Frank Sinatra and Friends: 60 Great Radio**

Shows, Schiller Park, IL: Radio Spirits, 2000; **("I can even get")** Laura Wagner, "Marilyn Maxwell."

225 **Marilyn Maxwell affair:** Four Sinatra relatives told the authors there was an affair: Sinatra's cousin Rose Paldino; his cousin Sam's widow, Rose Ellman Sinatra; and two second cousins, Marilyn Sinatra and Maryann Paldino Flannery. Maxwell's niece and namesake, Marilyn Gaffen, and her longtime secretary Jean Greenberg also said as much.

225 **Marilyn married:** Maxwell married the actor John Conte in late 1944, and divorced him in June 1946 ([**Clarinda, IA**] **Herald Journal,** Jun. 27, 1946); **("crazy about")** Kelley, 116.

225 **diamond bracelet:** The bracelet incident has been described in books by both Sinatra daughters, and featured in the 1992 TV movie **Sinatra: The Music Was Just the Beginning,** which Tina produced. In their books, Tina dated it to New Year's Eve 1945, Nancy to New Year's Eve 1946. The authors have opted for the 1945 dating, in part because of a passage in the singer Mel Tormé's autobiography. Tormé, who is rather specific about chronology, wrote that Maxwell was with him and the arranger Dean Elliott on New Year's 1946 (Sinatra with Coplon, 16–, Sinatra, **Legend,** 73, Tormé, **Velvet,** 94–); **(FS claimed)** ibid., Jack Holland clip; **(title fight) New York Journal-American,** Feb. 29, 1956, Shaw, **Sinatra,** 99—the fight, on June 19, 1946, was between heavyweight champion Joe Louis and Billy Conn; **(press had learned)** ibid., **Woman's Home Companion,** Jun. 1956, O'Brien, 25.

226 **Dietrich: (background)** Maria Riva, **Marlene Dietrich,** London: Bloomsbury, 1992, Charles Higham, **Marlene,** New York: Norton, 1977, Sheridan Morley, **Marlene Dietrich,** London: Sphere, 1978; **(trophies)** refs. in Riva, Higham, **Marlene,** 11, and re Wayne, Wills, **Wayne,** 104–; **(soldiers)** Riva, 547, (**London**) **Sunday Telegraph** magazine, Oct. 28, 2001; **(female lovers)** ibid., Riva, 52, 165–; **(husband)** Riva, 53, 763; **(knew FS in 1942)** Riva, 659.

226–227 **"I am eating":** ibid., 541. Many of Dietrich's diary entries and letters were made public in **Marlene Dietrich,** a biography written by her daughter Maria Riva following the actress's death at age ninety. Though not precisely dated in the book, the letter cited here was evidently written in early 1944. The diary entry mentioned is for February 2, 1955; **("Frankie's country")** ibid., 547; **("Sinatra's wife")** ibid., 552; **("swoon")** Higham, **Marlene,**

215; **("I know they had")** Freedland, 126; **("I was wrong")** Cahn, 144, Kelley, 112.

227 **"The day after":** Dwiggins, 86.

228 **"Keep Betty Grable":** In 1963, he updated the line to: "Keep Audrey Hepburn and keep Liz Taylor" (**Frank Sinatra: The Complete Studio Recordings,** Reprise, Master #2024, Apr. 29, 1963, and see **Where or When?** entry for V-Disc session, Jul. 8, 1944, Friedwald, 142–).

228–230 **Lana Turner: (background)** Cheryl Crane with Cliff Jahr, **Detour,** London: Sphere, 1989, 96–, Jeffrey Feinman, **Hollywood Confidential,** Chicago: Playboy Press, 1976, 143. Accounts of Turner's discovery vary. According to the actress, she was first noticed at the Top Hat Café—not at Currie's Ice Cream Parlor or Schwab's Drug Store, as originally claimed by press agents (Turner, **Lana,** 26, Joe Morella and Edward Epstein, **Lana,** New York: Dell, 1982, 6, Crane with Jahr, 40–, Feinman, 7, 143–, Taylor Pero and Jeff Rovin, **Always, Lana,** New York: Bantam Books, 1982, 16–); **("Sweater Girl")** Crane with Jahr, 42; **(attorney)** ibid., 47, Turner, **Lana,** 44–; **(Shaw/abortion)** ibid., 49–; **(other men)** Morella and Epstein, 89–; **(nonentity)** Crane with Jahr, 50—the new husband was J. Stephen Crane III, real name Joe Crane; **("The only thing")** Turner, **Lana,** 42; **("The closest things")** Turner, **Lana,** 98, picture caption after 184; **(original ms./"give him satisfaction")** Taraborrelli, 85fn; **(Ava "good friend")** Turner, **Lana,** 165, Gardner, 49; **("had a very serious")** Gardner, 125; **(met in 1940)** int. Joe Bushkin, O'Brien, 204; **(music)** Turner, **Lana,** 41, 49, 75; **(Holiday)** Morella and Epstein, 66–; **(Pearl Harbor)** Turner, **Lana,** 75; **(dated Dorsey/Sacks)** Morella and Epstein, 65, 88; **(Rich)** Tormé, **Traps,** 45–, Tormé, **Velvet,** 86.

230 **FS and Turner: (photographed together)** Shaw, **Sinatra,** 73, Morella and Epstein, 91; **(radio/FDR)** "**Where or When?** entries for Jun. 14, Nov. 6, 1944; **(Lana/Nancy close)** Turner, **Lana,** 98; **("When [Nancy] came")** Kelley, 92; **("They used to smooch")** Morella and Epstein, 92, 97, and see Dwiggins, 87, Kelley, 114, Freedland, 134, Romero, 78.

230 **began Lana Turner affair in New York:** Sinatra was making **It Happened in Brooklyn,** an indifferent movie about a demobbed GI in search of romance. Shooting took him to New York in mid-June. The date and location of the start of the Turner affair is

unclear in previous biographies of both stars, and unsubstantiated by contemporary clippings. Taking together the available information, the authors accept the version offered by Tina Sinatra in her book (Crane with Jahr, 105–, **Where or When?** entries for Apr. 3–10, 1946, O'Brien, 29, Sinatra with Coplon, 17; FS's other daughter, Nancy, has dated the New York shooting wrongly—as 1947—in her book **Legend,** p. 80).

231–233 **FS/Nancy separation: (Evans announced)** NYT, Oct. 7, 1946, Kelley, 120; **("the freedom")** LAT, Oct. 7, 1946; **("about trivial") American Weekly,** Jul. 20, 1952; **("dancing many") Los Angeles Examiner,** Oct. 7, LAT, Oct. 11, 1946; **(Palm Springs) Modern Screen,** May 1947, LAT, Oct. 24, 1946, Shaw, **Sinatra,** 102; **(Lana had a place)** Turner, **Lana,** 103, Taraborrelli, 84; **(Hollywood gossip columnists)** Feinman, 157–; **("morals clause")** Gardner, 45–, 51, Morella and Epstein, 199; **(Parsons/"to behave")** Crane with Jahr, 45; **(bosses agonizing)** ibid., 105–; **(troubleshooters)** Carpozi, 81, and see **New York Journal-American,** Oct. 26, 1946, Louella Parsons's column—Lana probably spoke not at a press conference as author Carpozi wrote, but with Louella Parsons; **(Hopper castigated)** LAT, Oct. 7, 1946; **("refuses to attend")** ibid., Oct. 17, 1946; **("I warned him") Modern Screen,** May 1947.

233 **FS/Nancy reconciliation:** Carpozi, 82, LAT, Oct. 24, 25, 26, 1946, **Modern Screen,** May 1947, unid. clip by Jack Stone, Robert Chester Ruark Papers, Southern Historical Collection, Wilson Library, University of North Carolina, Chapel Hill, int. Jo Carroll Dennison.

233 **Lana Turner affair continued: ("I was Frank's beard")** int. Phil Evans. According to author Richard Gehman, George Evans himself was on occasion recruited as beard, on the flimsy pretense—he, too, was a married man—that Lana was his date (Gehman, 198).

233 **FS "shuttling":** Gardner, 125, 173. It seems that Lana Turner had persisted in her contacts with Sinatra even though she was already months into a passionate involvement with the actor Tyrone Power. This would not have been out of character, given her emotionally volatile history. Sinatra stayed in touch with Turner over the years. He was "Uncle Frank" to her daughter, Cheryl, and was supportive after the 1958 fatal stabbing of Lana's mobster lover Johnny Stompanato, for which Cheryl was held

responsible. Lana was invited to dinner at Sinatra's home as late as 1972 (persisted—Fred Guiles, **Tyrone Power,** Garden City, NY: Doubleday, 1979, 216–, Crane with Jahr, 112; "Uncle"/supportive—ibid., 160, 291, 362; 1972—Pero and Rovin, 139–).

234 **"I haven't much":** Hedda Hopper int. of FS, **Chicago Tribune—NY News** syndicate, undat. 1947 draft, MHL.

234 **FS condition/conduct late 1946: (sick/impending breakdown)** Shaw, **Sinatra,** 103–; **(seventeen days) Where or When?** entries for Oct. 9–23, 1946; **("desperately tired")** Hedda Hopper int. of FS, **Chicago Tribune–NY News** syndicate, undat. 1947 draft, MHL; **(MGM memos)** Kelley, 116.

234–235 **"a long series":** Kelley, 119. MGM had first had problems with Sinatra two years earlier, during the making of **Anchors Aweigh.** He had high-handedly insisted on seeing the daily rushes, contrary to studio policy, then broken a promise not to let others share the viewing. Sinatra also threatened to quit the production unless Sammy Cahn and Jule Styne wrote the music. The studio had caved in (O'Brien, 23–, Cahn, 134); **("Just continue")** (LA) **Daily News,** Nov. 5, 1946; **("least cooperative")** Los Angeles **Daily News,** Dec. 21, 1946.

235 **No one "was going":** This remark is as reported on p. 101 of Arnold Shaw's excellent 1968 biography **Sinatra: Twentieth-Century Romantic.**

Chapter 13: A Handshake in Havana

236 **FS and gun: (license) LAT,** Jan. 31, Apr. 25, 1947, fingerprint record 3794610, FBI 25-244122. Sinatra's press spokesman said the gun was a Beretta, but the permit was issued for a Walther (unid. Robinson article); **("never left home")** Jacobs and Stadiem, 209. Jacobs aside, sources who have said Sinatra regularly carried a gun are Marilyn Sinatra, daughter of his first cousin—another Frank—Sinatra, who was raised with the singer and worked for him in the forties, the hostile columnist Lee Mortimer, and two future girlfriends (int. Marilyn Sinatra, **American Weekly,** Aug. 1951, int. Lois Nettleton, Marianna Case, **Another Side of Blue,** Running Springs, CA: self-published, 1997, 75–); **(souvenir)** unidentified article by Grace Robinson, probably **New York News,** Robert Ruark Papers, undat. article for **Movieland,** by David McClure, MHL; **("wanted Nancy")**

Hedda Hopper int. of FS, **Chicago Tribune–NY News** syndicate, undat. 1947 draft, MHL; **("to protect") Washington News,** Apr. 10, 1947.

237 **journey: (to NYC) LAT,** Jan. 31, 1947, Sinatra, **Legend,** 76; **(Miami) Where or When?, American Weekly,** Jul. 27, 1952; **(Wilson) New York Post,** Apr. 10, 1947.

237 **Fischetti: (host)** ibid.; **(mansion) Washington Times-Herald,** Feb. 28, 1947.

237 **"heirs to Al Capone": Miami Herald,** Apr. 12, 1951. The Fischettis have long been referred to in the press and elsewhere as cousins of Al Capone. Rocco and Joe, however, denied that to the FBI. A surviving relative told the authors the story arose because Capone sometimes introduced Charles Fischetti as a "cousin" from New York—an Italian-American way of referring to a close family friend (Rocco F., in Skokie, IL, memo, Feb. 12, 1963, FBI 92-HQ-2915, Joseph F., in Miami memo, Feb. 28, 1963, FBI 92-3024, int. David Fagen—Rocco F. nephew through marriage); **(Capone's funeral)** "Rocco Fischetti" memo, Apr. 24, 1964, FBI 92-HQ-2915; **(Charles background) Chicago Daily News, Chicago Sun-Times, Brooklyn Eagle,** Apr. 11, **Chicago Tribune,** Apr. 12, 1951, Jack Lait and Lee Mortimer, **Chicago Confidential,** New York: Crown, 1950, 182–; **(Rocco) Chicago Tribune,** Jul. 7, 1964, White to Williams, Bureau of Narcotics, Jan. 9, 1946, Box 36, Pegler Papers, Giancana and Renner, 76–; **(Joe)** Miami Field Office Report, Sep. 27, 1960, and Oct. 29, 1962, Jul. 24, 1972, FBI 92-3024, "Re: Joseph Fischetti," Jul. 16, 1957, FBI 62-96512-18, Lait and Mortimer, **Chicago,** 183, **Chicago Tribune,** Jul. 7, 1964; **("I'm the only")** Irv Kupcinet with Paul Neimark, **Kup,** Chicago: Bonus Books, 1988, 150; **(Rocco/Luciano and Charlie Moretti)** Peterson, **Barbarians,** 158–, and see Lait and Mortimer, **Chicago,** 115, SAC Newark to Director, Nov. 20, 1944, FBI 62-3312-13, "Miscellaneous Crime Survey," Aug. 12, 1946, FBI 62-8861-122, Aug. 8, 1946, FBI 62-8861-152.

238 **Luciano release/exile/arrival in Cuba: (released from prison)** There was prolonged controversy as to whether the mobster's release was a reward for using his influence to help the Allied cause during World War II. An exhaustive study by Rodney Campbell, drawing on the official postwar investigation of alleged collaboration between U.S. Naval Intelligence and the

Mafia, concluded flatly that Luciano did help. Governor Thomas E. Dewey, who commuted the mobster's sentence—and whose work as U.S. attorney had put Luciano in jail in the first place—publicly acknowledged the cooperation (Campbell, refs., and see Eisenberg, Dan, and Landau, 180–); **(Lercara Friddi)** Eisenberg, Dan, and Landau, 228, Gosch and Hammer, 295–, "Summary of Information re Lucania," Jan. 12, 1947, LLBN; **(associates)** Eisenberg, Dan, and Landau, 166, 174, **Miami Herald,** Feb. 24, 1947, Gosch and Hammer, 242, 245, and see chapter 5; **(Rome)** Gosch and Hammer, 304; **(in contact/plotting)** Siragusa to Oliva, and attached memo, Jun. 13, 1951, LLBN, "Activities of Top Hoodlums," Dec. 12, 1958, FBI 92-632-515; **(agreed Lansky)** Olivera to Williams, Mar. 21, 1947, J. Ray Olivera (Bureau of Narcotics) Papers, courtesy of Olivera family, Eisenberg, Dan, and Landau, 228, 232, Gosch and Hammer, 306; **(arrived Havana/connivance)** Luciano report summaries, 16–, LLBN, Olivera to Williams, Mar. 21, 1947, J. Ray Olivera Papers, **Commissione Parliamentare D'Inchiesta Sul Fenomeno Della Mafia in Sicilia,** vol. 4, pt. 2, 1209; **(a steady stream)** "Parties Participating in the Meeting with Luciano in Cuba, 1947," Luciano report summaries, 37, White to Anslinger, Feb. 5, 1951, and Siragusa to Anslinger, Feb. 19, 1951, LLBN; **("The guys")** Gosch and Hammer, 306.

238 **Rocco and Joe Fischetti/FS arrival Havana:** According to columnist Lee Mortimer, the three men traveled on Pan Am Flight 447 and their names were listed together on the passenger manifest. Sinatra is recognizable in the photograph, and according to Mortimer law enforcement officials identified the Fischetti brothers from file pictures. The identification has never been contested, and Sinatra himself acknowledged having traveled with the Fischettis. Another image, seen by attorneys for the Senate Committee to Investigate Organized Crime in 1951, showed him with a Fischetti brother to each side of him. The still frame has not been published since 1952, when it appeared in **American Weekly**—the authors obtained an original copy of the magazine at the Library of Congress. Some sources have suggested Sinatra was with the mobsters in Havana as early as December 1946, as opposed to early February 1947. Sinatra's known movements suggest he could have been in Cuba in December but, unless he made two visits, the authors see no way to reconcile the

two versions. On the evidence, including a photograph in the **Havana Post** recording Sinatra's arrival on February 11 and the dating of the contemporary reporting from Havana of Robert Ruark, the authors place the trip in February (photograph—**American Weekly,** Jul. 27, 1952; Mortimer on flight/identification—Mortimer to Westbrook Pegler, Sep. 26, 1947, attached to John F. Kelly to Pegler, Nov. 30, 1960, and undat. note re **Royal News** newsreel, and undat. letter Mortimer to Pegler—all in Box 73, Pegler Papers; Sinatra acknowledgment—**American Weekly,** Jul. 27, 1952; another image—transcript, Joseph Nellis interrogation of FS for Kefauver Committee, Mar. 1, 1951, published in **Gallery,** Sep. 1978, and Hank Messick with Joseph Nellis, **The Private Lives of Public Enemies,** New York: Dell, 1973, 234; December visit—Eisenberg, Dan, and Landau, 232–, Gosch and Hammer, 306–; Sinatra arrival photo—**Havana Post,** Feb. 12, 1947; Ruark—**Washington News,** Feb. 20, and memo, Ruark to Lee Wood, Feb. 25, 1947, Robert Ruark Papers).

238–239 **Ruark article: New York World-Telegram,** Feb. 20, 1947. Ruark was first with the story only in the United States. The news that Luciano was in Havana had broken first in the Cuban weekly **El Tiempo en Cuba** (**Tiempo en Cuba,** Feb. 9, 16, Mar. 2, [NY] **Sunday News,** Feb. 26, 1947).

239 **FS version of Havana: ("Any report")** (NY) **Sunday News,** Feb. 23, **New York World-Telegram,** Feb. 24, 1947.

239 **Fischetti fleetingly/"run into": American Weekly,** Jul. 27, 1952. According to his daughter Nancy, in her book **Legend,** Sinatra would later dismiss his own bylined article in **American Weekly**—which deals with the Cuba matter—as "crap" made up by the magazine's editors (Sinatra, **Legend,** 104). See note re "Most of my troubles," p. 452.

240–242 **Kefauver:** transcript, Joseph Nellis interrogation of FS for Kefauver Committee, Mar. 1, 1951, published in **Gallery,** Sep. 1978, int. Joseph Nellis, undat. Alfred Klein article, pt. 2, George White Papers, Stanford University, Messick with Nellis, 234. In 1951, after hearing some 800 witnesses, the Kefauver committee concluded that there was indeed "a national crime syndicate known as the Mafia." (Summers, **Official & Confidential,** 228–); **("not an ounce")** FS testimony, Nevada State Gaming Control Board, Feb. 11, 1981; **(Evans)** int. George Evans, Apr. 12, 1948, LLBN; **(already intended)** Joseph Nellis interrogation, and see Hedda Hopper int. of FS, **Chicago Tribune–NY News** syndicate, undat. 1947 draft, MHL; **(Nevada)** FS testimony, Nevada State Gaming Control Board, Feb. 11, 1981; **("I was brought up") New York World-Telegram,** Feb. 24, 1947; **("I dropped by")** Hedda Hopper int. of FS, **Chicago Tribune–NY News** syndicate, undat. 1947 draft, MHL; **("I was invited") American Weekly,** Jul. 27, 1952; **(FS on Immerman)** ibid., transcript, Joseph Nellis interrogation of FS for Kefauver Committee, Mar. 1, 1951, published in **Gallery,** Sep. 1978, Messick with Nellis, 234–; **(FS on Gross)** Miller to Hundley, Jan. 22, 1964, and attached memorandum, Jan. 3, 1964, Organized Crime and Racketeering Section, Criminal Division, Department of Justice, FS testimony, Nevada State Gaming Control Board, Feb. 11, 1981; **(companion explained)** transcript, Joseph Nellis interrogation of FS for Kefauver Committee, Mar. 1, 1951, published in **Gallery,** Sep. 1978—companion was Gross; **(knew no mobsters/Luciano's reputation)** Kelley, 394.

242 **FS and Fischettis: (visiting mother)** "Memorandum re Frank Sinatra," Feb. 26, 1947, FSFBI, "Indices Search Slip," Mar. 28, 1955, FBI NY 100-80275; **(Vernon Country Club) Chicago Sun,** Jan. 16, 1948; **(in touch with Joe)** "Summary Memorandum," Sep. 29, 1950, FSFBI, "Indices Search Slip," Mar. 28, 1955, FBI NY 100-80275; **(car dealership)** int. Joseph Nellis; **("had a financial interest")** "Summary Memorandum," Sep. 29, 1950, FSFBI.

242 **Cuba evidence: (FBI and Bureau of Narcotics had agents/had known Luciano)** Legal Attaché Havana to Director, Mar. 26, 1954, FBI 88-3277-2256, Olivera to Williams, Mar. 21, 1947, J. Ray Olivera Papers, "Summary of Information re Lucania," Jan. 12, 1947, and Luciano reports summary, 2–, 7–, 12, 23, 80, 92, and notes for Olivera, Mar. 27, 1947, LLBN; **(elevator/phone operators)** Frederic Sondern Jr., **Brotherhood of Evil,** New York: Farrar, Straus and Cudahy, 1959, 115; **(Luciano on eighth floor)** Dania Perez Rubio, **Hotel Nacional de Cuba,** Havana: Editorial José Martí, 1999, 16.

242 **Frank on seventh floor:** Mortimer to Pegler, Sep. 1947, Box 73, Pegler Papers. The recollection of the former Hotel Nacional employee interviewed in 2004—full name Jorge Miguel Jorge Fernandez—was that Luciano, too, was registered as using a suite not on the eighth floor but on the seventh and actually used

rooms on the second floor—for security reasons, as explained later in the text. His bodyguards used the suite on the upper floor (int. Jorge Jorge by PITV).

242–243 **"While in Havana":** Luciano reports summary, 37, LLBN. Bruce Cabot, named in White's report, was a friend of FS. A character actor who specialized in tough-guy roles, he was a veteran of World War II intelligence operations in Europe—including Sicily—and reportedly a "brawling roisterer" (Sinatra with Coplon, 136, Cabot entry at entertainment.msn.com/celebs, Lee Server, **Robert Mitchum: "Baby, I Don't Care,"** London: Faber and Faber, 2002, 123); **(Moretti in Cuba)** "General Crime Survey," Jul. 15, 1951, FBI 94-419, Peterson, **The Mob,** 248.

243–244 **FS would sue: Modern Screen,** May 1947. The authors found no indication that the suit went forward—it was almost certainly dropped. Ruark reported that he arrived in Havana while Sinatra was still in town, and got his initial tip from a senior executive at the Hotel Nacional; **("I was told"/"I wouldn't advise"/"*not* to file")** Ruark to Wood, Feb. 25, 1947, Robert Ruark Papers; **(Immerman background)** NYT, Oct. 25, 1967, Olivera to Williams, Mar. 21, 1947, J. Ray Olivera Papers, Luciano reports summary, 18, LLBN.

244–245 **"Sanchez threw a party"/"through a series of disastrous mistakes":** As did several accounts of the events in Havana, and probably to preempt a lawsuit, Sondern's 1959 book said only that the party had been given in honor of "a well-known Broadway and Hollywood star." In the circumstances, and in light of Ventura's letter to Ruark, this could refer to no one but Sinatra. The authors have not identified the Emilio Sanchez reported to have thrown the party ("Sanchez threw"—Ventura to Ruark, Mar. 17, 1947, Robert Ruark Papers, Sondern, 115–; "a well-known"—Sondern, 115–); **(informant/planeload)** "Summary Memo on Frank Sinatra," Mar. 1, 1955, FBI LA 100-41713-4.

245 **photographs/Kefauver staff confronted FS:** int. Joseph Nellis, Kelley, 159, M/G int. of Joseph Nellis. The Sinatra/Luciano photographs did once exist—once. A report in the FBI's Sinatra file indicates that by the mid-1950s they had been "stolen from the files of the Kefauver Crime Investigation." Other material also vanished ("File Review & Summary Check," Mar. 9, 1962, FBI LA 100-41413, ed. José Lizardo, **Records of the Senate Special**

Committee to Investigate Organized Crime in Interstate Commerce, 1950–51, Washington, DC: National Archives, 1959, 5).

246 **"We would come":** int. Jorge Jorge by PITV.

246–247 **money to Luciano: (developments/narcotics)** Luciano reports summary, 5–, 20, 35–, Luciano Files, LLBN, Eisenberg, Dan, and Landau, 233; **(cash to Havana)** ibid., 233, 251—the "Lansky associate" was Joseph Stacher, Luciano reports summary, 36–, 92, LLBN, Gosch and Hammer, 307, 312–, int. Joseph Nellis; **(Dempsey)** Luciano reports summary, 14, 37, LLBN; **(Fischettis $2 million)** Robinson to Olney, Kefauver Committee, Sep. 15, 1950, Alpha Names Files, "Sinatra, Frank," Kefauver Committee Files, NA, "Supplemental Correlation Summary," Feb. 25, 1969, FSFBI, report re Frederick J. Tenuto, Apr. 22, 1954, FBI 88-13277, **Wall Street Journal,** Aug. 19, 1968, int. Joseph Nellis; **(allegation in press) New American Mercury,** Aug. 1951; **(Luciano denied)** undat. article by Kefauver Associate Counsel Alfred Klein, pt. 2, George White Papers; **("Picture me") American Weekly,** Jul. 27, 1952, and see transcript, Joseph Nellis interrogation of FS for Kefauver Committee, Mar. 1, 1951, published in **Gallery,** Sep. 1978.

247 **FS took up painting?:** According to Nancy Sinatra, her husband hit on the idea of taking up painting, and rushed out to purchase art supplies, during the shooting of his movie **The Kissing Bandit. Bandit** did not start shooting until mid-May 1947, three months after Sinatra's trip to Havana (hit on the idea—"My Life with Frank Sinatra," article draft by Marva Peterson, Jul. 21, 1947, and see **Movie Show,** ms. by Lynn Peters, Jul. 31, 1947, MHL, and see intro. Tina Sinatra, **A Man and His Art,** refs.; **Bandit** shoot—AFI catalog details supplied by MHL); **("If you can find")** FS testimony, Nevada State Gaming Control Board, Feb. 11, 1981, FS testimony, Nevada State Gaming Commission, Feb. 19, 1981; **(Mailer) NYT,** Feb. 16, 1981, authors' corr. Norman Mailer, 2003; **(Lewis and FS)** int. Jerry Lewis, Sinatra, **Legend,** 177; **(Moretti wedding) Patterson** (NJ) **Call,** Sep. 22, 1947; **(knew Fischettis)** int. Jerry Lewis, Tosches, 156, 162–.

248 **"had to do with the morality":** int. Jerry Lewis. Former policeman and New York Crime Committee investigator William Gallinaro said he learned of Sinatra's courier role in 1947 from a Cuban police contact. As reported in another chapter, Sinatra's friend Brad Dexter later saw a briefcase containing a huge sum in

cash. Sinatra told him he was at the time involved in moving cash to and from Mafia operations in connection with the 1960 election campaign (ints. William Gallinaro, Brad Dexter).

248–250 **purpose of meeting/Siegel: (FS performed)** int. Jorge Jorge by PITV; **("Luciano was very fond")** Eisenberg, Dan, and Landau, 233; **(Siegel on agenda)** ibid., 237–, Katz, 157–, Gosch and Hammer, 315–; **(Siegel background)** "Final Report of the Special Crime Study Commission on Organized Crime," Sacramento, CA: State of CA, May 11, 1953, 22, Jennings, refs., Sifakis, 302; **(Flamingo)** W. R. Wilkerson, **The Man Who Invented Las Vegas,** Beverly Hills, CA: Ciro's Books, 2000, 99, 104; **(Fischettis contributed)** report re Rocco Fischetti, Feb. 14, 1963, FBI 92-3915, "Re Joseph Fischetti," Jul. 16, 1957, FBI 92-96512; **(FS exploring plans) Las Vegas Review-Journal,** Jul. 31, 1946, **Hollywood Citizen-News,** Apr. 3, 1946, "Correlation Summary," Jun. 8, 1964, and Rosen to Director, Feb. 26, 1947, and attached memo, FSFBI; **(Siegel had complained)** "Summary Memorandum," Sep. 29, 1950, and "Correlation Summary," Jun. 8, 1964, FSFBI; **(trying to get FS at opening)** "Memorandum re Frank Sinatra," Feb. 26, 1947, FBI O & C File 139, "Summary Memo on Frank Sinatra," Mar. 1, 1955, LA 100-41413; **(sentenced)** Eisenberg, Dan, and Landau, 238, Katz, 158, Gosch and Hammer, 317–, 328; **(Fischetti directed?)** ibid., 318.

250 **"We were with a couple":** int. Shirley Ballard. Siegel famously cultivated Hollywood stars, and initially Sinatra is said to have had a "natural respect" for him. A Bureau of Narcotics report placed him in Siegel's circle, with Lana Turner. Siegel's associate Allen Smiley said he knew Sinatra well, and at one point Sinatra rented an apartment in the same building as Smiley, at 8358 Sunset Boulevard. Los Angeles mobster Mickey Cohen said Sinatra was a friend, a claim corroborated by FBI reports ("natural respect"—David Thomson, **In Nevada,** New York: Knopf, 1999, 64; Narcotics Bureau and Siegel circle—Luciano reports summary, LLBN; Turner—Crane, 65, Rose, 105–; Smiley—"Summary Memorandum," Sep. 29, 1950, and "Correlation Summary," Jun. 8, 1964, FSFBI; apartment—"Summary Memo on Frank Sinatra," Mar. 1, 1955, FBI LA 100-41413; Cohen—Davidson, 20, Mickey Cohen with John Peer Nugent, **Mickey Cohen,** Englewood Cliffs, NJ: Prentice-Hall, 1975, 85–, 228,

Rosen to Director, Feb. 26, 1947, attached memo, and "Summary Memo on Frank Sinatra," Mar. 1, 1955, FSFBI); **(syndicate had taken over)** Wilkerson, 111, Reid, 222, Lait and Mortimer, 203.

250 **Luciano/FS relationship: (denied "was ever asked")** Gosch and Hammer, 312, and see **Washington Daily News**, Feb. 24, 1947, **Parade**, Jan. 12, 1964; **(FS insisted) American Weekly**, Jul. 27, 1952.

250–251 **Luciano after Cuba: (shipped back)** Anslinger and Oursler, 105–, Anslinger draft ms., Box 4, File 3, Harry Anslinger Papers, University of Pennsylvania, Director to Legal Attaché, Rio de Janeiro, Mar. 25, 1947, FBI 39-2171-110; **(in Italy)** Anslinger and Oursler, 107–, Luciano reports summary, 22, LLBN, **Commissione Parliamentare D'Inchieta Sul Fenomeno Della Mafia in Sicilia**, vol. 4, pt. 1, 405–, and vol. 4, pt. 2, 1393.

251 **cigarette case/lighter: ("When Italian police")** undat. column, ca. Sep. 1949, Alpha Names Files, "Sinatra, Frank," Kefauver Committee Files, NA; **(Anslinger's papers)** Anslinger draft ms., Box 4, File 3, Harry Anslinger Papers; **(later article) New American Mercury**, Aug. 1951—piece was by Lee Mortimer; **(no "gift") American Weekly**, Jul. 27, 1952, and see FS testimony, Nevada State Gaming Commission, Feb. 19, 1981; **("a few presents")** Gosch and Hammer, 312; **(Rizzo background)** Gosch and Hammer, 418–.

252 **"I had a gold lighter":** int. Adriana Rizzo. Official documents in Italian archives show that Luciano's brother Bartolo did come from the United States to deal with the Mafia boss's estate after his death. He apparently evicted Adriana Rizzo, allowing her to remove only her personal effects (**Rapporto Sulle Operazioni Di P.G.**, 1446, **Commissione Parliamentare D'Inchiesta Sul Fenomeno Della Mafia in Sicilia**, vol. 4, pt. 1, 377, and see **L'Ora**, Jan. 30, **Giornale di Sicilia**, Feb. 9, 1962, Gosch and Hammer, 449–).

252 **"large, gold cigarette case":** int. Fulvio Toschi, and research in **Rapporto Sulle Operazioni Di P.G. "Lucky Luciano,"** Rome: Nucleo Centrale Polizia Tributaria Della Guardia Di Finanza, Mar. 30, 1962, 1428. The information available to the authors, it will be noted, refers to a lighter inscribed to "Charlie" and a cigarette case inscribed to "Lucky." Luciano was christened "Salva-

tore" but changed to "Charlie" in early adulthood after friends called him "Sal," which he thought sounded effeminate. The "Lucky" tag was reportedly given him by fellow hoodlum Meyer Lansky, after Luciano narrowly escaped being killed. It has been said he later disowned the nickname—not least because he became **un**lucky when he was given a lengthy prison sentence. Sources suggest associates used both "Charlie" and "Lucky." The columnist Leonard Lyons, who interviewed Luciano in 1953, noted the initials C.L. on a lighter the mobster was using then.

Martin Gosch and Richard Hammer reported in their 1974 Luciano book that Italian police noted various personal items, including a gold cigarette **case** with a Sinatra inscription, during a search of Luciano's Naples apartment just days before his death ("Charlie"/"Lucky"—Sciacca, **Luciano,** 50, 87–, 168, Gosch and Hammer, 16, 109, 119, 148, Wolf with DiMona, 83, Katz, 88; C.L.—**Esquire,** Apr. 1953; police noted—Gosch and Hammer, 444, ints. Adriana Rizzo and Fulvio Toschi).

252 **Luciano knew FS's address:** The record indicates there were two separate address book seizures. The Anslinger document dates the seizure to "after Luciano's arrival in Italy in February of 1946." A 1949 report shows there was certainly a seizure in July 1949. Address lists are attached to both documents, and Sinatra appears in both lists—listed with his Toluca Lake, California, address. Numerous differences between the two lists are consistent with separate transcriptions at different times. There is a somewhat surprising reference in the 1946 document, however, to the simultaneous seizure of Luciano's lover Igea Lissoni's address book—and sources conflict as to whether the couple had become an item as early as 1946. Sinatra resided at the Toluca Lake address from spring 1944 to summer 1949 (Anslinger document—White to Anslinger, Feb. 5, 1951, LLBN; Lissoni—Sondern, 117, Gosch and Hammer, 335; other bureau documents—Luciano reports summary, 29, Manfredi "Affidavit" and attached address book entries, Nov. 21, 1952, and "Memorandum to District Supervisors," Aug. 15, 1949, LLBN, "Summary Information re Lucania," Jan. 12, 1947, J. Ray Olivera Papers; FS at Toluca Lake—Sinatra, **Legend,** 60, 91).

252–253 **later FS meetings with Luciano: (familiar figure)** John Davis, **Mafia Dynasty,** New York: HarperTorch, 1993, 120–, Wells and Bogdanovich, 312; **(bosses consulted)** Luciano reports summary, 28–, 45, 74, 83–, 87, Rizzo to Williams, May 4, 1948, and "Memorandum to District Supervisors," Aug. 15, 1949, LLBN, Henry Zeiger, **The Jersey Mob,** New York: Signet, 1975, 158–; **(remained power/drugs)** Cook, 125, 330, 346, 349–, **True,** Nov. 1952, and see Vizzini with Fraley and Smith, 154; **(Durante/Raft)** Luciano reports summary, 53–, Cusack to Anslinger, Mar. 2, 1961, LLBN.

253 **"close personal friends":** Cusack to Anslinger, Mar. 2, 1961, LLBN. Others named in Narcotics Bureau reports as having been in touch with Luciano were film director Roberto Rossellini, Ingrid Bergman's husband, actor Marc Lawrence, and actresses Lois Andrews and Ella Logan (Luciano reports summary, 57, 71, 51, 52, 63.

253 **FS carried money 1950/60?:** Memo to Mr. Boardman, Feb. 28, 1955, FSFBI, "File Review and Summary Check," Mar. 9, 1962, FBI LA 100-41413.

253 **expected in 1952:** Siragusa to Anslinger, Jan. 19, 1952, LLBN; **(following spring)** Siragusa to Anslinger, Jan. 5, 1954, but see Cusack to Anslinger, Apr. 7, 1961, LLBN; **(FS tour) "Where or When?"** Gardner, 189; **(new sorties)** Luciano reports summary, 63, 69, 72, 85, LLBN, Memo to Mr. Boardman, Feb. 28, 1955, FSFBI—report related to 1951, Legal Attaché Havana to Director, Mar. 26, 1954, FBI 88-3277-2256; **(nine times) Boston American,** Jan. 31, 1956; **(Mafia conclaves)** Memo to Mr. Boardman, Feb. 28, 1955, FSFBI; **("We used to meet")** Russo, 227, and see Cook, 349; **("present in 1951")** Memo to Mr. Boardman, Feb. 28, 1955, FSFBI; **("We walked into the suite")** Jacobs, who traveled the world with Sinatra for years, was no longer sure of the exact date of this encounter. He was clear, however, that it occurred in Rome—probably in the late 1950s—and Sinatra did visit Rome in 1958 (ints. George Jacobs, Jacobs and Stadiem, 191, Hanna, **Ava,** New York: Putnam, 1960, 221–).

254–255 **FS and Luciano in Havana at Christmas 1958?:** Chico Scimone, the Sicilian American who said he played piano at a mob "audition" of Sinatra in the late thirties, told the authors he heard from mob sources that both Luciano and Sinatra were in Havana at New Year's 1958, when Fidel Castro overthrew the Batista regime. Reports discussed earlier in this chapter indicate that the mobster made covert trips back from exile at various times, and, four years after imposing strict travel restrictions on Luciano, the Italian authorities had returned the mobster's passport to him on December 13.

It seems possible that Sinatra was in Havana at New Year's 1958. The authors located no indication of his precise whereabouts between December 29 and January 14. Shooting of final scenes for **A Hole in the Head**, meanwhile, was taking place in the first week of 1959 in the Miami area, a short airplane trip away from Havana. It was common, in those pre-Castro days, for pleasure-seeking Americans to make the trip for a couple of days or even less. A reference in Nancy Sinatra's book **Legend,** which places Sinatra in a recording studio in Los Angeles on January 2, appears to be inaccurate. Other sources indicate the recording sessions in question took place between October 13 and 15, 1958.

Sinatra's involvement in a Cuban casino deal features in an FBI report citing records of National City Bank. According to the report, he and six others were putting up $10 million to build the Monte Carlo Hotel and Casino—in association with a partner of Meyer Lansky. Lansky himself was in Havana on New Year's Eve 1958 (Luciano fretting—Fred Cook, **The Secret Rulers,** New York: Duell, Sloan and Pearce, 1966, 349–, Gosch and Hammer, 378–, 408–; Scimone—int. Chico Scimone; restrictions/passport—Gosch and Hammer, 408–, and see **L'Europeo** magazine, Jan. 11, 18, 25, 1959; FS whereabouts Dec. 29–Jan. 14—"**Where or When?**"; **Hole** shoot—O'Brien, 116, **LAT** magazine, May 24, 1959; in LA?—Sinatra, **Legend**, 140, but see Dec.–Jan., 1959, entries **Where or When?** Sayers and O'Brien, 240–; Monte Carlo casino—"Correlation Summary," Jun. 8, 1964, FSFBI, **Wall Street Journal**, Jan. 16, 1981; Lansky—Lacey, **Little Man,** 249–).

255–256 **"The crowd from from *Hole*":** Location shooting in Florida for **Hole in the Head** occurred between November 1958 and January 1959. The word "kadiddlehopper" refers to the type of hat worn by the comedian Red Skelton when portraying "Clem Kadiddlehopper," a character he created (ints. Bill Woodfield, 2001, and see **This Week,** May 24, 1959, O'Brien, 116–, Hersh, 142fn.); **("There are some people"/"He told it")** int. Peggy Connelly; **(FS "scared off")** Cusack to Anslinger, Mar. 2, 1961, LLBN; **(FS corresponded)** Siragusa to Anslinger, May

20, 1961, LLBN; **("Sinatra was a very close")** int. Adriana Rizzo.

Chapter 14: Courting Disaster

258 **"one of the dumbest":** Hamill, 145.

258 **Nancy/abortion: ("Will you be") Modern Screen,** May 1947; **(abortion)** Sinatra with Coplon, 18–.

259–260 **Mortimer attack: (basic incident)** Request for Investigation, Apr. 10, Investigator's Report, Apr. 14, 1947, and related docs., District Attorney, County of Los Angeles, courtesy of Gavin MacFadyen, Hedda Hopper int. of FS, **Chicago Tribune–NY News** syndicate, undat. 1947 draft, MHL int. Louanne Hogan Wilson, **New York Daily News,** Apr. 9, 15, (NY) **Daily Mirror,** Apr. 9, 11, 13, **New York World-Telegram,** Apr. 9, **New York Post,** Apr. 9, 11, (LA) **Daily News,** Apr. 9, **Daily Worker,** Apr. 9, AP, Apr. 9, UP, Apr. 9, 14, INS, Apr. 9, **Washington News,** Apr. 10, **LAT,** Apr. 10, 11, 12, 16, 17, **NYT,** Apr. 10, unid. article by Grace Robinson, probably **New York News,** Robert Ruark Papers, **New York Journal-American,** Apr. 12, 13, **Time,** Apr. 21, 1947; **(license withdrawn)** (NY) **Daily Mirror,** Apr. 15, 1947, **Chicago Herald-American,** Apr. 14, 1947, Carpozi, 93.

260 **song plugger Sam Weiss:** Weiss first met Sinatra on New York's 52nd Street, where he worked in the clubs. Sinatra was close to both him and his brother Irving "Sarge" Weiss, who was also present on the night of the Mortimer episode and became a key aide. (Weiss brothers background in int. and corr. Ric Ross, Sinatra with Coplon, 80, Sinatra, **My Father,** 58, int. Shirley Ballard; Irving present in Request for Investigation, Apr. 10, Investigator's Report, Apr. 14, 1947, and related docs., District Attorney, County of Los Angeles, courtesy of Gavin MacFadyen); **("He called me") Time,** Apr. 21, 1947. The word "sonofabitch" was deleted in many press reports and appears in the official record as "bastard." The account Harrison Carroll gave investigators and the text of his published report are also in the file; **(concocted)** Kelley, 125–, citing taped comments of Jack Keller.

260–261 **Mortimer background/sequel: ("squealing . . . juve delinqs")** Shaw, **Sinatra,** 79, 92, 93; **("until hostilities")** (NY) **Sunday Mirror,** Jul. 15, 1945; **("class struggle") New Republic,**

Mar. 31, 1986; **("much of his time") Los Angeles Examiner,** Apr. 10, 1947; **("(Lucky)")** (NY) **Daily Mirror,** Mar. 14, 1947; **("belt") New York Post,** Apr. 10, 1947, and see Kelley, 124; **("stick his head")** int. Sonny King, M/G int. of Sonny King, and see Wilson, **Sinatra,** 72; **("I'll kill you")** Investigator's Report; **(investigators concluded) New York Journal-American,** Apr. 13, 1947; **(never to trial) LAT,** (LA) **Daily News, Washington Times-Herald,** Jun. 4, 1947, DA Investigator's and Sheriff's Dept. Supplemental Reports, Jun. 5, 13, 1947; ***(U.S.A. Confidential)*** Jack Lait and Lee Mortimer, **U.S.A. Confidential,** New York: Crown, 1952, 21, and see Jack Lait and Lee Mortimer, **Washington Confidential,** New York: Crown, 1951, **Bergen** (NJ) **Record,** Jun. 21, 2000; **(beaten unconscious) Washington Times-Herald,** (NY) **Daily Mirror,** May 18, 1950; **(FBI 1960)** log of conv., Apr. 5, 1960, vol. 9, Misc. ELSUR Refs., HSCA Subject Files, Frank Sinatra, JFK, Zeiger, 200, and see (NY) **Daily Mirror,** Apr. 5, 1960; **("Frank and I")** int. Brad Dexter.

263–265 **Hearst papers & FS: (Hearst on FDR & "Reds")** W. A. Swanberg, **Citizen Hearst,** New York: Scribner's, 1961, 567, Vaughn, 41; **("wipe out") New York World-Telegram,** Apr. 2, 1947; **("almost fit") Time,** Apr. 21, 1947; **(Jefferson Award) New York Daily News,** Apr. 10, INS, Apr. 14, 1947, Carpozi, 91; **(Mortimer digging)** int. of George Evans by Charles Siragusa, Apr. 12, 1948, LLBN, "Memo for Mr. Tolson," May 12, Tolson to Director, May 13, 15, 1947, and "Summary Memorandum," Sep. 29, 1950, FSFBI; **(collate information)** Mortimer to Pegler, Sep. 26, 1947, and undat. letter, Box 73, Pegler Papers; **("hosstrade")** Ruark to Pegler, Mar. 14, 1947, Box 72, Pegler Papers; **(Pegler columns) New York Journal-American,** Sep. 10, 11, 12, 16, Oct. 1, 4, 1947, **Washington Times-Herald,** Nov. 14, 1947; **("Posing")** undat. column, Mar. 1947, Robert Ruark Papers; **("I don't know") Photoplay,** Nov. 1951; **("very contrite"/received)** Kelley, 127–, int. of George Evans by Charles Siragusa, Apr. 12, 1948, LLBN.

265 **FS status/working methods: (Old Gold)** UP, Apr. 24, 1947, **Chicago's American,** Sep. 25, 1966.

266–268 **Capitol audiences:** Shaw, **Sinatra,** 115, Wilson, **Sinatra,** 76, (NY) **Daily Mirror,** Nov. 28, 1947. A favorable review of the appearance by one of the big Hearst papers, it was said later, had been rewritten to read like dire criticism; **(ABC poll)** Shaw, **Sinatra,** 114; **(work in studio)** Granata, 35–, WP, Oct. 31, 1947; **(Quinlan) Metronome,** Oct. 1948; **("It drives me")** int. of FS by Arlene Francis, Sep. 25, 1981, WOR (NY) radio; **("It was stunningly")** Clooney with Barthel, 46, 8; **("He put a period")** Lees, 161; **(*Who's Who*)** LAT, Feb. 24, 1948; **("His voice")** int. Al Viola; **("darker hues")** Granata, 39; **("The songs that I sing") New York Daily News,** Jan. 23, 1978; **("felt")** Sinatra, **My Father,** 372.

268 **Sinatra Day: (appearance) New Jersey Monthly,** Feb. 1982, Frank, 61, int. Frank Monaco; **(squabbling)** ibid. and Gardner, 149–, int. Mearene Jordan; **(Francesco died)** NYT, Apr. 9, 1948, giving wrong age; **(FS "spit")** LAT, Feb. 4, 1998.

269–270 **FS family life: (fond memories)** Sinatra, **My Father,** 56–, 72, **Family Weekly,** Jun. 17, 1984; **("as traditional")** unid. article by Marva Peterson, Jul. 21, 1947, MHL; **(got away to Palm Springs)** int. Gloria Cahn, Sinatra, **My Father,** 58, 108; **(decided to build)** Davidson, 36–, "Twin Palms," www.locationsunlimited.com, **American Weekly,** Nov. 26, 1950; **(happy memories/As they drove)** Sinatra, **My Father,** 58–; **(baby) Los Angeles Examiner,** Nov. 10, 1947, **Movieland,** Sep. 7, 1948.

270 **Evans laboring: Los Angeles Examiner,** Oct. 6, 1947, Sinatra, **Legend,** 77, 90, int. of George Evans by Charles Siragusa, Apr. 12, 1948, LLBN, notes of int. of George Evans, Sep. 10, 1947, Box 72, Pegler Papers.

270 **Mob contacts: (Fischettis)** "Summary Memorandum," Sep. 29, 1950, FSFBI, **Chicago Sun,** Jan. 16, 1948; **("financial interest")** "Summary Memorandum," Sept. 29, 1950, FSFBI.

270 **Moretti "associated"/"kicked in":** "Summary Memorandum," Sep. 29, 1950, FSFBI. Columnist Lee Mortimer would report—and it has been widely repeated—that Sinatra sang at the wedding of one of Moretti's daughters. Moretti's daughter Angela told the authors, however, that he sang neither at her wedding nor at those of her two sisters. Mortimer report in **New American Mercury,** Aug. 1951, and see, e.g., Kelley, 172; and re Moretti daughters' weddings, int. Angela Marrocco, **Newark** (NJ) **Evening News,** Jun. 9, 1947, and **Paterson** (**NJ**) **Call,** Sep. 22, 1947, and see Dwiggins, 101.

271 **Cohen: (sordid story) Los Angeles Examiner,** Oct. 6, 1947, notes of int. George Evans, Sep. 10, 1947, Box 72, Pegler Papers.

271 **Cohen/boxing/criminal:** "Summary Memo," Mar. 1, 1955, FBI LA 100-41413, "Correlation Summary," Jun. 8, 1964, FSFBI, **Chicago's American,** Sep. 27, 1966, Robinson to Olney, Sep. 15, 1950, and Polski to McGill, Aug. 24, 1951, Alpha Names Files, "Sinatra, Frank," Kefauver Committee Files, NA, Peterson, **Mob,** 330–. The criminal in question was Jimmy Tarantino, who ran a scandal sheet FS apparently helped finance—as did Willie Moretti; **(FS had known the crook)** transcript, Joseph Nellis interrogation of FS for Kefauver Committee, Mar. 1, 1951, published in **Gallery,** Sep. 1978; **(address book)** "Summary Memorandum," Sep. 29, 1950, and Rosen to Director, Feb. 26, 1947, FSFBI, "Summary Memo," Mar. 1, 1955, FBI LA 100-41713; **("Why, he's a friend")** Davidson, 20.

271 **Palm Springs and mob: (Stables)** "Summary Memo," Mar. 1, 1955; FBI LA 100-41413, Pegler to Lloyd Felmly, Oct. 17, 1947, Box 72, Pegler Papers; **Chicago's American,** Sep. 28, 1966; **("favorite rendez-vous")** "The Special Crime Study Commission on Organized Crime," Final Report, Sacramento, CA: State of Calif., May 11, 1953, 21–, **Sacramento Bee,** Mar. 8, 1977; **(Smiley)** ibid., 35, 28; **(Smiley/FS)** int. Luellen Smiley, "Summary Memo," Mar. 1, 1955, LA 100-41413, "Summary Memorandum," Sep. 29, 1950, FSFBI; **("I've known these people")** Sinatra, **Legend,** 174.

272–274 **Hollywood status 1949: (MGM had paid)** Shaw, **Sinatra,** 124, Dwiggins, 104; **(pushed the patience)** Sinatra, **Legend,** 78, Sinatra, **My Father,** 16, Kelley, 127, O'Brien, 5–; **(FS behaved badly)** O'Brien, 29–, 51, 49–; **(*Miracle* premiere)** ibid., 38, Davidson, 38; **(movies lost money)** O'Brien, 31, 33, 38, 52; **(*Down Beat* poll)** Down Beat polls, Jan. 1, 1944–Dec. 30, 1949; **("decadent") Billboard,** Nov. 20, 1965; **("Is Sinatra Finished?") Modern Television & Radio,** Dec. 1948; **(did feel finished)** Nancy Sinatra, **Legend,** 87; **("When we had guests"/locked)** (LA) **Daily News,** Sep. 2, 1950.

Chapter 15: Lovers, Eternally

275–276 **MGM photograph:** John Springer Collection, Corbis photos—according to MGM's archivist, the picture was taken on Feb. 10, 1949, Gardner, 122; **Ava background: (as child)** Doris Cannon, **Grabtown Girl,** Asheboro, NC: Down Home Press,

2001, 12–, 31, undat. Ava int. by Charles Samuels, **Motion Picture,** MHL; **(barefoot as adult)** Roland Flamini, **Ava,** New York: Coward, McCann, 1983, 81; **(smoking at eight)** ibid., 28; **(beauty)** Cannon, 45, 54, 65; **(nails)** ibid., 52; **(could not afford)** Gardner, 18; **(acted/at ease)** Cannon, 35, 50–; **(movies)** taped 1988 interviews of Ava Gardner by Peter Evans, Gardner, 13, 24; **(dreamed)** Cannon, 43, 66; **(talked of singing)** Gardner, 29; **(wind up a secretary)** Evans tapes, Cannon, 63, **Look,** Dec. 11, 1956; **(local boy)** ibid., 51; **(demure shots)** ibid., 69–, undat. Ava int. by Charles Samuels; **(actress-in-waiting)** Evans tapes, Flamini, 21, 38–, Charles Higham, **Ava,** New York: Delacorte, 1974, 15–; **("I've never cared")** undat. Ava int. by Charles Samuels, Gardner, 188.

276–279 **Ava early lovelife: (strictly) Look,** Nov. 27, 1956; **(shy/"I played")** Evans tapes, Cannon, 46; **("the biggest")** Higham, **Ava,** 12; **(Rooney background)** Flamini, 44–, Mickey Rooney, **I.E.: An Autobiography,** New York: Putnam, 1965, refs., Mickey Rooney, **Life Is Too Short,** New York: Villard, 1991, refs., Cannon, 73–; **(far from L.A.)** Rooney, **Too Short,** 187; **("damn near")** Flamini, 53; **("Once he gets")** Higham, **Ava,** 24; **("I found evidence")** Evans tapes; **(Rooney said)** Rooney, **Too Short,** 192–; **(played field)** Higham, **Ava,** 41–; **(Hughes/breasts/"wet decks")** Higham, **Ava,** 46, Gardner, 67; **(never shared)** Gardner, 69, 127; **(believe otherwise)** e.g., Higham, **Ava,** 45–, 48—Charles Higham also wrote **Howard Hughes: The Secret Life,** London: Pan Books, 1994; **(Hughes pursues Ava)** Higham, **Ava,** 152, Gardner, 78–, 154, 158, Jane Ellen Wayne, **Ava's Men,** New York: St. Martin's, 1990, 185–; **(jitterbug)** Cannon, 58, **(Shaw "dysfunction")** Flamini, 75–; **(four wives)** Wayne, 81; **(psychoanalysis)** int. Artie Shaw, Higham, **Ava,** 57; **("the first intelligent"/"most perfect")** Gardner, 88–; **(living together)** Flamini, 80–; **("improve"/*Interpretation*/introduced)** Gardner, 90–; **(shut up)** ibid., 94; **(quarreling/divorced)** Higham, **Ava,** 58–; **(Tormé)** Tormé, **Velvet,** 89–; **(Duff)** Gardner, 106–, Higham, **Ava,** 72–; **(Taylor)** ibid., 117–; **(Mitchum)** Lee Server, **Robert Mitchum: "Baby, I Don't Care,"** New York: Faber and Faber, 2001, 251—but see Gardner, 119.

279–281 **Ava's problems: (Peter Evans)** Evans, a leading show-business writer, kindly permitted the authors to quote from the unpublished tapes of his interview with Gardner, for which he holds the copyright. Ava Gardner's memoir **My Story,** apparently drawn from subsequent taping sessions, was published after her death in 1990; **("revise")** int. Peter Evans; **("a tremendous capacity")** Rooney, **Too Short,** 184; **("like Coca-Cola"/Scotch and beer/"I got the blender")** Higham, **Ava,** 64, 61, 73; **("how much we drank")** Evans tapes; **("desperately insecure")** Higham, **Ava,** 89; **("could change")** Gardner, 284; **("When I lose")** Richard Hack, **Hughes,** Beverly Hills, CA: New Millennium, 2001, 139; **("taken a kitchen knife")** Rooney, **Too Short,** 195; **(knocked out Hughes)** Higham, **Ava,** 49, and see 73; **("The quality")** Rooney, **I.E.,** 137; **(puritan)** Gardner, 49; **(brothels)** Evans tapes, Gardner, 106–, Ted Quillin to authors, Apr. 18, 2002, Higham, **Ava,** 136, 154–; **("I think fucking's")** Messick, **Show Business,** 187; **("I want to be")** unid. article by Elsa Maxwell, MHL; **(never wanted)** Rooney, **I.E.,** 143; **(used contraception)** Flamini, 95; **("I don't think")** Evans tapes; **("operated on")** Higham, **Ava,** 76–. Author Charles Higham told the authors that he obtained the abortion account from the woman friend, whom he found credible.

281 **Tormé/Toxton party:** Tormé, **Velvet,** 64–.

281 **hit someone:** LAT, Mar. 22, 23, 1949, **Look,** May 14, 1957; **(bottle)** Carpozi, 99.

281 **FS & Ava early affair: (speeding car/"flirt")** Evans tapes, Gardner, 122.

282 **Palladium:** Evans tapes, undat. Ava Gardner interview by Thelma McGill, MHL, Gardner, 122. Other authors have dated Sinatra's first meeting with Gardner as 1945. She twice said, however, that it occurred earlier, during her marriage to Rooney and Frank's Dorsey period. She was divorced from Rooney in 1943, and Frank had left Dorsey by fall 1942. Re 1945 see Sinatra, **Legend,** 67, Freedland, 116; **("had eyes")** int. Artie Shaw; **(bat girl)** Kelley, 91, Sinatra, **Legend,** 81–; **(exchanged partners)** LAT, Oct. 24, 1946, Wilson, **Sinatra,** 88.

282 **"Just for mischief":** Cahn, 95. Cahn's memoirs suggest that this occurred as early as 1942, but that cannot be correct. Sinatra did not move to Hollywood until 1944, and Mearene Jordan—who according to Ava was with her at the Sunset Towers—did not start working for the actress until 1947 or 1948 (Gardner, 123, 283); **("conceited")** Higham, **Ava,** 91, and see int. Mearene Jordan; **("drank quite a bit")** Gardner, 123–; **("we drank")** Gardner, 125.

283 **shooting incident:** This incident is usually referred to as having occurred in late January/February 1950. Taken together, the evidence is that it occurred earlier—not least since it evidently occurred before the death, in late January 1950, of George Evans. In her 1986 Sinatra biography, author Kitty Kelley quoted Keller as saying the shooting spree occurred in Indio, California. The man who was Indio police chief in the late 1940s, Pat Cunningham, denied the incident occurred there while he was in office. The authors were unable to check the facts further with either Keller or Cunningham, since both are dead (Davidson, 5–, Kelley, 133–, and **Desert Sun,** Oct. 16, 1986); **(Nichols Canyon)** Higham, **Ava,** 79, Hanna, 131; **("We became lovers")** Gardner, 125.

284–285 **course of FS/Ava affair 1950: (Ava liberal)** Evans tapes, Gardner, 55; **(reds/Soviet consulate)** Evans tapes; **(broadcast)** Buhle and Wagner, 437–; **(jazz/African-American musicians)** Evans tapes, Cannon, 35; **(friends tried)** unid. article by Thelma McGill, circa Jul. 1952, MHL; **(Turner told Ava)** Gardner, 125–; **("watch it")** int. Jean Greenberg; **(Evans warned)** int. Phil Evans, Sinatra, **Legend,** 90–, and see int. Mearene Jordan; **(premiere/party)** Wilson, **Sinatra,** 89; **(threatened photographer)** LAT, Feb. 7, 1950, Gardner, 126; Flamini, 121, Bill Adler, **Sinatra: The Man and the Myth,** New York: NAL, 1987, 86–; **("My married life")** NYT, LAT, **Los Angeles Examiner,** Feb. 15, 1950; **("terribly"/press photos)** Sinatra, **My Father,** 75; **(FS troubled)** Sinatra with Coplon, 22, Gardner, 125; **("The battle I had") American Weekly,** Jul. 20, 1952; **(pills)** Flamini, 125, Higham, **Ava,** 95; **(jealousy/"If he looked")** Gardner, 129, 287; **("she would swear")** ibid., 287; **(FS worried)** ibid., 127, 154, 158.

285–287 **Shaw/Hampshire House incident:** Several versions of that night's events have surfaced over the years, differing in detail but telling the same core story. The authors have used the account offered by Artie Shaw in a 2002 interview, along with the gunshot finale as described in Ava Gardner's 1990 book **My Story,** at p. 130. For other versions see **Look,** Jun. 11, 1957, Gehman, 204–, Dwiggins, 106, Arnold Shaw, **Sinatra: The Entertainer,** New York: Delilah Books, 1982, 135–, Higham, **Ava,** 95–, Carpozi, 104, Flamini, 123, Kelley, 147–; **(Ava disliked mobsters)** int. Spoli Mills, MacLaine, **Lucky Stars,** 85,

Flamini, 123, 126; **(wanted to talk about sex)** int. Artie Shaw. By contrast, Earl Wilson, citing the singer Bricktop, reported Ava as having said: "It was always great in bed; the troubles were all out of bed." Bricktop herself made no mention of this in her published memoir (Wilson, **Sinatra,** 114, and see Bricktop with Haskins); **(Douglas)** Kirk Douglas, **The Ragman's Son,** New York: Pocket, 1988, 164–.

288 **Career slide 1950: ("A year from now")** Wilson, **Sinatra,** 84–; **(Evans death)** Shaw, **Sinatra,** 132; **("friendly parting")** LAT, Apr. 29, 1950; **(Mayer & FS)** O'Brien, 47–.

288–289 **joke:** FS int. by Zion. Sinatra made the joke during a conversation about an injury Mayer incurred when falling off a horse. Sinatra quipped that the MGM boss had fallen not off the horse but off Ginny Simms. Simms, a band singer, was a Mayer girlfriend at the time; **(told FS to get out)** Sinatra, **My Father,** 87. Sinatra's most recent movie, **On the Town,** had been a success, but that was not enough to change Mayer's mind. O'Brien, 48; **("He wanted to be"/"was no good")** Kelley, 149–; **("Every single night")** Evans tapes; **(no longer working)** Friedwald, 184, 192, Granata, 72; **(voice slurred)** (Chicago) **Sunday American,** Sep. 25, 1966; **(reached for a high note/blood) Life,** Apr. 23, 1965, Hamill, 148–, and see LAT, May 2, **Los Angeles Examiner,** May 3, **Metronome,** Jun. 1950.

290 **Mario Cabré episode: (basic story)** Shaw, **Sinatra,** 136–, Higham, **Ava,** 96–, Flamini, 129, Carpozi, 110–, Gardner, 136; **(FS phone calls)** Flamini, 131; **(necklace)** Shaw, **Sinatra,** 138–; **(accusations)** Flamini, 135; **("Nothing!")** Wilson, **Sinatra,** 93; **("The Ava thing")** int. Tony Mottola.

291 **Nancy separation: (wanted only separation)** Carpozi, 113, and see NYT, Feb. 15, 1950; **(judge awarded)** NYT, LAT, Sep. 29, 1950.

291–292 **FS/Ava in 1951: ("slow, vaguely")** Rosemary Clooney with Barthel, 107–; **(MGM pressure)** unid. clip by Elsa Maxwell, unid. article by Arthur Charles, both MHL; **(hate mail)** Flamini, 123, 144; **("People don't understand")** Granata, 71; **(not one song) Billboard,** Jan. 5, 1952; **(TV/radio)** entries, **Where or When?,** Shaw, **Sinatra,** 144–, Friedwald, 195; **(Laine et al.)** Rockwell, 102, Shaw, **Sinatra,** 23.

292–295 **FS gas episode:** The gas incident is reported in three books, the memoirs by Sinatra's daughters Nancy and Tina and

Earl Wilson's biography of the singer. Wilson quotes Sacks, but offers no date. Nancy dates the episode to mid-1952, while Tina seems to place it in 1950 or soon afterward. The detail in Tina's account suggests it occurred during Eddie Fisher's triumphant Manhattan appearances of early 1951 (Sinatra with Coplon, 22, Sinatra, **Legend,** 105, Wilson, **Sinatra,** 95; and re date of Fisher's 1951 appearance see Eddie Fisher, **My Life, My Loves,** New York: Berkley, 1982, 58–, Fisher with Fisher, 42–, **WP,** Mar. 25, 1951); **("Fool" session) Billboard,** Nov. 20, 1965, citing Ben Barton, Friedwald, 190–, Granata, 74–; **("in a voice numb") High Fidelity,** Aug. 1971; **("I am agreeing") NYT,** May 30, **LAT,** May 30, Jun. 2, 1951, Carpozi, 120; **(Hoboken/"sweet little photos")** Gardner, 150–; **(*Danny Wilson*)** O'Brien, 58; **(psychiatrists/priest)** Shelley Winters, **Shelley,** New York: Ballantine, 1980, 305–; **(Nancy psychiatrist/Kroger) Look,** Jun. 11, 1957, int. of William Kroger, 1994, courtesy of Dick Russell, **NYT,** Dec. 7, 1995; **("We vacillated")** Gardner, 151–; **(FS in Nevada) LAT,** Aug. 10, **Time,** Sep. 3, 1951; **("screaming")** int. Ralph Denton; **("I tried to evade"/"a single mistake"/"I told him")** Gardner, 154, 138, and see Sciacca, **Sinatra,** 168; **("He was drinking")** int. Brad Dexter; **(Tahoe rows)** Gardner, 154–.

295–296 **FS overdose: LAT, Los Angeles Examiner, New York World-Telegram,** Sep. 1, **WP,** Sep. 2, 1951. "Sinolo" was evidently an impromptu alias, based on the name of Frank's aide Hank Sanicola. Sanicola was present that night; **("I wanted to punch")** Gardner, 156; **("Suddenly, she got") Look,** Jun. 11, 1957; **("exhaustion"/abortion rumors)** Higham, **Ava,** 110–, Wayne, 145; **(MGM executives)** Flamini, 157; **(divorce decrees) Look,** Jun. 11, 1957, Kelley, 169, Higham, **Ava,** 111.

296 **FS & Ava wedding: ("from a woman")** Gardner, 159; **("We had arranged . . ." *et. seq.*)** Evans tapes.

Chapter 16: Busted

299–300 **Ava/FS early 1952: ("Bewitched")** Feb. 1952 entry, **Where or When?; (fix up house)** Shaw, **Sinatra,** 155; **(housewife)** Flamini, 154; **("At the last")** int. Janet Leigh; Janet Leigh, **There Really Was a Hollywood,** Garden City, NY: Doubleday, 1984, 153; **("Mrs. Sinatra"/"Mr. Gardner")** Evans tapes;

("Friends noticed") int. Gloria Cahn Franks; **("Frank didn't"/"He'd done")** Evans tapes—the "worst" track was the song "Castle Rock," Friedwald, 76, and see **Look,** Dec. 11, 1956; **("the worst thing")** Friedwald, 76.

300–301 **Career decline: (excellent work/not reflected)** Granata, 74–, O'Brien, 265; **(MCA took space)** Kelley, 176; **(Ava loathed)** Evans tapes, John Daniell, **Ava Gardner,** New York: St. Martin's, 1982, 21–, Flamini, 239–; **(railed at press) LAT,** June 1, 2, 1951, Evans tapes; **("This is a private"/Mexico incident) WP,** Aug. 6, 1951, **Look,** May 28, 1957; **(L.A. incident)** ibid., **LAHE,** Nov. 7, 1979.

301–302 **"Most of my troubles": American Weekly,** Jul. 20, 27, 1952. Sinatra disowned the article years later, claiming it was a fabrication. According to the columnist Earl Wilson, however, the truth was that Sinatra had a professional writer prepare the material for him—and approved it before publication. The writer he used was Irving Fine, Jack Benny's former press agent. Sinatra, **Legend,** 104, Wilson, **Sinatra,** 83–; **("be ready in case")** Shaw, **Sinatra,** 159–; **(Paramount)** Wilson, **Sinatra,** 99–; **(Paree)** ibid., 101; **("Sinatra had had")** Carpozi, 136– (Boyar, with his wife, Jane, went on to become a biographer of Sammy Davis Jr.); **("couldn't give away")** Granata, 72; **("one of the meanest") Look,** Jun. 11, 1957; **("Fuck him")** Granata, 76.

302–303 **"He hit some":** Kelley, 180–. It was probably this bitter experience in 1952, combined with the memory of the lukewarm reception some had given him five years earlier—on Sinatra Day 1947—that resolved Sinatra to make no more appearances in Hoboken. He would slip into town in the mid-1960s to show his daughter Tina key landmarks, but made no further public appearance until 1984. **New Jersey Monthly,** Feb. 1982, Freedland, 141, Sinatra with Coplon, 109, **Jersey Journal,** Jul. 27, 1984; **("looked like death") Woman's Home Companion,** May 1956, Taylor, 142—which places the conversation on 48th Street, and Wilson, **Sinatra,** 82; **("A pigeon") Hollywood Citizen-News,** Feb. 24, 1970; **(some second-rate) New Choices,** Dec. 1993/Jan. 1994; **(fan clubs disbanding)** Kelley, 176; **(female admirers) Photoplay,** Nov. 1951.

303–304 **Marriage troubles late 1952: ("Today is our seventh")** unid. Thelma McGill article, c. June 1952, MHL; **(Grimes)** Cannon, 100–; **("Anything could get")** Gardner, 162–; **("cute little**

gestures") Wilson, **Sinatra,** 104; **(ring)** undated Florabel Muir article, **Photoplay,** MHL, Flamini, 128; **("I hate")** Evans tapes.

304 **Farrow affair?:** Mia Farrow, **What Falls Away,** New York: Bantam: 1998, 24–, 87, Higham, **Ava,** 126. In her 1997 memoir, citing her mother, the actress Maureen O'Sullivan, Mia Farrow referred to the affair as fact. The allegation appears to contradict a report in one Gardner biography that she disliked John Farrow. There is no reference to the affair in Gardner's own posthumous memoir. Mia Farrow's dating of the affair as 1953 appears to be in error—**Ride Vaquero!** was filmed in 1952.

304–305 **Palm Springs fracas: (incident)** Kelley, 181–, citing interviews by Michael Thornton, Gardner, 171–, Lana Turner, 165–; **("sick rumors")** ibid., Morella and Epstein, 161, Higham, **Ava,** 128, Jane Ellen Wayne, **Lana: The Life & Loves of Lana Turner,** New York: St. Martin's Press, 1995, 95, Sciacca, **Sinatra,** 152–, int. Tita Cahn; **(FBI report)** "Summary Memo on Frank Sinatra," Mar. 1, 1955, FBI LA 100-41413.

306–307 **not credible:** Gardner claimed in one of her accounts that she climbed a perimeter fence and tried to peep through a window to catch Sinatra and Turner in flagrante. This makes no sense if, as claimed, she had moments earlier spotted Sinatra **outside** the house cruising about in his car. There are also great problems with the chronology. Gardner said she did not think of setting out for Palm Springs until "the hours after midnight." The trip would have taken more than two hours, yet she paints Turner as "looking lovely as ever" and Cole welcoming her and her sister and settling down for a "party," as though that were the normal way to greet unexpected guests in the middle of the night. Turner's version, meanwhile, has Gardner arriving in broad daylight when she and Cole were sitting sunbathing by the pool. A whole day and evening passed, according to Turner, before the dramatic nighttime arrival of the police. In an interview in 2003, Gardner's companion Reenie Jordan said she too was present during this episode—an assertion that adds to the confusion (Gardner's version—Kelley, 181–, citing interviews by Michael Thornton, Gardner, 171–; Turner's version—Turner, 165–); **(went to Van Heusen's)** Shaw, **Sinatra,** 165; **("in the bathroom")** Wilson, **Sinatra,** 103; **(changed phone)** Shaw, **Sinatra,** 165; **("close to a breakdown")** Wayne, **Ava,** 160–, Wilson, **Sinatra,** 104; **("You know")** Rose, 177, int. Milt Ebbins; **("Sinatra is**

frightening") Lee Israel, **Kilgallen,** New York: Dell, 1979, 214; **(FS asked/"he loves her"/Frascati's/rally)** Wilson, **Sinatra,** 104–, Shaw, **Sinatra,** 165; **(visit family)** Cannon, 101; **(no work/taxes)** LAT, Sep. 20, 1951, **LAHE,** Jan. 16, 1962, ints. Bob Neal, Peter Levinson; **("no money")** Evans tapes; **(airfare)** Flamini, 179.

307–309 ***Mogambo*: ("Are you married?")** (London) **Daily Telegraph,** Feb. 18, 2002; **(biggest safari)** Don Meredith, "The Last of the Great White Hunters," salon.com, Mar. 19, 1998; Higham, **Ava,** 129–, Flamini, 181; **(Africa fascinated)** ibid.; **(raged) Los Angeles Herald & Express,** Oct. 15, 1953, Flamini, 182; **(bottle)** James Spada, **Grace,** London: Sidgwick and Jackson, 1987, 126–; **(Ava/Kelly eventually)** Robert Lacey, **Grace,** New York: Putnam, 1994, 68; **("Ava is such")** Kelley, 190; **("treated him")** int. Eva Monley; **(killed time)** Dwiggins, 112; **("the figure")** Frank, 77.

309–310 **FS desire for *Eternity* role: (agents trying)** According to Sinatra, the idea that he could play Maggio came from him, after reading the novel. Not so, according to former William Morris agent Martin Jurow. Jurow recalled that he knew **Eternity** director Fred Zinnemann was looking for a suitable Maggio, thought Sinatra looked right for the role when he came to him for help, and put his name forward. Jurow's 2001 account is covered in chapter 17. For Sinatra's version see **Hollywood Citizen-News,** Apr. 16, 1953; for Jurow's account, see Martin Jurow as told to Philip Wuntch, **Martin Jurow Seein' Stars,** Dallas, TX: Southern Methodist University Press, 2001, 24–; **("I knew a hundred")** FS comments, 1987 Italian tour, RAI UNO and see **LAT,** Jun. 20, 1958, **Hollywood Citizen-News,** Apr. 15, 1953; **("I can act") Cosmopolitan,** May 1956; **(see Cohn)** Wilson, **Sinatra,** 109–; **("Who in the fuck?")** James Bacon, **Made in Hollywood,** Chicago: Contemporary Books, 1977, 4; **(cables)** Fred Zinnemann, **A Life in the Movies,** New York: Scribner's, 1992, 124; **(Ava putting in word)** Gardner, 177–, Wilson, **Sinatra,** 110, ints. Nick Sevano, Peggy Maley; **(summoned for test)** Zinnemann, 124, Flamini, 185–.

310 **Ava pregnancy/abortion: (At the time he left)** Wayne, **Ava,** 160, Flamini, 180; **(telling anyone)** unid. article by Arthur Charles, c. 1950–51, unid. article by Marsha Saunders, and undat. **Motion Picture** article by Linda Post, MHL, **Photoplay,**

Jun. 1951; **("At last I know")** undat. **Motion Picture** article by Charles Samuels, MHL; **("a dozen") Woman's Home Companion,** Jun. 1956; **("I couldn't go on")** Evans tapes, Gardner, 184; **("Ava hated Frank")** Higham, **Ava,** 134; **(Ford/traveled)** ibid., int. Spoli Mills, Kelley, 195–, George Carpozi, **Poison Pen,** Fort Lee, NJ: Barricade Books, 1991, 218.

311 **"eating lettuce": Look,** Feb. 10, 1953. Randy Taraborrelli stated in his book on Sinatra that Attwood interviewed Gardner not at the Savoy but at the "abortion clinic"—and that he was party to the "dysentery" deception. The authors have seen no evidence for these assertions (Taraborrelli, 153); **("All of my life")** Higham, **Ava,** 133–.

311–312 **Christmas 1952: (six other actors)** LAT, Jun. 20, 1958; **(rowed)** Higham, **Ava,** 135, M/G int. of Nick Sevano; **(miserable/Christmas)** Meredith, salon.com, Flamini, 187–, Higham, **Ava,** 135, Bobby Lamb int., RTE radio, Sep. 2002; **(mink/ring)** Sinatra, **Legend,** 107, Flamini, 188, Wayne, **Ava,** 166; **(FS promised)** int. Milt Ebbins—but see Jonathan Van Meter, 107–; **(Ava unimpressed)** Wayne, **Ava,** 166, Flamini, 188; **(night memorable/"She was drinking")** int. Eva Monley; **("He and Ava")** int. Lee Harragin.

312–313 **Second pregnancy: ("I got pregnant"/abortion)** Gardner, 186–; The precise date and location of this abortion is unclear. Interviewed for her memoir, Gardner said the second procedure, like the first, was performed at a nursing home in a London suburb. Safari leader Bunny Allen has been reported having mentioned both London and Paris as the location for the abortion. Gardner was reportedly briefly in Paris with Sinatra in early 1953, and, though she placed the second procedure in London, she said he was present. She awoke to see him seated by the bed in tears.

Available information indicates that the first abortion took place in late November 1952, after Gardner's departure for London on the 22nd. (Sinatra had left Africa on the 14th, on his way to the **Eternity** test.)

The second abortion likely occurred after Sinatra left for Boston—his shows there began on January 20, 1953—and probably in early February, when Gardner came free from location work in Africa.

Assuming a first abortion around November 22, medical advice is that the sexual encounter resulting in the second pregnancy could have occurred as soon as early December (abortion in London/FS present—Gardner, 196; Allen on London and Paris—**Bunny Allen: A Gypsy in Africa,** TV documentary, produced by Mark Macauley and Peter Hort for LVP International, London, int. Adrian Blomfield, and see Kelley, 196; Nov. 22/week after Frank left—dating is at Flamini, 187, Dwiggins, 112; Kelley, 196; re Nov. 14–22—Dwiggins, 112, Flamini, 187; FS in Boston—Jan. 20 entry, **Where or When?**; Ava came free—Flamini, 189; medical advice on dating—int. Theresa Swan); **(went on saying) Los Angeles Herald & Express,** Oct. 15, 1953; **("Pregnancy terrified")** Rooney, I.E., 142; **("thought she'd have")** int. Spoli Mills and see int. Mearene Jordan.

314–315 **Bunny Allen affair: (FS worried)** int. Sonny King; **(Gable/Kelly)** Spada, 63–, Flamini, 184, Lacey, 126–, ints. Lee Harragin, Mark Macauley, Evans tapes, Gardner, 103; **("We stuck")** Evans tapes; **(props man)** int. Eva Monley; **(Allen background)** Meredith, salon.com, **LAT,** Mar. 4, 2002, (**London**) **Daily Telegraph,** Feb. 14, 18, 2002, (**London**) **Daily Mail,** Feb. 14, May 2, 2002; **(managed all aspects)** Flamini, 181; Higham, **Ava,** 131; **(rhinos shoved)** ibid., 132, Wayne, **Ava,** 166–; **("the kind of man") LAT,** Mar. 4, 2002, and see Higham, **Ava,** 131; **("a lovely girl")** int. Bunny Allen, **A Gypsy in Africa**; **("She was running")** int. Eva Monley; **("It was common")** int. Lee Harragin.

316 **"Bunny didn't know":** int. Adrian Blomfield, and also int. Mark Macauley. If Ava had sex with another man not long before leaving for Africa—either **Ride, Vaquero!** director John Farrow or the unnamed man who by one report had sex with her on the night of the October furor in Palm Springs—she may even have had doubts as to who fathered the child involved in the first of the pregnancies.

316 ***Eternity*** **decision/filming: (still did not know) Hollywood Citizen-News,** Apr. 16, 1953; **(Adler)** Sciacca, **Sinatra,** 157–.

316–317 **"The test was all right":** int. Daniel Taradash, M/G int. of Daniel Taradash, Zinnemann, 124. Eli Wallach has said he was firmly selected for the part, that it opened up as an opportunity for Sinatra only after Wallach—offered a role in a Tennessee Williams play—begged off. "That paved the way for Sinatra," Sinatra's publicist Lee Solters told the authors. Cohn at first opposed the notion of using Sinatra, according to Ava Gardner's companion Reenie Jordan, saying, "I don't have money to invest in this man. He's a loser" (Wallach's version—Larry King with Peter Occhiogrosso, **Tell Me More,** New York: Putnam, 1990, 147–; other versions—ints. Lee Solters, Mearene Jordan).

317 **"He said, 'Pearl' ":** Levinson, **September,** 111. Sinatra was also quoted as saying he learned he had the part while in London and—another variation—Montreal. Boston seems more likely (re Boston—Jan. entries, **Where or When? LAT,** Jun. 20, 1958; London—**Hollywood Citizen-News;** Montreal—Sinatra, **My Father,** 96); **(FS/Clift)** Patricia Bosworth, **Montgomery Clift,** New York: Harcourt, Brace, Jovanovich, 1978, 224–, 232, Robert LaGuardia, **Monty,** New York: Avon, 1977, 110–; **(put FS to bed)** Sinatra, **My Father,** p. 97–; **("We would get")** Bosworth, 226; **(worrying/called/still talked)** ibid., 224, LaGuardia, 113.

318–320 **Marriage breakdown: (rushed to Europe)** Kelley, 201; **(disastrous tour) Hollywood Citizen-News,** May 8, 16, **LAT,** May 17, 19, 1953, **Giornale di Sicilia,** Jan. 26, 1962, Kelley, 203; **(booed in Naples) LAT,** May 17, 1953; **(Milan/Rome)** Flamini, 193, int. Abbe Lane; **(Scandinavia, etc.)** May-June 1953 entries, **Where or When?; ("I remember exactly")** Gardner, 191; **("more than anything") Los Angeles Herald & Express,** Oct. 15, 1953; **("exhausted") LAT,** Oct. 30, **Hollywood Citizen-News, (LA) Daily News,** Oct. 29, 1953, Shaw, **Sinatra,** 178; **(wrist slashing) Time,** Aug. 29, 1955, **Look,** May 14, 1957, Kelley, 207, Wilson, **Sinatra,** 95; **("thin cuts")** Fisher, **Been There,** 160, Nov. 29, 1953, entry, **Where or When?; (Ava psychiatrist/proof of love)** Kupcinet with Neimark, 214–; **(FS psychiatrist)** int. Hildi Greenson—widow of Dr. Ralph Greenson, Wilson, **Sinatra,** 120; **(118 pounds)** Flamini, 201; **(lose hair) Woman's Home Companion,** Jun. 1956, Higham, **Ava,** 92; **("I was busted")** FS int. by Zion.

Chapter 17: An Assist from the Boys

321–322 **Eternity Oscar: (Critics)** O'Brien, 65–, Frank, 92; **("Now I'm a star")** Taylor, 173; **("Although Mr. S.")** Jacobs and Stadiem, 58; **(Oscar night)** undat. 1954 Hedda Hopper column, MHL, Wilson, **Sinatra,** 117; **("greatest change")** Parsons, 156; **("It's funny") Motion Picture,** Aug. 1955; **("That's it")** int. Hildi Greenson; **(felt secure) Motion Picture,** Aug. 1955.

322 **Improvement on musical front: (Capitol)** Granata, 81; **("Ever see") Billboard,** Nov. 20, 1965, citing **Metronome,** Nov. 1953.

323–324 **FS and Mafia link: (Lanza)** Chappell to White, Nov. 27, 1956, Box 4, File 13, Harry Anslinger Papers, Strait and Robinson, 145–; **(no club appearances) Where or When?,** corr. Ric Ross—not five years as in Kelley, 146; **(Shamrock)** Jan. 28–Feb. 10, 1950, entry, **Where or When?; (Smiley)** int. Luellen Smiley, Peterson, **The Mob,** 387–, LAT, Apr. 28, 1951; **(Miller/godmother) Newsday,** Apr. 17, 1991; **("He was always")** Kelley, 194; **(Moretti/Fischetti at opening)** ibid., 146; **(Chez Paree)** ibid., 157, **Where or When?** and see Taylor, 41, Kupcinet with Neimark, 150–; **(Steel Pier)** Sep. 4, 1950, Aug. 1953, entries, **Where or When?**

324–325 **500 Club/D'Amato: (returned to sing)** Van Meter, 106–re '51 run, multiple entries, **Where or When?; (D'Amato background/Luciano)** Van Meter, 46–, 59–; **(sole owner)** ibid., 179–; **(Reginelli)** Ovid Demaris, **The Boardwalk Jungle,** Toronto: Bantam, 1986, 32–; **(Bruno)** ibid. and Van Meter, 77—but, re name of son, see also Van Meter, 173; **(FS/D'Amato)** ibid., 103–, 200, 278–, 107, 167; **("Sinatra was down") Philadelphia,** Sep. 1983.

325–326 **Mafia provided work: ("Before he made")** Vincent Teresa with Thomas Renner, **Vinnie Teresa's Mafia,** Garden City, NY: Doubleday, 1975, 125; **(Boston work)** Jan. 1953 entries, **Where or When?; (Palladino)** Teresa with Renner, 370, 390, **Boston Globe,** undat. 1943; **(Desert Inn)** Sep. 13, 1951, 1952 entries **Where or When?; ("At the time")** int. Sonny King; **(D'Amato call)** Van Meter, 107; **(Dalitz background)** undat. clip, "The Double Life of Moe Dalitz," **Las Vegas Review-Journal,** Roemer, 141–, Earley, 46; **(Dalitz/Luciano)** Peterson, **The Mob,** 159, 229, 247; **(intelligence report)** Peter Noyes, **Legacy of Doubt,** New York: Pinnacle, 1973, 242.

326–327 **Mafia and FS family divorce: (Cohen/lesser mobster/"go on home")** The Cohen associate arousing Sinatra's jealousy was Johnny Stompanato, the future lover of Lana Turner, who was stabbed to death in 1958 by Turner's teenage daughter. According to one of Ava Gardner's biographers she had dated Stompanato as early as 1948 (Cohen, 84–, Crane with Jahr, 33–, Wayne, **Ava,** 96); **("When Sinatra")** "Summary Memorandum," Sep. 29, 1950, FSFBI.

327 **telegram:** The full signature was "WILLIE MOORE," an anglicization of Moretti and one of several names the gangster used. The first reference to the telegram located by the authors appears in **The Green Felt Jungle,** the groundbreaking 1962 book on Las Vegas by Pulitzer winner Ed Reid. Reid reported that the telegram was on file at the U.S. Bureau of Narcotics, and had been sent "when the singer decided to divorce his wife Nancy." Other writers, including Nicholas Gage, have referred to the telegram in this context. That would date it to 1950. A search in available Bureau of Narcotics files failed to locate this telegram. William Gallinaro, however, a former New York police officer who became an investigator for the Senate Subcommittee on Investigations, told the authors he recalled having been shown the telegram by a law enforcement colleague (Reid and Demaris, 33; Gage, 91); **("The integrity")** Sterling, 72; **("showed a lack")** Katz, 220–, and see Sinatra with Coplon, 74, Nathan Glazer and Daniel Moynihan, **Beyond the Melting Pot,** Cambridge, MA: MIT Press, 1971, 197.

328 **"Luciano was tempted":** The Bureau of Narcotics report in question refers to Luciano having seen Sinatra in April 1953, but he almost certainly saw him in May—when Sinatra performed in Naples (Siragusa to Anslinger, Jan. 5, 1954, LLBN).

328 **Moretti dead/"Because of my dad's":** int. Luellen Smiley. Moretti was murdered in October 1951.

328–330 **Controversy over getting part in *Eternity:* (Fontane)** Mario Puzo, **The Godfather,** London: Pan, 1970, 8–, 41–, 38, 35, 37–; **(Woltz)** ibid., 60, 55, 35–, 68; **(Cohn parentage)** Cohn entry, **International Directory of Films and Filmmakers,** vol. 4, London: St. James Press, 1996; **(nickelodeon)** Bernard Dick, **The Merchant Prince of Poverty Row: Harry Cohn of Columbia Pictures,** Lexington, KY: University Press of Kentucky, 1993, 20–, Bob Thomas, **King Cohn,** Beverly Hills, CA: New Millennium, 2000, 20–; **(despot)** Dick, 13, Zinnemann, 117; **(sex appetite)** Thomas, 61–; **(horse racing/gambler/Omar Kiam)** ibid., 58–, Wilson, **Show Business,** 199; **(opposed casting FS)** LAHE, Mar. 14, 1976; **("What phony stuff!") New York Daily News,** Jan. 24, 1978, and see **TV Guide,** Apr. 16, 1977, and **Hour,** CBS TV, undat. 1985.

330 **Mafia pressure/*Eternity:* ("Hey, I got that part")** Jacobs and Stadiem, 102, int. George Jacobs; **(admitted to Dexter)** int. Brad Dexter.

330–332 **as did Ava:** Gardner was involved not least because, as reported in the previous chapter, she had herself urged Cohn to give Frank the part in **Eternity.** "For God's sake, Harry," she recalled saying, "I'll give you a free picture if you'll just test him" (Gardner, 178–, Dick, 183); **(Jurow)** ints. Erin Jo Jurow, Philip Wuntch, Jurow as told to Wuntch, 24–; **(Wood "connected")** Rose, 91–; **(Wood/Costello/Lansky)** ibid., 92–, 180, 190, Katz, 140; **(Alo power) Miami Herald,** Dec. 20, 1965, Sifakis, 6, "Correlation Summary," Jul. 28, 1965, FBI 92-2815-355; **(Alo knew FS & family)** ints. Carole Russo, Hector Saldana, and see chapter 2, p. 10, and chapter 3, p. 21; **("his closest friend")** int. Kenneth Roberts; **(Giné intimate)** ints. Carole Russo, Kenneth Roberts, Peter Levinson; **(Giné manager)** corr. Ric Ross, **Billboard,** Nov. 20, 1965; **(Alo/William Morris)** Messick, **Show Business,** 185, 234; **(Alo/Wood)** ints. Carole Russo, Erin Jo Jurow, Jurow as told to Wuntch, 29, Rose, 190–; **(Alo/Cohn)** Jurow as told to Wuntch, 30, int. Carole Russo.

332–333 **Joan Cohn acknowledged/"two gentlemen"/horse's head?:** int. Peter Evans. **Eternity** scriptwriter Dan Taradash, however, said he knew nothing of the mob involvement; and that he probably would never have been told. He and Cohn's widow dismissed the "horse's head on the bed" element of the **Godfather** novel as fiction. So did Cohn's former aide Jonie Taps and Abe Lastvogel of the William Morris Agency. Novelist Mario Puzo likely knew from his research that the planting of animal cadavers recurs in histories of the Mafia in Sicily. Delivery of a cadaver signaled that the recipient was under threat, and the gravity of the threat was indicated by the size of the animal delivered. Puzo likely saw the drama of this and made the horse-on-the-bed scene the climax of an episode of which he knew the outline from real-life sources (int. Dan Taradash; Joan Cohn, Lastvogel, Taps denials—int. Peter Evans, Kelley, 194–, **LAHE,** Mar. 14, 1976; planting of cadavers—Henner Hess, **Mafia & Mafiosi,** New York: New York University Press, 1996, 114, Sifakis, 159); **("he was the one who got")** Katz, 250. Costello was in prison, for contempt of the U.S. Senate during the Kefauver Committee hearings, between August 1952 and late October 1953. The mafioso, however, was not cut off from the outside world during that time (Katz, 195, Wolf with DiMona, 241–); **(Luciano authorized)** Charles Rappeleye and Ed Becker, **All American Mafioso,** New York: Doubleday, 1991,

69; **(Rosselli background)** Rappeleye and Becker, 58–, 130; **("was the one")** ibid., 133; **("Give Frank")** Richard Mahoney, **Sons & Brothers,** New York: Arcade, 1999, 63, 388, n 54.

333–334 **FS & Mafia from Nov. 1953: (Shenker/agents)** Kelley, 207; **(Shenker background) Life,** May 29, 1970, **Sacramento Bee,** Mar. 8, 1977, **Las Vegas Sun,** Jun. 17, 1985, **Las Vegas Review-Journal,** Feb. 18, 1989; **("When Frank ate") New York Journal-American,** Feb. 25, 1956; **(FS to be part of Sands)** Sinatra, **My Father,** 109, Pignone, 101, FS testimony, Nevada State Gaming Control Board, Feb. 11, 1981; **(IRS lien) LAT,** Aug. 20, 1953, **Nevada State Journal,** Oct. 31, 1953, **LAHE,** Jan. 16, 1962, Carpozi, **Sinatra,** 148–.

335 **paid only $10,000:** Sinatra's fee for **Eternity** is usually given as $8,000. The authors have accepted the $10,000 figure given by former William Morris agent Martin Jurow, who was involved in the deal (O'Brien, 63, Jurow as told to Wuntch, 30); **("until he has cleared") LAT,** Aug. 20, 1953; **(FS got license) Nevada State Journal,** Feb. 10, 1954; **(paying off debt)** ibid., **(Reno, NV) Evening Gazette,** Aug. 19, 1953, **LAHE,** Jun. 19, 1972.

335 **Costello/Alo/Sands:** Sifakis, 182, Rose, 189, int. Ed Walters. The principal owner of record was Jake Friedman, a Texas gambler, but sources agree that big-name mobsters shared the real ownership with him. (Rose, 189, James Bacon, **Hollywood Is a Four-Letter Town,** New York: Avon, 1976, 185, **LAHE,** Jun. 19, 1972); **(Alo monitoring)** Robert Lacey, **Little Man,** Boston: Little, Brown, 1991, 293–, John Tuohy, "The Sands," Aug. 2001, americanmafia.com; **(Entratter background)** Sifakis, 107, Reid and Demaris, 92, Sinatra, **Legend,** 52, 114, Fisher with Fisher, 30, "Sands Hotel," Jan. 21, 1963, FBI 92-6314-2, 35–.

336 **FS cavorting:** Ovid Demaris, **The Last Mafioso,** New York: Times Books, 1981, 63, 325. The enforcer, a suspected murderer, was Benedicto Macri, who was used by Luciano loyalist Albert Anastasia (Peterson, **The Mob,** 312, Sifakis, 12, Cook, 317–, Max Block with Ron Kenner, **Max the Butcher,** Secaucus, NJ: Lyle Stuart, 1982, 169); **(Oct. at Sands) Where or When?** Sinatra, **Legend,** 113; **(in style)** Wilson, **Sinatra,** 138–; **(Vegas home)** Sinatra, **Legend,** 113; **("King")** Wilson, **Sinatra,** 138.

336–342 **Nature of FS/mob relationship: (Kefauver/Nellis remembered)** ints. Joe Nellis, M/G int. of Joe Nellis; **("I've always felt")** M/G int. of Eddie Jaffe; **("Sinatra is a paradoxi-**

cal") Ezra Goodman, **The Fifty Year Decline and Fall of Hollywood,** New York: MacFadyen, 1962, 240; **("I remember")** Fisher with Fisher, 277–; **(*Brothers Rico*)** Peter Viertel, **Dangerous Friends,** New York: Doubleday, 1992, 135; **(FS told Coppola) Playboy,** Jul. 1975; **(*Godfather III*)** O'Brien, 209; **("The double doors")** Levinson, **September,** 136–; **("If anybody")** Davis, Boyar, and Boyar, 111, int. Tita Cahn, **People,** Jun. 1, 1998; **("Sometimes I wish")** Kelley, 439; **("I could have put")** Wilson, **Sinatra,** 6; **("When he said")** MacLaine, 71; **("I don't think") Las Vegas Review-Journal,** Dec. 9, 1998; **("Sicilians were proud")** Wilson, **Sinatra,** 17; **("Sinatra wanted")** Shaw, **Sinatra,** 289; **("If they remain") Esquire,** Apr. 1966; **("very obviously")** Puzo, **Godfather Papers,** 187; **("These are the guys"/factual background) LAT Calendar,** Jul. 26, 1992; **("The Boys")** int. John Smith; **(reports 1951–54)** "Correlation Summary," Jun. 8, 1964, FSFBI, Siragusa to Anslinger, Jan. 5, 1954, and "Int. of George Evans" by Charles Siragusa, Apr. 12, 1948, LLBN; **("It was a symbiotic")** int. John Smith; **("There's something"/"Sunday nights")** Tosches, 206, 152–; **("Tell the little")** Lewis with Gluck, 156–; **("Jerry got nervous")** Block with Renner, 129; **(Lanza episode)** Chappell to White, Nov. 27, 1956, Box 4, File 13, Harry Anslinger Papers, Strait and Robinson, 145–, 155–, 162–; **(Lucchese/Luciano)** Peterson, **The Mob,** 296, Hendrik De Leeuw, **Underworld Story,** London: Neville & Spearman Ltd., 1955, 50; **(Lucchese and FS)** Gage, **Mafia,** 89, "Frank Sinatra" memo, Feb. 10, 1961, FSFBI, Sinatra testimony, Select Committee on Crime, U.S. House of Representatives, 92nd Cong., 2nd sess., 1973.

342–343 **racetrack:** ibid. The racetrack was the Berkshire Downs, near Springfield, Massachusetts. Sinatra's involvement with the track was investigated by the House Select Committee on Crime in 1972 (**LAT,** Jul. 19, 1972); **(angered mob bosses)** Teresa with Renner, 125; **(spat with Bruno)** int. Jean Bruno; **("I told him")** Hamill, 146; **("He was always") Miami Herald,** Apr. 8, 2001.

Chapter 18: A Triumph of Talent

344–345 **Career recovery: (late in *Eternity* shoot)** Goldmine, May 3, 1991; **(Capitol)** Granata, 82; **(four songs/two not released)** Rednour, 239, 259, Scott Sayers and Ed O'Brien, **Sinatra: The**

Man and His Music, Austin, TX: TSD, 1992, 54, corr. Ric Ross; **(working with Riddle)** ibid., 86; **(chart successes)** Lees, 100, Sayers and O'Brien, 260, 264, Tom Rednour, **Songs by Sinatra,** Beacon, NY: Wordcrafters, 1998, 109; **(poll/music magazines)** Shaw, **Sinatra,** 192, **Billboard,** Nov. 20, 1965, John Howlett, **Frank Sinatra,** New York: Wallaby Books, 1979, 76; **(film offers)** O'Brien, 67; **(hits in eight years)** Sayers and O'Brien, 260; **("well away")** Time, Aug. 29, 1955; **("I was never") Good Housekeeping,** Jul. 1960; **("absolutely right")** LAT, Dec. 12, 1965; **("meek")** Friedwald, 207.

346–347 **Capitol: (Livingston/Dexter)** ibid., 206–, **Goldmine,** May 3, 1991; **(contract) Esquire,** Dec. 1987, **Rolling Stone,** Jan. 24, 1991, Friedwald, 207, Clooney with Barthel, 136; **("There must have been")** Granata, 82, Friedwald, 207.

346–347 **America of the 1950s and FS: ("Eisenhower Siesta")** Manchester, 772, 776; **(Monroe)** Anthony Summers, **Goddess: The Secret Lives of Marilyn Monroe,** New York: Macmillan, 1985, 59; **("sweet survivor"/"In the fifties")** undat. art. by Barbara Grizzuti Harrison, **Los Angeles Tattler; ("had produced") Playboy,** Apr. 1998; **("when a vocalist") M Inc.,** Feb. 1991.

348–352 **Nelson Riddle: ("Maestro")** Jacobs and Stadiem, 124; **(in-house)** Granata, 85; **(teeth)** Levinson, **September,** 64, Friedwald, 212; **(Bob Crosby et al.)** ibid., 213–; **(obscure)** ibid., 29, 208, 216; **("Do yourself a favor"/Stordahl)** ibid., 207–, and see Vern Yocum's taped recollections, supplied to authors by Vernise Yocum Pelzel; **("just conducting")** ibid., 217; **("Jesus Christ!")** Levinson, **September,** 113; **(good deal in common)** ibid., 17, 140, 217, 13, Friedwald, 254–; **(classics)** Hamill, 165, Levinson, **September,** 28, 26; **(Dorsey)** ibid., 46–; **("I watched")** Granata, 96–, **(FS rejected)** Douglas-Home, 34; **("a perfectionist")** Shaw, **Sinatra,** 174, and Vern Yocum's taped recollections; **("He'd have very definite")** Douglas-Home, 34; **(take notes/all night)** Friedwald, 29, 254, Levinson, **September,** 136; **(endless takes)** ibid., **Billboard,** Nov. 20, 1965; **("If I wasn't")** Kelley, 211; **("That gentle")** corr. Charles Higham, Sep. 18, 2003; **("There's no one")** Shaw, **Sinatra,** 173–; **("the greatest")** Douglas-Home, 35; **("the finest")** Levinson, **Trumpet Blues,** 252; **("with the biggest")** Frank Sinatra Jr., **As I Remember It.**

352–355 **FS and 1950s albums: (nine albums)** corr. Tom Rednour. The list of nine albums does not include four compilation albums, two movie soundtrack albums—for **Pal Joey** and **Can-Can**—or the five Riddle albums issued after 1963, when Sinatra was no longer with Capitol. Also not included is **Songs for Young Lovers,** which was a cocktail of orchestrations by Riddle and George Siravo—Riddle conducted (Tom Rednour—for more detail see Rednour, 234–, 249, Friedwald, 205; the Siravo-Riddle combination—Friedwald, 220–); **("First I decide"/"Tommy Dorsey did")** Douglas-Home, 36–; **(knew how to get the best)** Friedwald, 30–; **(Capitol equipment)** Granata, 23; **("lucid")** Hanna, 48; **("The ordinary") Music,** Spring 1955; **("the moment when") Stereo Review,** Nov. 1971; **("I changed record companies")** FS int. on CBS News special; **(hats)** ints. Peggy Connelly, Bob Neal, Zehme, 115–; **("the barometer")** Douglas-Home, 18.

355–358 **baldness:** Baldness ran in the family, and hair loss had been evident in Sinatra since the mid-1940s (int. Frank Monaco, Kahn, 37); **("spray hair")** Jacobs and Stadiem, 56; **(hairpieces)** Goodman, 239, Kelley, 131, **Woman's Home Companion,** Jun. 1956, **Look,** May 14, 1957; **("romantic"/"Even at the age")** Frank Sinatra Jr., **As I Remember It; ("I didn't care")** Levinson, **September,** 118, and see Lees, 100; **("up all night")** Taraborrelli, 175, and see ibid., 160, LaGuardia, 113; **(Frankie)** Frank Sinatra Jr., **As I Remember It; ("man"/"cat")** e.g., "Makin' Whoopee," on **Songs for Swingin' Lovers,** Capitol Records, 1956, rereleased on CD 1998, original "Makin' Whoopee" lyrics, **The Sinatra Songbook,** www.vex.net; **("darling"/"baby")** "Night and Day" on **A Swingin' Affair,** Capitol Records, 1957, rereleased on CD, 1998, "Night and Day," **The Sinatra Songbook; ("I've Got You"/"I've got, got,")** "I've Got You Under My Skin," **The Sinatra Songbook; ("Don't sing")** William McBrien, **Cole Porter,** New York: Random House, 1998, 151, and see George Eells, **The Life That Late He Led,** New York: Putnam's, 1967, 127; **(studied lyrics)** Douglas-Home, 34; **("I've always")** Granata, 98; **("He could practically")** Levinson, **September,** 118; **("Frank's personal")** WP, May 16, 1998; **(ballet/"stage-play")** ed. Mustazza, **Popular Culture,** 194; **("Music to me")** Douglas-Home, 35; **("points everything")** Granata, 11; **("plaintive") Playboy,** Apr. 1998, and see **New Yorker,** May 25, 1998, Charles Taylor, "Songs for Swingin' Lovers," www.salon.com; **("went beyond")** ibid.;

("darkness") Rolling Stone, Jan. 24, 1991; **("He can say")** Dwiggins, 140; **("It was Ava")** Kelley, 209.

Chapter 19: The Lonely Heart

360–365 **FS and Ava Dec. 1953–54: ("will risk")** Mark Twain, **Notebook,** 1906, cited at www.twainquotes.com; **(getting together/"Frank would call")** Gardner, 193; **("It'll be a mess"/Christmas 1953)** Hanna, 44–, Shaw, **Sinatra,** 182, Dwiggins, 114; **(New Year's Eve party)** Hanna, 48; **("was sitting")** Bricktop with Haskins, 269; **("trying to work")** Shaw, **Sinatra,** 182; **("not a chance")** Hanna, 49; **(Dominguín)** Higham, **Ava,** 145, Flamini, 196, and see int. Abbe Lane; **("Tell him")** Flamini, 204; **("very masochistic")** Jacobs and Stadiem, 61–; **(Bacall/cake)** Lauren Bacall, **Lauren Bacall: By Myself,** London: Jonathan Cape, 1979, 215; **("He would call")** int. Mearene Jordan; **(FS invited)** int. George Jacobs, Jacobs and Stadiem, 62–; **(apartment)** ibid., 30; **("There were pictures"/same at Palm Springs)** ibid., 46, 64; **(Styne move)** Taylor, 174; **("I come home"/FS tears/photograph)** Sciacca, **Sinatra,** 170–, **Look,** Jun. 11, 1957, Shaw, **Sinatra,** 186–; **("Frank was hunched")** Lazar with Tapert, 154, 149; **(statue)** Hanna, 44, Shaw, **Sinatra,** 182, Kelley, 527; **("You're the only") Look,** Jun. 11, 1957; **("Dad, all our love")** Sinatra, **Legend,** 114, Davidson, 42–; **(shirts/She hoped)** Sinatra with Coplon, 46, 34; **("Mr. S. was like")** Jacobs and Stadiem, 48–; **(Frank told Jacobs)** ibid., 202; **(told elder daughter)** Sinatra, **Legend,** 94; **(wandered streets) LAT,** May 16, 1998; **("Frank walked")** Kelly, 217.

365 **FS and women 1954–59: ("would keep")** Sinatra with Coplon, 160; **("Sinatra's Law") Look,** May 28, 1957.

365–366 **Jacobs:** No one was better placed than Jacobs to tell of the traffic in and out of Sinatra's bedroom in the 1950s and 1960s. The authors interviewed him before and after he found a publisher for his memoir, and it was clear he held his former employer in great affection. (ints. George Jacobs, 1983, 2001–04); **("the Casanova")** Jacobs and Stadiem, 67–; **("It was nightmare")** Kelley, 215; **("a pretty starlet")** Jacobs and Stadiem, 54–.

366 **FS and Dinah Shore:** Jacobs and Stadiem, 67–. Shore and Sinatra first sang together in 1937 on radio, then, on TV, in the 1950s

and '60s. They also appeared together in the 1970s, but then reportedly had a falling out over Shore's handling of former vice president Spiro Agnew—a Sinatra friend—on her show. They performed together again, however, as late as 1993 (sang in 1937—Dwiggins, 12–, Bruce Cassidy, **Dinah!** New York: Franklin Watts, 1979, 27–; in 1970s—**Where or When?, Hollywood Citizen-News,** Jul. 14, 1970; falling out—int. Jean Bach, Kelley, 438, and see **McCall's,** May 1973; 1993—Ridgway, pt. 2, 284, **Where or When?**).

366 **FS and Grace Kelly: (involved)** Steven Englund, **Grace of Monaco,** New York: Doubleday, 1984, 122; **(lasting friendship)** Evans tapes; **(agreed to see)** Englund, 122; **(FS drunk)** Taraborrelli, 191.

367 **"He held no": GQ,** Nov. 1999. Kelly and Sinatra nevertheless remained good friends after she became Princess Grace of Monaco. Sinatra often visited Monaco and sang at the principality's Red Cross Ball. George Jacobs suspected he and the princess had a sexual adventure during a visit in 1962. Shortly before her death, Kelly and Rainier celebrated their twenty-fifth wedding anniversary with Sinatra at Palm Springs (longtime friends—Lacey, **Grace,** 363, Sinatra, **My Father,** 112; Red Cross Balls—ed. Vare, 158, Bacon, **Four-Letter Town,** 259, Douglas-Home, 49; sexual adventure?—Jacobs and Stadiem, 195; anniversary—**LAT,** Apr. 20, 1981).

367 **Ava and FS 1954: (records)** Flamini, 203; **(cross)** Higham, **Ava,** 144; **(Dominguín)** Gardner, 201–, Higham, **Ava,** 145–, 148; **(divorce)** Higham, **Ava,** 149; Flamini, 212, Shaw, **Sinatra,** 188; **(photo on mirror)** Shaw, **Sinatra,** 189.

367–369 **FS and Gloria Vanderbilt: ("craved class")** Jacobs and Stadiem, 113; **($27 million)** authors' conversion from $4 million figure in Barbara Goldsmith, **Little Gloria, Happy at Last,** London: Macmillan, 1980, 585, and see **NYT,** Feb. 21, Mar. 1, 1945; **(forty-two years her senior)** Carol Matthau, **Among the Porcupines,** New York: Turtle Bay, 1992, 85; **(Van Heflin)** Gloria Vanderbilt, **Black Knight, White Knight,** New York: Fawcett, 1987, 41; **(Hughes)** ibid., 46–; **(De Cicco)** ibid., 124, 197; **(painting, etc.)** ibid., 208, 274–, 179, 227–, 290–; **("Stop!"/years earlier/"It was what")** ibid., 308, 229, 310–; **(stepped out)** (Bridgeport, CT) **Telegram,** Dec. 31, 1954, **Los Angeles Examiner,** Jan. 1, 1955, Shaw, **Sinatra,** 194–, **New York**

Journal-American, Feb. 29, 1956; **(St. Clair Pugh thought)** int. St. Clair Pugh; **(not true)** Matthau, 114; **("Very Good Year" conscious reference)** int. St. Clair Pugh, 7, see O'Brien with Wilson, 136, **Hi Fi/Stereo,** Nov. 1965.

369 **"during which":** Gloria Vanderbilt, **It Seemed Important at the Time,** New York: Simon and Schuster, 2004, 73–; **("I cannot imagine")** Vanderbilt, 312. Gloria Vanderbilt declined the authors' interview request in 2003, explaining that she was completing a further memoir. According to Sinatra's valet George Jacobs, Vanderbilt and Sinatra were on friendly terms in the 1960s (Jacobs and Stadiem, 221); **(star in a movie?) Los Angeles Examiner,** Oct. 27, 1955, O'Brien, 91, Howlett, 94, Dwiggins, 117, **Woman's Home Companion,** Jun. 1956.

370 **Ekberg: New York Journal-American,** Feb. 29, 1956, O'Brien, 153–, **People,** Dec. 7, 1987, and see int. Ekberg, **(London) Daily Mail,** Dec. 27, 1999.

370 **FS and Jill Corey: (FS at Copacabana) Washington Post & Times-Herald,** Jan. 12, 1955; **("I noticed")** int. Jill Corey; **(Corey background) Life,** Nov. 9, 1953, liner notes, **Sometimes I'm Happy, Sometimes I'm Blue,** CD, Collectables Records, 2003.

371 **FS took pains:** Jacobs and Stadiem, 50; **(discovery)** Sinatra, **My Father,** 107, Sinatra, **Legend,** 120, and Sinatra with Coplon, 58, FS introduction of colleagues, Melbourne concert, Jan. 1955, audiotape in collection of Alf Batchelder, Batchelder monograph.

372 **Ava 1954–55: ("Sinatra"/"my old man"/"greatest")** Hanna, 132; **(affair cooled)** Higham, **Ava,** 155, Hanna, 109; **("They'd be fighting")** M/G int. of George Jacobs, and see Gardner, 193; **(talking of moving)** Viertel, 233.

372 **FS sex/women: (women to "do")** Jacobs and Stadiem, 110; **(Van Heusen)** ibid., 110, 59–; **("Get me a goddamn")** ibid., 68; **(Renay background)** Ed Reid, **Mickey Cohen, Mobster,** New York: Pinnacle, 1973, refs.; **(Renay and FS)** int. Liz Renay and see Liz Renay, **My Face for the World to See,** New York: Lyle Stuart, 1971, 162, Liz Renay, **My First 2,000 Men,** Fort Lee, NJ: Barricade, 1992, 192–, and Dwiggins, 119.

373 **FS and Dietrich: ("Sinatra was half")** Clooney with Barthel, 247; **("keeping happy")** Riva, 632.

373 **Dietrich diary entries:** ibid., 658–, 680–. In **Blue Angel,** his 1992 book about Dietrich, Donald Spoto cited a diary entry

that—he said—reflected Sinatra's fear that he was "sexually out of practice." Dietrich, Spoto wrote, "soothed his fears." A Dietrich entry for the day in question, as published the same year by Dietrich's daughter, however, does not say quite this. It appears, moreover, to refer not to Sinatra but to Yul Brynner (Spoto, **Blue Angel,** 237, Riva, 686, entry for September 4).

375–376 **behaving callously: ("He showers")** unid. article by Joyce Simmons, MHL; **(Miss Ceylon) LC Information Bulletin,** vol. 55, Oct. 21, 1996; **(abandoned Corey)** Wilson, **Sinatra,** 320; **("Open up!") People,** Dec. 7, 1987, **(London) Daily Mail,** Dec. 27, 1999, and see Dwiggins, 121; **(FS and Zsa Zsa Gabor)** Zsa Zsa Gabor with Wendy Leigh, **One Lifetime Is Not Enough,** New York: Delacorte, 1991, 161–.

376–377 **Sandra Giles: (background)** www.dancersandromancers .com (Giles's Web site), www.glamorgirlsofthesilverscreen.com **Life,** Jun. 16, 1958; **("This is Frank")** int. Sandra Giles.

377–378 **FS and Shirley Van Dyke:** ints. Stan and Bob Levey, **LAT,** May 24, 1957.

379–380 **FS and Eva Bartok/daughter: (main sources)** transcript of 1976 taped interview of Bartok by Peter Evans, courtesy of Mr. Evans, ints. Peter Evans, Deana Sinatra, **(London) Sunday Mirror,** Nov. 7, 14, 1976, **(London) Mail on Sunday,** Aug. 14, **New York Daily News,** Aug. 16, **People,** Sep. 5, 1994, **(London) Daily Mail,** May 10, 1997; **(London charity)** main sources, Dwiggins, 123–, Sinatra, **Legend,** 139.

381–382 **name used/letters 1976 & 1994:** Deana changed her name to Deana Sinatra after Sinatra's death. She had previously used either her mother's name, Bartok, or Jurgens—her mother was divorced from the actor Curt Jurgens about a year before Deana's birth. That both the 1976 and 1994 letters to Sinatra existed is confirmed by Peter Evans, the writer Bartok first told about her child's alleged paternity. Evans supplied the authors with copies of the drafts of both letters, which he helped Eva Bartok and her daughter compose. He also supplied a delivery confirmation slip, dated July 5, 1976, showing that the 1976 letter was received by Sinatra's attorney Milton Rudin. Another Sinatra attorney, Harvey Silbert, confirmed that his client had received the 1994 letter and had discussed it (name change—Deana Sinatra letter to authors, Jan. 7, 2004; Bartok letter to FS—carbon copy of original, Jul. 5, 1976, with Red Arrow courier delivery slip 298437, courtesy of Peter Evans; Deana letter to FS is a draft, May 11, 1994, faxed to Peter Evans, and see **(London) Mail on Sunday,** Aug. 14, 1994; Silbert's comments—**People,** Sep. 5, 1994).

382 **FS and Jeanne Carmen: ("Nobody loved Frank")** ints. Jeanne Carmen, 1983, 2001.

382 **affair intermittently/"on-off"/"a stand-by":** George Jacobs and Brad Dexter remembered Carmen as having been a Sinatra girlfriend over a long period. The relationship is also documented to some extent. Ints. George Jacobs, Brad Dexter, Jacobs and Stadiem, 76–, 155; Twentieth Century-Fox release, 1959, Harrison Carroll column, May 22, 1961, undat. Carroll column, undat. Gene Carter column, circa 1963, MHL.

383–384 **Carmen background: (London) Sunday Mirror** magazine, Jun. 8, 1952, unid. article, circa 1952, "She Sells Shares . . . ," MHL, **Los Angeles Mirror-News,** Aug. 1, 1957, **TV Guide,** Jan. 11, 1958, brochure for "The Greatest Golf Show." Jack Redmond Enterprises—covers of magazines such as **Carnival, Gala, Dare, She,** etc. Anthony Summers's research for his book **Goddess** indicated that Carmen also became a friend of Marilyn Monroe, and that they occupied neighboring apartments at 882 Doheny Drive in West Hollywood. An old telegram sent to Carmen at that address confirms that she lived there (Summers's research—Summers, **Goddess,** 306, 394, 591, ints. Jeanne Carmen, 1983, 2001; telegram—Western Union message dated Jul. 31, 1961, in collection of Jeanne Carmen); **("We saw each other")** int. Jeanne Carmen. **("There was a 'Frank woman' ")** int. Brad Dexter.

Chapter 20: Peggy

385–387 **Peggy Connelly: (background and all quotes on FS relationship)** ints. and corr. Peggy Connelly, 2002, 2003, 2004; **(Club for Girls)** Peter Brown, **Kim Novak, Reluctant Goddess,** New York: St. Martin's, 1986, 49; **("There's a Flaw" background) NYT,** Oct. 7, 1990, Granata, 126.

387–388 ***Guys and Dolls:*** **("half destroyed"/Brando preferred over FS)** Jacobs and Stadiem, 51–, **New Choices,** Dec. '93/Jan. '94, **New Jersey Monthly,** Feb. 1982; **(refused "Good morning")** Sidney Skolsky, **Don't Get Me Wrong, I Love Hollywood,** New York:

Putnam, 1975, 41; **("most overrated") Look,** Jun. 11, 1957. In 1986, however, Sinatra acknowledged that Brando was "great . . . a tremendous performer" (FS int. by Zion); **(Method/"when Mumbles"/walked off set)** Bacon, **Four-Letter Town,** 190, Charles Higham, **Brando,** New York: New American Library, 1987, 158–.

388 ***Tender Trap:*** O'Brien, 82–.

388 **"Nembutal"/"Dexedrine":** ibid., 94.

388 **"I have to *go*": New Yorker,** Jun. 1, 1998.

391–395 **FS physical characteristics/clothing: (others on makeup)** e.g., Jacobs and Stadiem, 56; **(new home)** int. Peggy Connelly, Sinatra, **My Father,** 108–, Sinatra, **Legend,** 322; **(lawn furniture)** unid. article by Eleanor Harris, c. 1945, MHL; **(shirts)** Batchelder monograph; **(sweaters/blazers)** Jacobs and Stadiem, 46, 185; **(handkerchiefs) Philadelphia Daily News,** May 18, 1998, **Vanity Fair,** Dec. 1993; **(not ties) Paris Match,** May 28, 1998; **(apartment) LAHE,** Jan. 28, 1988; **(plane)** ints. pilot Johnny Spotts, Bob Neal, Farrow, 81; **(phone)** int. Bob Neal; **("He hated")** Jacobs and Stadiem, 186.

395 **"Take the hand off": Look,** May 14, 1957, Shaw, **Sinatra,** 229–, Gehman, 21, **Human Events,** May 4, 1963. The **Look** story had it that the politician in question was Speaker of the House Sam Rayburn, an allegation Sinatra was able to refute by citing a supportive telegram from Rayburn himself. A later report, however, suggests the encounter did indeed occur but involved not Rayburn but U.S. Senator Theodore F. Green (Green—**Chicago Tribune,** Jan. 7, 1961).

396 **"We'd been out":** int. Peggy Connelly. Nancy Sinatra, citing her father and pianist Joe Bushkin, wrote of an incident at Palm Springs in which—having arrived drunk—a woman "fell" through a window. Bushkin told the authors she "put her hand through a glass door" when thrown out by Sinatra. Peter Lawford was reported as saying he was present when Sinatra "got so mad . . . that he slammed her through a plate glass window. . . . Frank paid her off." Sammy Cahn's widow, Tita, said she understood Sinatra "got into a beef with the girl, threw her across the room, and she fell into plate glass" (Sinatra, **Legend,** 302–; int. Joe Bushkin; Lawford comments in Kelley, 256; int. Tita Cahn).

397–398 ***The Man with the Golden Arm:*** **(FS enthused)** FS comments, 1987 Italian tour, RAI UNO, Hamill, 29; **(lobbied)** Shaw, **Sinatra,** 207, O'Brien, 85; **(medical specialists)** FS comments, 1987 Italian tour, RAI UNO; **(peephole)** Bill Boggs int.; **(FS earned)** O'Brien, 89, and see FS at **New York Daily News,** Jan. 24, 1978, Bill Boggs int., FS int. by Arlene Francis, Oct. 1, 1977, WOR (NY); **(Connelly on awards)** Shaw, **Sinatra,** 213; **("manic-depressive") Playboy,** Feb. 1962.

398 ***caïd:*** In north Africa, the word **caïd** described a headman or leader, a man who kept order and dispensed justice (ed. Paul Vogé, **Larousse Universel,** Paris: Librairie Larousse, 1948, 267).

401–402 **Spain episode: (Ava left U.S.)** Gardner, 219; **(FS during *Pride & Passion*)** O'Brien, 95–, **Look,** May 14, 1957, Shaw, **Sinatra,** 217–, **NYT Magazine,** Feb. 10, 1957, Hanna, 180–, Nancy Nelson, **Evenings with Cary Grant,** New York: Wm. Morrow, 1991, 192–; **(Ava looked forward/viewing)** Shaw, **Sinatra,** 212–; **(car/records)** ibid., 213, 219, Flamini, 228, and int. Peggy Connelly.

404 **FS flew back:** Shaw, **Sinatra,** 218. Remaining scenes involving Sinatra would be filmed later, on a Hollywood soundstage. They looked phony compared to the authentic Spanish footage, and the movie suffered accordingly (O'Brien, 96).

404 **FS/Ava divorce: (Ava announced)** Shaw, **Sinatra,** 219; **(hinted Chiari)** Flamini, 229, and see Shaw, **Sinatra,** 176–, Carpozi; **("like a wild man") Look,** Jun. 11, 1957; **("like a whipped dog")** Shaw, **Sinatra,** 224; **("Mr. Sinada")** ibid., 212.

404 **Ellie Graham:** Sinatra began an affair with Ellie Graham Goldfarb, a fashion model, when she came to Las Vegas in late 1955 to establish the necessary residency to obtain a Nevada divorce. According to Graham in her 1994 book, Sinatra greeted her at the Sands—even before being introduced—by kissing her fingertips and saying, "I love you." After what she described as an "amiable" affair, of which neither of them expected much, she found herself pregnant and had an abortion. She continued to see Sinatra from time to time, but eventually met and married the actor David Janssen (Ellie Janssen, **David Janssen, My Fugitive,** Hollywood, FL: Lifetime, 1994, 1–, **Star,** undat. article, 1994).

404–405 **end of Connelly affair:** Sinatra did not readily accept the fact that Peggy Connelly had ended the affair. He came knocking at her door several times and later, when her marriage to Dick Martin broke up, telephoned repeatedly. Later still, just before Sinatra's marriage to Mia Farrow in 1966, they had dinner in New York. They last saw each other in about 1971 in Palm

Springs (int. Peggy Connelly); **("I'm a Fool")** Sayers and O'Brien, 47, Rednour, 47; **(Ava in Mexico)** Higham, **Ava**, 179–, Flamini, 229–; **("almost panicky")** Viertel, 318; **(Ava sued) Hollywood Citizen-News,** Jun. 15, 1957, Shaw, **Sinatra,** 231; **(decree issued) Newsweek,** Jul. 15, 1957, Flamini, 231–.

406 **FS 42/PR people:** Sinatra was born on December 12, 1915. A 1942 press release from George Evans stated that Frank had been born on that day in 1917. In 1947, in the wake of the Lee Mortimer episode, Frank gave his age as twenty-nine—when in reality he was thirty-one. His first **Who's Who** entry, in 1948, gave the incorrect 1917 birthdate. Entries are normally compiled on the basis of information supplied by the person listed (1942 press release in MHL, and see **Metronome,** May 1943, Dwiggins, 92).

406 **"My father":** Sinatra with Coplon, 160.

406–407 ***Tone Poems*:** Sickel had done rewrite work on the scripts for Sinatra's 1953–54 radio series, **Rocky Fortune.** They apparently got on well, for in 1956 Sinatra reportedly asked Sickel if he had an idea for a "different" sort of album. **Tone Poems of Color** was recorded on February 22 and 28 and March 7 and 15, 1956 (Sickel background and rewrite work—Dwiggins, 138, liner notes, **Tone Poems of Color,** CD, Capitol Records reissued, 1999; recording dates—Sayers and O'Brien, 238–, but see Sinatra, **Legend,** 126); **(Gigliotti)** Gilbert Gigliotti, **A Storied Singer: Frank Sinatra As Literary Conceit,** Westport, CT: Greenwood Press, 2002, 22–; **(orange "happiest") Paris Match,** May 28, 1998.

407–410 **FS emotional void: (dump)** e.g., the Lauren Bacall affair covered in chapter 21; **("lost a great")** FS int. by Zion; **("a lot of")** FS int. on **Suzy Visits; ("like my shadow") Newsday,** Jul. 24, 2002, draft article; **(refuge) LAT,** Jul. 26, 1992, Jacobs and Stadiem, 50, **Ladies' Home Journal,** Dec. 1993; **(fast asleep)** ibid., Sep. 1966; **(allowed in Nancy's bed?)** Sinatra with Coplon, 108; **(Chevrolet) Woman's Home Companion,** May 1956; **("One night")** Kelley, 260; **("no sleep")** Sinatra, **My Father,** 112–; **(FS downed) Look,** May 14, 1957; **(Kilgallen gushing)** Kahn, 105, Shaw, **Sinatra,** 73; **(series) New York Journal-American,** Feb. 25, 26, 27, 28, 29, Mar. 1, 2, 1956; **("ghastly likenesses")** int. Armand Deutsch, Deutsch, 115; **(abusing in public) Look,** May 14, 1957, ints. Sonny King, Tony Montana, M/G int. of Jay Bernstein, Israel, 275; **(long after dead)** Sinatra monologue, Caesars Palace, May 5, 1978, videotape in authors' collection; **(Sunset Strip incident) Look,** May 14, 1957, Davidson, 22–, Dwiggins, 117, int. Bob Neal, Shaw, **Sinatra,** 193—the journalist was Jim Byron, also described as a "publicist"; **(sued publisher)** ibid., 229–.

410–412 **"Bill was sitting":** ints. Maralynne Davidson and see Davidson, 13, Tosches, 313. There were other outbursts of temper and violence. On the set of **Not as a Stranger,** in 1954, when Sinatra threatened to "kick the shit" out of the photographer Billy Woodfield, costars Robert Mitchum and Broderick Crawford riposted by throwing him off a low terrace. In February 1957, when an airline could not provide one sleeping berth more than the two he had reserved, Sinatra canceled an entire tour to Australia. He was later obliged to settle with the tour promoter to the tune of $75,000. The same month, he got in a fight with Rex Harrison at a Hollywood party. Earlier, at a Palm Springs party, he had hit a man—with a bottle, allegedly—during a disagreement over how to mix a cocktail. The victim, businessman Jack Wintermeyer, required hospital treatment for a gashed forehead. (**Stranger** scrap—int. Billy Woodfield, but see Server, 337–; canceled tour—**LAT,** Feb. 5, 12, 1957; Rex Harrison—**LAT,** Feb. 19, 1957, Gehman, 180–; Palm Springs disagreement—**LAT,** Mar. 22, 23, 1949, **Look,** May 14, 1957, Carpozi, **Sinatra,** 99); **("should be available")** Sinatra, **My Father,** 119; **(favorite "Angel Eyes")** corr. Lois Nettleton, 2003; **("Angel" nickname)** int. Reenie Jordan; **(moved into house)** int. Peggy Connelly; **(sign)** Shaw, **Sinatra,** photo section at chap. 28; **(house described/music/telescope) Look,** May 14, 1957; **("I drove here")** Jan. 1, 1956, entry, eds. Graham Payn and Sheridan Morley, **The Noël Coward Diaries,** New York: Da Capo, 1982, 301; **(forlorn)** Bacall, 226.

Chapter 21: Betty

413 **FS and Bogarts: (radio)** Ridgway, pt. 1, 8, 31; **(yacht)** A. M. Sperber and Eric Lax, **Bogart,** New York: Wm. Morrow, 1997, 485; **(boozing)** Jeffrey Meyers, **Bogart: A Life in Hollywood,** Boston: Houghton Mifflin, 1997, 299; **("practically lived") McCall's,** Jul. 1966; **("the one guy")** int. Brad Dexter and see Jacobs and Stadiem, 40.

413 **"in awe":** int. of Bacall by Peter Bogdanovich, in **Süddeutsche Zeitung**, Aug. 16, 2002. The authors have drawn on Lauren Bacall's books **By Myself** (1978) and **Now** (1994), and on her **Süddeutsche Zeitung** interview. The actress declined the authors' repeated requests for an interview.

413–416 **pinnacle:** Though he had previously made many movies, Bogart didn't truly become a star until **High Sierra** and **The Maltese Falcon** in 1941; **(toupees)** Bacall, 152; **(drinkers)** ibid., 149, 152; **(Bogart early life)** Sperber and Lax, 1–; **(avoided fighting/moderated drinking)** Joe Hyams, **Bogart and Bacall: A Love Story**, New York: David McKay, 1975, 172–, 203; **("He just didn't")** **Süddeutsche Zeitung**, Aug. 16, 2002; **(well read/mentor/"I think")** Gehman, 42, 55; **("adult emotionally")** Carpozi, **Sinatra**, 95; **("stay away")** Gehman, 55; **("enjoyed")** Bacall, 218; **("a kind of endless")** Hyams, 170; **("a whirl")** Clooney with Barthel, 219; **("We dropped")** David Niven, **The Moon's a Balloon**, New York: Putnam's, 1971, 328.

416 **"Frankie did sing":** Melvyn Bragg, **Rich: The Life of Richard Burton**, London: Hoddard and Stoughton, 1988, 381. Burton's recollections notwithstanding, Bogart could also on occasion leap to the younger man's defense. "Don't you ever talk about a pal of mine like that again," he snarled when Joan Collins said something uncomplimentary about Sinatra at a party (Sammy Davis Jr., **Hollywood in a Suitcase**, New York: William Morrow, 1980, 15); **("four days")** Niven, 329; **(soon palled)** Bacall, 223.

417 **Holmby Hills Rat Pack: ("an organization with")** Hyams, 204, and see Nathaniel Benchley, **Humphrey Bogart**, Boston: Little, Brown, 1975, refs.; **("The Holmby Hills") New York Herald Tribune**, Dec. 15, 1955; **(pins)** Gerold Frank, **Judy**, New York: Da Capo, 1999, 415.

418–419 **"goddamned rat pack"/white rats:** Niven, 329. There were other versions of how the group got its name. Sammy Davis, who said he was part of the Bogart-era Rat Pack, said: "In those days teenagers hung around in 'rat packs,' and Bogie said we were the rat pack of Beverly Hills." According to the author Gerry Romero, the Bogarts' late-night guests at first referred to themselves as the "Freeloaders," but later changed to Rat Pack. A 1999 television documentary suggested that Hollywood studio bosses—exasperated by the Bogart group's aspirations to artistic freedom—dubbed them "the Rat Pack." The **New York Herald Tribune** list of founding members also included Judy Garland's husband Sid Luft, David Niven, Michael Romanoff, and Jimmy Van Heusen. Others who claimed or were said to be members included Spencer Tracy and Peter Viertel ("In those days"—**Star,** Dec. 15, 1981; "Freeloaders"—Romero, 120; 1999 documentary—**The Rat Pack,** New York, Praeses Productions for A&E, 1999, video in authors' collection; other members—**New York Herald Tribune,** Dec. 15, 1955, Davis, **Hollywood,** 13, Bacall, 222, **Viertel,** 238); **("adults who"/"I see the rat pack")** Joe Hyams, **Bogie,** New York: New American Library, 1966, 122; **(racing cars)** Howard Greenberger, **Bogey's Baby,** New York: St. Martin's, 1976, 122; **("Rats are for") High Times,** Jun. 1978; **("against the PTA") Bogart,** 55; **("that you and your")** Greenberger, 123; **("People have worked")** Kelley, 239; **(Barrymore/Flynn)** Michael Freedland, **Dino: The Dean Martin Story,** London: W. H. Allen, 1984, 91; **(only a joke)** Hyams, **Bogie,** 123; **(friends learned)** Bacall, 229.

419–420 **Bogart illness/death: (FS visited) Bogart,** 283, 288, Hyams, **Bogart and Bacall,** 221; **(phoned)** Bacall, 231, 244, 277; **(telegrams) Look,** May 14, 1957; **("He cheered")** Bacall, 244; **("I've slimmed")** Charles Hamblett, **The Hollywood Cage,** New York: Hart, 1969, 62; **("If Sinatra lost")** Bacon, **Made in Hollywood,** 67; **(watched FS movie)** Bacall, 254—but see **Süddeutsche Zeitung,** Aug. 16, 2002, which suggests the Sinatra movie was **On the Town; (canceled performances)** Davis, Boyar, and Boyar, 362, Sperber and Lax, 517; **(avoiding calls)** Greenberger, 156; **(funeral)** Bacall, 261, 267; **("He *never*")** int. Peggy Connelly.

420 **Verita Thompson:** Thompson's book about the affair is filled with persuasive detail, and Bogart biographers have treated her claim seriously (int. Verita Thompson, Verita Thompson with Donald Shepherd, **Bogie and Me,** New York: St. Martin's Press, 1982, Jeffrey Meyers, **Bogart: A Life in Hollywood,** Boston: Houghton Mifflin, 1997, refs., A. M. Sperber and Eric Lax, **Bogart,** New York: William Morrow, 1997, refs.).

420–421 **FS relationship with Bacall: (Ray)** Nicholas Ray, **I Was Interrupted,** Berkeley, CA: University of California Press, 1993, 159 and refs.; **("infatuation"/"His flirtatiousness")** Bacall, 204, 209; **("very attracted")** ibid., 217; **("If Lenny and I")** Lauren Bacall, **Now,** New York: Alfred A. Knopf, 1994, 168; **("I never**

dared") Bacall, **By Myself,** 217; **("Frank loved Bogart")** int. Peggy Connelly; **("It was no secret")** Kelley, 240; **(Bogart did not know)** int. Verita Thompson; **("That's the way")** Sperber and Lax, 462.

421–423 **birthday in Vegas:** According to Bacall in her 1978 memoir, Kim Novak was Sinatra's "date" during the birthday celebration at the Sands. There were rumors, never substantiated, that he and Novak had an affair. They had worked together on **The Man with the Golden Arm** the previous year and would work together again in 1957, on **Pal Joey.** Novak dismissed the gossip about her and Sinatra at the time as "nonsense." According to Tina Sinatra, she was one of her father's "flames." As late as 2004, however, on **Larry King Live,** Novak was saying nothing to support the notion that they were lovers ("date"/birthday—Bacall, **By Myself,** 241; rumors/"nonsense"—Brown, 52, 56, 120, **Los Angeles Examiner,** Oct. 6, 1957, and see O'Brien, 86; "flames"—Sinatra with Coplon, 114, and see Jacobs and Stadiem, 68; 2004—Novak int. on **Larry King Live,** CNN, Jan. 5, 2004); **("edgy"/"He was somewhat")** Bacall, **By Myself,** 240–; **("represented physical"/"wildly attractive"/"There must have always")** Bacall, **By Myself,** 277; **(going out)** ibid., 275; **(yacht/"After that"/"remote")** ibid., 280, **Süddeutsche Zeitung,** Aug. 16, 2002; **("Frank would feel"/rented house)** Bogart, 77–; **(clivia)** Bacall, **By Myself,** 281.

423 **marriage proposals/breakup: (Christmas) Süddeutsche Zeitung,** Aug. 16, 2002, referring to Fontainebleau appearance, which was December; **("like a maniac"/"he's really acting")** ibid.

423–425 **no contact: Süddeutsche Zeitung,** Aug. 16, 2002. Bacall heard nothing from Sinatra until the second week of February 1958, when he was on the East Coast for the funeral of Manie Sacks, his old mentor at Columbia (Sacks's death—**Gettysburg Times,** Feb. 10, 1958—the death is misdated in Sinatra, **Legend,** 136); **(proposed again & sequel)** ibid., and Bacall, **By Myself,** 283–; **(newspapers trumpeted) Los Angeles Examiner,** (LA) **Mirror, Hollywood Citizen-News,** Mar. 12, 1958; **(story leaked)** Bacall, **By Myself,** 284–, Lazar with Tapert, 156–, **Los Angeles Examiner,** Mar. 12, 1958; **("I don't know") Hollywood Citizen-News,** Mar. 12, 1958; **("Sinatra Won't Say") LAT,** Mar. 13, 1958; **("What for?") Chicago Sun-Times,** Mar. 19, 1958;

("My humiliation"/"like a complete shit"/not speak) Bacall, **By Myself,** 285–; **("because that's")** "Sinatra's Song," by John Lahr, Sinatra Music Society, 2000; **("married to a grown-up") Bogart,** 77–; **("incredibly juvenile")** ibid.

425 **"couldn't have lived": Süddeutsche Zeitung,** Aug. 16, 2002. According to Bacall's 1978 memoir, she and Sinatra eventually got back on to "some sort of friendly basis." Three years later, however, she told Barbara Walters that she did not see her former lover. "One of us is bound to leave, and it would probably be him. He has about as much humor as this floor. . . . No humor . . . I wish he'd just shut up and sing" (**The Barbara Walters Specials,** Jun. 2, 1981, ABC News, Liz Smith column, **New York Daily News,** May 1, 1981); **("a cross between")** Lazar with Tapert, 158.

Chapter 22: Leader of the Pack

426 **Rock 'n' roll/Presley: ("An electric guitar") Time,** Jun. 18, 1956; **(half the records)** Manchester, 724.

426 **"Sh-Boom"/Haley:** Evanier, 90. The Crew Cuts were a white group. A black group, the Chords, had been first out with "Sh-Boom" in April 1954. The Chords' version went to number five (Evanier, 90); **(not below waist)** Manchester, 759.

427 **Dorsey introduced:** Levinson, 124, Rose, 204. A better-known early television appearance by Presley was on Ed Sullivan's **Toast of the Town** show. His appearance on the Dorsey Brothers' **Stage Show** on January 28, 1956, however, preceded the **Toast of the Town** show by more than six months (Sullivan—Halberstam, 478–).

427 **Dorsey death:** Simon, 176, Shaw, **Sinatra,** 34. Frank, for his part, appeared again with Dorsey in August that year, at the Paramount in New York. He had not forgotten the rancorous parting with the bandleader in 1942, and declined to take part in a television tribute when the bandleader died three months later. In 1958, though, he devoted one of his own CBS shows to Dorsey. Then, at a concert as late as 1979, he railed against the way Dorsey had resisted his departure from the band back in the 1940s (declined/devoted—Friedwald, 113; railed—Kelley, 64); **($75,000)** David Halberstam, **The Fifties,** New York: Villard Books, 1993, 478.

427–428 **FS and rock 'n' roll: (FS letter)** Simon, vii; **("hated")** Jacobs and Stadiem, 124–; **("the most brutal")** AP, Oct. 29, 1957, Kelley, 254—, the magazine was **Western World; (FS worried)** FS interview, **Suzy Visits.**

428 **songs that rocked:** In 1955 Sinatra recorded two "doo-wop" singles, "Two Hearts, Two Kisses" and "From the Bottom to the Top." "Can I Steal a Little Love," an uncomfortable offering, got to No. 20 on **Billboard**'s singles chart for 1957 ("doo-wop"—Friedwald, 230; "Can I Steal?"—Rednour, 20, Frank Sinatra Jr. commentary, **As I Remember It**).

428–430 **FS work in 1957–59: (songs released 1957–59)** Rednour, refs., O'Brien and Sayers, refs.; **("Only the Lonely")** Rockwell, 132; **(best-selling albums)** ibid.; **(124 songs)** O'Brien and Sayers, 71–; **(TV/performances)** entries for 1957–59, **Where or When?; (movies)** O'Brien, 99–; **Kings Go Forth** was a clear failure, and the box office fate of **Pal Joey** remains unclear; **("the most fantastic"/"the love voice")** Shaw, **Sinatra,** 237, 256; **(Beatty) Hollywood Citizen-News,** (LA) **Mirror-News,** Oct. 21, 27, **LAT,** Oct. 22, 28, Nov. 4, **Los Angeles Examiner,** Oct. 27, **Newsweek,** Nov. 3, 1958, int. Shirley MacLaine, Gehman, 212–, 214, Dwiggins, 122–; **(Prowse)** int. Shirley MacLaine; **(one-night stands/hookers)** e.g., int. Jack Cione, Levy, 201, **Star,** Feb. 17, 1976.

430 **Australia/Ava wanted to see:** Gardner, 240, Higham, **Ava,** 195, Hanna, 254. Gardner was on location in Australia for the movie **On the Beach; ("We wanted to talk")** Gardner, 240; **("Come home"/key)** Evans tapes.

430–431 **"One for My Baby":** Sinatra first recorded an unremarkable version of "One for My Baby" in 1947. It bears no comparison with the virtuoso recording of 1958. The detailed history of the song as performed by Sinatra is in O'Brien with Wilson, 98; **("I've experienced") LAT,** Oct. 31, 1993; **("I wonder")** David Halberstam article, **Playboy,** Apr. 1998; **("Top male Singer") Down Beat,** poll results, Dec. 1956–59, Howlett, 101, Shaw, **Sinatra,** 258.

431 **TV deal:** The TV deal with ABC—for twenty-six half-hour shows plus some hour-long specials—got poor ratings (Shaw, **Entertainer,** 61, Shaw, **Sinatra,** 233); **($7 million/"highest paid") NYT Magazine,** Feb. 10, **Variety,** Nov. 13, 1957, citing NYT—but see **Newsweek,** Oct. 21, 1957, **Los Angeles Exam-**

iner, Nov. 29, 1956, suggesting lower figure; **("the hottest")** ibid., 259; **("the world's greatest") Chicago Sunday Tribune,** May 18, 1958.

432 **Sinatra Rat Pack:** Richard Gehman, author of the 1961 book that remains the most informative source on the subject, identified several others as members of the "Rat Pack Proper": Tony Curtis, who has described himself as a "mainstream player" in the group, Jimmy Van Heusen, Sammy Cahn, Irving Lazar, and the novelist and screenwriter Harry Kurnitz. **Life** reported that Judy Garland was a member, though Gehman did not. "Affiliates," Gehman wrote, were to include Eddie Fisher and Elizabeth Taylor, the comedian Milton Berle, Mike Romanoff of Romanoff's restaurant—and eventually President Kennedy. Orson Welles claimed a "sort of dim, out-of-town membership" (Gehman, 52–, Tony Curtis and Barry Paris, **Tony Curtis,** New York: William Morrow, 1993, 147, **Life,** Dec. 22, 1958, Welles and Bogdanovich, 27).

432–434 **Dean Martin: (Feb. 19 '57 appearances/three more)** 1957 entries, **Where or When?; ("There is something"/"simple") Look,** Dec. 26, 1967; **(background)** ibid., Tosches, refs., **Life,** Dec. 22, 1958, **Esquire,** Jul. 4, 1978; **(Steubenville gambling)** Messick, 192–, Messick with Nellis, 120; **(dabbled in gambling)** Tosches, 21; **("Your son's gonna") Look,** Dec. 26, 1967; **(bootleg whiskey) Esquire,** Jul. 4, 1978, Tosches, 47; **(met boss/record clean)** ibid., 51, 64; **(Martini) NYT,** Dec. 26, 1925; **(Riobamba)** Wilson, **Show Business,** 325–; **(early successes/Lewis)** Tosches, 102, 98, 109–, 120, 125; **("I'm no singer") Esquire,** Jul. 4, 1978; **(not real work) Look,** Dec. 26, 1967; **(FS first met)** int. Mort Viner, Van Meter, 97.

434–435 **Martin knew Fischettis:** The Fischettis' involvement with Martin and Lewis is reported at some length in Nick Tosches's biography of Martin. Columbia producer Morris Stoloff said he "knew that Martin had a set of heavy boys who tried to get him jobs. They came knocking at my door." The Amalgamated Meat Cutters union boss, Max Block, said the mob "made" Martin and that he later remained under mob control. FBI files indicate that Martin and Sinatra—accompanied by Joe Fischetti—visited a top Chicago Mafia boss in 1958. The FBI learned in 1960 that Fischetti was talking of getting Martin to make a record. There were more such references, showing for example that Martin was still playing golf with mobsters as late as 1977 (Fischetti brothers—Tosches; Stoloff—Freedland, 189; mob "made"—Block with Kenner, 129; visited Mafia boss—"Correlation Summary re Francis Albert Sinatra," Jun. 8, 1964, FSFBI; make record?—log of Oct. 20, 1960, Misc. ELSUR Refs., "Frank Sinatra," vol. 1, HSCA Subject Files, JFK Collection, NA.; more references—"Report re Samuel Giancana," Apr. 12, 1961, FBI 92-3171-185, HSCA staff log of FBI surveillance, Sep. 3, 1963, Demaris, 384); **(Moretti wedding) Patterson** (NJ) **Call,** Sep. 22 1947; **(careful not to flaunt)** int. Sonny King, Shawn Levy, **Rat Pack Confidential,** New York: Doubleday, 1998, 131.

435 **Wild oats/Martin self-control/drinking/marriage/golf: Look,** Dec. 26, 1967, Ricci Martin with Christopher Smith, **That's Amore,** New York: Taylor, 2002, 58, 3, int. Jeanne Martin, Rev. Robert Perrella, **They Call Me the Show Biz Priest,** New York: Trident, 1973, 143. Martin did resort to violence, he told Oriana Fallaci in 1967, when confronted with insults about his Italian heritage. He cited two incidents, one of them a notorious fracas in which Sinatra was also involved—to be covered later. He admitted having been a heavy drinker during his years with Lewis, but said that was in the past. Sinatra's valet, George Jacobs, however, has written of Martin having consumed "massive" amounts of alcohol in the late 1950s. Witnesses who knew Martin well said his stage "drunkie" image was just an act. The glass he clutched in his hand onstage was usually apple juice ("massive" drinking—Jacobs and Stadiem, 85; drinking just an act—ints. Jeanne Martin, Mort Viner, Jeanne Carmen, Martin with Smith, 55, MacLaine, 78, Michael Freedland, **Dino,** London: Allen, 1984, 92); **(Bogart's social circle)** int. Jeanne Martin, Tosches, 254; **(FS friend) Look,** Dec. 26, 1967; **("Uncle Dean")** Sinatra with Coplon, 93; **("Theirs was")** int. Jeanne Martin.

435 **"Those who entered":** Wil Haygood, **In Black and White,** New York: Knopf, 2003, 180; The Haygood biography and another by Gary Fishgall were published in 2003. Davis himself wrote or contributed to three autobiographical books, but they are not always reliable. An excellent additional source is a compendium of writing on Davis published in 2001 (Gary Fishgall, **Gonna Do Great Things,** New York: Scribner, 2003, Davis, Boyar, and Boyar, **Yes, I Can,** Davis, **Hollywood in a Suitcase,** Davis, Jane and Burt Boyar,

Why Me? New York: Warner, 1989, ed. Gerald Early, **Sammy Davis Jr. Reader,** New York, Farrar, Straus and Giroux, 2001).

436–437 **Sammy Davis, Jr.: (father fled)** Haygood, 47; **(early life)** ibid., 50—the childhood movie role was **Rufus Jones for President; (first FS meetings) Ebony,** Jul. 1958, **Star,** Dec. 15, 1981, **Down Beat,** Aug. 1998; **(New York theater)** May 1947 entry, **Where or When?** Shaw, **Sinatra,** 118; **("All the great")** Shaw, **Sinatra,** 118; **("Sammy might never")** int. Marilyn Sinatra.

437 **FS visited hospital '54:** Davis, Boyar, and Boyar, **Yes, I Can,** 220–, Davis, Boyar, and Boyar, **Why Me?,** 58. One of Sinatra's girlfriends, Cindy Bitterman, has said he delayed going to see the injured Davis and went only when shamed into doing so—Sinatra loathed hospitals (Haygood, 168, and see re FS/hospitals, Jacobs and Stadiem, 69); **(stay Palm Springs)** Jacobs and Stadiem, 69; **(took to parents)** Haygood, 180.

437 **accommodation:** According to Davis, the new place was a rented home in the Hollywood Hills. Other sources say Sinatra actually bought the house (Davis, Boyar, and Boyar, **Yes, I Can,** 220, 228, Sinatra, **Legend,** 316, **LAT Calendar,** Jul. 26, 1992, Fishgall, 89); **(idolatry)** int. Peggy Connelly.

438 **Davis/FS admiration: (imitated FS)** Haygood, 177, 180–, **Star,** Feb. 17, 1976; **("staggering talents") Ebony,** Jul. 1958; **(clipping/snapping)** Granata, 102.

438 **Davis and women: (promiscuous)** Haygood, 181, Fishgall, 154; **("Frank just beat")** Haygood, 200–. Maxwell House heir Bob Neal, who was close to Sinatra in these years, told the authors the singer "got tough" with prostitutes, as distinct from women of "quality." He recalled an episode in which Frank "hit one [prostitute] with a shoe, hit her with the heel of her shoe because she did something that displeased him." Two Sinatra books refer to a similar incident, but depict a furious Sinatra being hit on the head by the woman, rather than the other way around. A 1959 FBI document refers to an "escapade where a girl was assaulted by Sinatra and slightly injured in some kind of fracas." Recall too the earlier incident in which a woman was injured at Sinatra's Palm Springs house ("get tough"—int. Bob Neal; Sinatra hit woman—Dwiggins, with wrong date, 119–, Taraborrelli, 220–; document re "escapade"—"File Review & Summary Check," Sep. 19, 1960, 17, FBI LA 100-41413; earlier incident—see Chapter 20, p. 217).

438 **Davis and controversy: (embracing Judaism)** ibid., 79–, Haygood, 183–.

438–439 **Davis and Novak:** Haygood, 196–, Brown, 148–. Davis later acknowledged the affair, but Novak denied it—most recently in 2004 (Davis acknowledged—Davis, Boyar, and Boyar, **Yes, I Can,** 434–, **Why Me,** 81–; Novak denied—Brown, 160, Fishgall, 117, int. Kim Novak, **Larry King Live; (Cohn apoplectic)** Sam Kashner and Jennifer MacNair, **The Bad and the Beautiful,** New York: Norton, 2002, 209; **(Rand/hoodlum)** Haygood, 263; **(phony union)** Davis, Boyar, and Boyar, **Yes, I Can,** 460–; **("well-connected friend"/Mafia boss)** Davis, Boyar, and Boyar, **Why Me,** 93–, Rose, 477; **(Woodfield insight)** ints. Billy Woodfield.

439 **Joe Fischetti and Davis:** According to biographer Haygood, Davis had been beholden to the Mafia for some time, and to the Chicago mob in particular. Ever inept at handling his finances, he had borrowed mob money to settle old debts. FBI records reflect continued contact with Fischetti in the 1960s (Davis beholden—Haygood, 217; contact with Fischetti—report re "Joseph John Fischetti," Apr. 25, 1963, FBI 92-3024-60).

440 **Davis and Gardner:** The story about Davis and Ava, run in **Confidential** magazine, was a string of unsubstantiated insinuations built around a photograph of Davis in a Santa suit and beard and Ava in a red dress, an innocuous picture for the Christmas issue of another magazine. The story may have been without foundation, but former Davis aide Arthur Silber Jr. has claimed the pair slept with each other "on a few occasions" (**Confidential,** Mar. 1955, in ed. Early, 246—see also p. 575, Evans tapes, Gardner, 199—and, with an inaccurate timeline, Davis, Boyar, and Boyar, **Why Me,** 211–; Silber "a few"—Fishgall, 87); **(FS fury assuaged)** Jacobs and Stadiem, 68–; **(Bitterman)** Haygood, 28–.

440–441 **"Talent is not":** Dwiggins, 149, **Chicago's American,** Sep. 30, 1966. The offending interview, with celebrity radio host Jack Eigen, took place in the lounge of the Chez Paree in Chicago; **(retribution/apologized)** Shaw, **Sinatra,** 257, O'Brien, 121, James Spada, **Peter Lawford: The Man Who Kept the Secrets,** New York: Bantam, 1991, 210; **("disgusting")** Wilson, **Sinatra,** 140–; **("Charley")** Davis, Boyar, and Boyar, **Yes, I Can,** 111, 221, 229; **(catch-all name)** Gehman, 54, Shaw, **Sinatra: A Biography,** London: W. H. Allen, 1968, 367.

441–442 **Peter Lawford: ("Charley the Seal") Good Housekeeping,** Feb. 1962, Zehme, 38; **(halfway decent)** NYT, Dec. 25, 1984; **(early life)** Lawford with Schwarz, and Spada, **Lawford,** refs.; **("awful accident"/"Coogan")** Spada, **Lawford,** 29, 42; **("well-hewn god")** Twentieth Century-Fox PR profile, undat. 1952, MHL; **(Maxwell) Modern Screen,** Mar. 21, 1947, Lawford with Schwarz, 59; **(Turner)** ibid., 51, 58–; **(Gardner)** Evans tapes, Torme, **Velvet,** 98–; **(met FS) Modern Screen,** Mar. 21, 1947; **(skits)** int. Gloria Cahn Franks, Kelley, 113; **("singular temper") Modern Screen,** Mar. 21, 1947; **(Ava "date")** int. Milt Ebbins, Kelley, 206; **("I was in bed") Star,** Feb. 17, 1976.

443 **met at dinner party:** The dinner party, at the home of Gary Cooper and his wife, has been dated as August 1958, but other information (see below) makes it clear Sinatra and the couple were already close by that date. The dinner most likely occurred in late 1957 or early 1958 (August 1958—Spada, **Lawford,** 203); **(Dinah Shore)** Jan. 26, 1958, entry, **Where or When? (movies with FS) Never So Few,** 1959, **Ocean's 11,** 1960; **(restaurant)** Spada, **Lawford,** 205—the restaurant was Puccini's.

443 **"He looked up": Star,** Feb. 17, 1976, **American Weekly,** Nov. 12, 1961. The Sinatra-Lawford rift evidently occurred in spring 1954, when Ava Gardner returned to Los Angeles after making **The Barefoot Contessa.** Lawford's reference in a later interview to 1951 is in error. References that place the reconciliation in August 1958, or alternatively 1959, are also in error. Whatever the significance of the January 1958 appearance on the Dinah Shore show, they were clearly together as friends by June that year—during the first of two trips to Europe (rift—Kelley, 206, **Star,** Feb. 17, 1976, Lawford with Schwarz, 100–, but see Higham, **Ava,** 148, Carpozi, **Poison Pen,** 228–; reconciliation—Spada, **Lawford,** 483, **Star,** Feb. 17, 1976, but see Dwiggins, 122, Shaw, **Sinatra,** 247, **New York Herald Tribune,** Jun. 19, **New York Post,** Jun. 23, 1958, corr. Ric Ross); **(enthusing/aped)** ints. Peter Dye, George Jacobs, **Cosmopolitan,** Oct. 1961.

443 **"This is such": American Weekly,** Nov. 12, 1961. Peter and Pat Lawford were as subject to Sinatra's bad temper as anyone else. On New Year's Eve 1958, when they delayed a trip to see him in Palm Springs, he tried to set fire to the clothing they had left at his house. When the clothes did not burn easily, he threw them into the pool (Jacobs, 131, Lawford with Schwarz, 103–).

444–446 ***Some Came Running:*** **("typical American town")** High Times, Jun. 1978; **(boorish behavior)** Time, Aug. 25, **New York Daily News,** Sep. 2, 3, 1958, Carpozi, **Sinatra,** 190–, MacLaine, 84; **(ripped phone)** New York **Daily News,** Sep. 3, 1958; **(smashed TV)** Time, Aug. 25, 1958; **("Mr. Sinatra grabbed") New York Daily News,** Sep. 3, 1958; **(MacLaine account)** int. Shirley MacLaine, and MacLaine, 65–, 61, 74, 69, 84, 71, 109.

447–448 **"A *Life* magazine reporter":** Gehman, 50, **Star,** Dec. 15, 1981, and see Shirley MacLaine, **Don't Fall off the Mountain,** London: Bodley Head, 1971, 102. Shirley MacLaine later named the **Life** reporter with whom she and colleagues declined to cooperate as "Dave Zeitlin." **Time-Life** cover story veteran Paul O'Neil, however, wrote the landmark December 1958 "Clan" story; **("Noncomformity") Life,** Dec. 22, 1958, int. Michael O'Neil; **(Davis quoted/source)** Shaw, **Sinatra,** 262; **("He was our leader") Philadelphia Daily News,** May 18, 1998.

448–449 **Rat Pack name and behavior: ("Clan" label disowned)** FS in **Daily Variety,** Aug. 25, 1960, and cited in Tarraborrelli, 211, Lawford in **American Weekly,** Nov. 12, 1961, Davis in ed. Early, 238; **(change to Rat Pack)** Gehman, 36, 52; **("just a group") Pittsburgh Courier,** Mar. 3, 1962; **(FS definitions/"quim")** Gehman, 53–; **("bird")** Zehme, 39, **Philadelphia Daily News,** May 18, 1998; **("charlies")** ibid.; **("Mother")** Gehman, 54; **("I'm not a prude")** int. Keely Smith by Jim Raposa.

449–452 **"Summit at Sands": (Entratter took)** Davis, Boyar, and Boyar, **Why Me,** 107; **Variety,** Aug. 11, 1997; **(spoof telegrams)** Wilson, **Show Business,** 15, Ralph Pearl, **Las Vegas Is My Beat,** Secaucus, NJ: Lyle Stuart, 1973, 65; **(34,000/$100/$3) Playboy,** Jun. 1960, Pearl, 67; **("a wild iconoclasm") Playboy,** Jun. 1960; **("the Mount Rushmore") Vanity Fair,** May 1997; **("Hey, where the hell's"/"Dean, close"/undershorts)** Pearl, 66, **Playboy,** Jun. 1960; **("Here they are")** ibid.; **(ice bucket)** Starr, 57; **("*The Power*") Variety,** Aug. 11, 1997; **("the only cold-sober")** Davis, Boyar, and Boyar, **Yes, I Can,** 496; **("They were all")** corr. Ed Walters, by permission; **("glorification") Miami Herald,** Mar. 29, 1960; **("Drinking a great deal")** Davis, **Suitcase,** 83; **("*You* wanna dance")** Gehman, 73, **Playboy,** Jun. 1960; **("I'll dance wit' ya"/hurtful)** Fishgall, 154; **(mangling lyrics) Playboy,** Jun. 1960.

452–454 **Rat Pack & sex: (Clubhouse) Esquire,** Mar. 1996, corr. Ed Walters, by permission, Davis, Boyar, and Boyar, **Yes, I Can,**

498; **(initials) Las Vegas Review-Journal,** May 16, 1998; **(brown robe)** Sinatra, **My Father,** 134; **("I went")** Douglas, 400; **("I was like eighteen") Rolling Stone,** Jun. 25, 1998; **("The place was crawling")** Starr, 61; **("There were poker")** int. Count Guido Deiro; **("When Dean came")** int. Ed Walters; **("on-the-house")** Jacobs and Stadiem, 143; **("Women were treated")** int. Count Guido Deiro.

454 **Lawfords/FS and JFK: (weekending at Palm Springs) Star,** Feb. 17, 1976, Jacobs and Stadiem, 130; **(planned to seduce?)** ibid., 129; **(Victoria Frances)** Spada, **Lawford,** 204; **("I think we were") Star,** Feb. 17, 1976.

Chapter 23: The Guest from Chicago

455 **JFK image bogus: (chronic illness)** Robert Dallek, **An Unfinished Life,** Boston: Little, Brown, 2003, refs., Joan and Clay Blair Jr., **The Search for JFK,** New York: Berkley, 1976, esp. 635–; **("one of the best-kept") Atlantic Monthly,** Dec. 2002.

456 **celebrity quack:** That Kennedy resorted to treatment by the quack doctor, Max Jacobson, is now accepted as fact. "I don't care if it's horse piss," Kennedy said of the injections Jacobson administered, "it works." As president, he went so drugged to a meeting with Soviet leader Nikita Khrushchev (Jacobson—e.g., refs. in Dallek).

456 **recreational drugs:** The fragments of information now available about Kennedy's alleged drug use include a claim that he used cocaine during a visit to Las Vegas in early 1960, experimented with marijuana and LSD with a lover in the White House, and—with his brother-in-law Peter Lawford—fed amyl nitrate to a woman to see how it affected her sexual experience (drug use in Vegas—corr. Ed Walters, used by permission; drugs in White House—Nina Burleigh, **A Very Private Woman,** New York: Bantam, 1998, 11–, 212, 286, the lover was Mary Meyer; amyl nitrate—Lawford with Schwarz, 137–); **("lines of cocaine")** Jacobs and Stadiem, 140, 347; **JFK and sex: ("like God")** Richard Reeves, **President Kennedy: Profile of Power,** New York: Simon and Schuster, 1993, 291; **("I once asked")** Dallek, 152, and see Priscilla Johnson McMillan, **Marina and Lee,** New York: Harper and Row, 1977, 3.

456 **"Where sex":** Summers, **Goddess,** 240. There is fulsome coverage of Kennedy's sex life in Robert Dallek's study **An Unfinished Life,** in Joan and Clay Blair's **The Search for JFK**—often overlooked but invaluable—in Richard Reeves's **President Kennedy: Profile of Power** (all cited earlier) and in Nigel Hamilton's **Reckless Youth,** New York: Random House, 1992, and Sally Bedell Smith, **Grace and Power: The Private World of the Kennedy White House,** New York: Random House, 2004. It has been suggested that the medication he took for Addison's disease contributed—as it has in other patients—to heightened sexual desire (Blair, 648, Dallek, 213).

456–457 **Joe Kennedy background/bootlegging: ("partners" with Costello)** NYT, Feb. 27, 1973. Costello's remarks, made to the journalist Peter Maas, were reported in the **New York Times** in early 1973. In a book the following year, the mafioso's longtime attorney George Wolf seemed to suggest his client may merely have dropped Joe Kennedy's name mischievously—both to Maas and in an earlier comment to the State Liquor Commission about post-Prohibition activity—when in fact he had been referring to a different Joe Kennedy. Other information, however, indicates Costello was indeed speaking of the future president's father (Wolf comments—Wolf with DiMona, 146–, 202; other information—Katz, 68–, 13, Joseph Bonanno with Sergio Lalli, **A Man of Honor: The Autobiography of Joseph Bonanno,** New York: Simon and Schuster, 1983, 174); **(fell out)** Mahoney, 43; **(Stacher)** Eisenberg, Dan, and Landau, 108–; **(Dalitz)** Mahoney, 39, 383n83; **(Madden)** Graham Nown, **The English Godfather,** London: Ward Lock, 1987, 189, 195; **("I discussed")** Hersh, 50; **(Kohlert/customs report)** Russo, 361, 360.

457–459 **McLaney syndicate background:** In 1973, in testimony to the Senate Subcommittee on Investigations, a witness said McLaney "represents Meyer Lansky"—Luciano's close accomplice. With the go-ahead from Lansky, McLaney later purchased a large share in Havana's mob-controlled Hotel Nacional. A longtime McLaney aide backed up his assertion about Joe Kennedy (Hearings, HSCA, U.S. Government Printing Office, vol. 10, 185, and see Russo, 67–); **("controlled by Luciano")** information supplied to authors by Gus Russo, who interviewed McLaney; **(hijackings)** Eisenberg, Dan, and Landau, 109, Mark

A. Stuart, **Gangster: The Story of Longy Zwillman,** London: Star, 1987, 42, Morgan, 58, Russo, 361—the two bootleggers were Murray Humphreys and Joe Reinfeld, both prominent in the illicit trade; **("rum-running")** Hersh, 138, and see **supra.,** 19–; **(Cassara)** Fox, 315–, Hersh, 52–; **(Kennedy sold to bootleggers)** Richard Whalen, **The Founding Father,** Washington, DC: Regnery, 1993, 380–, Fox, 316, Hersh, 54, Sifakis, 353, Stuart, 40—partners were Moretti associate Longy Zwillman and Joseph Reinfeld; **("vaguely embarrassing")** Whalen, 380; **(Joe not run)** ibid., 137, 345, 358, Ralph G. Martin, **A Hero for Our Time,** New York: Macmillan, 1983, 41–; **("I told him")** ibid., 48; **(winning)** ibid., 22, Dallek, 36; **("Everything Joe"/at unprecedented rate)** Dallek, 130; **("I will work")** ibid., 169—the staffer was Frank Morrissey.

459 **Joe pinned his hopes:** Joe Kennedy had had presidential aspirations for his first-born son Joe Jr., but he had been killed during the war. "If it isn't Joe," Kennedy had said even before that loss, "it will be Jack." Martin, 41.

459 **Kennedys and Bonanno: (1954/1956 visits)** int. Bill Bonanno, Bill Bonanno, **Bound by Honor,** New York: St. Martin's, 1999, 5, 7, 27–. As Bill Bonanno told it in his 1999 book, Joe Kennedy visited Bonanno in late 1955 "looking to drum up support for his son." Scholarly studies of the 1956 campaign, however, indicate that the elder Kennedy was for months actively opposed to his son trying for the vice-presidential slot. It may be that—if authentic—Bonanno's recollection is of an early reconnaissance trip (Dallek, 206–, Parmet, 335–); **(Joe Bonanno background)** Sifakis, 40–, Brashler, 187, Bonanno with Lalli, refs.; **("skill")** ibid., 165–; **(Moretti)** int. Bill Bonanno, Bonanno with Lalli, 56–, 166, 172, 319.

460 **"No Democrat"/"Kennedy told":** Bonanno, 7, 27–. The author Gay Talese, who made Bill the subject of his book on the Mafia, **Honor Thy Father,** told the authors he found him a credible source. We note, however, that **Bound by Honor** and subsequent Bonanno interviews include dramatic, uncorroborated claims about the Mafia's alleged role in President Kennedy's assassination. Notwithstanding those claims, and given what else is now known about Joe Kennedy's crime links, Bonanno Jr.'s statements about the Kennedy visits to his father deserve inclusion here (int. Gay Talese, but see re assassination claims Bonanno,

299–, and Bill Bonanno ints., time.com, May 11, 1999, crime .about.com, Aug. 5, 1999); **(JFK/Battaglia at mass)** Rosen to Boardman, Mar. 4, 1958, Hoover O&C files, vol. 13.

460 **Battaglia Democratic official/Bonanno friend:** (Tucson) **Daily Citizen,** Jan. 22, 1970, Bonanno with Lalli, 307, Bonanno, 8. Though Battaglia's obituary merely identifies him as former vice chairman of the Arizona state Democratic Party, author Richard Mahoney has identified him as having been a Mafia underboss. Joe Bonanno's son Bill, who was once groomed to succeed his father, wrote of the Kennedy contacts in his 1999 memoir **Bound by Honor.** He told the authors that Battaglia was "part of our world" (Mahoney, 39, 383, and—re mob link—see Rosen to Boardman).

460 **Bonanno met JFK:** ibid. The agents' sighting of John F. Kennedy with Battaglia was in February 1958, while Bonanno referred in his memoir to having met the future president "in 1959–1960." It is not clear whether the Mafia boss misremembered the date of the encounter or whether there was more than one meeting.

460 **in touch FS/wedding/one of FS guests:** Bonanno said in a later interview that in the event Sinatra was unable to perform at the 1956 wedding—Tony Bennett performed instead (re-broadcast int.—Joe Bonanno on **60 Minutes,** CBS News, May 19, 2002, int. Bill Bonanno, Bonanno, 42 and photo, and see Bonanno with Lalli, 189–, Gay Talese, **Honor Thy Father,** Greenwich, CT: Fawcett, 1971, 24.

460–462 **Giancana: (background)** Brashler, Giancana, and Renner, and Roemer, refs.; **(sadistic streak)** Brashler, 44; **(at side of Accardo)** ibid., 120; **(power passed)** Roemer, 191; **(family man)** Brashler, 126, Giancana and Renner, 60–, 67–, 99–, 47, int. Antoinette Giancana, **Penthouse,** Mar. 1984; **("like someone")** ibid., 60–; **("a warm, vital")** Fisher with Fisher, 290–.

462 **"He's such great":** Demaris, **Mafioso,** 197. Shimon, who was also an electronics expert, met Giancana in 1961 through the mafioso's henchman Johnny Rosselli, when both men became involved in the CIA/Mafia plots to kill Castro (authors' ints. Joe Shimon, and see "Interim Report," Select Committee to Study Government Operations with Respect to Intelligence Activities, U.S. Govt. Printing Office, 94th Cong., 1st sess., 81); **("scary")** int. Rock Brynner; **("He was as serious")** Michael Corbitt with

Sam Giancana, **Double Deal,** New York: Wm. Morrow, 2003, 60–; **(beat daughter) Penthouse,** Mar. 1984; **(shot TV)** int. Sonny King; **("ruthless")** SAC Chicago to Director, Oct. 31, 1962, FBI 92-3171-917; **(lived by gun)** Brashler, 51–, 66, 151–, 156–, Giancana and Renner 32–, 75–.

463 **FS and Giancana: (FS would insist)** SAC Los Angeles to Director, Oct. 7, 1963, FBI 92-6667-6, Kelley, 394, FS testimony, Nevada State Gaming Commission and State Gaming Control Board, Feb. 11, 19, 1981; **(told FBI)** SAC Los Angeles to Director, Oct. 7, 1963, FBI 92-6667-6; **(after bureau established)** "Title: Samuel M. Giancana," Sep. 12, 1960, FBI 92-3171.

463 **mass of information:** ints. Peggy Connelly, Marilyn Sinatra, Gloria Cahn Franks, **NYT** int. of Antoinette Giancana, Feb. 2, 1984, Giancana and Renner, 101, Jacobs and Stadiem, 100–, Sinatra, **Legend,** 112, and see **LAT Calendar,** Jul. 26, 1992, report, May 5, 1961, FBI 92-636-3; **(De Carlo)** SAC Newark to SAC New York, Aug. 28, 1947, FBI 94–419535. See earlier exposition of the Sinatra/De Carlo connection at chapter 5, p. 47–, **supra.** The FBI document containing the lead refers to De Carlo as "Ray"—his preferred nickname. He was also known as "Gyp"; **("That hoodlum")** Sinatra, **Legend,** 112; **(charity)** Giancana and Renner, 81, 94–, 101, 104; **("very affectionate") NYT,** Feb. 2, 1984; **("My father")** int. Marilyn Sinatra.

464–465 **"special guest"/"thrilled"/"on perfect behavior"/"What he":** Jacobs and Stadiem, 103, 3, 105. Sinatra's lover Peggy Connelly, however, recalled that at one point Sinatra was avoiding Giancana's phone calls. The explanation may lie in the fact that, as she also recalled, the mobster was pestering Sinatra's secretary with unwelcome advances. Sinatra was helping fend him off (ints. Peggy Connelly); **(El Rancho)** "Frank Sinatra," Feb. 10, 1961, FSFBI; **(Giancana & *Some Came Running*) Las Vegas Review-Journal,** Dec. 14, 1995, int. John Smith—the man who cooked was Joe Pignatello; **(MacLaine incident)** int. Shirley MacLaine, MacLaine, **Lucky Stars,** 62–, 69; **("command performance")** "Correlation Summary," Jun. 8, 1964, and "Frank Sinatra," Feb. 10, 1961, FSFBI, "Joseph Fischetti," Sep. 27, 1960, FBI 92-3024-23; **(Armory Lounge)** "Samuel M. Giancana," May 5, 1961, FBI 92-636-3, "Samuel M. Giancana," Apr. 12, 1961, FBI 92-3171-185.

465 **FS at wedding:** Scatterday to Belmont, Mar. 30, 1960, FSFBI, AP, Aug. 31, 1963. An FBI report and a news clipping refer to Sinatra having been a guest at the wedding. Bonnie Giancana's sister Antoinette has said he was invited but did not attend. She cannot be relied on as a source on this, however, since she herself was not present (Giancana and Renner, 194–).

465 **"private party":** SAC Los Angeles to Director, Apr. 24, 1963, FBI 92-6667-1, Evans to Belmont, Apr. 17, 1964, FSFBI, "Samuel M. Giancana," Sep. 12, 1960, FBI 92-3171-72. In a sworn affidavit, Sinatra later denied Giancana had been present. FBI agents did not believe him, to the extent that they considered prosecuting him for fraud (Evans to Belmont, Oct. 9, 1963, FBI 92-6667-7).

465–466 **Giancana and Davis:** Davis, Boyar, and Boyar, **Why Me,** 87, 100; **(Worldwide Actors)** "Title: Samuel M. Giancana," May 5, 1961, FBI 62-636-3; **(distracted)** William Roemer, **Roemer: Man Against the Mob,** New York: Donald Fine, 1989, 189, Roemer, **Accardo,** 189, Brashler, 146–; **("in heat")** Brashler, 147, Giancana and Renner, 246; **(FS/Giancana & women)** "Title: Samuel M. Giancana," May 5, 1961, FBI 92-636-3, Brashler, 148; **(Keely Smith & FS)** int. Keely Smith by Jim Raposa, supplied to authors, Giancana and Renner, 232; **(Smith and Giancana)** Brashler, 149, "Samuel M. Giancana," Jan. 28, 1964, FBI 92-3171-1322, and "Title: Samuel M. Giancana," May 5, 1961, FBI 92-636-3; **(cigar supply)** M/G int. of Nick Sevano; **(ring)** int. and corr. Toni Shimon, "Taped Int. of Joe Shimon," Jul. 26, 1977, Rec. No. 180-10095-10496, HSCA, JFK; **(print of *Eternity*/"skinny little") Penthouse,** Mar. 1984; **("to further his own")** Giancana and Renner, 92; **("They're all rats") Penthouse,** Mar. 1984.

Chapter 24: The Candidate and the Courtesan

467–469 **FS and politics/JFK: (first met/"if it meant")** (LA) **Mirror,** Dec. 1, 1960, Shaw, **Entertainer,** 45. The 1955 dating is by Sinatra's own account, but he and Kennedy may have met even earlier. According to Sinatra's daughter Nancy, they met soon after Kennedy's marriage in late 1953, while Tina Sinatra said they met through Lawford. Taken together, the daughters' statements would date the first encounter as occurring before mid-

1954, when the Sinatra-Lawford friendship was interrupted by the rift between the two men (Sinatra, **My Father,** 132, Sinatra with Coplon, 71); **(registered Democrat)** Tina Sinatra int. for **Larry King Live,** CNN, 1993, int. Larry King, Sinatra, **My Father,** 219; **(campaigned FDR, Truman, Stevenson) Look,** May 14, 1957, **Human Events,** May 4, 1963, Sinatra with Coplon, 71; **(sang 1956)** (NY) **Daily Mirror,** Aug. 6, **Variety,** Jul. 23, 1956; Jon Wiener, **Professors, Politics and Pop,** New York: Verso, 1991, 265–; **("the real hero")** Parmet, 382; **("enthusing")** Sinatra, **My Father,** 133; **(Mayflower)** Robert Parker with Richard Rashke, **Capitol Hill in Black and White,** New York: Dodd, Mead, 1986, 84–, Christopher Andersen, **Jack and Jackie,** New York: Morrow, 1996, 156; **(JFK Palm Springs/"Does Shirley . . .")** Jacobs and Stadiem, 135–; **(loved gossip)** Kenneth O'Donnell and David Powers with Joe McCarthy, "**Johnny, We Hardly Knew Ye,**" Boston: Little, Brown, 1972, 18; **("I know that")** Bragg, 310; **(publicity)** Parmet, 437–, Whalen, 446; **("Senator Kennedy")** Dwiggins, 142; **("It was a mutual")** Freedland, **All the Way,** 271.

469 **Joe Kennedy effort for JFK: (visit FS)** Jacobs and Stadiem, 117–, 128; **("We're going to sell")** Whalen, 446; **(magazines/ limitless money)** Parmet, 482–, 435, 441; **("I have just")** ibid., 439; **(map)** Whalen, 447; **("who the bosses")** Ronald Kessler, **The Sins of the Father,** New York: Warner, 1996, 374.

470 **Joe sent intermediary/"Joe Kennedy had been":** In his 1999 book, Bill Bonanno named the Kennedy intermediary as " 'Skip' O'Brien." The authors have not been able to identify a Kennedy aide of that name (Bill Bonanno, 82, int. Bill Bonanno).

470–472 **Joe Kennedy and mob: (attempts on Luciano)** Gosch and Hammer, 387, 392–; **(met in Sicily)** Umberto Santino, **Storia del movimento antimafia,** Rome: Editori Riuniti, 2000, 205, Umberto Santino and Giovanni La Fiura, **Behind Drugs,** Turin, Italy: Edizioni Grouppo Abele, 1993, 140–, and see Bonanno with Lalli, 198–, Douglas Valentine, **The Strength of the Wolf,** New York: Verso, 2004, 165; **("I was instructed")** Bill Bonanno, 82–, int. Bill Bonanno; **(both on Mafia Commission)** Brashler, 187; **(heart attack)** Bonanno with Lalli, 222; **(did not get along)** ibid., 250, Brashler, 277.

472 **"Joe came to me early"/"Back in '59":** Anthony Summers interviewed Phil Regan in 1991, and he died in 1996. The

authors did not interview Alo until 1997, and thus had no opportunity to ask Regan about the alleged meeting with Joe Kennedy. Alo was also interviewed in 1997 by Gus Russo for his book on the Chicago mob, **The Outfit.** We have here combined what Alo said about the Phil Regan approach in the two interviews. Brooklyn-born Regan was a singer and actor who had sung the national anthem at President Truman's inauguration. He was close to East Coast mobsters Joe Stacher and Longy Zwillman and was involved in activities involving the mob and politicians as early as 1952 (Regan background—Louella Parsons column, Mar. 27, 1962, **Variety,** Jul. 10, 1963, **Boston Globe,** Jul. 19, 1988, **Collier's,** Feb. 25, 1950, Paul Fay, **The Pleasure of His Company,** New York: Harper and Row, 1963, 44–, Peterson, **The Mob,** 288; Regan prison—**NYT,** Mar. 24, Aug. 30, 1973, Apr. 17, 1975, **LAT,** Jan. 6, 1983; Russo on Alo—Russo, 367–).

472–474 **Giancana/Mafia/politics: (Luciano and Al Smith)** Gosch and Hammer, 97–, 156–, Wolf with DiMona, 97–, Stuart, 92–, 159; **(Llewella Humphreys/Truman/Eisenhower) There Was a Crooked Man,** TV documentary, HTV Wales, supplied to authors by director Don Llewellyn; **(Giancana "floater"/candidate shot)** Brashler, 58–, Peterson, **Barbarians,** 142–; **(Giancana and politicians end 1950s)** ibid., 312, Brashler, 210, ASA (name withheld) Chicago to Director, Dec. 20, 1962, FBI 92-3171, Memo to file by Max Goldshein, "Organized Crime and Rackets in Chicago and Cook Co., Ill.," Sep. 27, 1957, BN, NA, Mahoney, 49, and see Hearings, HSCA, 22–.

474 **Compromising officials:** An example of sexual entrapment is the ordeal of George Ratterman, who in 1961 was the reform candidate for sheriff in Newport, Kentucky. Mobsters rendered him semiconscious by spiking his drink, then put him in bed with a cooperative stripper and called the police. The plot backfired. Ratterman was able to prove his innocence and went on to win the election (Ratterman File, FBI 44-17593, Messick, 201–, 207, Messick, **Syndicate Abroad,** London: Macmillan, 1969, 232); **(Lansky's widow) 60 Minutes,** CBS News, Jun. 25, 1989, Lacey, **Little Man,** 340; **("Throw him a broad")** Bill Bonnano, 83–.

474 **Korshak: (Bea and Lawfords) Vanity Fair,** Apr. 1997; **(background)** NYT, Jun. 27, 1976; **(close to Giancana) NYT,** Jun. 28, 1976, "Samuel M. Giancana," May 5, 1961, FBI 92-636-3,

SAC Las Vegas to Director, May 21, 1963, FBI 92-5053-4, Scheim, 338n.

474 **Korshak close to FS:** The Korshaks were close to Sinatra by late 1959. Bea Korshak, a former Paramount starlet, had stayed at Sinatra's rented villa in Acapulco the previous year. She would still be a trusted friend decades later, when she acted as matron-of-honor at Sinatra's wedding to his fourth wife and helped refurbish his Palm Springs house. At one point, Frank was said to be a client of Korshak's (close by 1959—Jacobs and Stadiem, 107; starlet—**Vanity Fair,** Apr. 1997; at wedding—Sinatra with Coplon, 158; refurbishment—**Architectural Digest,** Dec. 1998; client?—"File Review & Summary Checks," Mar. 26, 1970, FBI LA 100-41413); **(confronting Kefauver) NYT,** Jun. 27, 1976, Russo, 258–, **Vanity Fair,** Apr. 1997.

475 **FS/JFK and sex: ("Jack's pimp")** Kelley, 269; **("indiscreet parties")** Scatterday to Belmont, Mar. 30, 1960, and "Correlation Summary," Jun. 8, 1964, FSFBI, "File Review & Summary Check," Sep. 19, 1960, FBI LA 100-41413-121; **("the most startling") Dallas Morning News,** Jun. 15, 1977.

475 **JFK Palm Springs 1959: ("music filled")** Kelley, 267; **("Kennedy Room") Architectural Digest,** Dec. 1998, **Look,** Nov. 30, 1965.

475 **plaque/"We had a great":** Kelley, 286, 531; the plaque commemorating Kennedy's stay was dated "November 6th and 7th 1960," but that cannot be right. Kennedy was moving around the country at a frantic rate on those days—the election took place on the 8th—but not in California. The senator was on a tour of the West Coast in early November 1959, but was in Oregon, not California, on the 6th and 7th. He was in Southern California, however, between October 30 and November 5, 1959, and press reports indicate that he had the opportunity to stay with Sinatra on the 3rd and 4th. Powers's reference to a stay at Sinatra's home that month remains the only evidence the authors found for such a visit, but can be considered reliable. Staff at the John F. Kennedy Library were unable to throw further light on the matter (JFK travel—Theodore White, **The Making of the President, 1960,** New York: Atheneum, 1962, 338–; West Coast swing—**LAT,** Nov. 1, 2, 4, 7, **NYT,** 8, **WP,** 2, 3, 10, 13, **Oregon Journal,** 6, 7, 8, 9, 10, 1959; JFK Library—Sharon Kelly, reference librarian, to authors, Feb. 5, 2003, and see Kelley, 267, 531).

475 **dined Puccini's/Campbell:** int. Nick Sevano. Sevano had recently rejoined Sinatra's team. Campbell never mentioned having met Kennedy as early as November 1959—she would claim they first met on February 7, 1960. Yet Sevano told the authors he was quite sure Kennedy was present at Puccini's. Press coverage shows Kennedy was in Los Angeles on November 1 and 2, and in Beverly Hills specifically on the 1st. Sevano's account, if accurate, would establish that the candidate's attention was first drawn to Campbell three months earlier than she claimed (Sevano rejoined—Shaw, **Sinatra,** 262; JFK Nov. 1–2—**LAT,** Nov. 2, 4, **WP,** Nov. 2, 3, **NYT,** Nov. 8, 1959).

476 **Campbell and FS: (Campbell background)** ints. Judith Exner, 1991, Judith Exner (Exner was Campbell's later married name) as told to Ovid Demaris, **My Story,** New York: Grove Press, 1977, 15–, testimony of Judith Exner, Sep. 20, 1975, Hearings, Select Committee to Study Government Operations with Respect to Intelligence Activities, U.S. Senate, vol. 1, Report of Proceedings; **("at parties")** int. of Campbell by Barry Farrell, courtesy of Tony Cook, Exner as told to Demaris, 49.

476 **Senate committee:** The Campbell episode was first probed by a Senate committee, formally titled the Select Committee to Study Governmental Operations with Respect to Intelligence Activities. Its interim report, issued on November 20, 1975, is often referred to as the Church Report, after the committee's chairman, Senator Frank Church. Alternatively, it is called the Intelligence Committee; **(Campbell on Puccini's/FS followed up/"idyllic")** Exner as told to Demaris, 49–.

477–478 **Hawaii trip/"massage":** According to Campbell, Sinatra's guests in Hawaii included Dr. Leon Krohn, a gynecologist, and City National Bank president Al Hart. Earlier in his career, Hart had worked for a mob-controlled liquor company in Chicago. Another former vacationer, Karen Dynan, corroborated the fact that Campbell was in Hawaii. She recalled encountering the Sinatra group, and said that it included Hart and a doctor (Krohn/Hart guests—Exner as told to Demaris, 50–; Hart banker—ibid., "File Review & Summary Check," Mar. 9, 1962, FBI LA 100-41413-148; Peter Dale Scott, **The Dallas Conspiracy,** unpub. ms., Reid, **Reapers,** 180; corroboration—int. Karen Dynan); **("We were having")** int. Karen Dynan; **(gossip columnist)** Harrison Carroll in **LAHE,** Nov. 17, 1959; **(saw FS**

again/Entratter/Formosa) Exner as told to Demaris, 61–; **(Formosa/Giancana)** "Samuel M. Giancana," Mar. 7, 1961, FBI 92-3171-146, Giancana and Renner, 107, Brashler, 212; **("I'll bet even")** Exner as told to Demaris, 64.

478–479 **"High Hopes":** Rednour, 37, Sayers and O'Brien, 83; **(new version)** Jan. 28, 1960, entry, **Where or When?**; **("I'm Jack Kennedy"):** Reeves, 160; **("Frank, what can we count") Rolling Stone,** Mar. 19, 1981; **(JFK and *Caroline*)** O'Donnell and Powers with McCarthy, 150, Parmet, 512.

479–481 **JFK at "Summit": (JFK flew in/relax)** NYT, Feb. 8, 9, 1960. As well as taking a break, Kennedy addressed the local Democratic Committee while in Las Vegas. This was on Monday, February 8, a day—his schedule indicates—that had been planned as a "day off." He apparently canceled a plan to fly to San Francisco (**Las Vegas Sun,** Feb. 9, 1960, corr. archivist Sharon Kelly, John F. Kennedy Library); **("There was no goddamn"/"We all figured")** Martin, 199, David Heymann, **A Woman Named Jackie,** London: Heinemann, 1989, 230; **("Ladies & gentlemen"/"The next president")** JFK at Sands, videotape in authors' collection, int. Bullets Durgom, 1986, int. Sonny King; **("What did you say")** Wilson, **Show Business,** 15; **("trophy"/"It's perfectly")** Pearl, 66–, Davis, **Suitcase,** 83; **(reboarded *Caroline*)** NYT, Feb. 10, 11, 1960; **(sat up talking)** Davis, **Suitcase,** 83; **(FBI informant)** "File Review & Summary Check," Sep. 19, 1960, FBI 100-41413-121. Given the information in the FBI report and the authors' knowledge of the informant's background, he was almost certainly Los Angeles private investigator Fred Otash. The owner of El Rancho was Beldon Katleman, the "campaign manager" probably Larry O'Brien.

An FBI report written soon after the Kennedy visit to the Sands included a specific allegation. "Senator Kennedy," an informant claimed, "had been compromised with a woman in Las Vegas." Other sources indicate that investigators for a scandal magazine succeeded in bugging Sinatra's suite and obtaining tapes of "Kennedy and a hooker." Months after the Vegas visit, according to press reports, there was a frantic effort to locate and destroy photographs taken of Kennedy in local nightspots. According to an unpublished manuscript by the author Ladislas Farago, who had interviewed senior FBI officials, J. Edgar Hoover obtained the tapes and passed them on to Kennedy when he became president (Kennedy compromised—New Orleans to Director, Mar. 23, 1960, FBI 94-37314-2; frantic effort—"Correlation Summary," Jun. 8, 1964, FSFBI, Shaw, **Sinatra,** 274; Hoover—Farago Collection, Mugar Library, Boston University).

481–482 **Campbell and JFK at Sands: (Blair classmate/"bimbos"/ "because we sensed")** Hersh, 224, Heymann, 231, Martin, 199; **("sampled the goodies")** int. John Daley, 1983; **(JFK and cocaine)** corr. Ed Walters, and see earlier reference to drug use, chapter 23, p. 247.

482–484 **"I was at a table":** int. Milt Ebbins. Ebbins told author Anthony Summers as early as 1983 that he "introduced" Campbell, in an interview that focused not on Campbell but on information for Summers's biography of Marilyn Monroe. Ebbins said virtually the same as here reported in the text to Laurence Leamer, author of the book **The Kennedy Women** (Laurence Leamer, **The Kennedy Women,** New York: Bantam, 1994, 489); **(three such women)** int. Count Guido Deiro; **("looked so handsome")** Exner as told to Demaris, 86–; **(JFK phoned/sex at Plaza/"a long")** ibid., 98–; **(FS urging)** Exner as told to Demaris, 99–; **(Fontainebleau performances)** corr. Ric Ross, **Miami Herald,** Mar. 27, 1960; **(introduced to Fischetti)** ibid., 107–; **("Come here, Judy"/"Flood's eyes")** ibid., 116–; **(next to Giancana)** ibid., 120–.

484 **Giancana paid bill:** Campbell claimed that she objected to Giancana settling the bill, and paid him back. Confirmation that Giancana was in Miami at the time comes from Gloria Cahn, who was there with her husband. In her interview for this book, Cahn recalled an incident involving the mobster and Frank's nineteen-year-old daughter Nancy. "Little Nancy was there," Cahn recalled. "She wasn't comfortable because her father had made arrangements for Giancana to take her to the airport. She said 'Daddy, I'd really rather go with Gloria and Sammy.' As we pulled away in the car with her she was very relieved." Nancy had been in Miami for the taping of an ABC show featuring Sinatra and Elvis Presley (paid money back—Exner as told to Demaris, 123; ABC show—**Where or When?** the taping was on Mar. 26, 1960, for showing in May, and see Sinatra, **Legend,** 147).

484 **Campbell claimed used as courier:** Campbell said in 1988 that Kennedy and Sam Giancana had prolonged contact with each other, and used her as a courier and go-between. Press agent and

reporter Johnny Grant, who had known Campbell as a teenager, has said Campbell told him the gist of this in 1963. A Chicago political operative who worked on the Kennedy campaign in 1960, Martin Underwood, was quoted in 1997 as saying that he stayed close to Campbell when she carried covert campaign funds to Giancana for Kennedy—on instructions from Kennedy aide Kenneth O'Donnell. Though Underwood later disowned the quote, his interviewer Gus Russo insisted in 2004 that Underwood told him and investigative reporter Seymour Hersh exactly that (1988 claims—**People,** Feb. 29, 1988; Grant—Hersh, 325; Underwood quoted—ibid., 304–; disowned—chapter 7, Final Report of Assassination Records Review Board, 1998; Russo—conv. with authors, 2004).

484 **"The only Campbell": Newsweek,** Dec. 29, 1975. Both former Kennedy aide Dave Powers and Kenneth O'Donnell denied all knowledge of Campbell. Powers insisted, moreover, that logs held at the Kennedy Library made no mention of the visits to the White House claimed by Campbell. The president's secretary, Evelyn Lincoln, claimed in the 1970s that Campbell had been just "a campaign worker." Not seen by outsiders until the 1990s, and first made public by the authors, were multiple Secret Service logs proving that Powers had lied. White House telephone logs, moreover, show that Campbell called Kennedy's office seventy-five times. Lincoln, for her part, admitted in a 1992 interview that she had in fact been aware of Campbell phone contacts with the president.

Richard Burke, who served as administrative assistant to Senator Edward Kennedy, has recalled seeing transcripts of some of President Kennedy's taped Oval Office phone conversations. "One," he said, "was a long, romantic conversation with the woman then named Judith Campbell." The screenwriter Bill Richmond, proven by phone records to have been in touch with Campbell during the presidency, told the authors she spoke at the time—though guardedly—of her relationship with Kennedy. Betsy Duncan, a girlfriend of Giancana associate Johnny Rosselli, said much the same (denials—Anthony Summers, "The Unmaking of a Myth," **(London) Sunday Times Magazine,** Oct. 6, 1991; White House logs—from JFK Library, in authors' files; "campaign worker"—int. Evelyn Lincoln, 1992; "romantic conversation"—Richard Burke with William and Marilyn Hoffer,

The Senator, New York: St. Martin's, 1992, 108; Richmond/ Duncan—authors' ints.).

484 **"Hell hath": Fort Worth Star-Telegram,** Jan. 19, 1976; **(claims credible/*private* confidences)** see above note.

485 **Campbell far from candid: (FS draft: "hooker")** Kelley, 538; **(Campbell denied)** Exner as told to Demaris, 13, ints. Judith Exner.

485 **libel action:** Campbell sued over a passage in Laurence Leamer's book **The Kennedy Women.** The judge in the case dismissed the suit because—pleading ill health—Campbell would not travel into Los Angeles to take part in a deposition. Though she later began a deposition, she walked out before it was completed. Campbell's appeal of the judge's ruling lapsed on her death in 1999 (corr. Campbell's attorney, James Lesar, 2004); **("definitely thought")** Hersh, 311.

485 **"call girl"/"she would date":** Jacobs and Stadiem, 134, 60–, 133, int. George Jacobs. According to Jacobs, Sinatra rated Campbell's sexual services highly, and—before she met John Kennedy—made her available to John's father, Joe; **("Campbell was notorious"/"because she was")** int. Count Guido Deiro.

486–487 **Campbell and Rosselli: (Rosselli/Vegas)** Rappeleye and Becker, refs.; **(and Joe Kennedy)** ibid., 202, Russo, 66, 126, 362, int. Joe Shimon, 1985; **("possibly in 1960")** Judith Exner testimony, Sep. 20, 1975; **(known no mobsters) People,** Feb. 29, 1988; **("once briefly")** Exner as told to Demaris, 215; **(Rosselli said had known)** John Rosselli testimony, Sep. 22, 1975, Hearings, Select Committee to Study Government Operations with Respect to Intelligence Activities, U.S. Senate, Report of Proceedings, JFK, **NYT,** Apr. 12, 1976, **LAT,** Dec. 19, **Newsweek,** Dec. 29, 1975; **(Breen)** Rappeleye and Becker, 208.

487 **Dexter:** int. Brad Dexter. Dexter had an intimate association with Sinatra—he was to play a key role in rescuing the singer from drowning in 1964, and worked for him for several years. An indication that he was well placed to know about Campbell's Mafia contacts is to be found in Campbell's own book. Dexter's then girlfriend, Betty Winikus, arranged Campbell's dinner with Giancana in Miami in March 1960 (Shaw, **Sinatra,** 338, Exner as told to Demaris, 120–); **("When Sam wanted")** int. George Jacobs.

487 **Judy "mob moll":** Lawford with Schwarz, 147. By Campbell's own account she met Lawford repeatedly—once in July 1960 at

the Democratic convention, when she was with John Kennedy. Lawford, for his part, said he had more than one encounter with Giancana (met Campbell—Exner as told to Demaris, 50–, 62–, 162; Lawford/Giancana—**Star,** Feb. 17, 1976).

488 **Campbell and Giancana: (Sinatra asked her)** Exner as told to Demaris, 75, 77, 82, 84.

488 **Davis/"We all knew": Newsweek,** Dec. 29, 1975. Davis had spoken with **Newsweek** on condition he not be named. In his memoir **Why Me?** published shortly before his death in 1990, he confined himself to writing: "Later the Senator and his party came upstairs and had drinks with us. . . . I was told there were four wild girls scheduled to entertain him." As discussed in chapter 22, Davis had repeated contact with Giancana when threatened by the mob because of his 1957 affair with Kim Novak (Davis as source—ints. **Newsweek** sources; loaned car—SAC Los Angeles to Director, Mar. 24, 1960, FBI 100-41413-96; "Later the Senator"—Davis, Boyar, and Boyar, 108).

489 **Cahn/"How can Frank?":** Campbell herself said Gloria Cahn was present, and prominent in the group around Kennedy, during his February 1960 visit to Las Vegas. As to the possibility that Giancana was present, the authors note that the Black Book—the list of reputed criminals banned from the casinos—did not come into existence until the following June. Note, moreover, that Giancana was to have no hesitation in defying the ban—he famously did so at the Cal-Neva Lodge in 1963 (Cahn present—Exner as told to Demaris, 84–, ints. Judith Exner; Black Book—Ronald Farrell and Carole Case, **The Black Book and the Mob,** Madison, WI: University of Wisconsin Press, 1995, 8, 44).

489 **"I met Jack Kennedy":** Sevano recalled this both in a filmed interview shot for the British ITV network and to the authors in 2004 (int. Nick Sevano, and M/G int., transcript supplied to authors); **("They talked about")** int. Taki Theodoracopulos, 1986.

489 **Possible evidence of Giancana role in Kennedy contacts:** The **Washington Post** reported that Senate files "indicate that several of Campbell's calls to the White House were made from the Oak Park, Illinois, residence of Giancana." Though White House phone logs reflect some calls by Campbell from Oak Park, they cannot be identified as having originated at Giancana's home. Campbell acknowledged having visited the house, but said she

never phoned Kennedy while there. It was possible, she suggested, that Giancana tried to reach the president by having a trusted female friend call using her name (visited Oak Park—Exner as told to Demaris, 261; name used?—taped ints. of Judith Campbell by Barry Farrell, 1977, and by authors' colleague, 1991); **"I don't think":** taped int. of Judith Campbell by Barry Farrell, 1977, and see Exner as told to Demaris, 142; **("They deliberately")** int. Brad Dexter.

490–492 **Intelligence Committee: (Giancana shot)** Blakey and Billings, 391; **(Rosselli refused)** John Rosselli testimony, Sep. 22, 1975, Hearings, Select Committee to Study Government Operations with Respect to Intelligence Activities, U.S. Senate, Report of Proceedings, JFK; **(Campbell questioned)** statement of Judith Campbell Exner, Sep. 20, 1975, Hearings, Select Committee to Study Government Operations with Respect to Intelligence Activities, U.S. Senate, Report of Proceedings, JFK; **(paragraph in report)** "Alleged Assassination Plots Involving Foreign Leaders," Interim Report, Select Committee to Study Government Operations with Respect to Intelligence Activities, U.S. Senate, Washington, DC: U.S. Gov't. Printing Office, 1975, 129; **(did not interview FS)** AP, LAHE, Jan. 19, **Variety**, Jan. 20, 21, **Chicago Tribune**, Feb. 11, 1976; **(Safire articles) NYT**, Dec. 15, 22, 1975, Jun. 13, 1977, **LAHE**, Jan. 11, 1976; **(Safire questions) NYT**, Jan. 7, 1976; **("slam the lid") NYT**, Dec. 22, 1975; **(FS "being made available")** SAC New Orleans to Director, Mar. 23, 1960, FBI 94-37314-2; **("Frank asked me")** as quoted in int. of Tita Cahn, Sammy Cahn's second wife.

Chapter 25: The Go-Between

493 **Joe Kennedy approaches mob: ("It's not the Pope")** Merle Miller, **Plain Speaking**, New York: Putnam, 1973, 187; **(courted Mafia)** Russo, 365–, Parmet, 521.

493–494 **lunch at Felix Young's:** Although the meeting reportedly resulted in a large campaign contribution, not all attendees were ready to give the Kennedy camp full support. Some, like New Orleans's Carlos Marcello, never would be (Summers, **Official & Confidential**, 269–, Mahoney, 43–, 386, Russo, 356–, 367); **(Giancana did not commit)** Jacobs and Stadiem, 140; **(Humphreys leery)** Hersh, 143, Russo, 372–; **(RFK targeted)**

Schlesinger, **RFK,** 164–; **(Illinois)** White, 124, 143, 160; **(approach to FS/TV version) Sinatra: The Music Was Just the Beginning,** Warner Bros. 1992.

495 **golf game:** Hersh, 137–, Sinatra with Coplon, 72–, and see Sinatra, **Legend,** 146. It is not clear exactly when Sinatra was summoned to see Joe Kennedy. Tina Sinatra has placed it both in "late 1959" and in early 1960. Her sister, Nancy, dated it as February 1960.

495 **West Virginia: (sure thing?)** Theodore White, **The Making of the President, 1960,** New York: Atheneum, 1962, 101–; **(95 percent Protestant) Memories,** Apr./May 1990; **(allegations)** Hubert Humphrey, **The Education of a Public Man,** Garden City, NY: Doubleday, 1976, 214–, Lawrence O'Brien, **No Final Victories,** New York: Ballantine, 1974, 69–, Hersh, 95–, Kessler, 380, James Hilty, **Robert Kennedy, Brother Protector,** Philadelphia: Temple University Press, 1997, 144–; **("I knew Joe")** int. Bob Neal.

495 **"talked up"/"to get that Joe":** Jeanne Humphreys's memories were supported by a more than 300-page journal she kept. She and Humphreys's grandson George Brady were interviewed in 1997 by authors Seymour Hersh and Gus Russo, as was Robert McDonnell, a former attorney for the mob who said he helped arrange a meeting between Joe Kennedy and Giancana in Chicago (Hersh, 135, 143–, Russo, 370–).

495–496 **D'Amato spreading money:** Demaris, **Boardwalk,** 33, int. of D'Amato by Ovid Demaris, 1983, Van Meter, 171, Michael Hellerman with Thomas Renner, **Wall Street Swindler,** Garden City, NY: Doubleday, 1977, 105–. The Mafia bosses hedged their bets, and also supplied money to the campaign of Kennedy's opponent, Richard Nixon (Anthony Summers with Robbyn Swan, **The Arrogance of Power,** New York: Viking, 2000, 213–); **("We got them in")** int. Skinny D'Amato, 1984; **(Malandra)** Van Meter, photo section and 173; **("one of the people")** int. Robert Blakey.

496 **FS "interested":** int. John Chernenko—a previously published account of this episode, Chernenko told the authors, was garbled.

496 **"If you want":** Davis, Boyar, and Boyar, **Why Me?** 108.

496 **"We got back":** int. Brad Dexter, 2001.

497 **"used to take messages and money":** Judith Campbell, for her part, claimed that she carried cash **to** Giancana on John

Kennedy's behalf. The first time she performed such a mission, she said, was on April 8, 1960, a month before the West Virginia primary, carrying what Kennedy told her was "a lot of money" in a "sort of briefcase made of very soft leather." The money was perhaps sent to Giancana in order to launder it (Anthony Summers's article, [**London**] **Sunday Times,** Oct. 6, 1991).

497 **"our errand boy":** interview of Joseph Shimon, HSCA files, JFK.

497 **convention: (Martin cared little)** int. Mort Viner, 2002; **(banquet)** Wilson, **Sinatra,** 157–, Davis, **Hollywood,** 84, **NYT,** Jul. 11, 1960; **("just prior")** Athan Theoharis and John Cox, **The Boss,** Philadelphia: Temple University Press, 1988, 333fn.

497–498 **Campbell:** Exner as told to Demaris, 162–, 72–. Campbell was certainly with Kennedy during the week of the convention—Los Angeles district attorney's investigators saw her in his party at a Los Angeles restaurant. She dated the episode with Kennedy and a second woman as having occurred on Monday, July 11. The second woman was perhaps supplied by the madam the police later interviewed (investigators—int. Bill Simcock, 1983); **(anthem)** Davis, Boyar, and Boyar, **Yes, I Can,** 556, **Los Angeles Examiner,** Aug. 20, 1960; **(jazzy)** David Heymann, **RFK,** New York: Dutton, 1998, 165; **(4,509 delegates)** White, 151; **(record)** Hilty, 149, corr. Ric Ross; **(bald patch)** Spada, **Lawford,** 228; **(FS "really loved")** int. Bob Neal and int. Fred Otash, 1985; **("I was placed")** Gore Vidal, **The Last Empire,** New York: Doubleday, 2001, 151–.

499 **"Well, Frank":** Mahoney, 63. Author Richard Mahoney, to whom Peter Lawford described this exchange, dated it as having occurred on July 16, 1960. A reading of Theodore White's book on the campaign, however, suggests it occurred on Saturday, July 17 (White, 179); **(Humphreys labored)** Russo, 378–.

499–500 **"hard, almost impossible"/Lucchese:** int. Bill Bonanno, Bill Bonanno, 85–. Unconvinced mafiosi were won over, Bonanno claimed, after Joe Kennedy agreed that Lyndon Johnson would be given the vice-presidential slot. So he was, in an unexpected development that has never been adequately explained. John Kennedy's secretary, Evelyn Lincoln, told the authors in 1992 that pressure over "womanizing, and things in Joe Kennedy's background" forced her boss to pick Johnson. Hy Raskin, a key Kennedy strategist, recalled John Kennedy telling him: "I was left with no choice. [Lyndon] and Sam Rayburn made it damn clear to me that Lyndon had to be the candidate. Those bastards were trying to frame me." The full truth, he told his press secretary, Pierre Salinger, "will never be known. And it's just as well it won't be" ("womanizing and things"—Summers, **Official & Confidential,** 271–; "I was left"—Hersh, 126; "will never"—Pierre Salinger, **With Kennedy,** Garden City, NY: Doubleday, 1966, 46, int. Pierre Salinger, 1997); **("what politicians had"/"We'll all get")** Russo, 382.

500–501 **FS in campaign: ("the one who really"/$50)** LAT, Aug. 13, 2000; **("He'd get")** Spada, **Lawford,** 226; **("If he asked"/plane)** LAT, Aug. 13, 2000; **("We'd spread out")** Davis, Boyar, and Boyar, **Why Me,** 111; **("Just a simple")** Shaw, **Entertainer,** 97; **(recipes) Hollywood Reporter,** Jul. 8, 1960; **(Hawaii)** O'Brien, **Film Guide,** 135; **("I wish I had")** Braden, 148; **("We want Sinatra!")** Wilson, **Sinatra,** 160; **(Eleanor Roosevelt)** Sinatra, **Legend,** 146, 148; **(offices burgled)** Dallek, 286fn, 755n.

501–502 **Hutschnecker/"a whole dossier":** The authors learned details of this episode in 1995 from the late Dr. Hutschnecker, and later—in 2002—from Milt Ebbins (Hutschnecker startled, etc.—ints. Dr. Arnold Hutschnecker, 1995–97, detail in Summers with Swan, 219, 520n4, and int. Milt Ebbins; FS leaker—Kelley, 530).

502 **election night: (FS at Curtis's)** int. Janet Leigh; **(Nixon saying privately)** Summers with Swan, 216, and see O'Brien, **No Final Victories,** 96, White, 24–; **("Frank was drunk")** int. Janet Leigh and see Messick, **Show Business,** 194.

503 **popular vote:** The precise number of votes cast for Kennedy varies somewhat in the literature. The authors have used the figures reported in Theodore White's **The Making of the President 1960** (White, 350, 386, but see Dallek, 294); **(line open)** Kelley, 281; **("It's gonna")** Jacobs and Stadiem, 167.

503–504 **"we're going to":** Mahoney, 81, 390n88. This is not quite the "few close friends" quote that Kennedy has been cited as having used the following day, but as he reportedly relayed it immediately after the call—according to his aide Ralph Dungan (Benjamin Bradlee, **Conversations with Kennedy,** New York: Norton, 1975, 33); **(Giancana had presided)** Mahoney, 81; **("Votes weren't bought")** Russo, 396; **("guys stood")** Sam and

Chuck Giancana, **Double Cross,** London: Macdonald, 1992, 290; **("I know")** Russo, 398, and see Wilson, **Sinatra,** 161.

504 **votes "stolen":** Hersh, 140–. Blakey was a special prosecutor under Attorney General Robert Kennedy, and later chief counsel of the House Select Committee on Assassinations. He went on to become director of the Cornell Institute on Organized Crime, and is currently a professor of law at Notre Dame.

504–505 **Joe Kennedy's deal with mob: ("lay off")** Hersh, 146; **("Eventually")** ibid., 139–, Roemer, **Man Against Mob,** 158; **(senator "with a yen")** Gosch and Hammer, 378.

505 **Luciano/"We were playing":** int. Sal Vizzini. Bureau of Narcotics Commissioner Harry Anslinger rated Vizzini "one of the most effective undercover agents the Bureau ever had." At great risk, he penetrated the Luciano organization for more than two years—from early 1959 to late 1961 (Anslinger—Vizzini with Fraley and Smith, foreword; penetration—ibid., 33, 216, int. Sal Vizzini, and see Valentine, xvi, 192); **(Adonis deported)** Cook, 347; **(Adonis murderer)** Cook, 139, Sterling, 87; **("hello & goodbye")** Messick with Nellis, 236, **American Weekly,** Jul. 27, 1952.

505 **records suggest:** SAC New York to Director, Apr. 15, 1954, FBI 62-83219-17, rereviewed and released to authors, 2004, "Correlation Summary," Jun. 8, 1964, FSFBI. One FBI document suggests Adonis was one of Sinatra's original backers—plausible because he was part of the Luciano mob, close to Willie Moretti, and long operated in New Jersey; **("do what he could")** Hellerman with Renner, 106.

506 **"Joe Adonis expects"/"Costello should":** Winchell syndicated column, Dec. 16, 1960. Costello had been jailed on tax evasion charges, and was in prison for much of the time from May 1956 until June 1961, when he was released after having served most of a five-year term (Katz, 199–).

506–507 **Kennedy family at odds: ("dangerous")** Peter Collier and David Horowitz, **The Kennedys,** London: Pan, 1985, 271–; **(family dispute)** Arthur Schlesinger Jr., **Robert Kennedy and His Times,** Boston: Houghton Mifflin, 1978, 142; **(RFK pursuing Giancana)** "Title: Samuel M. Giancana," Sep. 12, 1960, FBI 92-3171, section 4; **(interrogated/taken Fifth)** Schlesinger, 165; **("Can you believe?")** Jacobs and Stadiem, 126; **("really hated") Penthouse,** Mar. 1984; **(mobsters amazed)** Cohen as told to

Nugent, 236; **(RFK made clear)** Anthony Summers, **Not in Your Lifetime,** New York: Marlowe, 1998, 192.

507 **Pursuit of Giancana: (close to top)** Director to SAC New York, Apr. 12, 1961, FBI 92-3171-238; **(surveillance/"lockstep")** Blakey and Billings, 208–, 254, Roemer, **Mob,** 153–, 257–, Roemer, **Accardo,** 221–; **(double-crossed, as he saw it)** e.g., logs of convs., Dec. 6, 21, 1961, Jan. 4, 1962, Misc. ELSUR Refs., vol. 1, HSCA Subject Files, Frank Sinatra, JFK, int. Bill Roemer, 1985.

507 **Threat to FS: (knife Lewis?)** corr. Mark Gribben and see Giancana and Giancana, 167–; **(Lewis)** the Lewis maiming was covered earlier, as was the threat to Davis.

508 **order to kill Arnaz:** Demaris, **Last Mafioso,** 122–. Taking the relevant sources together, the chronology suggests spring 1961 as the most likely date for the Arnaz episode. Sinatra knew of Giancana's rage, confronted Arnaz, and at one point—in his cups—talked of killing the producer himself. In Italy, the Bureau of Narcotics discovered that Sinatra had written to Lucky Luciano about the Arnaz series. The fact that Sinatra had quarreled with Arnaz made the newspapers at the time (FS talked of killing—Kelley, 287; FS letter to Luciano—Siragusa to Anslinger, May 20, 1961, LLBN, int. Sal Vizzini; made newspapers—**Variety,** Dec. 8, 1960, Apr. 4, 1961, Russo, 353).

508 **Shavelson background:** Shavelson, refs., int. Melville Shavelson—Shavelson had written the screenplay for one of Sinatra's movies, **Double Dynamite** (1951), and would direct him in another, **Cast a Giant Shadow** (1966).

509 **lamb's head episode:** ints & corr. Melville Shavelson, M/G int. of Shavelson. The authors found Shavelson entirely credible, but it proved impossible to date the lamb's-head incident. Shavelson's colleague Jack Rose died in 1995, so could not be interviewed. Shavelson's best estimate was that the incident occurred in early 1961, and Sinatra did play the Fontainebleau—soon after the January inauguration—from February to March 13 that year (FS at Fontainebleau—corr. Ric Ross, Sinatra, **Legend,** 156).

509 **horse's head tradition:** Sifakis, 159–, Sinatra, **Legend,** 110, and see note at p. 460– **supra.**

509 **"sheep with its throat cut":** Hess, 114, int. Gino Spezia. There is some evidence that Giancana used symbols. He is believed to have had one of his men killed in 1948, for bungling a murder by leav-

ing behind evidence pointing to Giancana. The one item found on the corpse was a comb—a reference, investigators believed, to the man's failure to "comb clean" the body of his victim. Other murders covered by Giancana's biographer involved instances of a nickel left in the hand of a suspected informer, a valentine tossed on a corpse, and tiny coffins mailed as threats to a man who was eventually killed (Brashler, 156–); **(FS not abide smell)** undat. **National Enquirer** series, 1990, by former Sinatra valet Bill Stapely; **(back to wall)** int. Brad Dexter; **(what he did)** Sinatra with Coplon, 77.

Chapter 26: Friends Fall Out

510–511 **FS and inauguration: (evening at RFK's/"a god"/"That's enough")** Joan Braden, **Just Enough Rope**, New York: Villard, 1989, 146–, Heymann, 197; **(previous night)** (LA) **Mirror,** Jan. 18, 1961, Arthur Schlesinger, **A Thousand Days,** Boston: Houghton Mifflin, 1965, 166; **(gala success/only three thousand)** LAT, Jun. 21, 1998, NYT, Jan. 20, 1961, Taraborrelli, 238–; **(Jacqueline not approve/on arm)** Braden, 110, Heymann, 175, Sarah Bradford, **America's Queen,** London: Penguin, 2001, 219; **("indebted")** Kennedy remarks, JFK inaugural concert, videotape in authors' collection; **(area set aside)** Reeves, 36; **(FS not there/"Frank didn't want")** Spada, **Lawford,** 238.

511 **drunk/"There was a stand":** Henry Rogers of the Rogers & Cowan public relations firm later recalled trying, on Sinatra's instructions, to get the **Daily News** to retract the story, pointing out that Sinatra had watched the inauguration on TV at his hotel. Neal's account would indicate that Sinatra first visited Capitol Hill and then returned to his hotel suite at the Hilton, which adjoined Neal's. The **Daily News** did not retract the story. The authors could not locate the original story, and concluded that it appeared in an edition not filed at the Library of Congress (Henry Rogers, **Walking the Tightrope,** New York: William Morrow, 1980, 164, int. Bob Neal).

511–512 **FS dinner:** LAT, Jun. 21, 1998, Bradford, 224; **(boxes)** int. Brad Dexter; **("very much on edge")** Brownstein, 159; **("Tell him")** int. Mel Shavelson, Shavelson, 167–.

512 **FS not to Palm Beach/"Tony and I":** int. Janet Leigh. A contemporary newspaper report, probably based on an advance press

release, said Sinatra did make the journey. ([LA] **Mirror,** Jan. 21, 1961, and see Gehman, 85).

513 **FS movie and Maltz:** The movie in prospect was an adaptation of William Bradford Huie's bestseller **The Execution of Private Slovik,** the story of the real-life execution of an American World War II deserter. The project was shelved (O'Brien, **Film Guide,** 207); **(announced/conservative press) Science & Society,** Fall 2002, Wiener, 267, **Miami Herald, (NY) Daily Mirror,** Apr. 1, **New York Journal-American,** Apr. 2, **LAT,** Apr. 8, **Variety,** Apr. 13, 1960; **(FS fought) Variety,** Mar. 28, 1960, **Los Angeles Examiner,** Mar. 31, 1960; **(dropped Maltz)** (LA) **Mirror-News,** Apr. 9, **Variety,** Apr. 11, 1960; **(pressure from Joe and Bobby)** Sinatra with Coplon, 68, and see Gehman, 188; **(FS got drunk)** Jacobs and Stadiem, 145.

513 **Democratic concern re FS: ("Jack Pack")** Spada, **Lawford,** 226, and see **Hollywood Citizen-News,** Oct. 13, 1960; **("It is hoped")** Wilson, **Sinatra,** 169; **(word passed)** Braden, 110, Heymann, 175.

514 **FS, Davis & Kennedys: (booed) Los Angeles Examiner,** Aug. 20, 1960, Davis, Boyar, and Boyar, **Yes, I Can,** 556, Haygood, 304.

514 **press suggested/asked Davis to postpone:** Davis, Boyar, and Boyar, **Yes, I Can,** 565–, (LA) **Mirror,** Oct. 26, 1960, Fishgall, 165. Sinatra's daughter Nancy has said Joe Kennedy pressured her father to get Davis to postpone the marriage. According to George Jacobs, Davis put off the wedding as "a huge favor" to Sinatra. In his memoirs, Davis wrote of the episode as though the decision was his alone (Nancy on pressure—Sinatra, **Legend,** 150; "favor"—Jacobs and Stadiem, 146; Davis memoirs—Davis, Boyar, and Boyar, **Yes, I Can,** 566–, and **Why Me,** 116–); **("he does not want")** Davis, Boyar, and Boyar, **Why Me,** 130; **(Lawford call)** Sinatra, **Legend,** 151.

514 **FS appalled:** Sinatra, **My Father,** 145. Though not excusable, Kennedy's action should be seen in the context of the bigotry of the day. "There were tensions behind the scenes no one would have guessed," said the copyist Vern Yocum, who traveled to the capital with Frank and the Nelson Riddle orchestra to work on the inauguration gala. "They [Sinatra and Riddle] had a room in one of the best hotels in Washington. In the band we had two

black musicians, a saxophone player and a bass player. So they housed us across the river in a motel." The restaurant staff refused to serve the two black men, and at Frank's urging the entire party walked out and ate elsewhere. Such episodes were common in 1960 (Vern Yocum taped recollections); **(FS quarreled)** Sinatra with Coplon, 76; **(MLK benefit/FS drinking)** int. Peter Levinson, Levinson, **September**, 146.

515–516 **difficult FS/Kennedy relations: (phoned occasionally)** e.g., int. Mickey Finn, 1983, "Correlation Summary," Jun. 8, 1964, FSFBI; **("Happy Birthday!") Show Business Illustrated,** Sep. 5, 1961; **(White House visit once)** Sinatra with Coplon, 78; **(Joe Kennedy and film)** Spada, **Lawford,** 290; **(Côte d'Azur/"no room")** LAT, Aug. 3, 9, **Limelight,** Aug. 24, **New York Daily News, Hollywood Citizen-News,** Aug. 4, **Los Angeles Examiner,** Sep. 10, 1961, **Chicago's American,** Oct. 1, 1966, int. Bob Neal; **(FS at compound) Manchester Union Leader,** Sep. 26, **U.S. News & World Report,** Oct. 16, 1961; **(alcohol/"whores") Manchester Union Leader,** Sep. 26, 1961, Frank Saunders, **Torn Lace Curtain,** New York: Pinnacle, 1982, 79–; **("loud & obnoxious")** Barbara Leaming, **Mrs. Kennedy,** London: Orion, 2001, 177, 175; **(Salinger)** Michael Beschloss, **The Crisis Years,** New York: Edward Burlingame, 1991, 312, Kelley, 293; **(FS "is also coming")** Elise Kirk, "Music at the White House," JFK Library reprint, Jun. 29, 2001; **("showing off")** Smith, **Grace & Power,** 231; **("All the work")** Kelley, 292; **("was in a snit")** Granata, 151; **(not to Florida/bad throat)** Shaw, **Sinatra,** 308.

517 **No JFK stay at FS house: (extensive construction) Chicago Tribune,** Jan. 7, 1961, **New Yorker,** Nov. 3, 1997, Sinatra, **Legend,** 160; **("He spent thousands") Star,** Dec. 16, 1975; **(parties/guest lists)** Jacobs and Stadiem, 163.

517 **at Crosby's ranch:** LAT, Mar. 24, 1962. The president's aide Kenneth O'Donnell insisted later that the decision not to stay at Sinatra's home was dictated by security concerns. The Secret Service is said to have thought the house vulnerable because it was alongside a golf course. Crosby's home, by contrast, was more isolated and easier to guard. A memoir by former Air Force One pilot Ralph Albertazzie suggests the Secret Service did make such a recommendation. If so, it was convenient. The break with Sina-

tra was driven by more serious concerns (O'Donnell insisted—O'Donnell and Powers with McCarthy, 379; memoir—J. F. terHorst and Ralph Albertazzie, **The Flying White House,** New York: Bantam, 1980, 175, and see Bacon, **Hollywood,** 256, Reeves, 292; **(Lawford delivered/FS tore phone)** Jacobs and Stadiem, 163; **("Frank grabbed")** int. Sonny King, Van Meter, 186; **(rupture final) Star,** Dec. 16, 1975, **(Long Beach, CA) Southland,** Nov. 19, 1972, Collier and Horowitz, 428.

517–518 **FS laid blame:** ints. Milt Ebbins, Shirley MacLaine. The publisher Walter Annenberg later said it was Joe Kennedy who advised the president to "brush the Dago off." Though in character, this would be plausible only if Joe had offered the advice before December 19, 1961. He suffered a devastating stroke that day, and could not speak for months afterward ("brush the Dago"—John Clooney, **The Annenbergs,** New York: Simon and Schuster, 1982, 263–; stroke—Whalen, 479–); **("He was madder")** int. Shirley MacLaine; **(FS spoke fondly/mementos)** ints. Tony Oppedisano, Rock Brynner, Sinatra, **Legend,** 179, **Ladies' Home Journal,** Dec. 1975; **(red phone) Look,** Nov. 30, 1965.

518 **"Jack, you can't have":** Skolsky, 51–. This exchange likely occurred during a visit by the president to Los Angeles on the weekend of November 18–19, 1961. He and Monroe were at the Lawford beach house on the 19th, and he had seen Sinatra at a public function the previous day. There was a press rumor that week that the president had decided to distance himself from Sinatra (Nov. 18–19—**NYT,** Nov. 19, 1961, Summers, **Goddess,** 227, 228n; rumor—**New York Journal-American,** Nov. 15, 1961, and see **Photoplay,** Mar. 1962); **("Johnny, you just can't")** Collier and Horowitz, 371; **(Feldman)** Brownstein, 164.

518 **"It meant nothing":** ibid., 166. Former White House aide Dave Powers claimed years later that Kennedy would have been "displeased" by the suggestion that he had disassociated himself from Sinatra. There were some further contacts in the latter part of the presidency, but they were limited, so far as one can tell, to polite correspondence (**LAT,** Jan. 19, 1976).

518 **"I don't know":** int. Shirley MacLaine.

519 **"Peter told him":** int. Sonny King. Lawford, and Kennedy's former press secretary, Pierre Salinger, later acknowledged that this was indeed the gist of the message (**Star,** Dec. 16, 1975, Feb. 17, 1976, int. Pierre Salinger, in **Sinatra: Good Guy, Bad Guy,** Hart

Ryan Productions, for ITV [London], 2000); **("It was a question")** Brownstein, 164.

Chapter 27: Paying the Price

520–521 **pursuit of organized crime: (RFK announcing victories)** LAHE, Mar. 24, LAT, Mar. 25, 1962; **(indicted/convicted)** appen., HSCA, vol. 9, 20; **(D'Amato reminded)** Hellerman with Renner, 106; **(D'Amato indicted)** Hersh, 101; **(expel Costello/Rosselli)** Katz, 201, Rappeleye and Becker, 261, Mahoney, 97.

521 **Marcello:** Though deported less than three months into the presidency, Marcello sneaked back in within weeks (appendix., HSCA, vol. 9, 70–).

521 **action against Giancana: (vigorously pursued)** Director to SAC Las Vegas, Apr. 13, 1961, FBI 92-3171-196, Evans to Parsons, May 1, 1961, FBI 92-3171-211, and May 18, 1961, FBI 92-3171-240, Director to SAC Chicago, Jun. 22, 1961, FBI 92-3171-272, and Jun. 22, 1962, FBI 92-3171-626; **(RFK surprised)** Mahoney, 103; **("highly concerned")** Director to SAC Chicago, Feb. 8, 1962, FBI 92-3171-613; **("hoodlum lawyer")** int. Marion Phillips, 1983; **("unfair")** Hersh, 101; **("instructions")** Director to SAC Miami, Jul. 6, 1961, FBI 92-3024-25, "Title: Joseph Fischetti," Aug. 24, 1961, FBI 92-3024-27.

521–522 **FS spoke for Marcello:** Report of SA Furman Boggan, Jan. 14, 1963, HSCA Subject Files, LCN, Main File, 90- 6054, JFK, appen., HSCA, vol. 9, 70. According to this report, Sinatra spoke on Marcello's behalf on the initiative of Florida boss Santo Trafficante, whom he had met by the early 1950s. Trafficante, who suffered from baldness, reportedly used a hair-transplant surgeon recommended by Sinatra (Trafficante initiative—appendix, HSCA, vol. 9, 70, Report of SA Furman Boggan, Jan. 14, 1962, HSCA Subject Files, LCN, Main File, 92:6054, section 12; had known/hair transplants—int. Joe Nellis; "Supplemental Correlation Summary," Feb. 25, 1969, FS FBI, and see Ragano and Raab, 20, 115, 188, 214–; surgeon—ibid., 82); **(Giancana/Rosselli and Castro)** "Alleged Plots Involving Foreign Leaders," Interim Report, Select Committee to Study Government Operations with Respect to Intelligence Activities, 94th Cong., 1st sess., Nov. 1975, 74–; **("working for the government")**

Schlesinger, **RFK,** 495, Rappeleye and Becker, 231; **("Sinatra went to")** Cohen as told to Nugent, 235.

522–523 **" 'Johnny, I took Sam's name' "/" 'One minute he tells me' ":** The source the authors have used is the thirty-six-page FBI transcript of a series of conversations picked up by an FBI bug on the night of December 6–7, 1961. Giancana's interlocutor in this particular conversation is identified on the tape only as "John," and published sources differ as to his identity. The authors agree with those who conclude it was Formosa. Previous books, meanwhile, have referred to a conversation in which there was talk of "hitting" or "whacking" Sinatra and other Rat Pack members—language some have taken to refer to killing him. FBI transcripts at the National Archives contain no such dialogue. The "whacking" reference first appeared in a 1977 biography of Giancana, and may derive from the inexact memory or notes of Agent William Roemer, a lead member of the FBI's Chicago surveillance team. Roemer was probably misremembering Giancana's talk about giving Sinatra or Martin a "headache." The transcripts seen by the authors were not available until recently (Dec. 6 conversation—log of conv., Dec. 6, 1961, Misc. ELSUR Refs., vol. 1, HSCA Subject Files, Frank Sinatra, JFK; sources differ—e.g., Blakey and Billings, 383, Mahoney, 125, Ronald Goldfarb, **Perfect Villains, Imperfect Heroes,** New York: Random House, 1995, 137, Roemer, **Mob,** 189–; "hit"/"whack"—ibid., Brashler, 212–, and authors' corr. William Brashler, and see Blakey and Billings, 383).

523 **"punch the [obscenity]"/"They don't want him":** log of conv., Dec. 21, 1961, Misc. ELSUR Refs., vol. 1, HSCA Subject Files, Frank Sinatra, JFK.

524 **"Lying [obscenity]!":** log of Jan. 4, 1962, Misc. ELSUR Refs., Frank Sinatra, vol. 1, HSCA Subject Files, JFK, SAC Chicago to Director, Jan. 10, 1962, FBI 92-3171-58—the FBI thought the other associate was possibly Nick Civella. However great Giancana's frustration, the fact remained that Sinatra was an entrée to the Kennedys. As late as 1963, the mafioso would order an associate to pass a message to FBI agents outside his headquarters: "If Bobby Kennedy wants to talk to me, he knows who to go through." The associate made it clear that Giancana was referring to Sinatra (Director to Attorney General, Jul. 9, 1963, FBI 92-3171-1070, and see Roemer, **Mob,** 263).

524 **Joe K. felled:** Whalen, 479; **("Why oh why?")** Jacobs and Stadiem, 165.

524 **"Peel the banana":** NYT, Apr. 14, 1976.

524–525 **McMillan probe:** The authors had access to McMillan's final Sinatra memorandum, which was submitted in early 1964. Thirteen other related memos are still withheld. Though some details of the attorney's efforts to have Sinatra investigated have leaked out over the years, he has always been close-mouthed. McMillan gave limited interviews to the authors in 1983 and in 2002, and a longer interview—for the TV documentary linked to this book—in 2004 (Dougald McMillan to William Hundley, "Subject: Francis Albert Sinatra," Jan. 3, 1964, Department of Justice, Organized Crime Division—referencing eleven previous Sinatra memos, and two with the subject heading "Max Eder," also ints. Ron Goldfarb, Mrs. Edwyn Silberling, Robert Blakey, Messick with Nellis, 238–); **("Sinatra's affiliation")** int. Dougald McMillan; **(Silberling/Campbell/grand jury) NYT,** Apr. 12, 14, 1976; **("considered Sinatra")** Brownstein, 162; **("I believe there was")** int. Dougald McMillan for PITV; **("between a rock")** int. Dougald McMillan.

526 **FS and Fischetti: (saw time and again)** Burke to SAC Newark, Mar. 13, 1962, FBI 137-3514-234, SAC Miami to Director, Mar. 5, 1962, FBI 92-3024-38, "Joseph Fischetti," Apr. 24, 1962, FBI 92-3024-46, and Oct. 29, 1962, FBI 92-3024-55; **("Fischetti is")** "Joseph Fischetti," Jun. 18, 1962, FBI 92-3024-51.

526 **FS and Giancana together: ("in a private")** Van Meter, 194; **("the unlisted number")** "Samuel M. Giancana," Oct. 11, 1962, FBI 92-3171-904; **("Frank Sinatra's residence")** ibid.

526 **Villa Venice/capacity crowds:** Brashler, 213–, Giancana and Renner, 108–; "File Review & Summary Check: re Dean Martin," Feb. 2, 1974, FBI 62-4881-3, and see re Giancana's ownership role, "Special Summary Report, Samuel M. Giancana," May 5, 1961, FBI 92-636-3, FBI int. of Frank Sinatra, Jan. 17, 1963, FBI 92-962. A Sinatra attorney later denied claims that his client performed for free at the Villa Venice, saying he had been paid $15,000. A Nevada State Gaming Control Board investigator who checked the records testified that this appeared to be the case. Chicago FBI agent William Roemer and Sinatra's friend Sonny King concluded that he was paid "scale" or "minimum."

Tina Sinatra said her father "mollified" Giancana by performing, but not "out of fear." Her sister, Nancy, said the appearances were to pay the mobster back for his help in the 1960 election (free?—e.g., **LAHE,** Jan. 18, 1981; $15,000—Vincent Chieffo and Agent Weyland testimonies, Nevada State Gaming Control Board, Feb. 11, 1981; "scale"—Roemer, **Mob,** 191; "minimum"—int. Sonny King; "mollified"—Sinatra with Coplon, 76; payback?—Sinatra, **Legend,** 168).

526–527 **Acapulco:** int. Rock Brynner, Rock Brynner, **Yul: The Man Who Would Be King,** New York: Simon and Schuster, 1989, 148–; **("Dr. Moody")** Giancana's most common nickname was "Mooney." He used many aliases, and sometimes the title "Dr." In Mexico, Brynner thought, he called himself either "Moody" or "Goody" ("Mooney"—Brashler, 28–, 106; aliases—e.g., "Special Summary Report, Samuel M. Giancana," May 5, 1961, FBI 92-636-3; used "Dr."—e.g., int. Dan Arney, Fisher, 255; "Moody"/"Goody"—ints. and corr. Rock Brynner, Brynner, 148–); **(dined NY)** "Samuel M. Giancana," Apr. 30, 1963, FBI 92-3171, section 17; **(Palm Springs)** Exner as told to Demaris, 275–; **(Hawaii/J. J. Bracket)** SAC Honolulu to Director, Jun. 13, 1963, FBI 92-3171-1027, and Jul. 19, 1963, FBI 92-3171-1124; **(Perno)** SAC Honolulu to Director et al., Jun. 14, 1963, FBI 92-3171-1043, and Jun. 26, 1963, FBI 92-3171-1069; **(Giancana to NJ)** extract, Ralph Salerno summary re organized crime for HSCA, obtained by author.

527 **Cal-Neva: (described)** Anthony Summers's visit, 1983.

528–529 **Joe K. and Lodge:** Sally Denton and Roger Morris, **The Money and the Power,** New York: Knopf, 2001, 173, 183–, 187, Russo, 376–, "General Survey, Miami," Feb. 16, 1944, Joseph Kennedy FBI file rereviewed and released to authors, 2003; **(FS never acknowledged)** FS testimony, Nevada State Gaming Control Board, Feb. 11, 1981, "Nevada Gaming Industry, Cal-Neva Lodge," Jan. 18, 1963, FBI 190-HQ-1046581; **(Giancana true owner/admitted)** M/G int. of Joseph Nellis, int. Joe Shimon, 1985, ints. Robert Blakey, Tony Montana, John Smith, Demaris, **Mafioso,** 101, log of conv., Dec. 6, 1961, Misc. ELSUR Refs., vol. 1, HSCA Subject Files, Frank Sinatra, JFK, "Supplemental Correlation Summary," Feb. 25, 1969, FSFBI, SAC Chicago to Director, Aug. 31, 1962, FBI 92-3171-859, Russo, 389–; **(third season)** (Tahoe) **Daily Tribune,** Jun. 26, 29, 1962, Bethel Van

Tassel, **Wood Chips to Game Chips**, self-published, 1985, 37–; **(prostitution)** Edward Olsen Oral History, 1972, University of Nevada, Reno, 371–; **(D'Amato brought in)** ibid., 374, Demaris, **Boardwalk,** 33; **(Rosselli seen)** "File Review & Summary Check," Mar. 26, 1970, FBI LA 100-41413-179, SAC Las Vegas to Director, Jul. 6, 1962, FBI 62-9-65-243; **(Formosa seen/role)** Report of SA James Doyle (FBI), Dec. 19, 1962, HSCA Subject Files, LCN, Main File, 92:6054, section 12; **("the skim run"/"They'd call up")** int. Dan Arney; **("Giancana gave Joe")** int. Tony Montana and see re Pignatello background, Farrell and Case, 46–; **(Monroe was there)** Summers, **Goddess,** 395.

529 **"I developed the film":** Woodfield talked about the pictures in 1984 when author Summers was preparing his Monroe biography, **Goddess,** but asked then that his identity be concealed and only an abbreviated version of the story published. He was concerned about upsetting Sinatra, who was still very much alive at the time. Woodfield later retold the story to others and—again to Summers—shortly before his death in 2001. An element of corroboration came from Ruth Shavelson, the former wife of Woodfield's then partner John Florea, who recalled hearing about the episode soon after it occurred (ints. Billy Woodfield, 1984, 2001, and conv. Ruth Shavelson, Summers, **Goddess,** 396–).

529–530 **Giancana and Monroe sex?:** Russo, 432, int. Gus Russo. Peter Lawford is also quoted, by his agent Milt Ebbins, as having said Giancana had sex with Monroe at the Cal-Neva. Former FBI agent William Roemer, who ran the Giancana bugging operation in Chicago, recalled a conversation that may have referred to Monroe. "You sure get your rocks off," Rosselli told his fellow mafioso, "fucking the same broad as the brothers [Kennedy], don't you?" Judith Campbell, however, may also have slept with Giancana by July 1962, and—if so—Rosselli may have been referring not to Monroe but to Campbell. Campbell's memoir indicates that she first had sex with Giancana sometime after May 1962, a date she revised in an interview to as late as December of that year (Lawford—int. Milt Ebbins; Roemer—Roemer, **Mob,** 184, Exner as told to Demaris, 254, Exner int. with attorney contact of authors); **(Monroe disgust)** int. Jeanne Carmen.

530–532 **Giancana at Cal-Neva/licenses lost: (Black Book)** Farrell and Case, 8; **("He'd sneak in")** int. Nick Sevano; **(word reached authorities)** Edward Olsen Oral History, 377; **(left for Palm Springs)** int. George Jacobs; **(FS denied/D'Amato obstructed)** Edward Olsen Oral History, 381, 391; **(FS called Olsen)** ibid., 391, int. Guy Farmer, Farmer draft, "Frank Sinatra vs. the State of Nevada," 1998, supplied to authors; **(memorandum)** Edward Olsen Oral History, 388–; **(agents ejected/bribe)** ibid., 394–; **(complaint)** ibid., 396–; **(FS announced)** (Washington, DC) **Evening Star,** Oct. 8, 1963, SAC Las Vegas to Director, Oct. 7, 1963, FBI 92-6259-19.

532 **FS & Kennedy cutoff: ("If he would only")** Arthur Schlesinger, the former Kennedy aide and historian, noted Dickinson's comment in his journal on October 28, 1963—days after Sinatra was stripped of his gaming licenses (Schlesinger, **RFK,** 496, 975n104); **(JFK trip) Las Vegas Review-Journal,** Sep. 29, 1963; **("What are you guys?")** Grant Sawyer, **Hang Tough,** Reno, NV: University of Nevada Oral History Program, 1993, 94.

533 **"Is there anything":** eds. Michael Green and R. T. King, **A Liberal Conscience: The Oral History of Ralph Denton,** Reno, NV: University of Nevada Oral History Program, 2001, 243. It may be, too, that the president thought of Sinatra at a momentous time the following month. At the height of the Cuban Missile Crisis, when nuclear war seemed imminent, White House press secretary Pierre Salinger called Sinatra to warn him of the gravity of the situation. The singer's daughter Nancy recalled her father calling to tell her to pack some things and be ready to travel. He also phoned his lover Juliet Prowse, telling her to "get out of New York City because it's going to be blown apart" ("Pack"—Sinatra, **My Father,** 184, and see Sinatra with Coplon, 80; "get out"—Freedland, 285).

533 **"devastated":** M/G int. of Eddie Fisher; **("It was hurt")** int. Leonora Hornblow.

533 **pressure on Giancana: (FS had flown)** appen., HSCA, vol. 9, 34; **(intense surveillance/as if dictatorship)** log of conv., Dec. 6, 1961, vol. 1, Misc. ELSUR Refs., HSCA Subject Files, Frank Sinatra, JFK. A court order requiring the FBI to moderate its surveillance had been rapidly reversed (UP, AP, Jul. 17, 1963, Brash-

ler, 258–, Blakey and Billings, 255–); **(funds cut off)** log of conv., Sep. 19, 1963, Misc. ELSUR Refs., HSCA Subject Files, Sam Giancana, vol. 4, JFK, SAC Chicago to Director, Sep. 21, 1963, FBI 92-3171-1222; **($470,000)** int. Joe Shimon, 1985; **(might be ousted)** (Chicago) **Daily Tribune,** Jun. 4, 1962, SAC Chicago to Director, Sep. 11, 1963, FBI 92-3171-1205, notes of Giancana ELSUR, Oct. 16, 1963, supplied to authors, appendix, HSCA, vol. 9, 34; **(cursing the government)** SAC Chicago to Director, Oct. 17, 1963, 92-3171-1234; **(board stripped)** (Washington, DC) **Evening Star,** Oct. 23, 1963; **(Giancana with FS in November)** "Samuel M. Giancana," Jan. 28, 1964, FBI 92-3171, section 20.

533–534 **JFK assassination: (*Tom Jones*/"September Song")** O'Donnell and Powers with McCarthy, 387–; **(FS recorded)** Rednour, 82—FS recorded this song in 1946, 1961, and 1965; **(Campbell 1963)** Exner as told to Demaris, 272–; **(Campbell's calls/Giancana/FS)** NYT, Apr. 12, 1976; **("like I was"/Rosselli installed)** Exner as told to Demaris, 281, 286.

535 **FS reaction: (movie location)** O'Brien, **Film Guide,** 158, Gene Ringgold and Clifford McCarty, **The Films of Frank Sinatra,** New York: Carrol, 1993, 199. Another account had it that Sinatra heard about the assassination not at the Rosedale Cemetery in Los Angeles, but while filming a courtroom scene on the Warner lot. Most sources, including his costar Sammy Davis, said the news reached him at the cemetery (O'Brien, **Film Guide,** 158, Davis, Boyar, and Boyar, **Why Me,** 150–, Sinatra, **My Father,** 156–); **(gravestone)** ibid., 200, citing **Newsweek,** Sinatra, **My Father,** 156; **(walked off, etc.)** Davis, Boyar and Boyar, **Why Me,** 150–, Haygood, 316, Sinatra, **Legend,** 178; **(stayed in Palm Springs),** ints. George Jacobs, Sonny King, Sinatra with Coplon, 81, Jacobs and Stadiem, 205–; **(Thanksgiving)** Wilson, **Sinatra,** 200.

535–536 **Frank Jr. kidnapping:** Turner, **Gambler's Money,** 167, Shaw, **Sinatra,** 331–, **LAT,** Dec. 15, 1963, May 19, 1964, **New York Sunday News,** Oct. 31, 1965, "File Review & Summary Check," Mar. 26, 1970, FBI LA 100-41413-179. Attorneys for the accused tried to argue at the trial that this had been a bogus kidnapping, a hoax designed to get publicity for Frank Jr. One of the kidnappers, Barry Keenan, was quoted in 1998 as having admitted that this was a defense "perpetrated by me and our attorneys to confuse the jury and get us off the hook, plain and simple. It didn't work" (Shaw, Sinatra, 336, Taraborrelli, 316, **New Times,** Jan. 15, 1998); **("were only executing")** (LA) **Daily News,** Oct. 31, 1965.

536 **FS haunted:** The authors are indebted for this information to the author Dick Russell, who passed on the contents of a mid-1990s conversation with Tina Sinatra.

536–537 **Assassination findings: (lone gunman/Ruby loner)** "Report of the President's Commission on the Assassination of President John F. Kennedy," Washington, DC: U.S. Government Printing Office, 1964, 19, 21–, 801; **(poll)** Gallup Poll, Nov. 21, 2003, www.gallup.com, and see Report, HSCA, 1; **("the Mob did it")** Anthony Summers, **Not in Your Lifetime,** New York: Marlowe, 1998, 201; **("He meant")** Hersh, 450–, and see Richard Goodwin, **Remembering America,** Boston: Little, Brown, 1988, 465, Schlesinger, **RFK,** 615–; **(Campbell in hotel/to Palm Springs)** Exner as told to Demaris, 286; **("Sinatra wondered")** Jacobs and Stadiem, 205.

537 **Ruby and Reprise: (Assassinations Committee on crime connections)** appen., HSCA, vol. 9, iii, 149, 179; **(Ruby in Chicago)** Blakey and Billings, 283–, Summers, **Lifetime,** 332–; **(associates convened) The Third Decade,** vol. 1, no. 2, Jan. 1985, 15, Seth Kantor, **The Ruby Cover-Up,** New York: Kensington, 1978, 53–; **(discussing promotion)** Robert C. Patterson testimony, Warren Commission Hearings, vol. 14, 129, "Supplemental Correlation Summary," Feb. 25, 1969, FSFBI; **(Shore adviser and publicist for Frank)** Sinatra had recently assigned Shore—with William Woodfield—to draft his responses for a **Playboy** magazine interview. He then reviewed and approved the draft. (int. Billy Woodfield, Freedland, 292, 303–, Gigliotti, 106n6, int. Michael Shore for PITV, Kelley, 307, **Playboy,** Feb. 1963).

538 **Ruby calls to Shore:** appendix, HSCA, vol. 9, 198, 1088, 1098, 1079, Scheim, 220–. Shore was originally from Chicago, and had gone to school with Irwin Weiner and Ruby's brother Earl. "We all grew up on the West Side together," he said in a deposition to the House Assassinations Committee (origins/school—appendix, HSCA, vol. 9, 1044, 1047, 1050; "We all grew"—audiotape

of Michael Shore deposition, Jun. 14, 1978, HSCA, JFK); **(Shore testified calls re union)** Michael Shore deposition, June 14, 1978, Rec. No. 180-10131-10432, HSCA, JFK, appendix, HSCA, vol. 9, 1044, 198; **(AGVA then mob-dominated)** Blakey and Billings, 290, Scheim, 246–.

538 **call to Weiner:** ibid., 1098; **(Weiner background)** Report, HSCA, 159, Summers, **Lifetime,** 342; **(Giancana associate)** Hearings, HSCA, vol. 4, 497, 9, 1057; **(was not/was about union)** ibid., 1043; **(Shore and Woodfield re find attorney and Ruby interview)** Michael Shore deposition, ints. Billy Woodfield, int. Michael Shore for PITV, "Supplemental Correlation Summary," Feb. 25, 1969, FSFBI, appendix, HSCA, vol. 9, 1044, 1074, Alan Adelson, **The Ruby Oswald Affair,** Seattle, WA: Romar, 1988, 2, Blakey and Billings, 325–, John Kaplan and Jon Waltz, **The Trial of Jack Ruby,** New York: Macmillan, 1965, 25–, 31–, 63–; **(Shore never discussed)** int. Michael Shore by PITV.

539 **"things in confidence":** int. Tony Oppedisano.

539 **FS/Giancana continuing relations: (never forgave)** "Samuel M. Giancana," Nov. 5, 1975, FBI 92-3171, rereviewed and released to authors, 2003; **("That motherfucker")** Russo, 449, int. Gus Russo—the authors know the name of the family member, who does not wish to be named; **(socialized)** "Frank Sinatra," Feb. 18, 1972, and "Supplemental Correlation Summary," Feb. 25, 1969, FSFBI, SAC San Diego to Director, May 22, 1975, Sinatra FBI file, rereviewed and released to authors, 2003, FS testimony, Nevada State Gaming Control Commission, Feb. 19, 1981; **(Once, in Las Vegas)** int. Joseph Shimon, Aug. 13, 1977, HSCA, JFK; **(spoke of having Frank killed)** int. Jimmy Roselli, and see Evanier, 152.

539 **Murder of Giancana/arrangements to testify:** Blakey and Billings, 389–. Giancana's associate Johnny Rosselli, who did testify to the committee and who had begun to talk about the Kennedy assassination, was murdered the following year (Blakey and Billings, 383–).

540 **Safire questions: Dallas News,** Jan. 7, 1976. For most of the other questions, see chapter 24, p. 266–.

540 **"Put Your Dreams Away":** Sinatra, **My Father,** 353, Frank Sinatra Jr. commentary on **As I Remember It,** and Tina Sinatra com-

ments on **Sinatra: The Classic Duets,** Sinatra Enterprises, 2002, videotape in authors' collection, Rednour, 79, 249—Sinatra recorded the song in 1944, 1945, 1957, and 1963.

Chapter 28: The Lonely Millionaire

541–542 **Drowning incident:** ints. Brad Dexter, 2001, Ruth Koch. Dexter is credited with the rescue in one of Nancy Sinatra's two published accounts of her father's near-drowning, but not in the other. His name did not appear in the account published in the press the day after the accident. That account, however, was based on a statement by Sinatra's publicist. Piecing together the known details and various accounts, the authors believe that, though others played their part in the rescue, Dexter's was the most important. Ruth Koch was categorical in saying as much when interviewed by the authors in 2004. Fire Department lieutenant George Keawe, one of the rescuers, confirmed the gravity of the incident. He said Sinatra's "face was turning blue. . . . In another five minutes he would have been gone" (Nancy on rescue—Sinatra, **My Father,** 338, and **Legend,** 189; press accounts—**LAT, Hollywood Citizen-News** citing UPI, May 11, 1964; "turning blue"—**Hollywood Citizen-News,** May 11, 1964); **("Did you forget?")** Wilson, **Sinatra,** 184, **Orange County Register,** May 16, 1998.

542–543 **FS power: (Gehman/"The Enigma"/"If you know") Good Housekeeping,** Jul. 1960; **("It would be disturbing")** ibid., Gehman, 219; **("It does not matter")** ibid., 220.

544–546 **starts Reprise: ("I gotta right"/"as if he stood")** Sayers and O'Brien, 90, Jonathan Schwartz, "The Intimate Spirit," liner notes for **The Complete Reprise Studio Recordings; (ripped up)** Granata, 149; **("I helped")** Shaw, **Sinatra,** 283; **("to play")** Granata, 146; **("a new, happier") Billboard,** Nov. 20, 1965; **(creative freedom/money)** Granata, 145–, **Billboard,** Nov. 20, 1965; **(10 albums)** Rednour, 240–. One album, **Great Songs from Great Britain,** was recorded in London in 1962 and released there in 1965. It was not released in the United States until 1993 (Granata, 163, Rednour, 72, 241); **(jazz) High Fidelity,** Aug. 1971, Granata, 168–; **(performed/TV) Where or When?,** ed. Mustazza, **Popular Culture,** 228; **("not so much") Show Business Illustrated,** Sep. 1961;

(Woodfield photo) Lahr, 141, Shaw, **Sinatra,** 286; **(Another photo)** Lahr, 81.

546 **Chairman of the Board: (nickname/disc jockey)** Shaw, **Sinatra,** 317, **Billboard,** Nov. 20, 1965, **LAT,** Aug. 5, 1986.

546 **No Sinatra single:** Sayers and O'Brien, 265–. Seven Sinatra singles made the top forty between 1957 and 1963—"Can I Steal a Little Love," "All the Way," "Witchcraft," "High Hopes," "Talk to Me," "Ol' MacDonald," and "Pocketful of Miracles" (O'Brien and Sayers, 265–); **(Capitol was taking) Variety,** Jul. 31, 1961, Granata, 147, Shaw, **Sinatra,** 311–; **(Reprise in trouble)** Granata, 147, **(Washington, D.C.) Evening Star,** Oct. 14, 1963, Wilson, **Sinatra,** 152.

547 **FS had sold: Variety,** Aug. 7, 1963, **New Yorker,** Nov. 3, 1997, Granata, 147. The total amount involved in the deal was $3 million, or some $18 million at today's rates (**Variety,** Aug. 7, 1963); **(showing check)** Shaw, **Sinatra,** 327, Jacobs and Stadiem, 204; **(owed Warner)** "Correlation Summary," Jun. 8, 1964, FSFBI; **($250,000/15 percent) Look,** Dec. 14, 1965.

547 **nine movies/no more Rat Pack movies:** Of the nine movies, those involving Rat Pack members were **Sergeants 3, Come Blow Your Horn**—featuring a cameo appearance by Dean Martin—**4 for Texas, Robin and the 7 Hoods**—publicized with the risqué subtitle **Who Maid Marian?**—and **Marriage on the Rocks** (O'Brien, 133–74, 214–, and re **Who Maid?,** corr. Daniel O'Brien).

547–548 ***Manchurian Candidate:*** For Sinatra, **Manchurian Candidate** evoked a positive memory of his relationship with President Kennedy. The president had personally intervened to urge that the film be made at a time when United Artists boss Arthur Krim, who happened to be a senior member of the Democratic Party, was obstructing its development. Kennedy viewed the movie in August 1962, before its release in October on the eve of the Cuban Missile Crisis in October.

It was long said that Sinatra ensured that **Candidate** was kept out of circulation for years after Kennedy's assassination. He was supposedly appalled by the possibility that—because it involved the assassination of a presidential candidate—the movie might somehow have inspired events in Dallas. Both the singer and his daughter Nancy, however, maintained that the movie's withdrawal was not of his doing. Similarly, it was said Sinatra insisted on the withdrawal of the 1954 film **Suddenly**, in which he had played a would-be presidential assassin—because Lee Harvey Oswald had supposedly watched the movie on television a few weeks before the assassination in Dallas. Research indicates, however, that **Suddenly** was not shown on local television at the time alleged.

A remake of **Manchurian Candidate**, produced by Tina Sinatra, debuted in 2004 (JFK intervened—**Variety**, Nov. 12, 1987, Feb. 26, 1988, Sinatra with Coplon, 82; JFK viewed—**NYT**, Sep. 14, 2003; **Candidate** withdrawal—e.g., **Variety**, Feb. 8, 1980, O'Brien, 148, and see FS int. on **Larry King Live**, May 13, 1988, Sinatra, **Legend**, 168, **NYT**, Sep. 14, 2003; **Suddenly** withdrawal/Oswald—**Variety**, Nov. 12, 1987, McMillan, 380, Blakey and Billings, 361; **Suddenly** not shown—authors' corr. Gary Mack; **Candidate** remake—Paramount Pictures release, Jul. 2004).

548 ***Candidate* "without doubt":** Yarwood, 104; **(Queen of Diamonds/pool)** FS int. on **Suzy Visits**; **("special assistant")** Hollywood Reporter, Oct. 4, 1963; **(office/orange/photos/bust)** **Newsweek**, Sep. 6, 1965; **(Artanis, etc.)** ibid.

548–549 **planes in 1965:** ibid., int. Johnnie Spotts, Sinatra pilot. One of the planes was soon replaced by a British Hawker-Siddeley jet that Sinatra named **Christina II**, after his daughter Tina. **Christina I** was his yacht (ints. Johnnie Spotts, Bob Neal); **(jet commute)** **Newsweek**, Sep. 6, 1965, **Look**, Dec. 14, 1965; **(handy)** Sinatra with Coplon, 137, Farrow, 81; **(employs seventy-five)** **Life**, Apr. 23, 1965; **(homes)** **Newsweek**, Sep. 6, 1965; **($3.5 million)** **Look**, Dec. 14, 1965; **("lives like royalty")** **Newsweek**, Sep. 6, 1965; **(yacht/barber)** Globe Features notes for William Read Woodfield photos, int. Woodfield.

549–550 **FS generosity/charity: ("over-privileged adult")** Sinatra, **Legend**, 163. Sinatra gave thirty benefit performances in the two months of the 1962 World Tour for Children alone. Between 1965 and 1980, the Nevada State Gaming Commission was told, he made a further 250 appearances for charity. The authors were unable to calculate how many benefits he gave in the course of his long career (thirty in 1962–1965 entries, **Where or When?**; 250—comments of Commissioner Dodge, Hearing, Nevada State Gaming Commission, Feb. 19, 1981); **(World Tour/$6 million)** Shaw, **Entertainer**, 94, Ridgeway, pt. 1, 169, Douglas-

Home, 48–; **(Styne's mother)** Taylor, 123; **(Silvers)** int. Jo Carroll Dennison, **Variety,** Sep. 11, 1947, **Look,** May 14, 1957; **(Napoli)** int. Madeline Pucci; **(Miller)** Friedwald, 39, **McCall's,** Aug. 1989; **(Rich)** Levinson, **Trumpet Blues,** 211, **(Ireland) Sunday Independent,** Apr. 15, 2001; **(Louis)** ed. Vare, 210, **Ladies' Home Journal,** Oct. 1979, **People,** Nov. 21, 1977; **(Cobb)** int. Shirley Ballard, Carpozi, **Sinatra,** 300, Robert Stack with Mark Evans, **Straight Shooting,** New York: Macmillan, 1980, 264; **(Colbert's husband)** Shaw, **Sinatra,** 1, **Newsweek,** Jan. 15, 1968; **(Lee)** corr. Eve Quillen, Peggy Lee, "Frank-Lee," at www.sinatra-ms.com/article1; **(Mercer)** int. Leonora Hornblow.

550–551 **Billie Holiday:** ints. Brad Dexter, George Jacobs, Jacobs and Stadiem, 150–. **"Lady Day": Watertown** liner notes by Ed O'Brien. Sinatra first came upon the song "Lady Day" in August 1969 while recording the album **Watertown.** Oddly, the song's writers had not known that Billie Holiday was affectionately known as "Lady Day." Dissatisfied with his performance of the song on **Watertown,** Sinatra rerecorded it in the fall, and it appeared on the 1971 album **Sinatra and Company** (Friedwald, 442, 436, Rednour, 250).

551–552 **Other kindnesses: (maid's husband) Coronet,** Oct. 1964; **(bootblack) Boxing Monthly,** Jul. 1998, eulogy for FS by Sonny King, St. Viator's Church, Las Vegas, May 27, 1998; **(girl's leg)** int. Jerry Lewis; **(elderly couple)** LAHE, Dec. 25, 1970; **(child burned) McCall's,** Oct. 1974; **(truckload) (Long Beach, CA) Press-Telegram,** May 16, 1998; **("send them a nickel")** Sinatra with Coplon, 136; **("The one condition") (Long Beach, CA) Press-Telegram,** May 16, 1998; **(*padrone*)** e.g., Barzini, **Caesar,** 69–, Sterling, 48, Davis, **Mafia Dynasty,** 164–; **("In a certain way")** int. Peter Duchin.

552–553 **fiftieth birthday, etc.: (Talese/*Esquire* article)** "Frank Sinatra Has a Cold," **Esquire,** Apr. 1966; **("all set up")** int. of Gay Talese by David Talbot of **Salon,** kindly supplied to authors; **(article acclaimed)** eds. Petkov and Mustazza, 90, "The Greatest Story Ever Told," anniversary edition supplement to **Esquire; ("As a singer")** Douglas-Home, 42; **("try to nail")** int. of Gay Talese by David Talbot; **(NBC/CBS/major stories) Esquire,** Apr. 1966, **Where or When?** Howlett, 135, **Life,** Apr. 23, **Billboard,** Nov. 20, **Newsweek,** Nov. 29, **Look,** Nov. 30, 1965.

553 ***September of My Years:*** **September of My Years** was followed within months by **A Man and His Music,** packed with songs identified with Sinatra.

553–555 **voice lower/Camels: Billboard,** Nov. 20, 1965. Sinatra had previously smoked Lucky Strikes, but had switched to Camels by the mid-1960s (Strikes—Kahn, 113, Douglas-Home, photo caption; Camels—ints. Mort Viner, Tony Mottola, Hamill, 16); **("The silken") High Fidelity,** Aug. 1971; **(birthday party/"Tit Willow")** Sinatra, **Legend,** 197, Freedland, 319, "Tit Willow" lyrics for Nancy Jr., MHL; **(toupees/transplant) Esquire,** Apr. 1966, **Newsweek,** Jan. 19, 1987, Ragano and Raab, 82; **("nubby and raw") Esquire,** Apr. 1966; **(Jacobs/"I was ushered") Open House with Gloria Hunniford,** Channel 5 (UK), May 12, 2002, and tape of unid. BBC Radio 4 program, supplied to authors by Peggy Connelly; **("I'm a symmetrical") Life,** Apr. 23, 1965.

556–557 **FS and rock 'n' roll: ("Frank Sinatra lamenting")** Allen Ginsberg, **The Fall of America,** New York: City Lights, 1974, 4, Gigliotti, preface; **(Beatles/73 million)** Beatles, **The Beatles Anthology,** London: Cassell, 2000, 119, "1,000 Days of Beatle Mania," **Mojo Special Edition,** 2002, 89; **(FS "defeated rock") Newsweek,** Feb. 26, 1962; **(Beatles top singles/albums)** Chet Flippo, **McCartney,** London: Sidgwick and Jackson, 1988, 182; **(Capitol/Livingston)** "1,000 Days," 107; **("We came out of nowhere")** Beatles, 119; **("Long hair"/"He didn't care"/smash radio)** Jacobs and Stadiem, 233, 7; **("He genuinely")** int. Rock Brynner; **(repelled)** Taraborrelli, 427; **("miss the point") Look,** Oct. 31, 1967; **(Lennon/"Peggy Lee")** Beatles, 198; **(McCartney/"if anyone")** Beatles, 22, Flippo, 20.

557 **"I thought I was writing":** Beatles, 22. As well as having referred to writing the song for Sinatra, McCartney has separately suggested he had his own father in mind. His father was in his late fifties at the time his son has said he wrote the song. "When I'm Sixty-Four" was not copyrighted, however, until 1967 (Flippo, 20, Beatles, 360).

558–559 **"We must stop": Life,** Apr. 23, 1965; **(Starr's wife)** corr. Tita Cahn, lyrics kindly supplied to authors by Tita Cahn, **Rolling Stone,** Jun. 25, 1998; **(McCartney jet)** Flippo, 231; **(Harrison guest)** LAT, Nov. 19, 1968; **("Something"/"Yesterday")** Rednour, 85; **(praise)** LAT, Aug. 28, 1975, Dec. 1, 2001,

New York, Apr. 28, 1980, FS monologue at Caesars Palace, May 5, 1978, audiotape in authors' collection; **("it inspired"/"He needs") Esquire,** Apr. 1966.

Chapter 29: The Child Bride

560 **Ava and FS: (Vegas opening) Los Angeles Examiner,** Feb. 7, 1961, Shaw, **Sinatra,** 282; **(Los Angeles)** LAHE, Mar. 28, 1962.

560–561 **Madrid/"They went":** int. Dan Arney. "Dinner parties Ava gave," her friend Betty Wallers remembered, "often stretched to twenty-four- or even thirty-six-hour parties, and men used to drop exhausted like soldiers on a forced march. . . . She would call me at 3:00 a.m. and ask me to a 'marvelous party.' She would introduce me to a 'great flamenco singer' and it would turn out to be the elevator boy" (Higham, **Ava,** 208, and see Flamini, 242–); **(plane/"dry out")** ints. Dan Arney, Ben Tatar; **("Can you imagine?")** int. Sonny King.

561–562 **Other women: ("take out"/"I brought")** Hellerman with Renner, 101; **(hatcheck girl) Life,** Apr. 23, 1965; **(whore)** SAC Salt Lake City to SAC Los Angeles, Nov. 3, 1960, FBI 62-4867-9, "File Review & Summary Check," Sep. 19, 1960, FBI 100-41413-121, int. Al Porcino; **("First, there were"/"I don't understand") Good Housekeeping,** Jul. 1960; **("I'm supposed") Life,** Apr. 23, 1965.

562 **Prowse: (met *Can-Can*) Los Angeles Examiner,** Nov. 27, 1960; **(Prowse background) Coronet,** Oct. 1961, **(London) Times,** Sep. 16, 1996; **("He was singing")** int. Shirley MacLaine; **(British colonial family, etc.) Coronet,** Oct. 1961.

563–564 **"amazingly kind":** Freedland, 267. Juliet Prowse was interviewed by the author Michael Freedland shortly before her death, at the age of fifty-nine, in 1996. The quotations used here were first published in Freedland's Sinatra biography **All the Way,** published in the UK (Michael Freedland, **All the Way,** London: Orion, 1998, esp. chap. 20, and ints. and corr. Michael Freedland. The authors thank him for permission to quote from interviews.); **(knitted/gardened/painted)** ibid., 267, 283; **("She smothers") Newsweek,** May 25, 1998; **(proposed)** Freedland, 267, M/G int. of Jay Bernstein; **(FS to South Africa)** Jacobs and Stadiem, 170; **(parents to L.A.) Photoplay,** Apr. 1962, but see

Parsons, 158–; **(drunk/"throw things"/"never quarreled"/stop working)** Freedland, 267–; **("the big love")** ibid., 280; **(street corner/cartwheels/"really like a father")** ibid., 268.

564 **"I knew":** ibid., 281. Prowse also had a dalliance with Elvis Presley while both were performing in the movie **GI Blues.** This too, she said, infuriated Sinatra (**Los Angeles Examiner Magazine,** Sep. 18, **LAT,** Oct. 30, 1960, and Freedland, 282).

565 **FS and Monroe: (met 1954)** int. Milton Greene, 1984.

565 **bizarre incident/"It looked"/rushed into bedroom:** Summers, **Goddess,** 153–. Author Anthony Summers covered the break-in episode, generally known as the Wrong Door Raid, in his 1985 Monroe biography, **Goddess.** It now seems that Sinatra, not DiMaggio, recruited the detectives. An interview with the late former IRS agent John Daley, in particular, buttressed the allegation that Sinatra was one of those who broke into the apartment. Another interview, in 2002, further strengthened the claim. A former detective, the late John Danoff, moreover, told Summers he was involved—apparently in 1959 or early 1960—when DiMaggio tried to catch Sinatra with Monroe (Summers covered—Summers, **Goddess,** 153–; FS recruited—Robin Moore and Gene Schoor, **Marilyn & Joe DiMaggio,** New York: Manor, 1977, 222–, Jacobs and Stadiem, 95; Daley—int. John Daley, 1983; 2002 interview—int. with detectives' colleague, who is still working and requested anonymity; DiMaggio tried—int. John Danoff, 1983).

566 **Marilyn: (solicitous/"Maf"/use his house)** ibid., 312; **(Allan)** int. the late Rupert Allan, 1983; **("protector"/"little friend")** int. Sonny King; **("As physically beautiful")** Fisher with Fisher, 73, and see Earl Wilson, **Show Business Laid Bare,** New York: Signet, 1974, 63–.

566–568 **yacht/"I remember":** int. Jeanne Martin, Summers, **Goddess,** 313–. Author Summers first described the trip in his book **Goddess.** Jeanne Martin kept the album of photographs Sinatra sent his guests as a souvenir, and in 2001 kindly provided the authors with the photograph of Sinatra and Monroe aboard the yacht; **("She was taking")** Summers, **Goddess,** 434; **(Pepitone/"He pulled")** ibid., 314; **(Johnson/"the vapors")** Edwin Hoyt, **Marilyn: The Tragic Venus,** Radnor, PA: Chilton, 1973, 239; **("deeply saddened")** Summers, **Goddess,** 422, and see Fisher with Fisher, 254; **("in shock")** Jacobs and Stadiem, 173;

(Barred from funeral) int. Inez Melson, 1983, Summers, **Goddess,** 482; **("Who?")** Summers, **Goddess,** 310.

568–569 **Prowse break-up: (popped question/said yes/broke off)** Freedland, 281–, **LAT,** Jan. 10, Feb. 23, **Time,** Jan. 19, **New York Daily News,** Jan. 30, 1962. Just days before the announcement that he was engaged to Prowse, Sinatra had been in Australia with the actress Dorothy Provine. He had been seeing Provine during the hiatus in his courtship of Prowse (**Parade Magazine,** Apr. 1, **Time,** Jan. 19, 1962, Jacobs and Stadiem, 152, int. Dan Arney); **("He was")** int. Shirley MacLaine; **(Ava telegram)** Freedland, 282.

569–570 **Ava 1962–64: ("stayed very, very"/"If a pretty")** Gardner, 267; **(both in Italy)** O'Brien, **Film Guide,** 166–, **New York Daily News,** Sep. 10, 1964, Wayne, 234; **(Ava and Scott)** Gardner, 254–, John Huston, **An Open Book,** New York: Da Capo, 1994, 328–, Flamini, 262–; **("Frank and I")** int. Brad Dexter.

570–573 **Farrow affair: (parents' separate bedrooms/Ava affair)** For Gardner's affair with John Farrow, see page 166, **supra. (met FS/"you stay away")** Farrow, 78; **(FS met 1964)** O'Brien, **Film Guide,** 167; **(Parsons godmother)** Farrow, 34; **(Cukor godfather)** Edward Epstein and Joe Morella, **Mia,** London: Robert Hale, 1991, 35; **("wide-eyed sprite") Life,** May 5, 1967; **("waif") Mirabella,** Mar. 1997; **("heartbreaking") Photoplay,** Mar. 1965; **("impossibly naïve")** Farrow, 118; **("afraid of men") Photoplay,** Mar. 1965; **(only time in bed)** Farrow, 73, and see 80; **(5′5″ /20-20-20/falsies) Life,** May 5, 1967, Farrow, 72; **(Dalí/party)** Farrow, 66; **("a very clever")** Kelley, 345—Edie Goetz was the wife of producer William; **(Minnelli/"stronger")** Farrow, 94, unid. clip, "Mia Farrow's Secret Scheme to Keep Her Frank," Mar. 1968, MHL; **(FS initiative)** Farrow, 78–; **(screening/held hand/asked to fly)** ibid., 79–; **("googly eyes") GQ,** Nov. 1999; **(badgered FS)** Kelley, 344; **(arrived house/photos of Ava)** Farrow, 87; **("the cat slept alone")** ibid., 83; **(weekends/painted/sketched/crosswords)** ibid., 85–, unid. clip, "Mia Has Already Passed Sinatra's Marriage Test," Aug. 1965, MHL; **("diamond koala")** Farrow, 98; **(cigarette case)** Epstein and Morella, 80; **(Thunderbird)** Sinatra, **My Father,** 202; **("Charlie Brown")** int. Leonora Hornblow; **("Angel Face"/"Baby Face")** Farrow, 88; **("what a beautiful")** ibid., 90; **("The Impossible Dream") Look,** Oct. 31, 1967, Rednour, 52; **(kept Mia to him-**

self) Farrow, 89; **(not introduce to children)** ibid., Sinatra with Coplon, 112; **(not at fiftieth)** ibid., 111, Kristi Groteke with Marjorie Rosen, **Mia & Woody**, New York: Carroll and Graf, 1994, 53; **("Frank was really plastered")** int. Sonny King; **(befriended)** Sinatra with Coplon, 112, Sinatra, **My Father**, 203.

573–574 **"Frank had decided"/set included/"kids' table": Life**, May 5, 1967, Farrow, 91. Other Sinatra regulars were playwright Leonard Gershe, Gregory and Veronique Peck, actor Martin Gabel and his TV personality wife, Arlene Francis, and the writer Harry Kurnitz. Guests also included producer Leland Hayward and his wife, Pamela Hayward, a future U.S. ambassador to France. The men and women in the group were not all as old as suggested by **Life**'s interviewee, but they were indeed past their youth.

574–576 **3 compartments, etc.:** Farrow, 91–, 100–, 110; **("She would call")** int. Sonny King; **(throw money/Jack Daniel's)** Farrow, 91–, 100, 110; **("interminable"/hookers)** ibid., 92–, 112; **(whores who resembled Mia)** Jacobs and Stadiem, 8–; **(cruise) Time**, Aug. 20, 1965, Farrow, 95; **(Martin/Scotch)** ibid., 90; **("chasm"/went off traveling)** ibid., 101; **(MacRae)** Sheila MacRae with Paul Jeffers, **Hollywood Mother of the Year**, New York: Birch Lane, 1992, 158–; **("beautiful brunette")** "Joseph Fischetti," May 6, 1966, FBI 92-3024-88, "Supplemental Correlation Summary," Feb. 25, 1969, FBI 62-23219-60.

576 **Engagement/marriage: (ask to marry/ring/$85,000)** Farrow, 101–, Sinatra, **My Father**, 203, Kelley, 355; **("Marry Mia?") Chicago Daily News**, May 8–9, 1976. In July 1966, however, it was Farrow's mother who announced the engagement, declaring herself "delighted" (**NYT**, Jul. 14, 1966); **(not "emotionally prepared") Photoplay**, Oct. 1965.

576 **"My son is just": LAHE**, Aug. 13, 1965. Sinatra's mother had always gotten on with Ava Gardner, and was still welcoming her at her home in New Jersey as late as the mid-1960s (int. Ken Roberts, Jacobs and Stadiem, 98); **("couldn't seem to make up") Hollywood Citizen-News**, Apr. 24, 1967, **LAHE**, Aug. 22, 1965; **("He wanted")** int. Shirley MacLaine.

577 **"The Ava eyes brighten":** Sciacca, 19; Ava Gardner's comment was made on September 30, 1966, following the New York premiere of her film **The Bible** the previous night. Another source quoted her as having said, "I always knew Frank always (sic)

wanted a boy with a cunt." Gardner was drinking heavily during the interview with Reed, and may have delivered the barb in the second, cruder version—Reed may have cleaned the comment up for publication. Mia Farrow separately quoted Gardner as declaring that Mia "was the child she and Frank never had" (Ava's comment—Rex Reed, **Do You Sleep in the Nude?** New York: New American Library, 1968, 70; premiere—**NYT**, Sep. 29, 1966; "was the child"—Farrow, 95).

577–579 **continued to see Ava:** int. Peter Levinson; **("I went up")** Hellerman with Renner, 102; **("I guess")** Jacobs and Stadiem, 231–; **("The thing that triggered it")** int. Brad Dexter; **(dined with Peggy Connelly)** int. Peggy Connelly; **(MacRae)** MacRae with Jeffers, 175; **(prostitute)** Jacobs and Stadiem, 234; **(wedding) Hollywood Citizen-News,** Jul. 20, **Life,** Jul. 27, 1966; **(not told family)** Sinatra with Coplon, 113–, Farrow, 102; **("call Miss G.")** Kelley, 356; **("child bride")** Graham, 125; **("a little bit like")** Farrow, 118.

579 **differences with Mia: ("the Swinger and the Flower Child")** Sinatra, **My Father,** 202; **("cute"/Daisy)** Sinatra with Coplon, 116; **("When Frank walked")** int. Sonny King; **(Mia "was dancing")** int. Sandra Giles; **(Mia wanted children)** Sinatra with Coplon, 121, Epstein and Morrella, 152, **Life,** May 5, 1967; **(Vietnam)** ibid., Farrow, 115.

579 **Bolling dalliance:** Gossip also linked Sinatra at the time with the actress Jill St. John, with whom he had reportedly had a dalliance in 1963 (Bolling—int. in **Globe,** Dec. 23, 1997, O'Brien, **Film Guide,** 184; St. John, 1967—O'Brien, 184, Jacobs and Stadiem, 12; St. John, 1963—**Newsweek,** Oct. 28, 1963, Hellerman with Renner, 99, Wilson, **Sinatra,** 178).

580 **cage:** unid. article by Debbie Sherwood, Mar., 1968, MHL.

580 **Rift re career/"To lose"/Rudin/India/divorce:** Farrow, 107–, 112, 120–, 134–, and see Wilson, **Sinatra,** 227, **Newsweek,** Oct. 16, 1967. Burt Lancaster, who became close to Sinatra, said the singer "never mentioned" Mia in the years immediately after the divorce. Farrow has said, though, that he "remained a true friend, always there when I needed him." She recalled that in 1992, when her liaison with Woody Allen disintegrated amidst ugly allegations about Allen's sexual behavior, the Sinatra family rallied around her. "Frank," she wrote, "even offered to break Woody's legs." One measure of Farrow's lasting affection for Sina-

tra is that she named her Vietnamese-born adopted daughter Frankie-Minh ("never mentioned"—**Coronet,** Mar., 1972; "true friend"—**Philadelphia Inquirer,** May 17, 1998, and see Groteke with Rosen, 54; rallied/"even offered"/Frankie-Minh—Farrow, 280, 309).

580–581 **rumors of abuse:** Epstein and Morella, 137; **(Susskind/ "showed up")** Kelley, 370, 533; **(Mia repeatedly said)** LAT, Sep. 26, 1986, Groteke with Rosen, 54; **("If there's one guy") Photoplay,** Apr. 1965.

581 **Gabor:** Gabor with Leigh, 165. Gabor's reference to Mulholland Drive apparently relates to the house Sinatra had built in the 1950s on Bowmont Drive atop Coldwater Canyon. It had gated access to Mulholland. Other Los Angeles–area homes during the Farrow relationship included a rented apartment on Doheny Drive, a rented house on Sunset Boulevard, and—following the wedding—a Tudor-style house on Copa De Oro. For several months in the early 1970s, after the alleged powder-room incident and before his marriage to Barbara Marx, Sinatra had an affair with Zsa Zsa's sister Eva (Mulholland/Bowmont—**LAT,** Oct. 1, Dec. 16, 1989, Feb. 18, 25, Mar. 4, 1990, Sinatra with Coplon, 102, 187; Doheny—Farrow, 85; Sunset—Sinatra with Coplon, 112, Jacobs and Stadiem, 3; De Oro—Farrow, 104, Sinatra, 203, Sinatra with Coplon, 117; Eva—Gabor with Leigh, 166, **TV Guide,** Oct. 30, 1993, and see Sinatra with Coplon, 160).

581–582 **Rape allegation: (incident)** ints. Susan Murphy; the authors found Susan Murphy's account credible. As mentioned earlier, Sinatra used messages sent across restaurants to initiate contact with Sandra Giles, Judith Campbell, and Michael Hellerman's date. The same year he spotted Murphy in a restaurant, he used a similar ploy to approach the actress Patty Duke.

The industrialist Daniel Schwartz and others Murphy mentioned were indeed part of the Sinatra circle at the time. The ambience and activity she described is consistent with the authors' wider research. Murphy had been briefly married in her midteens, and was not without sexual experience. Yet even in 2003, when interviewed by the authors, she spoke of what happened that night as a "horrific" memory. Murphy is not now the woman's name (Duke—Patty Duke and Kenneth Turan, **Call Me**

Anna, New York: Bantam, 1987, 194–; Schwartz/FS circle—e.g., Sinatra, **My Father,** 218).

Chapter 30: Out of Control

586 **"A star":** CBS News special.

587 **edict: Look,** May 28, 1957.

588 **threats: ("Let me tell")** Kelley, 528; **(Prowse/"You'd better get")** (London) **Observer,** Dec. 13, 1998, Freedland, 281; **(Bolling re potential beating) Globe,** Dec. 23, 1997.

588–589 **threats/attacks on press: ("It's Sinatra")** Kelley, 370; **("In some segments"/Bacon friendly)** LAHE, Dec, 7, 1979, int. James Bacon, Freedland, 316, Shaw, **Entertainer,** 12.

589 **Vandergrift & Finkelstein:** A claim that Sinatra ordered his driver to "Run the bastard down!" was not substantiated. Finkelstein disowned it. The columnist Earl Wilson looked into the story, but could not resolve various inconsistencies (**LAT, (LA) Mirror-News,** Nov. 4, 1958, "Correlation Summary," Jun. 8, 1964, FSFBI, Wilson, **Sinatra,** 323–).

589–590 **throw *Time* journalist:** int. the late Billy Woodfield; **(wrestled photographer)** LAHE, Aug. 13, 1962; **(Spain/FS charged)** LAHE, Sep. 18, 21, LAT, Sep. 21, 1964; **(Paris/cherry bombs) LAHE,** Jul. 8, 17, **Time,** Jul. 17, 1964.

590 **"catastrophic"/"As the paparazzi's":** int. and corr. Rock Brynner. The companion in question was Jilly Rizzo, Frank's constant companion from the late 1950s on; **(weapon of choice)** SAC Miami to SA (deleted), Mar. 27, 1967, FBI 92-99-876, Kashner and MacNair, 293, **American Weekly,** Nov. 12, 1961, Farrow, 103; **(Engels)** Wilson, **Sinatra,** 224, Epstein and Morella, 110, LAT, Jul. 28, 1966.

591–593 **violent episodes: (Irwin/"very much afraid")** LAT, Feb. 28, Mar. 2, 27, **Hollywood Citizen-News,** Mar. 9, 1957; **("Frank took"/"Frank didn't")** int. Milt Ebbins; **(second parking attendant incident/"bodyguard"/FS settled) Hollywood Citizen-News,** Jul. 20, 1960, **Reno Evening Gazette,** Mar. 15, 1962, unid. articles circa 1960, FBI LA 62-4867-2, 3, 4, and 5, Gehman, 28, Kelley, 275–; **(Del Monte Lodge)** LAT, Jan. 21, Feb. 2, 1964; **("Whenever Frank")** int. Rock Brynner.

593–594 **Dunne: (FS drunk)** Kelley, 529, Bacall, 287, int. Peter Duchin, Lazar with Tapert, 159; **(abused wife)** ints. Dominick Dunne, Peter Duchin, Kelley, 529, Bacall, 287, **New Yorker,** May 25, 1998, Peter Duchin, **Ghost of a Chance,** New York: Random House, 1996, 270–, Lazar with Tapert, 158–; **(attack at Daisy)** int. Dominick Dunne, Dominick Dunne, **The Way We Lived Then,** New York: Crown, 1999, 131–.

594–595 **FS and alcohol: (flag)** Granata, 169; **(Alka-Seltzer)** Zehme, 9.

595 **"Jackie Daniel's": Esquire,** Mar. 1994. The oft-quoted statement "I'm for **anything** that gets you through the night, be it prayer, tranquilizers or a bottle of Jack Daniel's" did not necessarily originate with Sinatra. It first appeared in "his" 1963 **Playboy** interview that, as reported earlier, had been written for him by Reprise executive Mike Shore and journalist Billy Woodfield (**Playboy,** Feb. 1963); **(dressing room)** smokinggun.com; **(blazer/crest)** (**London**) **Daily Mail,** undat., May 1962; **(Squires)** int. office of Roger Brashears, Jack Daniel's Inc.; **(acre)** Perella, 274.

595–596 **carrying glass:** In Rat Pack days, according to Tina Sinatra, the glass her father carried on stage for the early show usually contained only iced tea or juice. During the second show, however, it might contain alcohol. Sources differ on what the glass contained in later years. Sinatra is said to have banned alcohol from the recording studio until a session was completed (iced tea—Sinatra with Coplon, 99; sources differ—Friedwald, 488, (**Irish**) **Sunday Independent,** Apr. 15, 2001; banned—Jacobs and Stadiem, 124); **(good for voice)** corr. Ed Walters, by permission; **("gasoline") Life,** Apr. 23, 1965; **(chocolate) Philadelphia Inquirer,** undat., May 1998; **("You're not drunk")** Zehme, 109; **("Drink, Dickie")** "Bird," as reported earlier, was Rat Pack-speak for penis. The friend was actor Dick Bakalyan (**Esquire,** Apr. 1966); **("bombed")** FS int. by Arlene Francis, Oct. 1, 1977, WOR (NY); **(Hawaii/"a bottle each")** int. Jack Cione; **("I feel sorry")** excerpts from Bill Zehme, "The Way You Wear Your Hat," at www.enteract.com, **The Rat Pack,** Praeses Productions for A&E, 1999, and see **Vibe,** Sep. 1995; **("I don't trust")** FS monologue, Caesars Palace, May 5, 1978, videotape in authors' collection. On the videotape, it is obvious that Sinatra was under the weather.

596–599 **quit drinking:** Yarwood, 32, Jacobs and Stadiem, 58, Farrow, 93; **("Drink, drink . . .")** Sinatra, **My Father,** xix; **(not big drinker)** ints. George Jacobs, George Sidney, Milt Ebbins, Sinatra, **My Father,** 137; **("More times than not") Ladies' Home Journal,** Nov. 1973; **("In all the long")** int. Leonora Hornblow; **(runs in families)** John Cooney, **Under the Weather: Alcohol Abuse and Alcoholism,** Dublin: Gill and Macmillan, 1991, 13; **("drinking man")** Yarwood, 52; **("a case of beer")** int. Marilyn Sinatra; **(doctor warned)** int. Peggy Connelly; **(Cahn)** int. Gloria Cahn Franks; **(Cooper/"someone") Las Vegas Review-Journal,** May 16, 1998; **(Hendrickson) Las Vegas Review-Journal,** May 16, 1998; **(Deutsch)** int. Armand Deutsch; **(FS admitted)** Zehme, 11; **("He needed it")** int. Leonora Hornblow; **("better professors"/"the outrageous"/"alcoholic shit")** ints. Rock Brynner; **(Schwartz treatment)** Jonathan Schwartz, **All in Good Time,** New York: Random House, 2004, 272–; **("a textbook case") Vanity Fair,** Jul. 1998, and see **New Yorker,** Nov. 3, 1997; **("There is little")** corr. and int. Dr. Robert Morse; **("Sinatra was an alcoholic")** int. James Graham. Graham is the author of **The Secret History of Alcoholism,** Shaftsbury, Dorset, UK: Element, 1996; **("personality change")** corr. and int. Dr. Robert Morse; **("Sinatra would get")** int. Mort Viner; **("Something would")** int. Bob Neal; **("The trick")** Lazar with Tapert, 158; **("It was predictable")** int. Rock Brynner.

600–601 **Weisman: (incident)** LAHE, Jun. 10, 11, 12, 13, 14, **NYT,** Jun. 11, **Hollywood Citizen-News,** Jun. 11, 28, **LAT,** Jun. 12, **Variety,** Jun. 13, 30, **Chicago's American,** Oct. 2, 1966, Jacobs and Stadiem, 230–, ints. Jeanne Martin, Carol Weisman Wilson, Kelley, 353–, Freedland, 330; **("in hiding")** LAHE, Jun. 10, 1966; **("We all drove")** Jacobs and Stadiem, 231; **("the only time")** Kelley, 354; **("no evidence") Variety,** Jun. 30, 1966; **("The guy was cursing")** Time, Jun. 17, 1966; **("I at no time") Chicago's American,** Oct. 2, 1966; **("discolored") LAT,** Jun. 12, 1966; **(fists or ashtray)** LAHE, Jun. 11, and see **NYT,** Jun. 11, 1966; **("some man") Hollywood Citizen-News,** Jun. 11, 1966.

602 **"to vent"/"I was standing"/*threw telephone:*** Kelley, 353. The valet George Jacobs, however, wrote: "Jilly . . . began beating Weisman in the head with one of the phones." "Jilly" is a reference to Sinatra's close friend and almost constant companion Jilly Rizzo, described in a later chapter. (Jacobs and Stadiem, 230, and

see 14) **("they just beat")** int. Carol Weisman Wilson; **("We were a little") Look,** Dec. 26, 1967, in an interview with Oriana Fallaci; **(Jeanne Martin nodding)** int. Jeanne Martin.

603 **Dexter/"He went crazy":** int. Brad Dexter, 2001, **Esquire,** Nov. 1999, and see Kelley, 356.

603 **Mason:** M/G int. of Jackie Mason, int. Myrna Lee Falk, Kelley, 364–. The author Kitty Kelley also interviewed Mason, in 1983 (Kelley, 364–, 533).

604 **FS in Miami 1967: (Fischetti/women)** SA (deleted) to SAC Miami, Mar. 16, 1967, FBI 92-99-868, Mar. 27, 1967, FBI 92-99-876, May 3, 1967, FBI 92-99-886, and May 4, 1967, FBI 92-99-889; **(smashed furniture, etc.)** ibid., SA (deleted) to SAC Miami, Jun. 9, 1967, FBI 92-99-902, and see "Sands Hotel," Nov. 11, 1967, FBI 92-6314-32.

604–605 **Shecky Greene: (drinking hard)** Kelley, 368, 533, SA (deleted) to SAC Miami, Mar. 16, 1967, FBI 92-99-868; **("As bad shape"/acid remarks) GQ,** Nov. 1999; **("things got"/"the bandage"/"Frank had so many")** Kelley, 368, and see **GQ,** Nov. 1999, "Joseph J. Fischetti," Jul. 28, 1967, FBI 92-3024-92.

605 **FS enraged/"Feeling no pain":** SA (deleted) to SAC Miami, May 3, 1967, FBI 92-99-887.

605–609 **Sands incident: (Hughes buys Sands)** Elaine Davenport and Paul Eddy, **The Hughes Papers,** London: André Deutsch, 1977, 76–, Charles Higham, **Howard Hughes: The Secret Life,** London: Pan, 1993, 279–; **(Hughes rival)** Gardner, 158; **(FS with astronauts)** Sinatra, **Legend,** 203; **(owed house/cut credit/Cohen row/all quotes unless specified)** Lt. W. Conger and Sgt. W. Adams to Sheriff R. Lamb, "Incident at the Sands Hotel," Sep. 18, 1967—kindly supplied to authors by David Robb, and see Bishop to DeLoach, Sep. 11, 1967, FSFBI, "Sands Hotel," Nov. 22, 1967, FBI 92-6314-32; **(Anka "got up")** eds. A. J. Hopkins and K. D. Evans, **The First 100: Portraits of the Men and Women Who Shaped Las Vegas,** Las Vegas: Huntington Press, 1999, 164; **("gonna break"/"I built") LAT,** Sep. 12, 1967, **Time,** Sep. 22, 1967; **(Mia/golf cart)** Farrow, 100–; **(Palm Springs/drinking)** Wilson, **Show Business Nobody Knows,** 20–, int. Ken Roberts; **(Cohen incident described)** Levy, 88–, **LAT,** Dec. 30, 1986; **("bewildered"/speech "unclear")** Farrow, 110–; **("get" Cohen)** int. Sonny King in **Sinatra: Good Guy, Bad Guy; ("In that town")** int. Ed Walters;

("just an argument") FS testimony to Nevada Gaming Control Board, Feb. 11, 1981 on Giuliano audiotape; **(FS call to Alo/"Jimmy was sitting")** int. Ken Roberts, Jimmy Roselli; **(contract with Caesars)** press release, Sep. 11, 1967, Sands Hotel Collection, University of Nevada, Las Vegas, **LAHE**, Sep. 12, **Variety**, Sep. 13, **Newsweek**, Sep. 25, 1967.

609 **Lees "All his jokes": High Fidelity**, May 1967.

Chapter 31: Looking for an Exit

611–612 **"Strangers in the Night": ("I don't want")** int. Brad Dexter, 2001; **("stick that violin")** Eve Quillen, **My Life in Shorts,** Las Vegas: self-published, 2003, 235; **("That's the worst")** corr. Ed O'Brien, Ric Ross re Concert for the Americas, Aug. 20, 1982; **("If you like")** FS monologue at Meadowlands concert, Dec. 12, 1983, supplied to authors by Ed O'Brien; **("You *still* like it") McCall's,** Aug. 1983; **("Just where my pants")** (Long Beach, CA) **Southland Sunday**, Mar. 10, 1974; **("dreck")** eds. Petkov and Mustazza, 140; **("lounge lizard") Esquire**, Dec. 1987; **("bad scatting . . . Alistair Cooke")** ibid.; **("He'd make fun")** int. Armand Deutsch, **McCall's,** Aug. 1983.

612 **number one:** Rednour, 11. "Strangers in the Night" originated as the score for the 1966 movie **A Man Could Get Killed,** with James Garner and Melina Mercouri. Sinatra's last number one single had been "Learnin' the Blues," in 1955. Once "Strangers" became a hit, it was tacked onto the front of the Sinatra album currently in the works—which duly went on sale as **Strangers in the Night** and became a number one album (movie—Granata, 180–, **A Man Could Get Killed** entry, imdb.com; previous No. 1—Rednour, 11; album—Granata, 181, Rednour, 249); **(fifteen weeks)** Sayers and O'Brien, 266; **(four Grammys)** ibid., 279, and see **Goldmine,** May 3, 1991; **("Michelle")** Sayers and O'Brien, 280.

613–614 **"My Way": ("I was thrilled")** int. Al Viola; **("national anthem")** Wilson, **Sinatra,** 3; **(Anka brought/"kooky"/"really had")** FS int. by Sid Mark, "Fridays with Frank," WWDB (Philadelphia), Dec. 31, 1979, audiotape in authors' collection; **("all him") Newsweek,** May 25, 1998; **("five words")** Frank Sinatra Jr. commentary, **As I Remember It; ("surly roar") Atlantic Monthly,** Jan. 1984; **("something Hitler")** (London)

Observer, May 17, 1998; **("the temper tantrums")** www.salon.com, Feb. 7, 1997, Vowell, 159–; **("Every time")** Granata, xvii; **("little Arab")** FS monologue, Caesars Palace, May 5, 1978; **("embarrassment"/"overplayed") Newsweek,** May 25, 1998, and see **New York Daily News,** Jan. 22, 1978.

614 **"My Way" not to top:** "My Way" reached only number twenty-seven in the **Billboard** Top 100 and vanished from the list after eight weeks. It was nominated for a 1969 Grammy—for Best Contemporary Male Vocal—but the award went to Harry Nilsson for "Everybody's Talkin'." In the U.K., however, "My Way" stayed in the top fifty for an astonishing 122 weeks. The original French hit on which Anka based the song was "Comme d'habitude," written by Jacques Revaux and Giles Thibaut and sung by Claude François (O'Brien with Wilson, 153, Sayers and O'Brien, 281, **(London) Observer,** May 17, 1998, Joy Williams, "Frank Sinatra," www.artistwd.com/joyzine).

614 **unsettled musically: ("How's your bird?")** Granata, 190; **("Some Enchanted Evening")** Rednour, 84, **Esquire,** Dec. 1987, Friedwald, 432.

614 **"Gunga Din":** Stan Cornyn with Paul Scanlon, **Exploding: The Highs, Hits, Hype, Heroes & Hustlers of Warner Music Group,** New York: Harper Entertainment, 2002, 74–, Sayers and O'Brien, 127, Ridgway, pt. 2, 277. The theme of "Gunga Din," transplanted from British Colonial India to Utah, had served as the inspiration for Sinatra's 1961 movie **Sergeants 3.** The movie flopped. Author Anthony Summers listened to the unreleased recording of "Gunga Din" courtesy of Ed O'Brien (Ringgold and McCarty, 177–, O'Brien, 138–).

615 **Jobim:** The two collections are **Francis Albert Sinatra and Antonio Carlos Jobim,** released in 1967, and **Sinatra and Company,** which appeared in 1971. Jobim's work features on only one side of the 1971 album, as the only published part of what was initially planned as a full second Sinatra-Jobim collection (O'Brien with Wilson, 150–, Rednour, 245); **(*A Man Alone*)** Friedwald, 437–; **(*Watertown*/"one more entry")** ibid., 442.

615 **"Fly Me to the Moon":** Research indicates that "Fly Me to the Moon" was not, as stated by Sinatra's daughter Nancy and the song's arranger Quincy Jones, played from the surface of the moon during the first lunar landing in July 1969. The authors contacted **Apollo 11** astronaut Buzz Aldrin, who has been cited by Jones as

saying he played a tape of the song after the landing. Aldrin responded saying that he had not played the song during the flight. According to the NASA History Office, however, the song **was** played during the **Apollo 10**'s earlier orbital flight. Andrew Chaikin's book on the **Apollo** voyages says the same, and states that astronaut Cernan played the tape (Nancy claim—Sinatra, **My Father,** 365; Jones claim—ints. of Jones in **Vibe,** Sep. 1995, **Rolling Stone,** Jun. 25, 1998; Aldrin denial—corr. with authors, 2004; NASA—Chronology of Music Flown in Space, compiled by Colin Fries of NASA History Office; book—Andrew Chaikin, **A Man on the Moon,** New York: Viking, 1994, 150–).

616–617 **FS and family: (Marty surgery/death)** Sinatra, **Legend,** 209, Sinatra with Coplon, 123, **Variety,** Jan. 29, 1969; **(Dolly tried to throw)** Sinatra, **My Father,** 218; **(reburied Palm Springs)** Sinatra with Coplon, 162; **(medical center)** Sinatra, **Legend,** 217, **Variety,** Jan. 13, 1971, **PR Newswire,** May 15, 1998; **(Dolly moved)** Sinatra with Coplon, 162, **LAT,** Mar. 24, 1971, **LAHE,** Jan. 8, 1977; **(loathed CA)** Jacobs and Stadiem, 256; **(fights)** Sinatra, **Legend,** 253, Sinatra, **My Father,** 234; **("adored")** Sinatra with Coplon, 162; **("He'd give")** ibid., 161; **(Tina adolescence/reproaching/"rock")** ibid., 101–, **LAT Calendar,** Jul. 26, 1992; **(Frank Jr./"away from inner")** **Esquire,** Apr. 1966, and see Kelley, 357; **("Is it genuine?")** **Good Housekeeping,** Jun. 1964, and see **Life,** Aug. 23, 1965; **("just one simple")** Harry Evans article for **TV Star Parade,** Jun. 1969.

617 **The younger Nancy:** Nancy had first married pop singer Tommy Sands, when she was twenty. In 1970 she married producer and choreographer Hugh Lambert, by whom she was to bear two daughters. Nancy's book on her father would not appear until 1985, when it was published as **Frank Sinatra: My Father.** This was followed, in coffee-table book form with many photographs, by **Frank Sinatra: An American Legend,** in 1995; **(*A Very Gentle*)** **Life,** May 5, 1967.

617–618 **FS dalliances:** Women linked with Sinatra from 1968 included Peggy Strasberg, a young model, the actresses Irene Tsu, Carol Lynley, Carol White—temporarily borrowed from her boyfriend—and Hope Lange (Strasberg—**Star,** Dec. 5, 1995, int. Josephine Alvarez; Tsu—unid. article, Paul Fjordsen, "The Girl Who Refuses to Marry Sinatra," and Dave Bryan, "How It Feels to Love Frank Sinatra," May 1970, MHL, Wilson, **Sinatra,** 196, authors' contacts with Irene Tsu; Lynley—int. Carol Lynley, Taraborrelli, 406, 415; White—"Sinatra Made Me Feel Like a Real Woman," unid. UK newspaper article by Carol White, MHL; Lange—int. Leonora Hornblow, Romero, 202, Wilson, **Sinatra,** 321–); **(Duke)** Patty Duke and Kenneth Turan, **Call Me Anna,** New York: Bantam, 1987, 194–; **(Ava/"a sacred monster")** Higham, **Ava,** 232.

618 **Hamill/"A song out":** Hamill, 13–, int. Pete Hamill. It was Billie Holiday's rendering of "I'm a Fool to Want You" that was playing on the jukebox at P. J. Clarke's in 1970.

618–619 **FS friendships: (concept of loyalty) LAT Calendar,** Jul. 26, 1992, FS int. on **Suzy Visits,** int. Milton Greene, 1983, int. Rock Brynner, **Esquire,** Apr. 1966, M/G int. of Jay Bernstein, **GQ,** Nov. 1999, ed. Mustazza, **Popular Culture,** 247–, MacLaine, **Lucky Stars,** 87; **("My son") Esquire,** Apr. 1966; **("ferocity") Family Weekly,** Jun. 17, 1984; **(Sanicola fight)** "File Review & Summary Check," Mar. 26, 1970, FBI LA 100-41413-179, Shaw, **Sinatra,** 311, **Variety,** Jan. 31, 1963, Sinatra, **Legend,** 165–; **(Entratter)** Kelley, 470, Jacobs and Stadiem, 87; **("capable of being")** int. Phyllis McGuire; **(Dexter fired)** int. Brad Dexter, 2001; **(Jacobs dumped)** Jacobs and Stadiem, 9–, 250, int. George Jacobs; **(Entratter dead)** Freedland, 353; **(Joe E. Lewis) NYT,** Jun. 5, 1971, Wilson, **Show Business Nobody Knows,** 246; **(Armstrong) NYT,** Jul. 7, 1971, refs. in **Where or When?,** O'Brien, **Film Guide,** 92; **(Romanoff)** Sinatra, **Legend,** 224, ints. Gloria Romanoff, 1983; **(Maxwell) LAT,** Mar. 24, **LAHE,** Mar. 25, 1972, ints. Jean Greenberg, Joseph Spaccavento, 1947, 1951 entries, **Where or When?; (Sanicola death) LAT,** Oct. 8, 1974; **("To be Frank's") Ladies' Home Journal,** Nov. 1973.

620 **Jilly Rizzo: ("Ermenigildo"/background/fighter)** "Jilly Rizzo," New York Field Office Report, Oct. 31, 1966, and Sep. 29, 1970, FBI 92-9522—correct spelling of name supplied by Tony Oppedisano; **(rhinoceros)** FS int. by Arlene Francis, Sept. 25, 1981, WOR (NY).

620–621 **bartender/Jilly's on 52nd:** "Jilly Rizzo," New York Field Office Report, Oct. 31, 1966, FBI 92-9522, undat. article for **Sound Track,** by John J. Miller. Other Jilly's would sprout in Miami Beach and Palm Springs, but by then Rizzo and Frank were bosom pals ("Jilly Rizzo," Oct. 27, 1967, FBI 92-9522-3, Sinatra with Coplon, 139, int. Marilyn Sinatra); **("Home of the King"/photos/chairs/customers evicted)** LAT, Nov. 19, 1968, NYT, Jul. 1965, **Modern Maturity,** Jan./Feb. 2000; **(at hand in crises)** Sinatra, **Legend,** 189, Kelley, 330, undat. article by John Miller; **("fuckface"/"belong") New Yorker,** Nov. 3, 1997, Sinatra with Coplon, 139; **(hookers)** int. Brad Dexter; **(Jackie O. et al./"clean up")** Kelley, 436, Sinatra with Coplon, 139, Joey Villa, **Living Well Is the Best Revenge,** Las Vegas: Comic Two Talent, 1998; **(orange jackets)** ibid., **New York,** Jul. 15, 1974; **("like a goddamn"/"the greatest"/"you purify") Esquire,** Apr. 1964, undat. article by John Miller; **(Artanis/movie parts/"Jilly loves you more")** Kelley, 533, "Jilly Rizzo," New York Field Office Report, May 27, 1970, FBI 92-9522, Granata, 190, Ringgold and McCarty, 248—the three movies were **Tony Rome, Cannonball Run,** and, for TV, **Contract on Cherry Street; ("poet")** Sinatra, **Legend,** 302.

621 **Rizzo & violence: (arrested)** "Jilly Rizzo," New York Field Office Report, Oct. 31, 1966, FBI 92-9522; **(bodyguard)** "Jilly Rizzo," May 27, 1970, New York Field Office Report, FBI 92-9522, Sinatra with Coplon, 138, ints. Marilyn Sinatra, Joey Villa; **("tractor") Esquire,** Apr. 1966—the comic was Don Rickles; **(Rizzo stomped)** int. Rock Brynner and see chapter 30, p. 323, **supra.; ("pulverized")** undat. article by John Miller, int. Jackie Jordan, and see **LAT,** Jul. 22, 1972, "Sinatra, Ol' Blue Eyes at 75," New York: Starlog, 1990, 45; **(punished drunk)** undat. article by John Miller.

622 **Palm Springs episode: (Rizzo took fall)** LAT, Jul. 9, 1973, Sep. 13, 1974, **LAHE,** Aug. 12, 1973, Sep. 13, 1974; **("Respect!"/ Rizzo guilty)** LAT, Sep. 11, **LAHE,** Sep. 14, **Variety,** Sep. 16, 1974, Jilly Rizzo testimony, Nevada State Gaming Commission, Feb. 19, 1981. According to the victim, insurance executive Frank Weinstock, Sinatra also struck him. Sinatra denied having done so—saying he had merely put his "finger on his chest"—and Rizzo backed him up. The case was settled out of court after attorneys for Rizzo filed for a new trial.

Rizzo was also at the Sands with Sinatra in 1967, when Sinatra got his front teeth punched out by Carl Cohen. On that occasion, warned by Cohen that he would wind up dead should he intervene, Rizzo prudently stepped aside. He took a more active role in 1970 in another violent incident at Caesars Palace, when Frank lunged at casino official Sanford Waterman. When Waterman pulled a gun, Rizzo jumped over the table and knocked the weapon from his hand. Though Waterman was initially arrested on a weapons charge, the district attorney concluded that Sinatra had been "the aggressor all the way." As the incident ended, by one account, the singer told Waterman, "The mob will take care of you." Years later, testifying to the Nevada State Gaming Control Board, Sinatra said of the episode: "If we hadn't stopped the people from wanting to take his head off, he would have been hurt very badly. . . . We actually saved his life" (FS first to strike/FS denied—**LAT,** Sep. 11, 13, 1974; Rizzo backed up/attorneys filed/settled—Carpozi, **Sinatra,** 326–, Wilson, **Sinatra,** 308; attorneys filed/settled—ibid.; Rizzo at Sands—Sheriff's Report, Sep. 18, 1967; wind up dead—M/G int. of Sonny King, int. Joey Villa; arrested/"Sinatra aggressor"—**LAHE,** Aug. 10, 1970, **LAT,** Sep. 7, 1970; "mob will take care"—ibid.; "If we hadn't"—FS testimony, Nevada State Gaming Control Board, Feb. 11, 1981).

622 **Rizzo & Mafia: ("made man"?)** "Jilly Rizzo," New York Field Office Report, Oct. 31, 1966, Feb. 27, 1969, FBI 92-9522, "Jilly Rizzo," Oct. 31, 1966, FBI 92-9522-2, May 27, 1970, FBI 92-4157-1, and Sep. 29, 1970, FBI 92-4157-3; **("LCN associate")** SAC Miami to SAC Los Angeles, Feb. 7, 1985, FBI 299-5245-80; **(Giancana/Fischetti)** "Jilly Rizzo," New York Field Office Report, Oct. 31, 1966, "Supplemental Correlation Summary," Feb. 25, 1969, FSFBI, FBI Wiretap Summary, Feb. 20, 1962, supplied to authors by HSCA staff member; **(Iacovetti friend)** Hellerman with Renner, 101; **(Iacovetti/Gambino)** Teresa with Renner, 226, **Wall Street Journal,** Aug. 19, 1968; **(Rizzo and FS socialized)** ibid., "Supplemental Correlation Summary," Feb. 25, 1969, FSFBI, Hellerman with Renner, 101; **(intimate with Bilottis)** ints. Joe Bilotti, Tony Montana, Mrs. James Bilotti, Kelley, 478; **(Bilotti/Gambino)** Sifakis, 33, Allan May, "Forgotten Man at Sparks," Feb. 2, 1999, http:americanmafia.com.

622 **Gambino/Rizzo stock scam:** In an FBI report on a subpoena relating to Rizzo, the scam is described as having been "an attempted manipulation of stock named Computer Fields Express . . . while attempting to inflate price of stock [the participants] ran short of funds . . . allegedly Carlo Gambino, Frank

Sinatra, and Jilly Rizzo invested in the stock." A later document cited Sinatra's attorney Milton Rudin as saying that, even if Sinatra did invest, he would probably not have been aware of the company's name. Rudin said he did not think there had been a Sinatra investment, but suggested there might have been a Rizzo involvement. Neither Sinatra nor Rizzo were charged with any offense. Rizzo was reportedly close long afterward to Joe Paterno, the capo who looked after Gambino interests in New Jersey (scam—SAC New York to Director, Nov. 21, 1973, FBI 166-5477-31, SAC Los Angeles to Director, Nov. 26, 1973, FBI 166-5477-32; close to capo—SA (deleted) to SAC Miami, Jul. 30, 1985, FBI 183A-2166-339; Paterno background—Sifakis, 278, 164).

623 **Rizzo mob connections:** Rizzo shared with Sinatra a Mafia connection that tracked back to the Luciano organization and to New Jersey. Bob Buccino, a former senior organized crime investigator for the state, told the authors Rizzo was "real friendly" with New Jersey Mafia figure Angelo De Carlo, whose relationship with Sinatra has been documented in this book. Rizzo reportedly owned a house in Mountainside, the mob boss's hometown ("real friendly"—int. Bob Buccino; Mountainside—"Jilly Rizzo," New York Field Office Report, Oct. 31, 1966, FBI 92-9522).

623 **$8 million fraud:** One of Rizzo's co-defendants was Michael Rapp, aka Michael Hellerman, who has featured elsewhere in these pages. Rapp/Hellerman, who had been in the restaurant business with Rizzo and met Sinatra on several occasions, had multiple Mafia associates. He was dubbed "the mob's stockbroker," and law enforcement officials described the list of those he had drawn into the case as "a **Who's Who** of organized crime"—from the Lucchese and Genovese families in particular (Rizzo convicted/spared jail—**NYT,** May 7, 1992; Stephen Pizzo, Mary Fricker, and Paul Muolo, **Inside Job: The Looting of America's Savings and Loans,** New York: McGraw-Hill, 1989, 141–, 144, 147; co-defendant Rapp/Hellerman—ADIC New York to Director, Apr. 20, 1990, FBI 290-17893-778, released to authors under FOIA, Hellerman with Renner, 97–, 102–; "mob's stockbroker"/**Who's Who**—Pizzo, Fricker, and Muolo, 131–).

623 **Jilly buried: NYT,** May 18, 1998, "Interments of Interest" fact sheet by Kathleen Jurasky, Palm Springs Cemetery District.

623 **Anti-Defamation League: ("taint")** "Why A.I.D.?" attachment to Di Lorenzo to Watson, Oct. 14, 1967, Frank Sinatra File, Box 320, White House Central Files, Lyndon B. Johnson Library; **(FS chairman) NYT,** May 4, 1967; **(18,000/Madison Square Garden) LAT,** Oct. 21, 1967; **(Salerno/"hardly matches") NYT,** May 12, 1967, and see **NYT,** May 13, 1967.

624 **board's Mafia associations/FS resigned:** Messick with Nellis, 242, Gage, 89. Anthony Scotto, an AID vice president, was son-in-law of Tony Anastasia, waterfront racketeer and brother of Albert "Lord High Executioner" Anastasia. He was later convicted of having taken more than $200,000 in payoffs from waterfront businesses. Informants told the FBI that he and fellow board member Dr. Mario Tagliagambe were "members of La Cosa Nostra." Former congressman Alfred Santangelo was the son-in-law of Vincent Rao, identified as a capo in the Lucchese family. Dr. Thomas J. Sinatra, apparently no relation to the singer, was Carlo Gambino's son-in-law. There was also Carmine DeSapio, the Tammany Hall boss whose strings had long been pulled by Mafia bosses. A probe of a Gambino cousin later led to AID president and cochairman, former congressman Ross Di Lorenzo, being prosecuted, but not convicted, for perjury. Henri Giné, Sinatra's East Coast representative and a close friend of Jimmy Alo, was also an AID board member (AID board—"Why A.I.D.?" attachment to Di Lorenzo to Watson, Oct. 14, 1967; Scotto—**Life,** Sep. 8, 1967, Sifakis, 13–, 263, 298, Cleveland to Gale, May 18, 1967, FBI 62-813217; Tagliagambe—ibid.; Santangelo—Ralph Salerno summary on organized crime for House Committee on Assassinations, 62, Sifakis, 127, 200; Dr. Sinatra—**Life,** Sep. 8, 1967; DeSapio—Sifakis, 90, 181, 198–; DiLorenzo—Salerno summary for HSCA, p. 68, and see Director to Attorney General, May 18, 1967, redacted document, FBI 62-83218, section 3; Giné—corr. Carole Cortland Russo.

624 **Italian-American Civil Rights League: (attendance/dollars/national attention) Staten Island Advance,** Oct. 19, **NYT,** Nov. 9, 1970, Apr. 4, 1971; **(not to use "Mafia") NYT,** Mar. 24, **Staten Island Advance,** Mar. 25, 1971.

624 **Colombo "founder": NYT,** Mar. 23, Apr. 4, 1971. Colombo was shot down by an assassin in June 1971 while addressing a league rally. By one speculation, Carlo Gambino ordered the attack in part as a personal reprisal, in part to snuff out league

activity—which he and mob associates considered too high profile. Colombo survived in a vegetative state, his brain damaged by the would-be assassin's bullets, for another seven years (Sifakis, 82–); **(FS leery/"Colombo was furious")** int. and corr. Hector Saldana—who was working on a biography of Alo, ints. Carole Cortland Russo, Ken Roberts, M/G int. of Eddie Jaffe, Villa.

625 **compromise:** "Joseph A. Colombo," Jan. 28, 1971, FBI 92-6210-65. A contemporary FBI report indicates that Sinatra was at first expected to perform at a league rally of Jun. 29, 1970. He did not appear, a fact that buttresses Alo's reference to a "no-show." He did appear, though, on Nov. 20, 1970, which would reflect the compromise arrangement reportedly made by Alo on his behalf. Several sources indicate that Sinatra also appeared at a benefit on behalf of the league in Nov. 1971. Checks of relevant press coverage, and of the FBI's running file on the league, however, reflect no such appearance (expected June 29—"Correlation Summary," Feb. 18, 1972, FSFBI; November 20—SAC New York to SAC Las Vegas, Dec. 9, 1970, FBI 92-6210-39, **NYT,** Apr. 4, 1971; 1971 appearance—corr. Ric Ross, Nov. 20, 1971, entry, **Where or When?**, Sinatra, **Legend,** 224, FBI 92-6210, refs.); **(skipped/"As far as")** handwritten letter sender and recipient names deleted, Mar. 19, 1971, FBI 166-3211-55.

625–626 ***The Godfather:*** **(FS rebuked)** NYT **Magazine,** Aug. 6, 1967; **(Puzo background/$1 million/$8 million)** Fox, 368–, **(most lucrative)** Robert Evans, **The Kid Stays in the Picture,** New York: Hyperion, 1994, 231; **(optioned in advance)** ibid., 217; **(attorneys demanded)** Mario Puzo, **The Godfather Papers,** New York: Putnam's, 1972, 53; **(get character written out?/"Sinatra still wasn't"/FS told to back off) Mean,** Sep. 2001; **(Chasen's/abused)** Puzo, **Godfather Papers,** 54–, and see **Chicago Sun-Times,** Sep. 11, 1970, Sciacca, 9.

626 **1969 revelations/De Carlo bugs: LAHE,** Jan. 7, 1970, logs of convs. Mar. 10, Dec. 5, 1961, Oct. 29, 1962, Apr. 22, Nov. 11, 1963, Jun. 12, 1964, vol. 9, Misc. ELSUR Refs., HSCA Subject Files, Frank Sinatra, JFK. Steve Lenehan, a mobster turned informant, recalled how in the mid-1960s, when told that De Carlo was on the phone, Sinatra immediately took the call. In old age, De Carlo kept a photograph of Sinatra on his office wall. Sinatra acknowledged only that he had "met" the gangster (Lenehan—int. Steve Lenehan and see "Interview with Steve Lenehan,"

americanmafia.com, Sep. 2001; photo—Sifakis, 98; "met"—LAT, Jan. 20, 1970).

626 **FS and crime probes: (served with subpoena)** LAHE, Oct. 15, 1969; **(fought to avoid)** LAHE, Oct. 15, 16, Dec. 18, 1969, Jan. 8, 14, 1970; **(Supreme Court) Philadelphia Inquirer,** Feb. 4, 1970; **(solemnly told)** LAT, Feb. 18, 1970, Kelley, 393–.

627 **Fontainebleau suit: (judge's order)** LAT, Apr. 11, 1968, "Joseph Fischetti," May 25, 1967, FBI 92-3024-92; **(left Florida)** int. Ralph Salerno, Ralph Salerno and John Tompkins, **The Crime Confederation,** Garden City, NY: Doubleday, 1969, 166; **(moot/suit dropped)** LAT, Apr. 24, 1968. The Miami case was a libel suit between the Fontainebleau Hotel and the **Miami Herald,** which in 1967 published articles alleging that the hotel was controlled by mobsters. The previous year, again after much ducking and weaving, Frank had been forced to testify before a federal grand jury investigating skimming by Las Vegas casino owners (grand jury—Kelley, 366); **(Four years later/prepared to appear) Hollywood Reporter,** NYT, Jun. 8, 1972; **(committee voted/FS vanished)** NYT, Jun. 8, 22, LAHE, Jun. 8, LAT, Jun. 9, 1972; **(belligerent appearance)** NYT, Jun. 28, Jul. 19, 23, 1972.

627 **"Let's dispense"/"From the standpoint":** FS testimony, Jul. 18, 1972, Hearings, Select Committee on Crime, U.S. House of Representatives, 92nd Cong., 2nd sess., Washington, DC: U.S. Government Printing Office, 1973. Sinatra won justified sympathy when the Crime Committee took hearsay testimony from a convicted felon, Joe Barboza. Barboza claimed that Sinatra had held an interest in the Fontainebleau, and had had an interest in the Sands and at Lake Tahoe, as a front for New England Mafia boss Raymond Patriarca. In the view of the American Civil Liberties Union, the airing of these allegations subjected Sinatra to "trial by publicity" and "character assassination." Before Barboza made his claims, however, the committee had planned to question Sinatra on a specific matter of unquestioned fact—his former investment and role as a vice president of the Berkshire Downs racetrack in Massachusetts. Coinvestors with Sinatra had been the mafiosi Patriarca and Lucchese. In his testimony, Sinatra denied knowing Patriarca. In his, Patriarca denied knowing Sinatra. When asked whether any of his associates had done business with or purchased stock from the singer on his behalf, however,

the Mafia boss pleaded the Fifth. Sinatra testified that he agreed to join the racetrack venture at the suggestion of a man named Salvatore Rizzo, whom he had met while performing in Atlantic City, apparently in 1962. Rizzo, for his part, repeatedly pleaded the Fifth when asked whether he knew Sinatra and, if so, how long he had known him. The former controller of the racetrack, however, quoted Rizzo as having told him: "I've known Sinatra since New Jersey. I was a neighbor of his . . . lived right next to them. I know his first wife and his children, and I know him." The **Providence Evening Bulletin** had reported as early as September 8, 1962, that Sinatra and Dean Martin were friends of Rizzo. As to Sinatra and Patriarca denying that they knew each other, an FBI report dated four years **before** they testified referred to Sinatra, at Caesars Palace, having "a message he wanted carried to Raymond Patriarca"—who was reportedly a hidden owner of Caesars. The Crime Committee's eventual report gave an acid account of Sinatra's version of events, but concluded that he had been an "unwitting front" in the corrupt Berkshire Downs scheme. It never cleared up the anomalies listed above (Barboza claim—Barboza testimony, Hearings, Select Committee on Crime, U.S. House of Representatives, 92nd Cong., 2nd sess., pt. 2, 752–, 756–, 763; ACLU—**Chicago Sun-Times,** Jun. 6, 1972; Berkshire Downs—**NYT,** Jun. 8, 1972; Sinatra testimony—Hearings, Select Committee on Crime, House of Representatives, 92nd Cong., 2nd sess., pt. 4, 1409–; Patriarca testimony—ibid., 1485; Rizzo—ibid., 1498, 1501, 1504; former controller—ibid., testimony of Charles Carson, 1447, 1451, 1457; **Evening Bulletin**—SA Boston to USA Boston, Nov. 6, 1962, FBI 92-2961; Las Vegas SA Aug. 29, 1968, FBI 92-1851-83; hidden owner—Dan Moldea, **Interference,** New York: William Morrow, 1989, 469n5; report—"Organized Crime Influence in Horse Racing," Report, Select Committee on Crime, U.S. Senate, 93rd Cong., 2nd sess., Jun. 25, 1973).

628 **sounded off in *NYT:*** NYT, Jul. 24, 1972; **("like Lear") New Times,** Oct. 19, 1973; **(echoed claim) NYT,** Apr. 4, 1971, and see **Hollywood Reporter,** Oct. 21, 1969, **NYT,** Jul. 24, 1972; **("If a man") New Times,** Oct. 19, 1973.

628–629 **1971 retirement: (Thompson/"try a little tenderness") Life,** Jun. 25, 1971; **(five thousand people/included)** ibid., and see **LAT,** Jun. 15, 1971. The "retirement" concert was in aid of the Motion Picture and Television Relief Fund, for which it raised $800,000 (Shaw, **Entertainer,** 43); **(two months earlier)** Sinatra with Coplon, 125; **(statement) New York Daily News,** Mar. 24, 1971; **("spectacular") Life,** Jun. 25, 1971.

629–630 **record sales dipped/movie flopped:** Sayers and O'Brien, 261, O'Brien, 186, 191, 195, 198, 205. The **My Way** album had placed number eleven in the charts in 1969, but the three albums released in the two years prior to 1971 had unexciting sales. The 1967 movie **Tony Rome** had decent audiences, as did **The Detective** and **Lady in Cement** in 1968. **Dirty Dingus Magee,** though, released in late 1970, was a commercial and critical disaster. Sinatra made no further movies until **The First Deadly Sin** in 1980, another failure. A 1984 cameo appearance in **Cannonball Run II** ended his movie career; **(nine hundred songs)** Rednour, 11–; **(eighty-seven albums)** ibid., 249–; **(forty-three movies)** O'Brien, **Film Guide,** 12—with cameo roles, the total would be fifty-five.

629–630 **"I've had enough": Life,** Jun. 25, 1971. Sinatra had undergone a surgical procedure the previous year for Dupuytren's contracture, a painful condition of the musculature of his right hand and palm, the hand in which he generally held the microphone. Its origin, Sinatra liked to say, was the bare-knuckle punch he had landed on columnist Lee Mortimer twenty-three years earlier. He had long since complained, too, that the Los Angeles smog affected his nose and throat. Rumors in 1971 that he was receiving secret treatment for throat cancer were unfounded. Sinatra sued one tabloid, which settled out of court by contributing a large sum to the medical facility established in memory of his father. There is no evidence that he had serious health problems at that time (Dupuytren's—**LAHE,** Jul. 9, Sep. 7, **LAT,** Sep. 8, 1970, **Screen Stars,** Jul. 1971; origin?—int. Al Viola; Los Angeles smog—**Time,** Nov. 22, 1968; rumors unfounded—**LAHE,** Jul. 21, 1971, SAC New York to Director, Sep. 15, 1971, FSFBI; tabloid settled—Shaw, **Entertainer,** 42); **("Being a public"/ "slobs"/"garbage collectors") TV Guide,** Nov. 17, 1973; **(Gage story) Wall Street Journal,** Aug. 19, 1968; **(confrontational)** see note re Rizzo in Caesars Palace incident; **(Giancana abroad)** Brashler, 294–, 304, 312–.

630 **De Carlo/Alo/Fischetti:** De Carlo, convicted on loan-sharking charges in 1970, was jailed for twelve years. The sentence was

commuted in 1972, amid reports that Sinatra had used influence with the Nixon White House to get his former New Jersey backer out of jail. A study of De Carlo's FBI file, and in particular reviews of his case by Bureau of Prisons personnel, do not support the allegation. De Carlo was suffering from cancer and other ailments, and died less than a year after his release.

Jimmy Alo was sentenced to five years in 1970 on charges arising from a Securities and Exchange Commission investigation, and went to jail in early 1971. He continued to be on friendly terms with Sinatra's parents following his release in 1973, but his relations with the singer himself cooled. Alo felt Sinatra had failed in several ways to reciprocate his support over the years—not least his part in securing Sinatra the role in **From Here to Eternity.**

Joe Fischetti was indicted on conspiracy and other offenses shortly before Sinatra's retirement, and in 1972 was sentenced to six months in jail. He remained the singer's friend until his death in 1979 (De Carlo—Angelo De Carlo File, FBI 179-195-82 through 156, Sifakis, 98; Alo—"Vincent Alo," May 28, 1971, FBI 92-2815-411, Jan. 10, 1975, FBI 92-2815-416, ints. Carole Cortland Russo, Ken Roberts, Hector Saldana; Fischetti—"Joseph J. Fischetti," Oct. 22, 1970, FBI 92-3024-106, Jan. 12, 1971, FBI 92-3024-108, Jul. 24, 1972, FBI 92-3024-112, FS testimony, Nevada State Gaming Control Board, Feb. 11, 1981).

630–631 **carried gun:** The women who saw the gun were the actress Lois Nettleton and the dancer Marianna Case, whose relationships with Sinatra are described in chapter 32 (ints. Lois Nettleton, Case, 75–); **("He was not")** int. Peggy Connelly; **("All of us") Coronet,** Mar. 1971; **(Streisand/tuxedo jacket) Life,** Jun. 25, 1971; **("I'm tired"/Everybody laughed)** ibid.

Chapter 32: "Let Me Try Again"

632–633 **FS in retirement: ("I'm finished")** Giuliano audiotape; **("Maybe I'm going"/"read Plato") Life,** Jun. 25, 1971; **(range of FS work)** Sinatra, **A Man and His Art,** ix, **Look,** Jun. 11, 1957; **("I wouldn't even hum")** Bill Boggs int.; **("I played")** "Sinatra in Egypt," unedited interview for **20/20,** ABC News, Oct. 4, 1979, videotape in authors' collection; **(galleries/Picasso)** Peter Malatesta, **Party Politics,** Englewood Cliffs, NJ:

Prentice-Hall, 1982, 45–, 117–; **(golf/"absolutely zero") Life,** Dec. 31, 1971; **(special Oscar)** LAT, Mar. 1, WP, Apr. 16, 1971; **(Senate tributes/"the greatest") Congressional Record,** Jun. 30, LAT, Jul. 1, 1971; **(Sinatra Day) Hollywood Reporter,** Jan. 18, 1971; **("Frank Sinatra Drive") Variety,** Aug. 19, 1971, **LAT,** Jan. 16, 2000; **(loneliest man)** Sinatra with Coplon, 150.

633 **Marianna Case:** Marianna Case, **Another Side of Blue,** Running Springs, CA: self-published, 1997, refs., int. Marianna Case.

633 **Walters:** Shaw, **Entertainer,** 102.

634 **FS deplored:** Hedda Hopper column, Jul. 20, 1965, MHL.

634–636 **Nettleton: (background/affair)** ints. & corr. Lois Nettleton and clippings 1971–72 in collection of Lois Nettleton. Sinatra and Nettleton had worked together in 1970 on the spoof western movie **Dirty Dingus Magee,** in which he played an outlaw and she an amorous schoolteacher (O'Brien, 196–); **(use of "Francis")** e.g., Case, 24, ints. Marianna Case, Carole Lynley; **(felt as though little boy)** Case, 63; **(painting clowns)** Wilson, **Sinatra,** 79, Malatesta, 45–, **Look,** Jun. 11, 1957; **(flour-white cheeks) Movie Show,** Jul. 31, 1947; **(over desk) Newsweek,** Sep. 6, 1965; **(dressed up)** Carpozi, **Sinatra,** 199; **(toothbrush glass)** int. Peggy Connelly; **(Emmett Kelly) Movie Show,** Jul. 31, 1947; **("sad & ragged")** Emmett Kelly with F. Beverly Kelly, **Clown,** New York: Prentice-Hall, 1954, 125; **(self-portraits)** int. Tina Sinatra, **A Man and His Art,** ix.

639–640 **FS politics: ("Long after")** JFK speech at inaugural gala, Jan. 19, 1961, videotape in authors' collection; **("lifelong Democrat")** int. of Tina Sinatra, **Larry King Live** CNN, Nov. 1992, and see Sinatra, **My Father,** 219; **(Agnew & Reagan at hospital)** LAHE, Jan. 13, 1971; **(Agnew at retirement)** Hank Messick, **J. Edgar Hoover,** New York: David McKay, 1972, 253; **("Nixon!") New York Journal-American,** Jan. 16, 1961; **("hated Nixon")** MacLaine, **Lucky Stars,** 86.

640 **Reagan/"friendly witness":** Wills, **Reagan,** 255; **("Bozo"/ "*Bonzo*")** Jacobs and Stadiem, 238. Reagan played a college professor who befriended a chimpanzee, his test subject, in the 1951 movie **Bedtime for Bonzo. ("stupid bore"/"a dumb broad")** MacLaine, **Lucky Stars,** 86, Kelley, 361; **(met Nancy)** Jacobs and Stadiem, 238, Sinatra, **My Father,** 60; **("leave the country")**

MacRae, 171; **("She dislikes California")** FS lyric at Oakland concert, May 22, 1968 cited in corr. Ed O'Brien.

640–642 **FS and 1970 Reagan campaign:** LAT, Jul. 13, 14, **Hollywood Citizen-News,** Jul. 14, 1970—the reference to Sinatra having supported Reagan as early as 1966, in a recent book by Charles Pignone, is surely an error; **("I support")** Taraborrelli, 384, and see Giuliano audiotape, **Hollywood Reporter,** Mar. 18, 1976; **("the outstanding"/"believes")** LAT, Jul. 13, 14, 1970; **(LBJ contempt/"It'll make a big")** Oliver Pilat, **Drew Pearson,** New York: Harper's, 1973, 282–; **(supported Humphrey/ "Bobby is just")** Variety, May 6, 1968, see **McCall's,** Jul. 1968; **(shed no tears)** Jacobs and Stadiem, 3, 249, and see Sinatra, **My Father,** 212; **("that fuckin' cop")** int. Michael Shore by PITV; **(report re FS and Hoffa aides)** Maxine Cheshire with John Greenya, **Maxine Cheshire, Reporter,** Boston: Houghton Mifflin, 1978, 106–, **McCall's,** May 1973; **(*Wall Street Journal*)** Aug. 19, 1968; **(Nellis warning)** int. Joe Nellis, Kelley, 386; **(FS faded)** WP, LAT, Aug. 25, 1968.

642 **FS and Nixon/Agnew: ("Nixon scares")** LAT, Jul. 14, 1970; **(Colson on wooing)** ed. Bruce Oudes, **Richard Nixon's Secret Files,** London: André Deutsch, 1989, 174.

642–643 **Agnew & FS met/hit it off:** Agnew dated his meeting with Sinatra as having occurred during the 1970 Thanksgiving holiday. According to Nancy Sinatra, they had met at a political event in Palm Springs as early as the summer of 1969. Agnew wrote as though they met on the golf course by chance, while his aide Peter Malatesta described the meeting as having been the result of an Agnew initiative (Agnew, 204–, Sinatra, **Legend,** 210, Malatesta, 15–); **(Agnew music/liked to sing)** Wilson, **Sinatra,** 280; **(houseguest)** WP, Feb. 25, 1972; **(eighteen visits) Newsweek,** May 25, 1998; **(*Deep Throat*)** (London) **Observer,** Apr. 28, 2002; **("Agnew House")** McCall's, Oct. 1974, **LAT,** Jul. 11, 1980, Shaw, **Entertainer,** 118; **("Sinatra is ready")** ed. Oudes, 211; **(FBI alerted)** Director FBI to Ehrlichman, Apr. 25, 1969, FSFBI; **("While Sinatra"/RN congratulations)** Moore to Hasek, Nov. 1, Nixon to Sinatra, Nov. 3, 1971, White House Central Files, Nixon Presidential Materials, NA; **(Mrs. Mitchell on FS jet)** Mohr to Tolson, Nov. 9, 1971, FSFBI; **(Agnew attempt to delay)** LAT, May 31, **Variety,** Jun. 1, 1972; **(presi-**

dent phoned) Kelley, 410, but see Freedland, 361; **("He's aboard")** H. R. Haldeman, **The Haldeman Diaries,** New York: Putnam, 1994, 491; **(FS supported reelection)** Mohr to Tolson, Nov. 9, 1971, FSFBI, **LAHE,** Feb. 4, 1973, Malatesta, 92; **(rented house)** Malatesta, 94–.

644 **Cheshire: ("cunt"/whore)** SA (deleted) to SAC Los Angeles, Feb. 2, 1973, FBI 92-1039-303, **Newsweek,** Feb. 5, 1973, Cheshire with Greenya, 124, **Time,** Feb. 5, 12, 1973, and see Malatesta, 99–; **("livid") New York Post,** Mar. 29, 1973.

644 **"two bits":** RN conv., Jul. 9, 1973, cited in Stanley Kutler, **Abuse of Power,** New York: Free Press, 1997, 621. The "two bits" comment was made later in private, to his friend Bebe Rebozo. It came to light only in the late 1990s, with the release of a new batch of White House tapes.

644–645 **asked FS to sing at the White House: LAHE,** Feb. 4, 1973, M/G int. of Al Viola. It was reported that Sinatra had entertained once previously at the Nixon White House, at a February 1970 tribute to the late Senator Everett Dirksen. That event in fact took place at the Washington Hilton (tribute at W. House?—**Hollywood Reporter,** Feb. 25, 1970, **Where or When?,** corr. Ric Ross; Hilton—**WP,** Feb. 28, 1970; **(ten songs/"The House")** Apr. 17, 1973, entry, **Where or When?** Vidal, 152; **("Washington Monument")** text from videotape of Nixon's comments, Apr. 17, 1973; **(switchboard)** Sinatra with Coplon, 143; **("Napoleon")** George Rush, **Confessions of an Ex–Secret Service Agent,** New York: Donald Fine, 1988, 193; **(FS gave refuge/urged to cling/legal costs)** Spiro Agnew, **Go Quietly . . . or Else,** New York: Wm. Morrow, 1980, 148–, 177–, 203–, Freedland, 362–, **WP,** Sep. 29, 1973, **New Times,** Oct. 19, 1973, Melvin Small, **The Presidency of Richard Nixon,** Lawrence, KS: University of Kansas Press, 1999, 287; **(one of the first) LAHE,** Feb. 23, AP, UP, Feb. 24, 1975, Robert Sam Anson, **Exile: The Unquiet Oblivion of Richard M. Nixon,** New York: Simon and Schuster, 1984, 99.

645 **"Nobody's perfect":** Sinatra, **My Father,** 226. Watergate investigators stumbled early on upon the fact that Sinatra knew Kenneth Dahlberg, the Midwest finance chairman of Nixon's reelection campaign, whose name was on a check that went to one of the Watergate burglars (Dahlberg—J. Anthony Lukas, **Nightmare: The Underside of the Nixon Years,** New York: Pen-

guin, 1988, 142, Barry Sussman, **The Great Cover-Up,** Arlington, VA: Seven Locks Press, 1992, 74).

645 **FS loyalties after RN: (state fund-raiser)** Nov. 1, 1974, entry, **Where or When?** ed. Vare, 115–; **(low profile Carter)** LAHE, Dec. 13, 1979, **Hollywood Reporter,** Mar. 18, 1976, **LAT,** May 8, 1979, Sinatra, **Legend,** 262; **("an incorrigible maverick"/Tina on FS liberal)** Sinatra with Coplon, 143.

645–646 **"He worked":** eulogy for FS, St. Viator's Church, Las Vegas, May 27, 1998, text provided by Sonny King. King made his remarks in a eulogy he gave at a service following the death of Sinatra, who had been godfather to one of his children. The authors have seen no published reports indicating that an ambassadorship was mooted during the Kennedy administration. Dean Martin's on-stage remark before the 1960 election, that if Kennedy got in, "You'll be Ambassador to Italy," came over as merely a joke. The mafioso John Rosselli, however, was overheard on an FBI wiretap grumbling that Sinatra had "big ideas . . . about being Ambassador, or something." In 1971, during President Nixon's first term, a long article headlined "Ambassadorship for Sinatra?" appeared in the **Los Angeles Herald-Examiner.** The same paper was to print a squib along the same lines early in Reagan's first term—only to state later that it had been "strictly a gag" (eulogy—given in St. Viator's Church, Las Vegas, text provided by Sonny King; Martin—Wilson, **Show Business,** 15; Rosselli—log of conv., Dec. 21, 1961, Misc. ELSUR Refs., vol. 1, HSCA Subject Files, Frank Sinatra, JFK; long article—**LAHE,** Jul. 2, 1971, Nov. 10, Dec. 9, 1980).

646 **"a neutered creature":** **(London) Observer,** May 17, 1998; **("I think Sinatra")** NYT, undat. piece by Robert Lindsey, Feb. 1981; **(pressure from mob?)** int. Shirley MacLaine.

647–648 **FS emerges from retirement: ("You must")** Shaw, **Entertainer,** 88; **("I didn't think")** liner notes, **The Complete Reprise Studio Recordings,** 51—there was a rift in Sinatra's relationship with Miller, lasting from 1978 to 1983, ibid., 37, Friedwald, 40; **("A great artist")** Time, Apr. 5, 1971; **(merely wanted rest/"figment"/pressure from children)** FS ints. by Arlene Francis, Oct. 1, 1977, and Sep. 25, 1981, WOR (NY), Larry King int. of FS, May 19, 1998 (rerun); **(thirty thousand letters/"people who")** Shaw, **Entertainer,** 90; **(FS "missed") Saga,** Nov. 1974, and see LAT, Nov. 18, 1973; **(Russell re bored) People,** May 3, 1976;

("He couldn't stand") Vern Yocum taped recollections, supplied to authors by his daughter Vernise Yocum Pelzel, and see **Saga,** Nov. 1974; **("private" appearances)** multiple entries, 1972–73, **Where or When?; (Palm Springs police show) Hollywood Reporter,** Jan. 20, 1972; **(Salute to Ted Agnew) WP,** May 20, 1972, Malatesta, 75; **(TV special announced)** LAHE, Apr. 20, 1973; **(return to Vegas)** Shaw, **Entertainer,** 91; **(Ol' Blue Eyes)** ed. Vare, 103—the art director was Ed Thrasher; **(concert began/rapturous welcome)** Shaw, **Entertainer,** 91–; **(less encouraging ratings)** ibid., Kelley, 421.

648–650 **album:** Sayers and O'Brien, 261. Though taping began on April 30, 1973, the recordings made that day were destroyed. Taping resumed in June (Sayers and O'Brien, 145, Granata, 191); **(voice "cracked"/apologized) WP,** May 20, 1972; **(vocalized) Sinatra in Egypt,** videotape; **("rusty"/lip trembled/blew lyric/"puffier") TV Guide,** Nov. 17, **LAT,** Nov. 18, 1973, **Newsweek,** Apr. 22, 1974; **("Let Me Try Again")** Rednour, 59—Sammy Cahn also had a hand in the lyrics; **(Madison Square Garden 1974)** Wilson, **Sinatra,** 1–, Oct. 13, 1974, entry, **Where or When? ("Ah, Frankie,") NYT,** Oct. 13, 1974; **("oldsters' Woodstock") Newsweek,** Apr. 22, 1974; **("That style") Rolling Stone,** Jun. 6, 1974.

650 **Thompson catalogued/"Frank is back": McCall's,** Oct. 1974. In Australia in 1974 Sinatra had called journalists "bums, and hookers and parasites." Such was the furor that Australian trade unionists prevented his plane from leaving, and the deadlock was resolved only when Labour Party leader Bob Hawke intervened. Sinatra also aimed puerile insults at the journalist Rona Barrett. An example, from a Las Vegas appearance: "She's so ugly that her mother had to put a pork chop around her neck just to get the dog to play with her. . . . I'm not going to mention her name. I'm also not going to mention Benedict Arnold, Aaron Burr, Adolf Hitler, Bruno Hauptmann, or Ilse Koch—she's the other $2 broad—the one who made the lampshades." In 1975 Frank was to call Barbara Walters "the ugliest broad in television," abuse he would renew in years to come. Sinatra or his bodyguards were accused of roughing up journalists in 1971, 1974, and 1975. Sinatra said in Toronto that the only use he had for newspapers was "to cover the bottom of my parrot's cage and to train my dog on" (Australia—**LAT,** Jul. 11, 1974, and **Melbourne Age,** Jul. 11,

12, 1974; Weinstock—as described in chapter 32; Barrett—**New York,** undat., 1974, Kelly, 423; Walters—Jerry Oppenheimer, **Barbara Walters,** New York: St. Martin's, 1990, 243–; roughing up/"to cover"—**LAHE,** Nov. 19, 1971, **LAT,** Jul. 11, 1974, May 12, 1975).

651 **"All your life":** Howlett, 152.

651 **"Don't worry":** Sinatra with Coplon, 213, 162.

Chapter 33: Barbara

652 **Barbara Marx: (Case aware/"uncomfortable")** Case, 120–, 144–; **("She was trying")** int. Lois Nettleton.

653 **FS would long date:** Sinatra did dally with other women in this period. Depending on which version one reads, he either pursued or was pursued by Pamela Hayward, the British-born former wife of Randolph Churchill and the widow of producer Leland Hayward. For a while in the fall of 1971 he reportedly took up briefly with Natalie Wood, with whom he had been involved years earlier. He would also have relationships of one sort or another with the actresses Eva Gabor, Victoria Principal, and—continuing an on-off liaison—Carol Lynley. The Eva Gabor affair lasted for some time (Hayward—**LAT,** Jun. 14, 1971, Jacobs and Stadiem, 224, Kelly, 431, Christopher Ogden, **Life of the Party,** Boston: Little, Brown, 1994, 324–, Sally Bedell Smith, **Reflected Glory,** New York: Simon and Schuster, 1996, 252–; Wood—Gavin Lambert, **Natalie Wood,** New York: Knopf, 2004, 212, 254, Suzanne Finstad, **Natasha,** New York: Harmony, 2001, 121–, 205–, 256, 268, Jacobs and Stadiem, 8; Gabor—**TV Guide,** Oct. 30, 1993, Gabor with Leigh, 166, Wilson, **Sinatra,** 320–, Sinatra with Coplon, 146, 160; Principal—int. of Victoria Principal in **National Examiner,** Oct. 18, 1983, int. Leonora Hornblow; Lynley—int. Carol Lynley, Taraborrelli, 415–).

653 **Marx background: (born 1927)** Sinatra with Coplon, 147, 267—we have accepted the date for Barbara Marx's birth given in her stepdaughter Tina's book; **(Missouri/father butcher)** ibid., 147, **LAT,** Mar. 27, 1983; **(hard times/settled Long Beach) LAT,** Mar. 27, 1983, Feb. 28, 1988; **(memoir)** int. Beverly Murphy, **New York Daily News,** undat. clip, c. 1990, and Jun. 12, 1990, **Chicago Tribune,** Aug. 11, 1991, corr. Ric Ross; **(fragment/"pursue a life")** Sinatra with Coplon, 147; **(tall/"long-**

stemmed") LAT, Jan. 9, 1975, Mr. Blackwell with Vernon Patterson, **From Rags to Bitches,** Los Angeles: General Publishing, 1995, 155; **(beauty contests)** Kelley, 432–; **(modeling/work NYC/married singer)** LAT, Feb. 28, 1988; **(School of Modeling Arts) Long Beach Magazine,** Winter 1983–84; **(Vegas/marriage to Zeppo Marx/"secret yearning")** LAT, Feb. 28, 1988; **(Riviera Mafia-run)** Turner, **Gambler's Money,** 246–, Denton and Morris, 127, 132, 164, Messick, **Mob in Show Business,** 169–, 178, 252.

653–654 **Riviera described:** Fred Basten and Charles Phoenix, **Fabulous Vegas in the Fifties,** Las Vegas: Angel City Press, 1999, 41, 59, 65, 105. Authors Ed Reid and Ovid Demaris wrote in their seminal 1963 book on Las Vegas that "showgirls are required by the house to sit in the lounge for at least an hour after each performance and 'dress up the room.' " In his 1980 memoir, Sammy Davis wrote that "mixing dates" were "a mandatory part of a showgirl's life . . . when they come down after the show to mix with the gamblers" (Reid and Demaris, 111, Davis, **Why Me,** 80); **(Becker entertainment director)** Rappeleye and Becker, vii; **("beautiful objects"/"had to spend"/"with his tongue")** int. Ed Becker; **("meeting place")** Basten and Phoenix, 52; **(Zeppo regular)** ed. Miriam Marx Allen, **Love, Groucho,** New York: Da Capo, 1992, 191–, 214; **(married 1959) Ladies' Home Journal,** Oct. 1976, Kelley, 433; **(golf/lunches)** LAT, Feb. 28, 1988.

654 **"I called the Racquet":** Gardner indicated in a taped interview that the meeting occurred while she was making the movie **The Angel Wore Red.** Shooting began in November 1959, and the movie opened in September 1960. The Ava interview aside, the authors were told of the meeting by Gardner's longtime companion Reenie Jordan and by her friend Spoli Mills (Gardner interview—Evans tapes, movie—Higham, **Ava,** 198, 254, www.imdb.com).

655 **FS and Barbara affair: ("Zeppo was in")** Jacobs and Stadiem, 255, int. George Jacobs. The visits referred to by Jacobs must have occurred before the summer of 1968, when Jacobs left Sinatra's employ.

655 **"a stopgap":** Sinatra with Coplon, 146. What Tina Sinatra has said of her future stepmother must be treated with caution. The book she wrote after her father's death is in large part a chronicle of bitter strife with Barbara. Nevertheless, as the only published

account of Sinatra's later years, it deserves serious attention; **("a stopgap")** ibid., 153; **(Barbara divorced from Marx)** Variety, May 1, 1973; **(not easy time)** Sinatra with Coplon, 151, 153, Sciacca, 20, Kelley, 435; **(liked a drink)** int. Leonora Hornblow, **Ladies' Home Journal,** Oct. 1976; **(sat in silence/cronies)** ibid. and int. Mel Haber; **("hang out")** int. Joey Villa.

655 **objected: Ladies' Home Journal,** Oct. 1976. There is a story relating to this period that links Sinatra with Jackie Kennedy Onassis and centers on an occasion in September 1975 when he and Jackie dined at the "21" Club in New York. In a book largely lacking in specific sources, Sinatra biographer Randy Taraborrelli wrote—after both had died—that they later "spent the night together" at Sinatra's Waldorf apartment. He cited a source he named only by a pseudonym, "Jim Whiting," as having said "they absolutely were intimate." The late Doris Lilly, who knew Onassis and wrote a book about Greek tycoons, has been quoted as saying Onassis "was convinced Jackie and Sinatra were having an affair. Onassis said he had caught them kissing." Lilly is also quoted as saying she remembered "seeing them going into her apartment late at night." The authors have seen nothing to substantiate such suggestions of a a sexual liaison. The bandleader Peter Duchin, who dined with Sinatra and Jackie Onassis in 1974, thought it improbable. "I got the impression," he told the authors, "that she didn't find him very attractive." When she was an editor for the publisher Viking, Jackie reportedly tried and failed to get Sinatra to write an autobiography (Sinatra/Onassis in New York—**LAHE,** Sep. 18, 1975; Taraborrelli—Taraborrelli, 408–, 524; Lilly—Christopher Andersen, **Jackie After Jack,** New York: Wm. Morrow, 1998, 215, 259, 324–; Duchin—Bradford, 515–, int. Peter Duchin; tried re autobiography—Andersen, **Jackie,** 312).

656–658 **"with a diamond":** Sinatra with Coplon, 153–, Sinatra, **Legend,** 244—the reference in Tina Sinatra's book to "1975" should evidently read "1976"; **("I don't want")** Kelley, 435, 437, Sinatra with Coplon, 152; **(FS sent attorney)** ibid., 155, Kelley, 437; **(marriage/"before a black"/guests/gifts) LAT,** Jul. 12, 16, **Canyon Crier,** Jul. 26, **Ladies' Home Journal,** Oct. 1976, John Cooney, **The Annenbergs,** New York: Simon and Schuster, 1982, 387; **(Bea Korshak) Hollywood Reporter,** Jun. 23, 1976, and see reference to Sidney Korshak at chapter 24, p. 260, **supra.;**

(daughters attended/not Frank Jr.) LAT, July 16, 1976, Kelley, 438; **(pen)** Sinatra with Coplon, 158, 197; **(Barbara balked)** ibid., 156; **(ex-wife Nancy at Tahoe)** LAHE, Oct. 22, 1974; **("take vacation"/"last romantic")** Sinatra with Coplon, 153–; **(reconcile)** ibid., 156; **(Ava in NY apartment)** Hamill, 176, int. Pete Hamill; **(FS "would ring")** int. Spoli Mills; **("called her several times")** Gardner, 287, int. Mearene Jordan, and see Cannon, 134; **("Darling")** Ava Gardner to Spoli Mills—original letter shown to the authors by the late Spoli Mills, in 2004; **("kind of wonderful")** TV Guide, Apr. 16, 1977.

658–659 **work in late 1970s: (ninety-two concerts)** Where or When?—from wedding, Jul. 11, 1976, to Apr. 12, 1977; **(more than a thousand)** ibid.—from wedding to Dec. 31, 1989; **("I'm sixty-one")** TV Guide, Apr. 16, 1977; **("I just cannot")** FS int. by Arlene Francis, Oct. 1, 1977, WOR (NY); **(albums on charts/only one a success)** Sayers and O'Brien, 261, Rednour, 250.

659 **"New York" background:** O'Brien with Wilson, 159, Friedwald, 481, Granata, 195. When released in 1980 as a single, "New York, New York" went to number thirty-two on the **Billboard** chart. "My Way," eleven years earlier, had gone to number twenty-seven. The three albums containing new material were the three-album set **Trilogy** (1980)—which included "New York, New York"—**She Shot Me Down** (1981), and **L.A. Is My Lady** (1984). **Trilogy,** with an album each for the themes "Past," "Present," and "Future"—with accompanying cumbersome subtitles—was too clever by far for the wider public. The **New Yorker** dismissed it as "the silliest venture the singer has ever got himself into." Jonathan Schwartz, a Sinatra enthusiast and a radio host at Metromedia, said of the "Future" album that "one must avert one's eyes when one hears it. . . . The ideas are so trite and clichéd." Such blasphemy led to Schwartz being temporarily suspended from his job, apparently because Sinatra complained to Metromedia chairman John Kluge. Schwartz has claimed, too, that Sinatra made bloodcurdling threats against him over the phone. Not all critics, however, damned **Trilogy.** The **Philadelphia Inquirer** reviewer thought the collection an "ambitious, flawed gem, but a gem nevertheless." The **She Shot Me Down** album was a collection of songs about lost love. It received decent reviews but failed to get major attention. **L.A. Is**

My Lady also misfired, suffering not least from the fact that the title track—planned as an anthem for Los Angeles as "Chicago" and "New York, New York" had been for those cities—did not take off. Sinatra reportedly feared the album would not work commercially, and it did rise only to number fifty-eight in the **Billboard** charts. The **Atlantic Monthly** critic Stephen Holden damned it as "probably the worst of Sinatra's career . . . slopped together." Others differed. Other Sinatra albums released between 1977 and 1990 were compilations of songs recorded years earlier (**New York, New York**—Rednour, 71, Sayers and O'Brien, 266; "silliest venture"—**New Yorker,** Oct. 4, 1982; "one must avert"—**People,** May 5, 1980; suspended—Schwartz, 248–; threats—**Vanity Fair,** Jul. 1998, but see Schwartz, 248; "ambitious"—**Philadelphia Inquirer,** Dec. 19, 1980; **Shot**—Rockwell, 221, Friedwald, 358; **Lady** misfired/title track—Friedwald, 494; FS feared—Granata, 200; No. 58—Sayers and O'Brien, 261; "probably worst"/differed—**USA Today,** Dec. 12, 1984, Rockwell, 222; compilations—Rednour, 250, 259, 264; "disappointingly subpar"—Friedwald, 268).

660 **"There it began": San Diego Union Leader,** Apr. 24, 1987; **(London/Francis Albert Hall)** Sinatra, **Legend,** 256; **(Egypt)** LAHE, Sep. 28, **Time,** Oct. 3, 1979.

660 **Rio de Janeiro:** Estimates of the numbers attending ranged from 150,000 to 180,000. Paul McCartney bettered the Sinatra figures somewhat, the **Guinness** record-keepers believed, when he performed at the same stadium in 1990 (estimates—**LAHE,** Jan. 28, **Variety,** Jan. 31, **Manchete,** Feb. 2, 1980; McCartney 1990—www.guinnessworldrecords.com); **(venues) Where or When?**

661 **"Barbara"/"disappointingly":** Friedwald, 268. Sinatra recorded "Barbara" in 1977 for **Here's to the Ladies,** an album that was never released. The song did not surface until 1995, when it appeared on a Reprise CD. Sinatra first sang it live, however, as early as 1979. From late 1987, after a long apparent gap, he sang it regularly (Rednour, 16, **Where or When?**).

661–663 **Marriage to Barbara: ("the sunshine")** "All Star Party for Frank Sinatra," Variety Clubs International benefit, Nov. 20, 1983, videotape in authors' collection; **(Brynner)** int. Rock Brynner, and see Kirk Douglas, **Climbing the Mountain,** New York: Simon and Schuster, 1997, 206; **(Rizzo persona non grata) Philadelphia Daily News,** Apr. 4, 1984, Jan. 23, 1985, Sinatra with Coplon, 179; **(Barbara remodeled/"Most of those"/ renamed) Architectural Digest,** Dec. 1998, **Buffalo News,** May 15, 1983, **LAT,** Mar. 27, 1983, Nov. 25, 1998, Sinatra, **Legend,** 322, FS int. on **Suzy Visits; ("All she wants") Ladies' Home Journal,** Oct. 1979; **(moderated drinking/sleeping better) LAT,** Feb. 28, 1988, Deutsch, 237, Shaw, **Entertainer,** 116; **("He seemed")** int. Charles Higham; **("Barbara began sorting")** int. Leonora Hornblow; **("Can you picture")** King with Occhiogrosso, 144; **(Griffin and lighter)** Matthau, 234–; **(planning adoption)** Sinatra, **My Father,** 260, **Us** magazine undat. late 2000.

663 **FS got annulment: Variety,** Nov. 5, **LAHE,** Nov. 9, 24, **Star,** Nov. 27, 1979. The Roman Catholic Church had in the past permitted few annulments—usually only on proof of one partner's mental illness, failure to consummate, or refusal to have children. By the time Sinatra got his annulment, however, the Church had become more lenient. Grounds now included immaturity at the time of the wedding or unwillingness to take on the responsibilities of a spouse. It is not clear what evidence Sinatra could have presented to justify annulment of his lengthy marriage to Nancy Barbato (**New York Post,** Jun. 11, 1971, **Newsweek,** Mar. 13, 1975, Garry Wills, **Structures of Deceit,** New York: Doubleday, 2000, 170–); **(first they knew)** int. Tina Sinatra for **60 Minutes,** CBS News, Oct. 8, 2000; **(Nancy "betrayed")** Sinatra with Coplon, 173.

663 **FS and Barbara marry in church:** According to the **National Catholic News Service,** Sinatra and Barbara exchanged vows in a private ceremony at St. Patrick's Cathedral in New York. **People** magazine, however, later reported that the ceremony took place in Palm Springs (NYC?—**Variety,** Nov. 5, 1979; Palm Springs?—**People,** Sep. 22, 1986); **(problems/separation) Star,** Jul. 5, 1983, **LAHE,** Jul. 11, **New York Post,** Jul. 12, 1985, **LAT,** Feb. 28, 1988, Kelley, 495, Sinatra with Coplon, 174–; **("Dad's legacy")** ibid., 186.

663–664 **Dolly's jet smashed: (Long Beach, CA) Press Telegram,** Jan. 9, **NYT, WP,** Jan. 10, 1977. News reports at the time, and even her granddaughter Nancy's book **Legend,** erroneously gave Dolly Sinatra's age at death as eighty-two. Official records in the United States and Italy, however, indicate that she was eighty. She was born on December 26, 1896, as cited in chapter 2 (**WP,**

Jan. 10, 1977, Sinatra, **Legend,** 248); **(FS grief-stricken)** Ladies' **Home Journal,** Oct. 1979, **Family Weekly,** Jun. 17, 1984; **("They'd fought")** Sinatra, **My Father,** 257–; **("He was a different")** int. Sonny King.

Chapter 34: The Photograph

665 **"He dials":** ints. senior hotel employee. Concerned about the many Sinatra associates who still live in his area, the employee asked that his name be withheld here. He was interviewed in person by Anthony Summers.

665 **Westchester Theater: (FS performed)** corr. Ric Ross, not as in Apr. 1–11 and Sep. 24–Oct. 2, 1976, May 16–29, 1977, entries, **Where or When?; (Theater folded/Mafia operation/investigation) New York Post,** Nov. 15, 1978, **New York Daily News,** Jan. 11, 1981, int. Nathaniel Akerman, int. Nathaniel Akerman for PITV; **(eleven jailed/paid fines)** int. and corr. Nathaniel Akerman, Demaris, **Last Mafioso,** 432, **NYT,** Mar. 30, **Facts on File,** Jun. 19, 1981, AP, Mar. 14, 1984, **LAT,** Feb. 1, 1985.

666 **FS and theater: (Rizzo skim/"tape recorded"/Rudin) New York Daily News,** Jan. 11, 1981; **(secretary/"knowledgeable")** ibid., Dec. 27, 1978, Carpozi, **Sinatra,** 342—the secretary was identified by the FBI agents only as "Dorothy."

666 **"accomplice witness": Chicago Sun-Times,** Apr. 15, 1980—attorney Akerman identified the witness to the authors as Jimmy Fratianno.

666–669 **Weisman & DePalma jailed:** Demaris, **Last Mafioso,** 432. Weisman was to work for Sinatra far into the future and be one of two executors of Sinatra's will (manager—**NYT,** Oct. 31, 1993, Sinatra with Coplon, 208; executor—Last Will and Testament of Francis Albert Sinatra, Los Angeles Superior Court, Case no. BP.051249); **("You should've seen")** ibid., 383; **(Exhibit 181) New York Daily News,** Dec. 27, 1978; **(photograph)** see second illustration section; **(Castellano)** Sifakis, 133, int. Nathaniel Akerman for PITV; **(Gambino's nephew) New York Daily News,** Jan. 11, 1981; **(Fratianno background) Look,** Sep. 23, 1969, Sifakis, 126; **(Fratianno informant)** Demaris, **Last Mafioso,** refs.; **(Spatola) New York Daily News,** Dec. 27, 1978, **NYT,** May 24, 1987, Jan. 28, 1989, (NY) **Newsday,** May 11, 1993; **(Fusco)** Demaris, **Last Mafioso,** 304, 432; **(DePalma)** ibid., 441, (Westchester County, NY) **Journal News,** May 6, Jun. 12, 1999; **(three in photo defendants)** New York Daily News, Dec. 27, 1978—the three were DePalma, Fusco, and Marson; **(photographer "scared shitless")** int. Nathaniel Akerman; **(FS no comment)** (Hudson/Bergen Counties, NJ) **Monday Dispatch,** Nov. 13, 1978; **("I didn't hear"/"I can't say")** New York Daily News, Dec. 27, 1978; **("Would you take"/"I was asked"/didn't know backgrounds)** FS testimony, Nevada State Gaming Control Board, Feb. 11, 1981, on Giuliano audiotape; **(FS never met Gambino)** FS testimony, Nevada State Gaming Control Board, Feb. 11, 1981; **(knew Marson/met "Jimmy")** ibid.; **(unaware of crooked goings-on)** ibid.; **(FS welcomed "with a kiss")** Demaris, **Last Mafioso,** 341; **(Gambino's son-in-law/board of league) Life,** Sep. 8, 1967, **NYT,** Oct. 16, 1976, Di Lorenzo to President Johnson, Aug. 30, 1967, Frank Sinatra File, Box 320, White House Central Files, Lyndon B. Johnson Library.

669 **Fratianno said had seen more of FS:** Demaris, **Last Mafioso,** 63, 312, 324–, 341, 343–, 349–, 354–. Fratianno made these statements not to the prosecutors but to the author Ovid Demaris, who wrote a book about him later. Demaris found Fratianno a credible source, as did U.S. Attorney Akerman.

Fratianno's claims aside, it is likely that Frank had known who Fratianno was well before meeting him with Marson. By a bizarre coincidence, Barbara's former husband Zeppo Marx had earlier been involved with Fratianno's wife—an involvement that culminated in an unpleasant lawsuit. Jean Fratianno had filed a suit against Marx alleging he had assaulted her. Marx claimed there had been merely a pushing incident as she tried to leave his Palm Springs house with his front-door key and company credit card. The case was tried in the late 1970s, and Marx was ordered to pay Mrs. Fratianno $20,690 in damages (Fratianno credible—Demaris, **Last Mafioso,** refs., int. Nathaniel Akerman; Zeppo Marx—Demaris, **Last Mafioso,** 258).

669–670 **DePalma and FS substantive conversations:** Demaris, **Last Mafioso,** 383; **(Pacella background) New York Post,** Nov. 19, 1978, Demaris, **Last Mafioso,** 445, Mickey Rudin testimony, Nevada State Gaming Commission, Feb. 19, 1981; **(Pacella jailed) NYT,** Jan. 11, 1981; **("involvement" of FS) Wall Street Journal,** Jan. 16, 1981, int. Nathaniel Akerman for PITV;

(refused to answer re FS/contempt) ibid., NYT, Jan. 11, Wall Street Journal, Jan. 16, 1981; **(FS admitted)** FS testimony, Nevada State Gaming Control Board, Feb. 11, 1981; **("You will find")** Wall Street Journal, Jan. 16, 1981; **(Pacella capo)** NYT, Jan. 11, Wall Street Journal, Jan. 16, 1981; **(heroin dealer)** Kelley, 450, and see int. Nathaniel Akerman for PITV.

670 **"After Sam Giancana":** "Investigation on 9/6–8/89," Mar. 27, 1990, FBI 183B-Z132-Sub. 2. Leonetti was an underboss in the Philadelphia mob, a nephew of mafioso Nicodemus "Nicky" Scarfo. Having agreed to cooperate with the FBI in 1989 following his conviction on a murder charge, he was held in protective custody and released after serving only five years. Leonetti's testimony resulted in the convictions of numerous top mobsters, and was used in the trial of John Gotti ("Illinois Police and Sheriff's News," at www.ispn.org, George Anastasia, **Blood and Honor,** New York: William Morrow, 1991, 339–, 347).

670–673 **FS and Reagan: ("We've heard those")** Philadelphia Inquirer, Jan. 17, 1981; **(asked FS to stage)** LAHE, Nov. 20, 1980; **(Reagan at wedding)** LAT, Feb. 9, 1981; **(at Dolly's funeral)** LAHE, Jan. 13, 1977; **("tooth fairy"/"Mickey Mouse")** Kelley, 455; **(large sums)** Newsweek, Jan. 19, **Philadelphia Inquirer,** Jan. 15, 20, 1981, Sep. 30, 1980, entry, Where or When?; **("It isn't every candidate")** Newsweek, Jan. 19, 1981; **("jubilant")** LAHE, Nov. 20, 1980; **("trashy Las Vegas show")** unid. Rex Reed column, Jan. 20, 1981, and see undat. Mike Royko column, Jan. 1981, **Chicago Daily News; ("Grecian Formula")** undat. Rex Winston article, Jan. 1981, **New York Daily News; ($5.5 million)** LAHE, Jan. 27, 1981; **(cigarette boxes) Hollywood Reporter,** Jan. 28, 1981; **(applied for license)** Wall Street Journal, Jan. 16, 1981; **("the burden of proof")** comments of Chairman Bunker, Nevada State Gaming Control Board, Feb. 11, 1981, 2; **(given easiest ride)** see transcripts, hearings of Nevada State Gaming Control Board, Feb. 11, 1981, and State Gaming Commission, Feb. 19, 1981; **(Peck & Douglas)** statements of Gregory Peck and Kirk Douglas, Nevada State Gaming Control Board, Feb. 11, 1981, 53–; **(Board member "satisfied")** ibid., comments of Mr. Askew, 181; **(some "change")** ibid., 184; **("in the gaming business")** ibid., 188; **("naively superficial"/"awe")** NYT, Feb. 15, 1981; **(French Smith at party/"totally unaware")** Philadelphia

Inquirer, Jan. 8, Newsweek, Jan. 19, 1981; **(Reagan referee)** Chicago Sun-Times, LAHE, Jun. 18, 1980; **(no more significance)** NYT, Jan. 2, 1981; **("an honorable")** NYT, Dallas Times-Herald, Feb. 19, 1981; **(Reagan shot/comfort Nancy)** LAT, Mar. 31, 1981, Sinatra, My Father, xx; **(bronco/"To the American")** LAT, Jun. 4, 1981.

673–674 **Second inaugural:** Jersey Journal, Jan. 18, 1985. Reagan also had Frank sing at a state occasion at the White House, and organize a show for Britain's Queen Elizabeth when she visited California in 1983. He and Sinatra appeared together in Hoboken, the singer's birthplace, when Reagan ran for a second term (state occasion—LAHE, Mar. 26, 1982; Queen Elizabeth—ibid., Jan. 9, 1983, Kitty Kelley, Nancy Reagan, New York: Simon and Schuster, 1991, 385; Hoboken—Jersey Observer, Jul. 7, 1984); **(Medal of Freedom/"one of our most")** LAT, Apr. 9, 1985, LAHE, Sep. 29, 1986.

674 **65th birthday party:** LAHE, Philadelphia Daily News, Dec. 15, 1980; **(64th birthday/40th anniversary)** LAHE, Dec. 13, 1979, Dec. 12, 1979, entry, Where or When?

674–676 **Kitty Kelley book: (working on autobiography)** TV Guide, Apr. 16, 1977; **("forced to write")** FS interview by William B. Williams, WNEW (NY), Dec. 6, 1983, audiotape in authors' collection; **(Kelley digging)** LAHE, Oct. 16, 1983; press release, Washington Independent Writers, Oct. 7, 1983, MHL; **(Kelley had written FS/except to sue/"presuming to write")** Kelley, ix, and see Frank Sinatra and Camden Enterprises v. Kitty Kelley, Superior Court of the State of California, County of Los Angeles, No. WEC082657, Sep. 21, 1983; **(suit came to nothing)** Variety, Sep. 20, 1984; **("so terrified")** Kelley, Nancy Reagan, 3; **(eight hundred others)** Kelley, xi; **(bestseller)** Columbia Journalism Review, Aug. 1991, Kitty Kelley entry, Du Plain International Speakers Bureau, www.duplain.com; **("I never read")** New York Daily News, Dec. 23, 1986; **("pimps and prostitutes"/ "parasites"/"crap")** Larry King int. of FS, May 19, 1998 (rerun), King with Occhiogrosso, 145–; **(name taboo/"nearly strangled")** LAHE, Oct. 29, 1986, Sinatra, Legend, 302–; **("the big C-word")** (London) Observer, Oct. 3, 2004; **(book made FS ill?)** TV Guide, Nov. 7, 1992, Ladies' Home Journal, Dec. 1993.

676 **FS health: (throat)** FS interview by William B. Williams, WNEW (NY), Dec. 6, 1983, transcript provided to authors by

Ed O'Brien, Sinatra, **Legend,** 259, 261; **(polyps) Time,** Jul. 7, 1986; **(cut back on cigarettes/drink)** Friedwald, 488, Sinatra, **My Father,** 276, **McCall's,** Aug. 1989, King with Occhiogrosso, 144; **(lapses)** Taraborrelli, 443, ints. Tony Posk, Ann Barak, Tita Cahn, Kelley, 495–, Brownstein, 363–; **(severe pain)** Larry King int. of FS, May 19, 1998 (rerun); **(surgery & colostomy) LAT,** Nov. 9, 1986, **Variety,** Nov. 25, 1986, **NYT,** Jan. 15, 1987, **Woman's Day,** Apr. 13, 1987, Sinatra, **Legend,** 304, Sinatra with Coplon, 188; **("If I hadn't")** Larry King int. of FS, May 19, 1998 (rerun); **(within two weeks)** Sinatra, **Legend,** 304.

677–678 **"Together Again" tour: (press conference/"As if replaying") LAT,** Dec. 2, 1987; **(Martin alcohol/painkillers)** Tosches, 256, 392, 403, 420–, 425, 427; **(ulcers/kidney trouble)** ibid., 433; **(son's death)** Martin with Smith, 208–; **(Davis alcohol/drugs/liver/hip operation)** Haygood, 443, 451, 455, 459, 463, 467, 470, Davis, Boyar, and Boyar, **Why Me,** 349–, **LAT,** Mar. 15, 1988; **(began tour/14,500/"String"/"Ipanema"/"Every time")** ibid., **Variety,** Mar. 16, 1988; **(FS cajole Martin)** Martin with Smith, 226, Tosches, 435; **(Martin had fallen)** int. Tony Posk; **(flicked cigarette/FS berated) LAT,** Mar. 15, 1988, Haygood, 467; **(FS wanted to party)** Martin with Smith, **People,** Jun. 1, 1998; **("They weren't in shape") People,** Jun. 1, 1998.

678 **harassed/flew back/sick/"He loved": (shouts)** Kupcinet, 212; Martin with Smith, 227. Martin's agent, the late Mort Viner, was still maintaining as late as 2002 that there were no confrontations in Chicago, that his client really did get sick. That claim is belied by what Martin's son has written and by several musicians in the orchestra, Ann Barak, Tony Posk, and Sol Schlinger, who were interviewed. There was also the announcement soon afterward that Martin was about to go back to work—on his own (Viner—int. of Mort Viner; musicians—ints. Ann Barak, Tony Posk, Sol Schlinger; announcement—**LAHE,** Apr. 15, 1988).

678–679 **Deaths: (Davis "scratchy throat"/refused surgery)** Haygood, 468–, 472–, Davis with Barclay, 202–; **(Van Heusen) LAT,** Feb. 8, 1990; **("in little pieces") People,** Dec. 17, 1990; **(visited/sobbed)** Davis with Barclay, 218–; **(gold watch)** Haygood, 480.

679–680 **Ava: (stroke)** Evans tapes, Cannon, 126–, corr. Peter Evans; **(smoking/drinking)** ibid., Evans tapes; **("I can't say")** ibid.; **(Dahl) People,** Feb. 12, 1996; **(bouquet)** Cannon, 103; **(photo of wedding)** Evans tapes; **(plane)** Sinatra with Coplon, 214; **(limousine)** Cannon, 126; **(FS broke down)** Sinatra with Coplon, 214, "Grieving Sinatra Tells Wife 'I Want to be Buried Next to Ava Gardner,' " unid. clip, 1990, MHL; **(not among mourners/"With my love")** int. Barbara Twigg (florist), Cannon, 130; **(Albany/Jack Daniel's/"Sinatra seemed")** Jan. 30, 1990, entry, **Where or When?**; int. & corr. Ed O'Brien.

Chapter 35: To the End of the Road

681–682 **performing in early 1990s: (world tour 1991)** Sinatra, **Legend,** 311, Taraborrelli, 491; **(number of concerts)** 1991–94 entries, **Where or When?**; **(Hackman) Heist,** directed by David Mamet, Warner Brothers, Nov. 9, 2001; **(TV special/"Physically")** Dec. 16, 1990, entry, **Where or When? NYT,** Dec. 31, 1990; **("cracked")** undat. Walter Scott "Personality Parade" column, late 1984; **("shook") L.A. Weekly,** Jan. 15, 1988; **("opaque") Élan,** Sep. 27–29, 1991; **("in a state")** ed. Mustazza, **Bibliography,** 77.

682–685 **physical decline: (hearing aid)** int. Ann Barak, **(Ireland) Sunday Independent,** Apr. 22, 2001; **(TelePrompTers not at every)** corr. Ric Ross; **("He was using")** int. Frank Fighera; **(cataract operation)** int. Tony Oppedisano, Sinatra with Coplon, 228, AP, undat., May 1998; **("forgot lyrics") Cue,** Oct. 28, 1978; **("I was in the midst")** Sinatra, **My Father,** 281–; **("We were doing")** int. Tony Mottola; **(walked off the stage) Philadelphia Daily News,** Sep. 4, 1984; **("incoherently rambling")** LAHE, Oct. 21, 1988; **(assumed drinking/"What the hell?") Variety,** Jan. 27, 1989; **("The sickness")** int. Frank Fighera; **(pill bottles / Elavil / sisters voiced concern / Tina and FS intellect)** Sinatra with Coplon, 195–, Oct. 29, 1988, entry, **Where or When?**; **(Bregman)** int. Buddy Bregman, provided to authors by Ed O'Brien; **(failed to recognize Liza)** int. Ann Barak; **("He was either")** int. Darrien Iacocca.

685 **side effects of medication or drink?:** Elavil entry, ed. William Kelly, **Drug Handbook,** 24th ed., Philadelphia: Springhouse, 2004, 439–, Sinatra with Coplon, 195, Granata, 200. The famous blue eyes now often looked "like marbles," violinist Tony Posk said. Fighera and violist Ann Barak, who knew Frank was on med-

ication, ascribed variations in Frank's condition to changes in the dosage (ints. Tony Posk, Ann Barak, Frank Fighera).

685 **Kennamer/"definitely had":** int. Dr. Rex Kennamer. In the late 1990s, brain scans would indicate dementia (Sinatra with Coplon, 259); **("If I were"/"no longer sustain") GQ,** Jun. 1989; **("the spontaneity")** eds. Petkov and Mustazza, 188; **("My guess") Esquire,** Dec. 1987.

687 **what drove FS to go on: ("God, give me")** Sinatra with Coplon, 231, and see int. Tina Sinatra for **60 Minutes,** CBS News, Oct. 8, 2000, ints. Tony Oppedisano, Leonora Hornblow.

687 **"A.J. and Amanda"/Michael:** Oddly, either because a grandchild born out of wedlock was not enough for him or because his mind was addled, Sinatra spoke as late as 1988—the year after Michael's birth—as though he had no grandson. (Michael's birth—Sinatra, **Legend,** 304; talk publicly 1988—Larry King int. of FS, May 19, 1998 (rerun).

687 **anxiety not outlandish:** Information from source close to FS advisers.

687–688 **decline: (Tina re acrimonious exchanges)** Sinatra with Coplon, 197–; **(Agreement to Rescind)** ibid., 198–; **(new will)** ibid., 291; **(As Tina saw it)** int. Tina Sinatra for **60 Minutes,** CBS News, Oct. 8, 2000; **("ridicule Dad")** Sinatra with Coplon, 194; **("openly dismissive")** ibid., 218; **(phoned ex-wife Nancy)** ibid., 177; **("the greatest")** int. Sonny King; **("the best thing")** int. Armand Deutsch; **("wonderful")** int. Rex Kennamer and see int. Abbe Lane.

689–690 **reading papers:** For news, Sinatra read the **New York Times** and the **New York Daily News.** He had an aversion to the **New York Post** and **The Wall Street Journal** (int. Tony Oppedisano); **(trains/"all the trains"/"an engineer's hat") People,** Dec. 17, 1990, Sinatra's Diamond Jubilee World Tour program, **USA Weekend,** Dec. 18, 1988; **("He asked")** int. Ann Barak; **("the strongest drug")** Newsweek, Mar. 21, 1994; **("It gives me") New York Daily News,** Jan. 23, 1978; **("a dribbling madman")** Frank Sinatra Jr. on **Showbiz Today,** CNN, Jul. 13, 1989, videotape in authors' collection; **("his life force")** Tina Sinatra int. for **Larry King Live,** CNN, Nov. 5, 1992; **("reduce the strain") LAT,** Sep. 16, 1990.

690 **Rizzo killed: LAT,** May 7, 1992, int. Tony Oppedisano, Sinatra with Coplon, 223.

691–692 **performing 1992: (concert tour)** Where or When; **(helped on stage)** Freedland, 409; **(MacLaine toured/"a ring ding . . .")** MacLaine, **Lucky Stars,** 97–, int. Shirley MacLaine; **(Clinton/"He and I")** int. Tony Oppedisano.

693 ***Duets:*** **(Ramone urging/Streisand et al./fiber optic system/ Olivier/"I'm singing")** Vanity Fair, Dec. 1993, NYT, Oct. 7, 1993, Granata, xi, 203–. Ramone said he first mentioned the duets concept to Sinatra's people in 1992, and Sinatra became involved the following year (Granata, 204); **("Tramp"/tears)** Pignone, 77–, conv. Henry Cattaneo; **("like Andy Warhol")** GQ, Mar. 1994; **(number two/two million)** int. Gordon Murray, **Billboard,** and figures supplied by Recording Industry Association of America, www.riaa.com—Sinatra believed erroneously that **Duets** went to number one (Sinatra, **Legend,** 318); **(largest selling) Down Beat,** Aug. 1998. **Duets II,** released a year later, sold more than a million copies (www.riaa.com); **("like a little kid")** Sinatra, **Legend,** 318.

693–694 **wonderful moments/confront reality: (danced in aisles)** eds. Petkov and Mustazza, 193; **(Queen of Sweden)** int. of Bobby Lamb, RTE (Ireland) radio, Sep./Oct. 2002; **("What the hell?")** eds. Petkov and Mustazza, 191; **(oxygen)** Sinatra with Coplon, 229; **(FS "is old") GQ,** Jan. 1994; **(FS shuffled)** Sinatra with Coplon, 239, Dec. 27–30, 1993 entries, **Where or When?; ("He well remembers")** eds. Petkov and Mustazza, 179–.

694–697 **performing in 1994: (handkerchief/"Legend"/toupee/ FS responded)** 36th Annual Grammy Awards, CBS-TV, Mar. 1, 1994, videotape in authors' collection; **("a man heavier") Philadelphia Inquirer,** May 17, 1998; **(FS vanished/cut off)** ed. Mustazza, 66, **New York Daily News,** Mar. 3, 1994, Sinatra with Coplon, 240; **(collapsed) Newsweek,** Mar. 21, 1994, (**London**) **Observer,** May 17, 1998; **("right through")** int. Tony Oppedisano; **(flew to California)** LAT, **Variety,** Mar. 7, **People,** Mar. 21, 1994, Zehme, 234–; **("You write") Time,** Mar. 21, 1994; **(Radio City/"This may be") Variety,** Apr. 25, 1994; **(Tokyo) Frank Sinatra in Japan,** Dec. 19–20, 1994, videotape of Japanese TV broadcast in authors' collection—the two appearances appear to have been edited together for the broadcast; **(musicians found painful)** ints. Ann Barak, Frank Fighera; **("Even before")** Natalie Cole with Digby Diehl, **Angel on My Shoulder,** New

York: Warner, 2000, 289; **(Palm Springs resort/golf tournament)** Feb. 25, 1995, entry, **Where or When?; Architectural Digest,** Dec. 1998; **(performed well)** int. Tony Oppedisano.

697–698 **eightieth birthday: (gestures/Empire State/Fifth Avenue) Commonweal,** Dec. 15, 1995, **Philadelphia Daily News,** May 18, 1998; **(TV special/"Patron Saint")** Variety, undat., Dec. 1995; **(Dylan song/trouble understanding)** LAT, Nov. 21, 1995, corr. Ric Ross; **("New York, New York")** int. George Schlatter, **Variety,** undat., Dec. 1995; **("*cent' anni*") Voices in Italian-Americana,** vol. 10, Fall 1992, e.g., Apr. 16, 1977, entry, **Where or When?** Anecdotal evidence suggests that **cent'anni** is a contraction of **a cento anni,** an old toast usually made at birthday parties (research by Livia Borghese, int. Ann Barak).

Chapter 36: Exit

699 **"You gotta love":** int. Tony Oppedisano.

699–700 **friends' deaths: (choked up)** undat. article by Robert Wolinsky, www.nj.com; **("gone to the mountains")** ibid.; **(Martin "brother")** Taraborrelli, 504; **("There was")** int. Tony Oppedisano; **(did not attend)** int. Mort Viner.

700 **Sands closure/"Frank took":** "La Rue's Sands," www.lvstriphistory .com.

700 **FS house move: (Fabergé/artists) LAT,** Jul. 28, 1991, catalogue for Christie's sale of Sinatra collection, Dec. 1, 1995.

700 **Fifth Avenue in snow:** ibid., 51, and see "My Life with Frank Sinatra," article draft by Marva Peterson, Jul. 21, 1947, MHL. The Christie's catalogue listed a painting entitled **Fifth Avenue in the Snow,** by Wiggins. In a 1947 magazine interview, Nancy Sinatra mentioned "special days like the time Frank brought me the painting of Fifth Avenue, N.Y., in a snow storm and had it hanging over the fireplace Christmas morning."

700–702 **gifts etc. in auction:** Christie's catalogue, 16, 14, 18, 93, 108, 91, 111, 91; **(he could play)** int. Tony Oppedisano, Frank, 77; **(caboose) Architectural Digest,** Dec. 1998; **(Christie's/$5 million)** Christie's catalogue, **Newsweek,** Dec. 11, 1995; **(house sold/$2 million) Architectural Digest,** Dec. 1998, **LAT,** May 7, 1995; **("everybody")** Sinatra, **Legend,** 322; **(devastated) Architectural Digest,** Dec. 1998; **("grieving"/allowed stay on/ twenty-six staff)** Sinatra with Coplon, 243–, int. Tony

Oppedisano, **Architectural Digest,** Dec. 1998; **(Beverly Hills spread)** (Newark, NJ) **Sunday Star-Ledger,** Mar. 22, 1998; **(Malibu/neighbors)** int. Shirley MacLaine, **LAT,** Sep. 2, 1990; **(sterile/"They must be doing"/ocean reminded)** Sinatra with Coplon, 245, int. Tony Oppedisano; **("When are we?")** Sinatra with Coplon, 244; **("Where am I?") Time,** May 25, 1998.

702–703 **renew vows/daughters not attend:** Such was the tension in the family that Tina did not see or even speak with her father for almost a year (Sinatra with Coplon, 251–).

703–704 **Final months: ("pinched nerve"/heart attack/pneumonia, etc.) LAT,** Nov. 2, 3, **(Long Beach, CA) Press-Telegram,** Nov. 3, **New York Post,** Nov. 10, 1996, Sinatra with Coplon, 253–; **(scans/psychiatrist/nurse)** ibid., 257–, 266, int. Dr. Rex Kennamer; **("He didn't know")** int. George Jacobs; **(Gold Medal)** (Long Beach, CA) **Press-Telegram,** Apr. 30, **People,** May 19, 1997, www.congressionalgoldmedal.com; **("wind up")** Sinatra with Coplon, 215; **(sauce/ties) LAT,** May 24, 1990, Apr. 15, 1995.

704 **"Sinatra's wife": Wall Street Journal,** Sep. 26, 1997. In 1999, less than a year after her father's death, Tina Sinatra would announce plans to market: a candle with her father's favorite fragrance, lapel pins, a miniature of a typical Sinatra hat, and a music stand with a hat dangling from a microphone boom. In 2001 she would attend a ceremony in Las Vegas to introduce a Frank Sinatra slot machine. Explaining these plans, Tina said the items would be sold to raise money for the Frank Sinatra Foundation, of which she was president. The project, she said, would "keep the flame alive" and raise money, in particular, for "youth education" (1999 plans—**Variety,** Apr. 22, 1999; 2001—**Las Vegas Review-Journal,** Dec. 7, 2001).

704–706 **Best moments: (Stern) USA Today,** Dec. 15, 1997; **(Clinton/Lewinsky/"Obviously")** int. Tony Oppedisano, Giuliano audiotape; **("I sat"/Old friends/"I went") People,** Jun. 1, 1998, and int. Sonny King; **("Barbara had gone")** int. Tony Oppedisano; **(until millennium)** Sinatra with Coplon, 278, Bill Boggs int.; **("This is not")** int. Tony Oppedisano; **(Catholic faith) Ladies' Home Journal,** Oct. 1979, **LAT,** Apr. 29, 1980, int. Tony Oppedisano; **("We had a talk")** int. Shirley MacLaine; **(previous life)** int. Tony Oppedisano; **("get my mother")** Sinatra with Coplon, 276.

707 **Churchill "closed":** LAHE, Apr. 29, 1980. Sir Winston, moreover, died on January 25, 1965, not at ninety-one but at ninety, following a series of strokes. Lord Moran, his physician, recalled that he had appeared not to recognize anyone, or to move, for some two weeks (Lord Moran, edited diaries, **Winston Churchill: The Struggle for Survival 1940–1965**, London: Constable, 1966, 788).

707 **death: (Barbara out dining)** int. Abbe Lane; **(complained)** cbsnews.com, May 16, 1998; **(sat up and screamed)** Sinatra with Coplon, 285; **(paramedics) Philadelphia Inquirer,** May 17, 1998; **("still very much")** int. Tony Oppedisano; **("very tired")** cbsnews.com, May 16, 1998; **("Fight") Philadelphia Daily News,** May 18, 1998, citing Jerry Vale; **("I'm losing it") Las Vegas Review-Journal,** AP, May 20, 1998, **Esquire,** Jan. 1999.

707–708 **"beyond talking":** int. Dr. Rex Kennamer. The Sinatra death certificate gives the cause of death as "cardiorespiratory arrest" due to "acute myocardial infarction" and "coronary atherosclerosis." The authors have reported Sinatra's dying moments on the basis of what seem to be the most reliable accounts. They discounted a version attributed in press reports to a man named Artie Funair. Funair, who said he had been a friend of Sinatra's, was reported in 1998 as saying that he learned Sinatra's last words had been, "Oh dear Lord, oh mother" (death certificate—County of Los Angeles, Department of Health Services, Certificate of Death no. 090097308; most reliable sources—cbsnews.com, May 16, 1998, reporting family statement, **Variety,** May 19, 1998, int. Tony Oppedisano, Sinatra with Coplon, 285, Sinatra, **Legend,** 323, int. Tony Oppedisano, Jerry Vale quoted in **Philadelphia Daily News,** May 18, 1998; Funair—ibid. and attempt to int. Artie Funair); **(daughters arrived)** Sinatra with Coplon, 281.

708 **reaction to death: (editors)** NYT, **Philadelphia Daily News,** May 18, 1998; **(broadcasters) Philadelphia Inquirer,** May 17, 1998; **(Empire State) Variety,** May 18, 1998; **(Capitol tower) Philadelphia Inquirer,** May 17, 1998; **(Vegas lights)** corr. Ed Walters, by permission, **Esquire,** Jan. 1999; **(Cal-Neva) Granta:76,** Winter 2002; **(Hoboken mass)** (Newark, NJ) **Star-Ledger,** May 19, **People,** Jun. 1, 1998, int. Rev. Michael Guglielmelli.

709–710 **vigil and funeral: (Miller played) New Yorker,** Jun. 1, 1998, Sinatra with Coplon, 294; **(those at mass) Las Vegas**

Review-Journal, May 20, **NYT, LAT, Variety,** May 21, 1998, Villa; **(ex-wife Nancy/Mia Farrow) Variety,** May 21, 1998; **(gardenias)** LAT, May 21, 1998, int. Peggy Connelly; **(five hundred people/photographers/plane)** NYT, LAT, May 21, **New Yorker,** Jun. 1, 1998.

710–711 **burial: (ceremony/flag)** Sinatra with Coplon, 298–, 292; **(others buried/epitaph)** authors' visit to cemetery, "Interments of Interest" fact sheet by Kathleen Jurasky, Palm Springs Cemetery District, **Las Vegas Review-Journal,** May 20, 1998; **("Babe, it's gonna") Sinatra in Japan,** Dec. 19–20, 1994, videotape of broadcast for Japanese TV in authors' collection.

711 **"because I'm not proud":** int. Marilyn Beck, Marilyn Beck, **Marilyn Beck's Hollywood,** New York: Hawthorn, 1973, 124, **New Yorker,** Nov. 3, 1997, (**"Westside," Los Angeles) Rave,** May 22, 1998.

711 **"to have succeeded":** int. of FS by William B. Williams, WNEW (NY) radio, Dec. 6, 1983, audiotape in authors' collection.

711 **"Whatever else": Playboy,** Feb. 1963.

Selected Bibliography

This list includes some three hundred books that are cited in the Notes and Sources. It does not include the many other books used for general reference and background only. Nor does it include newspaper and magazine articles or official documents, which are cited in full in the Notes and Sources.

Adler, Bill. **Sinatra: The Man and the Myth.** New York: NAL Penguin, 1987.

Andersen, Christopher. **Jack and Jackie.** New York: William Morrow, 1996.

Anslinger, Harry J., and Will Oursler. **The Murderers.** New York: Farrar, Straus and Cudahy, 1962.

Anson, Robert Sam. **Exile.** New York: Simon and Schuster, 1984.

Bacall, Lauren. **Lauren Bacall: By Myself.** London: Jonathan Cape Ltd., 1979.

———. **Now.** New York: Alfred A. Knopf, 1994.

Bacon, James. **Hollywood Is a Four-Letter Town.** New York: Avon, 1976.

Bartok, Eva. **Worth Living For.** London: Putnam, 1959.

Barzini, Luigi. **From Caesar to the Mafia.** New York: Library Press, 1971.

———. **The Italians.** New York: Atheneum, 1964.

Basten, Fred, and Charles Phoenix. **Fabulous Las Vegas in the Fifties.** Santa Monica, CA: Angel City Press, 1999.

Beschloss, Michael R. **The Crisis Years: Kennedy and Khruschev, 1960–1963.** New York: HarperCollins, 1991.

Bishop, George. **Frank Sinatra: A Photobiography.** Houston: Epps-Praxis, 1976.

Blair, Joan, and Clay Blair. **The Search for JFK.** New York: Berkley Publishing, 1976.

Blakey, G. Robert, and Richard N. Billings. **The Plot to Kill the President: Organized Crime Assassinated JFK.** New York: Times Books, 1981.

Block, Max, with Ron Kenner. **Max the Butcher.** Secaucus, NJ: Lyle Stuart, 1982.

Bonanno, Bill. **Bound by Honor: A Mafioso's Story.** New York: St. Martin's Press, 1999.

Bosworth, Patricia. **Montgomery Clift: A Biography.** New York: Harcourt Brace Jovanovich, 1978.

Bradford, Sarah. **America's Queen: The Life of Jacqueline Kennedy Onassis.** London: Penguin Books, 2001.

Bragg, Melvyn. **Rich: The Life of Richard Burton.** London: Hodder and Stoughton, 1988.

Branch, Taylor. **Parting the Waters: America in the King Years 1954–63.** New York: Simon and Schuster, 1988.

Brashler, William. **The Don.** New York: Ballantine, 1977.

Britt, Stan. **Frank Sinatra: A Celebration.** New York: Carlton Books, 1995.

Brownstein, Ronald. **The Power and the Glitter: The Hollywood-Washington Connection.** New York: Pantheon Books, 1990.

Brynner, Rock. **Yul: The Man Who Would Be King.** New York: Simon and Schuster, 1989.

Buhle, Paul, and Dave Wagner. **Radical Hollywood: The Untold Story Behind America's Favorite Movies!** New York: New Press, 2002.

Burleigh, Nina. **A Very Private Woman: The Life and Unsolved Murder of Presidential Mistress Mary Meyer.** New York: Bantam Books, 1998.

Cahn, Sammy. **I Should Care.** New York: Arbor House, 1974.

Callow, Simon. **Orson Welles: The Road to Xanadu.** London: Vintage, 1996.

Campbell, Rodney. **The Luciano Project.** New York: McGraw-Hill, 1977.

Cannon, Doris Rollins. **Grabtown Girl: Ava Gardner's North Carolina Childhood and Her Enduring Ties to Home.** Asheboro, NC: Down Home Press, 2001.

Carpozi, George, Jr. **Frank Sinatra: Is This Man Mafia?** New York: Manor Books, 1979.

———. **Poison Pen: The Unauthorized Biography of Kitty Kelley.** Fort Lee, NJ: Barricade Books, 1991.

Case, Marianna. **Another Side of Blue.** Running Springs, CA: Cyberwoman, 1997.

Caute, David. **The Great Fear.** New York: Simon and Schuster, 1978.

Cheshire, Maxine. **Maxine Cheshire: Reporter.** Boston: Houghton Mifflin, 1978.

Clarke, Donald. **All or Nothing at All: A Life of Frank Sinatra.** New York: Fromm, 2000.

Clooney, Rosemary, with Joan Barthel. **Girl Singer: An Autobiography.** New York: Random House, 1999.

Cohen, Mickey, as told to John Peer Nugent. **Mickey Cohen: In My Own Words.** Englewood Cliffs, NJ: Prentice-Hall, 1975.

Cohn, Art. **The Joker Is Wild.** New York: Random House, 1955.

Cole, Natalie, and Digby Diehl. **Angel on My Shoulder.** New York: Warner Books, 2000.

Coleman, Ray. **Sinatra: Portrait of the Artist.** Atlanta: Turner Publishing, 1995.

Collier, Peter, and David Horowitz. **The Kennedys: An American Drama.** London: Pan, 1985.

Consiglio, Albert. **Lucky Luciano.** Milan: Editrice A&G Marco, 1972.

Cook, Fred J. **The Secret Rulers: Criminal Syndicates and How They Control the U.S. Underworld.** New York: Duell, Sloan and Pearce, 1966.

Corbitt, Michael, and Sam Giancana. **Double Deal.** New York: William Morrow, 2003.

Crane, Cheryl, with Cliff Jahr. **Detour: A Hollywood Tragedy; My Life with Lana Turner, My Mother.** London: Sphere Books Ltd., 1989.

Cummings, John, and Ernest Volkman. **Goombata: The Improbable Rise and Fall of John Gotti and His Gang.** Boston: Little, Brown, 1990.

Dallek, Robert. **An Unfinished Life: John F. Kennedy 1917–1963.** New York: Little, Brown, 2003.

Daniell, John. **Ava Gardner.** New York: St. Martin's Press, 1982.

Davenport, Elaine, and Paul Eddy. **The Hughes Papers.** London: André Deutsch, 1977.

Davidson, Bill. **The Real and the Unreal.** New York: Lancer Books, 1962.

Davis, John H. **Mafia Dynasty: The Rise and Fall of the Gambino Crime Family.** New York: HarperTorch, 1993.

Davis, Sammy, Jr. **Hollywood in a Suitcase.** New York: William Morrow, 1980.

Davis, Sammy, Jr., Jane Boyar, and Burt Boyar. **Why Me?: The Sammy Davis, Jr., Story.** New York: Farrar, Strauss and Giroux, 1990.

———. **Yes, I Can: The Story of Sammy Davis, Jr.** New York: Farrar, Straus and Giroux, 1965.

Davis, Tracey, and Dolores Barclay. **Sammy Davis Jr.: My Father.** LA: General Publishing Group, Inc., 1996.

de Leeuw, Hendrik. **Underworld Story: The Rise of Organized Crime and Vice-Rackets in the USA.** London: Neville Spearman Ltd., 1955.

Dellar, Fred. **Sinatra: His Life and Times.** London: Omnibus Press, 1995.

Demaris, Ovid. **The Boardwalk Jungle.** Toronto: Bantam Books, 1986.

———. **The Last Mafioso.** New York: Times Books, 1981.

———. **The Lucky Luciano Story.** New York: Belmont Tower Books, 1974.

Denning, Michael. **The Cultural Front.** New York: Verso, 1998.

Denton, Sally, and Roger Morris. **The Money and the Power.** New York: Knopf, 2001.

Deutsch, Armand. **Me and Bogie and Other Friends and Acquaintances from a Life in Hollywood and Beyond.** New York: Putnam, 1991.

Doctor, Gary. **The Sinatra Scrapbook.** New York: Carol Press, 1991.

Douglas, Kirk. **The Ragman's Son.** New York: Pocket Books, 1988.

Douglas-Home, Robin. **Sinatra.** London: Michael Joseph, 1962.

Dwiggins, Don. **Frankie: The Life and Loves of Frank Sinatra.** New York: Paperback Library, 1961.

Earley, Pete. **Super Casino: Inside the "New" Las Vegas.** New York: Bantam, 2000.

Early, Gerald. **The Sammy Davis, Jr. Reader.** New York: Farrar, Straus and Giroux, 2001.

Eisenberg, Dennis, Uri Dan, and Eli Landau. **Meyer Lansky: Mogul of the Mob.** New York: Paddington Press, 1979.

Epstein, Edward Z., and J. Morella. **Mia: The Life of Mia Farrow.** London: Robert Hale Ltd., 1991.

Estrin, Mark W., ed. **Orson Welles: Interviews.** Jackson, MS: University Press of Mississippi, 2002.

Evanier, David. **Making the Wiseguys Weep: The Jimmy Roselli Story.** New York: Farrar, Straus and Giroux, 1998.

Evans, Harold. **The American Century.** London: Jonathan Cape, 1998.

Evans, Robert. **The Kid Stays in the Picture.** New York: Hyperion, 1994.

Exner, Judith, as told to Ovid Demaris. **My Story.** New York: Grove Press, 1977.

Farrell, Ronald, and Carole Case. **The Black Book and the Mob: The Untold Story of the Control of Nevada's Casinos.** Madison, WI: University of Wisconsin Press, 1995.

Farrow, Mia. **What Falls Away.** New York: Bantam Books, 1998.

Feinman, Jeffrey. **Hollywood Confidential.** Chicago: Playboy Press, 1976.

Finley, M. I., Denis Mack Smith, and Christopher Duggan. **A History of Sicily.** New York: Viking, 1987.

Fisher, Eddie. **Been There Done That.** New York: St. Martin's, 1999.

———. **Eddie: My Life, My Loves.** New York: Berkley, 1982.

Fishgall, Gary. **Gonna Do Great Things: The Life of Sammy Davis, Jr.** New York: Lisa Drew/Scribner, 2003.

Flamini, Roland. **Ava.** New York: Coward, McCann, 1983.

Fox, Stephen. **Blood and Power: Organized Crime in Twentieth-Century America.** New York: William Morrow, 1989.

Frank, Alan. **Sinatra.** New York: Leon Amiel, 1978.

Freedland, Michael. **All the Way: A Biography of Frank Sinatra.** London: Orion, 1998.

———. **Dino: The Dean Martin Story.** London: Comet, 1984.

Friedrich, Otto. **City of Nets: A Portrait of Hollywood in the 1940's.** New York: Harper and Row, 1986.

Friedwald, Will. **Sinatra: The Song Is You.** New York: Da Capo Press, 1997.

Gabor, Zsa Zsa, with Wendy Leigh. **One Lifetime Is Not Enough.** New York: Delecorte Press, 1991.

Gage, Nicholas. **The Mafia Is Not an Equal Opportunity Employer.** New York: Dell, 1972.

Gambino, Richard. **Blood of My Blood.** New York: Anchor Books, 1974.

Gardner, Ava. **My Story.** New York: Bantam Books, 1990.

Gehman, Richard. **Sinatra and His Rat Pack.** New York: Belmont Books, 1961.

Giancana, Antoinette, and Thomas Renner. **Mafia Princess.** New York: William Morrow, 1984.

Giancana, Sam, and Chuck Giancana. **Double Cross: The Story of the Man Who Controlled America.** London: MacDonald, 1992.

Gigliotti, Gilbert L. **A Storied Singer: Frank Sinatra as Literary Conceit.** Westport, CT: Greenwood Press, 2002.

Glazer, Nathan, and Daniel P. Moynihan. **Beyond The Melting Pot.** Cambridge, MA: MIT Press, 1971.

Goldfarb, Ronald. **Perfect Villains, Imperfect Heroes: Robert F. Kennedy's War Against Organized Crime.** New York: Random House, 1995.

Goldstein, Norm. **Frank Sinatra: Ol' Blue Eyes.** New York: Holt, Rinehart and Winston, 1982.

Goodman, Ezra. **The Fifty-Year Decline and Fall of Hollywood.** New York: MacFadden Books,1962.

Gosch, Martin, and Richard Hammer. **The Last Testament of Lucky Luciano.** Boston: Little, Brown, 1974.

Graham, Sheilah. **My Hollywood.** London: Michael Joseph, 1984.

Granata, Charles L. **Sessions with Sinatra: Frank Sinatra and the Art of Recording.** Chicago: A Cappella Books, 1999.

Green, Michael, and R. T. King, eds. **A Liberal Conscience: Ralph Denton, Nevadan.** Reno, NV: University of Nevada Oral History Program, 2001.

Halberstam, David. **The Fifties.** New York: Villard Books, 1993.

Haldeman, H. R. **The Haldeman Diaries.** New York: Putnam, 1994.

Hamblett, Charles. **The Hollywood Cage.** New York: Hart Publishing, 1969.

Hamill, Pete. **Why Sinatra Matters.** Boston: Little, Brown, 1998.

Hamilton, Nigel. **JFK: Reckless Youth.** New York: Random House, 1992.

Hammer, Richard. **The Illustrated History of Organized Crime.** Philadelphia, PA: Courage, 1989.

Hanna, David. **Ava: A Portrait of a Star.** New York: Putnam, 1960.

———. **Sinatra: Ol'Blue Eyes Remembered.** New York: Gramercy Books, 1990.

Haygood, Wil. **In Black and White: The Life of Sammy Davis Jr.** New York: Knopf, 2003.

Hellerman, Michael, and Thomas Renner. **Wall Street Swindler.** New York. Doubleday, 1977.

Hersh, Seymour. **The Dark Side of Camelot.** Boston: Little, Brown, 1998.

Hess, Henner. **Mafia & Mafiosi.** New York: New York University Press, 1996.

Heymann, C. David. **A Woman Called Jackie.** London: Heinemann, 1989.

Higham, Charles. **Ava.** New York: Delacorte Press, 1974.

———. **Howard Hughes: The Secret Life.** London: Pan Books, 1994.

———. **Marlene: The Life of Marlene Dietrich.** New York: W. W. Norton, 1977.

Howlett, John. **Frank Sinatra.** New York: Wallaby Books, 1980.

Hoyt, Edwin P. **Marilyn: The Tragic Venus.** Radnor, PA: Chilton Book Company, 1973.

Hyams, Joe. **Bogie: The Biography of Humphrey Bogart.** New York: Signet, 1967.

———. **Bogie: The Humphrey Bogart Story.** New York: Signet, 1966.

Israel, Lee. **Kilgallen: An Intimate Biography of Dorothy Kilgallen.** New York: Dell, 1979.

Jacobs, George, and William Stadiem. **Mr. S.: My Life with Frank Sinatra.** New York, HarperEntertainment, 2003.

Jennings, Dean. **We Only Kill Each Other: Bugsy.** New York: Penguin Books, 1992.

Jewell, Derek. **Frank Sinatra: A Celebration.** New York: Applause Books, 1999.

Jurow, Martin, as told to Philip Wuntch. **Marty Jurow Seein' Stars: A Show Biz Odyssey.** Dallas: Southern Methodist University Press, 2001.

Kahn, E. J. **The Voice.** New York: Harper and Brothers, 1946.

Kaplan, John, and Jon R. Waltz. **The Trial of Jack Ruby.** New York: Macmillan, 1965.

Kashner, Sam, and Jennifer MacNair. **The Bad & the Beautiful: Hollywood in the Fifties.** New York: W. W. Norton, 2002.

Katz, Leonard. **Uncle Frank: The Biography of Frank Costello.** New York: Drake, 1973.

Kelley, Kitty. **His Way: The Unauthorized Biography of Frank Sinatra.** New York: Bantam, 1986.

———. **Nancy Reagan: The Unauthorized Biography.** New York: Simon and Schuster, 1991.

Kennedy, Robert F. **The Enemy Within.** New York: Harper and Row, 1960.

Kerouac, Jack. **The Dharma Bums.** Great Britain: André Deutch Ltd., 1959.

Kessler, Ronald. **The Sins of the Father: Joseph P. Kennedy and the Dynasty He Founded.** New York: Warner Books, 1996.

Kupcinet, Irv, with Paul Neimark. **Kup.** Chicago: Bonus Books, 1988.

Kuntz, Tom, and Phil Kuntz, eds. **The Sinatra Files.** New York: Three Rivers Press, 2000.

Lacey, Robert. **Grace.** London: Sidgwick & Jackson, 1994.

———. **Little Man: Meyer Lansky and the Gangster Life.** Boston: Little, Brown, 1991.

LaGuardia, Robert. **Monty: A Biography.** New York: Avon, 1977.

Lahr, John. **Sinatra: The Artist and the Man.** New York: Random House, 1997.

Lambert, Gavin. **Natalie Wood: A Life.** New York: Knopf, 2004.

Lawford, Patricia Seaton. **The Peter Lawford Story.** New York: Carroll and Graf, 1988.

Lazar, Irving. **Swifty: My Life and Good Times.** New York: Simon and Schuster, 1995.

Leamer, Lawrence. **The Kennedy Women.** London: Bantam, 1994.

Lees, Gene. **Singers and the Song II.** New York: Oxford University Press, 1998.

Leigh, Janet. **There Really Was a Hollywood.** Garden City, NY: Doubleday, 1984.

Levinson, Peter J. **September in the Rain: The Life of Nelson Riddle.** New York: Billboard Books, 2001.

———. **Trumpet Blues: The Life of Harry James.** New York: Oxford University Press, 1999.

Levy, Shawn. **Rat Pack Confidential.** New York: Doubleday, 1998.

Lewis, Jerry, with Herb Gluck. **Jerry Lewis, in Person.** London: Robson Books, 1983.

Lukas, J. Anthony. **Nightmare: The Underside of the Nixon Years.** New York: Penguin, 1988.

MacLaine, Shirley. **Don't Fall Off the Mountain.** London: Bodley Head, 1970.

———. **My Lucky Stars.** New York: Bantam Books, 1995.

Mahoney, Richard D. **Sons & Brothers: The Days of Jack and Bobby Kennedy.** New York: Arcade Publishing, 1999.

Malatesta, Peter. **Party Politics.** Englewood Cliffs, NJ: Prentice-Hall, 1982.

Manchester, William. **The Glory and the Dream.** Boston: Little, Brown, 1973.

Martin, Ralph. **A Hero for Our Time.** New York: Macmillan, 1983.

Martin, Ricci, with Christopher Smith. **That's Amore: A Son Remembers Dean Martin.** New York: Taylor, 2002.

Matthau, Carol. **Among the Porcupines: A Memoir.** New York: Turtle Bay Books, 1992.

Mavaro, Giuseppe. **Dialogo tra un maestro ed i suoi alunni sulla storia di Lercara Friddi.** Lercara Friddi, Sicily: Biblioteca Comunale, 2002.

McBrien, William. **Cole Porter.** New York: Random House, 1998.

Messick, Hank. **John Edgar Hoover.** New York: David McKay, 1972.

———. **The Mob in Show Business.** New York: Pyramid, 1973.

Messick, Hank, with Joseph Nellis. **The Private Lives of Public Enemies.** New York: Dell Publishing, 1973.

Meyers, Jeffrey. **Bogart: A Life in Hollywood.** New York: Houghton Mifflin, 1997.

Monroe, Will. **The Spell of Sicily.** Boston: Page, 1909.

Moore, Robin, and Gene Schoor. **Marilyn and Joe DiMaggio.** New York: Manor Books, 1977.

Morella, Joe, and Edward Epstein. **Lana: The Public and Private Lives of Miss Turner.** New York: Dell, 1982.

Morgan, John. **The Prince of Crime.** Briarcliff Manor, NY: Stein and Day, 1985.

Morley, Sheridan. **Marlene Dietrich.** London: Sphere Books Ltd., 1978.

Mustazza, Leonard, ed. **Frank Sinatra and Popular Culture.** Westport, CT: Praeger, 1998.

———, ed. **Sinatra: An Annotated Bibliography, 1939–1998.** Westport, CT: Greenwood Press, 1999.

O'Brien, Daniel. **The Frank Sinatra Film Guide.** London: Butler and Tanner, 1998.

O'Brien, Ed, with Robert Wilson. **Sinatra 101: The 101 Best Recordings and the Stories Behind Them.** New York: Boulevard Books, 1996.

O'Donnell, Kenneth P., and David F. Powers, with Joe McCarthy. **"Johnny, We Hardly Knew Ye": Memories of John Fitzgerald Kennedy.** Boston: Little, Brown, 1972.

Ordway, Donald. **Sicily: Island of Fire.** New York: National Travel Club, 1930.

Parker, Robert. **Capitol Hill in Black and White.** New York: Dodd, Mead, 1986.

Parmet, Herbert S. **Jack: The Struggles of John F. Kennedy.** New York: Dial Press, 1980.

Parsons, Louella. **Tell It to Louella.** New York: Putnam, 1961.
Payn, Graham, and Sheridan Morley. **The Noël Coward Diaries.** New York: Da Capo Press, 1982.
Pearl, Ralph. **Las Vegas Is My Beat.** Secaucus, NJ: Lyle Stuart, 1973.
Peterson, Virgil W. **Barbarians in Our Midst: A History of Chicago Crime and Politics.** Boston: Little, Brown, 1952.
———. **The Mob.** Ottawa, IL: Green Hill, 1983.
Petkov, Steven, and Leonard Mustazza, eds. **The Frank Sinatra Reader.** New York: Oxford University Press, 1985.
Pignone, Charles. **The Sinatra Treasures.** New York: Bulfinch Press, 2004.
Pilat, Oliver. **Drew Pearson, An Unauthorized Biography.** New York: Pocket, 1973.
Powell, Hickman. **Lucky Luciano: His Amazing Trial and Wild Witnesses.** Secaucus, NJ: Arno Press, 1975.
Puzo, Mario. **The Godfather.** London: Pan Books, 1970.
Quirk, Lawrence, and William Schoell. **The Rat Pack: The Hey-Hey Days of Frank and the Boys.** Dallas: Taylor Publishing, 1998.
Ragano, Frank, and Selwyn Raab. **Mob Lawyer.** New York: Scribner's, 1994.
Rappeleye, Charles, and Ed Becker. **All American Mafioso.** New York: Doubleday, 1991.
Rednour, Tom. **Songs by Sinatra: A Unique Frank Sinatra Songography.** Beacon, NY: Wordcrafters, 1998.
Reeves, Richard. **President Kennedy: Profile of Power.** New York: Simon and Schuster, 1993.
Reid, Ed. **The Grim Reapers.** New York: Bantam, 1969.
———. **Mickey Cohen: Mobster.** New York: Pinnacle, 1973.
Reid, Ed, and Ovid Demaris. **The Green Felt Jungle.** New York: Trident Press, 1963.
Renay, Liz. **My Face for the World to See.** New York: Lyle Stuart, 1971.
———. **My First 2,000 Men.** Emeryville, CA: Barricade Books, 1992.
Ridgway, John. **The Sinatra File: Part One.** Birmingham, UK: John Ridgway Books, 1977.
———. **The Sinatra File: Part Two.** Birmingham, UK: John Ridgway Books, 1978.
———. **The Sinatra File: Part Three.** Birmingham, UK: John Ridgway Books, 1980.

Ringgold, Gene, and Clifford McCarty. **The Films of Frank Sinatra.** New York: Citadel Press, 1993.

Riva, Maria. **Marlene Dietrich.** London: Bloomsbury Publishing Ltd., 1992.

Rockwell, John. **Sinatra: An American Classic.** New York: Rolling Stone Press, 1984.

Roemer, William F., Jr. **Accardo: The Genuine Godfather.** New York: Donald I. Fine, 1995.

———. **Roemer: Man Against the Mob.** New York: Donald Fine, 1989.

Romero, Gerry. **Sinatra's Women.** New York: Manor Books, 1976.

Rose, Frank. **The Agency: William Morris and the Hidden History of Show Business.** New York: HarperCollins, 1995.

Russo, Gus. **The Outfit.** New York: Bloomsbury, 2001.

Sanford, Herb. **Tommy and Jimmy: The Dorsey Years.** New Rochelle, NY: Da Capo Press, 1972.

Sangiorgio, Nicolò. **Lercara Friddi: Itinerari storici e tradizionali.** Palermo, Sicily: Edizioni Kefagrafica, 1991.

Santino, Umberto. **Storia del movimento antimafia.** Rome: Editori Riuniti, 2000.

Santino, Umberto, and Giovanni La Fiura. **Behind Drugs: Survival Economies, Criminal Enterprises, Military Operations, Development Projects.** Turin, Italy: Edizioni Gruppo Abele, 1993.

Scheim, David. **Contract on America: The Mafia Murder of President John F. Kennedy.** New York: Shapolsky, 1988.

Schlesinger, Arthur M., Jr. **Robert Kennedy and His Times.** Boston: Houghton Mifflin, 1978.

———. **A Thousand Days: John F. Kennedy in the White House.** Boston: Houghton Mifflin, 1965.

Schoell, William. **Martini Man: The Life of Dean Martin.** Dallas: Taylor Publishing, 1999.

Sciacca, Tony. **Luciano: The Man Who Modernized the American Mafia.** New York: Pinnacle Books, 1975.

———. **Sinatra.** New York: Pinnacle Books, 1976.

Server, Lee. **Robert Mitchum: "Baby, I Don't Care."** London: Faber and Faber, 2002.

Shavelson, Melville. **How to Make a Jewish Movie.** Englewood Cliffs, NJ: Prentice-Hall, 1971.

Shaw, Arnold. **Sinatra: A Biography.** London: W. H. Allen, 1968.

———. **Sinatra: The Entertainer.** New York: Delilah Communications Ltd., 1982.

———. **Sinatra: Twentieth Century Romantic.** New York: Holt, Rinehart and Winston, 1968.

———. **The Street That Never Slept.** New York: Coward, McCann and Geoghegan, 1971.

Shepherd, Donald, and Robert Slatzer. **Bing Crosby: The Hollow Man.** New York: Pinnacle Books, 1981.

Shirak, Ed, Jr. **Our Way: In Honor of Frank Sinatra.** Hoboken, NJ: Lepore's Publishing, 1995.

Sifakis, Carl. **The Mafia File.** Wellington, UK: Thorsons, 1987.

Simon, George T., with foreword by Frank Sinatra. **The Big Bands.** Wellingborough, U. K.: Thorsons, Collier Macmillan, 1967.

Sinatra, Nancy. **Frank Sinatra: An American Legend.** New York: Reader's Digest, 1998.

———. **Frank Sinatra: My Father.** New York: Pocket Books, 1986.

Sinatra, Tina, introduction. **A Man and His Art: Frank Sinatra.** New York: Random House, 1991.

Sinatra, Tina, with Jeff Coplon. **My Father's Daughter.** New York: Simon and Schuster, 2000.

Sondern, Frederic, Jr. **Brotherhood of Evil: The Mafia.** New York: Farrar, Straus and Cudahy, 1959.

Spada, James. **Grace: The Secret Lives of a Princess.** London: Sidgwick and Jackson, 1987.

———. **Peter Lawford: The Man Who Kept the Secrets.** New York: Bantam, 1991.

Sperber, A. M., and Eric Lax. **Bogart.** New York: William Morrow, 1997.

Starr, Michael Seth. **Mouse in the Pack: The Joey Bishop Story.** New York: Taylor Trade Publishing, 2002.

Sterling, Claire. **The Mafia: The Long Reach of the International Sicilian Mafia.** London: Hamish Hamilton, 1990.

Strait, Raymond, and Terry Robinson. **Lanza: His Tragic Life.** Englewood Cliffs, NJ: Prentice-Hall, 1980.

Stuart, Mark A. **Gangster.** London: W. H. Allen, 1987.

Sullivan, Robert, and the Editors of **Life. Remembering Sinatra.** New York: Life Books, 1998.

Summers, Anthony. **Goddess: The Secret Lives of Marilyn Monroe.** New York: Macmillan, 1985.

———. **Official & Confidential: The Secret Life of J. Edgar Hoover.** New York: Putnam, 1993.

Sussman, Barry. **The Great Cover-Up.** Arlington, VA: Seven Locks Press, 1992.

Talese, Gay. **Honor Thy Father.** Greenwich, CT: Fawcett Publications, 1971.

Taraborrelli, J. Randy. **Sinatra: A Complete Life.** New York: Birch Lane, 1997.

Taylor, Theodore. **Jule: The Story of Composer Jule Styne.** New York: Random House, 1979.

Teresa, Vincent, with Thomas Renner. **My Life in the Mafia.** London: Grafton, 1974.

Theoharis, Athan, and John Stuart Cox. **The Boss: J. Edgar Hoover and the Great American Inquisition.** Philadelphia: Temple University Press, 1988.

Thomson, David. **Rosebud: The Story of Orson Welles.** London: Little, Brown, 1996.

Tormé, Mel. **It Wasn't All Velvet.** New York: Viking Penguin, 1988.

———. **Traps, the Drum Wonder: The Life of Buddy Rich.** Alma, MI: Rebeats Publications, 1991.

Tosches, Nick. **Dino: Living High in the Dirty Business of Dreams.** New York: Delta, 1992.

Turner, Lana. **Lana: The Lady, the Legend, the Truth.** New York: Dutton, 1982.

Turner, Wallace. **Gambler's Money.** Boston: Houghton Mifflin, 1965.

Valentine, Douglas. **The Strength of the Wolf: The Secret History of America's War on Drugs.** New York: Verso, 2004.

Vanderbilt, Gloria. **Black Knight, White Knight.** New York: Fawcett Gold Medal, 1987.

Vare, Ethlie Ann, ed. **Legend: Frank Sinatra and the American Dream.** New York: Boulevard Books, 1995.

Viertel, Peter. **Dangerous Friends: At Large with Huston and Hemingway in the Fifties.** New York: Doubleday, 1992.

Villa, Joey. **Living Well Is the Best Revenge: The Rat Pack and His Pals, the Friends of Joey Villa.** Las Vegas: Comic Two Talent, 1998.

Vizzini, Sal. **The Secret Life of America's No. 1 Undercover Agent.** Aylesbury, Bucks, Hazell Watson and Viney, 1972.

Wayne, Jane Ellen. **Ava's Men.** New York: St. Martin's Press, 1990.

Welles, Orson, and Peter Bogdanovich. **This Is Orson Welles.** New York: Da Capo Press, 1998.

Whalen, Richard J. **The Founding Father.** Washington, DC: Regnery Gateway, 1993.

White, Theodore H. **The Making of the President, 1960.** New York: Atheneum, 1962.

Wilkerson W. R., III. **The Man Who Invented Las Vegas.** Beverly Hills, CA: Ciro's Books, 2000.

Willoughby, Bob. **Sinatra: An Intimate Collection.** London: Vision on Publishing Ltd., 2002.

Wills, Garry. **Reagan's America: Innocents at Home.** Garden City, NY: Doubleday, 1987.

Wilson, Earl. **Show Business Laid Bare.** New York: Signet, 1974.

———. **The Show Business Nobody Knows.** New York: Bantam, 1973.

———. **Sinatra: An Unauthorized Biography.** New York: Signet, 1977.

Winters, Shelley. **Shelley, Also Known as Shirley.** New York: Ballantine, 1980.

Wolf, George, with Joseph DiMona. **Frank Costello: Prime Minister of the Underworld.** New York: William Morrow, 1974.

Yablonsky, Lewis. **George Raft.** New York: McGraw-Hill, 1974.

Yarwood, Guy, ed. **Sinatra in His Own Words.** London: Omnibus Press, 1982.

Zehme, Bill. **The Way You Wear Your Hat: Frank Sinatra and the Lost Art of Living.** New York: HarperCollins, 1997.

Index

Photographic Credits

Young Sinatra at microphone: Herbert Gehr/Time-Life Pictures/Getty Images

Lercara Friddi church and documents: photo courtesy Kathy Kirkpatrick

The S.S. **Spartan Prince** and documents: Ellis Island Foundation

Marty and Dolly Sinatra marriage portrait: Archive Photos

Child Sinatra in suit holding top hat: Hulton Archive/Getty Images

Sinatra family group: Hulton Archive/Getty Images

Dolly and Frank Sinatra next to car: Albert Lonstein Collection

Sinatra and friends in swimsuits: courtesy Edward Shirak

Sinatra in swimsuit, seated: courtesy Edward Shirak

The Hoboken Four: Culver Pictures

Sinatra in white tux with two other singers: Lucille Buccini

Mugshot: Bergen County., N.J. Sheriff's Department, now in FBI files

Frank and Nancy Sinatra marriage portrait: published in **Jersey Journal**, 1939, credited to Edward Davis

Waxey Gordon: John J. Binder collection

Willie Moretti: John J. Binder collection

Willie Moretti dead: AP/Wide World Photos

Sinatra and John Quinlan: Barry Kramer

Sinatra with Tommy Dorsey: AP/Wide World Photos

Sinatra being kissed by fans: © Peter Martin

Bobbysoxers in the street: © Bettmann/CORBIS

Swooning girls: © Peter Martin

Sinatra at youth rally: Ric Ross collection

Sinatra with portrait of Roosevelt: AP/Wide World Photos

Sinatra with Jo Davidson: courtesy Jacques Davidson

Bugsy Siegel dead: John J. Binder collection

Sinatra and Mortimer in court: AP/Wide World Photos

Lucky Luciano: © Bettmann/CORBIS

Chico Scimone playing piano: courtesy Chico Scimone

Adriana Rizzo with Luciano and Scimone: courtesy Chico Scimone

Marilyn Maxwell: © Bettmann/CORBIS

Lana Turner: © Bettmann/CORBIS

Sinatra and Ava Gardner: © Bettmann/CORBIS

Sinatra and Gardner on beach: © Bettmann/CORBIS

Sinatra, Cahn and Styne at piano: courtesy of Margaret Styne

Sinatra and Nelson Riddle: Murray Garrett/Getty Images

Sinatra and Bill Miller: © William Read Woodfield

From Here to Eternity still: © John Springer Collection/CORBIS

The Man with the Golden Arm still: AP/Wide World Photos

The Manchurian Candidate still: © Bettmann/CORBIS

George Wood: AP/Wide World Photos

Vincent Alo: © **The Miami Herald**

Harry Cohn: Allan Grant/Time Life Pictures/Getty Images

Frank Costello: John J. Binder collection

Sinatra and Gloria Vanderbilt: © Bettmann/CORBIS

Jill Corey: courtesy Jill Corey

Marlene Dietrich: © Motion Picture & Television Photo Archive

Sandra Giles: courtesy Sandra Giles

Jeanne Carmen: courtesy Brandon James

Peggy Connelly: courtesy Peggy Connelly

Connelly with Thunderbird: courtesy Peggy Connelly

Lauren Bacall, Sinatra, and Kim Novak: Sands Hotel collection, University of Nevada, Las Vegas

Eva Bartok: courtesy Deana Sinatra

Sinatra and Martin with signs: courtesy Jeanne Martin

Sands Hotel sign: Las Vegas News Bureau

Rat Pack in Sands steam room: © Bob Willougby/Motion Picture & Television Photo Archive

Joe Kennedy: Nevada State Archives

Skinny D'Amato and JFK: From the personal collection of Paulajane D'Amato

Sinatra singing at Kennedy rally: © Globe Photos, Inc. 2005

Sinatra and Marilyn Monroe: courtesy Jeanne Martin

Sinatra and JFK: Photofest

Judith Campbell: Photofest

Murray Humphreys: John J. Binder collection

Sinatra with Luella Humphreys: private collection, U.K.

Sam Giancana: FBI surveillance photo

Giancana dead: John J. Binder collection

Sinatra with chin in hand: © William Read Woodfield

Sinatra at meeting: © William Read Woodfield

Sinatra and Mia Farrow on set: © David Sutton/Motion Picture & Television Photo Archive

Sinatra and Farrow marry: © Bettmann/CORBIS

Susan Murphy: courtesy Susan Murphy

Sinatra drinking: courtesy of Jeanne Martin

Sinatra at baccarat table: Sands Hotel collection, University of Nevada, Las Vegas

Carl Cohen: Sands Hotel collection, University of Nevada, Las Vegas

Sinatra and Hubert Humphrey: Ric Ross collection

The Reagans, Agnew and Dolly, and Frank Sinatra: Palm Springs Historical Society

Sinatra and the Nixons: White House Photo Office Collection

Sinatra and Jilly Rizzo: Barry Talesnick/Retna Ltd.

Joe Colombo: Express/Getty Images

Lois Nettleton: courtesy Lois Nettleton

Frank and Barbara Sinatra: © Gunther/ Motion Picture & Television Photo

Dean Martin, Sammy Davis Jr., and Sinatra: © Bettmann/CORBIS

Sinatra smoking: the family of Carlo Mastrodonato

Elderly Sinatra singing: Ann Barak

Gravestone: courtesy Tony and Carol Pisciotta

The author and publisher regret that, despite their best efforts, it was not possible to identify the owners of some photographs used. They are therefore not credited here.

Permissions Acknowledgments

Grateful acknowledgment is made to the following for permission to reprint previously published material:

Bantam Books: Excerpt from **His Way, The Unauthorized Biography** by Kitty Kelley. Copyright © 1986 by H. B. Productions, Inc. Excerpt from **Ava, My Story** by Ava Gardner with Alan Burgess. Copyright © 1990 by C & J Films, Inc. Reprinted by permission of Bantam Books, a division of Random House Inc.

Jill Corey: Excerpt from "Tonight I've a Date with Sinatra" by Jill Corey. Reprinted courtesy of the author.

FranAm Publishing Administration: Excerpt from "When You Awake" by Henry Nemo. Copyright © 1968 by Indano Music Co. Renewed 1992. All rights reserved. International copyright secured. Reprinted by permission of FranAm Publishing Administration.

Hal Leonard Corporation: Excerpt from "One for My Baby (And One More for the Road)," lyric by Johnny Mercer, music by Harold Arlen. Copyright ©1943 (Renewed) by Harwin Music Co. All rights reserved. Reprinted by permission of Hal Leonard Corporation.

HarperCollins Publishers Inc.: Excerpts from **Mr. S.: My Life with Frank Sinatra** by George Jacobs and William Stadiem. Copyright © 2003 by George Jacobs and William Stadiem. Reprinted by permission of HarperCollins Publishers Inc.

Hobby Catto Properties LLC.: Excerpts from "Why Sinatra Hates the Press, part 1 & part 2," **Look Magazine** (May 28, 1957 and June 11, 1957). Excerpts from "Sinatra and Family," **Look Magazine** (December 26, 1967). Reprinted by permission of Hobby Catto Properties LLC.

Music Sales Corporation: Excerpt from "The House I Live In" by Earl Robinson and Lewis Allan. Copyright © 1942 (Renewed) by Music Sales Corporation (ASCAP). All rights reserved. International copyright secured. Reprinted by permission of Music Sales Corporation.

Peermusic: Excerpt from "I Get Along Without You Very Well" by Hoagy Carmichael. Copyright © 1938 by Songs of Peer, Ltd. Copyright renewed. All rights secured. Reprinted by permission of Peermusic.

Warner Brothers Publications U.S., Inc.: Excerpt from "Our Love" by Buddy Bernier, Larry Clinton, and Robert D. Emmerich. Copyright © 1939 (Renewed) by Chappell & Co., Bernier Publishing and Dulcet Music. Excerpt from "I'm a Fool To Want You" by Frank Sinatra, Jack Wolf, and Joel S. Herron. Copyright © 1951 (Renewed) by Sergeant Music Co., Integrity Music Corp. and Maraville Music Co. Administered by WB Music Corp. All rights reserved. Reprinted by permission of Warner Brothers Publications U.S., Inc., Miami, Florida 33014.

A NOTE ABOUT THE AUTHORS

ANTHONY SUMMERS covered the United States, the Middle East, and the Vietnam War for the BBC. His coups for television included smuggling cameras into the former Soviet Union to obtain an exclusive interview with the Nobel prize–winning physicist Andrei Sakharov when he was under house arrest. His best-selling books include **Goddess,** a life of Marilyn Monroe, **Not in Your Lifetime,** on the assassination of President Kennedy, **Official and Confidential,** on J. Edgar Hoover, **The Arrogance of Power,** on President Nixon, and **The File on the Tsar,** on the fate of the last imperial family of Russia. He won the Golden Dagger, the Crime Writers Association's top nonfiction award, for **Not in Your Lifetime.** ROBBYN SWAN worked with Summers on his last two books, and they have together contributed to **Vanity Fair** and various television documentaries. They are married, have five children between them, and live in Ireland.

A NOTE ON THE TYPE

THIS BOOK was set in Janson, a typeface long thought to have been made by the Dutchman Anton Janson, who was a practicing typefounder in Leipzig during the years 1668–1687. However, it has been conclusively demonstrated that these types are actually the work of Nicholas Kis (1650–1702), a Hungarian, who most probably learned his trade from the master Dutch typefounder Dirk Voskens. The type is an excellent example of the influential and sturdy Dutch types that prevailed in England up to the time William Caslon (1692–1766) developed his own incomparable designs from them.

Composed by North Market Street Graphics,
Lancaster, Pennsylvania
Designed by Virginia Tan